T0336857

Psychology, Pedagogy, and Assessment in Serious Games

Thomas M. Connolly
University of the West of Scotland, UK

Thomas Hainey
University of the West of Scotland, UK

Elizabeth Boyle
University of the West of Scotland, UK

Gavin Baxter
University of the West of Scotland, UK

Pablo Moreno-Ger
Universidad Complutense de Madrid, Spain

A volume in the Advances in Game-Based Learning (AGBL) Book Series

Information Science
REFERENCE
An Imprint of IGI Global

Managing Director:	Lindsay Johnston
Production Manager:	Jennifer Yoder
Publishing Systems Analyst:	Adrienne Freeland
Development Editor:	Allyson Gard
Acquisitions Editor:	Kayla Wolfe
Typesetter:	Christina Barkanic
Cover Design:	Jason Mull

Published in the United States of America by
Information Science Reference (an imprint of IGI Global)
701 E. Chocolate Avenue
Hershey PA 17033
Tel: 717-533-8845
Fax: 717-533-8661
E-mail: cust@igi-global.com
Web site: http://www.igi-global.com

Copyright © 2014 by IGI Global. All rights reserved. No part of this publication may be reproduced, stored or distributed in any form or by any means, electronic or mechanical, including photocopying, without written permission from the publisher. Product or company names used in this set are for identification purposes only. Inclusion of the names of the products or companies does not indicate a claim of ownership by IGI Global of the trademark or registered trademark.

Library of Congress Cataloging-in-Publication Data

CIP Data – Pending

ISBN 978-1-4666-4773-2 (hardcover)
ISBN 978-1-4666-4774-9 (ebook)
ISBN 978-1-4666-4775-6 (print & perpetual access)

This book is published in the IGI Global book series Advances in Game-Based Learning (AGBL) (ISSN: 2327-1825; eISSN: 2327-1833)

British Cataloguing in Publication Data
A Cataloguing in Publication record for this book is available from the British Library.

All work contributed to this book is new, previously-unpublished material. The views expressed in this book are those of the authors, but not necessarily of the publisher.

For electronic access to this publication, please contact: eresources@igi-global.com.

Advances in Game-Based Learning (AGBL) Book Series

ISSN: 2327-1825
EISSN: 2327-1833

Mission

The **Advances in Game-Based Learning (AGBL) Book Series** aims to cover all aspects of serious games applied to any area of education. The definition and concept of education has begun to morph significantly in the past decades and game-based learning has become a popular way to encourage more active learning in a creative and alternative manner for students in K-12 classrooms, higher education, and adult education. **AGBL** presents titles that address many applications, theories, and principles surrounding this growing area of educational theory and practice.

Coverage

- Curriculum Development Using Educational Games
- Digital Game-Based Learning
- Edutainment
- Electronic Educational Games
- Game Design & Development of Educational Games
- MMOs in Education
- Pedagogical Theory of Game-Based Learning
- Psychological Study of Students Involved in Game-Based Learning
- Role of Instructors
- Virtual Worlds & Game-Based Learning

IGI Global is currently accepting manuscripts for publication within this series. To submit a proposal for a volume in this series, please contact our Acquisition Editors at Acquisitions@igi-global.com or visit: http://www.igi-global.com/publish/.

The Advances in Game-Based Learning (AGBL) Book Series (ISSN 2327-1825) is published by IGI Global, 701 E. Chocolate Avenue, Hershey, PA 17033-1240, USA, www.igi-global.com. This series is composed of titles available for purchase individually; each title is edited to be contextually exclusive from any other title within the series. For pricing and ordering information please visit http://www.igi-global.com/book-series/advances-game-based-learning/73680. Postmaster: Send all address changes to above address. Copyright © 2014 IGI Global. All rights, including translation in other languages reserved by the publisher. No part of this series may be reproduced or used in any form or by any means – graphics, electronic, or mechanical, including photocopying, recording, taping, or information and retrieval systems – without written permission from the publisher, except for non commercial, educational use, including classroom teaching purposes. The views expressed in this series are those of the authors, but not necessarily of IGI Global.

Titles in this Series

For a list of additional titles in this series, please visit: www.igi-global.com

Psychology, Pedagogy, and Assessment in Serious Games
Thomas M. Connolly (University of the West of Scotland, UK) Thomas Hainey (University of the West Scotland, UK) Elizabeth Boyle (University of the West Scotland, UK) Gavin Baxter (University of the West Scotland, UK) and Pablo Moreno-Ger (Universidad Complutense de Madrid, Spain)
Information Science Reference • copyright 2014 • 356pp • H/C (ISBN: 9781466647732) • US $175.00 (our price)

Student Usability in Educational Software and Games Improving Experiences
Carina Gonzalez (University of La Laguna, Spain)
Information Science Reference • copyright 2013 • 439pp • H/C (ISBN: 9781466619876) • US $175.00 (our price)

Interactivity in E-Learning Case Studies and Frameworks
Haomin Wang (Dakota State University, USA)
Information Science Reference • copyright 2012 • 408pp • H/C (ISBN: 9781613504413) • US $175.00 (our price)

Handbook of Research on Improving Learning and Motivation through Educational Games Multidisciplinary Approaches
Patrick Felicia (Waterford Institute of Technology, Ireland)
Information Science Reference • copyright 2011 • 1462pp • H/C (ISBN: 9781609604950) • US $475.00 (our price)

Simulation and Gaming for Mathematical Education Epistemology and Teaching Strategies
Angela Piu (University of L'Aquila, Italy) and Cesare Fregola (Roma Tre University, Italy)
Information Science Reference • copyright 2011 • 256pp • H/C (ISBN: 9781605669304) • US $180.00 (our price)

Gaming for Classroom-Based Learning Digital Role Playing as a Motivator of Study
Young Kyun Baek (Korea National University of Education, Korea)
Information Science Reference • copyright 2010 • 358pp • H/C (ISBN: 9781615207138) • US $180.00 (our price)

Ethics and Game Design Teaching Values through Play
Karen Schrier (Columbia University, USA) and David Gibson (University of Vermont, USA)
Information Science Reference • copyright 2010 • 396pp • H/C (ISBN: 9781615208456) • US $180.00 (our price)

IGI GLOBAL
DISSEMINATOR of KNOWLEDGE

www.igi-global.com

701 E. Chocolate Ave., Hershey, PA 17033
Order online at www.igi-global.com or call 717-533-8845 x100
To place a standing order for titles released in this series, contact: cust@igi-global.com
Mon-Fri 8:00 am - 5:00 pm (est) or fax 24 hours a day 717-533-8661

Table of Contents

Section 1
Psychology and Serious Games

Elizabeth Boyle, University of the West of Scotland, UK

Elizabeth Boyle, University of the West of Scotland, UK
Melody M. Terras, University of the West of Scotland, UK
Judith Ramsay, University of the West of Scotland, UK
James M. E. Boyle, University of Strathclyde, UK

Michel Rudnianski, ORT, France
Milos Kravcik, RWTH Aachen University, Germany

Mireia Usart, Universitat Ramon Llull (ESADE), Spain
Margarida Romero, Universitat Ramon Llull (ESADE), Spain

Detailed Table of Contents

Section 1
Psychology and Serious Games

Over the past fifteen years there has been increasing interest in serious games as a new medium for learning, skill acquisition, and training. Developing and evaluating engaging and effective serious games presents an interdisciplinary challenge. Psychology is at the interface between hard science and social science and is uniquely placed to play an integrative role in advancing our understanding of the characteristics and impacts of serious games. As the diversity of the chapters in this book illustrates, psychologists have wide-ranging interests in serious games. The purpose of the current chapter is to introduce key concepts, constructs, theories, and research in psychology to examine areas where these are relevant to serious games and provide a context for subsequent chapters in the book.

Despite enhanced appreciation of the nature and scope of the cognitive advantages of playing games, our understanding of the actual mechanisms responsible for generating and maintaining these remains limited. In this chapter, the authors propose that viewing these changes from the information processing perspective of executive functions will help to elucidate the psychological infrastructure that underpins these gains. They apply Anderson's model of executive functions to understanding how games support visual-perceptual processing and higher-level thinking and problem solving. As well as extending our appreciation of how digital games can support learning, research on executive functions highlights the implications of the limitations of our cognitive systems for game design.

Chapter 3

Michel Rudnianski, ORT, France

Milos Kravcik, RWTH Aachen University, Germany

Several authors have suggested that serious games have the potential to be at their most useful in supporting higher level skills such as critical thinking and soft skills such as interpersonal and intrapersonal skills. In this chapter Rudnianski and Kravcik consider the problem of designing games from the perspective of the skill set required in the area of intelligence analysis. The specific example of the competences required by MBA graduates is considered with a focus on the hard and softer skills of data processing, empathy and critical thinking. Decision making and cognitive biases are discussed in the light of Prospect Theory, the Theory of Planned Behaviour and Game Theory. An overview of 'Games of Deterrence', a tool for representing argumentation based on game theory is discussed.

Chapter 4

Mireia Usart, Universitat Ramon Llull (ESADE), Spain

Margarida Romero, Universitat Ramon Llull (ESADE), Spain

From primary school levels to lifelong learning, the use of games for educational purposes has been an increasing focus of interest for instructional designers, teachers, and researchers. One of the factors that can be assessed in Game-Based Learning (GBL) is the time factor. In this chapter, time is considered as the time used by players (time-on-task) and as psychological time perceived by students (time perspective). Time Perspective (TP) is a cognitive aspect of players, defined as the manner in which individuals divide time into past, present, and future. This variable can be considered as an individual difference; players with a temporal perspective focused on the future may play games differently than students oriented to the past or present. This chapter aims to study how Serious Games (SG) can help in assessing time-on-task by learners and time perspective. After a theoretical review of these aspects, a case study of MetaVals is presented as an example of time assessment in SG. This game was designed by ESADE's learning innovation team and monitors player times for individual and collaborative phases of the game. The results focus on the key aspects for assessing time in the class use of GBL and offer designers and teachers a reliable instrument for better personalising and implementing of SG tasks in the context of time.

Chapter 5

Manuel Ninaus, University of Graz, Austria

Matthias Witte, University of Graz, Austria

Silvia E. Kober, University of Graz, Austria

Elisabeth V. C. Friedrich, University of Graz, Austria

Jürgen Kurzmann, University of Graz, Austria

Erwin Hartsuiker, Mind Media BV, The Netherlands

Christa Neuper, University of Graz, Austria & Graz University of Technology, Austria

Guilherme Wood, University of Graz, Austria

Neuroscience as well as computer gaming have rapidly advanced in the last decades. Yet, the combination of both fields is still in its infancy. One example of an emerging alliance is neurofeedback, where participants are required to learn controlling their own brain activity. So far, this kind of training is mostly applied in therapeutic settings, for example improving symptoms in epilepsy, attention-deficit/hyperactivity disorder, or autism spectrum disorder. However, there are some promising approaches that used neurofeedback in everyday situations for healthy subjects. This may prove especially valuable for serious games that aim to improve learning capabilities and cognitive aspects of individual users. The following chapter introduces the basic concepts and standards of neurofeedback. The different non-invasive imaging techniques are introduced along with successful applications in neurofeedback. Finally, benefits and pitfalls for future combinations of neurofeedback and games are discussed: while the former may profit from realistic and motivating video scenarios, the latter is expected to be a tool for evaluating and monitoring the direct effects on the user's brain.

Chapter 6

Bernd Remmele, Wissenschaftliche Hochschule Lahr, Germany

Nicola Whitton, Manchester Metropolitan University, UK

Studies on game-based learning often focus on positive motivations, behaviours, and outcomes. However, negative social behaviours are common in play. Game play is important for moral learning since players learn to comply with rules, fairness, and accountability. Games allow, and sometimes encourage, negative behaviours, which release players' obligations to behave in accepted ways and create new social situations where players learn to control behaviours as well as tolerate such behaviours in others. Sometimes this process fails and the magic circle of play is transgressed. Negative social behaviours, such as cheating, spoil-sporting, or sabotage, threaten to "break the magic circle" by disrupting the boundary between "game world" and "real world." Even if game rules encourage such behaviours, they can undermine the accepted social norms in both contexts. Educational game designers, researchers, and practitioners must appreciate and understand negative social behaviours and attitudes and the processes they can initiate.

Chapter 7

Gonçalo Pereira, INESC-ID, Portugal and Instituto Superior Técnico, University of Lisbon, Portugal

António Brisson, INESC-ID, Portugal and Instituto Superior Técnico, University of Lisbon, Portugal

João Dias, INESC-ID, Portugal and Instituto Superior Técnico, University of Lisbon, Portugal

André Carvalho, INESC-ID, Portugal and Instituto Superior Técnico, University of Lisbon, Portugal

Joana Dimas, INESC-ID, Portugal and Instituto Superior Técnico, University of Lisbon, Portugal

Samuel Mascarenhas, INESC-ID, Portugal and Instituto Superior Técnico, University of Lisbon, Portugal

Joana Campos, INESC-ID, Portugal and Instituto Superior Técnico, University of Lisbon, Portugal

Marco Vala, INESC-ID, Portugal and Instituto Superior Técnico, University of Lisbon, Portugal

Iolanda Leite, INESC-ID, Portugal and Instituto Superior Técnico, University of Lisbon, Portugal

Carlos Martinho, INESC-ID, Portugal and Instituto Superior Técnico, University of Lisbon, Portugal

Rui Prada, INESC-ID, Portugal and Instituto Superior Técnico, University of Lisbon, Portugal

Ana Paiva, INESC-ID, Portugal and Instituto Superior Técnico, University of Lisbon, Portugal

Serious Games rely on interactive systems to provide an efficient communication medium between the tutor and the user. Designing and implementing such medium is a multi-disciplinary task that aims at an environment that engages the user in a learning activity. User engagement is significantly related to the users' sense of immersion or his willingness to accept the reality proposed by a game environment. This is a very relevant research topic for Artificial Intelligence (AI), since it requires computational systems to generate believable behaviors that can promote the users' willingness to enter and engage in the game environment. In order to do this, AI research has been relying on social sciences, in particular psychology and sociology models, to ground the creation of computational models for non-player characters that behave according to the users' expectations. In this chapter, the authors present some of the most relevant NPC research contributions following this approach.

Chapter 8

Dawn G. Blasko, Pennsylvania State University, USA
Heather C. Lum, Pennsylvania State University, USA
Matthew M. White, Pennsylvania State University, USA
Holly Blasko Drabik, University of Central Florida, USA

Individuals differ in a myriad of ways and the promise of using a digital game format to teach or train new knowledge and skills is that they may be designed to allow each user to take their own path through the game and therefore create a more person-centered experience. The current chapter explores the research on some of the many individual differences that may be important to the design, use, and success of a serious game. These include factors that influence motivation to play and learn and learner characteristics such as age, gender, and ethnicity. Cognitive characteristics such as working memory and spatial skills can influence the play environment and may actually be improved by regular gaming. Finally, one area that has been much less studied is individual differences in teachers and trainers who often are charged with the implementation of the serious games.

Chapter 9

Ben Tran, Alliant International University, USA

Understanding the psychology of the gamer is important not just in studying video game players but also for understanding behaviors and characteristics of individuals who are non-players of video games. Currently, there is a gap in literature concerning the utilization of the gamer in selecting and training potential and current employees in organizational settings. The benefits of utilizing the gamer factor in selecting and training potential employees are: 1) identifying a qualified candidate who is a good fit to the organizational needs and 2) achieving and maintaining competitive advantage over competitors. Organizations are encouraged to utilize the Enneagram of Personality and Emotional Intelligence measures to identify gamers' other characteristics (O) and utilize the Tavistock method to assess gamers' factors. The Tavistock approach has been utilized in various formats including the Apprentice.

Chapter 10

Yulia Bachvarova, Cyntelix, The Netherlands
Stefano Bocconi, Cyntelix, The Netherlands

Social media and social networks have gained an unprecedented role in connecting people, knowledge, and experiences. Game industry is using the power of social networks by creating Social Network Games, which can be even more engaging than traditional games. In this chapter, the main characteristics of Social Network Games and their potential are discussed. This potentiality can also be used for serious games (i.e. games with purposes beyond entertainment) and especially games related to learning and behavioural changes. This leads to introducing the emerging field of Serious Social Network Games and their unique characteristics that make them suitable for serious applications. Finally, the rising phenomenon of Social TV is discussed, which combines the power of TV and social media. Based on a project by the authors, preliminary findings on the most engaging techniques of Social TV Games are presented, together with initial suggestions on what constitutes good game mechanics for such games. The chapter concludes with future research directions for Social Network Games to become even more engaging and effective for purposes beyond pure entertainment.

Section 2
Pedagogy and Assessment

Chapter 11

Karen Orr, Queen's University Belfast, Northern Ireland

Carol McGuinness, Queen's University Belfast, Northern Ireland

This chapter explores the nature of "learning" in games-based learning and the cognitive and motivational processes that might underpin that learning by drawing on psychological theories and perspectives. Firstly, changing conceptions of learning over the last few decades are reviewed. This is described in relation to the changes in formal learning theories and connections made between learning theory and GBL. Secondly, the chapter reviews empirical research on the learning outcomes that have been identified for GBL, with specific focus on cognitive benefits, school attainment, collaborative working, and the motivational and engaging appeal of games. Finally, an overview of the dominant theoretical perspectives/findings mostly associated with GBL is presented in an attempt to broaden understanding of the potential for GBL in the classroom.

Chapter 12

Peter van Rosmalen, Open University of The Netherlands, The Netherlands

Amanda Wilson, University of the West of Scotland, UK

Hans Hummel, Open University of The Netherlands, The Netherlands

With the advent of social media, it is widely accepted that teachers and learners are not only consumers but also may have an active role in contributing and co-creating lesson materials and content. Paradoxically, one strand of technology-enhanced learning (i.e. game-based learning) aligns only slightly to this development. Games, while there to experience, explore, and collaborate, are almost exclusively designed by professionals. Despite, or maybe because, games are the exclusive domain of professional developers, the general impression is that games require complex technologies and that games are difficult to organise and to embed in a curriculum. This chapter makes a case that games are not necessarily the exclusive domain of game professionals. Rather than enforcing teachers to get acquainted with and use complex, technically demanding games, the authors discuss approaches that teachers themselves can use to build games, make use of existing games, and even one step beyond use tools or games that can be used by learners to create their own designs (e.g. games or virtual worlds).

Chapter 13

Thomas Hainey, University of the West of Scotland, UK

Mario Soflano, University of the West of Scotland, UK

Thomas M. Connolly, University of the West of Scotland, UK

The literature suggests that every learner has a particular Learning Style (LS) and it is beneficial for the teacher and the learning approach to adapt to and accommodate these differences. The traditional classroom fails to motivate some learners and to maintain their engagement level during learning, possibly because of lack of interactivity. Computer games on the other hand seem to be able to engage participants for prolonged periods of time and motivate them to replay the game repeatedly. Some educationalists consider games as a potential platform to support learning and the term Games-Based Learning (GBL) has been introduced into the curriculum to reflect this approach. While many GBL applications have been developed, there is still a lack of empirical evidence to support its validity. Furthermore, there are very few adaptive GBL applications developed and adaptive GBL frameworks proposed. Another issue with GBL is that games engage the learners differently compared to traditional teaching approaches or eLearning and learning styles may differ inside and outside of the game. For the purpose of this research, a game with three game modes was developed. The modes were 1) non-adaptivity mode, 2) a mode that customises the game according to the learner's LS identified by a LS questionnaire, and 3) a mode with an in-game adaptive system based on a newly developed framework that can automatically adapt content according to the learner's interactions with the game. GBL has been used to teach various disciplines; however, this research focuses on teaching Structured Query Language (SQL) at Higher Education (HE). A Randomised Controlled Trial (RCT) was conducted with 30 students for each of the above game modes and another 30 students in a control group who learned SQL using a traditional paper-based approach. The results show that the game developed, regardless of mode, produced better learning outcomes than those who learned from a textbook. Particularly for adaptive GBL, learning effectiveness was identified to be higher while the learning duration was shorter compared to the other modes of the game.

Chapter 14

The last 10 years have seen explosive growth in the fields of online gaming. The largest of these games are undoubtedly the Massively Multiplayer Online Games (MMOG), such as World of Warcraft or City of Heroes, which attract millions of users throughout the world every day. The last 20 years have also seen the growth of a new field of physics known as Physics Education Research (PER). This field consists of physicists dedicated to improving how we learn and teach the subject of physics. In this chapter, the author discusses his personal quest to combine PER with a MMOG and create an online virtual world dedicated to teaching Newtonian physics.

Chapter 15

Serious Games (SG) are developing a reputation with some educationalists as a useful supplementary approach for teaching and learning. Two important issues for SG application developers and educationalists are how the learning is assessed and how assessment is integrated into a SG application. This chapter presents the results of a systematic literature review on assessment integration in SG and highlights the state of the literature in this area by outlining important papers to act as a guide for educationalists tackling this important issue. This chapter defines assessment and discusses formative and summative assessment and embedded and external assessment. A discussion of traditional assessment approaches and assessment approaches in SG are presented along with a discussion of existing frameworks for the integration of assessment into a SG application. The chapter presents a number of examples of assessment in serious games.

There is growing interest in assessment of student learning within education, not least because assessment practice within some sectors (the UK higher education sector for example) is stagnant: many courses designed independently to the assessment method and assessed through a small number of traditional methods. Games-based learning has shown little deviation from this pattern – games themselves often removed from assessment of the skills they are designed to teach, and in the worst cases from the intended learning outcomes: gamification being a particularly formulaic example. This chapter makes the case for an integrated approach to assessment within learning games and the wider curriculum, drawing on elements within game design that provide natural opportunity for such integration. To demonstrate and evaluate such an approach, integrated assessment case studies (including a full study from the University of Leicester) are presented and discussed.

In this chapter, the authors present a methodology for researching and evaluating Serious Games (SG) and digital (or other forms of) Game-Based Learning (GBL). The methodology consists of the following elements: 1) frame-reflective analysis; 2) a methodology explicating the rationale behind a conceptual-research model; 3) research designs and data-gathering procedures; 4) validated research instruments and tools; 5) a body of knowledge that provides operationalised models and hypotheses; and 6) professional ethics. The methodology is intended to resolve the dilemma between the "generality" and "standardisation" required for comparative, theory-based research and the "specificity" and "flexibility" needed for evaluating specific cases.

The objective of this chapter is to provide an overview of the different methods that can be used to evaluate the learning outcomes of serious games. These include Randomised Control Trials (RCT), quasi-experimental designs, and surveys. Case studies of a selection of serious games developed for use in higher education are then presented along with evaluations of these games. The evaluations illustrate the different evaluation methods, along with an assessment of how well the evaluation method performed. Finally, the chapter discusses the lessons learned and compares the experiences with the evaluation methods and their transferability to other games.

Foreword

As a technologist and as a researcher in serious games, it is my pleasure to write the foreword for this book, because from my work in the GALA Network of Excellence on Serious Games, I know the editors and many of the authors and their work and because I consider this book a great work in providing a novel and coherent approach to advancing our understanding of serious games. It could be surprising that a computer scientist was selected to write a foreword for a book that addresses psychology, pedagogy, and assessment in serious games, but I think that this reflects the editors' own diversity and their comprehensive view of serious games as a multifaceted and multidisciplinary topic.

This book provides an inclusive and multidisciplinary discussion of serious games that tries to provide a more holistic and coherent understanding of this emerging and fast-moving area of the educational applications of games. The aim is to try to better understand how interactive gaming technology can be utilised to enhance teaching and learning. This journey goes from the psychological theories of human behaviours, cognition, motives, and emotions that comprise the supporting body of knowledge necessary for understanding why and how serious games work to the actual application of games in real settings. While the relevance of theory and research in psychology to the design, development, and evaluation of serious games is recognised by computer scientists and technologists, it is not always clearly understood.

The pedagogical principles underlying serious games are also addressed, including the role of the teachers when using games and the new educational scenarios appearing (e.g. social interactions in games). Serious games have the potential to be at their most useful in supporting higher-level skills such as critical thinking and soft skills such as interpersonal and intrapersonal skills that are very difficult to acquire with more traditional educational approaches. Moreover, in this multidisciplinary topic, it is also necessary to examine new technological developments such as the application of artificial intelligence techniques to designing non-player characters in games or the use of players' brain signals (e.g. neurofeedback, brain computer interface) that have the potential to enhance the current applications of serious games.

However, this journey would not be complete without considering that the assessment of the learning experience is a key part of any learning process, allowing instructors to track the performance of students. Therefore, a crucial aspect for adoption of serious games in education is to incorporate or facilitate assessment and evaluation processes that can track effective learning while maintaining engagement. To address the practitioner's point of view, several examples and case studies covering different areas of serious games application are also provided.

This book was originally conceived within the framework of the EU-funded GALA Network of Excellence on Serious Games, but to increase coverage, the editors made an open call for contributions from external researchers from different parts of the world. GALA is composed of 30 research groups from universities, companies, and institutions from 14 European countries. This book reflects the efforts of GALA partners in articulating European research in this topic, identifying best practices, and combining different approaches and viewpoints.

Hopefully, this book will help you to better understand serious games and to provide new ideas about how and when serious games can be used to address educational problems in an innovative way. Enjoy the reading!

Baltasar Fernandez-Manjon
Complutense University of Madrid (UCM), Spain

Baltasar Fernández-Manjón *is associate professor in the Department of Software Engineering and Artificial Intelligence (DISIA) at the Complutense University of Madrid (UCM). Dr. Fernández-Manjón is also the Vice Dean of Research and Foreign Relationships at the Computer Science School of this university. He co-leads the Complutense e-learning research group (www.e-ucm.es). He is the former Academic Director of the Computer Science Technical School of Centro de Estudios Superiores Felipe II (Aranjuez, Spain) (2001-2006). He received his Bachelor in Physics (major in Computer Science) and a PhD in Physics from the UCM. He is a member of the Working Group 3.3 "Research on the Educational uses of Communication and Information Tecnlogies" of the International Federation for Information Processing (IFIP) and of the Spanish Technical Committee for E-learning Standarization (AENOR CTN71/SC36 "Tecnologías de la Información para el Aprendizaje"). He is also liason between IEEE Technical Committee on Learning Technology (LTTC) and IFIP WG3.3. His main research interests are e-learning technologies, educational uses of markup technologies, educational uses of serious games, application of educational standards and user modelling, on which he has published more than 60 research papers. He is also co-organizer and program committee member of several conferences (e.g. SIIE, ICALT, SCORM) and associate editor of several special issues about e-learning: Journal of Universal Computer Science (Springer, 2005 and 2007), Computers in Human Behaviour (2008), Simulation and Gaming (2008).*

Preface

INTRODUCTION

Since the 1970s, digital entertainment games have had a transformational impact on how we spend our free time. These games provide engaging and enjoyable activities and have become the world's most popular leisure activity. More recently, interest has turned to Serious Games, games that are intentionally designed for the purpose of learning, skill acquisition, and training. Serious Games are similar to games-based learning and the terms are sometimes used synonymously. However, it is more widely accepted that games-based learning is a subset of serious games and focuses on the use of games in educational contexts, while serious games are defined more broadly.

Despite the optimism about the potential of Serious Games, there remain a number of key challenges that need to be addressed to fully understand and demonstrate their applicability and limitations. While many papers have been published recently discussing the potential of Serious Games, there is still a gap in the literature concerning rigorous empirical evidence for their effectiveness in learning and training. At the same time, there are a number of gaps in the literature around three key areas:

1. **Psychology:** Serious Games provide activities that combine having fun with the more serious aims of learning or behaviour change. Theory and research in psychology are relevant to explaining the complex, subjective experiences such as flow, immersion, and presence that keep players engaged in games as well as explaining the different kinds of learning. For example, basic research in cognitive psychology can help to explain how players allocate attention to and remember information, construct simplified representations of mediated reality, and make decisions about different possible courses of action in games. Psychological research on individual differences such as gender, age, ability, personality, and learning styles may also be relevant in studying how players might use games most effectively. Understanding of psychological characteristics is important not just in studying players but also for designing realistic behaviours and characteristics of Non-Player Characters (NPCs).

2. **Pedagogy:** The use of games, virtual worlds, and simulations in learning must be based on established pedagogical theory. Games differ in their characteristics and the underlying models of learning that they will support. To encourage the use of games in learning, it is essential to develop a better understanding of the tasks, activities, skills, and operations that different kinds of games can offer and examine how these might match desired learning outcomes both within and out of the classroom. However, there is no uniform pedagogy within serious games; earlier games tended to be based on a behaviourist model while later games incorporate experiential, situated and socio-cultural pedagogical models.

3. **Assessment:** Assessment of the learning experience is a key part of any learning process, allowing instructors to track the performance of students. Therefore, serious games used in education should incorporate or facilitate assessment and evaluation processes. However, the interest for assessment in serious games goes further. Games are complex software artefacts that receive continuous input from the user and return immediate feedback. This exchange can be observed and logged, gathering vast amounts of information about how the students are interacting with the game.

These aspects of Serious Games will be covered in this edited book.

MISSION AND MAIN OBJECTIVES OF THE BOOK

The aim of this book is to disseminate knowledge on both the theory and practice of Serious Games, and to promote scholarly inquiry and the development/adoption of best practice in this area. The main objectives of the book are as follows:

1. To provide an understanding of three major topics (psychology, pedagogy, and assessment) underlying the successful use of Serious Games.
2. To help to provide a more coherent understanding of these key topics underlying the design, use, and evaluation of Serious Games, which will help to defragment the literature.
3. To provide an avenue for the publication of cutting-edge research that will inform both novice and expert readers about leading and emerging serious games pedagogy, technologies, and their applications to teaching and learning.
4. To showcase examples of current and emerging practice in innovative pedagogy and assessment and to discuss some of the key emerging psychological principles underlying serious games.
5. To contribute to the development of best practice in Serious Games through the evaluation and documentation of the successes and pitfalls of various techniques, approaches, and strategies.

While the focus of the book is on serious games, many of the issues discussed are also relevant to entertainment games.

INTENDED AUDIENCE

The intended audience for the book is broad, ranging from educationalists and researchers at all levels of education and training, particularly those with an interest in how serious games can be utilised to enhance teaching and learning. Game design is an interdisciplinary enterprise, involving those with a technical interest in game design, educationalists interested in learning and pedagogy, psychologists interested in motivational features of games, and sociologists interested in the impact of new technology on work practices. Researchers within the many subject areas in which games are being developed including health, business, engineering and science, and humanities will also be interested in the potential of games to support learning and change behaviour.

The book may also be adopted to support educational technology and e-learning courses at an undergraduate or postgraduate level. In addition, the book will be of interest to companies involved in the development of Serious Games applications, as it will provide an insight into some of the key challenges facing the industry and approaches to tackling these challenges.

Through a combination of theoretical pieces as well as practical cases or examples of "best practice" in the field, the novice reader will benefit from expert knowledge and learn from the experiences of both researchers and practitioners. Experts will stand to gain from reading the book to stay abreast of the latest developments and trends in this still nascent area and to obtain exposure to diverse perspectives and approaches to Serious Games.

OVERVIEW OF THE CHAPTERS

Section 1: Psychology and Serious Games

Serious games provide engaging activities that can help players to learn, acquire new skills, or change their behaviour. A key issue for serious games is how they can combine the engagement that games provide with effective learning. Psychologists have developed a wealth of theoretical and practical knowledge about learning, engagement, and behaviour, as well as a range of methods for studying these, which can help in developing a more coherent approach to understanding serious games. The diversity of the chapters in this book reflects the varied interests of psychologists in serious games. Chapter 1 provides an overview of key theories and constructs in psychology that are relevant to understanding serious games with a particular focus on those that are relevant to issues discussed in the chapters in this book.

Playing digital games is known to lead to a variety of perceptual and cognitive benefits, and there has been much optimism that serious games can support complex higher order thinking. Models of executive functions have recently been proposed as providing more coherent and coordinated accounts of cognitive processing. In chapter 2, Boyle et al. propose that applying Anderson's model of executive functions to games can help provide a more integrated framework for understanding the psychological infrastructure that underpins the cognitive benefits and constraints of playing digital games.

Several authors have suggested that serious games have the potential to be at their most useful in supporting higher-level skills such as critical thinking and soft skills such as interpersonal and intrapersonal skills. Chapter 3, Rudnianski and Kravcik consider the problem of designing games from the perspective of the skill-set required in the area of intelligence analysis. The specific example of the competences required by MBA graduates is considered with a focus on the hard and softer skills of data processing, empathy, and critical thinking. Decision-making and cognitive biases are discussed in the light of Prospect Theory, the Theory of Planned Behaviour, and Game Theory. An overview of "Games of Deterrence," a tool for representing argumentation based on game theory is discussed.

Usart and Romero argue in chapter 4 that it is useful to consider objective and subjective aspects of time as a factor in games. Objective time refers to the time that players take to carry out tasks in the game. Clearly, we might predict that the time that a learner devotes to learning, whether using a game or not, might be correlated with how much is learned. The subjective aspect of time (time perspective), refers to the player's perceptions of time in the game. This is a cognitive aspect of players, defined as the manner in which individuals divide time into past, present, and future. Players' perceptions of time is an important aspect of engagement in games since players frequently experience a distortion of their sense of time when they are engaged in playing games. Usart and Romero present a case study where they monitor player time for individual and collaborative phases of the Metavals game in order to discuss both objective and subjective time assessment in SG.

In chapter 5, Ninaus et al. discuss the potential for using Neurofeedback (NF) and Brain Computer Interfaces (BCI) in games. NF and BCI both detect the user's brain state, but in different ways. With BCI, brain signals are decoded to communicate with or control external objects such as a computer or computer game; with NF, users learn to modulate their brain signals directly coupled to feedback so as to ultimately affect behaviour. Ninaus et al. describe different neuroimaging techniques, such as Electroencephalography (EEG), Near-Infrared Spectroscopy (NIRS), and functional Magnetic Resonance Imaging (fMRI), and discuss their advantages and disadvantages as well as their application in games. Research on BCI and NF in combination with gaming is at an early stage but has potential in helping players to incorporate their brain states for a successful gaming experience.

Remmele and Whitton argue in chapter 6 that negative aspects of games, such as negative motives for playing games and negative behaviours in games, have been relatively neglected in the literature. They consider the "magic circle," which separates the game world from the real world, where different rules, behaviours, and codes of conduct apply, and they provide an interesting analysis of how negative behaviours can disrupt the magic circle, abruptly taking the player back out of the game where different systems of rules apply. Remmele and Whitton describe how games can help players understand the rules systems that apply in moral and social learning. They also consider examples of negative behaviours in games, such as cheating, spoil sporting, and trifling, which can disrupt the normal rules of a game.

Chapter 7 explores how user engagement in games is influenced by players' acceptance of Non-Player Characters (NPCs). In order for players to interact successfully with NPCs, these have to convey believable behaviours. The authors describe how research on the creation of computational models for NPCs in AI has been dependent on models developed in social sciences, especially psychological and sociological models. These models provide a basic understanding of human behaviours in specific domains that can be applied to generate believable behaviors in virtual, dynamic, and unpredictable environments. It also presents a series of examples describing theoretical models of emotions, emotion regulation, social identity, social power, and conflict resolution, and explains how these have been used in implementing autonomous NPCs.

Blasko et al. acknowledge that players differ along several dimensions, which are relevant to the enjoyment they experience and their learning in games. In chapter 8, Blasko et al. propose a categorisation of individual differences into personality and motivational factors, experiential factors, demographic characteristics, and cognitive factors such as learning styles, spatial skills, and working memory capacity. Consideration of these differences can help us to develop games that adapt to different players and provide personalised games and individualised learning.

Tran provides in chapter 9 a broad ranging account of players' motives for playing games. He then proceeds to examine the view that businesses are like games, concluding that this is an oversimplification of what a business is. He argues that MMORPGs support players in learning team and leadership skills that are key requirements for many jobs. He then examines how the Enneagram of personality and tests of Emotional Intelligence can help in personnel selection to assess the "o" factor, the knowledge, skills, and abilities that more established psychometric tests do not test. The Tavistock method is also examined as a means of collecting information about effective interactions in groups. These skills can be assessed by looking at gaming behaviours.

Early research looking at why players found entertainment games so engaging emphasised enjoyment, challenge, and competition, while neglecting social motives. However, the increasing popularity of Massively Multiplayer Online Games (MMOGs) and social network games has drawn attention to the importance of social reasons for playing games. Bachvarova and Bocconi describe in chapter 10 how game mechanisms used in social games, such as social interaction and the network effect principle, help to engage players in MMOGs and social network games. They also examine the combination of Web 2.0, games, and TV, and describe a prototype that was built to study the interdependencies between these. These social games can use their engaging power for purposes beyond pure entertainment, such as behavioral changes or learning.

Section 2: Pedagogy and Assessment

Chapter 11 explores the nature of "learning" in GBL and the cognitive and motivational processes that might underpin that learning by drawing on psychological theories and perspectives. The chapter first reviews changing conceptions of learning over the last few decades. Next, the chapter reviews empirical research on the learning outcomes that have been identified for GBL, with specific focus on cognitive benefits, school attainment, collaborative working, and the motivational and engaging appeal of games. Finally, the chapter presents an overview of the dominant theoretical perspectives/findings mostly associated with GBL to broaden understanding of the potential for GBL in the classroom.

The objective of chapter 12 is to present the view that games are not necessarily the exclusive domain of game professionals. Rather than requiring that teachers get acquainted with and use complex, technically demanding games, brief case studies are presented where teachers can build games themselves and games can be used by learners to create their own designs (i.e. games, worlds, or a-likes). For each case study, the learning objectives, the motivation to create the game, the design and the tools used, the game elements included, and the user experiences are discussed.

Chapter 13 provides important empirical evidence in the field of games-based learning and adaptive games-based learning by presenting the results of a randomised controlled trial to investigate learning effectiveness in relation to learning styles between adaptive games-based learning, games-based learning, and traditional teaching approaches. The chapter presents an extensive literature review to identify existing empirical evidence in adaptive games-based learning. The chapter then presents the results of the randomised controlled trial. The results suggest that games-based learning and adaptive games-based leaning are suitable teaching approaches for teaching Structured Query Language (SQL) at Higher Education (HE) level.

The last 10 years have seen an explosive growth in the fields of online gaming, the largest of these games being the Massively Multiplayer Online Games (MMOG), such as World of Warcraft or City of Heroes, which attract millions of users throughout the world every day. The last 20 years have seen the growth of a new field of physics known as Physics Education Research (PER). This field consists of physicists dedicated to improving how we learn and teach the subject of physics. In chapter 14, the author discusses his personal quest to combine PER with a MMOG and create an online virtual world dedicated to teaching Newtonian physics.

Chapter 15 addresses one of the key challenges associated with serious games, namely how assessment is integrated into serious games. The chapter provides an overview of assessment, formative assessment, summative assessment, and embedded and external assessment. The chapter also presents the results of an extensive literature review identifying the main approaches of integrating assessment into serious games. A number of case studies are then presented to discuss various forms of assessment integration including monitoring of states, quest types, use of assessment models or profiles, and micro-adaptive, non-invasive assessment of competencies, quizzes, and peer assessment.

Continuing the theme of assessment, chapter 16 makes the case for an integrated approach to assessment within learning games and the wider curriculum, drawing on elements within game design that provide natural opportunity for such integration. To demonstrate and evaluate such an approach, integrated assessment case studies (including a full study from the University of Leicester) are presented and discussed.

The final two chapters in the book (17 and 18) look not so much at assessment in games but at the evaluation of games. In the chapter 17, Mayer et al. explain that the emerging areas of serious games and games-based learning are complex and diverse and suffer from the absence of an overarching framework for executing and evaluating research. In this chapter, they propose a multidimensional framework for research and evaluation of games, suggesting that it should include an account of frames for evaluation (i.e. the philosophical positions to contextualise the research), the various kinds of evaluation methods that can be used, possible theoretical models to generate testable hypotheses, established tests, and measures of relevant variables and consideration of the ethical dimensions of games.

Chapter 18 complements the previous chapter by Mayer et al. by providing an overview of the different study designs that can be used to evaluate the learning outcomes of serious games, along with specific examples of these reported in the literature. Seven case studies are then presented of games that have been used by the authors to support their teaching in higher education across a range of subject disciplines, including business, health, and engineering manufacturing. These games had varied, and usually complex, learning objectives. Evaluations of the use of these games in teaching are discussed. These illustrate some of the pragmatic and ethical issues and constraints that arise for researchers and teachers in developing and using serious games in education.

Thomas M. Connolly
University of the West of Scotland, UK

Thomas Hainey
University of the West of Scotland, UK

Elizabeth Boyle
University of the West of Scotland, UK

Gavin Baxter
University of the West of Scotland, UK

Pablo Moreno-Ger
Complutense University of Madrid, Spain

Section 1
Psychology and Serious Games

Chapter 1
Psychological Aspects of Serious Games

Elizabeth Boyle
University of the West of Scotland, UK

ABSTRACT

Over the past fifteen years there has been increasing interest in serious games as a new medium for learning, skill acquisition, and training. Developing and evaluating engaging and effective serious games presents an interdisciplinary challenge. Psychology is at the interface between hard science and social science and is uniquely placed to play an integrative role in advancing our understanding of the characteristics and impacts of serious games. As the diversity of the chapters in this book illustrates, psychologists have wide-ranging interests in serious games. The purpose of the current chapter is to introduce key concepts, constructs, theories, and research in psychology to examine areas where these are relevant to serious games and provide a context for subsequent chapters in the book.

INTRODUCTION

The term "game" covers a very wide range of activities but, as Wittgenstein (1953) observed, games are difficult to define in term of a set of necessary and sufficient characteristics. Nevertheless several authors have tried to provide definitions of games, from Caillois (1961) in his influential book, Man, Play and Games, to Grendler (1996), Dempsey, Haynes, Lucassen, and Casey (2002) and Juul (2003). Most definitions identify key characteristics of games as voluntary, typically enjoyable physical or mental leisure activities which tend to be set apart from real life in some way and are essentially unproductive. In addition most definitions specify that games have goals and ways of achieving these goals by means of making allowable moves within specific constraints. Games can be played singly, in pairs or in teams.

Although computer and video games were developed initially as an entertainment medium primarily for fun and leisure, it gradually became clear that players were acquiring useful knowledge and skills while playing games. There has long been interest in the knowledge and skills acquired by players while they play traditional entertainment games such as Mastermind, Battleship and Chinese Checkers (Bottino, Ferlino, Ott, & Tavella, 2007). However reviews examining the educational potential of digital entertainment games (Kirriemuir & McFarlane, 2004; Mitchell & Savill-Smith, 2004) pointed out that it was difficult to integrate digital entertainment games into curricula as they frequently do not address the desired curricular learning objectives. It became

DOI: 10.4018/978-1-4666-4773-2.ch001

Copyright © 2014, IGI Global. Copying or distributing in print or electronic forms without written permission of IGI Global is prohibited.

clear that, if digital games were to be used for learning, they would have to be designed more carefully to match the desired learning outcomes.

Given the characteristics of games as fun, voluntary and essentially unproductive activities, combining the term "games" with the term "serious" made for even more definitional difficulties, since for many people these two terms are mutually contradictory. Serious games (SG) are clearly similar to games-based learning (GBL) in that both are intentionally designed for the purpose of learning, but as Hainey (2010) points out, GBL is a subset of serious games. Serious games are broader than GBL and include games to change attitudes and behaviour (Bogost, 2007) as well as games which are intentionally designed for the purpose of learning, skill acquisition and training (Boyle, Connolly, & Hainey, 2011). A number of definitions of serious games are proposed by the authors in this book but essentially they propose that (a) serious games include games for learning and behaviour change and (b) serious games have purposes which go beyond entertainment.

BACKGROUND

Serious games is a relatively new area of research, but there has been an explosion of interest in games over the past fifteen years as authors have speculated about their potential as an engaging new method for learning. The diverse nature of publications about serious games has led to criticisms that the area is fragmented and lacking in coherence (Ke, 2009). A number of researchers have aimed to develop organisational frameworks for serious games. With entertainment games, game genre provides a means of categorising games based on common activities required in these games (Herz, 1997). O'Brien (2011) attempted a similar categorisation for serious games distinguishing linear games, competitive games, strategy games and role playing games and tried to relate these game genres to the different cog-

nitive functions that they support. Sawyer and Smith (2008) developed a taxonomy of serious games, categorising games according to the game discipline/function of the game (games for health, education, business etc.) as well as the sectors in which the games might be used (government and defence, healthcare, advertising, education, industry etc.).

Psychology is an interdisciplinary subject at the interface between hard science and social science and, given this broad ranging scope, is uniquely placed to help in organising our understanding of serious games. Psychologists have developed a wealth of well-established and validated constructs, ways of measuring these, theoretical and practical knowledge about a wide range of human behaviours, cognitions, motives and emotions, as well as a range of quantitative and qualitative methods for studying these. Grounding our understanding of learning, behaviour change and engagement in games on existing research in psychology can help in developing a common language for discussing serious games and help to provide a more integrated and coherent approach to understanding serious games.

Many psychologists have applied their skills as hard scientists to provide physiological, biological, cognitive and computational explanations of mind and behaviour. Other psychologists are more interested in social behaviours and subjective experiences and they deal with the softer side of human nature, explaining human needs, wants, motives and emotions. As the varied topics addressed in this book illustrate, psychologists have broad ranging interests in serious games. There are chapters about cognitive, perceptual, neuropsychological, affective, motivational and social facets of players, as well as players' subjective experiences of games, individual differences between players and the relevance of psychological theory to designing realistic behaviours and characteristics for non-player characters (NPCs) in games. However most of these topics are relevant to two main issues: the first is in examining in what ways (if at all) serious games can support learning and the second is addressing the nature of engagement in games. The current chapter introduces key constructs from the psychological literature that have relevance to topics covered in the remaining chapters of the book, with a focus on learning and engagement in serious games.

Learning in Games

Theories of Learning: The chapters on pedagogy in this book review the relevance of theories of learning to establish which kinds of games are most appropriate for supporting which kinds of learning. However it is important to point out that most of the major theories of learning were developed by psychologists. The interests of psychologists and educationalists in learning clearly overlap but, where psychologists are more concerned with understanding the mechanisms that underlie learning, educationalists are more concerned with using these theoretical constructs for the practical goal of establishing whether learning a specific subject in a specific way in a specific context actually works. Theories of learning which have particular relevance for learning in games include behaviourism, Piagetian theory, Vygotsky's theory, Kolb's theory of experiential learning and cognitive theory.

Behaviourism or learning theory is an account of learning developed by Pavlov, Watson and Skinner which proposed classical and instrumental conditioning as fundamental mechanisms for learning. These accounts both view learning in terms of strengthening of connections via repeated associations between stimulus and response. Learning theory explains how physiological or emotional responses to "unnatural" stimuli might be elicited but does not apply well to explaining how we learn facts and skills. Learning theory does however have some relevance to learning in games, especially in understanding how rewards work (Howard-Jones, Demetriou, Bogacz, & Yoo, 2011). In Chapter V of this book, Ninaus et al.

argue that the learning which underlies the use of neurofeedback in games is based on operant conditioning of brain activation. The changes which arise as a result of making use of neurofeedback seem to operate as rewards.

Piaget's cognitive account of how children acquire knowledge has been influential in curricular design (Piaget & Inhelder, 1958). Piaget claimed that children are biologically programmed to understand the world in different ways at different stages in development. Through their actions on objects in the world, children develop increasingly complex cognitive schemas for representing and organising their knowledge of the world. Key tenets of Piaget's theory that are relevant to games are that understanding is gained via interactions with real world objects and that concrete understanding precedes understanding of abstractions. Actions in games allow players to operate on virtual but concrete representations of real world objects.

Vygotsky (1978) was a social constructivist who emphasised the importance of learning via social interactions with other people. Vygotsky proposed that learners make most progress when they are presented with tasks which are just beyond their current abilities but which they can complete with the help of a more experienced teacher. This idea of "scaffolding of learning in the zone of proximal development", i. e. presenting educational support just at the limits of learners' current level of understanding, has become a goal for many e-learning applications and games.

Kolb's (1984) theory of experiential learning has been influential in thinking about learning in games. Kolb proposed a cycle of four different stages in learning where different activities are carried out at each stage, from concrete experience to reflective observation, abstract conceptualisation and active experimentation. In Chapter XI, Orr and McGuinness point out that these stages are similar to the natural cycle of activities carried out by players as they play games.

Cognitive or information processing accounts view learning in terms of the flow of information about a stimulus into the perceptual system, the allocation of attention to relevant features of that stimulus, the transfer of information about the stimulus into long term memory and the use of a variety of problem solving and decision making strategies in deciding what to do with this information (Neisser, 1967). In Chapter II, Boyle, Terras, Ramsay and Boyle argue that cognitive accounts have the potential to provide more useful accounts of learning in games than other pedagogical theories since they focus on detailed mechanisms at the level of information processing which are of value to researchers and games developers.

Learning Outcomes: Teachers are increasingly encouraged to explain the effects of the teaching activities that they offer students in terms of learning outcomes and skills (QAA, 2006). These provide clear specifications of the knowledge and skills that a student should have acquired after having completed a specific activity.

A number of authors have aimed to provide some structure to the serious games literature by categorising the varied learning and behavioural outcomes that serious games address. Garris, Ahlers, and Driskell (2002) made a basic distinction between skills based learning outcomes (including technical and motor skills), cognitive outcomes (including declarative, procedural and strategic knowledge) and affective outcomes (beliefs or attitudes). Wouters, van der Spek, and Oostendorp (2009) proposed a model of four kinds of learning outcomes: cognitive learning outcomes, which they divided into knowledge and cognitive skills, motor skills, affective learning outcomes and communicative learning outcomes. O'Neill, Wainess, and Baker (2005) identified five "families of cognitive demands" in playing games: content understanding and problem solving which they viewed as content specific skills while collaboration/ teamwork, communication and self-regulation were regarded as content independent skills. With respect to cognitive outcomes, Dondlinger (2007) offered a finer grained analysis of the range of higher order thinking skills

that computer games for learning might support: critical thinking, problem solving, complex decision making, argumentation and deduction and hypothesis testing.

In a wide ranging literature review of empirical studies on the outcomes of playing games, Connolly, Boyle, Hainey, McArthur, and Boyle (2012) proposed that a multi-component analysis of games looking at the main purpose or intention of the game (entertainment or serious), game use, game genre, subject discipline and learning and behavioural outcomes would help to provide a framework for organising our understanding of games and their outcomes. Based on psychological theory, Connolly et al. categorised learning and behavioural outcomes as affective and motivational, knowledge acquisition /content understanding, perceptual and cognitive skills, behaviour change, physiological and social/soft skills outcomes.

Cognitive Approaches to Learning in Games: Three chapters in this book examine learning in games from a cognitive perspective. While learning outcomes are very useful for teachers, it seems likely that the cognitive approach offers an analysis of games at a more detailed level which may be useful for games researchers and designers. Boyle, Terras, Ramsay and Boyle discuss the perceptual and cognitive benefits of games from the perspective of Anderson's (2002) model of executive functions; Rudnianski and Kravcik examine how cooperative games might support the cognitive and affective competences required of MBA students and Usart and Romero look at players' perceptions of time in games.

In Chapter II, Boyle, Terras, Ramsay and Boyle argue that cognitive accounts can provide explanations of how learning in games operates at a detailed level of analysis. Playing games, even simple action games, requires the coordination of many different cognitive processes. Models of executive functions have recently been proposed which aim to provide more coherent and connected accounts of higher level cognitive processing and Boyle et al. propose that Anderson's model of executive functions can help to a more organised explanation of inter-related top down control processes required in tackling complex tasks such as playing games. Attentional and perceptual benefits which have been associated with playing entertainment games operate across the information processing, cognitive flexibility and attentional control components of Anderson's model, confirming the diversity of the effects from the perspective of this more organised model. The goal setting component of the model along with interactions between model components deal with the complex processing involved in higher level thinking, problem solving and self-regulation. Examples of serious games which support higher level cognitive functioning are also examined in this chapter. While there is much optimism in the literature that serious games will support higher order thinking such as problem solving, reasoning and decision making, Boyle et al. point out that there is an absence of high quality evaluations of games which support this claim.

In Chapter III Rudnianski and Kravcik approach the problem of using games to support higher level thinking by trying to characterise the nature of the competences required by those working in a specific area and then looking at games which might support these competences. The area that they examined was the field of intelligence analysis and they acknowledged the close interplay between hard and soft skills in the jobs available to 21st century graduates. The skills required by executive MBA graduates include data processing, empathy and critical thinking and these will be called upon in many of the cooperative decision making tasks that these graduates will undertake. Rudnianski and Kravcik describe how deterrence games, a variety of cooperative game of the kind used in game theory, provide good models of the decision making required in carrying out these complex tasks. The authors also remind us of some of the cognitive biases which psychologists such as Kahneman and Tversky (1979) identified which constrain rational decision making.

In Chapter IV Usart and Romero examine objective and subjective aspects of time in games. The objective aspect is the time taken by players to carry out a task in the game. Clearly the time that a learner devotes to learning, whether using a game or not, is typically important in determining how much is learned. The subjective aspect of time refers to the player's perceptions of time in the game. This is the psychological time perceived by students (time perspective). This time perspective (TP) is a cognitive aspect of players, defined as the manner in which individuals divide time into past, present, and future. Players' perceptions of time is an important aspect of engagement in games since players frequently experience a distortion of their sense of time when they are engaged in playing games. Both aspects of time have the potential to provide useful measures in games.

Engagement in Games

Serious games can potentially lead to a range of learning and behavioural outcomes, but one outcome of games which deserves closer consideration is the engagement that games provide. Much of the research on the appeal of games has focused on digital entertainment games. The popularity of these games is self-evident in terms of global sales, the large numbers of people who play and the amount of time they spend playing games. However the strong appeal of these games has been something of an enigma and is deceptively difficult to explain (Nabi & Kremar, 2004). Our understanding of why people like games so much has been advanced by two different strands of research. Firstly the motivational properties of the games have been examined, i. e. the reasons people have for playing games and secondly engagement has been examined with respect to the (largely enjoyable) subjective experiences that playing games provides.

Motivational Properties of Games: Many accounts of motives for playing games address why games are so engaging from the perspective of how games address human needs. Maslow (1943) proposed that human behaviours can be explained by examining how these behaviours address our fundamental human needs. According to Maslow, needs form a hierachy from lower level to higher level needs. In this framework, entertainment games would be viewed as leisure activities which address higher level human needs since leisure by nature is what human beings do with their time once lower level needs have been satisfied.

Self-determination theory (SDT) and uses and gratifications (U&G) theory provide more recent theoretical accounts of human needs which have been applied to playing games. Deci and Ryan's (1985) self-determination theory is an influential account of human motivation which proposes that human behaviours are determined by very general human needs for competence, autonomy and relatedness. The need for competence is related to the need for achievement which was characterised by McClelland (1961) as the human need to acquire and demonstrate competence and master skills across different domains. Consistent with this, many studies have shown that players view challenge as the number one reason for playing games. The need for autonomy refers to our need to feel in control of our lives and the decisions we make: games frequently offer players opportunities to experience autonomy in the decisions they make as they play. Relatedness refers to the need to feel a sense of connection to other people and this is increasingly evident in social games, such as Massively Multiplayer Online Games (MMOGs). Ryan, Rigby, and Przybylski (2006) applied SDT to explain engagement in digital entertainment games and found support for the claims that games can satisfy these self-determined needs.

Uses and gratifications (U&G) theory is another needs-based motivational theory which claims that people have specific needs for entertainment and will use a range of media to meet these needs. U&G theory was originally developed within the domain of media and mass communication to explain why people watch television and listen to music (Schramm, Lyle, and Parker, 1961) but has been extended to explain why people play computer games (Lucas and Sherry, 2004). These authors looked at competition, challenge, social interaction, diversion, fantasy and arousal as gratifications that students derive from playing entertainment games. Challenge was the top rated reason for both male and female students, with the need for arousal also rated highly by both genders. Males rated social motives as the second most important reason for playing while females rated them as least important, although online and browser games have changed this. Colwell (2007) identified companionship, preferring playing games to being with friends, fun/challenge and stress relief as needs that playing games meets for adolescents.

Another theory which has been applied to explaining why people play games is the Technology Acceptance Model (TAM) (Davis, 1989). This theory was developed to explain predictors of technology acceptance in the area of work and training. TAM proposes perceived usefulness and perceived ease of use as two key factors in this. While ease of use of a system may be a contributing factor to explaining engagement in entertainment games, perceived usefulness may be less important in determining the acceptance of games for leisure purposes. Hsu and Lu (2004) found that social norms, attitude, and flow experience were better predictors of the intention to use entertainment games than perceived usefulness and perceived ease of use.

Much of the optimism about the potential of serious games to support learning is based on the assumption that players will find serious games just as engaging as entertainment games. However rather than being complementary, engagement and learning may actually be in conflict. The features of games which lead to engaging experiences may work against rather than towards learning. Habgood and Ainsworth (2011) argued that, if the engaging features of games are to support learning, the learning activities in the game would have to be designed in this way. They proposed that the most intrinsically motivating games will occur when the learning content and game activities (rather than the game fantasy) are aligned with the activities in the game mechanics, since the game activities which give rise to flow ensure that flow is also directed at the educational goals.

We are beginning understand the many "engagement attributes" which contribute to engagement in games. From their qualitative study using semi-structured interviews to ask technology users about their engagement with technology O'Brien and Toms (2008) identified challenge, aesthetic and sensory appeal, feedback, novelty, interactivity, perceived control and time, awareness, motivation, interest, and affect as important features which contribute to engagement.

Social Motives in Games: Many early digital games were single player games but more recently Massively Multiplayer Online Games (MMOGs) have become increasingly popular. These games allow players to interact with people from all over the world. It would appear that MMOGs (as well as other social media) meet the social needs of humans described in SDT and U&G theory. Yee (2007) confirmed social motives in addition to the desire for achievement and immersion, as important reasons for playing online games. He identified three different kinds of social reasons for playing games: using games as a means of socialising by helping and chatting with other players; using games as a means of forming relationships with others and using games for teamwork and for the sense of achievement from working with others to tackle a problem. In a qualitative study of why players continue to play games, Schoenau-Fog (2011) found similar reasons with players reporting that games stimulate friendship, camaraderie and socialising as well as competition and comparing scores.

While MMOGs were developed as games for leisure, playing these games requires team work, social interaction and competition with other players. These are precisely the skills identified as soft skills or core skills for the 21st century workforce and there is interest in whether MMOGs can be used more formally to support soft skills (Beck, 2005). This issue is addressed by in Chapter IX by Tran who argues that players of Massively Multi-User Online Role-Playing Games (MMORPGs) are actually learning useful administrative and higher level business skills in playing these games. In Chapter X, Bachvarova and Bocconi look at how the growing popularity of social media and social networks has led to social games that can be even more engaging than traditional games. They describe the game mechanics used to create engaging social games and examine how serious social Network Games can be developed.

Subjective Experiences in Games: Vorderer, Klimmt & Ritterfield (2004) argued that the subjective experiences of players as they play games lie at the heart of explanations of engagement. Theoretical constructs such as flow (Sweetser & Wyeth, 2005; Cowley, Charles, Black, & Hickey, 2008), immersion (Jennett et al., 2008) and presence (Weibel, Wissmath, Habegger, Steiner, & Groner, 2008; Ivory & Kalyanaraman, 2007) have been proposed to explain these subjective feelings. Each of these constructs has a slightly different focus. Both flow and immersion are characterised as multi-factorial constructs. The concept of flow was explicitly developed by Csíkszentmihályi (1990) as an account of the enjoyment experienced while taking part in favoured activities and Sherry (2004) applied flow theory to explaining enjoyment felt in playing computer games. Flow focuses on cognitive features of an experience, highlighting the fit between the challenge of a task and the skills of a player, but also assessing concentration and focus, goals and feedback, control, loss of self-consciousness, transformation of time and the feeling that the activity has become autotelic. The balance between skills and challenge typical of flow experiences is very similar to Vygotsky's ideas about the zone of proximal development, where the best progress is made when learners are presented with challenging tasks which are just at the outer limits of their current level of skill.

Jennett et al. (2008) developed a questionnaire based measure of immersion which included affective and cognitive components, as well as a sense of real world dissociation, challenge and control while playing the game. Presence focuses on the feeling of being present in a game and physical and technological features of the game are especially important in this respect (Weibel et al., 2008).

Emotions are an important aspect of the subjective experiences players feel while playing games. The main emotion experienced in playing games is enjoyment and flow essentially provides an account of the component features which contribute to enjoyment felt while taking part in freely chosen activities. However Jennett et al. (2008) were also interested in the role of negative emotions in understanding immersion in games. They examined whether anxiety felt in playing fast paced games could add to player enjoyment, although their results were inconclusive. The role of negative emotions in contributing to enjoyment is an area where further research is required.

Negative Impacts of Playing Games

The main aim of serious games and educational games is to learn. Since learning is typically regarded in a positive light, interest in serious games tends to focus on positive aspects of games. In contrast, despite the immense popularity of entertainment games, much of the early interest in the impact of these games focused on the detrimental effects of video games on the behaviour of children and adolescents. The public perception of video games was that they promoted violence (Anderson & Bushman, 2001), were gender stereotyped (Dietz, 1998) and potentially addictive (Griffiths & Davies, 2002).

In Chapter VI, Remmele and Whitton argue that, apart from these less desirable effects of playing games, negative aspects of games, such as negative motives for playing games and nega-

tive behaviours in games, have been relatively neglected in the literature. They consider the "magic circle", which separates the game world from the real world and where different rules and behaviours and codes of conduct apply, and they provide an interesting analysis of how negative behaviours in games can disrupt the magic circle. Cheating, spoil sporting and trifling are examples of negative behaviours in games which can disrupt the normal rules of the game so that the player does not try to attain the goals of the game, the magic circle is broken and the game is typically abandoned. Negative aspects of games, such as bluffing in poker and losing in competitive games are also considered by Tran in Chapter IX. He considers the analogy which is often made between business and games, arguing that this analogy is not always useful since some negative behaviours, such as bluffing and taking risks, are expected behaviours in poker but not acceptable in business.

Measuring Player Behaviours and Characteristics in Games

Psychologists have extensive experience in operationalising and developing measures of many human characteristics, attitudes, traits and behaviours by means of valid and reliable questionnaires, tests and experiments. These include intelligence tests (Kaplan & Saccuzzo, 2009), cognitive and neuro-psychological tests (Phillips, 1997), personality tests (Costa & McCrae, 1992), as well as wider ranging tests of self-esteem (Rosenberg, 1965), emotional intelligence (Mayer, Salovey, Caruso, & Sitarenios, 2003), learning styles (Vermunt, 1994), team roles (Belbin, 1981), motives (Deci & Ryan, 2002) and positive and negative affective states (PANAS) (Watson, Clark, & Tellegen, 1988).

Several measures of engagement in games have been developed. Sweetser and Wyeth (2005) modified Csíkszentmihályi's eight component model of flow to develop their GameFlow model, although many studies used a subset of the features linked to flow. For example, Weibel et al.

(2008) measured involvement, concentration and challenge while Lee and LaRose (2007) assessed enjoyment, concentration and merging of action and awareness. Jennett et al. (2008) developed a subjective, questionnaire-based measure of immersion. IJsselsteijn, de Kort, Poels, Jurgelionis, and Bellotti (2007) described a model of user experience in games, while Brockmyer, Fox, Curtiss, McBroom, and Burkhart (2009) adopted a pragmatic and eclectic approach to characterising engagement in games in their Game Engagement Questionnaire by including questions about different aspects of subjective experience.

There is much interest in learning analytics in serious games (Nadolski et al, 2012). These provide a means of finding out about how players are learning from their behaviours as they play a game. Measures such as response times, responses, errors, patterns of responses, interest, enjoyment, as well as performance on and interest in games could be measured. The Horizon report (2011) defines learning analytics as "the interpretation of a wide range of data produced by and gathered on behalf of students in order to assess academic progress, predict future performance, and spot potential issues". For example, in Chapter III, Usart and Romero describe how data on the time taken by players in different phases of a game can inform us about effort and attention in learning. Tran, Chapter IX is also interested in how information about players' behaviours in games, especially when they are working on group tasks, can be utilized, in the domain of personnel selection and training in business. Tran proposes that, while psychometric tests are often used in personnel selection, there is an additional factor which he calls the "o" factor which refers to "other" characteristics that traditional psychometric tests used in personnel selection do not assess, such as personality, interest or motivational attributes. These characteristics play an important role in performance on the job but are known to be very difficult to assess. Psychologists trying to explain the gap between performance on occupational

selection tests and performance in the workplace have proposed constructs such as emotional intelligence (Goleman, 1996; Mayer & Salovey, 1997), practical intelligence (Sternberg, 1985), multiple intelligences (Gardner, 1999) and soft skills (Kantrowitz, 2005). Tran acknowledges emotional intelligence as a construct that has been developed to assess these "hidden" skills. Tests such as the Mayer-Salovey-Caruso Emotional Intelligence Test (MSCEIT) (Mayer, Salovey & Caruso, (2002) provide validated tests of emotional intelligence. Tran also proposes that personality measured via the Enneagram could also be used (Riso & Hudson, 1996). This is a rather esoteric approach to measuring personality which is less well validated than more mainstream measures such as the big five theory (Costa & McCrae, 1992), although Brown and Bartram (2005) have suggested strong overlaps between the Enneagram types and the Occupational Personality Questionnaires (OPQ32, a widely used occupational personality questionnaires. Tran also mentions the Tavistock method, or group relations method which looks at how people function in groups. While his Tran's about identifying useful characteristics of players from their gameplay behaviours is a useful area of research, it is imperative that measures of traits and behaviours in games are based on accurate, valid and reliable models of human traits and behaviours. It seems that there is still some way to go before these traits can be reliably identified through game playing.

Behavioural and Physiological Correlates: In addition to developing subjective, questionnaire based assessments, there is interest in whether behavioural and physiological measures can provide objective measures of engagement and performance. Intuitively the simplest behavioural measure of engagement would be the amount of time spent playing a game, since we might predict a strong correlation between engagement in a game and time spent playing it. However Lee and LaRose (2007) found that negative reasons for playing games, such as habit strength and using the game as a diversion, were better predictors of the amount of time spent playing entertainment games than the positive experiences associated with flow, since frequent players tend to play habitually and are poor at regulating the amount of time they spend playing games. This suggests a constraint on using time-based measures of engagement.

Jennett et al. (2008) found that both eye movements and time to re-engage in an activity following immersion provided promising objective measures of immersion. Liu, Agrawal, Sarkar and Chen (2009) used of a range of physiological correlates of emotions felt while gaming, including cardiovascular measures, electrodermal activity, skin conductance measures and EMG activity, to adapt the difficulty level of a game to players' needs. This suggests that these measures can provide reliable and useful indicators of engagement in games.

A variety of physiological measures have been studied as correlates of the emotions felt while playing games. These include increases in blood pressure (Baldaro et al., 2004), changes in heart rate and increases in skin conductance, muscle activity and skin temperature (van Reekum et al., 2004) and changes in facial expressions (Ravaja et al., 2005). However links between physiological and subjective measures of engagement are not always easy to interpret. Ravaja et al. pointed out that physiological measures can provide potentially ambiguous measures of arousal in computer games. Heart rate, for example, can either increase in response to emotional arousal or decrease in response to attentional engagement, both of which are relevant subjective indicators of engagement in games.

There is increasing interest in studying the activity recorded in players' brains while they play games as correlates of the emotions players experience. Salminen and Ravaja (2008) looked at oscillatory responses evoked by instantaneous violent events in a first-person shooter game. They found changes in theta wave activity in response to both violent game events. In a previous study they had found no similar responses when players were playing a non-violent game, SuperMonkey Ball 2. These results confirm the value of measuring electroencephalogram (EEG) responses in studying physiological responses to emotional stimuli. Beeli, Casutt, Baumgartner, and Jäncke (2008) also looked at physiological reactions in the brain to the engagement felt while playing games. They found that the feeling of presence in a virtual environment was enhanced when the excitability of the dorsolateral prefrontal cortex (dlPFC) was decreased.

Brain signals can also be used in interacting with games. In Chapter V, Ninaus et al. discuss the use of neurofeedback (NF) and brain computer interfaces (BCI) in games. NF and BCI both use the user's brain signals but they use them in different ways. With BCI the user's brain signals are used to communicate with or control external objects, while with NF users learn to use feedback from their brain states to change their behaviour. With NF users are provided with a visual or auditory representation of their brain signals as they carry out a task and the user tries to change these to a more desirable representation (linked to success). This then changes the brain signals, which in turn change the linked behaviour. Like other methods of biofeedback, NF has been used in an attempt to help individuals with dysfunctional brain signals to control their brain signals and consequently the accompanying behaviour. For example those with Attention Deficit Hyperactivity disorder (ADHD) were able to decrease the number of slow EEG frequencies, while increasing the number of faster EEG frequencies and this helps them to reduce impulsive behaviours while enhancing attentional capabilities (Gruzelier, Egner & Vernon, 2006). With respect to games we are more interested in how NF can change the behaviours of normal participants. Ninaus et al. describe different neuroimaging techniques, such as EEG, near-infrared spectroscopy (NIRS) and functional magnetic resonance imaging (fMRI), their application in

NF in games and the advantages and disadvantages of the different neuroimaging techniques. Research on BCI and NF is at an early stage but has potential in helping players to control external objects or change behaviours.

Individual Differences

As in other areas of life, game players differ with respect to their abilities, needs, expectations, styles and preferences and ideally these differences would be considered in the design, use and assessment of serious games. In Chapter VIII, Blasko and colleagues proposed four categories of individual difference variables which are relevant to player enjoyment of, preferences for and effectiveness in serious games. The first category includes personality and motivational factors such as learning self-efficacy; the second involves experiential factors such as gaming experience and video game self-efficacy; the third involves demographic characteristics such as gender, socio-economic status and age and the fourth focuses on cognitive factors such as learning styles, spatial skills and working memory capacity. Since games are typically viewed as an appealing way to learn, there has been interest in the use of serious games for learners with mental and physical disabilities and Blasko et al. discuss cognitive aspects of games from the perspective of players with Special Educational Needs such as dyslexia, autism and ADHD. An important reason for taking differences between players into account is the opportunity for personalisation of games, for example in presenting tasks to players at an appropriate level of difficulty (Liu et al., 2009).

Psychology and NPCs

So far we have examined how psychological theories have added to our understanding of how players learn, how games meet players wants and needs, players' behaviours in games and differences between players. Psychological theory is also relevant to Artificial Intelligence in games and in Chapter VII, Pereira et al. describe how psychological and social theories have been used in assisting the development of believable non-player characters (NPCs) in games. NPCs are characters in games which are controlled not by the player but by the AI system in the game. In order to develop NPCs which players find acceptable and believable and which they will interact with, the appearance and behaviours of these characters should be modelled on state of the art psychological and social theories and implemented using state of the art technology.

Pereira et al. present a series of case studies describing theoretical models of behaviours and how these have been used in implementing NPCs. These include Ortony, Clore, and Collins (1990) cognitive-based model of emotions, Gross and Thompson's (2007) theory of emotion regulation, Tajfel (1978) and Turner's (1978) social identity theory and Thomas's (1976) conflict resolution model. Pereira et al. describe how the success of state-of-the-art AI research depends heavily on the accuracy, validation and computability aspects of these social science models. A problem for this research is that in many areas foundational theory and research about how best to characterise and measure specific psychological traits and behaviours and how best to represent these in NPCs is still being developed and consequently the realism of NPCs is constrained by the accuracy of these theories and models.

CONCLUSION

Psychology is a very broad discipline covering diverse aspects of human behaviour and psychologists have developed a wealth of well-established constructs, validated ways of measuring these and expertise in both quantitative and qualitative research. In this chapter we have argued that grounding our understanding of serious games on existing research, theory and constructs developed in psychology can help to provide a more integrated and coherent approach to understanding serious games and establish a common language for discussion.

Grounding our understanding of learning, behaviour change and engagement in games on existing research in psychology can help to flesh out the framework proposed by Mayer et al. in Chapter XVII of this book. Mayer et al presented a coherent methodology for researching and evaluating serious games and game-based learning based on six key elements. The knowledge base in psychology can help to address some of these elements such as providing: "a dynamic body of knowledge identifying the state of the art and knowledge gaps leading to research questions, operationalised models, hypotheses for testing", "validated research instruments and tools, questionnaires, surveys and instruments", "research designs and data-gathering procedures" as well as an understanding of ethical issues in research.

The twin goals of serious games are to engage players and support their learning and this chapter focused on both goals. In recognition of the diversity of serious games and the wide ranging competences that games can support, we highlighted the importance of clearly specifying the learning outcomes and skills required in designing serious games. Effective learning and behaviour change are more likely to occur when there is a good match between the desired learning/behaviour change outcomes and the affordances of a game. We also proposed that cognitive theory in particular can play an important role in helping to explain how players process information and solve problems while playing games.

We looked at explanations of the appeal of games, highlighting the need for challenge, autonomy, competition and enjoyment as important reasons for playing games and recognising the increasing social impact of games. A variety of theoretical constructs, such as flow and immersion, which describe the intensely engaging subjective experiences of players as they play games were examined, while Remmele and Whitton examined negative behaviours in and reasons for playing games. Differences between players which might help to explain player preferences for and uses of different kinds of games were examined.

As well as considering the application of psychological theory to players and games, we looked at the importance of using psychological theories in the design of realistic and convincing NPCs. While psychology has the potential to advance research on serious games, it must also be acknowledged that human behaviour is complex and in some areas knowledge is contested. The effectiveness of games and the credibility of NPCs will be constrained by limitations on our understanding of human psychology.

Interestingly the link between psychology and games is not all a one-way street. As well as psychologists lending their expertise to the study of games, games can provide a new tool for testing psychological theories. van Reekum et al. (2004) argued that the ability of games to evoke strong emotional reactions makes them ideal as a method for studying self-reported emotions and underlying physiological measures. A similar point was made by Ninaus et al. in Chapter V who argued that serious games and NF can benefit each another. They described how NF techniques which have been developed in other areas, can be usefully applied to evaluating and monitoring cognitive aspects of serious games. However they also pointed out that games provide motivating and sensory-rich game environments which can assist in the study of conventional NF applications.

To summarise, existing theory, constructs and research in psychology can help to provide a base from which to develop a more coherent framework for research on serious games. As interest in serious games grows it seems likely that psychologists will continue to work in close collaboration with researchers in other disciplines in systematising our understanding of computer games and helping to overcome the fragmentation which is evident in this area.

ACKNOWLEDGMENT

This work was partially supported by the Games and Learning Alliance (GaLA) - Network of Excellence for Serious Games under the European Community Seventh Framework Programme (FP7/2007 2013), Grant Agreement no. 258169.

REFERENCES

Anderson, C. A., & Bushman, B. J. (2001). Effects of violent video games on aggressive behavior, aggressive cognition, aggressive affect, physiological arousal, and prosocial behavior: a meta-analytic review of the scientific literature. *Psychological Science*, *12*, 353–359. doi:10.1111/1467-9280.00366 PMID:11554666.

Anderson, P. J. (2002). Assessment and development of executive function (EF) during childhood. *Child Neuropsychology*, *8*(2), 71–82. doi:10.1076/chin.8.2.71.8724 PMID:12638061.

Baldaro, B., Tuozzi, G., Codispoti, M., Montebarocci, O., Barbagli, F., Trombini, E., & Rossi, N. (2004). Aggressive and non-violent videogames: Short-term psychological and cardiovascular effects on habitual players. *Stress and Health*, *20*(4), 203–208. doi:10.1002/smi.1015.

Beck, J. (2005). The impact of video gaming on decision-making and team-working skills. *Campus-Wide Information Systems*, *22*(5), 320–326. doi:10.1108/10650740510632226.

Beeli, G., Casutt, G., Baumgartner, T., & Jäncke, L. (2008). Modulating presence and impulsiveness by external stimulation of the brain. *Behavioral and Brain Functions*, *4*(33), 1–7. PMID:18173840.

Belbin, M. (1981). *Management teams*. London: Heinemann.

Bogost, I. (2007). *Persuasive games: The expressive power of videogames*. Cambridge, MA: The MIT Press.

Bottino, R. M., Ferlino, L., Ott, M., & Tavella, M. (2007). Developing strategic and reasoning abilities with computer games at primary school level. *Computers & Education*, *49*, 1272–1286. doi:10.1016/j.compedu.2006.02.003.

Boyle, E. A., Connolly, T. M., & Hainey, T. (2011). The role of psychology in understanding the impact of computer games. *Entertainment Computing*, *2*, 69–74. doi:10.1016/j.entcom.2010.12.002.

Brockmyer, J. H., Fox, C. M., Curtiss, K. A., McBroom, E., & Burkhart, K. M. (2009). The development of the game engagement questionnaire: a measure of engagement in video game-playing. *Journal of Experimental Social Psychology*, *45*, 624–634. doi:10.1016/j.jesp.2009.02.016.

Brown, A., & Bartram, D. (2005). *Relationships between OPQ and enneagram types*. Thames Ditton.

Caillois, R. (1961). *Man, play, and games*. New York: Free Press.

Colwell, J. (2007). Needs met through computer game play among adolescents. *Personality and Individual Differences*, *43*, 2072–2082. doi:10.1016/j.paid.2007.06.021.

Connolly, T. C., Boyle, E. A., Hainey, T., McArthur, E., & Boyle, J. M. (2012). A systematic literature review of empirical evidence on computer games and serious games. *Computers & Education*, *59*, 661–686. doi:10.1016/j.compedu.2012.03.004.

Costa, P. T. Jr, & McCrae, R. R. (1992). *Revised NEO personality inventory (NEO-PI-R) and NEO five-factor inventory (NEO-FFI) manual*. Odessa, FL: Psychological Assessment Resources.

Cowley, B., Charles, D., Black, M., & Hickey, R. (2008). Towards an understanding of flow in video games. *ACM Computers in Entertainment*, *6*(2), 1–27. doi:10.1145/1371216.1371223.

Csíkszentmihályi, M. (1990). *Flow: The psychology of optimal experience*. New York: Harper and Row.

Davis, F. D. (1989). Perceived usefulness, perceived ease of use, and user acceptance of information technology. *Management Information Systems Quarterly*, *13*, 319–339. doi:10.2307/249008.

Deci, E., & Ryan, R. (Eds.). (2002). *Handbook of self-determination research*. Rochester, NY: University of Rochester Press.

Deci, E. L., & Ryan, R. M. (1985). *Intrinsic motivation and self-determination in human behaviour*. New York: Plenum. doi:10.1007/978-1-4899-2271-7.

Dempsey, J. V., Haynes, L. L., Lucassen, B. A., & Casey, M. S. (2002). Forty simple computer games and what they could mean to educators. *Simulation & Gaming*, *33*(2), 157–168. doi:10.1177/1046878102332003.

Dietz, T. L. (1998). An examination of violence and gender role portrayals in video games: Implications for gender socialization and aggressive behavior. *Sex Roles*, *38*, 5–6, 425–442. doi:10.1023/A:1018709905920.

Dondlinger, M. J. (2007). Educational video games design: A review of the literature. *Journal of Applied Educational Technology*, *4*(1), 21–31.

Gardner, H. (1999). *Intelligence reframed: Multiple intelligence for the 21st century*. New York: Basic Book.

Garris, R., Ahlers, R., & Driskell, J. E. (2002). Games, motivation, and learning: A research and practice model. *Simulation & Gaming*, *33*(4), 441–467. doi:10.1177/1046878102238607.

Goleman, D. (1996). *Emotional intelligence, why it can matter more than IQ*. London: Bloomsbury.

Grendler, M. E. (1996). Educational games and simulations, a technology in search of a research paradigm. In D. H. Jonassen (Ed.), *Handbook of research for educational communications and technology*. New York: Simon & Schuster Macmillan.

Griffiths, M. D., & Davies, M. N. O. (2002). Excessive online computer gaming: implications for education. *Journal of Computer Assisted Learning*, *18*, 379–380. doi:10.1046/j.0266-4909.2002.00248.x.

Gross, J. J., & Thompson, R. A. (2007). Emotion regulation: Conceptual foundations. In J. J. Gross (Ed.), *Handbook of emotion regulation*. New York: Guilford Press.

Gruzelier, J., Egner, T., & Vernon, D. (2006). Validating the efficacy of neurofeedback for optimising performance. *Progress in Brain Research*, *159*, 421–431. doi:10.1016/S0079-6123(06)59027-2 PMID:17071246.

Habgood, M. P. J., & Ainsworth, S. E. (2011). Motivating children to learn effectively: Exploring the value of intrinsic integration in educational games. *Journal of the Learning Sciences*, *20*, 169–206. doi:10.1080/10508406.2010.508029.

Hainey, T. (2010). *Using games- based learning to teach requirements collection and analysis at tertiary education level*. (Thesis). University of the West of Scotland, Renfrewshire, UK.

Herz, J. C. (1997). *Joystick nation*. New York: Little, Brown and Company.

Howard-Jones, P., Demetriou, S., Bogacz, R., & Yoo, J. H. (2011). Toward a science of learning games. *Mind, Brain, and Education*, *5*(1), 33–41. doi:10.1111/j.1751-228X.2011.01108.x.

Hsu, C.-L., & Lu, H.-P. (2004). Why do people play on-line games? An extended TAM with social influences and flow experience. *Information & Management*, *41*, 853–868. doi:10.1016/j.im.2003.08.014.

Ijsselsteijn, W., de Kort, Y., Poels, K., Jurgelionis, A., & Bellotti, F. (2007). *Characterising and measuring user experiences in digital games*. Paper presented at the ACE 2007 Workshop. New York, NY.

Ivory, J. D., & Kalyanaraman, S. (2007). The effects of technological advancement and violent content in video games on players' feelings of presence, involvement, physiological arousal, and aggression. *The Journal of Communication, 57,* 532–555. doi:10.1111/j.1460-2466.2007.00356.x.

Jennett, C., Cox, A. L., Cairns, P., Dhoparee, S., Epps, A., Tijs, T., & Walton, A. (2008). Measuring and defining the experience of immersion in games. *International Journal of Human-Computer Studies, 66*(9), 641–661. doi:10.1016/j.ijhcs.2008.04.004.

Johnson, L., Smith, R., Willis, H., Levine, A., & Haywood, K. (2011). *The 2011 horizon report.* Austin, TX: The New Media Consortium.

Juul, J. (2003). The game, the player, the world: Looking for a heart of gameness. In M. Copier, & J. Raessens (Eds.), *Proceedings of level-up: Digital games research conference.* Utrecht, The Netherlands: University of Utrecht.

Kahneman, D., & Tversky, A. (1979). Prospect theory: An analysis of decisions under risk. *Econometrica, 47*(2), 263–291. doi:10.2307/1914185.

Kantrowitz, T. M. (2005). *Development and construct validation of a measure of soft skills performance.* (Ph. D. Dissertation). Georgia Institute of Technology, Atlanta, GA.

Kaplan, R. M., & Saccuzzo, D. P. (2009). Standardized tests in education, civil service, and the military. In *Psychological testing: Principles, applications, and issues.* Belmont, CA: Wadsworth.

Ke, K. (2009). A qualitative meta-analysis of computer games as learning tools. In R. E. Ferdig (Ed.), *Handbook of Research on Effective Electronic Gaming in Education* (pp. 1–32). Kent, OH: Kent State University.

Kirriemuir, J., & McFarlane, A. (2004). *Literature review in games and learning.* Retrieved from http://www.futurelab.org.uk

Kolb, D. A. (1984). *Experiential learning: Experience as the source of learning and development.* Englewood Cliffs, NJ: Prentice Hall.

Lee, D., & LaRose, R. (2007). A socio-cognitive model of video game usage. *Journal of Broadcasting & Electronic Media, 51*(4), 632–650. doi:10.1080/08838150701626511.

Liu, C., Agrawal, P., Sarkar, N., & Chen, S. (2009). Dynamic difficulty adjustment in computer games through real-time anxiety-based affective feedback. *International Journal of Human-Computer Interaction, 25*(6), 506–529. doi:10.1080/10447310902963944.

Lucas, K., & Sherry, J. L. (2004). Sex differences in video game play: A communication-based explanation. *Communication Research, 31*(5), 499–523. doi:10.1177/0093650204267930.

Maslow, A. H. (1943). A theory of human motivation. *Psychological Review, 50*(4), 370–396. doi:10.1037/h0054346.

Mayer, J. D., & Salovey, P. (1997). What is emotional intelligence? In P. Salovey, & D. Sluyter (Eds.), *Emotional development and emotional intelligence: Implications for educators* (pp. 3–31). New York: Basic Books.

Mayer, J. D., Salovey, P., & Caruso, D. R. (2002). *Mayer-Salovey-Caruso emotional intelligence test (MSCEIT).* Toronto, Canada: Multi-Health Systems, Inc.

Mayer, J. D., Salovey, P., Caruso, D. R., & Sitarenios, G. (2003). Measuring emotional intelligence with the MSCEIT V2.0. *Emotion (Washington, D.C.), 3,* 97–105. doi:10.1037/1528-3542.3.1.97 PMID:12899321.

McClelland, D. C. (1961). *The achieving society.* New York: Free Press.

Mitchell, A., & Savill-Smith, C. (2004). *The use of computer and video games for learning: A review of the literature.* Ultralab.

Nabi, R. L., & Kremar, M. (2004). Conceptualising media enjoyment as attitude: Implications for mass media effects research. *Communication Theory*, *14*(4), 288–310. doi:10.1111/j.1468-2885.2004. tb00316.x.

Nadolski, R., Baalsrud Hauge, J., Boyle, E., Riedel, J., Mayer, I., & Moreno Ger, P. (2012). *Are you serious? Evidence for learning using games*. Berlin: Online Educa.

Neisser, U. (1967). *Cognitive psychology*. New York: Appleton-Century-Crofts.

O'Brien, D. (2011). A taxonomy of educational games. In Information Resources Management Association (Ed.), Gaming and simulations: Concepts, methodologies, tools and applications (pp. 1–23). Hershey, PA: IGI Global.

O'Brien, H. L., & Toms, E. G. (2008). What is user engagement? A conceptual framework for defining user engagement with technology. *Journal of the American Society for Information Science and Technology*, *59*(6), 938–955. doi:10.1002/asi.20801.

O'Neil, H. F., Wainess, R., & Baker, E. L. (2005). Classification of learning outcomes: Evidence from the computer games literature. *Curriculum Journal*, *16*, 455–474. doi:10.1080/09585170500384529.

Ortony, A., Clore, G. L., & Collins, A. (1990). *The cognitive structure of emotions*. Cambridge University Press. Retrieved 6th May 2013 from http://www.amazon.com/Cognitive-Structure-Emotions-Andrew-Ortony/dp/0521386640

Phillips, L. H. (1997). Do frontal tests measure executive function? Issues of assessment and evidence of assessment and evidence from fluency tests. In P. M. A. Rabbitt (Ed.), *Methodology of Frontal and Executive Function*. Hove, UK: Psychology Press.

Piaget, J., & Inhelder, B. (1958). *The growth of logical thinking from childhood to adolescence*. New York: Basic Books.

Ravaja, N., Turpeinen, M., Saari, T., Puttonen, S., & Keltikangas-Jarvinen, L. (2008). The psychophysiology of James Bond: Phasic emotional responses to violent video game events. *Emotion (Washington, D.C.)*, *8*(1), 114–120. doi:10.1037/1528-3542.8.1.114 PMID:18266521.

Riso, D. R., & Hudson, R. (1996). *Personality types*. New York: Houghton Mifflin.

Rosenberg, M. (1965). *Society and the adolescent self-image*. Princeton, NJ: Princeton University Press.

Ryan, R. M., Rigby, C. S., & Przybylski, A. (2006). The motivational pull of video games: A self-determination theory approach. *Motivation and Emotion*, *30*, 347–363. doi:10.1007/s11031-006-9051-8.

Salminen, M., & Ravaja, N. (2008). Increased oscillatory theta activation evoked by violent digital game events. *Neuroscience Letters*, *435*(1), 69–72. doi:10.1016/j.neulet.2008.02.009 PMID:18325669.

Sawyer, B., & Smith, P. (2008). *Keynote address*. Paper presented at the Second European Conference on Games-Based Learning. Barcelona, Spain.

Schoenau-Fog, H. (2011). The player engagement process: An exploration of continuation desire in digital games. In *Proceedings of DiGRA 2011 Conference: Think Design Play*. Digital Games Research Association.

Schramm, W., Lyle, J., & Parker, E. (1961). *Television in the lives of our children*. Palo Alto, CA: Stanford University Press.

Sherry, J. (2004). Flow and media enjoyment. *Communication Theory*, *14*(4), 328–347. doi:10.1111/j.1468-2885.2004.tb00318.x.

Sternberg, R. J. (1985). *Beyond IQ: A triarchic theory of intelligence*. Cambridge, UK: Cambridge University Press.

Sweetser, P., & Wyeth, P. (2005). GameFlow: A model for evaluating player enjoyment in games. *Computers in Entertainment*, *3*(3), 1–24. doi:10.1145/1077246.1077253.

Tajfel, H. (Ed.). (1978). *Differentiation between social groups: Studies in the social psychology of intergroup relations*. Oxford, UK: Academic Press.

Thomas, K. W. (1976). Conflict and conflict management. In *Handbook of industrial and organizational psychology*. Chicago: Rand McNally.

Tran, B. (2008). *Expatriate selection and retention*. (Doctoral dissertation). Alliant International University, San Francisco, CA.

Turner, J. C. (1978). Social categorization and social discrimination in the minimal group paradigm. In H. Tajfel (Ed.), *Differentiation between social groups: Studies in the social psychology of intergroup relations*. Oxford, UK: Academic Press.

van Reekum, C. M., Johnstone, T., Banse, R., Etter, A., Wehrle, T., & Scherer, K. R. (2004). Psychophysiological responses to appraisal dimensions in a computer game. *Cognition and Emotion*, *18*, 663–688. doi:10.1080/02699930341000167.

Vermunt, J. D. (1994). *Inventory of learning styles in higher education*. Leiden, The Netherlands: Leiden University.

Vorderer, P., Klimmt, C., & Ritterfield, U. (2004). Enjoyment: At the heart of media entertainment. *Communication Theory*, *14*(4), 388–408. doi:10.1111/j.1468-2885.2004.tb00321.x.

Vygotsky, L. S. (1978). *Mind and society: The development of higher mental processes*. Cambridge, MA: Harvard University Press.

Watson, D., Clark, L. A., & Tellegen, A. (1988). Development and validation of brief measures of positive and negative affect: The PANAS scales. *Journal of Personality and Social Psychology*, *54*(6), 1063–1070. doi:10.1037/0022-3514.54.6.1063 PMID:3397865.

Weibel, D., Wissmath, B., Habegger, S., Steiner, Y., & Groner, R. (2008). Playing online games against computer-vs. human-controlled opponents: Effects on presence, flow, and enjoyment. *Computers in Human Behavior*, *24*(5), 2274–2291. doi:10.1016/j.chb.2007.11.002.

Wittgenstein, L. (1953). *Philosophical investigations*. Oxford, UK: Blackwell.

Wouters, P., van der Spek, E., & van Oostendorp, H. (2009). Current practices in serious game research: A review from a learning outcomes perspective. In Connolly, Stansfield, & Boyle (Eds.), Games-based learning: Techniques and effective practices. Hershey, PA: IGI Global.

Yee, N. (2007). Motivations of play in online games. *Journal of CyberPsychology and Behavior*, *9*, 772–775. doi:10.1089/cpb.2006.9.772 PMID:17201605.

KEY TERMS AND DEFINITIONS

Cognitive Psychology: The study of information processing that takes place in perceiving, understanding and remembering information and problem solving.

Engagement: A multicomponent quality of user experience characterized by attributes including challenge and positive affect.

Enjoyment: A complex construct with physiological, affective, and cognitive dimensions linked to pleasurable experiences.

Individual Differences: The study of how human beings differ in their cognition, behaviour, and actions.

Learning: The acquisition of knowledge or skills through experience, practice, or study, or by being taught.

Motives: Internal processes that activate, guide and maintain behaviour over time; very often linked to fulfilling needs and wants.

Psychology: A discipline that adopts a scientific approach to studying mental events and behaviours of individuals and behaviours and interactions in groups.

Serious Games: Games with a purpose beyond entertainment, such as learning or behavioural change.

Chapter 2
Executive Functions in Digital Games

Elizabeth Boyle
University of the West of Scotland, UK

Melody M. Terras
University of the West of Scotland, UK

Judith Ramsay
University of the West of Scotland, UK

James M. E. Boyle
University of Strathclyde, UK

ABSTRACT

Despite enhanced appreciation of the nature and scope of the cognitive advantages of playing games, our understanding of the actual mechanisms responsible for generating and maintaining these remains limited. In this chapter, the authors propose that viewing these changes from the information processing perspective of executive functions will help to elucidate the psychological infrastructure that underpins these gains. They apply Anderson's model of executive functions to understanding how games support visual-perceptual processing and higher-level thinking and problem solving. As well as extending our appreciation of how digital games can support learning, research on executive functions highlights the implications of the limitations of our cognitive systems for game design.

INTRODUCTION

It is well known that digital entertainment games provide highly engaging activities but more recent interest has focused on whether games can support learning. Research in this area has two main strands. The first concerns the accumulating evidence that playing digital entertainment games, especially action games, leads to improvements on a range of perceptual, attentional and memory skills. While the link between these skills and learning may not seem immediately obvious, it has been argued that successful performance on visual-spatial tasks underlies success on the key STEM subjects (science, technology, engineering and mathematics) taught at school and university (Subrahmanyam & Greenfield, 1994; Christou, Jones, Mousoulides & Pittalis, 2006; Hung,

DOI: 10.4018/978-1-4666-4773-2.ch002

Copyright © 2014, IGI Global. Copying or distributing in print or electronic forms without written permission of IGI Global is prohibited.

Hwang, Lee & Su, 2012) and necessary for many 21st century jobs. The second strand of research concerns whether games, either entertainment or educational, can improve problem solving and reasoning abilities. High level thinking skills such as problem solving are increasingly acknowledged as important to effective learning (McGuinness, 1997) as well as underpinning the 21st century skills necessary for success in the workplace (National Research Council, 2010).

Serious games are games which are intentionally designed to promote learning, skill acquisition and behaviour change more generally (Boyle, Connolly and Hainey, 2011). Although studies of the benefits of serious games have been informed by pedagogical theories such as experiential learning (Kolb, 1984) and constructivism (Kebritchi & Hiruni, 2008), less attention has been paid to the actual cognitive mechanisms that support the learning process in games. In this chapter we argue that concepts from cognitive psychology which provide explanations of the benefits of games at the level of information processing can advance our understanding of how games support learning.

To date, cognitive accounts have been relatively neglected in research on serious games despite the fact that they offer explanations of the psychological mechanisms at an information processing level which can inform game design, development and evaluation. Although the existing evidence base clearly indicates the benefits of games, no clear and consistent distinction is currently made between the underlying cognitive structures and the skills they support. We propose that examining these gains from the cognitive information processing perspective of executive functions will help elucidate the psychological infrastructure that underpins these gains. Cognitive research distinguishes between lower level and higher level processing, where lower level processing refers to perception, attention and working memory and higher level processing refers to problem-solving, reasoning and decision making. Any information processing system requires control

and co-ordination and recent models of cognition have proposed that such control is exercised via executive functioning.

BACKGROUND

'Executive functions' are not straightforward to define. In early theoretical accounts, such as that of Baddeley and Hitch (1974), the central executive was conceptualised as a unitary system. However, the unitary concept of the central executive has undergone 'fractionation' (Baddeley & Della Sala, 1996, p. 1402) into a much wider range of processes which are subsumed under the term 'executive function'. For example, Miyake, Friedman, Emerson, Witzki, & Howerter (2000) carried out a confirmatory factor analysis of performance data from adults and found evidence for inter-related but dissociable contributions from the executive functions of shifting of attention, updating of working memory representations, and inhibition. Andersson (2008) offers an even more fine-grained analysis: 'The key elements of executive function include (a) anticipation and deployment of attention; (b) impulse control and self-regulation; (c) initiation of activity; (d) working memory; (e) mental flexibility and utilisation of feedback; (f) planning ability and organisation; and (g) selection of efficient problem solving strategies' (Andersson, 2008, p. 4).

In short, 'executive processes are responsible for the control of cognition and regulation of behaviour and thought and are intertwined with the notion of volition: the freedom to make appropriate (or inappropriate) choices from a set of possible choices' (Phillips, 1997, p. 186). A further distinction is made by Zelazo and Muller (2002) between 'cool' and 'hot' executive functions (EF) which has implications for an understanding of the processes underlying digital gaming. 'Cool' EF are those which underpin cognitive tasks, while in contrast, 'hot' EF relate to decision-making where the outcomes have some emotional significance, such as in competitive game-play. A note of caution is required however. As a result of the inter-related nature of EF, tasks of EF generally measure more than one executive function, referred to as 'task impurity' (Booth, Boyle and Kelly, 2010). This may lead to problems of interpreting task performance in studies of EF and serious computer games.

Executive functions change across the lifespan with rapid development through childhood, due to processes of myelination and organisation of the frontal lobes, until adulthood (Blakemore & Choudhury, 2006; Davidson, Amso, Anderson & Diamond, 2006) and then they decline in old age (Salthouse, Atkinson & Berish, 2003). Although there are no overall gender differences in the rate of development (Jerman & Swanson, 2005; O'Shaughnessy & Swanson, 1998), evidence indicates that females perform more strongly on verbal tasks, information processing and tasks of organisation and males on visual-spatial tasks (see Anderson, 2002). With regard to developmental impairments, poor executive functions are a feature of autism (Rajendran & Mitchell, 2007), ADHD (Tillman, Eninger, Forssman & Bohlin, (2011), and learning difficulties more generally (Danielsson, Henry, Messer & Rönnberg, 2012). Social factors such as early exposure to maternal depression (Hughes, Roman, Hart & Ensor, 2013), early deprivation (Loman, Johnson, Westerlund, Pollak, Nelson & Gunnar, 2012) and maltreatment by parents (Cicchetti, 2002) also impact upon the development of executive functions in children.

Executive functions in children and young people underpin attainments across a wide range of curricular areas such as mathematics (Andersson, 2008), science (St Clair-Thompson & Gathercole, 2002), language (Ellis Weismer, Evans, & Hesketh, 1999) and literacy (Gathercole & Pickering, 2000). They are associated with performance in the National Curriculum Tests in England and Wales (Gathercole & Pickering, 2000) and in learning across domains more generally (Bull, Espy, &

Wiebe, 2008). Many tasks used to assess executive functions are also used in test batteries to measure cognitive abilities more generally. This raises the question: are executive functions therefore distinctive from intelligence? Some researchers have argued that reasoning ability and working memory capacity are one and the same (Kyllonen & Christal, 1990). However a recent meta-analysis of correlations between working memory and measures of general intelligence carried out by Ackerman, Beier & Boyle (2005) indicated an overall adjusted correlation of the order of 0.48, which supports the view that measures of executive functions and intelligence while correlated, tap into different constructs.

There is considerable interest in the extent to which interventions as diverse as physical activity and computer training can improve executive functions in populations ranging from typically developing children and young people, children with impairments such as ADHD, autism, and learning disabilities, and older adults. In a recent systematic review, Tomporowski, Davis, Miller and Naglieri, (2008) report the benefits of programmes of moderate to vigorous physical activity in schools for measures of children's executive functions and academic attainment. Shipstead et al. (2012) in their systematic review report the findings from computer training interventions, many of which utilize the Cogmed (2013) adaptive working memory training programme. There are also a number of studies of the Jungle Memory programme (Alloway, 2012; Alloway, Bibile & Lau, 2013). While there is evidence that intervention programmes improve scores on some measures of working memory and other executive functions, Shipstead and colleagues argue that there is a need for stronger evidence of transfer effects to a broader range of measures of working memory and executive function, an issue with implications for research in digital games to which we shall return.

Executive Functions: An Integrative Framework

Using converging evidence from neuropsychological research and factor analytic studies Anderson (2002) operationalized elements of executive functions into an 'Executive Control System'. This model identifies four distinct, but also inter-related, component of EFs: (i) attentional control, (ii) information processing, (iii) cognitive flexibility, and (iv) goal setting.

This model offers a general information processing framework to situate and help integrate existing research on the cognitive benefits of games as it encompasses both lower and higher level cognitive processing, which have been the focus of much research attention in recent years. It also provides an information processing account that specifies not only structures and processes but also the interconnections between them. An understanding of these interactions is essential to our understanding of the origin and transfer of games-related benefits. We will provide an outline of how the components of this executive function model are relevant to games before moving onto a detailed discussion of the research evidence indicating how the components of executive functions support, and may be developed by, game play.

Within this system, the attentional control components include *selective attention* (the ability to select specific stimuli to attend to and to concentrate on for sustained periods of time), *self-regulation* and *self-monitoring* (the ability to initiate, monitor and terminate processes) and *inhibition* (the ability to inhibit both irrelevant information and 'pre-potent' (i.e. dominant) responses which are not appropriate to the task in hand). Problems with these attentional control components will be associated with impulsivity, problems in task completion, poor error correction and inappropriate responding which would have an adverse impact upon performance in serious computer games. The information-processing components include *fluency*, *efficiency* and *speed*

of processing. These components reflect the individual's reaction times to stimuli as a function of efficiency of the brain and nervous system. Problems here in slow reaction times will also adversely affect performance in computer games. The cognitive flexibility components include *divided attention* (the ability to split attentional processes and resources across different sources of information and responses at the same time), *working memory* (a limited-capacity and time-limited active memory system with the ability to store and simultaneously process information), *conceptual transfer* (the ability to transfer a solution from one problem to another and hence to develop alternative strategies) and *feedback utilisation* (the ability to adapt to and learn from feedback). Problems with these components will be associated with persisting with unsuccessful strategies and hence in problems in learning from experience. Finally, the goal-setting components include *initiative* (the ability to generate new ideas), *conceptual reasoning* (problem-solving abilities), *planning* (the ability to devise the implementation of actions) and *strategic organisation* (the ability to coordinate strategies). Problems with these components will be associated with poor problem-solving, planning and lack of co-ordination.

Executive Functions and Digital Games

There is a growing evidence base showing that players of digital action games perform better on a range of attentional and perceptual skills than non-game players. Given the number, unpredictability and fast paced nature of the visual stimuli within action games, it is unsurprising that players improve in these skills.

Several studies have compared game players and non-game players on a variety of cognitive tasks. Green and Bavelier (2006a) showed that action gaming enhances visual-spatial attention both in peripheral vision and in more central vision, while Green and Bavelier (2006b) found that game players performed more accurately than non-game players on an enumeration task where players had to say how many squares were present when an array of squares was flashed up quickly on a screen. They also found that game players were better than non-players at tracking multiple objects simultaneously, with game players being able to track on average two more items than non-players. Green and Bavelier (2003) investigated performance on a flanker compatibility task, where players had to respond to a stimulus in the presence of a compatible or incompatible distracting stimulus. They found that, as the task became more difficult, game players' performance did not decline, whereas non-game players' performance did decline, suggesting that game players have greater attentional capacity than non-game players. Boot, Kramer, Simons, Fabiani and Gratton (2008) examined whether the benefits of playing games extended to a broader range of cognitive abilities. They found advantages for game-players on visual short term memory and task switching tasks, but they also found non-significant differences on several tasks where previous research had reported differences between game players and non-game players.

Rather than comparing game players and non-game players, another approach to studying the impact of playing games on cognition has been to train non-game players on games to establish whether practice leads to improvements in performance on visual perceptual tasks. Barlett, Vowels, Shanteau, Crow & Miller (2009) found that playing video games for even a short time led to improvements in performance on working memory, addition, auditory perception and selective attention tasks. Feng, Spence & Pratt (2007) found that giving females experience in playing an action video game reduced gender differences in mental rotation and useful-field-of-view (UFOV) tasks. This UFOV task assesses how players perceive objects in the periphery of vision and the extent of the field of vision over which information can be extracted.

While there is evidence that playing games alters varied aspects of visual and attentional processing, there is no agreement about the source and explanations of these effects (Green & Bavelier, 2012). We argue here that progress can be made in providing a more coherent explanation of the effects of games by examining them from the perspective of Anderson's model of executive functions. Playing action games impacts on all four of the components of Anderson's model of executive functioning: information processing, attentional control, cognitive flexibility, and goal setting. We will consider each of these in turn.

Information Processing: One of the best documented benefits of playing action games is the speeding of reaction times, with action game players showing a 10%-12% reaction time advantage over non-players (Dye, Green, & Bavelier, 2009), with no detrimental effect on accuracy. This would suggest that playing action games makes game players faster, more efficient, more fluent processors of information than non-gamers. There is evidence too that playing games can reduce or eliminate the attentional blink (Green and Bavelier, 2003). This is a hiatus in information processing experienced when individuals are asked to process a second target item 200–500 ms after having identified the first one. Recovery from the attentional blink is faster in game-players, again suggesting that game players are faster, more efficient processors of information.

The rapid processing required in action games has been examined as one of the factors that lead to the feelings of immersion that players experience in playing games. Jennett, Cox, Cairns, Dhoparee, Epps, Tijs and Walton (2008) carried out a preliminary investigation looking at the relationship between the pace of a game and immersion in the game, but found inconclusive evidence. However temporal processing in games is clearly worth further investigation. Game players frequently report that their experience of time is altered while playing games to the extent that they are unaware of time passing (Sweetser and Wyeth,

2005). This is regarded as a key characteristic of subjective experiences of immersion and flow reported in the literature. Psychological research on attention and executive functioning may offer insights into the experiential dimension of time and the psychological infrastructure that supports our temporal abilities may offer insight into issues concerning immersion and flow (Terras & Ramsay, in press). Although there is a substantial knowledge base in psychology concerning temporal processing in traditional learning contexts, our understanding remains limited with respect to the processing of temporal information within games and in on-line contexts. Given that attention and executive functioning play a major explanatory role in explanations of the subjective experience of time, most notably the Attentional Gate Model (Zakay, 2000), it is likely that these mechanisms also support the ability to monitor and make temporal judgements in virtual contexts (Terras & Ramsay, in press). There is a need to consider both physical (objective) time and psychological (subjective) time. Physical time is linear, continuous and measured in standardised units such as seconds, hours, and days. Psychological time is non-linear, discrete and unique as it is context dependent (Zakay, 2012). Understanding how time is experienced, monitored and allocated in on-line and virtual contexts might allow links to be made between cognitive processing and affective experience in games.

Attentional Control and Cognitive Flexibility: Theories of attention are central to cognitive explanations of the impact of entertainment games. Two of the components of Anderson's EF model, attentional control and cognitive flexibility, focus on attention. Attention is traditionally sub-classified as either focused or divided with each conception having its own specific theoretical explanations. Research on focused attention explores issues concerning our ability to focus attention on a single task or object or location in space and our ability to cope with irrelevant information and inhibit distractions (List & Robertson, 2007). In

Anderson's model focused attention is located in the attentional control component. In contrast, divided attention research examines issues concerning automaticity and dual task performance, more generally known as multitasking. Within Anderson's system, divided attention is located in the cognitive flexibility component. The fact that attention is a flexible resource that can utilised in a variety of ways to support the information processing demands of a task makes it an important process that must be monitored and controlled by executive functioning. There is evidence that playing games might lead to improvements in both the attentional control and cognitive flexibility systems.

There is much debate in the literature over the control of attention - how much attention is under our conscious control and how much is unconscious? Such issues are reflected by the distinction between endogenous and exogenous attention where attention is intentionally controlled or automatically captured by environmental stimuli (Posner, 1980). This distinction reflects the flow of control, top-down or bottom-up, with attention being capable of being goal directed or stimulus driven. This distinction is further defined with reference to neuropsychological data, with the identification of the posterior (stimulus-driven) attention system responsible for the shifting and engagement and disengagement of attention, and the anterior attention system, a more goal directed system akin to the central executive component of working memory (Posner & Peterson 1990). This complexity and flexibility of attentional control is what makes it such an essential cognitive mechanism.

Insight into the cognitive basis of games-related benefits may be derived from an understanding not only of the factors that facilitate the allocation of attention and dual task performance but also from an appreciation of the processes underlying the development of automaticity. Findings indicate that automatic processes often come with practice and that the automatic performance of tasks/skills is less resource intensive. Shiffrin and Schneider (1977) discussed how controlled processing requires attention, is capacity limited and can be used flexibly to meeting changing task or environmental demands. On the other hand, automatic processes are not so constrained by capacity, do not require attention, and lack flexibility and variability once acquired. Although it is possible to make this distinction in theory, evidence suggests that in practice such a division is not so clear cut, with many tasks involving a mix of automatic and controlled processes.

Understanding of factors that support the development of automaticity may inform our understanding of the games-related benefits and their possible transfer. Playing games also leads to the increased ability of players to focus attention and ignore irrelevant distracters. For example the superior performance of game players on the flanker compatibility task reported by Green and Bavelier (2003) suggests that game players are better at ignoring irrelevant distractors than non-game players. This is consistent with the inhibition sub-component of Anderson's attentional control component.

Effective attentional control is a key component of executive functioning and Green and Bavelier (2012) have recently argued that many of the attentional effects found in games are related to greater control of top-down attention, rather than increases in automatic processing of visual stimuli. Green and Bavelier propose that action game play enhances top-down aspects of attention by allowing gamers to allocate their resources more flexibly. Consistent with this proposal is that several of the benefits of playing action games fit best into the cognitive flexibility subcomponent of Anderson's EF model. Divided attention research examines issues concerning automaticity and dual task performance, more generally known as multitasking. For example Colzato, van Leeuwen, van den Wildenberg and Hommel (2010), Karle, Watter and Shedden (2010) and Boot et al (2008) found that experience with action video games

improves the ability to proficiently task switch. Further, Colzato et al. reported that game players performed better than non-game players on a task switching paradigm that provides a relatively well-established diagnostic measure of cognitive flexibility. Participants were required to manually press a button in response to either a global (large) or a local (small) stimulus. The target response was cued by figures presented to the sides of a target stimulus and the cues changed from one stimulus to another.

This task switching ability may generalise beyond action-based manual responses to different modality responses such as vocal responses and even to wider level cognitive activities such as goal related switching. A controlled training study indicated a causal relationship between game play and the reduction in the cognitive costs associated with switching (Green, Sugarman, Medford, Klobusicky, & Bavelier, 2012). The accumulating evidence highlights the usefulness of action game-based interventions generally for improving reaction time and task switching in particular.

While task switching has been studied more extensively in the visual domain, it seems likely that it may also operate across modalities. The bulk of cognitive research has addressed attentional modalities separately, with the majority being focused on visual attention. More recently cross modal attention has been explored with renewed interest and enthusiasm with research exploring how information from two or more sensory modalities is integrated and co-ordinated (Driver & Spence, 1998). Findings highlight the importance of visual information, and that sounds can be misperceived as coming from their apparent visual source as demonstrated by the ventriloquist illusion. The importance of visual information in auditory processing is also shown in the 'McGurk Effect' (McGurk and MacDonald, 1976), an illusion whereby the pairing of the auditory component of one sound with the visual component of a second sound results in the perception of a third sound. An appreciation of the processes that underlie and influence our cross-modal perceptual abilities may help inform the design of both action and serious games.

The cognitive flexibility that games support is becoming an ever more important skill. In recent years the availability and the sophistication of technology have led to increasing simultaneous use of multiple forms of media. Over the past 10 years there has been a 20% increase in media use and a 120% increase in media multitasking by American youths (Becker, Alzahabi & Hopwood, 2012). This changing behaviour places increased demands on our executive ability to allocate attention across a range of tasks/inputs. As discussed earlier, research on dual task performance has a long established history within cognitive psychology as a research strand within attentional research and recently, research has begun to systematically evaluate whether the multitasking skills used during video game play generalise to other tasks. Current research findings are contradictory, potentially attributable to methodological variations. Findings from some recent methodologically rigorous studies indicate that experimentally controlled experience with action games improved multi-tasking ability via increased attentional capacity (Chiappe, Conger, Liao, Caldwell, & Vu, 2013). Less encouraging are the findings of Donohue, James, Eslick and Mitroff (2012) who demonstrated that although action gamers showed an advantage in single task performance on tasks tapping the coordination of visual and motor skills, they showed a decline in performance when dual tasking. However, it should be noted that gamers showed less decline on performance on the primary task than non-gamers. Interestingly, both gamers and non-gamers displayed a similar drop in their ability to multitask in task involving multiple-object tracking and visual search.

Although lab-based studies with their high degree of experimental control and standardisation are essential, it is also informative to explore multi-tasking in more ecologically valid settings. Insight into the reasons why people engage in multi-tasking in everyday life highlight the importance of appreciating people's motivations for doing so and their ability to assess the disadvantages of multitasking. Sanbonmatsu, Strayer, Medeiros-Ward and Watson (2013) examined participants' actual and perceived multi-tasking ability and found that people tended to overestimate their competence at multi-tasking and that this overconfidence was related to the amount of multitasking they engaged in everyday life. Interestingly, the participants with the best objectively measured ability to multi-task were less likely to do so, while those who are less able were more likely to do so. They explained their findings with reference to the participants' ability to control their attention (links to executive functioning) and proposed that individuals may engage in frequent multi-tasking because they are easily distracted, therefore finding it difficult to concentrate on a single task. Their findings also indicate that high levels of multitasking are significantly correlated with sensation-seeking personality traits, suggesting that certain individuals may choose to engage in multi-tasking behaviour as it offers stimulation and challenges and that such stimulation may be prioritised. Such findings are important because they highlight the significant contribution of individual differences. Traditionally cognitive research has focused on group level behaviour and has been criticised for neglecting the influence of socio-emotional and personality factors, as well as general individual variation in cognitive abilities. In recent years the benefits that can be gained by considering individual differences is being recognised (Kane & Engle, 2002). With respect to multitasking, recent evidence indicates a high degree of variation with a small number of individuals, so- called "supertaskers", being highly proficient at allocating their cognitive resources across a number of tasks (Watson & Strayer, 2010).

Working Memory: Working memory is a further sub-component of cognitive flexibility in Anderson's model. The most widely accepted view of working memory is that proposed by Baddeley (1998) where working memory is conceptualized as an active "scratch pad" that supports the active processing of information. It comprises two "slave" systems, namely a phonological loop that processes verbal and written information and a visuo-spatial scratch pad that processes visual and spatial data. Crucially it also comprises an executive or supervisory facility that oversees this processing. In particular, it prioritises information to which attentional resources should be allocated, and integrates new information with previously stored material in long-term memory. This model of the central executive was an early model of executive functions. Working memory plays a central role in the processing of incoming information in the forms of text (written words or full sentences), sounds, speech, images (static or dynamic) and in guiding the individual's response to such information. Clearly, these constitute activities that are commonplace when engaging with multimedia, multimodal, digital learning materials such as digital games.

A number of studies have suggested that some of the visual-perceptual benefits of games are attributable to the superior visual short-term memory of gamers. Boot et al. (2008) found that game players outperformed non-gamers on a visual short term memory task where players had to detect change on a multiple object tracking task at higher speeds. Green and Bavelier (2006) attributed the improvements that they found on object enumeration and tracking tasks to improvements in working memory. They found that the benefits of games appear to be due to enhanced counting ability rather than to improvements in the number of items which can be immediately apprehended and argued that this was possibly due to a longer lasting visual memory trace. An alternative explanation was that not all items are kept active in working memory at the same time, but rather that

items are refreshed in a cyclic refreshing process where attention is focused on each item in turn and gamers have a faster rate of cycling through the items in memory than non-gamers.

The discussion so far has highlighted the well-documented visual-perceptual and attentional benefits of playing games and argued that these are evident in three of the four components of Anderson's EF model: games lead to faster, more efficient information processing, greater top-down attentional control, greater cognitive flexibility and improved working memory. The advantages of games in these three components have been studied in entertainment games, although the games were not intentionally designed to support these skills.

Goal Setting and Higher Level Cognitive Functioning: The fourth component of Anderson's EF model, the goal setting component, includes the sub-components: initiative, planning, conceptual reasoning and strategic organization. These skills underlie higher order thinking and problem solving. Goal setting reflects the literature on problem solving which suggests that setting goals provides an important means of constraining the search space for a problem and this helps to focus on a solution. Initiative is a creative component helping to generate new approaches to tackling problems. Planning and strategic organization provide a means of thinking ahead and organizing available resources and strategies to tackle problems.

Researchers have looked for evidence of these higher level thinking and problem solving skills in entertainment games (Bottino, Ferlino, Ott & Tavella, 2007), but the ability of games to support these skills is the focus of research in serious games and educational games. Several authors have claimed that digital games have the potential to be at their most useful in supporting higher level thinking such as problem solving, critical thinking, decision making, argumentation and hypothesis testing (Dondlinger, 2007; Dede, 2000; Beck, 2005; Gee, 2003, 2005; Barab & Dede, 2007). Johnson et al (2011) claimed that "the greatest potential of games for learning lies in their ability to foster collaboration, problem-solving, and procedural thinking". Razak et al (2012) found that problem solving was the top-rated skill that primary school teachers felt that digital games could support. Despite these optimistic claims, much of the existing evidence concerning the effectiveness of educational games in learning relates to how well they support content understanding and knowledge acquisition rather than reasoning and problem solving (Connolly et al, 2012).

One of the difficulties which has to be tackled in looking at how games support higher level thinking and problem solving lies in characterizing exactly what we mean by problem solving. This difficulty was evident in the earliest research carried out by Newell and Simon (1972). In their ground-breaking research, reported in their book "Human Problem Solving", these authors aimed to identify very general approaches to problem solving which would operate across different subject disciplines, domains and types of problems. Despite their optimism, it soon became clear that Newell and Simon's goal of developing a "general problem solver" was elusive since both the kinds of problems that people face and the strategies they use to solve them are very diverse and frequently domain specific.

Cognitive research on problem solving has identified two generic approaches to solving problems which are widely used in education and business as a way of tackling complex problems and are of relevance to thinking about problem solving in games. The first approach is the cyclic approach to solving problems which proposes that it is useful to view problem solving as a cyclic process with different stages where different subproblems are tackled at each stage. The very simple "plan, do, review" heuristic is consistent with this idea, and Kolb's (1984) theory of experiential learning which proposes four different stages in the learning process also reflects the cyclic nature of tackling problems. The second general approach is problem space theory, which proposes

that in solving problems it is frequently useful to construct a mental representation of the problem and all possible "states" of the problem, called the problem space (Newell and Simon, 1972). Solutions to the problem would be viewed as ways of getting to the goal state from the starting state in the state space representation.

These two generic approaches to problem solving have been applied to many different kinds of problem and can also be applied to the thinking required in digital games. The cycle of activities in games with different activities relevant at different stages in the game seems to reflect the cyclic problem solving structure well, so much so that Kiili and Ketamo (2007) view the cyclic process as at the heart of problem-based learning in games. Similarly problem space theory describes the different possible states in playing a game and the different paths through a game. Spires et al (2011) examined how players explored and worked their way through the "hypothesis space" of a scientific problem solving game and found that the extent to which players did this was predictive of successful learning in the game.

Similar difficulties in characterizing higher level thinking and problem solving emerged for educators aiming to identify the thinking skills promoted by non-digital entertainment games such as chess, Go, Monopoly, crosswords, Suduko and logic puzzles. While there is optimism that these games support "generic" cognitive and problem solving skills, we still lack a clear understanding of the precise skills and operations that these games support and a systematic mapping of these with respect to curricular outcomes. Huang, Chen and Chang (2007) acknowledged that although puzzles can facilitate forms of thinking which are valuable, they are not necessarily the skills required in the curriculum. Games in the classroom have been used more as an extension activity mainly to engage pupils or as a reward for completing work. There has also been concern that skills learned in games are not transferable to thinking about problems in the real world. Chase and Simon (1973) showed that expert chess players' memories for board positions of pieces was better than that of non-players but only for "real" games and not for randomly placed pieces.

Related to the lack of general problem solving strategies, the diverse nature of problems raises a further difficulty in this area. It has been useful to categorise different kinds of thinking and cognitive psychologists have distinguished problem solving, reasoning, creativity and judgement and decision making as requiring different kinds of thinking with respect to the structure of the problems addressed and the operations required (Eysenck and Keane, 2010).

Jonassen (1997) made an important contribution to problem solving research by categorising different kinds of problems in terms of their structuredness, complexity, dynamicity, and domain specificity or abstractness. Well-structured problems are clearly stated, the solution follows clearly and unambiguously from the information given and the solver has knowledge of a solution procedure. Ill-structured problems tend to be complex problems where neither the problem itself nor the solution is evident. Many of the problems which we face in everyday life are of the latter kind, although Jonassen viewed problems as existing on a continuum from well-structured to ill-structured. Using these dimensions and others, Jonassen (2004) categorized different kinds of problems with respect to similarities in the characteristics that they might have. He distinguished logical problems, algorithm problems, story problems, rule-use problems, decision making problems, troubleshooting problems, diagnosis–solution problems, strategic performance problems, case analysis problems, design problems and dilemma problems. These problems differ with respect to how well or ill-structured they are, how abstract they are, the contexts in which they would typically be encountered, what would be regarded as a successful solution and, most importantly from the perspective of executive functioning, the operations required to solve them.

While the goal setting component of Anderson's EF model is most relevant to higher level thinking and problem solving, the EF model is an integrative model which looks at how different components work together in tackling problems. Processes across all components of the EF model will be required to tackle many complex problems of the kind included in digital games. Different combinations of component skills will be required to tackle different kinds of problems. The EF model highlights the relationship between other elements of executive functions and offers insight into how low-level processing may support higher level thinking skills, e. g. how effective information processing, self-regulation and cognitive flexibility support conceptual reasoning and planning.

Meta-Cognition and Self-Regulation

It is increasingly recognized that an important aspect of successful problem solving and learning is our awareness of how we process information and our ability to reflect on how we learn, i. e. meta-cognition and self-regulation. Meta-cognitive learners will plan how they will approach a task, monitor their performance as the execute it and evaluate their success on the task when they have completed it. Self-regulation (SRL) is a related construct which specifies that the learner has to take responsibility for their own learning (Zimmerman, 2002). Learners who have good meta-cognitive and self-regulation skills will be more effective learners and problem solvers.

Models of metacognition and self-regulation are similar to models of executive functions in that both are models of higher order regulatory and control processes that coordinate lower level information processing and underlie complex thinking and learning. The difference between Anderson's EF model and Zimmerman's model of self-regulation is that Anderson's EF model is a structural model of different cognitive components, whereas Zimmerman's model is a temporal model of different stages in learning. In Anderson's EF model, characteristics of self-regulation are distributed across the different components: planning is included in the goal setting component of Anderson's EF model, while self-regulation and self-monitoring are viewed as part of the attentional control system and feedback utilisation is part of the cognitive flexibility component.

The planning, monitoring and evaluation activities carried out by self-regulated learners are like the scaffolding provided by more able learners in helping novice learners to progress to higher levels of understanding as described by Vygotsky (1978). Self-regulated learners are able to provide their own scaffolding by asking themselves key questions as they proceed. The use of metacognitive strategies should provide learners with an effective means of coordinating information in tackling complex ill-defined problems, testing hypotheses and making effective decisions.

There is much optimism that digital games can help players to self-regulate by providing scaffolding for them as they carry out tasks. Zap and Code (2009) propose that "electronic games are unique in that they initiate self-regulatory processes through their inherent design". Games provide goals which help players to set targets. They also provide continuous feedback about performance by allowing players to evaluate how close they are to attaining their goals. Games can also provide opportunities for players to reflect on their learning. Games can include prompts, hints, tips and other features at key points during play which can make players more aware of their learning and can help in transferring knowledge from the game to the real world. In this way games can provide support for students in solving more difficult problems than they would otherwise be able to.

A number of studies have examined how digital games incorporate scaffolding for learning. Kim, Park and Baek (2009) found that introducing support in the form of the modeling and thinking aloud strategies helped to increase students' performance in learning basic economic concepts. Lee and Chen (2009) found that specific prompts were

more useful than and led to better performance than general prompts, especially on a more difficult version of a "frog leaping" task. Kiili and Ketamo (2007) found that conflicts, competition, visualization of performance, communication with other players and challenging comments of game characters acted as triggers for reflection in a game.

Games and Problem Solving

Progress in understanding how games can support higher level thinking will be made by examining how specific kinds of games can support specific kinds of thinking. O'Brien (2011) applied Jonassen's categorization of problems to games examining which kind of problem solving different types of game might support. Game genre provides an established classification of entertainment games based on common activities required in games and we have examined how one genre, action games, supports faster, more efficient processing of information. There is less agreement in the literature about how to categorise genre with respect to educational games. However, O'Brien distinguished linear games, competitive games, strategy games and role playing games and tried to relate these games genre to the different cognitive functions which they support. Linear games such as puzzles and first person shooter games require linear logic; competitive games such as sports and combat games require logic plus prediction of the actions of other players; strategy games such as war and management games require strategic planning and management of a complex system and role playing games, including Massively Multiplayer Online Games (MMOGs), require complex problem solving in a complex environment. O'Brien proposed that all game types have the potential to support problem solving and reasoning but that strategy and role play games are better suited for supporting poorly structured problems and complex decision making. Role playing games provide concrete activities which support domain specific problem solving.

A few empirical studies have examined higher level thinking in entertainment games. Bottino et al (2007) identified some of the general cognitive abilities and skills that playing mind games such as Mastermind, Minefield, Battleship, Chinese Checkers and Labyrinth supports: adapting to different situations according to changing data and constraints, formulating and verifying a hypothesis, looking forward and anticipating, conceiving a solution strategy, generalizing from concrete and specific cases, using the feedback provided, revising the work done and orienteering in the space and discriminating visual stimuli. Bottino, Ott and Tavella (2008) compared the performance of experimental groups of fourth grade primary school children who had played the games with that of control groups who had not on language, science and mathematics tests which included items on logical reasoning. They found higher means for the experimental groups, although they did not report whether these differences were statistically significant. They concluded that the evidence suggests reasons to be optimistic "about the positive impact of the proposed activities on pupils' logical and strategic reasoning skills."

Blumberg, Rosenthal & Randall (2008) looked at whether playing the digital entertainment game, Sonic the Hedgehog 2, helped players to develop successful problem solving strategies. Using think aloud protocols, comments made by frequent and infrequent adult video game players while playing this game, were collected and coded according to the categories: cognitive processes, goal orientation, affective evaluation, game orientation and context orientation. Comments made as a result of encountering an impasse in the game were of particular interest as these might suggest that games can help players to think of new solutions to problems. The results indicate that frequent players made significantly more insight and game strategy comments during game play than infrequent players but they did not seem to apply their game knowledge to tackling impasses in the game.

Scientific reasoning requires complex thinking in the area of hypothesis testing or developing arguments supported by evidence. It requires consideration of multiple perspectives on an issue where frequently the evidence and the arguments are disputed. Research has explored the benefits of both entertainment games and educational games on these skills. Ramler and Chapman (2011) described the use of the popular entertainment game, 'Guitar Hero', to teach the different stages in the design and execution of a research project. Playing this game provided students with an opportunity to develop hypotheses, collect and analyse data, and draw conclusions. For example, participants could test a hypothesis about the distribution of missing notes in playing such as: "Notes are missed completely as random". While this paper reports an innovative use of an entertainment game in teaching higher order thinking, the game was not evaluated.

Steinkuehler and Duncan (2008) carried out an in-depth qualitative study to examine whether playing an entertainment game could support higher level scientific reasoning and argumentation skills. They analysed the scientific reasoning skills displayed by players in their contributions to the online discussion boards while they played the popular Massively Multiplayer Online Role-playing game (MMORPG), World of Warcraft (WoW). Steinkuehler and Duncan developed a rigorous coding system for these contributions based on the benchmarks of the AAAS (1993) for scientific reasoning and Chinn and Malhotra's (2002) theoretical framework for evaluating enquiry tasks. They found that WoW players demonstrate an impressive variety of higher order scientific reasoning skills in these fora, such as using data and argument, building on others' ideas and using system based reasoning. Contributions to discussion boards provided evidence of the kind of higher level evaluative thinking demonstrated in discussion, knowledge sharing and debate. The study did not include a control condition, and in fact it is difficult to specify a suitable control.

Several papers examined educational games which were specifically designed to teach reasoning and scientific reasoning skills. Ko (2002) found that most 10 year olds used logical strategies rather than simply guessing in a logical inference game, whereas 7 year olds were just as likely to guess. Lanzilotti and Roselli (2007) tested the impact of a Hypermedia Tutoring System on helping 9-10 years old children to learn basic concepts of logic, such as understanding conditional statements. They found that children in the game group were more highly motivated than those taught by the teacher, but performance of the hypermedia group on the logical test was no better than the control group. Similar results were found by Wang, Tsai, Chou and Hung (2010) in using educational games to teach logic. They found an improvement in motivation but not performance. Kordaki (2012) found more encouraging results in using a card game to teach primary children basic principles of analogical reasoning in the binary system, but only a qualitative analysis was conducted.

The promotion of scientific literacy amongst the general population is a topical issue. Scientific literacy is defined as "solving personally challenging yet meaningful scientific problems as well as making, responsible socio-scientific decisions" (Holbrook & Rannikmae, 2009, p 275). Halpern, Millis, Graesser, Butler, Forsyth and Cai (2012) cite the example of fitness shoes which claim that they help to develop "more shapely legs and a better butt" (sic). In 2010, consumers spent $1.1 dollars on these shoes, despite the fact that there was no evidence to support this claim. Halpern et al argue that people need to be encouraged to acquire more evaluative and better evidenced approaches to making everyday judgements of this kind.

Halpern et al (2012) described the development of the game, Operation ARA, which aims to teach critical thinking and scientific reasoning skills to undergraduates. Halpern is well-known for her contribution to research on critical thinking and the game was explicitly designed using principles derived from the literature on effective learning and critical thinking. Operation ARA was an adventure/mystery game aimed at teaching players statistical and methodological concepts. Early evaluation of the game was encouraging with students who played the game having significantly higher proportional learning gains than students who did not play the game.

Asbell-Clarke et al (2012) were influenced by their observations that players of MMOGs are actively engaged in activities which have close parallels with the problem solving and reasoning activities of professional scientists in tracking down and analysing data. They developed a mystery game, Martian Boneyards, which aimed to help players develop skills of systematic scientific enquiry in the area of paleontology. The results showed that players spend a lot of time gathering data, but also have opportunities to analyse data and look at how the evidence that they collected supported specific theories. This study was interesting in showing that a collaborative game could be used in the same way as science develops by players collaborating to collect evidence which might support or contradict specific theories. The use of games in scientific reasoning is at an early stage in development and high quality evaluation of games is required.

There is a long history of using non-digital simulations and role-playing games in businesses and organisations to support complex decision making. Typically complex scenarios are presented and players have to make decisions, solve problems or develop strategies to deal with these multifaceted problems from different perspectives. For example, Schwartz and Teach (2002) described the congruence game, a non-digital game, which illustrated the importance of making decisions which consider congruence between personnel and strategy in maximising performance in business environments. Digital games provide ideal opportunities to support and extend these complex decision making environments. Jonasson's categorization of problem solving suggested that strategy and role play games will be more useful in complex decision making because these problems tend to be ill-structured and frequently present opposing views. Mayer, Carton, de Jong, Leijten and Dammers (2004) demonstrated that games can provide complex scenarios which support real world real decision-making and higher level thinking and planning skills in the domain of development planning and urban networks. Similarly Zwikael and Gonen's (2007) Project Execution Game (PEG) was targeted at improving students' project management knowledge by training them to manage the kind of unexpected, real life problems that might crop up during a project's execution. In a before/after study, Zwikael and Gonen showed that students who played PEG gained more practical relevant experience and consequently showed improvements in project management knowledge after the game compared with before. Decision making games have also been developed to train military decision making. Again the diversity of problems which emerge is a challenge, but Caird-Daley and Harris (2007) propose that decision making skills such as situation awareness, metacognition and resource management, as well as more situation specific skills, can be trained. The existing evidence clearly indicates the potential of digital games for creating immersive, experiential learning environments for decision making, but as Caird-Daley et al point out, this potential has yet to realized.

Another potential area for development is the creation of games. Although most attention has been paid to how playing games might improve players' performance in the areas supported by the game, a few researchers have examined how creating games can help players to think more effectively. Vos, van der Meijden and Denessen (2011) compared intrinsic motivation, the use of deep learning strategies and achievement in understanding Dutch proverbs in children who played a game with children in a group who constructed their own game. They found that the children who constructed games were more motivated along

the dimensions competence, interest and effort, used more deep learning strategies and performed better than those who simply played games. This suggests that children find the active experience of creating a game engaging and that this helps them to apply themselves to the task resulting in improved performance.

The Utility of the Information Processing Approach of Executive Functions

In this chapter we have argued that adopting the cognitive perspective of executive functions can help to provide a finer grained understanding of the advantages that games can offer, clarify the mechanisms that underlie the benefits of playing digital games and extend our understanding of how digital games support learning. Furthermore applying models of executive functions to digital games can help to develop a more coherent and integrated framework for understanding the cognitive gains linked to playing games. We have focused on two main areas where games benefit learning, attention and perceptual skills and problem solving and metacognition.

The strongest and most rigorous evidence for the benefits of games comes from the studies which show that playing action video games leads to improvements in performance on a range of attentional and perceptual tasks. This literature has been rather fragmented and we have argued that Anderson's model of executive functions can help to provide a more organised theoretical framework for understanding these gains. The perceptual and attentional advantages linked to playing games can be located within three of the four components of Anderson's model of executive functioning: games lead to more efficient information processing, greater cognitive flexibility and improved attentional control.

While there is now a large pool of evidence about these gains, it should be pointed out that concerns about the quality of the research on the cognitive effects of action games have been raised. For example, Boot et al (2008) found null results on many of the tasks where others had previously reported effects of action games and, more recently, Boot et al (2012) have suggested that most of the research in this area includes design flaws of various kinds. It is clear that further carefully controlled research needs to be carried out in the area to clarify the exact nature and scope of games-derived benefits.

Methodologically the evidence about the effectiveness of games in supporting higher order thinking tends to be of lower quality than the evidence about the impact of games on visual-perceptual skills. Cognitive research has highlighted the complex nature of problem solving and difficulties in identifying generalisable problem solving skills. Anderson's EF theory helped to explain why problem solving is complex. It highlights the goal setting component as key to problem solving but also shows how metacognitive components, which are key to the control and regulatory aspects of cognition, are dispersed throughout the different components of the model. Executive functions play an important supervisory role in controlling and managing lower level cognitive processing and in the deployment of effective strategies. Different kinds of problem will require different components of the model, leading to distinctive patterns of interactions between components.

With respect to entertainment games, Bottino et al (2008) identified a number of skills that mind games can support, while Steinkuehler and Duncan's (2008) qualitative analysis indicated that players of World of Warcraft are engaging in high level argument about the game in their discussion boards. However there have been few rigorous quantitative studies looking at how entertainment games support problem solving. Studies looking at how serious games can support problem solving have been even more piecemeal. We looked at examples of educational games which support problem solving, reasoning, hypothesis testing, scientific reasoning and decision making. The

skills and strategies which are supported in games seem to depend on the precise characteristics of the problem domain under study and exactly how the game is implemented in terms of game mechanics, feedback etc. There has been an absence of guidelines about which kinds of games might be useful for which kinds of thinking, although O'Brien's attempt to identify game types which might support specific kinds of problems provides a useful initial framework. Consideration of metacognition and self-regulation in games showed how opportunities can be provided to support more effective problem solving in games via prompts, hints, reflections and feedback.

FUTURE RESEARCH DIRECTIONS

As noted earlier, although the evidence base demonstrating the benefits of games for developing both low and high level skills is rapidly expanding, it contains not only methodologically flawed evidence but also lacks coherence and integration. It is necessary not only to clearly specify the nature and extent of the outcomes of games that are being assessed but also to recognise that an understanding of the reasons (i.e. psychological basis) for these benefits is required. Such an in-depth understanding of the source of game-derived benefits is required if the educational potential of games is to be realised. When outcomes are considered from an information processing perspective, the specification of the psychological infrastructure (structures, knowledge and processes) is essentially the aim of contemporary cognitive psychology. Therefore there is a need to raise awareness of the theories that are available and the insights that they may offer.

While we focused upon Anderson's model of executive functioning in this chapter, there are alternative accounts, such as that of Diamond (2013), for example, which proposes inhibitory control, working memory and cognitive flexibility as key components feeding into the higher level executive functions of reasoning, problem solving and planning which are linked to fluid intelligence. Future research should explore how such models can account for the benefits of games.

The current apparent lack of cross-fertilisation in terms of approaches and theories most likely reflects the developing nature of the field, with more integration and appreciation of the strengths of contributing disciplines occurring over time. In addition further integration and understanding of the benefits of games could come from broader consideration of the kinds of evidence to support claims about games.

To date evaluations of higher level thinking in games have been largely qualitative, largely due to the complex nature of decision making, difficulty in clearly articulating what the outcomes might be and possible difficulties in identifying suitable controls. A potential way forward for research in higher level thinking in games lies in better methods of evaluations and design with clearly specified and testable outcomes. Just as theories of executive functioning serve to co-ordinate our understanding of information processing, a framework is needed to integrate and assimilate research and theory concerning the evaluation and development of games.

Research in neuroscience is relevant here. A recent review of neuro-science paradigms used to evaluate the attentional and working memory benefits associated with games and game-based training highlights the importance of developing a shared understanding of rigorous methodology in order to promote comparability in research findings and subsequent meta-analysis (Mishra, Bavelier & Gazzaley, 2012). We support and fully endorse these proposals and further argue that psychologically driven insights should lie at the core, making a major contribution in addressing the issues concerning the use, application, advantages and disadvantages from a multidisciplinary perspective which supports the use of converging evidence from different methodologies and theoretical perspectives to help promote understanding

of the process that underpin benefits and inform the development of educational uses of games and their associated interventions.

Maximising the Benefits of Games: Transfer and Overcoming Constraints

If the learning potential of games is to be maximized then we must understand why these benefits occur and how the positive impacts, especially skills, may transfer. Interestingly, and in contrast to other forms of training, such as working memory training that have limited long term benefits (Melby-Lervag & Hulme, 2013), research indicates that the skills acquired in playing games do seem to transfer out of the game to tasks in the real world (Green & Bavelier, 2012). The ability of games to develop transferable skills is of huge interest to educationalists as understanding and promoting factors that support the transfer of skills is the Holy Grail of education (Perkins & Salomon, 1989). Green and Bavelier (2012) recently offered an interesting insight into the transferability of action video game-based skills. These authors have been at the forefront of research in this area and they also argue that we need to adopt a more integrated approach to trying to understand the cognitive benefits linked to playing games. They demonstrate that the benefits of games are evident across a wide range of tasks and they suggest that the explanation may lie in the capacity of games to support new learning: "Game playing may not convey an immediate advantage on new tasks (increased performance from the very first trial), but rather the true effect of action video game playing may be to enhance the ability to learn new tasks." (Green & Bavelier, 2012, pg 197). This enhanced ability to learn occurs as a result of enhanced attentional control and the superior ability of players to "predict" on the basis of previous experience. Further, skill generalisation may be supported by effective use of attention and executive control (Lustig, Shah, Seidler & Reuter-Lorenz, 2009;

Green & Bavelier, 2012). These proposals draw upon the development of automaticity in the performance of skills. The importance of practice and the automatic performance of skills which place less demand on limited resources have long been recognised within psychology as an essential component in the development of expertise across a number of domains (Ericson et al., 2006). The proposal that games support learning because they support the ability to learn highlights the need for future research to address the underlying cause of games-based benefits in greater detail. Such research is likely to draw heavily upon existing psychological explanations of learning and will benefit from the application of an information processing perspective such as Anderson's model of executive functioning, specifically the components of attentional control and cognitive flexibility.

The focus of this paper has been on providing cognitive explanations of how the activities inherent in playing games can help players to learn more easily by improving visual-perceptual skills, providing practice in developing efficient problem solving strategies and coordinating sequences of actions. However the limited nature of our cognitive capabilities, especially attention and working memory, also impose constraints on information processing. Recognition of these inherent constraints may offer two potentially interesting directions for future research and development. Firstly, it may be informative to consider the benefits of games from a constraint-based perspective i.e. what are the specific aspects of game-play that allow players to maximise their limited abilities and enable them to carry out operations faster and on more stimuli? What cognitive mechanisms support the development of such skills?

Secondly, from a design perspective, the development of educational technologies such as game-based learning environments will benefit significantly from reflecting on and accommodating cognitive limitations (Sweller, 1999). Cognitive Load Theory (CLT) is concerned with the limitations of human working memory and has

had an important impact in thinking about how we can design games for more effective processing of information. As Sweller, van Merrienboer and Paas (1998) observe, human working memory can only be deployed efficiently if the chasm between information format and human cognitive architecture is successfully bridged. The challenge is to create the conditions in a games-based learning environment that enable human working memory to be utilised to maximal effect, whilst avoiding cognitive overload. Game designers and developers should also take into account heuristics and cognitive biases used in problem solving and decision making (Kahneman & Tversky, 1979). These can make certain decisions very difficult, and therefore a suitable choice architecture is crucial.

It is important to recognize that although game-based learning environments offer promising learning opportunities, they are sufficiently complex in nature to the place additional cognitive demands on the learner (Huang & Johnson, 2008; Huang, 2011). The simultaneous demands placed upon the learner's cognitive resources are quite considerable, ranging from the game task itself, the elements of the game and the other game players (Ang, Zaphiris & Mahmood, 2007). This might also involve searching for items or information, looking for clues and trying to decode contextual information and understand narratives. Kalyuga and Plass (2009) note that cognitive load considerations are especially important in the development of educational games as they generally require not only cognitive but also motor activity. Furthermore, characteristics that are unique to gaming such as high degrees of interactivity and immersion may detract from learning (Lim et al, 2006). For example, although immersion may provide many contextual cues that assist in navigating one's way through a game towards the learning goal, if executed ineffectively, it may hinder learning.

Over the past decade, the growing awareness of the necessity of understanding and addressing cognitive load has led to the development of a number of techniques for the measurement of cognitive load. These include subjective ratings of mental effort (Paas et al, 2003), using verbal protocols (Kalyuga & Plass, 2009) or by using the dual-task technique (Brünken et al, 2002, where the learner is required to carry out two tasks and performance on the secondary task indicates the extent of the cognitive load that is being demanded by the primary task. In addition to the development of measurement techniques, the field has seen a growing appreciation of the way(s) in which working memory capacity and cognitive load is handled in group work settings. For example, Kirschner, Ayres, & Chandler (2011) demonstrated that group learning is more effective than individual learning when the information to be learned is complex. This may be due to the fact that in a group setting, it is possible to distribute the demands placed on working memory across several members of the group. This clearly has implications for the design of game-based learning. There is clear evidence of a growing appreciation by learning technology developers of the impact of a finite working memory capacity and associated cognitive load. The challenge now is to further inform this understanding with empirical studies of the relationship between working memory, cognitive load and game-based learning.

CONCLUSION

To conclude, this chapter has outlined the advantages of applying Anderson's model of executive functions to extend our understanding of the learning potential of digital games from a cognitive perspective. Anderson's model of executive functions has helped to provide a more coherent and integrated framework for understanding the cognitive gains linked to playing games. We have focused on two main areas of cognition where games benefit learning: attention and perceptual skills and problem solving and metacognition. While these skills ultimately underlie learning, the exact relationships between these skills and

learning require further clarification. Future research should aim to clarify these relationships with respect to both entertainment and serious games. Games may have pedagogical value not only within traditional educational contexts; they may also inform more clinically orientated rehabilitation and interventions for individuals with cognitive deficits such as poor attentional skills and impaired decision making and problem solving abilities, given that game-derived benefits appear to be more enduring and transferable than more traditional forms of cognitive training.

Considering how information processing accounts can help to explain learning in games highlights that an information processing framework may also offer interesting insights into the underlying cognitive processes and structures that support engagement in games. The framework clearly identifies that further exploration of the role of attention, the pace or speed of games and the different challenges that games present may help to explain why games are so engaging are key areas for future research.

While we have considered how playing games can improve aspects of cognitive processing, we can also use games as a new methodology for studying cognitive skills and executive functioning. The complex information processing demands of games can provide an exciting but controlled environment where specific task features can be systematically manipulated and the resulting changes in information processing examined. The importance of executive functioning to human cognition is widely accepted within psychology and cognitive science, therefore it essential that it is fully explored and understood with respect to games-based learning. The information processing outlined in this chapter offers an exciting direction for future research that not only offers integration but also affords predictive potential with an associated methodology. Games-based research raises interesting questions about the nature of human cognition and the information processing framework of executive functions offers a stimulating perspective to situate future research.

ACKNOWLEDGMENT

This work was partially supported by the Games and Learning Alliance (GaLA) - Network of Excellence for Serious Games under the European Community Seventh Framework Programme (FP7/2007 2013), Grant Agreement no. 258169.

REFERENCES

Ackerman, P. L., Beier, M. E., & Boyle, M. O. (2005). Working memory and intelligence: The same or different constructs? *Psychological Bulletin*, *131*(1), 30–60. doi:10.1037/0033-2909.131.1.30 PMID:15631550.

Alloway, T. P. (2012). Can interactive working memory training improve learning? *Journal of Interactive Learning Research*, *23*(3), 197–207.

Alloway, T. P., Bibile, V., & Lau, G. (2013). Computerized working memory training: Can it lead to gains in cognitive skills in students? *Computers in Human Behavior*, *29*, 632–638. doi:10.1016/j.chb.2012.10.023.

American Association for the Advancement of Science. (1993). *Benchmarks for science literacy*. New York: Oxford University Press.

Anderson, P. J. (2002). Assessment and development of executive function (EF) during childhood. *Child Neuropsychology*, *8*(2), 71–82. doi:10.1076/chin.8.2.71.8724 PMID:12638061.

Andersson, U. (2008). Working memory as a predictor of written arithmetical skills in children: The importance of central executive functions. *The British Journal of Educational Psychology*, *78*, 181–203. doi:10.1348/000709907X209854 PMID:17535520.

Ang, C. S., Zaphiris, P., & Mahmood, S. (2007). A model of cognitive loads in massively multiplayer online role playing games. *Interacting with Computers*, *19*(2), 167–179. doi:10.1016/j.intcom.2006.08.006.

Asbell-Clarke, J., Edwards, T., Rowe, E., Larsen, J., Sylvan, E., & Hewitt, J. (2012). Martian boneyards: Scientific inquiry in an MMO game. *International Journal of Game-Based Learning*, *2*(1), 52–76. doi:10.4018/ijgbl.2012010104.

Baddeley, A. (1998). *Human memory*. Boston: Allyn and Bacon.

Baddeley, A. (1998). The central executive: A concept and some misconceptions. *Journal of the International Neuropsychological Society*, *4*, 523–526. doi:10.1017/S135561779800513X PMID:9745242.

Baddeley, A., & Della Sala, S. (1996). Working memory and executive control. *Philosophical Transactions of the Royal Society of London. Series B, Biological Sciences*, *351*, 1397–1404. doi:10.1098/rstb.1996.0123 PMID:8941951.

Baddeley, A. D., & Hitch, G. (1974). Working memory. In G. H. Bower (Ed.), *The psychology of learning and motivation: Advances in research and theory* (Vol. 8, pp. 47–89). New York: Academic Press.

Barab, S., & Dede, C. (2007). Games and immersive participatory simulations for science education: An emerging type of curricula. *Journal of Science Education and Technology*, *16*(1), 1–3. doi:10.1007/s10956-007-9043-9.

Barlett, C. P., Vowels, C. L., Shanteau, J., Crow, J., & Miller, T. (2009). The effect of violent and non-violent computer games on cognitive performance. *Computers in Human Behavior*, *21*(1), 96–102. doi:10.1016/j.chb.2008.07.008.

Beck, J. (2005). The impact of video gaming on decision making and team working skills. *Campus-Wide Information Systems*, *22*(5), 320–326. doi:10.1108/10650740510632226.

Becker, M. W., Alzahabi, R., & Hopwood, C. J. (2013). Media multitasking is associated with symptoms of depression and social anxiety. *Cyberpsychology, Behavior, and Social Networking*, *16*(2), 132–135. doi:10.1089/cyber.2012.0291 PMID:23126438.

Blakemore, S. J., & Choudhury, S. (2006). Development of the adolescent brain: implications for executive function and social cognition. *Journal of Child Psychology and Psychiatry, and Allied Disciplines*, *47*(3-4), 296–312. doi:10.1111/j.1469-7610.2006.01611.x PMID:16492261.

Blumberg, F. C., Rosenthal, S. F., & Randall, J. D. (2008). Impasse-driven learning in the context of video games. *Computers in Human Behavior*, *24*(4), 1530–1541. doi:10.1016/j.chb.2007.05.010.

Boot, W. R., Blakely, D. P., & Simons, D. J. (2011). Do action video games improve perception and cognition? *Frontiers in Psychology*, *2*. PMID:21738514.

Boot, W. R., Kramer, A. F., Simons, D. J., Fabiani, M., & Gratton, G. (2008). The effects of video game playing on attention, memory, and executive control. *Acta Psychologica*, *129*(3), 387–398. doi:10.1016/j.actpsy.2008.09.005 PMID:18929349.

Booth, J. N., Boyle, J. M., & Kelly, S. W. (2010). Do tasks make a difference? Accounting for heterogeneity of performance of children with reading difficulties on tasks of executive function: Findings from a meta-analysis. *The British Journal of Developmental Psychology*, *28*(1), 133–176. doi:10.1348/026151009X485432 PMID:20306629.

Bottino, R. M., Ferlino, L., Ott, M., & Tavella, M. (2007). Developing strategic and reasoning abilities with computer games at primary school level. *Computers & Education*, *49*, 1272–1286. doi:10.1016/j.compedu.2006.02.003.

Bottino, R. M., Ott, M., & Tavella, M. (2008). The impact of mind game playing on children's reasoning abilities: Reflections from an experience. In *Proceedings of the 2nd European Conference on Games-Based Learning* (ECGBL). Barcelona, Spain: ECGBL.

Boyle, E. A., Connolly, T. M., & Hainey, T. (2011). The role of psychology in understanding the impact of computer games. *Entertainment Computing*, *2*, 69–74. doi:10.1016/j.entcom.2010.12.002.

Brünken, R., Steinbacher, S., Plass, J. L., & Leutner, D. (2002). Assessment of cognitive load theory in multimedia learning using dual-task methodology. *Experimental Psychology*, *49*(2), 109–119. doi:10.1027//1618-3169.49.2.109 PMID:12053529.

Bull, R., Espy, K. A., & Senn, T. E. (2004). A comparison of performance on the Towers of London and Hanoi in young children. *Journal of Child Psychology and Psychiatry, and Allied Disciplines*, *45*(4), 743–754. doi:10.1111/j.1469-7610.2004.00268.x PMID:15056306.

Caird-Daley, A., & Harris, D. (2007). *Training decision making using serious games*. Human Factors Integration Defence Technology Centre.

Chase, W. G., & Simon, H. A. (1973). The mind's eye in chess. In W. G. Chase (Ed.), *Visual Information Processing*. New York: Academic Press.

Chi, M. T. H. (1997). Quantifying qualitative analyses of verbal data: A practical guide. *Journal of the Learning Sciences*, *6*(3), 271–315. doi:10.1207/s15327809jls0603_1.

Chiappe, D., Conger, M., Liao, J., Caldwell, J. L., & Vu, K. P. L. (2013). Improving multi-tasking ability through action videogames. *Applied Ergonomics*, *44*(2), 278–284. doi:10.1016/j.apergo.2012.08.002 PMID:22981314.

Chinn, C. A., & Malhotra, B. (2002). Epistemologically authentic inquiry in schools: A theoretical framework for evaluating inquiry tasks. *Science Education*, *86*(2), 175–218. doi:10.1002/sce.10001.

Christou, C., Jones, K., Mousoulides, N., & Pittalis, M. (2006). Developing the 3DMath dynamic geometry software: Theoretical perspectives on design. *The International Journal for Technology in Mathematics Education*, *13*(4), 168–174.

Cicchetti, D. (2002). The impact of social experience on neurobiological systems: Illustration from a constructivist view of child maltreatment. *Cognitive Development*, *17*, 1407–1428. doi:10.1016/S0885-2014(02)00121-1.

Cogmed. (2013). *Cogmed working memory training*. Retrieved from http://www.cogmed.com/program

Colzato, L. S., van Leeuwen, P. J., van den Wildenberg, W. P., & Hommel, B. (2010). DOOM'd to switch: Superior cognitive flexibility in players of first person shooter games. *Frontiers in Psychology*, *1*, 8. doi:10.3389/fpsyg.2010.00008 PMID:21833191.

Connolly, T., Boyle, E., MacArthur, E., Hainey, T., & Boyle, J. (2012). A systematic literature review of empirical evidence on computer games and serious games. *Computers & Education*, *59*, 661–686. doi:10.1016/j.compedu.2012.03.004.

Danielsson, H., Henry, L., Messer, D., & Rönnberg, J. (2012). Strengths and weaknesses in executive functioning in children with intellectual disability. *Research in Developmental Disabilities*, *33*(2), 600–607. doi:10.1016/j.ridd.2011.11.004 PMID:22155533.

Davidson, M. C., Amso, D., Anderson, L. C., & Diamond, A. (2006). Development of cognitive control and executive functions from 4 to 13 years: Evidence from manipulations of memory, inhibition, and task switching. *Neuropsychologia*, *44*(11), 2037–2078. doi:10.1016/j.neuropsychologia.2006.02.006 PMID:16580701.

Dede, C. (2000). A new century demands new ways of learning: An excerpt from the digital classroom. In D. T. E. Gordon (Ed.), *The Digital Classroom*. Cambridge, MA: Harvard Education Letter.

Diamond, A. (2013). Executive functions. *Annual Review of Psychology*, 64. PMID:23020641.

Dondlinger, M. J. (2007). Educational video games design: A review of the literature. *Journal of Applied Educational Technology*, *4*(1), 21–31.

Donohue, S. E., James, B., Eslick, A. N., & Mitroff, S. R. (2012). Cognitive pitfall! Videogame players are not immune to dual-task costs. *Attention, Perception & Psychophysics*, *74*(5), 803–809. doi:10.3758/s13414-012-0323-y PMID:22669792.

Driver, J., & Spence, C. (1998). Cross modal links in spatial attention. *Proceedings. Biological Sciences*, *353*, 1–13.

Dye, M. W. G., Green, C. S., & Bavelier, D. (2009). Increasing speed of processing with action video games. *Current Directions in Psychological Science*, *18*, 321–326. doi:10.1111/j.1467-8721.2009.01660.x PMID:20485453.

Ellis Weismer, S., Evans, J., & Hesketh, L. J. (1999). An examination of verbal working memory capacity in children with specific language impairment. *Journal of Speech, Language, and Hearing Research: JSLHR*, *42*(5), 1249–1260. PMID:10515519.

Ericsson, K. A., Charness, N., Feltovich, P. J., & Hoffman, R. R. (Eds.). (2006). *The Cambridge handbook of expertise and expertise performance*. Cambridge, UK: Cambridge University Press. doi:10.1017/CBO9780511816796.

Eysenck, M. W., & Keane, M. T. (2010). *Cognitive psychology: A student's handbook* (6th ed.). New York: Psychology Press.

Feng, J., Spence, I., & Pratt, J. (2007). Playing an action video game reduces gender differences in spatial cognition. *Psychological Science*, *18*(10), 850–855. doi:10.1111/j.1467-9280.2007.01990.x PMID:17894600.

Gathercole, S. E., & Pickering, S. J. (2000). Working memory deficits in children with low achievements in the national curriculum at 7 years of age. *The British Journal of Educational Psychology*, *70*, 177–194. doi:10.1348/000709900158047 PMID:10900777.

Gee, J. P. (2003). *What video games have to teach us about learning and literacy*. New York: Palgrave Macmillan. doi:10.1145/950566.950595.

Gee, J. P. (2005). Learning by design: Good video games as learning machines. *E-learning*, *2*(1), 5–16. doi:10.2304/elea.2005.2.1.5.

Green, C. S., & Bavelier, D. (2003). Action video game modifies visual selective attention. *Nature*, *423*, 534–537. doi:10.1038/nature01647 PMID:12774121.

Green, C. S., & Bavelier, D. (2006a). Effect of action video game playing on the spatial distribution of visual selective attention. *Journal of Experimental Psychology*, *32*, 1465–1478. PMID:17154785.

Green, C. S., & Bavelier, D. (2006b). Enumeration versus multiple object tracking: The case of action video game players. *Cognition*, *101*, 217–245. doi:10.1016/j.cognition.2005.10.004 PMID:16359652.

Green, C. S., & Bavelier, D. (2012). Learning, attentional control, and action video games. *Current Biology*, *22*, 197–206. doi:10.1016/j.cub.2012.02.012 PMID:22226749.

Green, C. S., Sugarman, M. A., Medford, K., Klobusicky, E., & Bavelier, D. (2012). The effect of action video game experience on task-switching. *Computers in Human Behavior*, *28*, 984–994. doi:10.1016/j.chb.2011.12.020 PMID:22393270.

Halpern, D. F., Millis, K., Graesser, A. C., Butler, H., Forsyth, C., & Cai, Z. (2012). Operation ARA: A computerized learning game that teaches critical thinking and scientific reasoning. *Thinking Skills and Creativity*, *7*(2), 73–100. doi:10.1016/j.tsc.2012.03.006.

Holbrook, J., & Rannikmae, M. (2009). The meaning of scientific literacy. *International Journal of Environmental and Science Education*, *4*(3), 275–288.

Huang, H.-W. (2011). Evaluating learners' motivational and cognitive processing in an online game-based learning environment. *Computers in Human Behavior*, *27*, 694–704. doi:10.1016/j.chb.2010.07.021.

Huang, H.-W., & Johnson, T. (2008). Instructional game design using cognitive load theory. In R. Ferdig (Ed.), *Handbook of Research on Effective Electronic Gaming in Education* (pp. 1143–1165). Hershey, PA: IGI Global. doi:10.4018/978-1-59904-808-6.ch066.

Huang, O. W. S., Cheng, H. N. H., & Chan, T. (2007). Number jigsaw puzzle: A mathematical puzzle game for facilitating players' problem-solving strategies. In T. W. Chan, A. Paiva, & D. W. Shaffer (Eds.), *Proceedings of the First IEEE International Workshop on Digital Game and Intelligent Toy Enhanced Learning* (pp. 130-134). Los Alamitos, CA: IEEE Computer Society.

Hughes, C., Roman, G., Hart, M. J., & Ensor, R. (2013). Does maternal depression predict young children's executive function? A 4-year longitudinal study. *Journal of Child Psychology and Psychiatry, and Allied Disciplines, 54*(2), 169–177. doi:10.1111/jcpp.12014 PMID:23171379.

Hung, P.-H., Hwang, G.-J., Lee, Y.-H., & Su, I.-H. (2012). A cognitive component analysis approach for developing game-based spatial learning tools. *Computers & Education, 59*, 762–773. doi:10.1016/j.compedu.2012.03.018.

Jennett, C., Cox, A. L., Cairns, P., Dhoparee, S., Epps, A., Tijs, T., & Walton, A. (2008). Measuring and defining the experience of immersion in games. *International Journal of Human-Computer Studies, 66*(9), 641–661. doi:10.1016/j.ijhcs.2008.04.004.

Jerman, O., & Swanson, H. L. (2005). Working memory and reading disabilities: A selective meta-analysis of the literature. In T. E. Scruggs & Mastropieri (Eds.), Advances in Learning and Behavioural Disabilities, Cognition and Learning in Diverse Settings (Vol. 18, pp. 1-31). Oxford, UK: Elsevier.

Johnson, L., Smith, R., Willis, H., Levine, A., & Haywood, K. (2011). *The 2011 horizon report*. Austin, TX: The New Media Consortium. Retrieved from http://net.educause.edu/ir/library/pdf/HR2011.pdf

Jonassen, D. H. (1997). Instructional design model for well-structured and ill-structured problem-solving learning outcomes. *Educational Technology Research and Development, 45*(1), 65–95. doi:10.1007/BF02299613.

Jonassen, D. H. (2004). *Learning to solve problems, an instructional design guide*. San Francisco, CA: Pfeiffer.

Kahneman, D., & Tversky, A. (1979). Prospect theory: An analysis of decision under risk. *Econometrica, 47*(2), 263–292. doi:10.2307/1914185.

Kalyuga, S., & Plass, J. (2009). Evaluating and managing cognitive load in games. In R. E. Ferdig (Ed.), *Handbook of Research on Effective Electronic Gaming in Education* (pp. 719–737). Hershey, PA: IGI Global.

Kane, M. J., & Engle, R. W. (2002). The role of prefrontal cortex in working memory capacity, executive attention and general fluid intelligence: An individual-differences perspective. *Psychonomic Bulletin & Review, 9*, 637–671. doi:10.3758/BF03196323 PMID:12613671.

Karle, J. W., Watter, S., & Shedden, J. M. (2010). Task switching in video game players: Benefits of selective attention but not resistance to proactive interference. *Acta Psychologica, 134*(1), 70–78. doi:10.1016/j.actpsy.2009.12.007 PMID:20064634.

Kebritchi, M., & Hiruni, H. (2008). Examining the pedagogical foundations of modern educational computer games. *Computers & Education, 51*, 1729–1743. doi:10.1016/j.compedu.2008.05.004.

Kiili, K., & Ketamo, H. (2007). Exploring the learning mechanism in educational games. In *Proceedings of the ITI 2007 29th Int. Conf. on Information Technology Interfaces*. Cavtat, Croatia: IEEE.

Kim, B., Park, H., & Baek, Y. (2009). Not just fun, but serious strategies: Using meta-cognitive strategies in game-based learning. *Computers & Education, 52*, 800–810. doi:10.1016/j.compedu.2008.12.004.

Kirschner, P. A., Ayres, P., & Chandler, P. (2011). Contemporary cognitive load theory research: The good, the bad and the ugly. *Computers in Human Behavior, 27*(1), 99–106. doi:10.1016/j.chb.2010.06.025.

Ko, S. (2002). An empirical analysis of children's thinking and learning in a computer game context. *Educational Psychology, 22*(2), 221–233. doi:10.1080/01443410120115274.

Kolb, D. (1984). *Experiential learning: Experience as the source of learning and development.* Englewood Cliffs, NJ: Prentice Hall.

Kordaki, M. (2012). A computer card game for the learning of basic aspects of the binary system in primary education: Design and pilot evaluation. *Education and Information Technologies, 16,* 395–421. doi:10.1007/s10639-010-9136-6.

Kyllonen, P. C., & Christal, R. E. (1990). Reasoning ability is (little more than) working-memory capacity?! *Intelligence, 14*(4), 389–433. doi:10.1016/S0160-2896(05)80012-1.

Lanzilotti, R., & Roselli, T. (2007). An experimental evaluation of Logiocando, an intelligent tutoring hypermedia system. *International Journal of Artificial Intelligence in Education, 17*(1), 41–56.

Lee, C.-Y., & Chen, M.-P. (2009). A computer game as a context for non-routine mathematical problem solving: The effects of type of question prompt and level of prior knowledge. *Computers & Education, 52*(3), 530–542. doi:10.1016/j.compedu.2008.10.008.

List, A., & Robertson, I. C. (2007). Inhibition of return and object-based attentional selection. *Journal of Experimental Psychology. Human Perception and Performance, 33,* 1322–1334. doi:10.1037/0096-1523.33.6.1322 PMID:18085946.

Loman, M. E., Johnson, A. E., Westerlund, A., Pollak, S. D., Nelson, C. A., & Gunnar, M. R. (2012). The effect of early deprivation on executive attention in middle childhood. *Journal of Child Psychology and Psychiatry, and Allied Disciplines, 54*(1), 37–45. doi:10.1111/j.1469-7610.2012.02602.x PMID:22924462.

Lustig, C., Shah, P., Seidler, R., & Reuter-Lorenz, P. A. (2009). Aging, training, and the brain: A review and future directions. *Neuropsychology Review, 19,* 504–522. doi:10.1007/s11065-009-9119-9 PMID:19876740.

Mayer, I. S., Carton, L., de Jong, M., Leijten, M., & Dammers, E. (2004). Gaming the future of an urban network. *Futures, 36*(3), 311–333. doi:10.1016/S0016-3287(03)00159-9.

McGuinness, C. (2005). BJEP monograph series II, number 3 – Pedagogy. *Teaching for Learning, 1*(1), 107–126.

McGurk, H., & MacDonald, J. (1976). Hearing lips and seeing voices. *Nature, 264*(5588), 746–748. doi:10.1038/264746a0 PMID:1012311.

Melby Lervag, M., & Hulme, C. (2013). Is working memory training effective? A meta analytic review. *Developmental Psychology, 49*(2), 270–291. doi:10.1037/a0028228 PMID:22612437.

Mishra, J., Bavelier, D., & Gazzaley, A. (2012). How to assess gaming-induced benefits on attention and working memory. *Games for Health Journal: Research. Development and Clinical Applications, 3*(1), 192–198.

Miyake, A., Friedman, N. P., Emerson, M. J., Witzki, A. H., Howerter, A., & Wager, T. D. (2000). The unity and diversity of executive functions and their contributions to complex frontal lobe tasks: A latent variable analysis. *Cognitive Psychology, 41*(1), 49–100. doi:10.1006/cogp.1999.0734 PMID:10945922.

National Research Council. (2010). *Exploring the intersection of science education and 21st century skills: A workshop summary.* Washington, DC: National Academy Press.

Newell, A., & Simon, H. A. (1972). *Human problem solving.* Englewood Cliffs, NJ: Prentice-Hall.

O'Brien, D. (2011). A taxonomy of educational games. In *Gaming and simulations: Concepts, methodologies, tools and applications* (pp. 1–23). Hershey, PA: IGI Global.

O'Shaughnessy, T. E., & Swanson, H. L. (1998). Do immediate memory deficits in students with learning disabilities in reading reflect a developmental lag or deficit? A selective meta-analysis of the literature. *Learning Disability Quarterly, 21*(2), 123–148. doi:10.2307/1511341.

Perkins, D. N., & Salomon, G. (1989). Are cognitive skills context bound? *Educational Researcher, 18*(1), 16–25. doi:10.3102/0013189X018001016.

Phillips, L. H. (1997). Do frontal tests measure executive function? Issues of assessment and evidence of assessment and evidence from fluency tests. In P. M. A. Rabbitt (Ed.), *Methodology of Frontal and Executive Function*. Hove, UK: Psychology Press.

Posner, M. I. (1980). Orienting of attention. *The Quarterly Journal of Experimental Psychology, 32A*, 3–25. doi:10.1080/00335558008248231 PMID:7367577.

Posner, M. I., & Peterson, S. E. (1990). The attention system of the human brain. *Annual Review of Neuroscience, 13*, 25–42. doi:10.1146/annurev.ne.13.030190.000325 PMID:2183676.

Rajendran, G., & Mitchell, P. (2007). Cognitive theories of autism. *Developmental Review, 27*(2), 224–260. doi:10.1016/j.dr.2007.02.001.

Ramler, I. P., & Chapman, J. L. (2011). Introducing statistical research to undergraduate mathematical statistics students using the guitar hero video game series. *Journal of Statistics Education, 19*(3), 1–20.

Razak, A. A., Connolly, T. M., & Hainey, T. (2012). Teachers' views on the approach of digital games-based learning within the curriculum for excellence. *International Journal of Game-Based Learning, 2*(1), 33–51. doi:10.4018/ijgbl.2012010103.

Salthouse, T. A., Atkinson, T. M., & Berish, D. E. (2003). Executive functioning as a potential mediator of age-related cognitive decline in normal adults. *Journal of Experimental Psychology. General, 132*(4), 566–594. doi:10.1037/0096-3445.132.4.566 PMID:14640849.

Sanbonmatsu, D. M., Strayer, D. L., Medeiros-Ward, N., & Watson, J. M. (2013). Who multi-tasks and why? Multi-tasking ability, perceived multi-tasking ability, impulsivity, and sensation seeking. *PLoS ONE, 8*(1), e54402. doi:10.1371/journal.pone.0054402 PMID:23372720.

Schwartz, R. G., & Teach, R. D. (2002). The congruence game: A team-building exercise for students of entrepreneurship. *Simulation & Gaming, 33*(1), 94–108. doi:10.1177/1046878102033001006.

Shiffrin, R. M., & Schneider, W. (1977). Controlled and automatic human information processing: Perceptual learning, automatic attending, and a general theory. *Psychological Review, 84*, 127–190. doi:10.1037/0033-295X.84.2.127.

Shipstead, Z., Redick, T. S., & Engle, R. W. (2012). Is working memory training effective? *Psychological Bulletin, 138*(4), 628–654. doi:10.1037/a0027473 PMID:22409508.

Spelke, E. S., Hirst, W. C., & Neisser, U. (1976). Skills of divided attention. *Cognition, 4*, 215–230. doi:10.1016/0010-0277(76)90018-4.

Spires, H. A., Rowe, J. P., Mott, B. W., & Lester, J. C. (2011). Problem solving and game-based learning: Effects of middle grade students' hypothesis testing strategies on learning outcomes. *Journal of Educational Computing Research, 44*(4), 453–472. doi:10.2190/EC.44.4.e.

St. Clair-Thompson, H. L., & Gathercole, S. E. (2006). Executive functions and achievements in school: Shifting, updating and inhibition, and working memory. *Quarterly Journal of Experimental Psychology*, *59*(4), 745–759. doi:10.1080/17470210500162854 PMID:16707360.

Steinkuehler, C., & Duncan, S. (2008). Scientific habits of mind in virtual worlds. *Journal of Science Education and Technology*, *17*(6), 530–543. doi:10.1007/s10956-008-9120-8.

Subrahmanyam, K., & Greenfield, P. M. (1994). Effect of video game practice on spatial skills in girls and boys. *Journal of Applied Developmental Psychology*, *15*, 13–32. doi:10.1016/0193-3973(94)90004-3.

Sweetser, P., & Wyeth, P. (2005). GameFlow: A model for evaluating player enjoyment in games. *ACM Computers in Entertainment*, *3*(3), 1–24. doi:10.1145/1077246.1077253.

Sweller, J. (1999). *Instructional design in technical areas*. Camberwell, Australia: ACER Press.

Sweller, J., Van Merriënboer, J., & Paas, F. (1998). Cognitive architecture and instructional design. *Educational Psychology Review*, *10*(3), 251–296. doi:10.1023/A:1022193728205.

Terras, M. M., & Ramsay, J. (2013). *A psychological perspective on the temporal dimensions of e-learning*. E-Learning and Digital Media.

Tillman, C., Eninger, L., Forssman, L., & Bohlin, G. (2011). The relation between working memory components and ADHD symptoms from a developmental perspective. *Developmental Neuropsychology*, *36*(2), 181–198. doi:10.1080/87565641.2010.549981 PMID:21347920.

Vos, N., van der Meijden, H., & Denessen, E. (2011). Effects of constructing versus playing an educational game on student motivation and deep learning strategy use. *Computers & Education*, *56*(1), 127–137. doi:10.1016/j.compedu.2010.08.013.

Vygotsky, L. S. (1978). *Mind in society: The development of higher psychological processes*. Cambridge, MA: Harvard University Press.

Wang, H.-S., Chou, C.-H., Tsai, S.-N., & Hung, H.-J. (2012). The study of motivation and reasoning faculties of game-based learning in elementary school students. In *Proceedings of 2010 2nd International Conference on Education Technology and Computer (ICETC)*. ICETC.

Zakay, D. (2000). Gating or switching? Gating is a better model of prospective timing. *Behavioural Processes*, *50*, 1–7. doi:10.1016/S0376-6357(00)00086-3 PMID:10925031.

Zakay, D. (2012). Experiencing time in daily life. *The Psychologist*, *25*(8), 578–581.

Zap, N., & Code, J. (2009). Self-regulated learning in video game environments. In R. E. Ferdig (Ed.), *Handbook of Research on Effective Electronic Gaming in Education* (pp. 738–756). Hershey, PA: IGI Global.

Zelazo, P. D., Qu, L., & Muller, U. (2004). Hot and cool aspects of executive function: Relations in early development. In W. Schneider, R. Schumann-Hengsteler, & B. Sodian (Eds.), *Young children's cognitive development: Interrelationships among executive functioning, verbal ability and theory or mind* (pp. 71–93). Mahwah, NJ: Erlbaum.

Zimmerman, B. J. (2002). Becoming a self-regulated learner: An overview. *Theory into Practice*, *41*(2), 64–70. doi:10.1207/s15430421tip4102_2.

Zwikael, O., & Gonen, A. (2007). Project execution game (PEG), training towards managing unexpected events. *Journal of European Industrial Training*, *31*(6), 495–512. doi:10.1108/03090590710772668.

KEY TERMS AND DEFINITIONS

Cognitive Flexibility: Refers to the mental ability to switch between thinking about two different concepts or to carry out two different aspects of a task at the same time.

Divided Attention: The ability to attend to different sources of information and responses at the same time.

Executive Functions: A superordinate term used to refer to a range of higher level cognitive processes that regulate, control, and manage other cognitive processes. These components include selective and divided attention, working memory, planning, problem solving, verbal reasoning, inhibition, mental flexibility, task switching, and self-regulation. In this chapter we use Anderson's (2002) model of executive functions but other models such as Diamond's (2013) have been proposed.

Information Processing: In cognitive psychology information processing is an approach to understanding human thinking which draws an analogy with how computers work, discussing the structures and operations involved in attending to, remembering and thinking about stimuli.

Problem Solving: The attempt to find solutions to challenges.

Selective Attention: The ability to select and focus on specific stimuli to the exclusion of others over a sustained period of time.

Self-Regulation: The ability to plan, monitor, terminate and evaluate processing.

Chapter 3

The Road to Critical Thinking and Intelligence Analysis

Michel Rudnianski
ORT, France

Milos Kravcik
RWTH Aachen University, Germany

ABSTRACT

In an environment characterized by an ever-increasing flow of data and resulting complexity, the development of intelligence analysis is of core importance. After a brief analysis of three core competences (data processing, empathy, critical thinking), decision making issues are addressed through considering on the one hand cognitive and psychological biases, and on the other hand methodologies based on instrumental rationality. Core factors for the development of critical thinking are then discussed before a specific tool of Game Theory, called Games of Deterrence, is introduced based on bounded rationality. An example of Games of Deterrence's application to critical thinking is given through using these games to model argumentation. Finally, on the basis of the method adopted, a framework is proposed for building a serious game devoted to critical thinking and intelligence analysis.

INTRODUCTION

Intelligence analysis is a 'hot' topic due to the acceleration of change and the volume of information flow stemming from the constant progress of information technologies. The activity of intelligence analysis can be considered as the transformation of a set of raw data into meaningful information, which will enable decision-makers who have requested that analysis, to take appropriate actions. Good examples are those concerning criminality or economic intelligence.

Efficient intelligence analysis requires several skills and competences, from understanding and knowledge of specific application fields to the mastering of some information technologies and critical thinking. In turn, as far as critical thinking is concerned, various competences are required, which include methods of both logical and psychological analysis, enabling for instance the determination of cognitive biases (Heuer, 1999).

On the basis of the literature available on each of these topics the present chapter develops a

DOI: 10.4018/978-1-4666-4773-2.ch003

Copyright © 2014, IGI Global. Copying or distributing in print or electronic forms without written permission of IGI Global is prohibited.

combined approach for developing serious games to form experts in intelligence analysis. More precisely, starting from an analysis of relevant competences, the chapter will propose a methodology to support their development accordingly. As addressing comprehensively all issues concerning intelligence analysis is out of scope of a single chapter, we shall focus on key cognitive biases as analysed by Kahneman and Tversky (1979) in their Prospect Theory, and the approaches that should be developed to deal with these. Then, a specific branch of Game Theory, called 'Games of Deterrence', which has been already used to model argumentation, will serve as a supporting tool for a serious game devoted to intelligence analysis (Rudnianski, 2012; Rudnianski & Bestougeff, 2008; Rudnianski & Lalonde, 2009).

RELEVANT COMPETENCES

According to the European Qualification Framework (European Commission, 2008) *competence* means "the proven ability to use knowledge, skills and personal, social and/or methodological abilities, in work or study situations and in professional and personal development". Thus for instance the competences of an Executive MBA include the tasks that the MBA graduate should be able to accomplish as a company top executive manager; i.e., define the vision, the value and the strategy of the firm, take advantage of the opportunities offered by the environment, efficiently manage crises, supervise the company's organisation and governance, develop corporate social responsibility, team spirit, etc. It can be seen from this example that the capabilities expected from an Executive MBA graduate are diverse: in particular, some require 'hard' skills such as the ability to develop a corporate financial plan, while others pertain more to 'soft' skills, like leadership, persuasion, etc.

Similarly, what is expected from an expert in intelligence analysis covers a variety of fields. Berkowitz and Goodman (1989) define intel-

ligence analysis as "the process of evaluating and transforming raw data into descriptions, explanations and conclusions for intelligence consumers". It follows that the following three fields, representing each one a particular stage in the elaboration of the solution to the issue under scrutiny are of particular importance:

- Data processing.
- Empathy.
- Critical thinking.

Data Processing

According to the Business Dictionary (2013), data processing can be defined as "operations performed on a given set of data to extract the required information in an appropriate form". It follows that the operations can be structured under the form of a four stage process:

- **Data Search,** which consists in looking for data sources that are meaningful with respect to the issue under consideration.
- **Data Selection,** during which the data found in the data sources will be separated between those which are relevant for the issue and those which are irrelevant.
- **Data Connections,** during which connections between relevant data will be built.
- **Data Translation,** during which the connections established between the relevant data will be interpreted with respect to the issue under consideration.

However, such a linear account fails to reflect the complexities of the interplay between these processes. For example, data selection may intervene during data search. Similarly, the information that is looked for at the stage of data translation might impact the connection between data. Furthermore, although data processing looks very much like a hard skill, it includes various subjective evaluations of information, such as meaningfulness, relevance, or interpretations. It has also been observed that emotions play an important role in decision-making (Damasio, 2005). Most of our decisions are done automatically and fast based on the acquired skills and heuristics, in order to efficiently deal with vast amounts of information (Kahneman, 2011).

Empathy

To "step in another's shoes" is a familiar expression which means to look at the situation through adopting the point of view of another party. This is nothing more than a form of empathy and is not an easy process. In fact human beings have a natural tendency to consider that actions taken by other parties and which do not look consistent with respect to the rationality of the observer(s) are necessarily irrational. In other words there is a natural tendency to equate differences of rationality with absence of rationality. Such conclusion may be true some times, but other times it is not. In this respect it has been shown by Kahneman (2011) that human behaviour is not well described by a rational model. Therefore, to be able to "step in another's shoes" entails being fully aware that the existence of significant distance between the observed behaviour and the observer's rationality does not mean that this behaviour is irrational. In fact, deciding whether the observed behaviour is rational or not requires that the observer develops an elicitation process enabling to determine the preferences of the stakeholder under observation. A vast literature has explored this subject (see Rubinstein & Salant, 2012). Of course, one of the problems regarding this process is that by nature it is based on observation of actions taken by the stakeholder under consideration. These actions are then connected like the pieces of a puzzle with the aim of reconstituting the preference system of the stakeholder. But the preferences can change according to the context, which makes this process even more complex. This raises an epistemological question: when can we draw conclusions about others' rationality? Actually, it seems difficult to do it completely, as human decision making is often driven not only by rational reasoning, but also by emotions (including ethics, morality, etc). In addition, rational thinking depends also on mental energy (Vohs et al., 2008), which can also vary over time. An alternative and more modest approach to resolving this question would be to limit in practice the field of rationality to the perimeter of the issues at stake; in other words to the issues that are of interest for the intelligence analysis within the task received. While this will not guarantee that the assessment of the other's rationality is not erroneous, it will limit the consequences of such error, and be helpful despite the epistemological question above. One way to minimize the probability and the consequences of a rationality assessment error is to gather as much data as possible about the issue at stake and derive a preference elicitation.

Critical Thinking

For intelligence analysis, as in many other fields related to decision making, critical thinking is a core competence. Many definitions of critical thinking exist. Most would agree with the following one proposed by The Critical Thinking Co. (2005) on its website: "Critical thinking is the identification and evaluation of evidence to guide decision making." Furthermore, according to the same source, "a critical thinker uses broad in-depth analysis of evidence to make decisions and communicate his/her beliefs clearly and accurately." This "broad in-depth analysis of evidence" encompasses both data processing and empathy.

Given a dataset – which may include the results of a preference elicitation process taking into account the rationality specific to each stakeholder – what consistent and relevant conclusions can be drawn? To answer this question one needs first to draw from the case analysis a possible set of relevant conclusions. Often, cases are complex, in particular those in which the intelligence analyst has no predefined goal, but has, on the basis of the available data set, to sketch possible scenarios and the associated conclusions. In other words, under such circumstances targets are not given to the intelligence analyst but have to be derived from the available dataset. This will be the case for instance for teams of some large multi-national corporations, such as oil companies, which have devoted significant resources to develop both short- and long-term scenarios, some concerning features that at first sight do not appear directly connected to their present activity.

However, whether the targets are set or still need to be elicited, the meta-method for addressing the issue at stake requires an analysis at two different, albeit connected, levels. The first one is the level of relevance. Given the data set, the analyst needs to determine which data are relevant for the given context. If the targets are set prior to the analysis, then the analyst needs to associate with each target a description and a categorization of the relevant factors with respect to these sets. This is not necessarily an easy task. An example of such task's complexity is how an organization should develop appropriate procedures for crisis management. It is widely accepted that such procedures should be continuous and recursive in nature due to uncertainty as well to whether all factors relevant to such crisis management have been taken into account (Schauster, 2012). This level of uncertainty is further related to the fact that the set of all possible crises is not known in advance, which would be the case if targets were set prior to intelligence analysis.

The second level aim is to determine whether contradictions that may exist between the factors associated with the available dataset. If two contradictory factors are deemed to be irrelevant, the analyst may discard both. But a problem arises when these two contradictory factors are relevant. It is then necessary to sketch an inference scheme in order to determine which factor is true and which is not.

Sketching such an inference scheme requires that the analyst takes into account all relevant factors and simultaneously looks at all existing contradictions (this will be considered in more detail below). One could ask, of course, what would happen if one of the contradicting factors was relevant and the other irrelevant. In fact, the two subcases need to be distinguished, depending on whether the irrelevant factor is true or not. In the subcase where the irrelevant factor is true, the occurrence of the situation considered above is logically impossible since the contradiction between that irrelevant factor and the relevant one implies the fallacy of the latter. Accordingly, the a priori irrelevant factor is in fact relevant. However, if the irrelevant factor is not true, then it no longer needs to be taken into account.

The overall process can be described by Table 1 in which given a factor A deemed to be relevant for the intelligence analysis process, the analyst further considers a factor B that can be either (a) relevant or irrelevant, or (b) consistent or inconsistent with factor A.

COGNITIVE AND DECISION-MAKING BIASES

A substantial literature has developed especially in economic sciences and applied mathematics about how to model decisions. A striking example is that of the 19th Century French scientist

Table 1.

Factor B	Consistent	Inconsistent
Relevant	The pair (A,B) raises no problem	Which of the two factors is true has to be determined by taking other factors into consideration
Irrelevant	The pair (A,B) raises no problem	If B is false the pair (A,B) raises no problem If B is true, this is impossible

Augustin Cournot, whose vision was that the laws of Mechanics and more generally, mathematical formulae, would provide an appropriate framework for rational decision making (Cournot, 1838). The literature dealing with optimization theory, i.e. with mathematical methods that aim at finding optimal solutions to decision problems, stems from this vision (Dixit, 1990) However, since the second part of the 20th century, theoretical understandings have become more diverse. On the one hand, rigidity associated with the Cournot's concept of mechanical organization led to the development in Japan of the concept of 'Bunsha', a view of organization based on the biological concepts of flexibility and adaptability (Sakai & Russel, 1994). On the other hand, behavioural studies have shown that there might be significant divergences between observed behaviours and behaviours predicted by mathematical theories of rational decision making, leading to questioning the development of an economic science built on mathematical laws (Camerer, 2003). Some authors, like Ariely (2009), regard human behaviours as predictably irrational, while research in experimental psychology has led Kahneman & Tversky (1979) to develop their Prospect Theory, which emphasises the importance of cognitive and decision-making biases. An illustrative example of such bias is the higher sensitivity of human beings to losses than to gains (i.e. the degree of dissatisfaction generated by the loss of 100 € is higher than the degree of satisfaction generated by a gain of 100 €).

If Prospect Theory focuses mainly on biases with no explicit references to cultural specificities (like anchoring biases, or greater sensitivity to losses than to gains) Ajzen's Theory of Planned Behaviour (Ajzen, 1991) introduces a cultural dimension by highlighting the importance not only of personal attitude toward the behaviour and perceived behavioural control for explaining behavioural intention, but also of subjective norms which represent the perception of the behaviour reflected by the social environment of the individual under consideration. Similarly, the Ultimatum Game of Güth et al. (1982) shows that strict economic utility cannot by itself be predictive of human behaviour. This game concerns the interaction of two players, the proponent who proposes a share of a given amount of money, say for instance 100 €, and the respondent, who can accept or reject the proposal. In case of acceptance the 100 € are shared according to the proposal made by the proponent. In case of rejection by the respondent, each one gets nothing. Strict economic utility would determine that whatever the proposal made, the respondent should accept it on the grounds that getting little is better than getting nothing. However, experiments have shown that this is not the case. If the share proposed to the respondent is too small, he will refuse it. The findings from these experiments have led some analysts to conclude that rationality can no longer be regarded as the core factor underpinning human decision making. New fields of research such as Neuro-Economy have also emerged, which relate economic decisions taken by human beings with neural activity (Pinker, 2009; Schmidt, 2010).

Psychology also tells us that people change their views of events so that they can feel better about them (Gilbert, 2006). Thinking allows us to change our views of the world in order to change our emotional reactions to it. Rationalization is largely an unconscious process. There are dozens of fallacies and cognitive biases in human nature (Gilbert, 2006; Taleb, 2007), for instance:

- **Confirmation Bias:** A tendency for people to prefer information that confirms their preconceptions or hypotheses, independently of whether they are true.
- **Hindsight Bias:** The inclination to see events that have occurred as more predictable than they in fact were before they took place.
- **Optimism Bias:** The demonstrated systematic tendency for people to be over-

optimistic about the outcome of planned actions.

- **Impact Bias:** The tendency for people to overestimate the length or the intensity of future feeling states.
- **Observation Bias:** As people usually see just the winners, not the losers, they may misattribute the causes that led to the winning.
- **Planning Fallacy:** The tendency to underestimate task-completion times.
- **Narrative Fallacy:** Creating a story post-hoc so that an event will seem to have an identifiable cause.
- **Ludic Fallacy:** Believing that the unstructured randomness found in life resembles the structured randomness found in games.

Taking into account a whole variety of biases and fallacies, three basic categories can be distinguished (Thaler & Sunstein, 2008):

- **Bounded Rationality:** Our rationality is delimited.
  - Unrealistic optimism is a pervasive feature of human life.
  - Humans fear loss more than they love gain.
  - People have a tendency to stick with their current situation.
  - Choices depend on the way in which problems are stated.
  - **Priming:** Subtle influences can increase the ease with which certain info comes to mind (channel factors).
- **Self-Control:** Our rationality and temptation may be in conflict.
  - An individual is containing two semi-autonomous selves, which means there is a two-system conception of self-control: planner and doer.

- **Social Influences:** We are influenced by the behavior of other people.
  - **Information:** On actions and thoughts of others (we tend to conform).
  - **Peer Pressure:** Considering what other people think to avoid their disapproval.

CRITICAL THINKING DEVELOPMENT

Critical thinking is a broad concept, which includes clarification of goals, evaluation of evidence, accomplishment of actions, and assessment of conclusions. It has its roots thousands of years ago in the Socratic method of Ancient Greece as well as in the Buddha's teachings. The list of core critical thinking skills includes observation, interpretation, analysis, inference, evaluation, explanation, and meta-cognition (Ennis, 1987).

Some psychologists (Kahneman, 2011) describe human mental processes by the metaphor of two agents, System 1 and System 2, which respectively produce fast and slow thinking. System 1 is fast, impulsive and intuitive, but prone to cognitive biases. If System 1 is involved in cognitive processes, the conclusion comes first and the arguments follow. System 2 is capable of reasoning, cautious, but in some cases "lazy". Self-control and cognitive effort are forms of mental work and System 2 controls thoughts and behaviours. This means that System 2 monitors and controls actions "suggested" by System 1. Various activities compete for the limited resources of System 2, so self-control and deliberate thought draw on the same limited budget of effort. This leads to the law of 'least effort'. One of the key observations in the field of psychology is that many people are overconfident, prone to place too much faith in their intuitions. They find cognitive effort unpleasant and try to avoid it (Frederick, 2005).

'Intelligence', in the sense of cognitive abilities (Burt, 1931), generally includes the ability to reason as well as the ability to retrieve relevant material in memory and to deploy attention when needed. The search for relevant information in memory is performed by System 1, but System 2 can be used for deliberate checking and search. This is an important ability that varies among individuals. Based on System 2 usage for self-monitoring, two types of people can be distinguished: 1. "lazy" and 2. "engaged" or "more rational" (Stanovich, 2011) – in the second case, those who are more alert, intellectually active, sceptical about intuitions.

Measures of cognitive abilities, such as IQ scores, display only weak correlations with thinking dispositions (Stanovich, 2011). If people are provided with the rules they need to follow in order to solve a thinking problem (well-defined problems), then those with higher IQ scores do better. But in the absence of given rules they do not. Mental dispositions that contribute to real world performance include (Stanovich, 2009): "The tendency to collect information before making up one's mind, the tendency to seek various points of view before coming to a conclusion, the disposition to think extensively about a problem before responding, the tendency to calibrate the degree of strength of one's opinions to the degree of evidence available, the tendency to think about future consequences before taking action, the tendency to explicitly weight pluses and minuses of a situation before making a decision, and the tendency to seek nuance and avoid absolutism."

Pinker (2009) asserts that our minds are made rather for 'fitness' (i.e. survival), than for truth. Indeed, evidence from behavioural and cognitive psychology supports this view. As Gilbert (2006) points out, the meaning or interpretation of sensory stimuli can be subjectively ambiguous and depends on the context, frequency, recency, as well as preferences of the concrete person (i. e. we see what we want to see). Memory plays tricks on us when we try to look backwards in time and imagination does it when we try to look forward. People neither remember nor predict events correctly.

However, such cognitive biases have a pattern – they are lawful, regular, and systematic. We can utilize these findings to enhance our understanding, for when humans err predictably, this knowledge can be harnessed to help them (Thaler & Sunstein, 2008).

A GAME THEORY BASED SUPPORTING TOOL

In this section we introduce a supporting tool based on Game Theory. The aim is that the tool is based on serious games and helps to develop critical thinking and intelligence analysis.

Description and Prescription: The Use of Game Theory

Game Theory (Eatwell et al., 1989) is a scientific tool for analysing rational behaviours of interacting decision makers. It is essentially a normative and prescriptive instrument. Its relevance to the description of observed behaviours may at first sight be considered as irrelevant, but nevertheless three branches of Game Theory have some utility for closing the gap between description and prescription.

The first, Behavioural Game Theory, takes into account players' emotions and limited foresight, and combines them with rational thinking (Camerer, 2003). If we consider the case of the Ultimatum Game, this means that conclusions drawn from experiments will not necessarily militate against the usefulness of rational thinking when trying to describe decision makers' behaviours: they may possibly lead to wider definitions of utility. Such definitions may, for example, take into account feelings like pride, humiliation, sense of fairness etc, which constitute supplementary dimensions of utility with respect to those traditionally taken into account in instrumental rationality (Kolodny & Brunero, 2013).

Beyond these problems related to emotions and feelings, a second branch of Game Theory, Evolutionary Games, describes the evolution of behaviours inside a given population broken down into species, such that each species is characterized by a specific behaviour. The premise of Evolutionary Games is that in the long run, the population as a whole will tend to adopt the behaviours that are the most efficient with respect to the goals pursued by the individuals composing that population. Evolutionary Games also help us to understand why 'evolution' may not always be optimal by means of the concept of 'Evolutionary Stable Equilibrium' which indicates the conditions under which evolution might stop (Maynard-Smith, 1982). Based on a Darwinian selection principle, Evolutionary Games thus enable to give a quite appropriate description of behaviours and cultures' evolutions within a given society. In that sense, just like Behavioural Game Theory, Evolutionary Game Theory builds bridges between behavioural description and prescription.

A third branch of Game Theory which focuses on building such bridges is the one that links Neural Networks and Game Theory. A vast literature has already been developed concerning the representation of the brain starting from observations about how the mind works (Pinker, 2009) and modelling the system under the form of Artificial Neural Networks (ANN). In turn these ANN have been used to model players' behaviours. Such has been the case for instance for modelling the behaviours of players in a repeated Prisoners' Dilemma (Chellapilla & Fogel, 1999). Conversely some attempts have been made to use Game Theory to analyse the functioning of ANN (Schuster & Yamaguchi, 2010). As we shall see below, beyond describing the functioning of the brain, Game Theory can also be used to foster creativity and intelligence analysis. However to this end, we need first to introduce a particular class of games called 'Games of Deterrence'.

Games of Deterrence: An Introduction

The previous section devoted to cognitive and decision making biases has argued that in real life human beings often do not adopt rational behaviours, as would be predicted by the classical framework of instrumental rationality (Kolodny & Brunero, 2013). Accordingly, human behaviour cannot be adequately predicted by the instruments of standard Game Theory based on the principle of utility maximization. A case that led to an in-depth exploration by Simon (1982), is that of decision makers equipped with a bounded rationality, whose decision making is driven by the goal of obtaining not the optimal outcome, but more modestly, merely a satisficing one. In game theoretic terms, this means that the games to be used within the framework of bounded rationality would be more qualitative than quantitative.

More precisely, Rufus Isaacs' theory of Qualitative Games analyzes, analyses situations in which the players' objective is to reach a target that can be defined as a particular set of states of the world, irrespective of the cost required to reach that target (Isaacs, 1965). Games of Deterrence stem from this approach. They consider that the set of states of the world (i.e. the situations to which the players may be confronted) can be clustered in two categories: (a) states of the world that are acceptable to the player under consideration, and (b) states of the world that are unacceptable to her. The notation '1' will be used here to indicate acceptable states, and '0' to indicate unacceptable states.

In a Game of Deterrence, the aim of each player is to get a 1, which in terms of bounded rationality means to get a *satisficing* outcome (Simon, 1982). As in Isaacs' Qualitative Differential Games, Games of Deterrence focus on the strategies' playability properties. In Isaacs' approach every strategy that guarantees that the player under consideration will reach her target is called 'playable'. In Games of Deterrence, things are a little more complex. Let us consider for instance the two player game involving 'Roger' and 'Eve' which is represented by the matrix of Table 2.

Strategies e_1 for Eve and r_2 for Roger guarantee the players who select them an acceptable outcome. Therefore, they will be termed *safe*. In contrast, strategies e_2 and r_1 bear a risk. Thus, if Roger chooses r_1, while Eva chooses e_1, Roger will be put in an unacceptable situation. Similarly, if Eve chooses e_2 while Roger chooses r_1, Eve will be put in an unacceptable situation. Therefore e_2 and r_1 are termed *dangerous*. In this elementary game, it seems obvious that the good decision for each player is to select her / his safe strategy. In other words, there is a one to one correspondence, between safe strategies and playable ones. But the example of Table 3 shows that this is not always the case.

We see here that due to Eve's strategy e_1, both of Roger's strategies are now dangerous. Nevertheless, as in a game a player must play, and given that the two strategies of Roger are equivalent (they give Roger the same outcome, whatever the strategy selected by Eve), Roger will choose one of the two. Consequently both strategies of Roger are simultaneously dangerous and playable (in the sense explained below).

Now it seems obvious that the nature of these two strategies' playability is not the same. In the first example r_2 was playable because it was in

Table 2. Example 1

		Roger	
		r_1	r_2
Eve	e_1	(1,0)	(1,1)
	e_2	(0,1)	(1,1)

Table 3. Example 2

		Roger	
		r_1	r_2
Eve	e_1	(1,0)	(1,0)
	e_2	(1,1)	(1,1)

some sense a "good" strategy, while in example 2 r_2 is not a "good" strategy, but Roger has no better choice. So we shall distinguish between two types of playability:

1. A strategy will be termed *positively playable* if it guarantees the player who selects it an acceptable outcome, provided that the other player plays rationally (i.e. takes decisions that are consistent with her / his goal, i.e. to get an acceptable outcome).
2. If a player has no positively playable strategy, then all her / his strategies will be termed *playable by default*.

A strategy which is either positively playable or playable by default will thus be termed *playable*.

Before being able to apply Games of Deterrence to the development of critical thinking and intelligence analysis, two further steps are required. The first one deals with the introduction of the concept of deterrence. Thus, given a strategic pair (e,r) we shall consider Eve's strategy e as *deterrent* vis-à-vis Roger's strategy r if the following three conditions apply:

1. e is playable.
2. Implementation of strategic pair (e,r) leads to an unacceptable outcome for Roger.
3. Roger has an alternative strategy r' that is positively playable.

For instance in Example 1, e_1 is deterrent vis-à-vis r_1. Indeed:

1. e_1 is safe, hence playable.
2. Implementation of (e_1,r_1) is unacceptable for Roger.
3. Roger's strategy r_2 is safe hence positively playable.

Conversely, in example 2, e_1 is not deterrent vis-à-vis r_1 because Roger has no positively playable strategy, and hence the third condition is not satisfied.

Now there is a one to one relation between deterrence and playability. More precisely, it has been shown (Rudnianski, 1991) that a strategy s of a player is playable if and only if there is no strategy of the other player which is deterrent vis-à-vis s. So playability and deterrence are like two faces of the same coin, and therefore deterrence can be used for determining the strategies' playability properties. Thus in example 1, r_1 is not playable since there Eve has strategy (e_1) which is deterrent vis-à-vis r_1.

We can then introduce the concept of game *solution*. With each player's strategy s, let us associate a positive playability index J(s), such that J(s) = 1 if s is positively playable, and J(s) = 0 otherwise. A solution of the Game of Deterrence can be defined as the set of values taken by all J(s). We further define a strategic pair (e,r) as an *equilibrium* of the Game of Deterrence if e and r are playable.

In example 1 the solution is {$J(e_1)$ = 1; $J(e_2)$ = 1; $J(r_1)$ = 0; $J(r_2)$ = 1}, and then the Game displays two equilibria (e_1,r_2) and (e_2,r_2). It can be shown (Rudnianski, 1991) that a game may have several solutions, and that several equilibria may be associated with the same solution.

The second step to the application of Games of Deterrence to Critical Thinking and Intelligence Analysis is the introduction of Graphs of Deterrence, which are in a one-to-one relation with each matrix Game of Deterrence[1]. More precisely with each matrix Game of Deterrence, we shall associate a graph such that:

1. The graph vertices are the players' strategies.
2. The graph is bipartite (i.e. a graph such that the origin and extremity of any arc are strategies that do not belong to the same player).
3. There is an arc of origin e (respectively r) and of extremity r (respectively e) if implementation of strategic pair (e,r) leads to an unacceptable outcome for Roger (respectively for Eve).

Now it has been shown (Rudnianski, 1991) that every graph of deterrence can be broken down into connected parts, each one being a path or a graph without root. Let us further define:

- An *E-path* (respectively an *R-path*) as a path which root is a strategy of Eve (respectively of Roger).
- A *C-graph* as a graph without root.

The rationale for distinguishing between different categories of graphs lies in the fact that each category can be associated with specific properties of the corresponding game solutions. Thus it has been shown (Rudnianski, 1991) that:

- If the graph of deterrence reduces to a path, the only positively playable strategy is the root, all other strategies of odd rank are not playable, with all strategies of even rank being playable by default[2].
- If the graph of deterrence is a circuit[3], all the players' strategies are playable by default.
- More generally, depending whether the breakdown of the graph includes E-paths, R-paths or C- graphs, one can distinguish between 7 types of matrix Games of Deterrence: E,R,C, E/R, E/C, R/C, and E/R/C[4] and the game type defines the properties of the solution set.

Returning to example 1, the graph of deterrence associated with the matrix is the following:

$$e_1 \rightarrow r_1 \rightarrow e_2 \, r_2$$

Similarly, the graph of deterrence associated with the matrix of example 2 is:

$$r_1 \leftarrow e_1 \rightarrow r_2 \, e_2$$

We can conclude that graphs of deterrence can be used to facilitate the determination of the solutions and equilibria of Games of Deterrence.

Application to Critical Thinking and Intelligence Analysis

The representation of matrix Games of Deterrence by graphs of deterrence, presents another advantage focused on a specific type of application, which is argumentation (Rudnianski, 2012; Rudnianski & Bestougeff, 2008; Rudnianski & Lalonde, 2009).

Let us return to example 1 above. It can be seen either from the game matrix or from the associated graph of deterrence that the game is of type E/R with a unique solution characterized by: $J(e_1) = 1$; $J(e_2) = 1$; $J(r_1) = 0$; $J(r_2) = 1$.

Suppose that Roger is a photographer and Eve is the chief editor of the magazine 'The World' that has published one of Roger's photographs. Suddenly, Roger discovers that Eve has sold the photograph to a foreign magazine 'The Globe Today', believing that, as it was taken for 'The World', the latter is entitled to transfer its rights of use (argument e_2).

Roger denies this argument on the basis that he did not give any authorization to Eve (argument r_1). But Eve replies that Roger is an employee of 'The World' and that the photography has been taken by him under the terms of his contract with the magazine and following a specific demand from Eve (argument e_1).

Roger replies that he has been taken many photos before becoming an employee of the World (argument r_2). One can consider that argument r_1 defeats argument e_2: the fact that the photo taken by Roger has been reproduced by 'The World' does not enable the magazine to transfer the rights of use to a third party. But in turn, argument r_1 is defeated by argument e_1: the photo was taken by Roger under the terms of his employment contract and in response to a specific demand from Eve, and as a result, the work belongs to the magazine. Finally, the fact that Roger has taken many photos for 'The World' before the sell-on of his work to another magazine has no impact on the issue under consideration.

Now if two arguments x and y are such that x defeats y, we can represent the corresponding inference scheme by: **x -> y**

We can then see that the above case of intellectual property rights (IPR) concerning the use of Roger's photograph can be represented by the graph of deterrence of example 1, and hence that the argumentation case can be associated with the corresponding matrix Game of Deterrence. This means more generally that any bilateral argumentation issue can be represented under the form of a matrix Game of Deterrence, the solutions of which will provide the clue for the conclusions about the argumentation under consideration.

More precisely, as in the present example, and under the assumption that the charge of proof belongs to the one who wants to deny the validity of an argument:

- Arguments that are associated with positively playable strategies are not defeated and hence are deemed to be true.
- Arguments that are associated with non playable strategies are defeated, and hence are deemed to be false.

Given the above associations, one question has to be addressed: what about argumentation cases in which the arguments of one party are associated with strategies that are playable by default (remember that such is the case if the party has no positively playable strategy)?

This case is dealt by ensuring that it never occurs! How? By adding a consistency condition associated with a safe strategy, which therefore guarantees that the game associated with the argumentation does not include strategies that are playable by default. Indeed in this case, the strategies which in the original game were playable by default, become not playable.

How should we choose the consistency condition? In the framework of binary logic, take any proposition x and its negation ¬x. Then the proposition x ∨ ¬x (either x is true or non x is true) is always true, therefore cannot be defeated, and hence in the Game of Deterrence representation is associated with a safe strategy.

A possible extension which has already been explored is to consider, not binary logic (in which an argument is either true or false), but fuzzy logic in which arguments can be *more or less* true. It has been shown that such argumentation can be associated with a fuzzy Game of Deterrence, i.e. a game in which solutions display indices of positive playability which take non binary values (Rudnianski & Lalonde, 2009).

Without entering into technical details that are out of scope in this chapter, let us just note that it has been demonstrated (Rudnianski & Lalonde, 2009) that if the graph of deterrence is a path, the positive playability index of strategies of odd rank decreases with the distance to the root of the path, while on the opposite the positive playability index of strategies of even rank increases with the distance to that root. In particular, if the number of strategies grows endlessly, the positively playability indices of strategies of even and odd rank tend toward .5. Translated into terms of argumentation, this means that an inference scheme will be such that the further the distance between two arguments on the corresponding graph, the lower the impact of the upward argument on the other. Thus, playability analysis enables to draw conclusions about the truthfulness of arguments within the framework of the available information (in other words, of the set of possible arguments as known by the stakeholder under consideration).

Now argumentation can be considered as a specific example of intelligence analysis, which deals with interpretation of available data, transforming them into meaningful information, i.e. information that can be used to build, confirm or infirm hypotheses. Therefore the game theoretic tools introduced here can be used to develop intelligence analysis.

One possibility is to use these tools to support the development of a serious game in which the goal of the trainee(s) is to draw conclusions about

a case presented in the form of various bits of data presented either simultaneously or not, either upon the trainee's demand or generated by the system. Let us return to the case of the photograph:

1. A first set of bits of data is presented to the trainee (the photo, a portrait of Roger, a portrait of Eve, Roger's claim r_1).
2. The trainee is asked: is Roger's claim justified?
3. The trainee can have access upon demand to legal texts.
4. After a moment, Eve's argument e_2 is sent to the trainee.
5. Then Roger's argument r_2 is presented.
6. Last Eve's argument e_1 is presented.

What is expected from the trainee is the construction of an inference scheme which allows conclusions to be drawn. More generally, the serious game may start with a narrative characterized by imperfect information, and the trainee required (a) to select a set of potential conclusions between which she will have to choose on the basis of further information and then (b) to construct the inference scheme.

CONCLUSION

The aim of this chapter is to highlight that intelligence analysis is a challenging topic, as psychology has shown that humans are not only rational beings, but also emotional ones. Nevertheless, especially when making important decisions, rationality will play an important role in the process. Hard skills such as ordinary data processing do not suffice solely in themselves to comprehend and analyse the decisions of others. Instead, soft skills such as empathy and critical thinking have to be cultivated. Serious games have the potential to serve as a supporting tool for the development of these skills. We have tried to outline how one particular type of game, Games of Deterrence, might be used to represent argumentation and cultivate intelligence analysis across a wide range of applications.

REFERENCES

Ajzen, I. (1991). The theory of planned behavior. *Organizational Behavior and Human Decision Processes*, *50*(2), 179–211. doi:10.1016/0749-5978(91)90020-T.

Ariely, D. (2009). *Predictably irrational: The hidden forces that shape our decisions*. New York: Harper.

Berkowitz, B. D., & Goodman, A. E. (1989). *Strategic intelligence for American national security*. Princeton, NJ: Princeton University Press.

Burt, C. (1954). The differentiation of intellectual ability. *The British Journal of Educational Psychology*, *24*(2), 76–90. doi:10.1111/j.2044-8279.1954.tb02882.x.

Camerer, C. (2003). *Behavioral game theory: Experiments in strategic interaction*. Princeton, NJ: Princeton University Press.

Chellapilla, K., & Fogel, D. B. (1999). Evolution, neural networks, games, and intelligence. *Proceedings of the IEEE*, *87*(9), 1471–1496. doi:10.1109/5.784222.

Cournot, A. A. (1838). *Recherches sur les principes mathématiques de la théorie des richesses*. L. Hachette.

Damasio, A. (2005). *Descartes' error: Emotion, reason, and the human brain*. New York: Penguin Books.

Dixit, A. K. (1990). *Optimization in economic theory*. Oxford, UK: Oxford University Press.

Eatwell, J., Milgate, M., & Newman, P. (Eds.). (1989). *The new palgrave: Game theory*. New York: Macmillan Reference Books.

Ennis, R. H. (1987). A taxonomy of critical thinking dispositions and abilities. In J. B. Baron, & R. J. Sternberg (Eds.), *Teaching thinking skills: Theory and practice* (pp. 9–26). New York: Freeman.

European Commission. (2008). *The European qualifications framework for lifelong learning (EQF)*. Luxembourg: Office for Official Publications of the European Communities.

Frederick, S. (2005). Cognitive reflection and decision making. *The Journal of Economic Perspectives*, *19*(4), 25–42. doi:10.1257/089533005775196732.

Gilbert, D. (2006). *Stumbling on happiness*. New York: Vintage.

Gilboa, I. (2010). *Making better decisions: Decision theory in practice*. Oxford, UK: Wiley-Blackwell.

Güth, W., Schmittberger, R., & Schwarze, B. (1982). An experimental analysis of ultimatum bargaining. *Journal of Economic Behavior & Organization*, *3*(4), 367–388. doi:10.1016/0167-2681(82)90011-7.

Heuer, R. J. Jr. (1999). *Psychology of intelligence analysis*. Washington, DC: US Government Printing Office.

Issacs, R. (1955). *Differential games: A mathematical theory with applications to warfare and pursuit, control and optimization*. Academic Press.

Kahneman, D. (2011). *Thinking, fast and slow*. New York: Farrar, Straus and Giroux.

Kahneman, D., & Tversky, A. (1979). Prospect theory: An analysis of decision under risk. *Econometrica*, 263–291. doi:10.2307/1914185.

Kolodny, N., & Brunero, J. (2013). Instrumental rationality. In E. N. Zalta (Ed.), *The Stanford Encyclopedia of Philosophy*. Palo Alto, CA: Stanford University. Retrieved from http://plato.stanford.edu/archives/spr2013/entries/rationality-instrumental/

Maynard Smith, J. (1982). *Evolution and the theory of games*. Cambridge, UK: Cambridge University Press. doi:10.1017/CBO9780511806292.

Pinker, S. (2009). *How the mind works*. New York: Norton Publishers.

Rubinstein, A., & Salant, Y. (2012). Eliciting welfare preferences from behavioural data sets. *The Review of Economic Studies*, *79*, 375–387. doi:10.1093/restud/rdr024.

Rudnianski, M. (1991). Deterrence typology and nuclear stability: A game theoretical approach. *Defense Decision Making*, 137-168.

Rudnianski, M. (2012). From argumentation to negotiation: The game of deterrence path. *Rivista Quadrimestrale*, (17).

Rudnianski, M., & Bestougeff, H. (2008). Deterrence and defeasibility in argumentation process for ALIS project. In *Computable Models of the Law* (pp. 219–238). Berlin: Springer. doi:10.1007/978-3-540-85569-9_14.

Rudnianski, M., & Lalonde, T. (2009). Argumentation and time in IPR issues: the ALIS project game of deterrence approach. *Game Theory and Applications*, *14*, 114–140.

Sakai, K., & Russell, D. (1994). *To expand, we divide: The practice and principles of Bunsha management*. Intercultural Group.

Schauster, E. (2012). The structuration of crisis management: Guiding a process of repair. *Journal of Professional Communication*, *2*(1), 77–88.

Schmidt, C. (2010). *Neuroéconomie: Comment les neurosciences transforment l'analyse économique*. Odile Jacob.

Schuster, A., & Yamaguchi, Y. (2010). Application of game theory to neuronal networks. *Advances in Artificial Intelligence*, 1–13. doi:10.1155/2010/521606.

Simon, H. A. (1982). *Models of bounded rationality*. Cambridge, MA: MIT Press.

Stanovich, K. (2011). *Rationality and the reflective mind*. Oxford, UK: Oxford University Press.

Stanovich, K. E. (2009). *What intelligence tests miss: The psychology of rational thought*. New Haven, CT: Yale University Press.

Taleb, N. N. (2007). *The black swan: The impact of the highly improbable*. New York: Random House.

Thaler, R. H., & Sunstein, C. R. (2008). *Nudge: Improving decisions about health, wealth, and happiness*. New Haven, CT: Yale University Press.

The Critical Thinking Co. (2005). Retrieved from http://www.criticalthinking.com/company/articles/critical-thinking-definition.jsp

Vohs, K. D., Baumeister, R. F., Schmeichel, B. J., Twenge, J. M., Nelson, N. M., & Tice, D. M. (2008). Making choices impairs subsequent self-control: A limited-resource account of decision making, self-regulation, and active initiative. *Journal of Personality and Social Psychology*, *94*(5), 883. doi:10.1037/0022-3514.94.5.883 PMID:18444745.

KEY TERMS AND DEFINITIONS

Cognitive Bias: A pattern of deviation in judgment, whereby inferences of other people and situations may be drawn in an illogical fashion.

Critical Thinking: The identification and evaluation of evidence to guide decision making.

Data Processing: Operations performed on a given set of data to extract the required information in an appropriate form.

Empathy: The capacity to recognize emotions that are being experienced by another sentient or fictional being.

Game Theory: The study of mathematical models of conflict and cooperation between intelligent rational decision-makers.

Games of Deterrence: Games, which consider that the set of states of the world (i.e. the situations to which the players may be confronted) can be clustered in two categories: (a) states of the world that are acceptable to the player under consideration, and (b) states of the world that are unacceptable to her.

Intelligence Analysis: The transformation of a set of raw data into meaningful information, which will enable decision-makers who have requested that analysis, to take appropriate actions.

ENDNOTES

[1]   A matrix Game of Deterrence is a two player Game of Deterrence represented by a table called matrix and such that the rows represent the strategies of one player while the columns represent the strategies of the other player. Examples 1 and 2 above are matrix Games of Deterrence.

[2]   The various vertices are ranked, the first one being the root. The second strategy is the one which is at the extremity of the arc, which origin is the root. Likewise the third strategy is the one located at the extremity of the arc which origin is the second one etc. So for instance given a path such that the root is a strategy of Eve (E-path), the strategies of Eve will be of odd rank while the strategies of Roger will be of even rank. Similarly if we consider an R-path, i.e. a path with root is a strategy of Roger, all strategies of Roger on that path will be of odd rank, while all strategies of Eve will be of even rank (see examples below).

[3]   A circuit is the simplest form of graph with no root. For instance a circuit can be obtained from a path through adding an arc which origin is the strategy of highest rank and the extremity is the root.

[4]   For instance a game which graph of deterrence includes only E-paths will be called a game of E-type, while a game which graph of deterrence includes both R-paths and C-graphs will be called a game of type R/C.

Chapter 4
Time Factor Assessment in Game-Based Learning:
Time Perspective and Time-on-Task as Individual Differences between Players

Mireia Usart
Universitat Ramon Llull (ESADE), Spain

Margarida Romero
Universitat Ramon Llull (ESADE), Spain

ABSTRACT

From primary school levels to lifelong learning, the use of games for educational purposes has been an increasing focus of interest for instructional designers, teachers, and researchers. One of the factors that can be assessed in Game-Based Learning (GBL) is the time factor. In this chapter, time is considered as the time used by players (time-on-task) and as psychological time perceived by students (time perspective). Time Perspective (TP) is a cognitive aspect of players, defined as the manner in which individuals divide time into past, present, and future. This variable can be considered as an individual difference; players with a temporal perspective focused on the future may play games differently than students oriented to the past or present. This chapter aims to study how Serious Games (SG) can help in assessing time-on-task by learners and time perspective. After a theoretical review of these aspects, a case study of MetaVals is presented as an example of time assessment in SG. This game was designed by ESADE's learning innovation team and monitors player times for individual and collaborative phases of the game. The results focus on the key aspects for assessing time in the class use of GBL and offer designers and teachers a reliable instrument for better personalising and implementing of SG tasks in the context of time.

DOI: 10.4018/978-1-4666-4773-2.ch004

Copyright © 2014, IGI Global. Copying or distributing in print or electronic forms without written permission of IGI Global is prohibited.

INTRODUCTION

In educational contexts, the time factor is an implicit perspective that some approaches have tried to make explicit by defining typologies of academic time. The time factor and quality of time are important aspects for understanding learning activities (Barberà, Gros & Kirschner, 2012; Romero, 2010), and especially in active learning methodologies such as Game Based Learning (GBL), where students have a central role in the development of the game and the regulation of their time-on-task. The allocated time for a game activity set by the instructional designers also represents an important factor that must be taken into account, especially regarding student performances, when integrating games in the curriculum and, in particular, when designing how and what aspects should be assessed in learning activities.

GBL can be defined as a computer-based learning methodology intended for educational purposes that supports student-centred learning in a significant way (Sica, Delli Veneri, & Miglino, 2011). Also called Serious Games (SG), this methodology is designed to help learners achieve a balance between fun and educational value (Zyda, 2005; Klopfer, Osterweil & Salen, 2009). In particular, following Connolly and colleagues (2012) there is a need to pay attention to psychological and pedagogical aspects of SGs. As a computer-based methodology, one of the aspects highlighted as an important factor in GBL is time (Gee, 2009). Time has also been highlighted as an important factor in computer-based learning methodologies (Barbera, Gros & Kirschner, 2012). Therefore, in this chapter we will focus on how to assess time in GBL, in particular, we will present a case study of SG MetaVals to help us understand the new needs that GBL creates for practitioners and SG designers when compared to non-game-based learning methodologies relating to time. With the aim of giving a wide perspective to the assessment of the time factor in learning, we will focus on engagement time (defined as time-on-task; Fisher et al., 1980; Romero, 2011), as an objective measure of time in a learning task; as well as studying the assessment of time as a subjective or psychological variable such as the Time Perspective (TP) of students (Zimbardo & Boyd, 1999).

The main aim of this chapter is to understand how student time can be assessed during the different stages of an SG learning activity: the preparation phase before the start of the game; the SG playing activity; and the subsequent analysis of the SG activity. Moreover, we give tips on how instructional designers and teachers can help learners regulate their time when playing SG. To achieve this objective, we focus on how two factors impact on learning in the GBL methodology: 1) time-on-task as the objective time students spend in a GBL activity or task; and 2) student time perspective (TP) as the psychological time each player contributes. Figure 1 shows an overview of the typological assessment of time according to the various stages of SG activity addressed in this chapter.

TIME ASSESSMENT IN GBL

Time in learning has been mostly studied as a factor related to academic achievement. Following Carroll (1963), students can learn optimally when the time they spend learning is the time required by the task in relation to the current stage of development, ability, and knowledge of each learner. The time invested in learning by students is nevertheless framed by their personal and social temporal constrictions, time constrictions in their learning institutions (institutional time), and the time constrictions introduced by teachers (time allocated to learning the task). The time a student decides to invest in learning has been related to student engagement and motivation (Lewis, 2007; Wagner, Schober & Spiel, 2008). Focusing on computer-based learning in general and on GBL in particular, time could be a key factor in assess-

Figure 1. Time assessment scheme for GBL activities. (© 2013 Margarida Romero and Mireia Usart. Used with permission.)

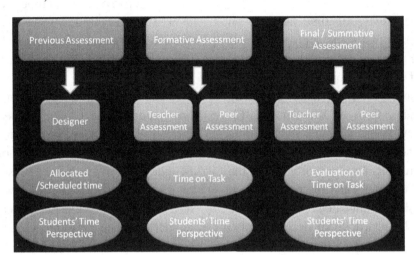

ment, due to the fact that SG can promote a more active role for students, and the amount of time they spend in these activities could be related to an improved learning rate (Cooley & Lohnes, 1976; Lewis, 2007). From a metacognitive standpoint, Metcalfe (2002) claims that existing results in computer-based methodologies seem to sustain the idea that these methodologies could help learners manage time while learning. Furthermore, learners' TP (Zimbardo & Boyd, 1999) have also been related to academic achievement in GBL (Romero & Usart, 2012). This intrapsychological variable has historically been assessed through the use of self-reported tests – such as the Zimbardo Time Perspective Inventory (ZTPI) measuring the TP (Zimbardo & Boyd).

We could therefore approach the assessment of time in GBL from the institutional side; from the teacher standpoint, or as the time (objective and subjective) learners are engaged in a SG task. The focus of this chapter is to understand how to assess student use of time spent in the learning task, and player psychological time in the field of GBL activities.

In this chapter, we will start by studying learner time in GBL as an objective and directly measurable variable: time-on-task, defined as the time

an individual spends in a learning activity (Fisher et al. 1980). This concept is part of instructional time, and following Berliner (1990), it is less molar than allocated instructional time. Therefore, it may be more related to learning achievement than the institutional time variable. Furthermore, time-on-task is not the exact learning time a student is effectively learning (effective learning time), as this latter concept is framed by time-on-task and it is still difficult to measure from an educational standpoint (most research and assessment on student learning time is based on measurements of the time-on-task variable).

Secondly, we will focus on learner subjective time; each student has an individual time perspective (TP) that enables him or her to play and interact with other students in a very different manner, depending on his or her particular TP factor distribution. TP, as we will show in the following sections, can be considered a subjective variable (Zimbardo & Boyd, 1999), defined as the way individuals and cultures divide their experience into three different temporal categories: past, present and future. These three categories are divided by Zimbardo and Boyd into five factors (past positive, past negative, present hedonism, present fatalism, and future).

Both aspects of time should be assessed in three time intervals: before the game (designers must build a temporal framework within the game where students can play and interact, and define the limits of the gameplay in terms of time); during the game (teachers allow a certain amount of time for the activity, and players interact with the game during a certain time-on-task, while they perceive time in a subjective manner); and after the GBL activity (teachers can evaluate the time spent in the task and the student results). This sequence must be followed to evaluate the correct design of an SG activity; for the individual and collaborative use of time during this learning task by students; and finally, once the task has ended, to help evaluate and improve the learning process.

Time-on-Task Assessment in GBL

The measure of time in learning has been studied and defined through different models and theories; we will focus on the widely used ALT model (Fischer et al. 1980; Harnischfeger & Wiley, 1985). In particular, we will study GBL using the ALT model adaptation to computer-based learning by Romero (2010) (see Figure 2). This model focuses on time, both from instructional and student perspectives. Within the ALT model, students can devote more or less time to the learning activity (engaged time or time-on-task) within the bounds of the time allocated by the teacher (allocated time). Within this time range, students have an amount of effective learning time.

- **Instructional Time:** Instructional time is defined as the theoretical time-on-task required for achieving the learning objectives of a designed learning task (Berliner, 1990). It can be set by the game designer based on the educational objectives, but teachers can differently allocate it at the beginning of the GBL activity to adapt the needs of the GBL task to each particular group. It has been observed in computer-

Figure 2. The ALT model for computer-based learning (© 2013 Margarida Romero and Mireia Usart. Used with permission.)

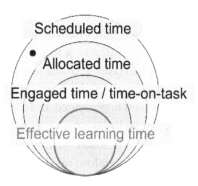

assisted learning that external time allocation could help students optimise their learning and metacognitive assessment (Metcalfe, 2002).

- **Game Temporality:** There is also a game temporality, framed by the implementation of the interaction delays and lapses in the game dynamics, time-outs for finishing certain tasks within the game, SG chronemics related to the way students perceive and value time structure, and delays and time-outs during game interaction.

- **Time-on-Task by Students:** The expected relationship between the time-on-task investment by students and the performance of the time lapses between the different screens or phases of an SG that could increase the amount of playing time within a GBL task, without relating this increased playing time to a longer period of effective learning time for students (Gee, 2003).

- **Effective Learning Time for Students:** This is defined as the effective learning time that occurs within the time-on-task frame, when the learners effectively develop learning objectives (Fisher et al. 1980). This learning time differs from time-on-task, as there is an off-learning time-on-task when the learner is playing the game without developing any of the learning objectives. In terms of the cognitive load theory (Sweller, 1994; Van Merriënboer & Sweller, 2005), this time is defined as the extraneous cognitive load, and could be anything that distracts a learner from the learning objective. Extraneous cognitive load is the result of the way the interface or information is presented and structured. In SGs, a well-designed game dynamic should ensure a lower extraneous cognitive load, and therefore maximise effective learning time.

Furthermore, time-on-task in GBL can significantly vary from time-on-task in other educational activities where there is a minimum of extraneous cognitive load, and long time lapses do not occur (Lewis, 2007; Romero, 2010). Therefore, assessing time-on-task in these GBL contexts demands new strategies. SG characteristics differ from those associated with other learning tasks. Firstly, these learning activities, when computer-based, demand a certain degree of ICT ability and skill from students; secondly, GBL is a student-centred, active learning methodology that enables social and collaborative learning (Romero, Usart, Ott & Earp, 2012). Time-on-task in collaborative learning can differ from individual learning, as there is a shared learning temporality within the SG that must be taken into account. Finally, games in general and SG in particular, are designed to bring students to a state of flow (Kiili & Lainema, 2010). This state of flow changes the perception of time by the player, and could be related to higher time-on-task as learners lose their perception of time and are absorbed in the game activity.

In the following sections we explain three aspects of computer-based GBL that should be considered in relation to time factor assessment: (a) the ICT perspective; (b) social interaction and group management; and (c) the concept of flow.

1. **ICT Elements of Computer-Based GBL:** Student skills, technical issues, and online access to computer-based SGs can influence the amount and quality of time spent in a GBL task and the manner in which we assess it. Previous research on computer-based learning methodologies, such as SGs (Metcalfe, 2002), claimed that results seem to sustain the idea that these learning methodologies could help learners manage time while learning (and so enjoy an optimal allocation of time for difficult to easier items) by providing students with fixed-time tasks (as we will see in the case study described in the third section of this chapter). Furthermore, recent studies on time-on-task and GBL by Schaaf (2012), in which different Digital GBL (DGBL) activities were examined and compared with effective, research-based learning strategies, resulted in significant differences in student engagement and time-on task behaviour. In particular, students in primary schools were observed while playing and surveyed to determine which student groups had higher levels of engagement and time-on-task behaviour. Results showed higher levels of student enjoyment, attention, scores, and a higher time-on-task while experiencing DGBL. The author suggests that DGBL could be as effective as other instructional strategies. Moreover, time flexibility in online learning tasks is usually less important than the initial expectations of online learners (Levinsen, 2006), and therefore a high degree of temporal self-regulation in GBL could cause less regulated students to fail to set aside enough time-on-task, so reducing their effective learning times and performance (Romero, 2010). Following Schaaf, while the use of DGBL is not always the best teaching practice, it should be used in lesson plans where appropriate. Teachers should consider incorporating SGs to provide fun and engaging experiences for students.

Designers and teachers should decide when to utilise SGs appropriately, after an evaluation of each gameplay.

2. **Social Interaction and Group Management in Computer-Based GBL:** In collaborative and multiplayer SGs, the quality and quantity of time-on-task depends on the temporal nature of the game. In asynchronous games, learners must coordinate their time-on-task in turns, and be more flexible in their time-on-task allocation than learners playing collaborative synchronous games that require players to be sharing time-on-task (Romero & Usart, 2013). Playing together for learning can be a synchronous or asynchronous activity. If the gameplay is synchronous, it could require an adequate level of joint cognitive quality time that could be difficult to achieve in computer-based learning contexts in general, and in online contexts in particular, as time flexibility allows a higher degree of temporal flexibility for the distributed learning groups engaged in GBL activities. Nevertheless, if a multiplayer or collaborative SG is played asynchronously, the amount of joint time decreases and individual time-on-task is the variable to be assessed. When assessing collaborative times, practitioners should be able to monitor their class (Berliner, 1990) and catch any mismatches between student objectives and tasks assigned by spotting any unusually high error rates. Correcting that problem could result in higher success rates. The author affirms that attention and success rates are two important instructional time variables affecting ALT, so it is no wonder that higher levels of monitoring appear to be an effective teaching behaviour when assessing learning tasks. In the case of DGBL, this can be conducted easily through the use of accessible game databases where student

(time) logs can be retrieved and analysed after the SG task (Romero, Usart, Popescu & Boyle, 2012).

3. **The Concept of Flow in GBL:** Defined as a state of deep absorption in an activity that is intrinsically enjoyable (Csikszentmihalyi, 1990), student focus on performance has been related to greater time-on-task in GBL activities, when compared to non-GBL learning tasks. As Admiraal, Huizenga, Akkerman and ten Dam (2012, p. 1186) affirm: "In GBL, the game activity must balance the inherent challenge of the activity and the player's ability to address and overcome it in order to maintain a player's flow experience. If the challenge is beyond that ability, the activity becomes so overwhelming that it generates anxiety. If the challenge fails to engage the player, the player quickly loses interest and tends to leave the game." Therefore, designers must foresee the optimal amount of difficulty and time needed for a GBL task to assure flow. In the complete review from Connolly et al. (2012), we find that flow is a variable impacting on attitude and the intention of use for online GBL activities. In particular, a field survey of online game users (Hsu et al. 2004) looked at different elements, including flow, and results from structural equation modelling showed that flow experience directly impacts on student intentions to play games. Furthermore, Weibel and colleagues (2008) examined the links between presence, flow, and enjoyment in an online multiplayer game when compared to a virtual-opponent game. Participants who played against a real opponent reported stronger experiences of presence, flow, and enjoyment in a regression analysis, in particular, flow mediated the relationship between presence and enjoyment. These results could help designers

and practitioners when deciding on the kind of collaboration (real or virtual) that could lead to a better flow and a more balanced time-on-task in a DGBL task.

Admiraal, Huizenga, Akkerman and ten Dam (2012) studied engagement in gaming by relating flow to game performance and student learning outcomes among secondary school students. Although distracted by solving problems in technology and navigation, students showed flow with game activities. Distractive activities and competition among teams showed an effect on learning outcomes, in particular, the fewer students distracted from the game and the more they were engaged in group competition, the more the students learned. Therefore, assessing these temporal aspects should help practitioners when designing and implementing collaborative DGBL activities that require minimal technical expertise, and this should enhance performance and learning through the use of flow. We therefore accept that flow in a GBL context could help students engage and spend more time-on-task; nevertheless, it does not ensure a better performance by learners if the additional time-on-task is not an effective learning time. Therefore, we must be very careful when measuring time-on-task in GBL. Experience shows that extraneous cognitive load (Sweller, 1994; Van Merriënboer & Sweller, 2005) could, in fact, lead to students learning less. In SGs, a well-designed game dynamic should enable a lower extraneous cognitive load, and therefore maximise effective learning time.

In brief, the point of using both the concept of ALT and DGBL characteristics to interpret and assess SG temporal data is now clearer: instructional time variables that are observable or relatively simple to measure through game databases and time logs, such time-on-task, can provide an understanding of instructional processes that reasonably accounts for the effects that have been found in many empirical research studies on SGs.

Subjective Time Assessment in GBL

Time is not only objective, but it has also a subjective dimension: intrapsychological time (Nuttin & Lens, 1985). This dimension of time is composed of individual variables related to the concept of time, and how it is perceived by humans – and has been related to different learning processes and outcomes. Three individual constructs are defined as the generators of psychological time: orientation to multitasking or polychronism; time orientation; and time perspective (Zimbardo & Boyd, 1999). Polychronism is based on change and flexibility, and attention is diverted among various possible activities, contrary to monochronism (defined as the ability to concentrate on one activity at a time, with an emphasis on the development and adherence to schedules (Hall & Hall, 1987). Polychronism is found in high-context cultures, where punctuality is less important, and flexibility and changes of activity are common and expected. Time orientation is described as being part of the wider TP context, but contrary to this variable, it is a one-dimensional trait that is independent of the situation or life domain.

TP is probably the aspect of psychological time that has been most related to learning processes and outcomes in formal education (Schmidt & Werner, 2007). Therefore, we must learn how to assess this subjective time variable in GBL. Most of the existing studies on TP have been focused on lecture-based, face-to-face learning environments (Romero & Usart, 2012); and TP has been approached in teacher-centred methodologies rather than in student-centred, active learning tasks such SGs. However, it is relevant to study TP assessment in GBL because in these learning scenarios, students are no longer in a future-based environment, but are given immediate feedback from the gaming activity (Wassarman, 2002) that, together with the fostering of social interaction and collaboration (EDUCAUSE, 2012) in GBL, could lead to different relations regarding TP by students and learning outcomes.

Time Perspective

Time perspective (TP) has historically been defined and measured from a wide range of approaches and using different methods. The authors of this chapter use the definition given by Zimbardo, Keough, and Boyd (1997, p. 1008): time perspective is 'the manner in which individuals, and cultures, partition the flow of human experience into distinct temporal categories of past, present and future'. From this definition, TP can be understood as a cognitive construct that can be assessed through the use of self-reported instruments; in particular, one of the most studied and validated instruments in the field of TP and learning is the Zimbardo Time Perspective Inventory (hereinafter ZTPI) developed by Zimbardo and Boyd (1999). This test measures an individual's orientation towards the five factors composing TP, where the past, present, and future temporal frames are subdivided into five subscales or factors: present hedonism; present fatalism; past positivism; past negativism; and future time perspective (Figure 3). A high score for past positivism, present hedonism, and future defines a balanced TP. This instrument consists of 56 items or statements such as: 'It upsets me to be late for appointments'. Each statement has to be rated using a 5-point Likert scale (1 = strongly disagree,

to 5 = totally agree). ZTPI provides researchers with a quantitative value for an individual's TP. It has been tested by different authors in various contexts and results have shown its reliability when used in Western cultures (Apostolidis & Fieulaine, 2004; Díaz-Morales, 2006). There are two temporal orientations that seem strongly related to learning; present hedonism (defined as seeking immediate pleasure, with little regard to risk or consequences), and future time perspective (FTP; characterised by delayed reward, as a result of the desire to achieve specific long-term goals). In particular, present-oriented individuals may show lower academic achievement when compared to future-oriented students (Adelabu, 2007), while future-oriented individuals tend to engage in more learning activities (Simons, Vansteenkiste, Lens & Lacante, 2004).

Time Perspective Assessment in GBL

Assessment of TP in GBL could lead to better adaptation of SG activities; awareness in advance of student TPs could help designers and teachers implement an SG activity and meet student needs (e.g. support collaboration processes through the design of more temporal balanced teams that could optimise the learning task). As measured by Romero and Usart (2012), future-oriented students are more likely to intend playing games in the near and distant future (3 months to 1 year), and a field survey of online game users (Hsu et al. 2004) showed that flow experience impacted directly on the intention to play games.

In conclusion, we may assume that student intrapsychological time in general, and TP in particular, must be assessed through the introduction of self-reported tests, as these perceptions could play a role in student performance during GBL activities. Furthermore, these scenarios may help students who are not future-oriented in terms of knowledge acquisition (and less engaged in learning activities) but are attracted to SGs. Therefore,

Figure 3. Time perspective factors following the theory of Zimbardo and Boyd (© 2013 Margarida Romero and Mireia Usart. Used with permission.)

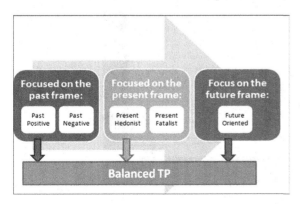

TP must be taken into account when deciding on the implementation of SGs in the curriculum, as it is related to motivation and learning performance in GBL (Adelabu, 2007; Romero & Usart, 2012).

METAVALS CASE STUDY

In the following section the MetaVals case study is presented. MetaVals is an SG designed by the ESADE Learning Innovation Unit (Usart, Romero & Almirall, 2011). It was designed while bearing in mind temporal aspects such time-on-task and student TP assessment. We will focus on how time is assessed before, during, and after the gameplay; and further analyse the results of student time-on-task (both for collaborative and individual phases of the SG) and TP. Finally, general proposals for implementing time assessment in GBL tasks are given.

MetaVals Game

MetaVals is a computer-based classification game designed by the ESADE Learning Innovation team. It can be considered as a decision-making activity initially developed with the pedagogical objective of studying assets and liabilities in the field of finance. The design of MetaVals is based on human computer interaction user-centred methodologies, which are in turn based on iterative prototyping (Lambropoulos, Romero, & Culwin, 2010). This SG was designed with a view to adapting the decision-making dynamics involved in classification to other fields of knowledge. The present release of the MetaVals game allows the content of the items presented to students to be personalised, together with the look and feel of the game.

MetaVals is a web-based DGBL classification game (see Figure 4) that consists of three stages, one individual, and two collaborative (a correction phase and a discussion phase). The game is

Figure 4. Image of the individual phase of the MetaVals SG (© 2013 Margarida Romero and Mireia Usart. Used with permission.)

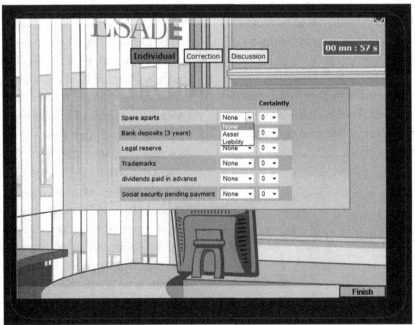

played in pairs – who must collaborate to win against other pairs in the gameplay.

This game-based activity design allows students to interact in two ways: collaborating in pairs and competing with the rest of the class (Romero, Usart, Ott & Earp, 2012). The game engine allows teachers to choose if students play in real pairs (for face-to-face contexts) or with virtual peers (in online scenarios). The present case study was run with real dyads, and students had to classify 12 items into assets or liabilities, sharing their level of certainty for each answer. Each phase of the game was set with a time-out of five minutes.

Context and Participants

The target population is composed of adult life-long learning professionals attending blended-learning master courses at ESADE Business and Law School. This university has more than 50 years of experience training professionals to become highly-competent in their work. After a complete study of the population (students from various management courses that fit the requirements) the sample was chosen from those attending courses that began in the first term of the 2011-12 academic year. These programs use a blended learning approach. The initial number of participants in the sample was the sum of two groups of adult learners' engaged in postgraduate programs (N=39). The first group (N_1= 15) is enrolled in the Executive Master in Marketing and Sales (EMMS hereinafter) a postgraduate program including an introductory course in Finance. The second group of participants (N_2= 24) is enrolled in a similar course, the Corporate Master (CM hereinafter), also including an introductory course in Finance. As completing the questionnaires and learning activities was not compulsory, some of the participants in the EMMS and CM groups have not completed all the required activities: the pre-test and post-test questionnaires and the MetaVals game activity. In this study, only the

participants having completed both questionnaires and the Metavals activity has been considered in the final sample. For this reason the final sample size is composed by 24 students instead of 39 students, which represents a mortality of 38.46% of the participants on the EMMS and CM courses.

The 24 students in the final sample (9 women, 15 men, M=31.90, age range: 26-42 years) were all Spanish, with three exceptions (students from Italy, France, and Argentina). The professional profile of the participants in the EMMS and CM programs is composed of marketing, sales, law, and operations experts. Despite the fact that the two groups studied were chosen because of their similarity; the majority of the CM students had previously attended a course on accounting.

Research Design

MetaVals was tested in a quasi-experimental design with a pre- and post-test, where student TP, time, performance logs, and conversations were monitored and analysed. Time-on-task was measured during three phases of the game, as the time each student spent at the game screen. TP was measured in the ZTPI before gameplay, voluntarily completed online by students using the two programs. ZTPI is a self-reported test on TP that was validated for Spanish by Diaz-Morales (2006).

To study time assessment in MetaVals, we divide the case study into the three stages of implementation of the SG in the class (as shown in Figure 1). That is, before the SG (where we find scheduled or institutional time); during the activity (where there is time-on-task); and finally, after the SG task (where analysis and assessment can be made of the different temporal variables).

Before the MetaVals Game

When deciding how to implement a SG task, the first temporal variable to look at is institutional or scheduled time. In ESADE, this time strongly frames the number of hours for each program, and the amount of time a teacher can devote to face-to-face lessons. In our example, the teacher has four days for face-to-face classes in the introductory finance course where MetaVals is implemented. The teacher decides, within this frame, the amount of allocated time allocated for MetaVals.

Also before the task, MetaVals allows personalised time-outs in each of the three screens of the game. These counters can be fixed by the teacher or designer prior to gameplay accessing the game interface. The specific experience presented in this chapter was fixed at five minutes per each screen or phase. Finally, depending on the context, designers set a virtual or real pair scenario for the task. In this case study, as a face-to-face experience, students were paired.

Concerning TP, once logged in the MetaVals game and before the first individual phase, students are invited to access a previous test screen, with the ZTPI and a knowledge pre-test consisting of three questions related to basic financial concepts. These tools are directly implemented in the MetaVals interface to help students become more aware of their initial level and give them information on their peer's basic data – such as age and level of knowledge. The objective is to give students important clues for guiding their performance and set a base for peer-assessment and time awareness during the game.

During the MetaVals Gameplay

When the SG tasks starts, the variables to assess are time-on-task (individual and collaborative) and flow. Due to the fact that each screen is guided by a virtual character, and that there is only one possible path for the game, MetaVals can be considered as a structured SG. This guide enables students to play the game face-to-face or online (Romero, Usart, Popescu, & Boyle, 2012), without the risk of feeling unattended or lost in the process of gameplay. Nevertheless, designers aim to balance this scaffolding with self-directed

stages, where students choose their own actions under time pressure to maintain the engagement and flow during the MetaVals activity.

Peer assessment is allowed and even reinforced in the MetaVals SG. Students, playing in real or virtual pairs, see their partner's answers for each item together with a confidence level for each answer. This may enable them to better assess their time-on-task during the discussion phase through the process of sharing cognitive and metacognitive awareness. Finally, concerning TP, the teacher's role in assessment during the gameplay should be focused on the creation of balanced pairs that can achieve good game performances and optimal time-on-task.

After the MetaVals Gameplay

After the SG task, there is time for analyzing the temporal variables of the participants in order to further understand and decision-making process on the learning experience. When a MetaVals gameplay has finished, the game database enables teachers to retrieve game logs and ZTPI data to assess game performance and TP for each phase. A simple Excel file is generated from a Mysql database for each gameplay. All student logs and data are organised and enable teachers with even a low ICT level to use the data. Following Caldwell, Huitt and Graeber (1982) the measure of the time-on-task variable is operationalised in our case study as the amount of time a student is actively engaged in MetaVals, that is, as the sum of the time spent for each student in each of the three phases of the game. MetaVals enables measuring each phase time-on-task in order to have a more in-depth view of this variable and study the differences among individual and collaborative performances.

Concerning TP, results from the ZTPI are also retrieved from the survey spreadsheet and given to the teacher if needed. Researchers can use this data to study the TP of each student and pair to assess these variables and relate them to time-on-task, game performance, or other variables. Furthermore, if the teacher aims to repeat an SG experience, this TP data can be useful for helping in the creation of pairs, or furthermore, personalising other learning activities according to the participants' TP.

RESULTS

We briefly describe the results of the MetaVals experience in the two face-to-face contexts studied. Results for both TP and time-on-task variables are further analysed in the discussion section to better understand the assessment of these variables in our case study.

Before the MetaVals Gameplay

The previous theoretical allocated time by the teacher for the MetaVals experience in this case study was 40 minutes. As the teacher had not used this SG, he calculated the time period based on the time used in the previous face-to-face activity for studying assets and liabilities. The teacher located this learning task at the beginning of the first face-to-face class, immediately after the welcome and introductory parts of the lesson. Nevertheless, the real experiences lasted up to 50 minutes. This difference was due to the fact that ICT problems were reported by students when trying to connect to the ESADE Wi-Fi. These problems required the presence of an ICT expert and were solved before the game started; nevertheless, these difficulties increased the initially predicted allocated time for the task. As there were no previous data on students' TP, dyads were set randomly by the teacher. Students had access to their peer's information at the beginning of the gameplay and had the possibility to take into account this information during the game.

During the MetaVals Gameplay

The direct observation of both groups (EMMS and CM) during the SG task, together with results from the post-test, enabled researchers to qualitatively assess student engagement during the activity. Despite initial ICT problems when the game started, students tended to engage in the activity and comments among pairs were directly observed. Students engaged in the activity both individually and in dyads, and they discussed with their partners during the two collaborative phases (peer assessment and discussion phases), showing more time-on-task in this later screens, as we will discuss. A relaxed atmosphere and conversation about the game accompanied all the activities and the final ranking screen. The students were focused on the task and some discussion was made on the time-outs, as pairs feared not having enough time to classify all the items. Finally, students commented on the results of the gameplay in the ranking screen, some of them being anxious because they expected higher scores. All the students were able to finish the game, and most of the students filled the pre and post questionnaires.

The measure of individual time-on-task shows an average value for the first group (EMMS) of $M_{11}=103.47$ (seconds), $SD_{11}=36.32$. For the second group (CM), $M_{21}=64.19$ seconds, $SD_{21}=29.80$. Average time-on-task for the collaborative phases in the MetaVals game was $M_{12}=250.33$, $SD_{12}=64.19$; and for the second group: $M_{22}=143.82$, $SD_{22}=68.15$ (seconds).

We can observe that, even though each screen or phase had a five minute time-out, the average time-on-task spent in these phases was less, and only in the EMMS group (and for the sum of the two collaborative phases) did students spend more than four minutes classifying the 12 items.

Student TP was measured from the web-based version of the ZTPI, which was introduced in the game interface and could be accessed before starting the game. Participants in the two courses were classified as present, future, and balanced (taking into account that the average score for each TP factor on the ZTPI for the sample presents a TP structure close to the mean of the two groups). Present fatalism (M=2.24; SD=0.57) and past negative scores (M=2.32; SD=0.74) were low; while past positive (M= 2.98; SD=0.45), present hedonist (M=3.06; SD=0.53), and future orientation factors (M=3.45; SD=0.42) were high.

After the MetaVals Gameplay

Student reports retrieved from the post-test (based on the TAM questionnaire; Davis, 1989) show high scores for ease of use (PEU) and usefulness (PU) in the game experience (see Table 1). In the open question about the game experience, students said they felt engaged in the gameplay, and highly rated the inclusion of a computer-based SG in their learning curriculum.

DISCUSSION

Before the MetaVals Game

In the design and implementation of SG tasks in the curriculum, we studied how time assessment can be made using the ALT model, and took into account that while game characteristics may facilitate flow and engagement, they can also introduce ICT issues and distractive activities that increase the extraneous cognitive load. The MetaVals case study showed how to use time-outs in the MetaVals game to help students engage in the experience through the concept of flow (Schaaf, 2012), in particular, students retrieved a motivat-

Table 1. Results of the TAM questionnaire

Results of the TAM Questionnaire	PEU *M SD*	PU *M SD*
EMMS and CM	4.48 (1.62)	4.48 (1.38)

ing temporal pressure when playing MetaVals, especially in the discussion screen, where they had to reach consensus before 5 minutes. The total allocated time for the SG task was higher than the time initially scheduled by the teacher. This fact may be due to the teacher's lack of experience in implementing SGs, and ICT problems when accessing Wi-Fi. These two factors finally increased the real amount of allocated time, as predicted by the theory. DGBL activities highly depend on ICT and so teachers and designers must be aware of these issues in order to allow enough time for the game task. However, we cannot affirm that ICT difficulties in the use of the MetaVals SG directly influenced time-on-task during the game.

The decision to implement time-outs in this case study could also help learners in the allocation of learning time during the game. As Metcalfe (2002) stated, people allocate their time to the items they judge to be difficult, but a computer-based scaffolding of time could help them optimise their learning time during a task. We implemented these time-outs for each phase of the MetaVals and measured the time-on-task for each student. However, further analysis must be made to confirm this hypothesis measuring the real effective learning time for each student and relating it to the measured time-on-task.

During the MetaVals Gameplay

The fact that the average time-on-task spent in MetaVals SG was less than five minutes for the different phases can be related to the fact that the five-minute time-outs were set theoretically, without knowing the prior knowledge level of the participants – nor their TPs. MetaVals is, as we defined, a structured SG. Following Weppel, Bishop and Muñoz-Avila (2012), these activities were perhaps made less engaging by the amount of information and corrective assessment required during the game. Therefore, having all the student information available before setting the time-outs could help teachers adjust the time for each screen, and consequently, increase student levels of engagement and flow (Levinsen, 2006).

Furthermore, social interaction during the collaborative phases of MetaVals in our case study may result in a less flexible time-on-task for individuals, as the game was set synchronically, and according to Romero and Usart (2012), these contexts demand a higher collaborative time-on-task that could significantly increase the total amount of this variable for gameplay, as seen in our results. Nevertheless, when deciding on the implementation of real or virtual pairs, we have taken into account the results from Weibel et al. (2008): namely, that real pairs can help increase enjoyment, and therefore heighten the flow experience.

Peer assessment, as seen in the literature review, may allow students to better assess the knowledge level of the pair partner. This could help pairs manage time in the discussion phase; in fact, Chiang, Shih, Liu and Lee (2011) showed that GBL and interactive peer assessment are viable combinations to motivate colleague students to collaborate and improve career goals and objectives. In the MetaVals experience, results point to the fact that students prefer collaborating with peers rather than simply listening to the teacher and using the classic case-study methodology in class. These results will be used to implement peer-assessment in the next MetaVals gameplays.

Time perspective results confirm that all the TP profiles could similarly engage in GBL activity, therefore, assessing TP is more useful for team building, as it could facilitate collaboration among peers with similar TP factors. Time invested in the MetaVals game does not show significant differences among TP groups. This result is explained by the fact that present-hedonists engage in games and instantly rewarding activities (Wassarman, 2002) and see GBL as an amusing and competitive activity. However, future-oriented students may be engaging in GBL not for fun, but with a focus on the learning and future outcomes of playing the game in an educational context. Finally,

balanced individuals adapt their time orientation to the needs of the present moment, both having fun and thinking about the future learning gains (Boyd & Zimbardo, 2005).

After the MetaVals Gameplay

After an SG task, a profound analysis of individual and collaborative (dyads) time-on-tasks, together with game performance and results of the post-test could help teachers and instructional designers understand the relationships between these variables. Following Berliner (1990), not only time-on-task, but also the error-rates of students during a learning task can be directly related to learning performance. From a first, qualitative standpoint, we could suggest that participants in MetaVals with real dyads engage in task-oriented discussions on the learning objectives thanks to the metacognitive sharing of certainty and to the information each partner has from his peer. These tools could therefore help optimizing discussion time and therefore time-on-task in the SG, nevertheless, more research with discourse analysis should be done.

Following Admiraal, Huizenga, Akkerman and ten Dam (2012), competition is related to game engagement. In MetaVals, students have access to the final ranking scores in pairs – depending on both the correct items and the time spent in the collaborative or discussion phase. Therefore, MetaVals SG can enhance student self-reflection and competition with other pairs via time spent or collaborative time-on-task. This is also observed in the post-test results; students give high scores when asked about the usefulness of the game.

In conclusion, as summarized in Table 2, after the gameplay designers were provided with all the necessary information to implement, if needed, the changes in the SG time settings; furthermore, teachers could personalise the game activity for the subsequent gameplays with MetaVals, according to the results and data analysis. Teachers can vary time pressure by changing the time-out depending

Table 2. Summary of the temporal variables results in the MetaVals case study

Time Assessment in GBL	Key Finding in MetaVals Study
Time-on-task	This temporal variable was studied and measured as defined in the ALT model, in particular, for adult students in a face-to-face SG activity:
Instructional time	• Time was strongly framed by the institution, with fixed hours for the teacher to devote to face-to-face lessons. • A theoretical time-on-task of 40 minutes was scheduled by the teacher, based on his experience in previous, no SG tasks.
Game temporality	• In particular, time outs for each game screen were set by designers in 5 minutes per phase as a higher limit for time-on-task in MetaVals. • Students in the case study perceived the time boundaries as enough for the objectives of the activity in the first phases of the gameplay; nevertheless, some students report time pressure during discussion.

Time-on-task by students	• Time-on-task was measured as the amount of time student were actively engaged in MetaVals, in particular:
	    Students needed between one and two minutes to complete the individual phase.
	    The collaborative phases of the game took more than two minutes but less than four.
	• The total time-on-task for the MetaVals activity was 50 minutes, it was higher than the scheduled due to the ICT issues, in particular, the Wi-Fi connection.

Effective learning time for students	• This variable does not coincide with time-on-task and cannot be directly measured from a direct observation of a learning activity. The effective learning time refers to the time where the conceptual change is produced, a time that only some neuroscientific approaches aiming to measure the electrochemical brain activity are starting to explore. Nevertheless:
	    Social interaction among peers increases effective learning
	    Flow is decreased due to ICT issues and little experience of the teacher on SG, this could decrease effective learning time.

Time Perspective	• Students fill in the web-version of the ZTPI before they access the game. • TP profiles for case study students was high in past positivism, present hedonism and future, that could be considered as balanced TP.

on how knowledgeable students are, with the objective of reaching an optimal flow level (Admiraal, Huizenga, Akkerman & ten Dam, 2011).

Concerning TP, awareness of student temporal factors could help teachers when creating more effective groups or pairs, in terms of time and performance, for further learning activities and games.

CONCLUSION AND FURTHER RESEARCH

This chapter shows that the time factor is a key element in education in general, and GBL in particular. Because many perspectives of the time factor influence the gaming and learning experience, game designers, instructors, and teachers

should be aware of each of these perspectives. The ALT model should help define the curricular integration of the game in instructional times, and enable learners to invest a certain time in the use of the GBL activity (time-on-task). Temporal intrapsychological factors of monochrony/polychrony, and temporal perspectives should be also considered as we have seen how they influence learner activity and outcomes. For all of these aspects, time assessment within these different perspectives should be taken into account in GBL to ensure the success of the GBL objectives and the adaptation of GBL activities to the inter-individual differences of the learners.

We have focused our analysis on two temporal variables, and studied the three steps of implementing an SG. Firstly, objective time before the SG activity has been studied in the design and personalisation of the task, and measured as scheduled and allocated time. Differences among expected and real data have been analysed in the context of DGBL theory, enabling us to conclude that preparation is a key aspect for the successful implementation of these SG tasks. Secondly, during the learning activity, we have studied both peer assessment and the formative assessment of individual and collaborative time-on-task. Finally, we have focused on the assessment that teachers and practitioners can make after the learning activity, as a final or summative time assessment.

Concerning student temporal perspectives, we have to admit that TP cannot be changed in such a limited learning task (Zimbardo & Boyd, 1999), but it can be assessed by implementing ZTPI in games as a part of the screens that players have to go through, allowing researchers to use the game interface in an efficient manner. Nevertheless, implementing various social or collaborative SGs and student-centred activities during a whole semester may help students reflect on their TPs and adapt them to improve their performances. However, more research is needed to confirm this hypothesis. In addition, an analysis of pair chat logs could be very useful to better understand how students distribute time during the game: following Metcalfe (2002), as those students who are metacognitively aware can allocate time to the items they judge to be difficult.

LESSONS LEARNT AND TIPS FOR PRACTITIONERS

Our case study has been based on and analysed previous theoretical studies in the field of DGBL and temporal assessment. Results point to the importance of the temporal variables in general, and learning time and temporal perspective in particular, during the process of designing, implementing, and running an SG task. Although the focus of this chapter is on formal adult learning, we can adapt the results for other learning contexts where DGBL can be used in lesson plans if appropriate. Therefore, practitioners should consider incorporating SG tasks into instruction to provide a fun and engaging experience for students, and decide when to use them after an evaluation of temporal variables in a particular context.

We could give a brief list of guiding tips to help in time assessment before, during, and after the completion of an SG task (see Table 3).

When setting the institutional and scheduled time framework for the activity, learning institutions, instructional designers and teachers, have to allow enough time for the learning activity to be implemented. DGBL tasks differ from other learning activities, as they demand an ICT-based context that can increase allocated time. Previous experience and knowledge of SGs may help in this prior analysis of the time allocated for imple-

Table 3. Tips for implementing time assessment in SGs

Guiding Tips Before, During and After the SG		
Before	**During**	**After**
• Setting time-outs in the different game screens as a temporal framework could help players experiencing time pressure and facilitate flow and engagement. • Access to peers' information such prior knowledge could optimize the time required for interaction among players and increase the task-oriented discussions. • The implementation of the ZTPI in the SG interface, before the gameplay, can maximize the retrieval of TP data. • Teachers can use ZTPI results for creating temporally optimal teams.	• The use of metacognitive awareness tools in the SG could help students optimizing gameplay time through the focusing of discussions during the game. • Minimizing ICT difficulties and using a SG with a balanced level of difficulty may help learners increasing their effective learning time. • Students' self awareness on TP could help them in a better distribution of time during the game.	• The use of post-tests can give teachers qualitative data on the students' temporal experience in the SG. • Teachers can use the results from the gameplay to distribute students in future activities and redesign time-outs. • Researchers can relate TP to performance and Time-on-task to study relations among these variables.

menting SG activities in the learning curriculum. We have seen that well-designed SGs can lead students to a state of flow, and that good GBL design can improve student engagement (e.g., just two minutes per screen could be set when a group has a high prior knowledge level). Correctly set difficulty levels can help students engage and spend more time-on-task; however, setting the right difficulty level does not ensure more effective learning time, nor higher learning performances.

We have to be careful when measuring time-on-task during an SG activity. There are many elements unrelated to learning that can increase the amount of measured time-on-task in DGBL (such as the time students spend learning how to play, or discussing off-content subjects with peers). These elements can be minimized with a balanced amount of collaboration and competition, as shown in our case study. This could help designers and practitioners when deciding on the type of collaboration (real or virtual) that could lead to a better flow and a more balanced time-on-task in a DGBL task.

TP has been measured and assessed after the SG activity, as students complete the ZTPI during the activity, but it is after the task that teachers can analyse TP results. The implementation of previous TP assessments could be a future research line, as it is intended to help individuals and teachers increase performance during the task through the implementation of balanced TP groups.

After the SG activity, we must evaluate the results from a GBL activity and the reports of the formative assessment. These results must be used to improve and adapt new releases of the SG in the curriculum.

Finally, because of the importance of time during the whole process of teaching and learning with SG, we recommend that game designers, practitioners, teachers, and curriculum designers invest time in the consideration of the time factor in the design, implementation, and evaluation of SG activities. Optimising learning times is one of the best investments for 21st century lifelong learners.

REFERENCES

Adelabu, D. H. (2007). Time perspective and school membership as correlates to academic achievement among African American adolescents. *Adolescence*, *42*(167), 525–538. PMID:18047236.

Admiraal, W., Huizenga, J., Akkerman, S., & ten Dama, G. (2011). The concept of flow in collaborative game-based learning. *Computers in Human Behavior*, *27*, 1185–1194. doi:10.1016/j.chb.2010.12.013.

Apostolidis, T., & Fieulaine, N. (2004). Validation française de l'e'chelle de temporalite´ the zimbardo time perspective inventory. *European Review of Applied Psychology*, *54*, 207–217. doi:10.1016/j.erap.2004.03.001.

Barbera, E., Gros, B., & Kirschner, P. (2012). Temporal issues in e-learning research: A literature review. *British Journal of Educational Technology*, *43*(2), 53–55. doi:10.1111/j.1467-8535.2011.01255.x.

Berliner, D. C. (1990). What's all the fuss about instructional time? In M. Ben-Peretz, & R. Bromme (Eds.), *The nature of time in schools* (pp. 3–35). New York: Teachers College Press.

Boyd, J., & Zimbardo, P. (2005). Time perspective, health, and risk taking. In Strathman & Joireman (Eds.), Understanding behavior in the context of time: Theory, research, and application. Mahwah, NJ: Lawrence Erlbaum Associates.

Caldwell, J. H., Huitt, W. G., & Graeber, A. O. (1982). Time spent in learning: Implications from research. *The Elementary School Journal*, *82*, 471–480. doi:10.1086/461282.

Carroll, J. B. (1963). A model of school learning. *Teachers'. College Record, 64*, 723–733.

Chiang, T., Shih, R., Liu, E. Z., & Lee, A. J. (2011). Using game-based learning and interactive peer assessment to improve career goals and objectives for college students edutainment technologies. *Lecture Notes in Computer Science, 6872*, 507–511. doi:10.1007/978-3-642-23456-9_91.

Connolly, T., Boyle, E., MacArthur, E., Hainey, T., & Boyle, J. (2012). A systematic literature review of empirical evidence on computer games and serious games. *Computers & Education, 59*(2), 661–686. doi:10.1016/j.compedu.2012.03.004.

Cooley, W. W., & Lohnes, P. R. (1976). *Evaluation research in education*. New York: Irvington publishers.

Davis, F. D. (1989, September). Perceived usefulness, perceived ease of use, and user acceptance of information technology. *Management Information Systems Quarterly*, 318–340.

Díaz-Morales, J. F. (2006). Estructura factorial y fiabilidad del inventario de perspectiva temporal de zimbardo. *Psicothema, 18*(3), 565–571. PMID:17296088.

Fisher, C., Berliner, D., Filby, N., Marliave, R., Cahen, L., & Dishaw, M. (1980). Teaching behaviors, academic learning time, and student achievement: An overview. In C. Denham, & A. Lieberman (Eds.), *Time to learn*. Washington, DC: National Institute of Education.

Gee, J. P. (2003). *What video games have to teach us about learning and literacy*. New York: Palgrave Macmillan. doi:10.1145/950566.950595.

Gee, J. P. (2009). Video games, learning, and content. In C. Miller (Ed.), *Games: Purpose and potential in education*. Boston, MA: Springer. doi:10.1007/978-0-387-09775-6_3.

Hall, E. T., & Hall, M. R. (1987). *Hidden differences: Doing business with the Japanese*. Garden City, NJ: Anchor Books Doubleday.

Harnischfeger, A., & Wiley, D. E. (1985). Origins of active learning time. In C. W. Fisher, & D. C. Berliner (Eds.), *Perspectives on instructional time* (pp. 133–156). New York: Longman.

Hsu, C.-L., & Lu, H. P. (2004). Why do people play on-line games? An extended TAM with social influences and flow experience. *Information & Management, 41*, 853–868. doi:10.1016/j.im.2003.08.014.

Kaufman-Scarborough, C., & Lindquist, J. D. (1999). Time management and polychronicity: Comparisons, contrasts, and insights for the workplace. *Journal of Managerial Psychology*, 288–312. doi:10.1108/02683949910263819.

Kiili, K., & Lainema, T. (2010). Power and flow experience in time-intensive business simulation game. *Journal of Educational Multimedia and Hypermedia, 19*(1), 39–57.

Klopfer, E., Osterweil, S., & Salen, K. (2009). *Moving learning games forward*. Retrieved from http://education.mit.edu/papers/Moving-LearningGamesForward_EdArcade.pdf

Lambropoulos, N., Romero, M., & Culwin, F. (2010). HCI education to support collaborative e-learning systems design. *eLearn Magazine, 9*.

Levinsen, K. (2006). Collaborative on-line teaching: The inevitable path to deep learning and knowledge sharing? *Electronic Journal of E-learning, 4*(1), 41–48.

Lewis, M. W. (2007). Analysis of the roles of serious games in helping teach health-related knowledge, skills, and in changing behavior. *Journal of Diabetes Science and Technology, 1*(6). PMID:19885166.

Metcalfe, J. (2002). A region of proximal learning model of study time allocation. *Journal of Memory and Language, 52,* 465–477.

Nuttin, J., & Lens, W. (1985). *Future time perspective and motivation: Theory and research method.* Hillsdale, NJ: Erlbaum.

Romero, M. (2010). Gestion du temps dans les activités projet médiatisées à distance. Ed.s Européenes Universitaires.

Romero, M. (2011). *Students' temporal perspectives, participation, temporal group awareness and grades: Are future oriented students performing better?* Paper presented at the FP7 IAPP Euro-CATCSCL Scientific Results' Workshop. Toulouse, France.

Romero, M., & Usart, M. (2012). Game based learning time-on-task and learning performance according to the students' temporal perspective. In *Proceedings of the 6th European Conference on Games Based Learning.* Waterford Institute of Technology.

Romero, M., & Usart, M. (2013). Time factor in the curriculum integration of game based learning. In *New pedagogical approaches in games enhanced learning curriculum integration.* Hershey, PA: IGI Global. doi:10.4018/978-1-4666-3950-8.ch013.

Romero, M., Usart, M., Ott, M., & Earp, J. (2012). Learning through playing for or against each other? Promoting collaborative learning in digital game based learning. Retrieved from http://aisel.aisnet.org/ecis2012/93

Romero, M., Usart, M., Popescu, M., & Boyle, E. (2012). Interdisciplinary and international adaption and personalization of the metavals serious games. *Lecture Notes in Computer Science, 7528,* 59–73. doi:10.1007/978-3-642-33687-4_5.

Schaaf, R. (2012). Digital game-based learning improve student time-on-task behavior and engagement in comparison to alternative instructional strategies? *Canadian Journal of Action Research, 13*(1), 50–64.

Schmidt, J. T., & Werner, C. H. (2007). Designing online instruction for success. *Future Electronic Journal of e-Learning, 5*(1), 69-78.

Sica, L. S., Delli Veneri, A., & Miglino, O. (2011). Exploring new technological tools for education: Some protime-on-taskypes and their pragmatical classification. In *E learning.* São Paulo, Brazil: Technological Research Institute of São Paulo.

Simons, J., Vansteenkiste, M., Lens, W., & Lacante, M. (2004). Placing motivation and future time perspective theory in a temporal perspective. *Educational Psychology Review, 16*(2), 121–139. doi:10.1023/B:EDPR.0000026609.94841.2f.

Sweller, J. (1994). Cognitive load theory, learning difficulty, and instructional design. *Learning and Instruction, 4*(4), 295–312. doi:10.1016/0959-4752(94)90003-5.

Usart, M., Romero, M., & Almirall, E. (2011). Impact of the feeling of knowledge explicitness in the learners' participation and performance in a collaborative game based learning activity. *Lecture Notes in Computer Science, 6944,* 23–35. doi:10.1007/978-3-642-23834-5_3.

Van Merriënboer, J., & Sweller, J. (2005). Cognitive load theory and complex learning: Recent developments and future directions. *Educational Psychology Review, 17*(2).

Wagner, P., Schober, B., & Spiel, C. (2008). Time students spend working at home for school. *Learning and Instruction, 18,* 309–320. doi:10.1016/j.learninstruc.2007.03.002.

Wassarman, H. S. (2002). The role of expectancies and time perspectives in gambling behaviour. *Dissertation Abstracts International. B, The Sciences and Engineering*, *62*(8B), 3818.

Weibel, D., Wissmath, B., Habegger, S., Steiner, Y., & Groner, R. (2008). Playing online games against computer- vs. human-controlled opponents: Effects on presence, flow, and enjoyment. *Computers in Human Behavior*, *24*(5), 2274–2291. doi:10.1016/j.chb.2007.11.002.

Weppel, S., Bishop, M., & Munoz-Avila, H. (2012). The design of scaffolding in game-based learning: A formative evaluation. *Journal of Interactive Learning Research*, *23*(4), 361–392.

Zimbardo, P. G., & Boyd, J. N. (1999). Putting time into perspective: A valid, reliable individual differences metric. *Journal of Personality and Social Psychology*, *77*, 1271–1288. doi:10.1037/0022-3514.77.6.1271.

Zimbardo, P. G., Keough, K. A., & Boyd, J. N. (1997). Present time perspective as a predictor of risky driving. *Personality and Individual Differences*, *23*, 1007–1023. doi:10.1016/S0191-8869(97)00113-X.

Zyda, M. (2005). From visual simulation to virtual reality to games. *IEEE Computer*, 25-32.

KEY TERMS AND DEFINITIONS

ALT Model: This temporal pattern focuses on time, both from instructional and from student's perspectives. Within the ALT model, students can devote more or less time to the learning activity (engaged time or time-on-task) within the bounds of the time allocated by the teacher (allocated time). Within this time range, students have an amount of effective learning time.

Future Time Perspective: Orientation toward future events and outcomes simultaneously referred to person-related and contextual properties. "FTP is the degree to which and the way in which the chronological future is integrated into the present life-space of an individual through motivational goal-setting processes. It can be defined as the present anticipation of future goals."

Game Temporality: It is the framed time during the game by the implementation of interaction delays and lapses in the game dynamics. E.g. time-outs for finishing certain tasks within the game, SG chronemics related to the way students perceive and value time structure, and delays and time-outs during game interaction.

Instructional Time: The theoretical time-on-task required for achieving the learning objectives of a designed learning task. It can be set by the game designer based on the educational objectives, but teachers can differently allocate it at the beginning of the GBL activity to adapt the needs of the GBL task to each particular group.

Time Assessment: The measurement of the different temporal variables that can be measured before, during and after a learning activity in order to provide useful feedback to the students' performance.

Time-on-Task: The amount of time when a student is actively engaged in a learning task, in particular, in a Serious Game.

Time Perspective: The manner individuals and societies partition time into past, present, and future. It is related to learning performance, motivation and self-regulation processes in face-to-face educational contexts.

Chapter 5
Neurofeedback and Serious Games

Manuel Ninaus
University of Graz, Austria

Matthias Witte
University of Graz, Austria

Silvia E. Kober
University of Graz, Austria

Elisabeth V. C. Friedrich
University of Graz, Austria

Jürgen Kurzmann
University of Graz, Austria

Erwin Hartsuiker
Mind Media BV, The Netherlands

Christa Neuper
University of Graz, Austria & Graz University of Technology, Austria

Guilherme Wood
University of Graz, Austria

ABSTRACT

Neuroscience as well as computer gaming have rapidly advanced in the last decades. Yet, the combination of both fields is still in its infancy. One example of an emerging alliance is neurofeedback, where participants are required to learn controlling their own brain activity. So far, this kind of training is mostly applied in therapeutic settings, for example improving symptoms in epilepsy, attention-deficit/hyperactivity disorder, or autism spectrum disorder. However, there are some promising approaches that used neurofeedback in everyday situations for healthy subjects. This may prove especially valuable for serious games that aim to improve learning capabilities and cognitive aspects of individual users. The following chapter introduces the basic concepts and standards of neurofeedback. The different non-invasive imaging techniques are introduced along with successful applications in neurofeedback. Finally, benefits and pitfalls for future combinations of neurofeedback and games are discussed: while the former may profit from realistic and motivating video scenarios, the latter is expected to be a tool for evaluating and monitoring the direct effects on the user's brain.

DOI: 10.4018/978-1-4666-4773-2.ch005

Copyright © 2014, IGI Global. Copying or distributing in print or electronic forms without written permission of IGI Global is prohibited.

INTRODUCTION

In recent years, the number of neuroscientific studies trying to modify either behavioral or cognitive performance of people via the use of feedback training is rising enormously. There is ample evidence that the successful regulation of one's own brain activity can lead to improvements in either of those domains (Coben & Evans, 2010). As the term "feedback training" already suggests users are required to gain control over brain activity in repeated training sessions. This continued learning process can take about ten training sessions to achieve positive effects on cognitive performance (Vernon, 2005), whereas up to 30 or 40 training sessions are necessary to improve behavior such as attentional and self-management capabilities in children with attention-deficit/hyperactivity disorder (ADHD) (Gevensleben et al., 2010). Keeping the user's motivation high over prolonged time periods is thus one of the main challenges. Yet, traditional neurofeedback trainings generally use rather simple visual feedback modalities such as two-dimensional moving bars on a computer screen representing brain activity in real-time.

In this context, games offer a motivating, entertaining, innovative, and sensory rich alternative to traditional feedback modalities and seem to be well suited for feedback applications. While the primary purpose of conventional games is entertainment, we will refer to the term "serious games" as games that have educational and/or health-related aims besides entertainment (Wang, Sourina, & Nguyen, 2010, Breuer & Bente, 2010). The implementation of these kind of games or game elements in neurofeedback applications might proof beneficial in terms of maintaining motivation over repeated training session.

On the other hand, serious games may also benefit from neurofeedback: Physiological parameters of users can be recorded during gaming and directly fed back to the user. For instance, brain activation patterns can provide the user with feedback about one's current affective or arousal state, so that the user can determine whether he or she is in the right mood for learning. In this way, the ultimate goal of serious games, which is to optimize learning success, is further supported.

The aim of the present review is to discuss the usefulness of combining neuroscience and gaming. First, we will elaborate on neurofeedback concepts and their history. Second, we will elaborate on the benefits of combining serious games or game-elements and neurofeedback. In the third part of this review, we will describe different neuroimaging techniques and their application to neurofeedback. A comprehensive examination of the neuroscientific literature combining neurofeedback and game-like feedback modules will be presented. In the last part of this article we summarize our findings, present some possible limitations of neurofeedback and outline future perspectives.

BACKGROUND

Neurofeedback (NF) is a kind of biofeedback, also called neurotherapy in the literature (Lofthouse, Arnold, & Hurt, 2012). In NF applications, the user's brain activation is depicted in real-time with the goal of helping the user to gain control over specific aspects of the activity in his/her central nervous system. Hence, the user receives direct feedback about his/her actual brain activation pattern and consequently can learn to gain voluntary control over neural signals. By watching and listening to real-time multi-media representations of its own activity, the brain can modify its functionality and even its structure (Budzynski, Budzynski Kogan, Evans, & Abarbanel, 2009). The theory of NF often refers to these mechanisms as operant conditioning of brain activation (Kropotov, 2009): healthy, age appropriate brain activity is rewarded with visual, auditory or even tactile stimulation. In contrast, undesirable patterns of brain activity are ignored or even penalized (Coben & Evans, 2010).

NF is often confused with brain computer interface (BCI). BCI provides an independent non-muscular channel for communication and control by means of translating signals of the brain into an output that reflects the user's intent (Wolpaw, Birbaumer, McFarland, Pfurtscheller, & Vaughan, 2002). While in both, NF and BCI the user's brain signals are directly displayed to the participant in real-time, these applications differ conceptually. BCI can be seen as a direct communication pathway between a human brain and external devices such as a wheelchair, a computer, or prosthesis (Kropotov, 2009). In BCI applications, the recorded brain signals are translated in real-time into commands that operate a computer display or other devices (Wolpaw et al., 2002). In contrast, in NF applications, the feedback parameters are used for self-regulation of the brain itself (Kropotov, 2009). Participants learn to control their own brain activity by means of contingent feedback of measures of the brain activity during NF experiments (Weiskopf, 2012). In recent studies, both, NF and BCI approaches have been used to control games without muscular activity (e.g. Wang et al., 2011; Yan et al., 2008; Zhao et al., 2009).

Different neuroimaging techniques have been used in NF research and a detailed review of the major features will be given later in this chapter. For now, we want to introduce some of the main applications. Historically, electroencephalography (EEG) based NF was first applied in clinical practice for treatment of epileptic patients. Epilepsy patients who learned to control their electrical brain activity using EEG based NF training showed a reduced seizure rate (Kotchoubey et al., 1999). Later, NF was mainly applied to reduce attention deficit-hyperactivity disorder (ADHD) symptoms in children, such as inattention and overactivity (Gruzelier & Egner, 2005). There is ample evidence that children with ADHD show an excess of slow EEG frequencies (4-7 Hz) and a lack of faster EEG frequencies (15-20 Hz) compared to normal kids. Therefore, ADHD kids are trained to enhance fast EEG frequencies combined with inhibiting slow frequencies. This EEG based NF training shows positive effects on behavior, such as a reduction of negative hyperactive/impulsive behaviors with simultaneous improvement of attentional capabilities (Gruzelier & Egner, 2005). Nowadays, NF approach is used to regulate a variety of brain dysfunctions and psychiatric disorders, such as schizophrenia, addiction, depression, or obsessive-compulsive disorder (Kropotov, 2009). Generally, when participants become successful in regulating their own brain activity, e.g. increasing voluntary specific EEG frequency bands, improvements in cognition and behavior usually follow (Coben & Evans, 2010). However, NF is not only useful for people with deficits in specific cognitive domains. In specific situations healthy people can benefit from NF as well. Recent studies were able to show that EEG based NF is useful to improve memory performance in healthy young students (e.g. Nan et al., 2012). This confirms findings of prior studies indicating that EEG NF training leads to improvements in cognitive performances in healthy adults (Angelakis et al., 2007; Gruzelier, Egner, & Vernon, 2006; Hoedlmoser et al., 2008; Vernon, 2005; Vernon et al., 2003). The majority of NF studies are based on EEG signals, but the derived EEG parameters are not the only physiological parameters that reflect functioning of the brain. Recently, the number of NF studies using hemodynamic/metabolic activity of the brain measured by functional magnetic resonance imaging (fMRI) or near-infrared spectroscopy (NIRS) as NF signal is rising (Yoo et al., 2008). The fMRI and NIRS signal can be fed back to the participants and, consequently, can be used for voluntary control of brain functions (Kropotov, 2009).

AN EMERGING NEW FIELD: HOW NEUROFEEDBACK AND SERIOUS GAMES CAN BENEFIT FROM ONE ANOTHER

Cognitive capacity of our brain and performance in computer games are tightly coupled (Feng, Spence, & Pratt, 2007; Green & Bavelier, 2003; Green, Pouget, & Bavelier, 2010; Oei & Patterson, 2013). With the increasing complexity of modern games one has to process huge amounts of sensory information, make ultra-fast decisions, memorize previous events of the game and finally react with an appropriate motor response. This human-computer interaction is interactive and due to highly realistic scenarios the popular media has begun to speak of a 'new sensory reality'.

Research combining neuroscience and gaming is a very young discipline that faces a lot of challenges. The following section is aimed at introducing potential benefits for these two fields. First, we will consider the role of attention in NF and how game design could help to ensure a focused, motivated user. Second, we will discuss how one can incorporate different brain states into serious games to improve learning. Finally, critical issues will be outlined, especially with respect to the complexity of multimodal feedback. As we will see, some of these issues may actually relate to discrepancies in the general conceptualization in both disciplines.

Cognitive Aspects Determining the Individual Ability to Learn from Neurofeedback

As defined earlier in this chapter, NF is based on training paradigms that enable users to gain voluntary control over brain signals. This is usually achieved with a direct, ongoing sensory feedback. Two stages of this learning process can be roughly outlined: In the beginning of the NF training, the user most probably does not know how to control his brain activity. He may thus ask questions like

'How should I act to make it work?' or 'What does it feel like to control the task?' Of course the instructor will provide information on the general task design and what the user is supposed to do. However, as typical for procedural learning, verbal instructions alone are not sufficient to reach mastery (i.e. being able to describe how to ride a bicycle does not imply any ability driving one on the streets in reality). Instead, the way to master NF initially involves a lot of 'trial-and-error' learning. That is, desirable brain states may appear by chance but because of the immediate positive feedback manifest themselves over time. During later stages of NF training this link between brain signals and feedback has consolidated so that users can intuitively switch between desirable and undesirable brain states.

The crucial point here is to establish the electrophysiological signature of a desirable brain state and how to activate and maintain it. The pattern of brain activation should be highly specific, distinct and reproducible. These characteristics will greatly facilitate the reliable detection using non-invasive neuroimaging methods and therefore help to ensure a consistent brain-feedback link. Producing such patterns is not straightforward: The NF literature has mostly suggested a state of relaxed but focused mind of the user (Gruzelier, Egner, & Vernon, 2006; Gruzelier, Inoue, Smart, Steed, & Steffert, 2010; Pfurtscheller, 1992; Serruya & Kahana, 2008). Let us thus briefly review what is known about motivational and attentional factors and their influence on NF performance.

In his seminal book 'Rhythms of the Brain' (Buzsáki, 2006) Buzsáki nicely outlined the beginning of NF: the so called 'alpha movement' in the 1970s tried to commercialize a feedback therapy where enhancement of 8-12 Hz brain oscillations was promised to promote a state of deep relaxation. The idea was somehow inspired by meditation techniques, like Zen or Yoga training, and indeed these mental practices can influence brain rhythms to some degree (Fell, Axmacher, & Haupt, 2010; Green & Turner, 2010). However, relaxation and a state of enhanced attention, or so to say focused mind, may not represent the same processes. Moreover, there are different components of attention (Posner & Raichle, 1994) which are associated to the activity in partially segregated neural networks: one for orienting towards sensory stimuli, another that is maintaining a state of alertness and a third one involved in executive control of goal-directed behavior. The neural correlates of these attentional processes are not localized in a single brain area but instead emerge in large networks that additionally interact with each other. For this reason, enormous scientific efforts have been made since the 1990s to describe the cognitive constructs in their complexity and specificity. Solving these open questions may thus help to identify the objective physiological and psychological predictors of the individual's ability to voluntarily regulate brain activity.

First insights came from slow cortical potentials, large amplitude fluctuations that reflect threshold modulations of local networks (Birbaumer et al., 1999; Daum et al., 1993). These oscillations play a crucial role in setting the excitability level of the brain and have been employed in the treatment of pathological states of oscillatory activity, like epilepsy and ADHD. However, there are large inter-individual differences in both healthy and diseased participants so that the training duration and effectiveness of NF paradigms using slow cortical potentials can vary a lot. Neuropsychological tests have suggested that general attentional abilities correlate, at least partly, with the variations seen during NF (Daum et al., 1993; Holzapfel, Strehl, Kotchoubey, & Birbaumer, 1998; Roberts, Birbaumer, Rockstroh, Lutzenberger, & Elbert, 1989). A plausible interpretation of these results is that we only possess a limited amount of attentional resources that can be allocated and reallocated during cognitive tasks. For successful NF control this means that users have to focus on the task and have to develop and retrieve certain mental strategies that result in the desired patterns of brain activity.

Two studies on self-regulation of 12-15 Hz and 15-18 Hz EEG components showed a direct feedback effect on attention and behavior in healthy participants (Egner & Gruzelier, 2001, 2004). The P300b, an event-related EEG potential reflecting processes that update stimuli information in working memory, was evaluated as output measure in a continuous performance task. This task required participants either to respond to auditory target stimuli by pushing a switch or to withhold motor response. Following NF training of only ten sessions using the signals mentioned above, these authors found increased amplitudes of the P300b component that correlated with the success of the training. Moreover, it was shown that errors rates were reduced and participants responded faster. The important conclusion is that successful NF learners showed selective enhancement in attentional processing that ultimately resulted in better behavioral performance.

With the growing interest in BCI in the last 15 years, many additional factors have been considered that may influence brain activity and the interaction with computerized feedback. Although researchers have applied all recording techniques available, different algorithms to extract brain activations and various types of feedback signals, one problem is omnipresent: BCI illiteracy, i.e. the finding that about 10-40% of users fail to gain significant BCI control (Blankertz et al., 2010; Guger, Edlinger, Harkam, Niedermeyer, & Pfurtscheller, 2003). The reasons for this failure are still unknown and only weak and unsystematic relations between factors like mood, motivation, intelligence and personal traits have been found (Hammer et al., 2012; Nijboer et al., 2008) . However, two interesting points were raised in these studies. First, Hammer and colleagues reported that inefficiency in a BCI using motor imagery (n=84 participants) could be best predicted by a test of fine motor skills. This may indicate that learning to regulate physiological parameters, like the amplitude of EEG components, is linked to processes of motor learning. Second, the work of

Nijboer and colleagues dissociated four different motivational factors: mastery confidence, incompetence fear, challenge and interest. Although the user population in these studies was a small group of paralyzed patients revealing ambiguous results, an important issue was raised, for the influence of psychological factors may also depend on the initial level of performance. For example, users who can perform well from the beginning of the training could be hampered by incompetence fear while initially worse users may in fact experience a motivational boost driven by this fear. Related to this idea is the concept of the 'locus of control of reinforcement' (LOC; (Beier, 2004; Rotter, 1966). That is, people with an external LOC tend to attribute results of their actions to external sources such as luck, chance or unpredictable circumstances. In contrast, people with an internal LOC attribute the results of their actions to their own capacity and abilities. In terms of technical environments, people with an internal LOC feel more comfortable and confident to control devices. So far, there is only one study that demonstrated a correlation between LOC and BCI feedback performance (Burde & Blankertz, 2006) but the general idea stating that trust in technologies is an important factor seems convincing and thus needs further exploration.

To summarize, we have seen evidence for an important contribution of different psychological factors, like motivation or attention, to the ability to self-regulate brain signals in NF and BCI paradigms (Figure 1). However, there is no general rule guiding these influences but any effect seems highly specific to the respective paradigm and individual user. One important empirical question is how to overcome current limitations. Developments from the field of serious games could provide valuable tools in several respects. As described earlier, a key point is to maintain or even increase motivation and attention of potential users so that their engagement in the task is consistently high without increasing the amount of motor artifacts and eye movements. While

Figure 1. Summary of possible factors influencing NF performance

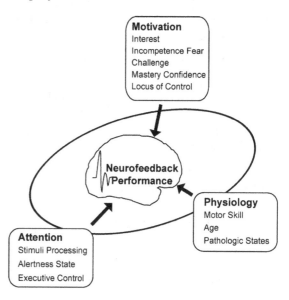

neuroscience has mostly relied on simple visual feedback, like a moving bar, gaming design can contribute more vivid scenarios which in itself might ensure high attentional involvement of users. Indeed, there is ample evidence that increased engagement or involvement in a game can spur motivation and can also improve training and learning outcome (Garris & Driskell, 2002; Ott & Tavella, 2009). The level of engagement in games with a graphic surface is mainly influenced by technology-related factors such as stereoscopy, image motion, a realistic and detailed design, display devices, etc. (Kober, Kurzmann, & Neuper, 2012). Positive consequences of increased engagement are that the user enjoys what he/she is doing, and persists over a longer time (Garris & Driskell, 2002; Ott & Tavella, 2009; Rowe, Shores, Mott, & Lester, 2010). All of this is of central relevance for transferring results from laboratory experiments to applications for home use, where there are many sources of distraction and monitoring by an instructor is missing. A milestone in this development is to tailor such gaming-inspired tasks to the cognitive capacities and personal needs of individuals: the optimal training would thus constantly adjust the level of difficulty to balance challenging and rewarding aspects for each individual user. Another limitation is that a clear connection between NF training and enhanced performance is often hard to validate (Vernon, 2005), especially when one aims to report long-term effects. Here serious games offer additional criteria, for example the amount of training it takes to progress to the next level of the game. Because users presumably spend significant time playing games this will facilitate future exploration of a potential causal relationship.

Incorporating Brain States into Serious Games

So far we considered basic principles and issues from the field of neuroscience and cognitive psychology. But how is that relevant for the gaming industry in any way? The answer for serious games is straightforward: if one wants to go beyond the mere 'fun factor' of commercial video games and aims at beneficial training effects in terms of health, well-being or education, one definitely needs to acknowledge how the human nervous system responds to gaming. Human brains do have an immense capacity for plastic changes throughout the whole lifespan and this is where one wants to make a difference.

Recent advancements in neuroscience have demonstrated that we are able to decode different brain states, for example dissociating periods of resting from preparatory activity and action-related brain signals. This is especially important for neuroprosthetics, i.e. when technical devices are used to substitute dysfunctional modalities of the body. Indeed, first successful approaches in monkeys have been reported that allow for automatic detection of the transition from one state to another during arm reaching movements (Kemere et al., 2008). This kind of real-time monitoring of fluctuations between different mental states is a promising tool for serious games to detect when the user is in an optimal condition for suc-

cessful learning. This is often independent from conscious perception so that instead of verbal reports by users one can rely on more objective patterns of brain activity. Going one step back, a second way to incorporate knowledge from NF is to carry out pre-training screens (Blankertz et al., 2010; Maeder, Sannelli, Haufe, & Blankertz, 2012). Short recordings of brain activity during rest may help to assess the overall level of relaxation and arousal. In turn, this could have two important consequences: first, it indicates when to avoid lengthy but ineffective training sessions and second, it indicates and adjusts for the most appropriate initial level of difficulty.

As we have learned in the previous sections, the participants' internal motivation and the expected reward have been shown to modulate brain signals. For example, oscillatory 4-8 Hz activity in fronto-parietal brain areas does not only indicate whether an event is subsequently remembered but also seems to be related to the anticipated reward (Fell et al., 2012; Gruber, Watrous, Ekstrom, Ranganath, & Otten, 2013; Musallam, Corneil, Greger, Scherberger, & Andersen, 2004). These kinds of signals can help evaluating whether a given game design produces the desired effects: a highly motivating feedback recruits those brain regions helping to enhance memory. Altogether, physiological signals and tools from the field of neuroscience and psychology can provide additional information for the implementation and evaluation of serious games.

DIFFERENT NEUROIMAGING TECHNIQUES AND THEIR APPLICATION IN NEUROFEEDBACK

A reasonable application of gaming elements in NF supposes that developers have a solid understanding of the resources and limitations of neuroimaging techniques. That is, all people involved – from engineer to software programmer to medical assistant - should know the strengths and weaknesses of a given technique and find a common language to communicate emerging problems from their field to the other disciplines. We therefore will introduce the most common neurophysiological methods here and give some examples on feedback paradigms that have been realized so far (see Table 1.)

EEG

The most frequently applied neurophysiological method for NF and BCI applications is the electroencephalogram (EEG). This technique uses electrodes to measure the electrical activity of the brain at the scalp surface, which is reflecting the summed potential of ionic currents across membranes of single cells. The EEG contains a wide frequency spectrum that can be split up in different frequency sub-bands. From a psychophysiological viewpoint, the most important sub-bands which are clinically relevant are: Delta (below 3.5 Hz), Theta (4-7.5 Hz), Alpha (8-13 Hz), Beta (14-30 Hz), and Gamma (above 30 Hz) (Niedermeyer & Lopes da Silva, 2005). These EEG frequencies are associated with specific brain functions: Delta is prevalent in the EEG of infants or during sleep, Theta is associated with drowsiness but at the same time Theta is generally increased during spatial navigation, memory and language processes, Alpha is prevalent in the EEG during relaxation, Beta is associated with attentional processes and concentration, and Gamma is linked to problem solving and memory work (Birbaumer & Schmidt, 2006; Kober & Neuper, 2011). For NF studies, the power in different EEG frequency bands can be fed back to the user, but there are also EEG based NF applications using event-related potentials (ERP), such as slow cortical potentials (SCP), as feedback signal (Budzynski et al., 2009; Coben & Evans, 2010; Kropotov, 2009). ERP are defined in the time domain as the electrical activity of the brain that is triggered by the occurrence of particular events or stimuli (Niedermeyer & Lopes da

Silva, 2005). Generally, averaging techniques are used to detect such ERP (Pfurtscheller & Lopes da Silva, 1999). SCPs reflect changes in cortical polarization, such as negative and positive trends in the EEG, lasting from about 300ms to several seconds after an eliciting event. Several studies have demonstrated associations between electro-cortical negativity and behavioral measures such as short-term memory performance or reaction time (Birbaumer, Elbert, Canavan, & Rockstroh, 1990).

In the following we will discuss some of the most interesting and promising NF and BCI-applications for serious games and virtual environments using EEG. In most cases game elements have been integrated in traditional NF or BCI protocols to increase participants' motivation. One reason is that NF is often used for the treatment of clinical disorders e.g. ADHD, anxiety-disorders, phobias and social problems where a substantial part of the treatment involves an active contribution of participants. Thus, a combination of NF and games is highly promising particularly since traditional feedback screens are often monotonous consisting of two-dimensional moving bars, spots, or lines. These modalities of training may quickly become boring, what in turn can lead to decreased training performance or a stagnated progression of the clinical treatment.

There is empirical evidence that the implementation of simple game elements as feedback modality can improve NF or BCI performance. For instance, Ron-Angevin and Díaz-Estrella (2009) compared two different visual feedback protocols: One group of participants received a conventional visual feedback consisting of a horizontal bar on a computer screen, which extends in varying degrees to the left or to the right depending on the classification result of the BCI classifier. The second group saw a car via a head mounted display, which was driving down the middle of three lanes. Additionally the participants had to avoid obstacles appearing on the left or right lane. Participants were able to control the car's position by means of voluntary changes in their EEG signal.

Table 1. Summary of NF studies using game-like feedback modalities

Reference	Neuroscientific Method	NF/ BCI	Physiological Parameters Used as Feedback Signal	Mental Task	Game-Like Feedback
Ron-Angevin & Díaz-Estrella (2009)	EEG	BCI	EEG power in different frequency bands	Mental relaxation vs. motor imagery	Virtual car driving game, (visual)
Zhao et al. (2009)	EEG	BCI	EEG power in different frequency bands	Motor imagery (left hand-, right hand- and foot-imagery) vs. resting period	Virtual car driving game (visual)
Cho et al. (2004)	EEG	NF	Controlling EEG beta wave ratio		Virtual classroom (visual)
Wang et al. (2011)	EEG	NF	EEG power in different frequency bands	Relaxation vs. concentration	2D ("Pipe" and "Brain Chi") and 3D ("Dancing robot" and "Escape") NF games (visual)
Doud et al. (2011)	EEG	BCI	Controlling EEG SMR (12-15 Hz) frequency	Motor imagery	Navigating a virtual helicopter through a virtual space (visual)
Gruzelier, Inoue, Smart, Steed, & Steffert (2010)	EEG	NF	Controlling different EEG frequency bands		Interaction with virtual theatre auditorium (visual)
Yan et al. (2008)	EEG	NF	EEG power in different frequency bands		Controlling different games
Matsuyama et al. (2009)	NIRS	BCI	Relative concentration changes in oxy-Hb	Mental arithmetic task vs. resting period	Moving a humanoid robot (visual)
Coyle et al. (2007)	NIRS	BCI	Relative concentration changes in oxy-Hb	Motor imagery	"Mindswitch" Game (visual)
Power et al. (2012)	NIRS	BCI	Relative concentration changes in oxy-Hb	Mental arithmetic task vs. mental singing task vs. "no-control" state	Answer multiple choice questions (visual)
Ayaz et al. (2011)	NIRS	BCI	Relative concentration changes in oxy-Hb	Intention-related cognitive activity	Controlling of objects in 3D virtual environment (visual)
DeCharms et al. (2005)	fMRI	BCI	BOLD signal in rostral anterior cingulate cortex (rACC)		Brightness of virtual fire image and movement of scrolling line graph (visual)
Yoo et al. (2004)	fMRI	BCI	BOLD signal	Mental calculation, mental speech generation, left and right hand motor imagery	Navigation through a simple 2D maze (visual)
Mueller et al. (2012)	fMRI	BCI	BOLD signal		Virtual 3D maze and a virtual 3D city environment (visual)
Sorger et al. (2009)	fMRI	BCI	BOLD signal	Motor imagery, mental calculation, inner speech	Answer multiple choice questions (visual)

In both groups, the BCI training was carried out discriminating between two mental tasks: mental relaxation and imagining a movement of the right hand. Ron-Angevin and Díaz-Estrella (2009) were able to show that there were significant differences in classification error rates between both visual feedback protocols. The visual feedback protocol that contained the car produced higher accuracy than the conventional visual horizontal bar protocol. These results demonstrate that even slight changes of a conventional protocol can produce significant effects for BCI. By integrating further game elements or by implementing virtual reality technology (e.g. head mounted displays) into traditional protocols it is even possible to improve therapeutic outcomes and increase the participants' perceived motivation (e.g. Leeb et al., 2007).

More complex scenarios have already been implemented and may provide an additional level of control in future serious games. One example is the study by Zhao, Zhang, & Cichocki (2009), where participants were able to control a virtual car in 3D dynamically changing virtual environment. The researchers implemented a BCI system which was able to distinguish between four mental states: motor imagery states of left hand-, right hand- and foot-imagery as well as relaxation. These different mental tasks were decoded and used to control the virtual car in the virtual environment: turning left or right, speedup and none command, respectively. Doud and colleagues (2011) trained participants to modulate their EEG activity through motor imagery to achieve three-dimensional movement of a virtual helicopter. Participants successfully learned to control the helicopter with the goal of flying through rings in a 3D space.

The examples mentioned so far can be considered as a proof-of-principle and one can foresee different applications in everyday life. With respect to serious games, users may experience an increased awareness of the learning content and higher motivation due to the enriched feedback. Furthermore, controlling BCI systems with im-

agery tasks can enhance motivation and mental toughness (Mahmoudi & Erfanian, 2006). Additionally motor-imagery tasks can also improve real motor skills (e.g. Mahmoudi & Erfanian, 2006), which could be a relevant implication for rehabilitation purposes. However, conventional rehabilitation tools or protocols are often monotone and the success of rehabilitation relies on patients' compliance (Cameirao, Bermudez i Badia, & Verschure, 2008). Adding game elements could enhance therapy by increasing the motivation of the patients to participate in the rehabilitation process.

An important issue in paradigms of increased complexity is how to design a vivid feedback while at the same time controlling for possible side effects. As one step in this direction, the successful application of virtual reality to NF protocols has been demonstrated (e.g. Cho et al., 2002), especially for cognitive training. A NF study by Cho and colleagues (2004) examined the effectiveness of NF, along with virtual reality, for reducing the level of inattention and impulsiveness in male participants with social problems. To this end, the researchers created a virtual classroom. One group of participants used a head mounted display to visually orient themselves in the virtual world (VR group). Another group only used a computer monitor for their NF training. Both groups should learn to control the beta activity of their brain signal (15-18Hz). Beta activity is closely related to attention and impulsiveness. When the beta activity of the participants' EEG signal was greater than a baseline threshold, participants earned a score for a positive reinforcement outcome in the virtual environment. The environment used in this NF training was similar to a game. By increasing the beta wave ratio a dinosaur's egg rose from a desk in the virtual classroom, which then split in two. From the broken egg, each part of a dinosaur picture puzzle gradually appeared on a whiteboard, if the participants were able to further increase the beta wave ratio. The game ended when all the puzzle pictures of the dinosaur egg were completed on the whiteboard. The VR group with the head mounted display achieved better results than the group without VR in a test that was able to measure the ability to respond and pay attention. Furthermore, the VR group paid more attention and made their decisions more rapidly in a continuous performance task. The results of this study imply that NF training within an immersive virtual reality is helpful in attention enhancement. Similar results, regarding a better training outcome with more immersive NF training, have also been shown by Othmer and Kaiser (2000) in a retrospective data analysis. The researchers examined different 2D and 3D applications used for different NF trainings. They discovered that 3D applications outperformed 2D applications. The researchers conclude that some tests of cognitive function show better outcomes with 3D applications. These findings imply that participants could benefit from a more complex and information-rich feedback compared to conventional NF trainings. Virtual reality applications for NF training seem to improve training outcome and should therefore be considered as an important part for future NF protocols.

Recent studies took advantage of these promising findings and implemented game elements and virtual reality technique for their NF trainings (e.g. Wang, Sourina, & Nguyen, 2011; Yan et al., 2008). While most paradigms mentioned above have been driven by questions from a neuroscientific view, one can also recognize an increasing interest from game-inspired research. As mentioned in the study by Wang and colleagues, EEG is widely used in serious game design and becomes even more prominent since more wireless headsets that meet consumer criteria for affordability, portability and ease-of-use are available at the consumer market. For game implementation researchers have used different sorts of game engines, which provide different tools and utilities designing and creating games. In a study by Wang, Sourina and Nguyen (2011) 2D and 3D NF games have been implemented to help the user to improve concentration

ability. The authors applied two 2D-("Pipe" and "Brain Chi") and two 3D-games ("Dancing robot" and "Escape") in combination with a commercial EEG system that detected the level of concentration. All these games used the same general game strategy: points could be earned or lost by the user depending on whether concentration was in- or decreased (game examples are given at http://www3.ntu.edu.sg/home/EOSourina/projects.html; Sourina, 2013). Changing the game strategy in this setup, that is either enhancing concentration or relaxation, provided a way of flexible training.

Based on this common design, games may implement different virtual environments and different tasks. The game "Brain Chi" for example is a 2D single-player game, where the player controls a little boy hero by using his/her "brain power" (e.g. concentration level). The task was to help this little boy hero to fight against evil bats using a protection ball. The size of the protection ball is actually controlled by the "brain power" of the player: by increasing the size of the protection ball the player can eliminate all the bats and win the game.

A sophisticated variant of this approach is "Escape" by Wang, Sourina and Nguyen (2011). This 3D single-player game has an educational purpose. The game-story requires the player to solve different educational puzzles. If the player is able to solve the puzzle he or she could get a password to unlock doors in the virtual environment to escape. However, when the player is not able to solve the puzzle in a conventional way an alternative possibility is to analyze the concentration level of the player via the EEG. The player has to stay concentrated for a specified amount of time to get the password that he/she needs to pass through the door. In case the player uses his "brain power" to get the password, the overall game time allocated for the player to escape is reduced.

These examples provide insight on how NF and games may be combined in future training approaches. NF might use game design principles to make such training more fun, immersive and engaging. At the same time, future games and especially serious games can incorporate brain and other physiological signals as new control mechanisms.

To make these future perspectives come true an intensive exchange between researchers and companies such as Mind Media BV (http://www. mindmedia.nl) is needed that play an important part in developing new, efficient and engaging NF applications as well. In the early 1990's, Mind-Media developed one of the first applications offering true multimedia feedback on a standard PC (NeuroTrace software; V1.0 1994, Mind Media). NeuroTrace for instance allowed controlling video and bitmap animations to play or pause when user definable physiological thresholds were met (see Figure 2.)

The objects shown in the animations were pre-rendered in 3D graphics software and played back to the user, providing a new sort of feedback. The user was rewarded by interesting and colorful computer graphics, rather than a simple line graph.

The first computer games used in commercially available neuro- and biofeedback systems were relatively simple and still rather close to animated sequences. The client could move backward and forward freely, while the environment would also provide some interaction. An example is shown below (Figure 3). In this game, a rabbit makes a journey through a horizontally scrolling landscape

Figure 2. Example of first generation of bitmap animations used for feedback training (Mind Media)

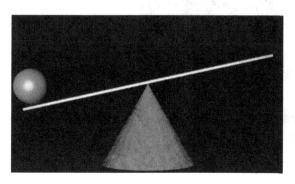

Figure 3. Walking rabbit game with scrolling background and interaction with environment (Mind Media, 2003)

and collects points when certain landmarks are 'discovered'. The movement of the rabbit was driven by physiological signals.

When the first computer game elements were used for NF, a new generation of feedback technology was introduced. As game technology improved, new elements were introduced and biofeedback driven games became more intelligent and more versatile. A (flash based) game, which Mind Media introduced in the year 2005, may serve to illustrate this. In this game Mind Media introduced the idea that up to three individual programmable signals control up to three moving objects in the game (Figure 4). This game is a race where each caterpillar has their own color and signal attached to it. For a single person this could mean training three EEG frequency bands such as Theta, Beta and the Sensory Motor Rhythm (SMR; 12-15 Hz). In the example below, the green caterpillar (SMR) is supposed to win, by having more time over threshold, than Theta and Beta. This game could however also be used to connect two or three people and do Biofeedback on EMG, respiration, HRV and so on, where each caterpillar represents a person. So they would be playing 'against' each other or more positively put: 'with' each other.

In these flash games the user was also allowed to define how the physiological signals would impact the parameters of the game and environment. So a signal could drive movement of objects,

Figure 4. Neurofeedback driven games controlling up to 3 objects

their speed, direction, color, brightness and so on. This introduces many degrees of freedom of how the brain signal could be fed back and was another step forward in NF driven computer games in the commercial sector of NF.

Another example of a NF-game is space invaders (Figure 5). In this game, the movement of the laser gun (ship at the bottom of the screen) was controlled either by the user or therapist (via the keyboard) or automatically by the computer. The laser gun would shoot whenever all criteria were met. Example: the laser gun would shoot when SMR activity went over threshold (enough neurons firing in that frequency) and when Theta and EMG artifact was low enough (below threshold).

Besides 2D games, games with a 3D environment were developed by Mind Media and other companies. The graphics were improved as well as the game play, but the essence did not change. The physiological signals are used to drive elements of the game such as the main objects and the environment and the game present new challenges and rewards in various ways, such as through new levels. As long as the game sticks to the principles of operant conditioning and provides meaningful feedback, game technology can enrich NF training and will continue to do so.

By highlighting also the perspective of an industrial company devoted to the manufacturing of NF-devices and software we can be confident that game elements become more and more important for serious applications such as NF, especially for commercially available devices. As already mentioned above, the most frequently

Figure 5. Space Invaders: firing the laser gun is driven by brainwave activity

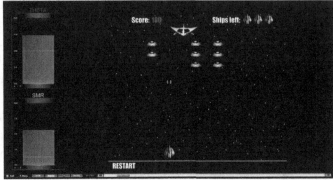

applied neurophysiological method for NF and BCI applications is EEG. Due to its affordability, portability and ease-of-use EEG is also the most popular neurophysiological method for NF in the industry. Nevertheless EEG is not the only method to fed back neurophysiological signals.

MRI

There are also attempts to use other neurophysiological methods than EEG for feedback studies. Hemodynamic activity of the brain measured by functional magnetic resonance imaging (fMRI) or near-infrared spectroscopy (NIRS) is an additional candidate signal for NF in this sense (S. Yoo, Lee, O'Leary, Panych, & Jolesz, 2008).

Magnet resonance imaging (MRI) is a non-invasive brain imaging method that uses strong magnetic fields to create images of biological tissue. With functional MRI (fMRI) changes in brain function, typically increases or decreases in blood oxygenation, are measured during mental activation by assessing changes in magnetization between oxygen-rich and oxygen-poor blood. Hence, fMRI measures brain activity by detecting associated changes in blood flow in the brain. fMRI uses the blood-oxygen-level-dependent (BOLD) contrast as its basic measure. The BOLD hemodynamic response is defined as the relative concentration change of deoxygenated hemoglobin (oxygen-poor blood) following neural stimulation. After stimulus onset the concentration of deoxygenated hemoglobin increases rapidly peaking at about two seconds after stimulus onset, and then declines to a minimum value about six seconds after onset, before returning to baseline about ten seconds after stimulus onset (Huettel, Song, & McCarthy, 2009). One advantage of fMRI over EEG is its spatial resolution, which allows researchers to target at the activation in anatomically specific regions of the brain.

Real-time fMRI is a relatively new feedback technique compared to well-established EEG based feedback applications. Therefore, the focus of fMRI based feedback studies lies mainly on the implementation of the continuous monitoring of the BOLD response in real time rather than on how these changes in the BOLD response can be fed back to the user optimally. Hence, only a few fMRI based feedback studies implemented gaming elements as feedback modality. Goebel and colleagues for example created a computer game based on table tennis that people can play via self-regulated brain activity (Goebel, Sorger, Kaiser, Birbaumer, & Weiskopf, 2004).

DeCharms and colleagues (2005) trained participants to gain control over the endogenous pain modulatory system to enable voluntarily control over pain by using real-time fMRI. Therefore, participants learned to increase or decrease activity in the rostral anterior cingulate cortex (rACC), a region putatively involved in pain perception and regulation. Activity in the rACC was fed back to participants by means of visual feedback. Participants received real-time fMRI information from the target brain region in the rACC as a scrolling line graph of BOLD signal from the entire brain region and a continuous video display depicting the same information as a larger or smaller virtual fire image. Hence, whenever the BOLD signal in the rACC increased the scrolling line graph moved up and the virtual fire got brighter. When participants deliberately induced increases or decreases in rACC fMRI activation, there was a corresponding change in the perception of pain caused by an applied noxious thermal stimulus.

Spatial navigation by thoughts is also a hot topic in the context of real-time fMRI applications. Yoo et al. (2004) used fMRI based BCI for navigation through a simple 2D maze solely through thought processes. For navigation control, four different mental tasks were used: mental calculation for moving up, mental speech generation for moving down, right hand motor imagery to move to the right side, and left hand motor imagery to move to the left in the maze. These different mental tasks activate specific regions in the brain. When a participant wanted for instance to turn left in the virtual maze, he/she imagined a left hand movement which led to an increase of activation in the right (contralateral) motor cortex. This change in the BOLD signal in the right motor cortex is detected online by the BCI system and consequently the curser moves to the left side in the maze. Hence, real-time fMRI applications can be used to detect specific brain activation patterns and to translate these patterns into distinct BCI commands. In the context of spatial navigation by thoughts, Mueller and colleagues (2012) developed neuroinformatics techniques that enable real-time fMRI studies in virtual reality (VR) environments. They designed a virtual 3D maze and a virtual 3D city environment which could be combined with real-time fMRI.

Real-time fMRI is also used to answer multiple-choice questions. By using different mental tasks (motor imagery, mental calculation, inner speech), participants voluntarily changed their BOLD signal in specific brain regions to answer simple questions. For instance, they were asked which color did they like most. They could choose one of four different answers, in this case red, blue, green, or black. The participants' task was to select one of the four response options displayed at a screen and encode the corresponding letter (A, B, C, or D) by performing a certain mental task in a specific time window. In 94.4% of all questions the participants' answers were encoded correctly (Sorger et al., 2009).

NIRS

NIRS is a new non-invasive optical neuroimaging technique. With this method, relative concentration changes of oxygen-rich and oxygen-poor blood on the surface of the brain can be measured, which are indicative of local changes in brain activation. More precisely, NIRS measures changes in oxygenated hemoglobin (oxy-Hb) and deoxygenated hemoglobin (deoxy-Hb) in the cerebral vessels based on their different absorption spectra for light in the near-infrared range (Villringer

& Chance, 1997). Activation in a specific brain area leads to a localized vascular response that causes an inflow of oxygen-rich blood to the active brain area and its surrounding tissue. Thus, oxy-Hb increases and deoxy-Hb decreases in the active brain region (Matthews et al., 2008). Such a decrease in deoxy-Hb in active brain areas is the major source of the BOLD contrast as measured with fMRI (Telkemeyer et al., 2011). Hence, NIRS represents an adequate alternative to measure the BOLD effect in cortical areas (Weiskopf, 2012).

There is only a handful of NIRS based NF or BCI studies using other feedback modalities than moving bars. In one of these rare studies, a NIRS based BCI was developed, which was used to generate motion of a humanoid robot. Relative concentration changes in oxy-Hb were assessed over frontal and temporal brain regions while participants performed mental arithmetic tasks compared to a resting period. Whenever the oxy-Hb concentration level exceeded a specific threshold during the mental task, the brain machine interface sent a control signal to a humanoid robot that was raising its right arm as visual feedback (Matsuyama, Asama, & Otake, 2009).

Moreover, Coyle and colleagues (2007) used NIRS based BCI to control a simple game called "Mindswitch". Mindswitch presents a basic "on/off" switching option to the user, where selection of either state takes 1 min by using motor imagery strategies. NIRS optodes were placed over the motor cortex to detect changes in oxy-Hb during motor imagery.

Power et al. (2012) extended this two-choice BCI system (Coyle et al., 2007), in which only two mental states (e.g., a mental task and rest) are discriminated, and used three different mental states for controlling a game. Participants had to either perform mental arithmetic tasks, a mental singing task, or they had to allow natural thought patterns to occur without restriction ("no-control" state) and change their oxygenation level in the prefrontal cortex voluntarily. With these mental strategies they could answer multiple choice questions. For instance, participants saw three different animals at a screen, such as a turtle, a dog, and a fish. The task was to name those animals capable of walking. The three animals were highlighted one after each other. To choose the turtle and the dog for the correct answer, participants had to perform the mental strategies as long as these animals were highlighted. When the fish was highlighted, participants had to relax themselves to indicate that they did not want to select the fish. With this three-choice NIRS BCI system they reached classification accuracies of 62.5% at maximum. Hence, in 62.5% of all possible answers the participants could successfully change their oxygenation level in prefrontal brain regions to give the correct answer.

There are also attempts to use NIRS based BCI systems for environmental control. Ayaz et al. (Ayaz, Shewokis, Bunce, & Onaral, 2011) developed and tested a new BCI design that utilizes intention-related cognitive activity within the dorsolateral prefrontal cortex recorded by functional near infrared spectroscopy (fNIRS). NIRS signals were used to augment interactive behavior within the 3D environment. Navigation through the virtual environment was controlled by using a keyboard, but interaction with virtual objects was controlled via the NIRS based BCI. Participants consistently utilized the NIRS based BCI with an overall success rate of 84% and volitionally increased their cerebral oxygenation level to trigger actions within the virtual environment.

In one of our NF studies (unpublished data) we developed a NIRS based NF protocol implementing a game-like feedback modality to increase motivation and entertainment during repeated NF training sessions. The aim of the feedback game was to navigate a penguin either to the left or the ride side of a feedback screen to catch a fish and avoid crashing into a barrier (see Figure 6.) Participants could move the penguin to the right side when imaging a right hand movement or to the left side of the screen when imaging a left hand movement. Changes in blood oxygenation during

movement imagery were assessed in real-time over the motor cortex using NIRS. There is ample evidence that motor imagery activates motor areas similar to those activated during motor execution of the same movement (Neuper, Scherer, Reiner, & Pfurtscheller, 2005; Wriessnegger, Kurzmann, & Neuper, 2008). Hence, imagery of a left hand movement leads to increased brain activation over the contralateral (right) motor cortex and vice versa. After ten NF training sessions, the majority of participants successfully learned to control the penguin. Hence, participants learned to play this simple game, in which no muscular activity is needed for controlling the penguin (unpublished data) (see Figure 7.)

Pros and Cons of Different Neuroimaging Techniques Used for NF

In summary one can see that different neurophysiological methods can be used successfully for NF and BCI applications. However, a critical comparison of these brain imaging techniques commonly used for NF applications reveals that each method is associated with various advantages and disadvantages. For instance, a crucial point for NF applications is the temporal resolution of the feedback signal. EEG has a high temporal resolution compared to NIRS and fMRI, which are based on relatively slow metabolic changes. When using EEG as NF signal, changes in electrical brain activity can be detected immediately and fed back to the user with no time delay. In contrast, NIRS and fMRI based NF systems have a latency of several seconds in responding to a change in users' behavioral or mental states. This delayed feedback response limits the practical use of these systems (Cui, Bray, & Reiss, 2010).

A further important issue is the spatial resolution of the brain imaging technique. The big advantage of fMRI based NF over EEG and NIRS based approaches is the whole-brain coverage, overcoming limitations of most EEG-based NF

Figure 6. Feedback screen of a NIRS based NF paradigm. The arrow indicated whether a participant should imagine a right hand movement to steer the penguin to the right side of the screen or a left hand movement to steer the penguin to the left. The aim was to catch the fish. The penguin moved in a constant speed forward, left and right movements of the penguin corresponded to the oxygenation level in the left and right motor cortex.

Figure 7. Projections of the 24 NIRS channel positions on the cortical surface (over the left and right motor areas). NIRS positions are overlaid on a MNI-152 compatible canonical brain that is optimized for NIRS analysis according to a procedure of (Singh, Okamoto, Dan, Jurcak, & Dan, 2005). The left panel shows relative concentration changes in oxy-Hb over the right motor cortex during a left hand movement, whereas the right panel pictures increased activation over the left motor cortex during movement of the right hand.

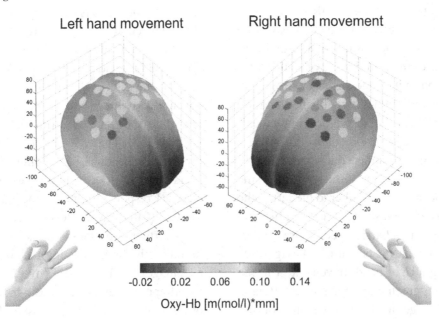

studies (Weiskopf, 2012). Using fMRI, it is possible to measure activity in deep brain structures such as the hippocampus or the amygdala. In the majority of EEG based NF studies only a rather small number of electrodes were used to accelerate the measurement preparation process. Such a small number of electrodes allows only for unreliable localization of active brain areas and results in limited access to deep sub-cortical brain areas. Even with modern multi-channel EEG systems electric source localization in the brain is an intrinsically ill-posed problem (Weiskopf, 2012). Using NIRS, it is only possible to measure changes in hemodynamic responses at the surface of the brain. The penetration is a limitation of NIRS, because one can only measure changes in oxy- and deoxy-Hb a few centimeters (0.5 – 2 cm) from the surface of the head, with a relatively low signal-to-noise ratio (Huppert, Hoge, Diamond, Franceschini, & Boas, 2006).

The quality of the assessed neurophysiological data is also crucial for NF applications. Compared to fMRI and EEG, NIRS has the big advantage of a reduced sensitivity to motion-artifacts and can accommodate a higher degree of movement (Lloyd-Fox, Blasi, & Elwell, 2010; Nambu et al., 2009). For instance, NIRS can be adequately used to measure brain activation patterns during playing a dance video game, where participants had to move extensively (Tachibana, Noah, Bronner, Ono, & Onozuka, 2011). While lying in the narrow space inside the MR-scanner, participants should not move their head to avoid motion artifacts which can confound the fMRI results.

In neuroscientific studies, factors such as measurement preparation or comfort for participants should be considered as well. The montage of the NIRS optodes is very fast and repeated NIRS measurements are also more comfortable for participants compared to EEG measurements since there is no abrasive gel needed, which could lead to skin irritations. Compared to fMRI, EEG and NIRS are more flexible and portable (Huppert et al., 2006; Sitaram, Caria, & Birbaumer, 2009).

Recently, wireless and portable instruments are available which might be useful when using NIRS or EEG in the gaming context (Muehlemann, Haensse, & Wolf, 2008; Sitaram et al., 2009). While lying in a MR-scanner, some participants even experience discomfort because of the noise and the narrow scanner. Additionally, fMRI is locally bounded to the installation site and restricted in study design due to the limitation of the participant's free moving (Weiskopf, 2012).

The last point refers to the costs of the different brain imaging methods. While fMRI is the most expensive technique, both in terms of purchase and maintenance, EEG is highly cost-effective. Table 2 summarizes the above mentioned advantages and disadvantages of the different neurophysiological methods used for NF and BCI applications. NIRS seems to have great potential for future NF studies.

FUTURE RESEARCH DIRECTIONS

As outlined so far, the different neuroimaging techniques have various advantages and disadvantages. However, improvements in technology will increase the possibilities of using neuroimaging techniques during serious gaming especially when devices become more user friendly and meet consumer criteria for affordability, portability and ease-of-use. In general the combination of NF and serious games can lead to major advance-

Table 2. Advantages and disadvantages of EEG, NIRS, and fMRI for NF applications

	EEG	NIRS	fMRI
Spatial resolution	-	±	+
Temporal resolution	+	-	-
Portability	+	+	-
Costs	+	±	-
Motion tolerance	-	+	-
Measurement preparation	-	+	+
Comfort for participants	-	+	-

ments in both fields. Intuitively, one could come to the conclusion that the best way to increase game efficiency is to provide as much feedback information as possible to the user. There is indeed evidence that multimodal sensory feedback allows reaching the threshold of a given neural activation faster and therefore enhances learning (Shams & Seitz, 2008). This finding relates to theories that suggest a distributed cognitive load in multimodal tasks (Burke et al., 2006; Sigrist, Rauter, Riener, & Wolf, 2012).

However, one should be careful not to generalize this concept. Firstly, the amount and complexity of feedback seems to have different effects depending on the task complexity (for a review see Sigrist et al., 2012). For instance, in simple visuomotor tasks a vivid, real-time feedback approach can actually interfere negatively with learning processes. Secondly, the impact of artifacts has to be considered with great care. Eye movements and muscle activity, for example, can produce large amplitude signals superimposed to brain activity reflecting the genuine activation of cognitive functions. These kinds of artifacts, often not consciously perceived by users, can easily provide an effective way of control over feedback and mimic the recruitment of cognitive functions. The failure to detect and isolate the influence of this kind of artifact on signal may completely prevent effective use of NF to optimize learning. Therefore, more than simply trying to combine feedback on EEG signal with games, one should check for plausibility and aim for an artifact-free control signal that presumably will result in more targeted impact on brain functions.

Ultimately, one may be able to take advantage of the 'optimal' sources, i.e. one can combine sensory modalities in a task-specific manner. One can take into consideration the fine spatial details our visual system is able to resolve and add to that the high temporal resolution of the hearing system. The challenge is to create individual solutions: which feedback is optimal for different tasks and different users? And will this change during the learning process? Evidence from motor learning

(Salmoni, Schmidt, & Walter, 1984; Schmidt, Young, Swinnen, & Shapiro, 1989) suggests that practice with concurrent feedback results in the fusion of them: the feedback becomes a central part of the task as the new skill consolidates. Future work will thus have to assess long-term effects of individualized, multimodal NF strategies on cognitive improvements in serious games approaches.

CONCLUSION

In the present review, we focused on the combination of NF and serious games. We outlined the benefits of this combination such as improved learning outcomes and increased motivation and attention of users. But we also tried to point out its limitations, for instance highly complex games can interfere with the learning outcome. Overall, we foresee that neuroscience and gaming will become more tightly coupled but future studies are mandatory to address remaining issues. We particularly identified shortcomings in a common language and a coherent study design between both disciplines. Overcoming this limitation will likely be a key point for success.

After an extensive literature search it turned out that feedback studies using games as feedback modality are rare. The majority of studies used simple two-dimensional moving objects as feedback modality. For instance, voluntary changes in EEG power spectra were visually fed back to the participant as a bar moving up and down on a computer screen. Nevertheless, there are some promising approaches that started to implement game-like aspects. So far, those examples have often focused on spatial aspects, for example producing a control signal in virtual reality environments. The next step is to develop true 'serious games' that incorporate knowledge about attention and memory capacities coming from the cognitive neurosciences. This novel aspect should take us one step closer to the ultimate goal of boosting human brain performance.

To be maximally successful in combining neuroscience and games, feedback studies in this area require collaborative efforts among a team of engineers and neuroscientists. We believe that (i) it is important to choose the right and appropriate neurophysiological method for the feedback signal, (ii) it is mandatory to determine exactly the desired brain activation patterns, which should be voluntarily increased with feedback training by the users, and (iii) the design and elements of the game, used as feedback modality, need careful considerations as they are distinctly contributing to the training outcome.

Due to the fast evolving computer and gaming industry it becomes even more important to keep in mind, that operant conditioning as one of the main principles of NF, does not require very complex or highly interesting auditory or visual feedback in order to be effective. In fact in some cases complex feedback or game-play elements can also distract attention, introduce stress, movement and other artifacts. Nevertheless, the practical experience of some therapists is that particularly young people appreciate game elements which facilitate getting started with NF.

Therefore, much work remains to be done, for example identifying which types of users will benefit most from combining games and NF, which system features are critical, and what types of games will work best. However, promising findings from the first combined NF-games studies indicate a common result: game elements implemented in feedback modalities increase motivation, interest, attention, engagement, and training outcome.

ACKNOWLEDGMENT

This work was supported by the Games and Learning Alliance (GaLA) - Network of Excellence for Serious Games under the European Community Seventh Framework Programme (FP7/2007 2013), Grant Agreement no. 258169.

REFERENCES

Angelakis, E., Stathopoulou, S., Frymiare, J. L., Green, D. L., Lubar, J. F., & Kounios, J. (2007). EEG neurofeedback: A brief overview and an example of peak alpha frequency training for cognitive enhancement in the elderly. *The Clinical Neuropsychologist, 21*(1), 110–129. doi:10.1080/13854040600744839 PMID:17366280.

Ayaz, H., Shewokis, P. A., Bunce, S., & Onaral, B. (2011). An optical brain computer interface for environmental control. In Proceedings - IEEE Engineering in Medicine and Biology Society (pp. 6327–6330). IEEE.

Beier, G. (2004). *Kontrollüberzeugungen im umgang mit technik: Ein persönlichkeitsmerkmal mit relevanz für die gestaltung technischer systeme.* Retrieved from http://www.dissertation.de

Birbaumer, N., Elbert, T., Canavan, A., & Rockstroh, B. (1990). Slow potentials of the cerebral cortex and behavior. *Physiological Reviews, 70*(1), 1–28. PMID:2404287.

Birbaumer, N., Ghanayim, N., Hinterberger, T., Iversen, I., Kotchoubey, B., & Kübler, A. et al. (1999). A spelling device for the paralysed. *Nature, 398*(6725), 297–298. doi:10.1038/18581 PMID:10192330.

Birbaumer, N., & Schmidt, R. (2006). *Biologische psychologie* (6th ed.). Heidelberg, Germany: Springer-Verlag.

Blankertz, B., Sannelli, C., Halder, S., Hammer, E. M., Kübler, A., & Müller, K.-R. et al. (2010). Neurophysiological predictor of SMR-based BCI performance. *NeuroImage, 51*(4), 1303–1309. doi:10.1016/j.neuroimage.2010.03.022 PMID:20303409.

Breuer, J., & Bente, G. (2010). Why so serious? On the relation of serious games and learning. *Journal for Computer Game Culture, 4*(1), 7–24.

Budzynski, T., Budzynski Kogan, H., Evans, J., & Abarbanel, A. (2009). Introduction to quantitative EEG and neurofeedback. *The Journal of Head Trauma Rehabilitation*.

Burde, W., & Blankertz, B. (2006). Is the locus of control of reinforcement a predictor of brain-computer interface performance. In *Proceedings of the 3rd International Braincomputer Inferface Workshop and Training Course 2006* (pp. 76–77). IEEE.

Burke, J., Prewett, M., Gray, A., Yang, L., Stilson, F., Coovert, M., et al. (2006). Comparing the effects of visual-auditory and visual-tactile feedback on user performance: A meta-analysis. In *Proceedings of the 8th International Conference on Multimodal Interfaces* (pp. 108–117). IEEE.

Buzsáki, G. (2006). *Rhythms of the brain*. New York: Oxford University Press. doi:10.1093/acprof:oso/9780195301069.001.0001.

Cameirao, M. S., Bermudez i Badia, S., & Verschure, P. F. M. J. (2008). Virtual reality based upper extremity rehabilitation following stroke: A review. *Journal of CyberTherapy & Rehabilitation*, *1*(1), 63–73.

Cho, B.-H., Kim, S., Shin, D. I., Lee, J. H., Lee, S. M., Kim, I. Y., & Kim, S. I. (2004). Neurofeedback training with virtual reality for inattention and impulsiveness. *Cyberpsychology & Behavior: The Impact of the Internet. Multimedia and Virtual Reality on Behavior and Society*, *7*(5), 519–527.

Cho, B.-H., Ku, J., Jang, D. P., Kim, S., Lee, Y. H., & Kim, I. Y. et al. (2002). The effect of virtual reality cognitive training for attention enhancement. *Cyberpsychology & Behavior: The Impact of the Internet. Multimedia and Virtual Reality on Behavior and Society*, *5*(2), 129–137.

Coben, R., & Evans, J. (2010). *Neurofeedback and neuromodulation techniques and applications*. London: Elsevier Academic Press.

Coyle, S. M., Ward, T. E., & Markham, C. M. (2007). Brain-computer interface using a simplified functional near-infrared spectroscopy system. *Journal of Neural Engineering*, *4*(3), 219–226. doi:10.1088/1741-2560/4/3/007 PMID:17873424.

Cui, X., Bray, S., & Reiss, A. L. (2010). Speeded near infrared spectroscopy (NIRS) response detection. *PLoS ONE*, *5*(11), e15474. doi:10.1371/journal.pone.0015474 PMID:21085607.

Daum, I., Rockstroh, B., Birbaumer, N., Elbert, T., Canavan, A., & Lutzenberger, W. (1993). Behavioural treatment of slow cortical potentials in intractable epilepsy: Neuropsychological predictors of outcome. *Journal of Neurology, Neurosurgery, and Psychiatry*, *56*(1), 94–97. doi:10.1136/jnnp.56.1.94 PMID:8429329.

deCharms, R. C., Maeda, F., Glover, G. H., Ludlow, D., Pauly, J. M., & Soneji, D. et al. (2005). Control over brain activation and pain learned by using real-time functional MRI. *Proceedings of the National Academy of Sciences of the United States of America*, *102*(51), 18626–18631. doi:10.1073/pnas.0505210102 PMID:16352728.

Doud, A. J., Lucas, J. P., Pisansky, M. T., & He, B. (2011). Continuous three-dimensional control of a virtual helicopter using a motor imagery based brain-computer interface. *PLoS ONE*, *6*(10), e26322. doi:10.1371/journal.pone.0026322 PMID:22046274.

Egner, T., & Gruzelier, J. H. (2001). Learned self-regulation of EEG frequency components affects attention and event-related brain potentials in humans. *Neuroreport*, *12*(18), 4155–4159. doi:10.1097/00001756-200112210-00058 PMID:11742256.

Egner, T., & Gruzelier, J. H. (2004). EEG biofeedback of low beta band components: Frequency-specific effects on variables of attention and event-related brain potentials. *Clinical Neurophysiology*, *115*(1), 131–139. doi:10.1016/S1388-2457(03)00353-5 PMID:14706480.

Fell, J., Axmacher, N., & Haupt, S. (2010). From alpha to gamma: Electrophysiological correlates of meditation-related states of consciousness. *Medical Hypotheses*, *75*(2), 218–224. doi:10.1016/j.mehy.2010.02.025 PMID:20227193.

Fell, J., Staresina, B., Do Lam, A., Widman, G., Helmstaedter, C., Elger, C., & Axmacher, N. (2012). Memory modulation by weak synchronous deep brain stimulation: A pilot study. *Brain Stimulation*. PMID:22939277.

Feng, J., Spence, I., & Pratt, J. (2007). Playing an action video game reduces gender differences in spatial cognition. *Psychological Science*, *18*(10), 850–855. doi:10.1111/j.1467-9280.2007.01990.x PMID:17894600.

Garris, R., & Driskell, J. E. (2002). Games, motivation, and learning: A research and practice model. *Practice*, 1–17.

Gevensleben, H., Holl, B., Albrecht, B., Schlamp, D., Kratz, O., & Studer, P. et al. (2010). Neurofeedback training in children with ADHD: 6-month follow-up of a randomised controlled trial. *European Child & Adolescent Psychiatry*, *19*(9), 715–724. doi:10.1007/s00787-010-0109-5 PMID:20499120.

Goebel, R., Sorger, B., Kaiser, J., Birbaumer, N., & Weiskopf, N. (2004). BOLD brain pong: Self regulation of local brain activity during synchronously scanned, interacting subjects. In *Proceedings of 34th Annual Meeting of the Society for Neuroscience*. IEEE.

Green, C. S., & Bavelier, D. (2003). Action video game modifies visual selective attention. *Nature*, *423*(6939), 534–537. doi:10.1038/nature01647 PMID:12774121.

Green, C. S., Pouget, A., & Bavelier, D. (2010). Improved probabilistic inference as a general learning mechanism with action video games. *Current Biology*, *20*(17), 1573–1579. doi:10.1016/j.cub.2010.07.040 PMID:20833324.

Green, R., & Turner, G. (2010). Growing evidence for the influence of meditation on brain and behaviour. *Neuropsychological Rehabilitation*, *20*(2), 306–311. doi:10.1080/09602010903172239 PMID:20204915.

Gruber, M. J., Watrous, A. J., Ekstrom, A. D., Ranganath, C., & Otten, L. J. (2013). Expected reward modulates encoding-related theta activity before an event. *NeuroImage*, *64*, 68–74. doi:10.1016/j.neuroimage.2012.07.064 PMID:22917987.

Gruzelier, J., & Egner, T. (2005). Critical validation studies of neurofeedback. *Child and Adolescent Psychiatric Clinics of North America*, *14*(1), 83–104. doi:10.1016/j.chc.2004.07.002 PMID:15564053.

Gruzelier, J., Egner, T., & Vernon, D. (2006). Validating the efficacy of neurofeedback for optimising performance. *Progress in Brain Research*, *159*, 421–431. doi:10.1016/S0079-6123(06)59027-2 PMID:17071246.

Gruzelier, J., Inoue, A., Smart, R., Steed, A., & Steffert, T. (2010). Acting performance and flow state enhanced with sensory-motor rhythm neurofeedback comparing ecologically valid immersive VR and training screen scenarios. *Neuroscience Letters*, *480*(2), 112–116. doi:10.1016/j.neulet.2010.06.019 PMID:20542087.

Guger, C., Edlinger, G., Harkam, W., Niedermeyer, I., & Pfurtscheller, G. (2003). How many people are able to operate an EEG-based brain-computer interface (BCI)? *IEEE Transactions on Neural Systems and Rehabilitation Engineering, 11*(2), 145–147. doi:10.1109/TNSRE.2003.814481 PMID:12899258.

Hammer, E. M., Halder, S., Blankertz, B., Sannelli, C., Dickhaus, T., & Kleih, S. et al. (2012). Psychological predictors of SMR-BCI performance. *Biological Psychology, 89*(1), 80–86. doi:10.1016/j.biopsycho.2011.09.006 PMID:21964375.

Hoedlmoser, K., Pecherstorfer, T., Gruber, G., Anderer, P., Doppelmayr, M., Klimesch, W., & Schabus, M. (2008). Instrumental conditioning of human sensorimotor rhythm (12-15 Hz) and its impact on sleep as well as declarative learning. *Sleep, 31*(10), 1401–1408. PMID:18853937.

Holzapfel, S., Strehl, U., Kotchoubey, B., & Birbaumer, N. (1998). Behavioral psychophysiological intervention in a mentally retarded epileptic patient with brain lesion. *Applied Psychophysiology and Biofeedback, 23*(2), 189–202. doi:10.1023/A:1022299422116 PMID:10384250.

Huettel, S. A., Song, A. W., & McCarthy, G. (2009). *Functional magnetic resonance imaging* (2nd ed.). Boston: Sinauer Associates, Inc.

Huppert, T. J., Hoge, R. D., Diamond, S. G., Franceschini, M. A., & Boas, D. A. (2006). A temporal comparison of BOLD, ASL, and NIRS hemodynamic responses to motor stimuli in adult humans. *NeuroImage, 29*(2), 368–382. doi:10.1016/j.neuroimage.2005.08.065 PMID:16303317.

Kemere, C., Santhanam, G., Yu, B. M., Afshar, A., Ryu, S. I., Meng, T. H., & Shenoy, K. V. (2008). Detecting neural-state transitions using hidden Markov models for motor cortical prostheses. *Journal of Neurophysiology, 100*(4), 2441–2452. doi:10.1152/jn.00924.2007 PMID:18614757.

Kober, S. E., Kurzmann, J., & Neuper, C. (2012). Cortical correlate of spatial presence in 2D and 3D interactive virtual reality: An EEG study. *International Journal of Psychophysiology: Official Journal of the International Organization of Psychophysiology, 83*(3), 365–374. doi:10.1016/j.ijpsycho.2011.12.003 PMID:22206906.

Kober, S. E., & Neuper, C. (2011). Sex differences in human EEG theta oscillations during spatial navigation in virtual reality. *International Journal of Psychophysiology: Official Journal of the International Organization of Psychophysiology, 79*(3), 347–355. doi:10.1016/j.ijpsycho.2010.12.002 PMID:21146566.

Kotchoubey, B., Strehl, U., Holzapfel, S., Blankenhorn, V., Fröscher, W., & Birbaumer, N. (1999). Negative potential shifts and the prediction of the outcome of neurofeedback therapy in epilepsy. *Clinical Neurophysiology: Official Journal of the International Federation of Clinical Neurophysiology, 110*(4), 683–686. doi:10.1016/S1388-2457(99)00005-X PMID:10378738.

Kropotov, J. D. (2009). *Quantitative EEG, event-related potentials and neurotherapy.* San Diego, CA: Elsevier Academic Press.

Leeb, R., Scherer, R., Friedman, D., Lee, F., Keinrath, C., Bischog, H., et al. (2007). Combining BCI and virtual reality: Scouting virtual worlds. In G. Dornhege, J. del R. Millán, T. Hinterberger, D. J. McFarland, & K.-R. Müller (Eds.), Toward brain computer interfacing (pp. 393–408). Cambridge, MA: MIT Press.

Lloyd-Fox, S., Blasi, a., & Elwell, C. E. (2010). Illuminating the developing brain: The past, present and future of functional near infrared spectroscopy. *Neuroscience and Biobehavioral Reviews, 34*(3), 269–284. doi:10.1016/j.neubiorev.2009.07.008 PMID:19632270.

Lofthouse, N., Arnold, L., & Hurt, E. (2012). Current status of neurofeedback for attention-deficit/hyperactivity disorder. *Current Psychiatry Reports, 14*(5), 536–542. doi:10.1007/s11920-012-0301-z PMID:22890816.

Maeder, C. L., Sannelli, C., Haufe, S., & Blankertz, B. (2012). Pre-stimulus sensorimotor rhythms influence brain-computer interface classification performance. *IEEE Transactions on Neural Systems and Rehabilitation Engineering: A Publication of the IEEE Engineering in Medicine and Biology Society, 20*(5), 653–62. doi:10.1109/TNSRE.2012.2205707

Mahmoudi, B., & Erfanian, A. (2006). Electro-encephalogram based brain-computer interface: Improved performance by mental practice and concentration skills. *Medical & Biological Engineering & Computing, 44*(11), 959–969. doi:10.1007/s11517-006-0111-8 PMID:17028907.

Matsuyama, H., Asama, H., & Otake, M. (2009). Design of differential near-infrared spectroscopy based brain machine interface. In *Proceedings of 18th IEEE International Symposium on Robot and Human Interactive Communication*, (pp. 775–780). IEEE. doi:10.1109/ROMAN.2009.5326215

Matthews, R., Turner, P. J., McDonald, N. J., Ermolaev, K., Manus, T. M., Shelby, R. A., & Steindorf, M. (2008). Real time workload classification from an ambulatory wireless EEG system using hybrid EEG electrodes. In *Proceedings: Annual International Conference of the IEEE Engineering in Medicine and Biology Society*. IEEE. doi:10.1109/IEMBS.2008.4650550

Muehlemann, T., Haensse, D., & Wolf, M. (2008). Wireless miniaturized in-vivo near infrared imaging. *Optics Express, 16*(14), 10323–10330. doi:10.1364/OE.16.010323 PMID:18607442.

Mueller, C., Luehrs, M., Baecke, S., Adolf, D., Luetzkendorf, R., Luchtmann, M., & Bernarding, J. (2012). Building virtual reality fMRI paradigms: A framework for presenting immersive virtual environments. *Journal of Neuroscience Methods, 209*(2), 290–298. doi:10.1016/j.jneumeth.2012.06.025 PMID:22759716.

Musallam, S., Corneil, B. D., Greger, B., Scherberger, H., & Andersen, R. A. (2004). Cognitive control signals for neural prosthetics. *Science, 305*(5681), 258–262. doi:10.1126/science.1097938 PMID:15247483.

Nambu, I., Osu, R., Sato, M., Ando, S., Kawato, M., & Naito, E. (2009). Single-trial reconstruction of finger-pinch forces from human motor-cortical activation measured by near-infrared spectroscopy (NIRS). *NeuroImage, 47*(2), 628–637. doi:10.1016/j.neuroimage.2009.04.050 PMID:19393320.

Nan, W., Rodrigues, J. P., Ma, J., Qu, X., Wan, F., & Mak, P.-I. et al. (2012). Individual alpha neurofeedback training effect on short term memory. *International Journal of Psychophysiology: Official Journal of the International Organization of Psychophysiology, 86*(1), 83–87. doi:10.1016/j.ijpsycho.2012.07.182 PMID:22864258.

Neuper, C., Scherer, R., Reiner, M., & Pfurtscheller, G. (2005). Imagery of motor actions: Differential effects of kinesthetic and visual-motor mode of imagery in single-trial EEG. *Brain Research. Cognitive Brain Research, 25*(3), 668–677. doi:10.1016/j.cogbrainres.2005.08.014 PMID:16236487.

Niedermeyer, E., & Lopes da Silva, F. H. (2005). *Electroencephalography: Basic principles, clinical applications, and related fields*. Academic Press.

Nijboer, F., Furdea, A., Gunst, I., Mellinger, J., McFarland, D. J., Birbaumer, N., & Kübler, A. (2008). An auditory brain-computer interface (BCI). *Journal of Neuroscience Methods*, *167*(1), 43–50. doi:10.1016/j.jneumeth.2007.02.009 PMID:17399797.

Oei, A. C., & Patterson, M. D. (2013). Enhancing cognition with video games: A multiple game training study. *PLoS ONE*, *8*(3), e58546. doi:10.1371/journal.pone.0058546 PMID:23516504.

Othmer, S., & Kaiser, D. (2000). Implementation of virtual reality in EEG. *Biofeedback*, *3*(3).

Ott, M., & Tavella, M. (2009). A contribution to the understanding of what makes young students genuinely engaged in computer-based learning tasks. *Procedia - Social and Behavioral Sciences*, *1*(1), 184–188. doi:10.1016/j.sbspro.2009.01.034

Pfurtscheller, G. (1992). Event-related synchronization (ERS): An electrophysiological correlate of cortical areas at rest. *Electroencephalography and Clinical Neurophysiology*, *83*(1), 62–69. doi:10.1016/0013-4694(92)90133-3 PMID:1376667.

Pfurtscheller, G., & Lopes da Silva, F. H. (1999). Event-related EEG/MEG synchronization and desynchronization: Basic principles. *Clinical Neurophysiology: Official Journal of the International Federation of Clinical Neurophysiology*, *110*(11), 1842–1857. doi:10.1016/S1388-2457(99)00141-8 PMID:10576479.

Posner, M., & Raichle, M. (1994). *Images of mind*. New York: Scientific American Library.

Power, S. D., Kushki, A., & Chau, T. (2012). Automatic single-trial discrimination of mental arithmetic, mental singing and the no-control state from prefrontal activity: Toward a three-state NIRS-BCI. *BMC Research Notes*, *5*(1), 141. doi:10.1186/1756-0500-5-141 PMID:22414111.

Roberts, L., Birbaumer, N., Rockstroh, B., Lutzenberger, W., & Elbert, T. (1989). Self-report during feedback regulation of slow cortical potentials. *Psychophysiology*, *26*(4), 392–403. doi:10.1111/j.1469-8986.1989.tb01941.x PMID:2798689.

Ron-Angevin, R., & Díaz-Estrella, A. (2009). Brain-computer interface: Changes in performance using virtual reality techniques. *Neuroscience Letters*, *449*(2), 123–127. doi:10.1016/j.neulet.2008.10.099 PMID:19000739.

Rotter, J. (1966). Generalized expectancies for internal versus external control of reinforcement. *Psychological Monographs*, *88*(609). PMID:5340840.

Rowe, J. P., Shores, L. R., Mott, B. W., & Lester, J. C. (2010). *Integrating learning and engagement in narrative-centered learning environments*. Academic Press. doi:10.1007/978-3-642-13437-1_17.

Salmoni, A., Schmidt, R., & Walter, C. (1984). Knowledge of results and motor learning: A review and critical reappraisal. *Psychological Bulletin*, *95*(3), 355–386. doi:10.1037/0033-2909.95.3.355 PMID:6399752.

Schmidt, R., Young, D., Swinnen, S., & Shapiro, D. (1989). Summary knowledge of results for skill acquisition: Support for the guidance hypothesis. *Journal of Experimental Psychology. Learning, Memory, and Cognition*, *15*(2), 352–359. doi:10.1037/0278-7393.15.2.352 PMID:2522520.

Serruya, M. D., & Kahana, M. J. (2008). Techniques and devices to restore cognition. *Behavioural Brain Research*, *192*(2), 149–165. doi:10.1016/j.bbr.2008.04.007 PMID:18539345.

Shams, L., & Seitz, A. R. (2008). Benefits of multisensory learning. *Trends in Cognitive Sciences*, *12*(11), 411–417. doi:10.1016/j.tics.2008.07.006 PMID:18805039.

Sigrist, R., Rauter, G., Riener, R., & Wolf, P. (2012). Augmented visual, auditory, haptic, and multimodal feedback in motor learning: A review. *Psychonomic Bulletin & Review*. doi: doi:10.3758/s13423-012-0333-8 PMID:23132605.

Singh, A. K., Okamoto, M., Dan, H., Jurcak, V., & Dan, I. (2005). Spatial registration of multichannel multi-subject fNIRS data to MNI space without MRI. *NeuroImage*, *27*(4), 842–851. doi:10.1016/j.neuroimage.2005.05.019 PMID:15979346.

Sitaram, R., Caria, A., & Birbaumer, N. (2009). Hemodynamic brain-computer interfaces for communication and rehabilitation. *Neural Networks: The Official Journal of the International Neural Network Society*, *22*(9), 1320–1328. doi:10.1016/j.neunet.2009.05.009 PMID:19524399.

Sorger, B., Dahmen, B., Reithler, J., Gosseries, O., Maudoux, A., Laureys, S., & Goebel, R. (2009). *Another kind of bold response: Answering multiple-choice questions via online decoded single-trial brain signals*. London: Elsevier. doi:10.1016/S0079-6123(09)17719-1.

Sourina, O. (2013). *Emotion-based personalised digital media experience in co-spaces (EmoDEx Project)*. Retrieved January 5, 2013, from http://www3.ntu.edu.sg/home/EOSourina/projects.html

Tachibana, A., Noah, J. A., Bronner, S., Ono, Y., & Onozuka, M. (2011). Parietal and temporal activity during a multimodal dance video game: an fNIRS study. *Neuroscience Letters*, *503*(2), 125–130. doi:10.1016/j.neulet.2011.08.023 PMID:21875646.

Telkemeyer, S., Rossi, S., Nierhaus, T., Steinbrink, J., Obrig, H., & Wartenburger, I. (2011). Acoustic processing of temporally modulated sounds in infants: Evidence from a combined near-infrared spectroscopy and EEG study. *Frontiers in Psychology*, *1*, 62. doi:10.3389/fpsyg.2011.00062 PMID:21716574.

Vernon, D. (2005). Can neurofeedback training enhance performance? An evaluation of the evidence with implications for future research. *Applied Psychophysiology and Biofeedback*, *30*(4), 347–364. doi:10.1007/s10484-005-8421-4 PMID:16385423.

Vernon, D., Egner, T., Cooper, N., Compton, T., Neilands, C., Sheri, A., & Gruzelier, J. (2003). The effect of training distinct neurofeedback protocols on aspects of cognitive performance. *International Journal of Psychophysiology: Official Journal of the International Organization of Psychophysiology*, *47*(1), 75–85. doi:10.1016/S0167-8760(02)00091-0 PMID:12543448.

Villringer, A., & Chance, B. (1997). Non-invasive optical spectroscopy and imaging of human brain function. *Trends in Neurosciences*, *20*(10), 435–442. doi:10.1016/S0166-2236(97)01132-6 PMID:9347608.

Wang, Q., Sourina, O., & Nguyen, M. K. (2010). EEG-based serious games design for medical applications. In *Proceedings of 2010 International Conference on Cyberworlds* (pp. 270–276). Singapore: IEEE. doi:10.1109/CW.2010.56

Wang, Q., Sourina, O., & Nguyen, M. K. (2011). Fractal dimension based neurofeedback in serious games. *The Visual Computer*, *27*(4), 299–309. doi:10.1007/s00371-011-0551-5.

Weiskopf, N. (2012). Real-time fMRI and its application to neurofeedback. *NeuroImage*, *62*(2), 682–692. doi:10.1016/j.neuroimage.2011.10.009 PMID:22019880.

Wolpaw, J. R., Birbaumer, N., McFarland, D. J., Pfurtscheller, G., & Vaughan, T. M. (2002). Brain-computer interfaces for communication and control. *Clinical Neurophysiology: Official Journal of the International Federation of Clinical Neurophysiology*, *113*(6), 767–791. doi:10.1016/S1388-2457(02)00057-3 PMID:12048038.

Wriessnegger, S. C., Kurzmann, J., & Neuper, C. (2008). Spatio-temporal differences in brain oxygenation between movement execution and imagery: A multichannel near-infrared spectroscopy study. *International Journal of Psychophysiology: Official Journal of the International Organization of Psychophysiology*, *67*(1), 54–63. doi:10.1016/j.ijpsycho.2007.10.004 PMID:18006099.

Yan, N., Wang, J., Liu, M., Zong, L., Jiao, Y., & Yue, J. et al. (2008). Designing a brain-computer interface device for neurofeedback using virtual environments. *Journal of Medical and Biological Engineering*, *28*(3), 167–172.

Yoo, S., Lee, J., O'Leary, H., Panych, L. P., & Jolesz, F. A. (2008). Neurofeedback fMRI-mediated learning and consolidation of regional brain activation during motor imagery. *International Journal of Imaging Systems and Technology*, *18*(1), 69–78. doi:10.1002/ima.20139 PMID:19526048.

Yoo, S.-S., Fairneny, T., Chen, N.-K., Choo, S.-E., Panych, L. P., & Park, H. et al. (2004). Brain–computer interface using fMRI: Spatial navigation by thoughts. *Neuroreport*, *15*(10), 1591–1595. doi:10.1097/01.wnr.0000133296.39160.fe PMID:15232289.

Zhao, Q., Zhang, L., & Cichocki, A. (2009). EEG-based asynchronous BCI control of a car in 3D virtual reality environments. *Chinese Science Bulletin*, *54*(1), 78–87. doi:10.1007/s11434-008-0547-3.

ADDITIONAL READING

Angelakis, E., Stathopoulou, S., Frymiare, J. L., Green, D. L., Lubar, J. F., & Kounios, J. (2007). EEG neurofeedback: a brief overview and an example of peak alpha frequency training for cognitive enhancement in the elderly. *The Clinical Neuropsychologist*, *21*(1), 110–129. doi:10.1080/13854040600744839 PMID:17366280.

Birbaumer, N., Elbert, T., Canavan, A., & Rockstroh, B. (1990). Slow potentials of the cerebral cortex and behavior. *Physiological Reviews*, *70*(1), 1–28. PMID:2404287.

Birbaumer, N., Ghanayim, N., Hinterberger, T., Iversen, I., & Kotchoubey, B., Kübler, a, Perelmouter, J., et al. (1999). A spelling device for the paralysed. *Nature*, *398*(6725), 297–298. doi:10.1038/18581 PMID:10192330.

Birbaumer, N., & Schmidt, R. (2006). *Biologische Psychologie* (6th ed.). Heidelberg: Springer-Verlag.

Blankertz, B., Sannelli, C., Halder, S., Hammer, E. M., Kübler, A., & Müller, K.-R. et al. (2010). Neurophysiological predictor of SMR-based BCI performance. *NeuroImage*, *51*(4), 1303–1309. doi:10.1016/j.neuroimage.2010.03.022 PMID:20303409.

Buzsáki, G. (2006). *Rhythms of the Brain* (1st ed.). New York, USA: Oxford University Press. doi:10.1093/acprof:oso/9780195301069.001.0001.

Cho, B.-H., Kim, S., Shin, D. I., Lee, J. H., Lee, S. M., Kim, I. Y., & Kim, S. I. (2004). Neurofeedback training with virtual reality for inattention and impulsiveness. *Cyberpsychology & behavior: the impact of the Internet, multimedia and virtual reality on behavior and society*, *7*(5), 519–527. Retrieved from http://online.liebertpub.com/doi/abs/10.1089/cpb.2004.7.519

Coben, R., & Evans, J. (2010). *Neurofeedback and neuromodulation techniques and applications* (R. Coben, & J. Evans, Eds.). 1st ed.). London: Elsevier Academic Press.

Green, C. S., & Bavelier, D. (2003). Action video game modifies visual selective attention. *Nature*, *423*(6939), 534–537. doi:10.1038/nature01647 PMID:12774121.

Green, C. S., Pouget, A., & Bavelier, D. (2010). Improved probabilistic inference as a general learning mechanism with action video games. *Current biology: CB, 20*(17), 1573–9. doi:10.1016/j.cub.2010.07.040

Gruzelier, J., Egner, T., & Vernon, D. (2006). Validating the efficacy of neurofeedback for optimising performance. *Progress in Brain Research, 159*, 421–431. doi:10.1016/S0079-6123(06)59027-2 PMID:17071246.

Huettel, S. A., Song, A. W., & McCarthy, G. (2009). *Functional Magnetic Resonance Imaging* (2nd ed., pp. 147–154). Massachusetts: Sinauer Associates, Inc.

Kober, S. E., Kurzmann, J., & Neuper, C. (2012). Cortical correlate of spatial presence in 2D and 3D interactive virtual reality: an EEG study. *International journal of psychophysiology: official journal of the International Organization of Psychophysiology, 83*(3), 365–74. doi:10.1016/j.ijpsycho.2011.12.003

Kober, S. E., & Neuper, C. (2011). Sex differences in human EEG theta oscillations during spatial navigation in virtual reality. *International journal of psychophysiology: official journal of the International Organization of Psychophysiology, 79*(3), 347–55. doi:10.1016/j.ijpsycho.2010.12.002

Kropotov, J. D. (2009). *Quantitative EEG, event-related potentials and neurotherapy* (1st ed.). San Diego: Elsevier Academic Press.

Leeb, R., Scherer, R., Friedman, D., Lee, F., Keinrath, C., Bischog, H., et al. (2007). Combining BCI and Virtual Reality: Scouting Virtual Worlds. In G. Dornhege, J. del R. Millán, T. Hinterberger, D. J. McFarland, & K.-R. Müller (Eds.), Toward brain computer interfacing (pp. 393–408). Massachusetts: MIT Press.

Niedermeyer, E., & Lopes da Silva, F. H. (2005). *Electroencephalography: Basic Principles*. Clinical Applications, and Related Fields.

Oei, A. C., & Patterson, M. D. (2013). Enhancing Cognition with Video Games: A Multiple Game Training Study. (J. J. Geng, Ed.)PLoS ONE, 8(3), e58546. doi: doi:10.1371/journal.pone.0058546.

Othmer, S., & Kaiser, D. (2000). Implementation of Virtual Reality in EEG Biofeedback, *3*(3).

Pfurtscheller, G. (1992). Event-related synchronization (ERS), An electrophysiological correlate of cortical areas at rest. *Electroencephalography and Clinical Neurophysiology, 83*(1), 62–69. doi:10.1016/0013-4694(92)90133-3 PMID:1376667.

Pfurtscheller, G., & Lopes da Silva, F. H. (1999). Event-related EEG/MEG synchronization and desynchronization: basic principles. *Clinical neurophysiology: official journal of the International Federation of Clinical Neurophysiology, 110*(11), 1842–57.

Ron-Angevin, R., & Díaz-Estrella, A. (2009). Brain-computer interface: changes in performance using virtual reality techniques. *Neuroscience Letters, 449*(2), 123–127. doi:10.1016/j.neulet.2008.10.099 PMID:19000739.

Sigrist, R., Rauter, G., Riener, R., & Wolf, P. (2012). Augmented visual, auditory, haptic, and multimodal feedback in motor learning: A review. *Psychonomic Bulletin & Review*. doi: doi:10.3758/s13423-012-0333-8 PMID:23132605.

Vernon, D. (2005). Can neurofeedback training enhance performance? An evaluation of the evidence with implications for future research. *Applied Psychophysiology and Biofeedback, 30*(4), 347–364. doi:10.1007/s10484-005-8421-4 PMID:16385423.

Vernon, D., Egner, T., Cooper, N., Compton, T., Neilands, C., Sheri, A., & Gruzelier, J. (2003). The effect of training distinct neurofeedback protocols on aspects of cognitive performance. *International journal of psychophysiology: official journal of the International Organization of Psychophysiology, 47*(1), 75–85.

Wang, Q., Sourina, O., & Nguyen, M. K. (2010). EEG-Based Serious Games Design for Medical Applications. *2010 International Conference on Cyberworlds* (pp. 270–276). Singapore: Ieee. doi:10.1109/CW.2010.56

Wang, Q., Sourina, O., & Nguyen, M. K. (2011). Fractal dimension based neurofeedback in serious games. *The Visual Computer*, *27*(4), 299–309. doi:10.1007/s00371-011-0551-5.

Weiskopf, N. (2012). Real-time fMRI and its application to neurofeedback. *NeuroImage*, *62*(2), 682–692. doi:10.1016/j.neuroimage.2011.10.009 PMID:22019880.

Yan, N., Wang, J., Liu, M., Zong, L., Jiao, Y., & Yue, J. et al. (2008). Designing a Brain-computer Interface Device for Neurofeedback Using Virtual Environments. *Journal of Medical and Biological Engineering*, *28*(3), 167–172.

KEY TERMS AND DEFINITIONS:

Biofeedback: Using Biofeedback, one gets direct feedback about different physiological functions and processes such as brain activity, muscle tone, skin conductance, heart rate, etc. and consequently can learn to control them voluntarily.

Brain-Computer Interface: A direct communication pathway between a human brain and external devices such as a wheelchair, a computer, or prosthesis.

Neurofeedback: A type of biofeedback. The user's brain activation is depicted in real-time with the goal of helping the user to gain control over specific aspects of the activity in his/her central nervous system.

Neuroscience: An interdisciplinary science that studies the nervous system.

Non-Invasive Neuroimaging: Various techniques to directly or indirectly image the function or structure of the brain without penetrating the body of the participant.

Serious Games: Games that have educational and/or health-related aims besides entertainment.

Virtual Reality: A computer generated environment that simulates physical presence in real or artificial worlds.

Chapter 6
Disrupting the Magic Circle:
The Impact of Negative Social Gaming Behaviours

Bernd Remmele
Wissenschaftliche Hochschule Lahr, Germany

Nicola Whitton
Manchester Metropolitan University, UK

ABSTRACT

Studies on game-based learning often focus on positive motivations, behaviours, and outcomes. However, negative social behaviours are common in play. Game play is important for moral learning since players learn to comply with rules, fairness, and accountability. Games allow, and sometimes encourage, negative behaviours, which release players' obligations to behave in accepted ways and create new social situations where players learn to control behaviours as well as tolerate such behaviours in others. Sometimes this process fails and the magic circle of play is transgressed. Negative social behaviours, such as cheating, spoil-sporting, or sabotage, threaten to "break the magic circle" by disrupting the boundary between "game world" and "real world." Even if game rules encourage such behaviours, they can undermine the accepted social norms in both contexts. Educational game designers, researchers, and practitioners must appreciate and understand negative social behaviours and attitudes and the processes they can initiate.

INTRODUCTION

The potential of games to support learning is recognized by teachers and academics alike (e.g. Felicia, 2009; Poulsen & Køber, 2011). There are examples of their use in formal education from early years (Sung, Chang, & Lee, 2008), through primary and secondary school settings (Huizenga, Admiraal, Akkerman, & Dam, 2009; Miller & Robertson, 2010; Tuzun et al., 2009), to further

and higher education (Connolly, Stansfield, & Hainey, 2007; Piatt, 2009). Playing games can also support informal learning, such as the development of social skills (Ducheneaut & Moore, 2005) or creating interest in the game topics themselves (Turkay & Adinolf, 2012).

While the benefits of games for learning are implicitly related to socially acceptable or desirable behaviours in the literature, the implications of negative social motivations and behaviours, both for learning and game play, receive less attention.

DOI: 10.4018/978-1-4666-4773-2.ch006

Copyright © 2014, IGI Global. Copying or distributing in print or electronic forms without written permission of IGI Global is prohibited.

The game-based learning literature focuses on positive social game-playing behaviours, such as community-building and sharing, but commonly ignores negative ones, such as cheating, sabotaging other players, or spoil-sporting. However, these negative behaviours are commonplace, some being legitimate within the game structure (for example, sabotaging other players in the game *Ludo*, or lying in *Poker*), while others take place outside of the 'magic circle' of the game (for example, throwing the *Chess* board in the air or stealing money from the *Monopoly* bank). There is a growing body of research relating to violent motivations and the impacts of aggressive gaming (see Anderson & Bushman, 2001; Gentile & Gentile, 2007, for example) but this is out of the scope of this chapter because the focus here is on negative *social* behaviours that impact on other players and threaten to disrupt the very basis of the game world. The player of a violent video game may be learning behaviours that are negative within the real world, but they are entirely consistent within the game world.

The idea of a 'magic circle' (Huizinga, 1955; Salen & Zimmerman, 2004) that separates the real world from the game, is a key aspect of game play. It allows players to enter an 'other world' with different rules and codes of practice, moral and ethical structures, and ways of behaving. This magic circle of play is important for learning with games because it provides a safe space in which mistake-making is not only accepted, but is customary. However, negative social behaviours can disrupt the circle, undermining the learning benefits of the game; they threaten the social dynamics that support the game because they cross or move the boundary of the magic circle. In this chapter, the authors will argue that the circle can be viewed as a 'fuzzy band', not quite 'of the game' and yet not quite 'of the real world', in which play norms and rules are not explicitly discussed or agreed.

In the discourse of game studies, these negative social aspects of game-playing, and their effects on the magic circle of play, are often neglected. This is particularly true in the field of games and learning, where it is crucially important, and it is vital that these behaviours are understood and managed. In this chapter, the authors will argue that an understanding of negative gaming motivations and behaviours is crucial to appreciate the potential drawbacks of games for learning, and address the impact of these behaviours. In this chapter, the authors explore these issues in depth, starting with a discussion of games in relation to rule frames and morals, and a consideration of motivations for game-playing. Different types of negative behaviours will be presented and explored in relation to the magic circle of play. The chapter concludes with a consideration of the implications of the preceding discussions on the field of games and learning.

MORALS AND GAMES

To look at social negativity in games means to shift the primary focus from individual immersion to social framing, because negativity needs to be understood as an interaction between a player who shows a certain behaviour, and a second player who constructs it as negative because of its effect on him or her. As such, disruption can only be judged against a certain social norm that defines 'proper' conduct, otherwise there would not be negativity. Accordingly, although game theorists and philosophers disagree on an exact definition for games (see, for example Crawford, 1984; Prensky, 2007; Suits, 1978; Wittgenstein, 1958), one feature that is remarkably common throughout the definitions is the importance of rules. Hence games are a powerful vehicle for moral and social learning, as this is all about rules at its heart, and the interaction of people within rules. This can be traced back to animals: for example, when young dogs or cats play-fight they change the frame of reference, i.e. the set of rules, from 'this is real' to 'this is play' by indicating this to their peers.

Such framing is used to create a context for game-based learning (Bekoff, 2002); and here one can already see the close relation between learning and playing in that both can support transfer from one context or frame of reference (the world of 'as if') to another (the 'real' world).

For animals, these changes of frames of reference are, of course, limited to the forms of interaction that are constitutive of each species (e.g. subordination or hunting). It can be argued that humans, however, permanently live in the 'as if' frame of reference because social rules *could* always be different (cf. Plessner, 1968). So the ability to play games is a consequence of the human necessity to live a cultural life. Culture means to live within rules, but rules that have to be learned and can be changed. Accordingly, social interaction in 'real life' is only a playing of roles (e.g. Goffman, 1959); and culture is interlaced with play (Huizinga, 1955).

As culture is based on communication, another important issue here is that this change of frame of reference, i.e. from the 'real' to the 'as if' of the magic circle, is signaled – more or less consciously. Like animals, humans affirm to one another that they are now changing the rule frame (cf. Bateson, 1972). However, such signals can be ambivalent or ambiguous and the communication, particularly about whether to stop a game, can be uncertain. Signs inherent in negative behaviors (like cheating or spoil-sporting) create an uncertainty about whether to stop or continue, or whether there is already another secondary game taking place. Negative gaming behaviour constitutes an interesting self-referential dialectic: it creates an uncertain situation, as it brings into question whether the game has already stopped or should be stopped, because the behaviour of one player might be understood as a signal of his discontent, which is likely to increase the discontent and anxiety of the other player(s) as well. The negative behaviours can also be understood as a signal for playing another game (for example, a cheating or swearing battle) and this complex structure makes negative gaming behaviour an interesting phenomenon for game studies.

Due to its rule-based character, play enables people to take on roles in different ways. As such, it is an essential method of learning – not only when humans are young but as mature adults and beyond, for example by using playfulness to examine, test and determine personal moral frameworks and codes (Mead, 1934). Playing games not only helps people to learn more and more complex rule sets, it also supports the structural development of validity of rules. Piaget (1932), observing children playing games, identified a cognitive development in the understanding of the validity of rules, from 'heteronomous' rules, where the rules are perceived as given by some authority (God, parents, teacher, etc.) and are hence static, to 'autonomous' rules, that are simply conventions and can be changed by the participants. However, even agreed rules demand accord: as long they are not changed, they still have to be complied with. The problem of negative social behaviours is more apparent when rules are construed as autonomous; when rules are considered to be 'God-given' then there is no scope for negotiation, and those who transgress them receive appropriate 'punishment'. However, when the rules are based on common agreement, be it explicit or implicit, there is always room for movement although the mechanisms by which changes can be implemented may be unclear. This creates uncertainty as to whether negative behaviours are being undertaken as part of a rule renegotiation process or for some other purpose. There would also be uncertainty about the appropriateness of punitive action.

To complete this shift of game analysis to social framing, in addition to the cultural basis of rules, the consequences of those rules must also be considered. This clarifies the relationship between motivation and behaviour to a certain extent. Rules are of crucial importance when considering games as tools for learning morals, because it is these rules that create accountability. Games have rules that allow actions or decisions to be taken within a known framework in a way that intended consequences follow in an explicit and open way (modern legal frameworks try to do the same). As this relationship between decision and consequence is evident, self-reflection, moral development and the development of expertise becomes possible (Kahnemann, 2011). Of course, moral learning takes place in the real world, too, but the complexity of the real world can create attribution problems, where it becomes difficult to relate an effect to a specific cause and therefore learn from it. The development of superstitions, for example, shows how easily cause and effect in the real world can be misconstrued. It is very difficult to tell who, or what, is accountable for a certain situation, and why, or whether the original intention for an action was realized. So what the rules of a game do is to solve the attribution problem and allow for a clear relationship between a certain (intentional) action and a particular result.

Further, having a limited set of rules makes it possible to decide what the most 'reasonable' move is in term of achieving desired outcomes. In this respect, economic game theory (used in the context of payoff matrices, Nash-equlibria, and so on) is appropriately named as it reduces a social situation to a clear set of rules that define the reasonable moves and choices (in most other respects economic game theory is not related to games). Accordingly, social rationalists like to reduce society to a framework of rational decisions, for example based on a set of individual property rights (e.g. Demsetz, 1967; Hardin, 1968). Similarly, classical utopias are construed in a way that presupposes that complete reason is possible because of the new order (e.g. More, 1516). Then, one may add, if everything is reasonable, only changing the frame of reference and playing games, as voluntarily overcoming unnecessary obstacles, remains as desirable (Suits, 1978).

As mentioned previously, in a given framework of interaction, if a clear relationship between intention and result is made possible, an actor or player can have the impression of accountability and hence a certain sense of freedom. He or she can perceive his or her efficacy. This idea of contingency (that one action is contingent upon another, leading to a feeling of control) can be an important motivational aspect of game-play (Malone & Lepper, 1987); similarly the perception of autonomy and competence is essential for intrinsic motivation according to self-determination theory (Deci & Ryan, 1985). However, one can perceive this also if the action, which is in accordance with rules, has negative consequences for others. This may be common in competitive games where the aim is to win and inevitably involves others losing. However, because this type of behaviour takes place within the rule set it would not be considered as 'negative' in the context of this chapter: although it may have negative consequences for the other players it does not threaten to break the magic circle.

In addition, the idea that conventional rules have to be universally complied with has a negative side. Compliance with the rules tends to imply that it is morally sufficient to stick to the given set of rules without question or critical consideration. This then unburdens the player from further supererogatory duties, so because the moral code lies in the (agreed) rules (Homann & Lütge, 2005) no further moral expectation is addressed to the actor within these rules. This also applies to the real social world. This is, for example, the argument of Adam Smith (1776) who declares that people should address their objectives to the self-interest and not the benevolence of others and that individuals not only *can* do this, but *should* do this in order to improve the functioning of the market. This model also applies to certain games, where the rules allow (or even encourage) the players to be selfish, aggressive or mean in order to increase the thrill of the game

From a motivational point of view, this is of crucial importance. Human beings are, to a certain extent and in certain situations, intrinsically selfish (Fehr & Schmidt, 2005) and by nature aggressive. This dimension is neglected in intrinsic motivational theories like self-determination theory (Deci & Ryan, 1985) or Malone and Lepper's (1987) taxonomy of intrinsic motivation. Negative intrinsic motivations are treated as deviation, disruption of social order, or as animal instincts. The perceptions of autonomy and competence, and partly even social relatedness (cf. Deci & Ryan, 1985) can be created by negative behaviours. How the other players, who are outperformed, bullied, or damaged, relate to the experience is another question; but one that is very important for the development of the common rule frame. For good or bad, this is the nature of play, and this will be discussed in more detail in the following section.

This moral disburdening based on compliance has its limits; there are also rules that define the range of rules and of their compliance (cf. Wittgenstein 1958). In the same way as greedy managers and financial speculators endanger the validity of the rules of the market, and thus their morally disburdening effect, gaming behavior that is 'too' negative endangers the willingness of play partners to stay within the magic circle. In German, *Ludo* is named 'Mensch ärgere Dich nicht' ('Don't get angry'). Examining the social-constructivist definition of anger, this makes sense. Anger can be understood as "a socially constituted response which helps to regulate interpersonal relations through the threat of retaliation for perceived wrongs" (Averill, 1979, p. 71), i.e. it is a necessary construction in order to uphold standards of conduct. If the perceived wrongs are too big, anger ceases to be regulative but becomes disruptive, transgressing the social situation, in the case of games, the magical circle. Learning how to control anger, as well as other emotions such as fear and frustration, is a valuable lesson that game playing can teach. So, games play an important role in the development of social and moral learning and provide a mechanism for gaining an understanding of boundaries and the implications of rule transgression, but negative social behaviours can impact on this learning process. In gaining insights into negative game-playing

behaviours, it is first necessary to understand the range of motivations that people have for playing games, and where negative motivations might fit within them.

MOTIVATIONS FOR GAME-PLAYING

There are a wide variety of different reasons why people choose to play games, at different times and under a range of circumstances. People do not necessarily undertake game-play with the straightforward motivation to win the game or to play it well. It is often assumed that games are intrinsically motivating, and that players will play them for their own sake (e.g. Oblinger, 2004; Prensky, 2007), simply for the enjoyment inherent in the game. However this is not always the case, certainly not in the context of games for learning. Understanding players' motivations for game playing is crucial for understanding why negative behaviours occur.

The idea of 'motivation' in the context of games is used in two related, but distinct, ways. There is the motivation to play a game in the first place. This is what Salen and Zimmerman (2004) refer to as the 'seduction' into the magic circle that must necessarily occur before a player is willing to take part in the gaming activity at all. Secondly, there is sustained motivation to continue to participate in the game, commonly termed 'engagement'. Often in the literature no distinction is made between these two types of motivation, but it is important to recognise the difference, particularly concerning the different function of negative motivations in relation to the two conceptions.

From a pure game design perspective, Ferrara (2012) describes motivations for playing digital games, including immersion (flow), a feeling of autonomy and control, a feeling of competence, accomplishment at no personal risk, social image and reputation within the game community, social interaction, and as an outlet for creativity. It is interesting that he also highlights catharsis and an outlet for aggressive impulses as a motivation, as this angle is uncommon in the literature on games and learning. Crawford (1984) differentiates between a motivation to play games in general, and motivations to play a specific game. He argues that people play games for fantasy fulfillment, to overcome the social restrictions of real life, to demonstrate competence or prowess, for social lubrication, mental or physical exercise, or to satisfy a need for acknowledgement. When selecting a specific game, he suggests that there are two factors at play: the game play itself, and the sensory gratification inherent in the game. As most games do not tap only one of these motivations there can be contradictory drives in relation to single moves or actions in a game. For example, social lubrication can direct a player to move in one direction whereas self-affirmation can lead to the other, particularly if it conveys negative or aggressive elements against the ones with whom the game is played.

A key question is when does the motivation to play a specific game (or willingness to continue engagement in the game play) cease? One reason for play ending is that negative behaviours of one or more other players become so intrusive, unfair or inappropriate in relation to standards of conduct, that the game ceases to be engaging. Balancing the tension of motivations to continue playing and for motivations for stopping the game is a game in itself; this motivational ambivalence can create an arc of suspense (Heckhausen, 1964). However, the motivations for negative social gaming behaviours that are the focus of this chapter are seldom referenced in the literature on games and learning. They are however sometimes discussed in relation to habit-formation, avoidance techniques, and lack of behaviour regulation (Lee & LaRose, 2007) and multiplayer game design, see for example, Schell's (2008) discussion of 'griefing' or Bartle's (1996) description of the 'killer' player type.

Tensions between different forms of intrinsic motivation can also be inferred from the 'taxonomy of intrinsic motivations'. Malone and Lepper (1987) identified four internal motivations – challenge, curiosity, control and fantasy – and three interpersonal motivations – cooperation, competition and recognition. Appropriate challenge can be created by the use of obvious, compelling and adaptable goals, with an uncertainty of whether these goals can be met and a belief that they are achievable. Curiosity is the ability of a game to arouse and then satisfy interest, either cognitive or sensory. Control has three elements: actions leading to logical consequences (contingency); availability of a large number of options (choice); and a decision having a strong effect (power). Fantasy can be intrinsic, where the fantasy is closely interwoven and fundamental to the structure of the game (e. g. an adventure game set on a space ship), or extrinsic, where the fantasy is unrelated to the game structure (e. g. a card game with space-themed playing cards). There is evidence that intrinsic fantasies are better for learning (Habgood, Ainsworth, & Benford, 2005). In terms of the interpersonal motivations, cooperation involves playing together to achieve a common goal (such as competing with other teams), competition involves playing against one or more people in order to win, and recognition refers to the ways in which games make achievements visible for others to see. Competition implies satisfaction from the (relative) detriment of others, which could be seen as a negative motivation, depending on whether the aim of a game is constructed as 'winning' or 'others are losing' and the degree of pleasure the player gets from each event. In either case, however, the magic circle remains intact as both winning and losing are bona fide outcomes of the game. The desires for cooperation and recognition are more positive and can also be understood as motivations to play games in general and to balance disruptive impulses.

Self-determination theory distinguishes between three main forms of intrinsic motivation: first, the perception of autonomy; second the perception of competence; and third the perception of social relatedness (Deci & Ryan 1985). The third aspect is of particular relevance to negative social behaviours. By creating the feeling of affiliation, of being part of a social group or community, playing a (social) game can be intrinsically motivating for those motivated by social interactions; hence, the potential motivation to play games in general, i.e. enter the magic circle, is given. This also provides an insight into the nature and development of social games. Before there were computer games, solitaire-type games formed a real exception to the norms of game playing since games primarily existed to facilitate social interaction. So it is not surprising that "despite the [digital game] industry's initial (pre-networking) focus on single-player games or games played against the machine ... just about all of today's computer games have become multiplayer in one form or another" (Prensky, 2007, p. 123).

In a small-scale phenomenographic study with gamers and non-gamers, Whitton (2007) identified three primary and two secondary motivations for game playing. All of the interviewees who considered themselves to be game players exhibited one (or more) of the primary motivations for game playing: mental stimulation, social interaction, and physical challenge. The participants who did not consider themselves to be game players, still played games under certain circumstances: killing time and social facilitation. In the case of these two motivations, the game was seen as a means to achieving another end (i.e. passing time or making a social occasion easier) rather than being motivational in itself. Unsurprisingly the game players were intrinsically motivated to play, while non-gamers required extrinsic motivation.

Also highlighted in the study were a range of other factors that affected motivation for different individuals. There emerged two factors that seemed to be motivating for all those who mentioned them, four that were universally de-motivational, and a further fifteen factors that were either motivational or de-motivational depending on the individual. The two motivating factors were: continual improvement, being able

to see swift and steady advances; and perceived proficiency, a feeling of being skilled and adept. The four factors that were considered by all to be demotivating were: difficulty starting, problems beginning to play, understanding the concept or mastering the rules; getting stuck, reaching a dead end and being unable to make progress; unfairness, a lack of trust in the game, where it is seen as being inequitable or unjust; and boredom, intrinsic lack of interest with the subject matter or game itself. The idea of unfairness hints at negative behaviours, but this was contructed as unfairness by the 'system' (i.e. the game itself) rather than by unfairness by the other players. This reinforces the idea of the game rules as being perceived as inscrutable by players, and the ideas of releasing responsibilty to 'the rules'.

In addition, fifteen elements emerged, each of which were seen by two or more respondents as being opposed as positively or negatively motivational. The fifteen additional elements were: 1) cerebral activity, the extent to which the game is seen to be intellectually challenging; 2) chance, the degree of random input into the game; 3) collaboration, whether the activity is undertaken collaboratively or individually; 4) competition – the importance of playing against others and winning; 5) complexity, the degree to which the rules are hard or easy to master; 6) difficulty, whether the games is easy or hard to play; 7) involvement, the degree of active participation required; 8) length, whether the game is quick or time-consuming; 9) open-endedness, whether the game has a fixed end or could continue indefinitely; 10) playfulness, whether the game is serious or light-hearted; 11) physical activity, the extent to which the game requires physical exertion; 12) realism, whether the game is realistic or fantastic; 13) sociability, whether the game is played alone or with others; 14) Speed-dependence, the degree to which speed of action is important; and 15) stimulation, whether the game is relaxing or stimulating.

Each individual who mentioned an element found it to be either motivating or demotivating to different degrees. Some preferences seemed to be realtively static for an individual, while others were more fluid depending on the particular circumstances and context of the game playing (e.g. mood, purpose, other players). An individual's preferences determine whether he or she is generally more likely to play games (as opposed to other leisure activities) as well as influencing the types of games played. These motivational preferences also contribute to the explanation of whether, and when, a person stops playing a game, because for example, one player exploits the collaboration of the other players. On reflection, what is striking about these results, which look at both positive and negative motivations, is that negative behaviours do not feature at all, when negative behaviour such as cheating or spoilsporting must surely negatively impact on some players. Perhaps it is simply that the sample size (12 interviews) was small that such issues were not highlighted, or even that the action of what might be seen as 'complaining about others' was not seen by participants in the interviewees as appropriate behaviour, or perhaps the very use of the word 'motivations' implies a positive framing . A fourth hypothesis relates to the nature of negative behaviours within the magic circle: that they are either perceived as an intrinsic part of the game and therefore ignored ('there's always someone who cheats') or that they are seen as being 'other' from the game and outside of the magic circle, and therefore not being within the sphere of critique.

Overall, some of these motivations can include negative aspects, however what is lacking in the research on games and motivation is a systematic consideration of the more negative reasons why people are motivated to play games (and withdraw from games) and behave in certain ways in social gaming situations, for example why players cheat or even risk spoiling the game experience for other people. A possible explanation for the lack of reference to negative motivations in the literature could be because it is not necessarily something that people would willingly admit to or openly discuss in interviews, and questions have not been asked with sufficient focus. However there are a whole range of negative behaviours that need to be considered because of their impacts on the game play, and the learning experience of games, which will be considered in the forthcoming section.

NEGATIVE BEHAVIOURS IN GAMES

There are a wide variety of behaviours that can be considered to be 'negative' in the context of game playing. Five of the most commonly occurring negative behaviours, and their relationship to the magic circle of gaming are discussed below.

Cheating: Occurs when a player intentionally and covertly breaks the formal rules of the game. In some games, such as the card game *Cheat* (or *Mäxle* or *Schummeln*), cheating is itself part of the formal rule set, but then only cheating in prescribed ways. It would be possible to genuinely cheat at these games, for example, by introducing cards from another deck, or by turning the dice. Cheating can also be part of customary gaming practice, for example moving pieces to let a small child win, or in the case of poorly-designed games where everyone agrees to transgress the rules so that the game can become more playable. There can also be an 'in-game' competition to cheat best, e.g. who is most creative in circumventing the rules. However cheating can also destroy the gaming motivations of the players who realize that they have been cheated. Thus cheating may be considered to be on the ambivalent rim of the magic circle.

Spoil-Sporting: Occurs when a player refuses to play or plays the game in such a way that spoils the game for others (for example, taking longer than required, exaggerated sighing). On the one hand a spoil-sport might not want to take part in the game activity at all but is being 'forced' to for social or other reasons. On the other hand the act of spoil-sporting can be a game itself by displacing the magic circle away from a bad or boring game into the direction of teasing game. Whether the spoil-sporting will break or displace the magic circle is at least partly dependent on the reaction of the other players. Spoil-sporting is relatively common in the context of educational gaming, particularly with adults. A student may refuse to play, or play grudgingly because the activity is not perceived as being appropriate, worthy enough for formal education, or motivating enough. Whether a displaced, more motivating (i.e. more fun) version of the game is still educational is another question.

Trifling: Occurs when a player is engaging in a game, and going through the motions, but with different goals to the other players (for example, the *Chess* player who makes patterns with his pieces). Once the other players realise that the trifler is playing another game there is set of potential developments: stop playing, or sustain the magic circle either by trying to tune in into the 'other' game or by continuing to play both games at once, i.e. creating a new one, whatever is more fun.

Suits (1978) draws attention to these three behaviours, describing the differences as "triflers recognise rules but not goals, cheats recognize goals but not rules, players recognize both rules and goals, and spoilsports recognise neither rules nor goals; and that while players acknowledge the claims of both the game and its institution, triflers and cheats acknowledge only institutional claims, spoilsports acknowledge neither" (p. 60). Huizinga (1955) comments that "it is curious to note how much more lenient society is to the cheat than to the spoil-sport. This is because the spoil-sport shatters the play-world itself" (p. 11). The authors also want to draw attention to two further behaviours (without claiming that the list is complete and mutually exclusive), which are more clearly directed in a negative way to the other players then to the formal structure of the game.

Sabotage: Occurs when one player wilfully disrupts and diminishes the performance or achievements of other players in the game. Intended sabotage (i.e. sabotage intended by the game designer) is a common game mechanic (for example in the board games *Sabotage* and *Ludo*) and is also used in educational gaming (e.g. Forsyth, Whitton, & Whitton, 2011) to add tension and dynamics. Unintended sabotage (i.e. sabotage that is unintended by the game designer) occurs when a player spoils the game for another player or all players outside of the rules; it differs from cheating in that the aim is not necessarily to win but to inflict damage on an opponent. For the line of argument of this chapter it is the moment when the 'victim' realizes the sabotage, whether it was secret at first place or directly visible, that is important. The intentionality of the damage is likely to create anger (depending on the degree of the loss) and thus again an ambivalent situation concerning the continuation of the game; and it is only a marginal difference whether the sabotage is part of the game and increasing the thrill, like in *Ludo*, or a result of improper playing.

Schadenfreude: Is simply the pleasure in other people losing or suffering, for example going into prison in *Monopoly*. Koster (2005) lists schadenfreude as a gaming motivation, describing it as "the gloating feeling you get when a rival fails at something" (p. 92). The main difference to sabotage is that for schadenfreude the occurring damage does not have to be inflicted intentionally – the occasional 'banana peel' or drawing the wrong card will suffice. Nevertheless showing schadenfreude demonstrates to the damaged player that one's general solidarity with gaming partners is at least limited. This can be perceived as a breach of confidence.

Other less common types of negative gaming behaviour include sadism, direct aggression and offensive behaviour. Sadism is the pleasure in causing actual physical or emotional pain to another player. There are not many games that provide the opportunity for this (e.g. boxing, contact sports) and fewer that are explicitly designed with a sadistic purpose: the children's game of *Saulöffel* or *Raps* provides an example, where the object of the game is to hit the other players as hard as possible with a pack of playing cards, causing as much pain and dermatological damage as possible. Aggression includes both physical and verbal assaults, and can occur in, for example contact sports or live action role playing games. Offensive behaviour includes bad language and inappropriate behaviours (e.g. groping, swearing) that are quasi-legitimised by the medium of the game. Verbal aggression and/or offensive language are often part of the framework programme of certain games (swearing battles), which hence become an implicit part of the game. In all these instances it can be considered part of gaming suspense when, or if, the other players will be offended so much that they will exit the game.

There are a wide variety of negative gaming behaviours that can occur, and a few of the most prevalent have been discussed here. It is the relationship between the negative behaviours and the transgression of the magic circle that is the real issue here; the ability of these behaviours to break the trust and illusion of solidarity within the game world, and to highlight differences in understanding about the nature of game playing and suspension of disbelief, and what amounts to acceptable and appropriate practices within the game space.

NEGATIVE GAMING AND THE MAGIC CIRCLE

Huizinga (1955) sees the magic of the magic circle mainly in a symbolical over-determination of a concrete place, like a playground, a stage or a table, which is "marked off beforehand" (p 10). Salen and Zimmerman (2004) miss this sequence that starts with the initial marking or social framing: "In a very basic sense, the magic circle of a game is where the game takes place" (p 95). For them, the magic of the magic circle is that something happens to things within the circle: "within the magic circle, special meanings accrue and cluster around objects and behaviors" (Salen & Zimmer-

man, 2004, p 96). This approach is either circular, or mixing the cause with the symptom; it is not that there is a place and then players agree to enter it but that it is the agreement that makes the place or has marked it in a previous encounter ('this is our football field'). A reason for this imprecision might be found in the metaphorical structure of the term.

The 'magic circle' is a metaphor for the common creation of a specific social situation, in which participants cross a virtual boundary into a secondary world or 'playspace'. Until now in this chapter the authors have used this metaphor naively, but now a short reflection seems appropriate. Spatial metaphors for social phenomena are almost inevitable (e.g. Casasanto & Boroditsky, 2008), but are also always deficient because they tend to eliminate the temporal dimension of social processes (Remmele, 2003). Thus, though spatial connotations, like 'breaking the circle', 'the rim of the circle' or 'displacing the circle' have to be used, it is better not only to think of some enclosed physical space. A more appropriate way would be to think of something happening through time, like circling together on a more or less fuzzy band or course.

The magic circle that is created during the play of some games (and, for example, during religious rituals) can be considered to be a *liminal* space; it is "a step outside mundane reality, yet exist in continuity with it, and have the capacity to facilitate significant social and cognitive changes, such as life transitions and the transmission of secret knowledge" (Harviainen, 2012, p. 508). Harviainen (2012) differentiates between the engrossment of, for example, a chess match and the liminal state created by a game that takes players to a new reality. He argues that it is the continual boundary control of these liminal games that is essential to preserve the game reality. The authors also believe that the boundary between the game world and the real world is a crucial space in understanding the motivations and behaviours of players in a game; particularly in the case of (unintended) negative behaviours. While the 'rules' of both the real-world and game-world are to a major degree fixed and explicit, it is in the boundary zone that anomalies arise, owing to different constructions of rules at the limits of the game, notions of acceptability and appropriateness and the existence of inexplicit and tacit knowledge and understanding. The magic circle can thus be viewed a 'fuzzy' boundary between the game world and the real world.

The magic circle is thus 'fuzzy' in a certain sense, because of the double contingency of social situations (Luhmann 1995). It is never fully clear if the participants in a situation mean or want the same things, if they interpret the potential signals of entry and exit in the same way the others do, or if the move they make in relation to the previous one is the one expected. To deal with this problem, institutionalized interaction sequences or rites of passage are commonly used: sitting down at the table, distributing pawns, asking for the potentially different interpretations of certain game specifics, re-iteration of the rules. However, this does not fully address the issue, as many of the behaviours that occur at the boundaries occur because of unquestioned assumptions on the part of the players. In some cases this may be addressed during game play ('Oh, you're playing like that') but on other occasions behaviours may go unaddressed because of a lack of understanding by other players whether certain behaviours lie within or outside of the magic circle. A similar uncertainty arises with the question whether to play another round or not. These boundary rules are not explicit but are embedded in the particular context of play, and they are usually not explored in game studies. Taking the magic circle as a fuzzy social process implies – metaphorically – that the circle is neither a thin line or solid handrail but that it is rather a thick and squashy, perhaps somewhat foggy, rim or band one stumbles onto, around on and off.

The analysis of negative social motivations and behaviours only makes sense in a social situation, as the negativity is determined in relation to the moral framework of the specific situation.

As seen previously, the usual analysis of gaming motivations has an individualistic or psychological starting point, which makes it impossible to judge the tensions between different motivational traits concerning the upkeep of the magic circle or the transgressive power of specific motivations in relation to it. As long as individual immersion is the dominant paradigm any motivation is similarly functional. However the shift from individual immersion to social framing allows different behaviours to be discerned, which are brought forth by different motivations. Seeing the behaviours also from the point of view of the other players requires taking the mentioned dialectics (such as the tension between social cohesion and self-fulfillment) into account.

Negative behaviours, such as cheating and sabotage in particular, present a motivational dilemma for the player, for exhibition of these behaviours may meet the player's motivations in terms of game-play strategy but are likely to lead to transgression of the magic circle and ultimate break-up of the game (with reduction of offers of future games). Being bad, i.e. overtly breaking, bending, and destructing the rules, or taking satisfaction from others' damage, can break the social ties of the magic circle, but as legitimate negativity it can also be part of the rules of another game, i.e. of a displaced magic circle. This adds to the gamefulness: people play games in different ways, and for some the rules are gospel, for others subversion is part of the fun. It is when these unspoken rules conflict that problems arise. Thus, from this sociological perspective one can question the threshold level where negative gaming breaks the magic circle. An understanding of this is important from a game studies perspective, but crucial when games are used in other contexts where intrinsic motivation is not the only or dominant motivation to play, as in the context of game-based learning. A discussion of the implications of negative behaviours in relation to game-based learning follows in the concluding section.

IMPLICATIONS FOR GAME-BASED LEARNING

In this chapter, the authors have tried to show that negative social gaming behaviours and their specific consequences have been neglected in analyses of gaming. As theoretical approaches to game based learning build on these analyses this aspect is important here also. In this final section, the authors will consider the practical implications of the preceding analysis on the use of games for learning, and conclude by exploring ways forward in this context.

First of all, the mentioned ambivalence of transgressing or displacing the magic circle has to be understood against the backdrop of the general tension between the framing of learning (this is for a future external effect, i.e. learning as a transfer to somewhere) and the framing of game-playing (this is just for now and here). Thus this general tension is due to the latent contradiction of the two goals inherent in educational games seen from the player's/learner's perspective. Educational games are usually marked as such, by the teacher or by the packaging, and the player/learner knows that he or she ought to learn while playing.

As we adapt games for serious purposes, we must be aware of this tension between the world of play and the world of work. Thus, in one sense, the term instructional game is an oxymoron. Game play is voluntary, nonproductive, and separate from the real world. Instruction or training is typically non-voluntary, undertaken to achieve certain learning outcomes, and related to life or work skills. (Garris et al., 2002, p495)

Thus, even if the game allows for playful immersion (which is of course the major problem of many so-called educational games) there will be an ambiguity whether the conceived goals of learning and playing do sufficiently coincide (cf. Remmele et al., 2009). There is always the danger that the magic circle will become a learning (but a

boring) circle. The necessity for a 'ludic attitude' for game play (Suits, 1978) breaks down in a context where game play is 'forced' upon the players for means other than playing the game for its own sake. Particularly in the context of adult learners, students may be reluctant to play a game to learn because it is seen as frivolous or inappropriate; however, where learners are convinced that it is an appropriate and effective (ideally the most effective) way to learn then they will be much more ready to accept the use of a game (Whitton, 2007). The impact of negative behaviours in this context applies both to gaming and learning (in effect the overlapping of two magic circles), which adds to the complexity of the situation with unspoken social norms from both contexts. More than ever, this strengthens the argument for appropriate briefing and debriefing in game-based learning contexts.

So, what happens if the precarious ambivalence of transgressing or displacing the magic circle, which in an assured state can be very powerful for learning, hits the tense magic learning circle? The combination of social learning as well as social game playing can be sustainable if it is perceived as a situation of (mutual) generosity – giving knowledge, skills, or time and attention to each other – because in this way intrinsic motivations (e.g. perception of relatedness and competence) for learning and gaming can coincide. Negative behaviour, both in the contexts of learning and gaming, is likely to destroy this tie. Overall this is not so much of an issue in games with exogenous goals, but these do not reach full benefit of game-based learning, because here the frames of learning and gaming are separated anyway. One can still be motivated to answer a question correctly while misusing a bingo-card or suggesting less metaphorical usages of the gallows in *Hangman*.

In the case of endogenous goals, where the frames clearly intersect, the question of how to learn from playing a game is evident. If one is cheating or trifling it is obvious that another game is being played. Apart from the fact that attention of the other players is distracted, the intended learning effect for all is in danger. However, the participants might learn something completely different. Spoil-sporting as well as joy from others' damage will harm the intrinsic intersection of learning and gaming because the dissatisfaction with the common interpersonal relationship is brought to the fore. There is also the possibility of displacing the magic circle by adding another game mechanism to those that are explicit, e.g. a swearing battle, will distract the attention and potentially the learning to another field, such as quick-wittedness.

From the specific perspective of game based learning, a further negative behaviour has to be added: learning resistance. Apart from a general attitude of rejection, reasons for resistance could be found here in a disjunction between the personal learning style and the game-based teaching style or the assumption that gaming is an irrelevant learning activity in the given case (cf. Brookfield, 2006). If the goal of learning is not present for the player then of course everything (and anything) is possible. Understanding the precarious nature of the social situation can even be the actual learning target.

To conclude, it is crucial that the impacts of negative behaviours in games, both intended and unintended within the 'fuzzy' magic circle, are given more attention in the research, both within game studies in general and the specific implications for the field of game-based learning. Gaining a greater understanding of the motivations behind these behaviours will enable a more sophisticated understanding of the processes and practices at work when games are used in learning contexts, and support the design of games that account for, and even exploit, these behaviours.

REFERENCES

Anderson, C. A., & Bushman, B. J. (2001). Effects of violent video games on aggressive behavior, aggressive cognition, aggressive affect, physiological arousal, and prosocial behavior: A meta-analytic review of the scientific literature. *Psychological Science, 12*(5), 353–359. doi:10.1111/1467-9280.00366 PMID:11554666.

Averill, J. (1979). Anger. In H. Howe & R. Dienstbier (Eds.), *Nebraska Symposium on Motivation* (pp. 1–80). Lincoln, NE: University of Nebraska Press.

Bartle, R. (1996). Hearts, clubs, diamonds, spades: Players who suit muds. *Journal of MUD Research, 1*(1), 1–24.

Bateson, G. (1972). *Steps to an ecology of mind.* New York: Ballantine Books.

Bekoff, M. (2002). *Minding animals: Awareness, emotions, and heart.* Oxford, UK: Oxford University Press.

Brookfield, S. (2006). *The skillful teacher: On technique, trust, and responsiveness in the classroom.* San Francisco, CA: Jossey-Bass.

Casasanto, D., & Boroditsky, L. (2008). Time in the mind: Using space to think about time. *Cognition, 106*, 579–593. doi:10.1016/j.cognition.2007.03.004 PMID:17509553.

Connolly, T. M., Stansfield, M., & Hainey, T. (2007). An application of games-based learning within software engineering. *British Journal of Educational Technology, 38*(3), 416–428. doi:10.1111/j.1467-8535.2007.00706.x.

Crawford, C. (1984). *The art of computer game design.* New York, NY: McGraw-Hill.

Deci, E., & Ryan, R. (1985). *Intrinsic motivation and self-determination in human behavior.* New York: Plenum. doi:10.1007/978-1-4899-2271-7.

Demsetz, H. (1967). Towards a theory of property rights. *The American Economic Review*, *57*(2), 347–359.

Ducheneaut, N., & Moore, R. J. (2005). More than just XP: Learning social skills in massively multiplayer online games. *Interactive Technology and Smart Education*, *2*(2), 89–100. doi:10.1108/17415650580000035.

Fehr, E., & Schmidt, K. (2005). *The economics of fairness, reciprocity and altruism: Experimental evidence and new theories*. Retrieved 17 April, 2013, from http://epub.ub.uni-muenchen.de/726/1/Fehr-Schmidt_Handbook(2005-Munichecon).pdf

Felicia, P. (2009). *Digital games in schools: A handbook for teachers*. Brussels, Belgium: European Schoolnet.

Ferrara, J. (2012). *Playful design: Creating game experiences in everyday interfaces*. New York: Louis Rosenfeld.

Forsyth, R., Whitton, N., & Whitton, P. (2011). Accreditation! The responsive curriculum game. In D. Gouscos & M. Meimaris (Eds.), *Proceedings of the 5th European Conference on Games Based Learning* (pp. 176–182). Reading, MA: Academic Publishing Limited.

Garris, R., Ahlers, R., & Driskell, J. (2002). Games, motivation, and learning: A research and practice model simulation gaming. *Simulation & Gaming*, *33*(4), 441–467. doi:10.1177/1046878102238607.

Gentile, D. A., & Gentile, J. R. (2007). Violent video games as exemplary teachers: A conceptual analysis. *Journal of Youth and Adolescence*, *37*(2), 127–141. doi:10.1007/s10964-007-9206-2.

Goffman, E. (1959). *The presentation of self in everyday life*. New York: Doubleday.

Habgood, M. P. J., Ainsworth, S. E., & Benford, S. (2005). Endogenous fantasy and learning in digital games. *Simulation & Gaming*, *36*(4), 483–498. doi:10.1177/1046878105282276.

Hanneforth, D., & Mutschke, A. (1991). *Ärgerspiele: Varianten und verschärfungen von mensch-ärgere-dich-nicht bis malefiz*. Reinbek: Rororo.

Hardin, G. (1968). The tragedy of the commons. *Science*, *162*, 1243–1248. doi:10.1126/science.162.3859.1243 PMID:5699198.

Harviainen, J. T. (2012). Ritualistic games, boundary control, and information uncertainty. *Simulation & Gaming*, *43*(4), 506–527. doi:10.1177/1046878111435395.

Heckhausen, H. (1964). Entwurf einer psychologie des spielens. *Psychologische Forschung*, *27*, 225–243. doi:10.1007/BF00424560 PMID:14114184.

Homann, K., & Lütge, C. (2005). *Einführung in die wirtschaftsethik*. Münster: LIT-Verl.

Huizenga, J., Admiraal, W., Akkerman, S., & Dam, G. T. (2009). Mobile game-based learning in secondary education: Engagement, motivation and learning in a mobile city game. *Journal of Computer Assisted Learning*, *25*(4), 332–344. doi:10.1111/j.1365-2729.2009.00316.x.

Huizinga, J. (1955). *Homo ludens: A study of the play element in culture*. Boston: Beacon Press.

Kahneman, D. (2011). *Thinking, fast and slow*. New York: Farrar, Straus and Giroux.

Koster, R. (2005). *Theory of fun for game design*. Scottsdale, AZ: Paraglyph Press.

Lee, D., & Larose, R. (2007). A socio-cognitive model of video game usage. *Journal of Broadcasting & Electronic Media*, *51*(4), 632–651. doi:10.1080/08838150701626511.

Luhmann, N. (1995). *Social systems*. Stanford, CA: Stanford University Press.

Malone, T., & Lepper, M. (1987). Making learning fun: A taxonomy of intrinsic motivations for learning. In R. Snow & M. Farr (Eds.), Aptitude, Learning and Instruction: Volume 3: Conative and Affective Process Analyses (pp. 223-253). Hillsdale, NJ: Lawrence Erlbaum.

Mead, G. H. (1934). *Mind, self, and society.* Chicago: University of Chicago Press.

Miller, D. J., & Robertson, D. P. (2010). Using a games console in the primary classroom: Effects of brain training programme on computation and self-esteem. *British Journal of Educational Technology*, *41*(2), 242–255. doi:10.1111/j.1467-8535.2008.00918.x.

More, T. (1516). *Utopia.* Retrieved 17 April, 2012, from http://www.gutenberg.org/files/2130/2130-h/2130-h.htm

Oblinger, D. (2004). The next generation of educational engagement. *Journal of Interactive Media in Education*, *8*, 1–18.

Piaget, J. (1932). *The moral judgment of the child.* London: K. Paul, Trench, Trubner & Co. ltd.

Piatt, K. (2009). Using alternate reality games to support first year induction with ELGG. *Campus-Wide Information Systems*, *26*(4), 313–322. doi:10.1108/10650740910984646.

Plessner, H. (1968). *Der kategorische konjunktiv.* Frankfurt/M.

Poulsen, M., & Køber, E. (2011). *The GAMEiT handbook: A framework of game based learning pedagogy.* Oslo, Norway: GAMEiT.

Prensky, M. (2007). *Digital game-based learning.* St Paul, MN: Paragon House Publishers.

Remmele, B. (2003). *Die entstehung des maschinenparadigmas.* Opladen: Leske & Budrich.

Remmele, B., Seeber, G., Krämer, J., & Schmette, M. (2009). Game-based teaching - Dimensions of analysis. In M. Pivec (Ed.), *Proceedings of the 3rd European Conference on Games-Based Learning* (pp. 325-331). Reading, MA: Academic Publishing Limited.

Salen, K., & Zimmerman, E. (2004). *Rules of play: Game design fundamentals.* Cambridge, MA: The MIT Press.

Schell, J. (2008). *The art of game design: A book of lenses.* Boca Raton, FL: CRC Press.

Suits, B. (1978). *The grasshopper: Games, life and utopia.* Peterborough, Canada: Broadview Press.

Sung, Y.-T., Chang, K.-E., & Lee, M.-D. (2008). Designing multimedia games for young children's taxonomic concept development. *Computers & Education*, *50*(3), 1037–1051. doi:10.1016/j.compedu.2006.07.011.

Turkay, S., & Adinolf, S. (2012). What do players (think they) learn in games?. *Procedia - Social and Behavioral Sciences, 46*, 3345–3349.

Tuzun, H., Yilmazsoylu, M., Karakus, T., & Inal, Y., KIzIlkaya, G., Tüzün, H., & YIlmaz-Soylu, M. (2009). The effects of computer games on primary school students' achievement and motivation in geography learning. *Computers & Education, 52*(1), 68–77. doi:10.1016/j.compedu.2008.06.008.

Whitton, N. (2007). *An investigation into the potential of collaborative computer game-based learning in higher education.* (Unpublished doctoral dissertation). Edinburgh Napier University, Edinburgh, UK.

Wittgenstein, L. (1958). *Philosophical investigations.* Oxford, UK: Basil Blackwell.

ADDITIONAL READING

Bateson, G. (1972). *Steps to an ecology of mind.* New York: Ballantine Books.

Bekoff, M. (2002). *Minding animals. Awareness, emotions, and heart.* Oxford: Oxford University Press.

Deci, E., & Ryan, R. (1985). *Intrinsic motivation and self-determination in human behavior.* New York: Plenum. doi:10.1007/978-1-4899-2271-7.

Fehr, E., & Schmidt, K. (2005). *The Economics of Fairness, Reciprocity and Altruism. Experimental Evidence and New Theories.* Retrieved 17 April, 2013, from http://epub.ub.uni-muenchen.de/726/1/Fehr-Schmidt_Handbook(2005-Munichecon).pdf.

Goffman, E. (1959). *The presentation of self in everyday life.* New York: Doubleday.

Harviainen, J. T. (2012). Ritualistic Games, Boundary Control, and Information Uncertainty. *Simulation & Gaming, 43*(4), 506–527. doi:10.1177/1046878111435395.

Huizinga, J. (1955). *Homo Ludens: A Study of the Play Element in Culture.* Boston: Beacon Press.

Kahneman, D. (2011). *Thinking, fast and slow.* New York: Farrar, Straus and Giroux.

Koster, R. (2005). *Theory of Fun for Game Design.* Scottsdale, AZ: Paraglyph Press.

Luhmann, N. (1995). *Social systems.* Stanford, CA: Stanford University Press.

Mead, G. H. (1934). *Mind, Self, and Society.* Chicago: University of Chicago Press.

Piaget, J. (1932). *The moral judgment of the child.* London: K. Paul, Trench, Trubner & Co. ltd.

Salen, K., & Zimmerman, E. (2004). *Rules of Play: Game Design Fundamentals.* Cambridge, MA: The MIT Press.

Schell, J. (2008). *The Art of Game Design: A book of lenses.* Boca Raton, FL: CRC Press.

Suits, B. (1978). *The Grasshopper: Games, Life and Utopia.* Peterborough, Canada: Broadview Press.

Wittgenstein, L. (1958). *Philosophical Investigations.* Oxford: Basil Blackwell.

KEY TERMS AND DEFINTIONS

Cheating: When a player deliberately and covertly acts outside of the formal rules of the game.

Magic Circle: The imaginary barrier between the the game world and the real world.

Sabotage: When one player wilfully disrupts and diminishes the performance or achievements of other players in the game.

Schadenfreude: The pleasure taking in seeing other people lose or suffer.

Spoil-Sporting: When a player refuses to play a game 'correctly' play or plays the game in such a way that spoils the game for others.

Trifling: When a player is engaging in a game, and going through the motions, but with different goals to the other players.

Chapter 7
Non–Player Characters and Artificial Intelligence

Gonçalo Pereira
INESC-ID, Portugal and Instituto Superior Técnico, University of Lisbon, Portugal

Joana Campos
INESC-ID, Portugal and Instituto Superior Técnico, University of Lisbon, Portugal

António Brisson
INESC-ID, Portugal and Instituto Superior Técnico, University of Lisbon, Portugal

Marco Vala
INESC-ID, Portugal and Instituto Superior Técnico, University of Lisbon, Portugal

João Dias
INESC-ID, Portugal and Instituto Superior Técnico, University of Lisbon, Portugal

Iolanda Leite
INESC-ID, Portugal and Instituto Superior Técnico, University of Lisbon, Portugal

André Carvalho
INESC-ID, Portugal and Instituto Superior Técnico, University of Lisbon, Portugal

Carlos Martinho
INESC-ID, Portugal and Instituto Superior Técnico, University of Lisbon, Portugal

Joana Dimas
INESC-ID, Portugal and Instituto Superior Técnico, University of Lisbon, Portugal

Rui Prada
INESC-ID, Portugal and Instituto Superior Técnico, University of Lisbon, Portugal

Samuel Mascarenhas
INESC-ID, Portugal and Instituto Superior Técnico, University of Lisbon, Portugal

Ana Paiva
INESC-ID, Portugal and Instituto Superior Técnico, University of Lisbon, Portugal

ABSTRACT

Serious Games rely on interactive systems to provide an efficient communication medium between the tutor and the user. Designing and implementing such medium is a multi-disciplinary task that aims at an environment that engages the user in a learning activity. User engagement is significantly related to the users' sense of immersion or his willingness to accept the reality proposed by a game environment. This is a very relevant research topic for Artificial Intelligence (AI), since it requires computational systems to generate believable behaviors that can promote the users' willingness to enter and engage in the game environment. In order to do this, AI research has been relying on social sciences, in particu-

DOI: 10.4018/978-1-4666-4773-2.ch007

Copyright © 2014, IGI Global. Copying or distributing in print or electronic forms without written permission of IGI Global is prohibited.

lar psychology and sociology models, to ground the creation of computational models for non-player characters that behave according to the users' expectations. In this chapter, the authors present some of the most relevant NPC research contributions following this approach.

INTRODUCTION

Non-player characters (NPCs) are entities that embody a role in a game context that is usually performed by a person. For example, in a bullying scenario in which a player plays the role of a bullied child, diverse NPCs are needed to play the roles of the bully, the bully's friends and the teacher (Vannini et al., 2011). These characters are controlled by artificial intelligence (AI) algorithms, which generate behaviours based on different human characteristics according to the design goals. The modelled behaviours can range from simple wandering entities that populate a scenario (Thalmann et al., 2004; Ulicny & Thalmann, 2001), e.g., members of a crowd, to more complex and human-like entities that intelligently interact with a player (Gratch et al., 2002; Magnenat-Thalmann & Kasap, 2009).

However, at its core, what is a Non-Player Character? The answer is an autonomous agent (for games) that senses its environment and acts intelligently and independently from the player. In fact, different types of characters[1] represent attempts to mirror human behaviours either at a specific or a holistic level depending on the game's requirements.

Common approaches to modelling of NPCs result in the creation of different types of entities: scripted (Spronck, Ponsen, Sprinkhuizen-Kuyper, & Postma, 2006), reactive, deliberative and hybrid (Wooldridge, 2002). Each of these approaches contains different design purposes and applications. From a designer's point of view, to establish a parallel with real people, we can conceptualise others in different ways according to the context of the situation at hand. For example, if we consider the management of exits in a stadium, we focus on people's steering and the resulting flow behaviours through bottleneck points in the environment. In this situation, people are usually more adequately modelled in NPCs by reactive characters that can exhibit emergent crowd behaviours based on simple rules (Thalmann et al., 2004; Ulicny & Thalmann, 2001). In another example, if we consider a situation of emotional support for a learning situation, we are interested in the advisor's (character) knowledge, skill and ability to help the user (João Dias & Paiva, 2005). In this case, modelling of the advisor person in an NPC role is better achieved by means of a deliberative or hybrid (combining different types of behaviours) entity that contains the required mental models necessary to respond to the situation. Beyond these examples, several other focused behaviours can be applied, e.g., genetic algorithms (Krovi, Graesser, & Pracht, 1999), to evolve behaviours or machine learning used to exhibit human-like learning capabilities (Spronck et al., 2006).

Another important aspect of NPCs is their form. Given the game-like types of scenarios, the NPCs we discuss in this chapter are usually virtual characters. The visual representation of the characters aims to approximate the experience of player-character interaction with that of human-human interaction. If we combine the virtual characters with the previously described creation of intelligent behaviours, we create intelligent virtual characters. These virtual characters are intended to give the illusion of human behaviour by simulating many human aspects (physical and cognitive) and modalities (perceptions and action) for dynamic social environments. To many, the ultimate goal is the creation of synthetic characters that "are not only believable but also as remarkable and unforgettable, as humans are"[2].

The fundamental contribution of NPCs to serious games stems from the interactive experience they provide to the player. The inclusion of NPCs in virtual environments fosters the creation of highly interactive and socially vivid scenarios that can provide more socially realistic experiences. Such environments aim to achieve "suspension of disbelief" in the players (J. Bates, 1992; Joseph Bates, Loyall, & Reilly, 1994) with respect to the virtual environment and to immerse them in the narrative, tasks and challenges provided by the game designers. In the context of a serious game, NPCs can be used to enhance immersion, engage players and create characters that can intelligently interact with the users. Intelligent NPCs can act to guide players in the achievement of specific learning goals associated with a given serious game (e.g., bullying awareness (Aylett, Paiva, Dias, Hall, & Woods, 2009) or conflict resolution skills (Joana Campos, Martinho, & Paiva, 2013)) in a pedagogically driven manner.

NPC behaviours are frequently designed to address character believability at different levels, such as physical behaviour generation, psycho-physiological-based responses and social intelligent interactions, which are a subset of the most relevant elements to consider when generating believable behaviour. The goal of the first category of behaviours is to generate believable physical interactions between the NPCs' body representations, their avatars and the environment in general. Examples of such behaviours can be observed in crowd simulation systems, where NPCs must coherently navigate a scenario (e.g., walk on a sidewalk and not on a road) and also demonstrate awareness (e.g., avoid collisions) (Ulicny & Thalmann, 2001) of the other characters and objects in the environment. The second category of behaviours aims at maintaining character and personality consistency by generating the proper responses based on complex human cognitive processes. An example is the simulation of emotional reactions (e.g., the NPC emotionally appraises the environment events) (J. Dias, Mascarenhas, & Paiva, 2011) and certain types of in-game situations (e.g., failure of a task). A

third category is directly related to the agents' social awareness of themselves, others and their relationships with others. NPC social behaviour includes interaction models used in the dialogue process and the ability to behave according to the NPC's sense of social identity (Rui Prada et al., 2012) and positioning in a particular social system (Mascarenhas, Dias, Prada, & Paiva, 2010; Pereira, Prada, & Santos, 2013).

Because the ultimate goal is to generate behaviours for a believable user/NPC interaction, i.e., human/virtual human interaction, we must address the creation of the computational models that operate these human specific processes. Such models should be inspired by theoretical background research, which has studied these subjects for a long time. As such, AI algorithms that support the different levels of believability of NPCs are often inspired by psychology and sociology theories that describe human behaviour. The effectiveness of the artificial intelligence modelling and its operationalisation is therefore inherently dependent on how accurately the psychological model and its artificial intelligence representation are connected.

The benefits of successful NPC implementation in serious games are enormous. Based on the physical and cognitive capabilities that can be conferred to NPCs, many types of user/NPC interactions can be explored to maximise the users' engagement (W. L. Johnson, Vilhjalmsson, & Marsella, 2005). Scenarios created with these NPCs can be used to simultaneously enhance the interactive experience and guide the user towards the learning goals of a serious game. For example, in the context of artificial tutors, NPCs are used to pedagogically guide players towards the acquisition of knowledge or the competences required to achieve a set of learning goals.

Many games require NPCs to play the role of an adversary (e.g., military tactical training) or several adversaries against the player. To create this situation, artificial intelligence techniques are applied in the NPCs to provide interesting and believable challenges to players. These techniques take into account the player's capabilities and generate behaviours that create the desired learning challenges (e.g., a specific tactical situation) in which players can learn and train the strategies required to tackle those challenges. For example, in a military training scenario, an NPC that behaves as a citizen of an occupied territory triggers the required adversarial behaviour to challenge the player and enhances the believability of the situation.

Another area is companion NPCs in which characters are used to provide players with companions that accompany them during long-term learning experiences. Companions often have the ability to appraise situations emotionally, understand the players learning styles and react accordingly by offering emotional and didactic support.

In this chapter, we analyse a subset of the benefits that NPCs can provide in the learning context of a serious game by presenting a series of case studies and discussing their contributions. Using theories of human behaviour from psychology and sociology, it is possible to create agents that can increase user engagement while also offering pedagogical support, either by aiding the user or creating the necessary conditions for learning to occur.

CASE STUDIES

In this section, we present a series of case studies based on our research at GAIPS/INESC-ID[3] that illustrate different computational models of agents that can be applied in NPC characters for serious games. Although each case study embodies its own specificities, we aim to describe the problem that each study addresses and in which context. Additionally, we relate that work to the supporting social sciences background and briefly overview how it is implemented. Finally, we also discuss the benefits or possible benefits in terms of en-

gagement, believability and support for learning and pedagogy that the presented models offer to a serious game-learning context.

Modelling Emotion For Intelligent Virtual Agents

Intelligent virtual environments embrace the presence of intelligent virtual agents (IVAs) that "autonomously" act in an intelligent and believable manner with the users. A key success element for IVAs is their believability, which according to (Joseph Bates et al., 1994; Ortony, Clore, & Collins, 1990), goes beyond physical appearance to include emotional behaviours and personality. As such, the development of IVAs must consider not only the physical aspect of the characters but also that the agent's reasoning and behaviour selection processes must be influenced by its personality and emotional state.

The OCC (Ortony et al., 1990) is a cognitive based theory that structures emotions in a hierarchical organisation according to emotion types. An emotion type defines a category of emotions that are similar in terms of intensity and manifestation. Furthermore, according to the model, emotions are defined as valenced reactions to events, which can be positive (e.g., joy) or negative (e.g., distress and fear). The association of the characters' emotions with the events is determined by appraisal functions, which are subject to the characters' goals, standards and attitudes.

To create believable and emotional virtual agents, we created the FAtiMA (FearNot! Affective Mind Architecture) (João Dias & Paiva, 2005) in which the generation of emotions is heavily inspired by the OCC model. The architecture includes 22 different emotions with configurable activation thresholds and decay rates.

By following this model of emotions, the FAtiMA appraisal process allows characters to react according to perceived events, which may be players' actions, other characters' actions or other occurrences. FAtiMA implements two main behavioural processes: reactive and deliberative. Reactive behaviour allows the agent to react rather quickly but corresponds to simple action tendencies that are triggered by particular emotional states. In contrast, deliberative behaviour is slower but allows for more complex goal-based behaviour. Moreover, an effort was made to design FAtiMA's architecture in a modular manner (J. Dias et al., 2011) that allows the incorporation of new components, models and features. FAtiMA was recently extended with several models, including empathy, theory of mind, emotional intelligence and social relations, among others.

Hence, FAtiMA's characters can be imbued with behaviours that allow them to detect and respond sensitively to the player's affective state and to proactively assess the social relationships among the character, the player and others. Figure 1 shows a diagram of the architecture with the components used to create agents with emotional intelligence skills and social relationships.

FAtiMA's implementation is open source and is available on SourceForge[4]. Since its first implementation, this model has been applied in several different scenarios with serious goals, such as anti-bullying (Vannini et al., 2010, 2011),

Figure 1. FAtiMA architecture with emotional intelligence components

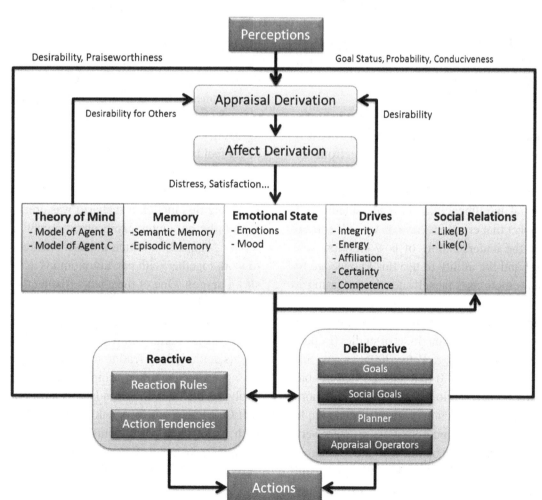

empathy (Rodrigues, Mascarenhas, Dias, & Paiva, 2009) and cultural awareness (Mascarenhas, Dias, Afonso, Enz, & Paiva, 2009). A subset of the following case studies presents more recent examples of how FAtiMA is currently extended by the community with new features to enhance the believability of the virtual agents.

Emotionally Intelligent Agents

One important aspect of virtual agents is that they should portray intelligent social and emotional behaviour. The establishment of social relationships becomes more critical if we want the user to interact with an agent in an engaging interactive narrative or role-playing game in which the relationship between the two takes a preponderant role in the plot. With this in mind, we must create embedded features that will allow the characters to automatically and autonomously establish believable social relationships with one another or even with the user.

To achieve this goal, we explored mechanisms that mimic the way in which relationships between real people evolve and drew inspiration from the concept of emotional intelligence studied by (Salovey & Mayer, 1990). These researchers define emotional intelligence as the understanding of the impact that emotions have on the self and on others, the understanding of how emotions are created and the ability to use this knowledge to regulate emotions of the self and others. Aiming at understanding the connection between emotional intelligence skills and the development of social relations, Lopes performed a set of studies (Lopes, Salovey, Côté, Beers, & Petty, 2005; Lopes, Salovey, & Straus, 2003) that showed that people who have higher emotional intelligence have more positive social interactions with peers and people who are better at managing emotions in others were more liked and valued by the opposite sex. Thus, it appears that the highly emotionally intelligent individual is indeed successful at establishing social relationships with others.

Based on Gross's model of emotion regulation (Gross & Thompson, 2007), we proposed a generic model for emotionally intelligent agents (João Dias & Paiva, 2013) that is able to generate emotions, perform backwards reasoning of emotions using two emotional meta-operators and perform interpersonal emotion regulation. The model also contains an explicit model of social relationships that evolves according to the experienced emotions. For instance, if someone does something nice for the agent to make him or her feel a positive emotion, the agent's relationship towards such a person will increase proportionally. The model works with a set of domain-independent emotion regulation goals to aid the agent in deciding when to perform Interpersonal Emotion Regulation. For the proactive positive regulation goal, the agent takes the initiative to regulate emotions in others (even if they themselves do not necessarily feel bad) to make others like him or her. In contrast, the reactive positive regulation goal is activated when someone the agent likes is feeling a negative emotion. In these situations, the agent will try to identify a possible plan of action to make the target feel better, e.g., making predictions of the effects of actions towards the target's emotional state and selecting the most appropriate choice.

Using this model, a scenario was created on top of the computer game environment *Never Winter Nights 2*[5] in which the user was required to work together with two autonomous agents to slay a dragon. One of the agents frequently tried to befriend the player by making him feel better (see Figure 2). One evaluation was performed to test if the social behaviour generated by the agents could indeed lead to the establishment of stronger affective relationships with the user. By applying the McGill Friendship Questionnaire (MFQ)(Mendelson & Aboud, 1999) in a study with twenty-two participants, we were able to show that when one of the agents employed interpersonal emotion regulation strategies, the agent was perceived as more friendly, with a better score

Figure 2. Validation strategy used by Varsuvius to make the user feel better

Varsuvius: I care about you Uthgard

on four out of six friendship functions (intimacy, self-validation, help and emotional security).

This study allowed us to show that endowing agents with emotional intelligence skills can indeed help us to establish certain aspects of friendship relationships with synthetic characters. This topic is of particular importance for the virtual agent community because it will lead to increased flexibility in the creation of these types of agents. We can easily build intelligent virtual agents that (by simple authoring) can dynamically change the relationships they establish with the users.

NPCs as Actors

Our Artificial Intelligence approach to NPCs for Interactive Storytelling (IS) goes beyond the creation of NPCs for bystander roles. Our NPCs are designed to integrate with and adapt to user actions to enhance the users' effective participation in the story that is generated in the game. Our main assumption is that this effect can be achieved by endowing our NPCs with acting abilities that allow them to proactively affect the story development. In this case study, we report research undertaken to address the proactive ma-

nipulation of emotions to establish the pace of a comical sketch in a process known as Emotional Escalation (Carvalho, Brisson, & Paiva, 2012).

As presented by Schulz (Martin, 2007), Incongruence-Resolution theory refers to comical punch lines (ending) as the creation of an incongruity that contrasts with what was suggested by the setup of the joke. One must go back and search for an ambiguity in the setup and interpret it in a different way to get the joke. At first, we are surprised by the incongruence and subsequently find an explanation for the incongruence that elicits the laugh. Additionally, according to this theory, failing to demonstrate the incongruence will lead spectators to become confused and consequently, the comical effect will fail.

In this project, we consider the generation of incongruence as the process of building up an inconsistency gap that can be explored to create a comic reality, i.e., a caricature of reality. Others have previously integrated incongruence theory with NPCs (Cavazza, Charles, & Mead, 2001, 2003; Olsen & Mateas, 2009) and have done so by modifying action planning algorithms to generate incongruent actions with a comic purpose. Nonetheless, we take a step forward by considering the timing of the build-up process and the emotional incongruence that arises from the characters' behaviours.

Inspired by Vorhaus' comical perspective concept (Vorhaus, 1994), which is defined as the point of view of a character that is quite different from that of a normal person, we can deliberately author a character to include goals that are clearly inconsistent with his or her character, e.g., a pastry seller who refuses to sell a cake to an overweight client. Because we use an agent-architecture-inspired OCC model of emotions and appraisal, we can author the appraisal variables to generate emotional states that are incongruent with the non-comical character. Furthermore, these states will influence the character's planning, action, decisions and expressiveness.

In addition, because timing is an essential element of the comic effect, we endow our NPCs with the ability to set the timing to create just the right tension before delivering a joke in a process that we refer to as Emotional Escalation.

To this end, we extended FAtiMA by implementing the concept of Emotional Goals, which are emotional guidelines as a function of time. When defining an Emotional Goal, the authors establish a desired value of emotion for any character as a function of time. At the end of the planning process, the agent simulates the effects of the action candidates and selects the option that maximises the proximity to the desired emotional goals.

In a case study presented in (Carvalho et al., 2012), we designed the comic character of a pastry seller who aims to gradually provoke distress in a client before delivering the punch line (see Figure 3).

We evaluated the result in a small study with 75 participants (Carvalho et al., 2012). Our main results point towards success with respect to the evaluator's perception of a gradual intensification of the emotions in the scene and of its contribution to the comic effect.

Emotional Escalation is the main contribution towards providing NPCs with an emotional perspective through the story development and relieving the authorial burden. We aim to further study the relationship between emotions and story development to create additional generative models that could allow agents to adapt emotional goals to the story circumstances.

Social Identity in Agents

Our identities play important roles in our lives because they regulate our thoughts, feelings and actions. Our identities allow others to recognise us as unique and consistent individuals but without freedom from changes and variations throughout time and space.

In virtual worlds, the importance of the agent's identity has not gone unnoticed. Because of its significance, many researchers have given attention to identity and the way in which it can impact the agent's processes and reactions. Certain works have focused on the development of the agent's identity through the implementation of personalities (Rizzo, Veloso, Miceli, & Cesta, 1997), whereas more recently, others have focused on cultural traits (Mascarenhas et al., 2009). Although these approaches provide a certain amount of consistency in the agent's behaviour in a specific scenario, the personality-driven or culture-based agent identity remains unchanged across different social contexts. We intend to provide agents with a dynamic identity that not only influences the agent's decisions and behaviour but also adapts to new social contexts.

Figure 3. Left image presents the implementation of an emotional goal with two guidelines used by the seller agent to select actions A, B, C, D and E to progressively provoke distress in the client. Right image shows a screenshot of the prototype.

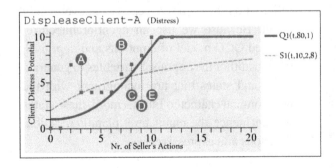

According to Social Identity (Tajfel, 1972, 1978) and Self-Categorisation (J.C. Turner, 1978; John C. Turner, Oakes, Alexander, & McGarty, 1994) theories, one of the processes that greatly influences a person's identity is how one sees oneself and others within each other's social groups. Seeing a person as a distinct individual or as a member of a group that shares the same interests and norms with all of its members will impact how one perceives oneself and will also impact one's behaviour towards others.

These different perceptions with respect to the self and others are dependent on several factors and many are related to the social situation in which the person is located (Smith & Mackie, 2000). One of the most frequently studied aspects is the presence of in-group or out-group members. In the presence of members of a person's own in-group, the person becomes aware of the others' uniqueness and specific personal attributes and relates to others in an interpersonal manner that depends on personality traits and close personal relationships. However, in the presence of an out-group, the perception as a group member strengthens because a person tends to focus his or her perception on the shared features with other in-group members. The person will subsequently see himself/herself as less distinct from the rest of his/her own group and when that occurs, there is a shift of the person's own motives and values from self-interest to group interests.

As a member of a group with shared interests among its members or as unique and distinctive individual, the perception of group membership will determine if one's behaviour will be influenced by one's social identity or personal identity. When social identity is salient, people tend to cooperate more fully with members of their group, even when the group's goals differ from their own personal goals. With this in mind, we developed a Dynamic Identity Model for Agents (Dimas & Prada, 2013).

The Dynamic Identity Model for Agents (DIMA) aims to provide the agents with an identity that is adaptive to their social situation, while at the same time, it allows the agents to be influenced by the situation. According to this approach, instead of displaying a fixed personality, the agent features a sub-set of characteristics that represents the portion of the self that is currently salient to the agent. The agent will not only express his or her individual identity, but for each social group to which an agent belongs, the agent will embody a social identity that can be expressed if the situation requires it.

In the presence of other agents, several factors from the context (represented in DIMA with a theme) will help the agent to perceive if he or she is in the presence of in-group or out-group members and behave accordingly. If the agent perceives himself or herself as in the presence of only in-group members, the identity will be determined by the agent's personal identity. If the agent is in the presence of out-group members, the identity will be determined by a social identity.

One of the interesting applications for such a model is a social dilemma situation because it represents the paradoxes of individual rationality in which group interests are at odds with individual interests (Rui Prada et al., 2012).

To explore the situation described above, we developed a multi-player game within the Project INVITE (social Identity and partNership in VIrTual Environments)[6] in which both humans and virtual agents participate. Although this project is intended to explore the role of social identity and social dilemmas in mixed-motive tasks, this platform is fully parameterised and allows the exploration of different scenarios and case studies (see Figure 4).

Because social identity has a great impact on a wide range of fields and settings, i.e., group formation, cohesiveness, prejudice, conformity, social influence and crowd behaviour, etc. (Hogg, 2003; John C. Turner et al., 1994), we believe that the study of these other phenomena could also benefit from DIMA. However, simulations are not the only scenarios that could take advantage

Figure 4. Screenshot of the island from the Project INVITE game

of agents with dynamic identities. Another possible application area is entertainment because many video games revolve around social categorisations, offering worlds populated by a great variety of characters in the form of genres, professions, classes or even factions.

Culturally Adaptive Agents

Contact between individuals with distinct cultural backgrounds is becoming increasingly more frequent in the modern world. One of the main reasons for this is that people more easily move to other countries in search of better life conditions. This process is not always smooth because the vast cultural diversity between nations can become a source of social conflicts that lead to the creation of negative stereotypes and discrimination. As such, improved and more easily accessible methods of raising intercultural awareness are becoming increasingly important in our societies. With this in mind, researchers have begun to explore the potential of using Intelligent Virtual Environments (IVEs) as a novel intercultural training tool.

Traveller is a recent IVE designed for intercultural training that has been developed in the

context of the EU-funded project known as eCute[7]. This project aims to give young adults a generic understanding of how national cultures differ from one another. To fulfil its goal, Traveller is designed as an interactive-storytelling application in which the user plays the role of a young character who receives a letter from a deceased grandfather. In the letter, the grandfather explains that he wants his grandson/granddaughter to find a lost treasure. In a quest to find this treasure, the player must embark on a journey to visit several fictional countries, collecting pieces of the grandfather's journal in each location. In the final country, the last page mentions that the actual treasure is the life experiences that the player obtained in his or her travel.

The learning experience in Traveller is structured around Critical Incidents (CIs), which correspond to situations that require the user to address a practical problem with the aid of synthetic characters. These situations are designed to evoke cultural misunderstandings that result from the mismatch between the user's own cultural assumptions and those shared by the characters, which will differ in each country. Figure 5 shows an example of a CI that takes place in a museum. In this scene,

Figure 5. Traveller Screenshot of a Critical Incident at a Museum

the player's mission is to find a supervisor of a wild park and ask his permission for a visit. At the start of the CI, the player re-encounters a guard who works for the supervisor and subsequently explains the identity of the supervisor to the player. Players must subsequently decide whether to approach the supervisor directly or to ask the guard to speak on their behalf. Both options, which are illustrated in Figure 5, can be performed as natural gestures using a Kinect sensor. More importantly, depending on their ascribed culture, the characters will respond differently to the user's choices. This allows the scenarios to be replayed from different cultural perspectives simply by changing the cultural profile of the characters.

The advantage of a system such as Traveller is that it allows a person to be confronted with distinct cultural behaviour in a safe environment as a result of the interaction with intelligent characters that are able to act in a believable manner. However, several challenges remain in the development of an artificial intelligence for such characters that must be properly addressed by the autonomous agent community. An issue that is particularly relevant in the case of Traveller is how best to endow characters with the ability to adapt their cultural behaviour in a flexible manner. To achieve this goal, we investigate the development of an agent architecture based on a parameterisable model of cultural manifestations found in human behaviour.

Initially, we began by formalising the notion of cultural rituals, which are defined in (Hofstede, Hofstede, & Minkov, 2010) as essential symbolic activities carried out in a predetermined fashion. Based on this definition, the resulting model (Mascarenhas et al., 2009) implements rituals as a particular type of goal in which success is tied to the execution of a series of symbolic steps in a given order. Regular goals are different in the sense that the actions needed to achieve a certain outcome are interchangeable as long as the same result is obtained in the end.

In addition to rituals, we included an explicit representation of two dimensions of cultural variation in our model derived from a large empirical study across several countries (Hofstede et al., 2010). The two dimensions (Individualism versus Collectivism and Power Distance) are used to influence the processes of decision-making (selecting between alternative goals) and emotional appraisal (synthesising emotions in response to a subjective evaluation of events). As detailed in (Mascarenhas et al., 2010), both of these processes have a strong impact on the agent's behaviour, thus further augmenting the desired link between culture and behaviour.

Finally, we are currently in the process of extending our architecture with a model of social behaviour dynamics that pertains to the ways in which agents perceive others from a relational perspective and influences how much they are willing to do for other agents and how much it is appropriate to ask of them. In humans, these perceptions are heavily influenced by shared cultural assumptions, as proposed in the status-power theory of Kemper (Kemper, 2011). The resulting model (Mascarenhas, Prada, Paiva, Degens, & Hofstede, 2013) is based on the aforementioned theory and enables a different encoding of such assumptions in different group of characters, thus affecting their patterns of behaviour.

Social Power in Agent-Based Modelling

Social power is one of the most pervasive concepts in human societies due to its function as a social heuristic (Keltner, Van Kleef, Chen, & Kraus, 2008) in decision making and its effects can be observed in a multitude of social situations, such as friend interactions (Keltner et al., 2008), organisations (Pfeffer, 1981) or even laboratory experiments (Milgram, 1974), among others. Given the widespread impact of power in people's decisions and consequent behaviours, it is fundamental to understand such power-based social dynamics and emulate them in socially intelligent agents to improve their social interaction capabilities.

Although power has been previously explored as a social heuristic for agent behaviour, significant research gaps still exist with respect to social intelligence for intelligent virtual agent believability in both inter-agent (Marsella & Pynadath, 2005) and agent-human interactions (R. Prada & Paiva, 2009). Our main goal is to create an agent architecture that extends the current socially intelligent agent models to include social-power-specific reasoning processes.

To model social power interactions into agent-based applications, we needed to define the fundamental properties behind power and identify the cognitive stages involved in power-based reasoning. In defining the fundamental properties of power, we based our conceptualisations on French and Raven's (French Jr & Raven, 1959)

bases of social power. Their work introduced a differentiation and dynamics of social power grounded on five bases of power: reward, coercion, legitimate, referent and expert. We used this basis due to the simplicity, repeated acknowledgment by the research community and expressive behaviour potential.

Given our focus on interaction, we additionally sought inspiration for our agent architecture in Raven's (Raven, 1992) Power Interaction Model of Interpersonal Influence. The authors represented the process of influence and its connection to the bases of power in two simple fluxograms. Each fluxogram illustrates the main cognitive stages for an individual who either provides influence or is influenced.

Before modelling social power processes, we must first define them. In this research, we follow the conceptualisation of power as a potential influence: "Social Power of A over B regarding a possible change in B is the resultant potential force that A can induce on B towards that change." However, to mobilise power, we also must clearly identify and conceptualise the diverse forces that constitute this potential. To do so, we formalised (Pereira et al., 2013) four bases of power based on French and Raven's work (French Jr & Raven, 1959): welfare, legitimate, referent and expert.

Welfare power conceptualises the ability to mediate rewards or punishments to someone. This power results from the abstraction of the reward and coercive power bases because these present symmetric dynamics. Legitimate power conceptualises internalised values (norms, contracts, etc.), which gives an individual the authority to influence another. Referent power conceptualises power stemming from a relationship of identification. Finally, expert power conceptualises the acknowledgment of a skill difference. These different power bases are at the core of interaction-oriented social-power-based reasoning.

In our work, we designed an agent architecture intended for inter-agent and agent-human interactions. Inspired by Raven's Power Interaction

Model of Interpersonal Influence (Raven, 1992), we identified three main social power specific components for an agent's mind: Power Situational Analysis, Power Effects Assessment and Power Interaction Planner. Based on the processes associated with these components, we can simulate influence and attempt situations grounded in social power forces.

The Power Situational Analysis component evaluates the different bases of power available in any given situation using the agent's beliefs. We conceptualise the agent's decision as a resultant force that is generated by combining and weighting the diverse power bases and utilities (Pereira et al., 2013). The Power Effects Assessment maps the different bases of power usage to the effects (e.g., relationship changes) in an agent's power bases. The Power Interaction Planner component devises plans for how to strategically influence others by taking into account the possible different power strategies, the underlying bases of power and their effects.

At the time of writing, the described architecture is in the design and development stage and will be used to simulate situations in which agents must influence other agents and human-controlled agents.

Several areas might benefit from using agents capable of adapting and responding to social situations in which interactions are strongly influenced by social power forces. One example is education/support; our agents can be used to analyse the power forces involved in social situations and propose strategies to resist the negative influence of peer pressure. Another possible application area is entertainment because many games involve rich worlds and aim to create increasingly believable societies of agents. Our model would enable non-player characters to become socially intelligent with respect to social power and could be used to create agents capable of acting as either friend or foe, depending only on the relationships and interactions between the player and the agents.

A Tool for Teaching Conflict Resolution

Conflict and conflict dynamics are phenomena that are intertwined with social change and are often related to problematic structures in society. For the ability to recognise conflict situations and respond effectively for their resolution, social skills should be fostered early in life to lead to a healthier and peaceful society.

Educational interventions in schools have taken different forms (e.g., peer mediation programs or drama workshops) and have proven to have a positive impact on student behaviour ((D. W. Johnson & Johnson, 1996) and (T. S. Jones, 2004)). However, these training programs are rarely adapted to a child's individual needs because they promote in-class learning. To address this issue, game-learning environments are thought to offer untapped potential for education (e.g., (Gibson, Aldrich, & Prensky, 2007) and (Kirriemuir & Mcfarlane, 2004)). Not only do they promote a safe setting in which to explore different perspectives of a complex issue, but they also offer tools for a more personalised learning experience.

In the SIREN project[8], we explore the use of a virtual environment to support learning and conflict resolution by giving the player the opportunity to take on different roles and perspectives and to help him or her evaluate the consequences of actions. In particular, the "My Dream Theatre" (MDT) scenario is a single-player game designed to prepare for and teach conflict resolution skills to 10-to-12-year-old children. In MDT, the player takes on the role of the director of a school theatre club and manages the actors, their needs and the conflicts that arise among them.

The three parallel forces of conflict theory, user research and principles from game design have shaped the design of MDT (see (J. Campos, Martinho, Ingram, Vasalou, & Paiva, 2013) for additional details). By bringing together these three perspectives, our aim was to create a set of finely tuned mechanics that weave the three influences together to deliver the serious messages we believe to be important: broadening children's vocabulary, conveying that conflicts can be positive, supporting training for critical thinking, perceiving that different people have different styles in handling conflict and ensuring sensitivity to others' emotional changes.

At the core of MDT is the existence of the Non-Player Characters (NPCs) that are the actors in the theatre club. These agents have personalities and preferences for roles and will react emotionally when they perceive that their goals are threatened. It is the task of the player to mediate the conflicts that arise among the actors to guarantee success in the end.

Conflict in real life has a strong emotional component reflected in one's actions. The intense emotions associated with conflict episodes are the factors that make those involved feel so overwhelmed. Thus, emotion is a central element in the definition of conflict in MDT and we believe that more naturalistic approaches to defining agent behaviour are necessary. Despite the large amount of research on conflict in the social sciences that gives direction on how to define such behaviours, little is known of methods that translate the theory

to more specific parameters that will provide an adequate description of conflict ((Joana Campos et al., 2013)). To achieve a better representation of conflict from an agent point of view, we rely on findings and perspectives from various lines of research and suggest that conflict is a dynamic process that evolves from latent forms of conflict to states of awareness until a trigger occurs and the agent formulates an intention that hampers or promotes conflict resolution ((Joana Campos et al., 2013)). This process is followed by a loop in which conflict escalation and de-escalation may occur depending on the actions that the agents take for conflict resolution.

Our approach to conflict resolution in MDT falls in line with the Thomas-Kilmann model ((Thomas, 1976)). Although the Thomas-Kilmann model has been applied only to organisational settings, this theoretical model represents a clean and simple approach to illustrate the decisions taken by the agents in the theatre scenario. The model states that conflict-handling modes are defined according to the individual actor's assertiveness and cooperativeness. The former refers to the satisfaction of one's own goals and the latter refers to

Figure 6. My Dream Theatre" screenshot of the mini game. Graphics produced by Serious Games Interactive (SGI)

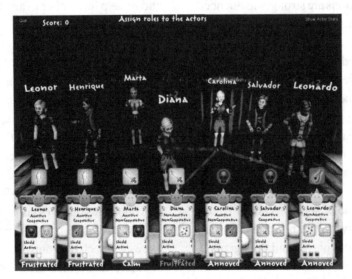

the extent to which one tries to satisfy the others' goals (see Figure 6.)

To take advantage of the virtual environment, an important component in MDT is its adaptation system, which aims to help players to gain the most from the game and optimise their learning gains. For example, the system may promote scenarios in which the player is forced to use a certain conflict resolution strategy and reinforce a certain learning aspect. This component allows us to control aspects of the game and to tailor the game experience to the player.

Throughout this project, theories of conflict and conflict resolution have guided our decision-making process. Overall, the theory represents a scaffold of many of the methods employed both in the requirements gathering (e.g., interviews, cultural probes) and design phases to ensure that that the content and practice are finely tuned. This issue is at the forefront of the main challenges in designing this type of tool. Not only must a designer and developer base their decisions on the gamers' practices, but it is also essential to build a good scaffold based on theory and sound educational principles. This balance was one of our main concerns when developing MDT in view of a successful and serious game.

Embodiment

Embodiment is a major aspect in the development of NPCs because embodiment defines how the characters look and how the players (or users of the application) perceive them. The concept of an embodied agent has been widely explored in both robotics and computer science (Cassell et al., 1999; Dautenhahn, 1999; Poggi, Pelachaud, De Rosis, Carofiglio, & De Carolis, 2005). The traditional computational approach uses a continuous sense-reason-act loop in which the "mind" of the agent has full control over the "body". The "mind" receives sensory information from the "body", analyses that information and activates

the effectors. The "body" is a passive collection of sensors and effectors.

However, certain further questions are compelling. Could the "body" play a more active role in the process? Does embodiment have any impact on how the cognitive "mind" reasons and decides?

Embodiment encompasses a wide field of research. The classical perspective of Descartes' Dualism, in which our bodies are separated from our minds, is being progressively replaced by Embodied Cognition theories, which state that the nature of our minds is largely determined by the form of our bodies. Damasio (Damasio, 2011) presents recent findings in neuroscience that describe how our bodies are important in shaping the conscious mind and its role in such key processes as emotional phenomena. Pfeifer (Pfeifer, Bongard, & Grand, 2007) also point out that entities we view as intelligent are always compliant with the physical and social rules of the environment and exploit these rules to create diverse behaviour; therefore, we cannot dissociate intelligence from our body as a whole.

The main idea behind our research is to enrich the aforementioned sense-reason-act loop with an explicit model of the body (Ribeiro, Vala, & Paiva, 2012; Vala, Ribeiro, & Paiva, 2012). The model defines the following entities: a physiological space (Bernard, 1974), which represents the current state and condition of the body; a set of internal sensors, which monitor the body's physiological condition (interoception (Craig, 2002)) and gather feedback from the effectors (proprioception (L. A. Jones, 1988)); a set of internal effectors, which can execute changes within the body; and an implicit memory (Schacter, 1987), which stores procedural memories (reactions that are executed in certain conditions). These mechanisms are a component of a secondary control loop, a "subconscious mind" that runs in parallel with the "conscious mind" (see Figure 7).

We used a subset of these ideas in a case study using Starcraft, a well-known Real-Time Strategy (RTS) game from Blizzard[9]. In RTS (Real-Time

Figure 7. Our model of embodied cognition

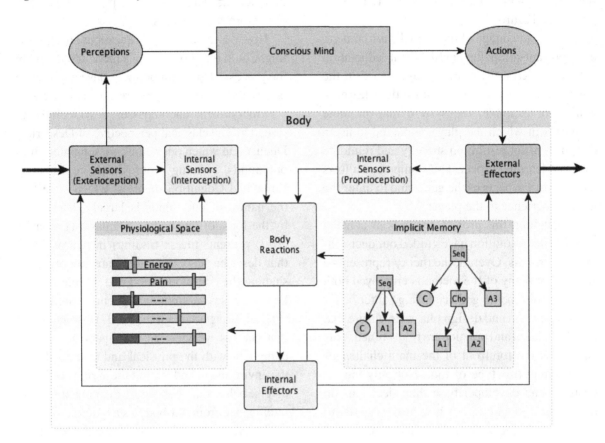

Strategy) games, each player represents a faction and controls units to secure areas of the map and to defeat their opponents.

The original Starcraft AI uses a single centralised control for all units. We explored a decentralised approach and examined each unit individually. The goal was to create emergent coordination between units and to compare the results against the original AI in terms of effectiveness and also in terms of engagement and believability.

We modelled each unit with an internal state of the body focused on the unit's health and self-preservation. The unit will follow general goals, e.g., teaming with other units to destroy a target, but it will also contain a "subconscious" process that may lead to a retreat if the unit is at risk. Therefore, the state of the body affects the behaviour of the unit and its future decisions.

The evaluation process contained two phases. First, we measured the effectiveness of our AI against the original AI using simulations across several scenarios. Next, we used both AIs against human players and used questionnaires to evaluate the players' perception.

The results show that our AI can defeat the original AI, especially in situations in which the number of units is limited and self-preservation is important. More importantly, the human players rated our AI as superior to the original AI in a perceived intelligence questionnaire. They also found it less "artificial" and less predictable in terms of behaviour, which leads to a more satisfying game experience.

The main contribution of this work is the idea that the body of an NPC can be more than a graphical representation of the character. It can contain regulation and reaction mechanisms that perform "subconscious" tasks in parallel with higher-level behaviours. The mind controls what the body does, but the body may also affect and condition how the "mind" reasons and decides. As a consequence, both mind and body continuously adapt to each other, creating a richer behaviour that, in the end, is perceived as less "artificial".

We believe that these results can also be useful in different contexts. In a serious game context, embodiment can definitely play an important role, especially in situations in which the body of the NPC is important in itself, e.g., medical training scenarios. NPCs with different "bodies" should behave differently not only in terms of graphical animations but also in the ways in which they reason and decide. Possessing richer bodies might increase the overall believability and engagement.

Empathic Companions

Robots are becoming a reality in our daily lives, but as they move outside of the lab and are deployed in people's homes and workplaces, several challenges remain that must be addressed. For example, how can robots engage users for extended periods of time? In what types of tasks can users benefit from the assistance of social robots? How do the interactions between users and robots develop and evolve over time?

In our research, we are interested in investigating these issues with children as our target users. To this end, we have developed a scenario consisting of a Philips' iCat robot that plays chess with children using an electronic chessboard (see Figure 8 and Figure 9). The iCat provides feedback on the children's moves by conveying facial expressions determined by its affective state. One of the first studies conducted with this scenario showed that the affective behaviour expressed by the iCat increased the children's perception of the chess game (I. Leite, Pereira, Martinho, & Paiva, 2008). However, in this experiment, the participants only interacted with the robot once and as mentioned

previously, we are interested in understanding what happens after the novelty effect wears off. To investigate, we performed a pilot study to examine the changes in children's behaviours and perceptions of the robot after several interactions. In this study (I. Leite, Martinho, Pereira, & Paiva, 2009), we analysed the same group of children who played a chess game with the iCat over five sessions (once per week). The children filled out a social presence questionnaire in both the first and last week of interaction. The results suggest that the social presence decreased over time, especially in terms of perceived affective and behavioural interdependence (the extent to which users believe that the behaviour and affective state of the robot is influenced by their own behaviour and affective state). We also observed that the amount of time children spent looking at the robot decreased over

Figure 8. iCat robot

Figure 9. Child playing with the iCat

the sessions, especially between the second and third interactions.

In interactions between humans, it is expected that social presence remains constant over time. The outcomes of our long-term pilot study strengthened the hypothesis that the ability to understand and respond to the affective state of users is relevant in long-term interactions. To further investigate this hypothesis, we conducted another experiment (Iolanda Leite et al., 2013) to evaluate the influence of empathic behaviours on the user's perception of a social robot. For this study, a slight variation of our application scenario was implemented in which the iCat observes and comments on a chess match between two human players. The robot exhibits empathic behaviours towards one of the players and neutral comments to the other player via facial expressions and verbal comments. The results of this study suggest that players to whom the iCat displayed empathic behaviour perceived the robot as more friendly. These two studies inspired our current work in distinct ways. Although the long-term study was important to acknowledge that perceptual and empathic capabilities are important for a social robot intended to engage users for extended periods of time, the empathy study showed that by the manipulation of simple empathic behaviours, people might perceive the robot differently.

We believe that by adapting the robot's affective behaviour to the preferences of a particular user over time, the relationship between the child and the robot can improve. Consequently, children will be more willing to play chess with the iCat and eventually, their chess skills will improve. Therefore, our aim is to study the effects of an empathic model on the long-term interactions between users and social robots. The inputs of the proposed empathic model are the user's affective state and the contextual information of the task that the robot performs with the user. Using a database of several empathic and supportive behaviours inspired by the literature of social support

(Cutrona, Suhr, & MacFarlane, 1990), the model includes a decision-making mechanism that allows the robot to select the most appropriate empathic behaviours based on the history of interactions with that user.

The empathic model was developed using an iterative approach that was continuously evaluated and refined in several user studies. The preliminary results raise the possibility of a link between empathy and higher perceived social presence, engagement, help and self-validation in users who interact with social robots for extended periods of time (Iolanda Leite, Castellano, Pereira, Martinho, & Paiva, 2012). These observations mean that empathic robots will be more likely to engage children in long-term interactions.

DISCUSSION

In the previous section, we presented a series of case studies that illustrate how our contribution towards more believable behaviour generation has been supported by social sciences research. A summary of these contributions is presented in Table 1.

One of our most relevant contributions is the FAtiMA. The fact that its architecture is heavily based on a solid cognitive model of emotions (i.e., OCC) contributes towards FAtiMA's vast dissemination across many different projects that require high character consistency. The benefits that FAtiMA receives from the detail of the OCC model in terms of functions and variables greatly facilitate transposition from the theoretical model to the AI architecture. The benefits for Serious Games are primarily related to ease of the authoring process. The parameterisation of the agents' emotional variables and goals influences agent planning and reactions to the environment, thus maintaining character consistency and relieving the author of the need to foresee every action in detail.

Table 1. Summary of contribution chain Social Sciences -> AI for NPCs -> Serious Games

Social Sciences	AI for NPCs	Serious Games
OCC (Ortony et al., 1990) Cognitive-based model of emotions	FAtiMA (João Dias & Paiva, 2005), emotional mind architecture for NPCs.	NPCs react and plan according to their expected emotional state, facilitating authoring and increasing believability.
Emotional regulation (Gross & Thompson, 2007)	Model for emotionally intelligent agents (João Dias & Paiva, 2013) to generate emotions, backwards reasoning via emotions using two emotional meta-operators and performance of interpersonal emotion regulation.	Creation of NPCs that apply befriend strategies to engage the user.
Incongruence-Resolution theory as presented by Schulz (Martin, 2007)	Adaptation of acting techniques for manipulating the emotional development of a story in an interactive environment.	Online influence of the user's emotional engagement.
Social Identity (Tajfel, Turner) (Tajfel, 1972; J.C. Turner, 1978)	Dynamic Identity Model for Agents (Dimas & Prada, 2013).	Behaviour generation for social dilemma contexts (Rui Prada et al., 2012).
Rituals (Hofstede et al., 2010), Cultural variation (Hofstede et al., 2010), Status-Power (Kemper, 2011)	Ritual models (Mascarenhas et al., 2009, 2010) and impact on behaviour generation (Mascarenhas et al., 2013).	Generation of inter-cultural interaction scenarios for cultural awareness and education
Social Power (French Jr & Raven, 1959), Power Interaction Model of Interpersonal Influence (Raven, 1992)	Model for agent/agent and agent/human interaction that considers Power Situational Analysis, Power Effects Assessment and Power Interaction Planner elements.	Facilitates the generation of scenarios with strong social pressures that can be used for training and education.
Conflict resolution model (Thomas, 1976)	Conceptualisation of conflict and development of a model for conflict resolution implemented.	Representation of conflict that can be used in real-life learning scenarios, such as a tool for conflict resolution.
Body and intelligence (Damasio, 2011; Pfeifer et al., 2007)	Regulations of "subconscious" tasks using the body.	Dynamic body / behaviour adaptation with a clear positive impact on the character's believability and reduction of character design effort. (Vala et al., 2012)
Social support behaviours	Empathic companions for long-term tutoring.	iCat chess tutor increases user engagement in learning. (Iolanda Leite et al., 2012)

FAtiMA provides a strong model for emotional cognitive support in agents. However, given its extensibility, it also provides a starting framework for other cognitive components that can increase believability based on expansion of the agents' social capabilities. Current extensions to the existing architecture already address certain research areas, such as emotional regulation, social identity, cultural elements or conflict resolution.

Character consistency is a crucial element for NPC believability and for fostering engagement. This goal can be achieved by constraining NPCs to portrayal of well-defined characters. Nevertheless, we treat NPCs as privileged story participants that can also proactively contribute to generating the best user experience possible. As such, the NPC perceptions and intentions should extend beyond character boundaries to include a critical perspective of the story development and of their possible contributions within the character space. We believe that this behaviour is similar to acting and as such, we entertain the possibility of endowing our agents with acting abilities.

Emotional escalation is our first explicit contribution towards this new paradigm of NPCs as actors. The fact that our agents are able to proactively provoke specific emotional tension encourages us to speculate on the possibilities of integrating other acting techniques in our mind architecture.

The inclusions of NPCs that adapt their bodies and associated behaviours to affective situations and dynamic social environments (identity, power, culture, conflict) should provide a major contribution towards the reusability and increased efficiency of game design in general. Additionally, for serious games in particular, social simulations are frequently used to make NPCs aware of their environment and capable of responding to diverse social stimuli. We argue that the successful application of social sciences models in the implementation of intelligent agents presents a major contribution towards the definition of new technologies for serious games that benefit all stakeholders. Users will feel more engaged when presented with believable interactions among all game elements. An increase in user engagement supports the tutors' intentions towards the users' learning achievements, while at the same time, more efficient and adaptive technologies will be put the disposal of serious games developers.

CONCLUSION

Research on NPCs plays an important role in the application of social sciences to serious games. Our goal of achieving believable behaviours using state-of-the-art technology has led to the creation of pioneering integration between the social sciences and AI. From an AI perspective, it is particularly relevant to underline the pioneering aspect of our research because it exposes a clear lack of benchmarks for comparative analysis of our models. This context increases our demand for validated and detailed[10] models from the social sciences.

The success of state-of-the-art AI research depends heavily on the accuracy, validation and computability aspects of social science models (see Table 2). Accurate models will allow us to more precisely integrate new aspects of behaviour generation and at the same time, it will contribute towards enhancement of character believability.

Table 2. Social sciences, AI and serious games dependencies

Social Sciences	NPCs	Serious Games
Accurate	Naturalistic behaviour generation	Believability enhancement
Validation	Theoretical support	Successful impact
Computable	Increases consistency between technical implementation and the original model	Increases development efficiency.

The lack of benchmarks for comparative AI analysis increases the relevance of the theoretical implementation of the applied models. We also stress the fact that the adaptation of social sciences models to AI formalisms is not a straightforward process and could also introduce unexpected problems (e.g., loss of detail due to computation constraints). Thus, it is highly important to AI researchers that social scientists understand the AI need for models described using operational representations (including functions and parameterisation) that can be more easily transformed into computational models and in this way, could mitigate problems from conversion of the models.

Although the use cases presented in this text represent only a small glimpse of a larger collection of relevant research contributions that occurred in the past 10 years, there is still a long way to go before we integrate all of the relevant social sciences contributions. We view this future as a rich and exciting research area that results from mixed contributions of Social Sciences, Artificial Intelligence and Serious Games. By studying and presenting new models, Social Sciences provide a theoretical grounding for Artificial Intelligence research that can enhance Serious Games technologies by improving the user experience, enhancing the learning achievements and improving the production efficiency. At the same time, we view Serious Games as an opportunity for Social Sciences to test and improve their models in a constrained and controlled scenario.

REFERENCES

Aylett, R., Paiva, A., Dias, J., Hall, L., & Woods, S. (2009). Affective agents for education against bullying. In *Affective Information Processing* (pp. 75–90). London: Springer. Retrieved from http://link.springer.com/chapter/10.1007/978-1-84800-306-4_5

Bates, J. (1992). Virtual reality, art, and entertainment. *Presence: The Journal of Teleoperators and Virtual Environments*, *1*(1), 133–138.

Bates, J., Loyall, A. B., & Reilly, W. S. (1994). An architecture for action, emotion, and social behavior. In *Selected papers from the 4th European Workshop on on Modelling Autonomous Agents in a Multi-Agent World, Artificial Social Systems* (pp. 55–68). London: Springer-Verlag. Retrieved from http://dl.acm.org/citation.cfm?id=646907.710645

Bernard, C. (1974). *Lectures on the phenomena of life common to animals and plants*. Thomas. Retrieved from http://books.google.pt/books?id=zMhqAAAAMAAJ

Campos, J., Martinho, C., Ingram, G., Vasalou, A., & Paiva, A. (2013). My dream theatre: Putting conflict in center stage. In *Proceedings of 8th International Conference on the Foundations of Digital Games (FDG 2013)*. Foundations of Digital Games.

Campos, J., Martinho, C., & Paiva, A. (2013). Conflict inside out: A theoretically-based approach to conflict from an agent's point of view. In *Proceedings of the 12th International Conference on Autonomous Agents and Multiagent Systems (AAMAS 2013)*. AAMAS.

Carvalho, A., Brisson, A., & Paiva, A. (2012). Laugh to me! Implementing emotional escalation on autonomous agents for creating a comic sketch. In *Proceedings of the 5th Joint International Conference on Interactive Digital Storytelling: Interactive Storytelling*. Berlin: Springer-Verlag.

Cassell, J., Bickmore, T., Billinghurst, M., Campbell, L., Chang, K., Vilhjálmsson, H., & Yan, H. (1999). Embodiment in conversational interfaces: Rea. In *Proceedings of the SIGCHI Conference on Human Factors in Computing Systems: The CHI is the Limit* (pp. 520–527). New York, NY: ACM. doi:10.1145/302979.303150

Cavazza, M., Charles, F., & Mead, S. J. (2001). Character-driven story generation in interactive storytelling. In *Proceedings 7th International Conference in Virtual Systems and Multimedia* (pp. 609–615). IEEE.

Cavazza, M., Charles, F., & Mead, S. J. (2003). Generation of humorous situations in cartoons through plan-based formalisations. In *Proceedings of CHI-2003 Workshop: Humor Modeling in the Interface*. ACM.

Craig, A. D. (2002). How do you feel? Interoception: The sense of the physiological condition of the body. *Nature Reviews. Neuroscience*, *3*(8), 655–666. PMID:12154366.

Cutrona, C. E., Suhr, J. A., & MacFarlane, R. (1990). Interpersonal transactions and the psychological sense of support. *Personal Relationships and Social Support*, 30–45.

Damasio, A. (2011). *Self comes to mind: Constructing the conscious brain*. New York: Random House. Retrieved from http://books.google.pt/books?id=2ILun_SB4NIC

Dautenhahn, K. (1999). *Computation for metaphors, analogy, and agents*. Berlin: Springer-Verlag. Retrieved from http://dl.acm.org/citation.cfm?id=1830925.1830936

Dias, J., Mascarenhas, S., & Paiva, A. (2011). *Fatima modular: Towards an agent architecture with a generic appraisal framework*. Paper presented at the Workshop in Standards in Emotion Modeling. Leiden, The Netherlands.

Dias, J., & Paiva, A. (2005). Feeling and reasoning: A computational model for emotional characters. In C. Bento, A. Cardoso, & G. Dias (Eds.), *Progress in Artificial Intelligence* (pp. 127–140). Berlin: Springer. Retrieved from http://link.springer.com/chapter/10.1007/11595014_13

Dias, J., & Paiva, A. (2013). I want to be your friend: Establishing relations with emotionally intelligent agents. In *Proceedings of the 12th International Conference on Autonomous Agents and Multiagent Systems (AAMAS 2013)*. AAMAS.

Dimas, J., & Prada, R. (2013). You are who you hang out with: Agents with dynamic identity. In *Proceedings of the 12th International Conference on Autonomous Agents and Multiagent Systems (AAMAS 2013)*. AAMAS.

French, J. R. P. Jr., & Raven, B. (1959). The bases of social power. In Studies in social power (pp. 150–167). Oxford, UK: University of Michigan.

Gibson, D., Aldrich, C., & Prensky, M. (2007). *Games and simulations in online learning: Research and development frameworks*. Information Science Publishing.

Gratch, J., Rickel, J., Andre, E., Cassell, J., Petajan, E., & Badler, N. (2002). Creating interactive virtual humans: Some assembly required. *IEEE Intelligent Systems*, *17*(4), 54–63. doi:10.1109/MIS.2002.1024753.

Gross, J. J., & Thompson, R. A. (2007). Emotion regulation: Conceptual foundations. Handbook of Emotion Regulation, 3, 24.

Hofstede, G., Hofstede, G. J., & Minkov, M. (2010). *Cultures and organizations: Software for the mind* (3rd ed.). New York: McGraw-Hill.

Hogg, M. A. (2003). Social Identity. In M. R. Leary, & J. P. Tangney (Eds.), *Handbook of Self and Identity*. London: Guilford Press.

Johnson, D. W., & Johnson, R. T. (1996). Conflict resolution and peer mediation programs in elementary and secondary schools: A review of the research. *Review of Educational Research*, *66*(4), 459–506. doi:10.3102/00346543066004459.

Johnson, W. L., Vilhjalmsson, H., & Marsella, S. (2005). Serious games for language learning: How much game, how much AI. In *Artificial Intelligence in Education: Supporting Learning Through Intelligent And Socially Informed Technology* (pp. 306–313). Amsterdam: IOS Press.

Jones, L. A. (1988). Motor illusions: What do they reveal about proprioception? *Psychological Bulletin*, *103*(1), 72–86. doi:10.1037/0033-2909.103.1.72 PMID:3279446.

Jones, T. S. (2004). Conflict resolution education: The field, the findings, and the future. *Conflict Resolution Quarterly*, *22*(1-2), 233–267. doi:10.1002/crq.100.

Keltner, D., Van Kleef, G., Chen, S., & Kraus, M. (2008). A reciprocal influence model of social power: Emerging principles and lines of inquiry. *Advances in Experimental Social Psychology*, *40*, 151–192. doi:10.1016/S0065-2601(07)00003-2.

Kemper, T. D. (2011). *Status, power and ritual interaction: A relational reading of Durkheim, Goffman and Collins*. London: Ashgate Publishing, Ltd.

Kirriemuir, J., & Mcfarlane, A. (2004). *Literature review in games and learning*. Retrieved from http://telearn.archives-ouvertes.fr/hal-00190453

Krovi, R., Graesser, A. C., & Pracht, W. E. (1999). Agent behaviors in virtual negotiation environments. *Trans. Sys. Man Cyber Part C*, *29*(1), 15–25. doi:10.1109/5326.740666.

Leite, I., Castellano, G., Pereira, A., Martinho, C., & Paiva, A. (2012). Long-term interactions with empathic robots: Evaluating perceived support in children. In S. S. Ge, O. Khatib, J.-J. Cabibihan, R. Simmons, & M.-A. Williams (Eds.), *Social Robotics* (pp. 298–307). Berlin: Springer. Retrieved from http://link.springer.com/chapter/10.1007/978-3-642-34103-8_30

Leite, I., Martinho, C., Pereira, A., & Paiva, A. (2009). As time goes by: Long-term evaluation of social presence in robotic companions. In *Proceedings of the 18th IEEE International Symposium on Robot and Human Interactive Communication,* (pp. 669 –674). IEEE. doi:10.1109/ROMAN.2009.5326256

Leite, I., Pereira, A., Martinho, C., & Paiva, A. (2008). Are emotional robots more fun to play with? In *Proceedings of the 17th IEEE International Symposium on Robot and Human Interactive Communication,* (pp. 77–82). IEEE. doi:10.1109/ROMAN.2008.4600646

Leite, I., Pereira, A., Mascarenhas, S., Martinho, C., Prada, R., & Paiva, A. (2013). The influence of empathy in human–robot relations. *International Journal of Human-Computer Studies, 71*(3), 250–260. doi:10.1016/j.ijhcs.2012.09.005.

Lopes, P. N., Salovey, P., Côté, S., Beers, M., & Petty, R. E. (2005). Emotion regulation abilities and the quality of social interaction. *Emotion (Washington, D.C.), 5*(1), 113. doi:10.1037/1528-3542.5.1.113 PMID:15755224.

Lopes, P. N., Salovey, P., & Straus, R. (2003). Emotional intelligence, personality, and the perceived quality of social relationships. *Personality and Individual Differences, 35*(3), 641–658. doi:10.1016/S0191-8869(02)00242-8.

Magnenat-Thalmann, N., & Kasap, Z. (2009). Virtual humans in serious games. In *Proceedings of the International Conference on CyberWorlds,* (pp. 71 –79). CW. doi:10.1109/CW.2009.17

Marsella, S. C., & Pynadath, D. V. (2005). Modeling influence and theory of mind. In *Artificial Intelligence and the Simulation of Behavior* (pp. 199–206). IEEE.

Martin, R. A. (2007). *The psychology of humor: An integrative approach*. Academic Press.

Mascarenhas, S., Dias, J., Afonso, N., Enz, S., & Paiva, A. (2009). Using rituals to express cultural differences in synthetic characters. In *Proceedings of the 8th International Conference on Autonomous Agents and Multiagent Systems* (Vol. 1, pp. 305–312). Richland, SC: International Foundation for Autonomous Agents and Multiagent Systems. Retrieved from http://dl.acm.org/citation.cfm?id=1558013.1558055

Mascarenhas, S., Dias, J., Prada, R., & Paiva, A. (2010). A dimensional model for cultural behavior in virtual agents. *Applied Artificial Intelligence, 24*(6), 552–574. doi:10.1080/08839514.2010.492163.

Mascarenhas, S., Prada, R., Paiva, A., Degens, N., & Hofstede, G. J. (2013). Can I ask you a favour? A relational model of socio-cultural behaviour. In *Proceedings of the 12th International Conference on Autonomous Agents and Multiagent Systems (AAMAS 2013)*. AAMAS.

Mendelson, M. J., & Aboud, F. E. (1999). Measuring friendship quality in late adolescents and young adults: McGill friendship questionnaires. *Statistics, 31*(2), 130–132.

Milgram, S. (1974). *Obedience to authority: An experimental view*. New York: Harper & Row.

Olsen, D., & Mateas, M. (2009). Beep! Beep! Boom! Towards a planning model of coyote and road runner cartoons. In *Proceedings of the 4th International Conference on Foundations of Digital Games* (pp. 145–152). IEEE.

Ortony, A., Clore, G. L., & Collins, A. (1990). *The cognitive structure of emotions*. Cambridge, UK: Cambridge University Press. Retrieved from http://www.amazon.com/Cognitive-Structure-Emotions-Andrew-Ortony/dp/0521386640

Pereira, G., Prada, R., & Santos, P. A. (2013). Bases of social power for agents. In *Proceedings of the 12th International Conference on Autonomous Agents and Multiagent Systems (AAMAS 2013)*. AAMAS.

Pfeffer, J. (1981). *Power in organizations*. Boston: Pitman Marshfield.

Pfeifer, R., Bongard, J., & Grand, S. (2007). *How the body shapes the way we think: A new view of intelligence*. Cambridge, MA: MIT Press. Retrieved from http://books.google.pt/books?id=EHPMv9MfgWwC

Poggi, I., Pelachaud, C., De Rosis, F., Carofiglio, V., & De Carolis, B. (2005). GRETA: A believable embodied conversational agent. In O. Stock & M. Zancanaro (Eds.), *Multimodal Intelligent Information Presentation* (Vol. 27, pp. 1–23). Boston: Kluwer Academic Publishers. Retrieved from http://www.springerlink.com/index/vg369201254923n7.pdf

Prada, R., & Paiva, A. (2009). Teaming up humans with autonomous synthetic characters. *Artificial Intelligence*, *173*(1), 80–103. doi:10.1016/j.artint.2008.08.006.

Prada, R., Raimundo, G., Dimas, J., Martinho, C., Peña, J. F., & Baptista, M. … Ribeiro, L. L. (2012). The role of social identity, rationality and anticipation in believable agents. In *Proceedings of the 11th International Conference on Autonomous Agents and Multiagent Systems* (vol. 3, pp. 1175–1176). Richland, SC: International Foundation for Autonomous Agents and Multiagent Systems. Retrieved from http://dl.acm.org/citation.cfm?id=2343896.2343907

Raven, B. H. (1992). A power/interaction model of interpersonal influence: French and Raven thirty years later. *Journal of Social Behavior and Personality*, *7*(2), 217–244.

Ribeiro, T., Vala, M., & Paiva, A. (2012). Thalamus: Closing the mind-body loop in interactive embodied characters. In *Proceedings of IVA* (pp. 189–195). IVA.

Rizzo, P., Veloso, M., Miceli, M., & Cesta, A. (1997). Personality-driven social behaviors in believable agents. In *Proceedings of the AAAI Fall Symposium on Socially Intelligent Agents* (pp. 109–114). AAAI. Retrieved from http://www.aaai.org/Papers/Symposia/Fall/1997/FS-97-02/FS97-02-026.pdf

Rodrigues, S. H., Mascarenhas, S. F., Dias, J., & Paiva, A. (2009). I can feel it too! Emergent empathic reactions between synthetic characters. In *Proceedings of Affective Computing and Intelligent Interaction and Workshops, 2009*. ACII. doi:10.1109/ACII.2009.5349570.

Salovey, P., & Mayer, J. (1990). Emotional intelligence. In Imagination, Cognition and Personality (pp. 185–211). Baywood Publishing.

Schacter, D. L. (1987). Implicit memory: History and current status. *Journal of Experimental Psychology. Learning, Memory, and Cognition*, *13*(3), 501–518. doi:10.1037/0278-7393.13.3.501.

Smith, E. R., & Mackie, D. M. (2000). *Social psychology* (2nd ed.). Philadelphia: Psychology Press.

Spronck, P., Ponsen, M., Sprinkhuizen-Kuyper, I., & Postma, E. (2006). Adaptive game AI with dynamic scripting. *Machine Learning*, *63*(3), 217–248. doi:10.1007/s10994-006-6205-6.

Tajfel, H. (1972). La catégorisation sociale. *Introduction à la psychologie sociale*, *1*, 272–302.

Tajfel, H. (Ed.). (1978). *Differentiation between social groups: Studies in the social psychology of intergroup relations.* Oxford, UK: Academic Press.

Thalmann, D., Hery, C., Lippman, S., Ono, H., Regelous, S., & Sutton, D. (2004). Crowd and group animation. In *ACM SIGGRAPH 2004 course notes* (p. 34). Retrieved from http://dl.acm.org/citation.cfm?id=1103934

Thomas, K. W. (1976). Conflict and conflict management. In *Handbook of industrial and organizational psychology.* Chicago: Randy McNally.

Turner, J. C. (1978). Social categorization and social discrimination in the minimal group paradigm. In H. Tajfel (Ed.), *Differentiation between social groups: Studies in the social psychology of intergroup relations.* Oxford, UK: Academic Press.

Turner, J. C., Oakes, P. J., Alexander, S., & McGarty, C. (1994). Self and collective: Cognition and social context. *Personality and Social Psychology Bulletin, 20*(5), 454–463. doi:10.1177/0146167294205002.

Ulicny, B., & Thalmann, D. (2001). Crowd simulation for interactive virtual environments and VR training systems. In P. D. N. Magnenat-Thalmann & D. D. Thalmann (Eds.), *Computer Animation and Simulation 2001* (pp. 163–170). Vienna: Springer. Retrieved from http://link.springer.com/chapter/10.1007/978-3-7091-6240-8_15

Vala, M., Ribeiro, T., & Paiva, A. (2012). A model for embodied cognition in autonomous agents. In *Proceedings of IVA* (pp. 505–507). IVA.

Vannini, N., Enz, S., Sapouna, M., Wolke, D., Watson, S., & Woods, S. et al. (2010). FearNot! A computer-based anti-bullying-programme designed to foster peer intervention. *European Journal of Psychology of Education.*

Vannini, N., Enz, S., Sapouna, M., Wolke, D., Watson, S., & Woods, S. et al. (2011). FearNot! A computer-based anti-bullying-programme designed to foster peer intervention. *European Journal of Psychology of Education, 26*(1), 21–44. doi:10.1007/s10212-010-0035-4.

Vorhaus, J. (1994). *The comic toolbox: How to be funny even if you're not.* Los Angeles, CA: Silman-James Press.

Wooldridge, M. (2002). *An introduction to multiagent systems.* Hoboken, NJ: John Wiley & Sons.

ADDITIONAL READING

Isbister, K. (2006). *Better game characters by design: a psychological approach.* Elsevier and Morgan Kaufmann.

Kemper, T. D. (2011). *Status, Power and Ritual Interaction: A Relational Reading of Durkheim, Goffman and Collins.* Ashgate Publishing, Ltd.

Prendinger, H., & Ishizuka, M. (2004). *Life-Like Characters: Tools, Affective Functions, and Applications.* Springer. doi:10.1007/978-3-662-08373-4.

Reeves, B. (1998). *The Media Equation.* Cambridge University Press.

Sawyer, R. K. (2003). *Improvised dialogues: emergence and creativity in conversation.* Greenwood Publishing Group. Retrieved from http://books.google.com/books?id=fMiTmZqPL0kC&pgis=1

Stedman, N. (2009). *Affective Robotics as Device Art.* State University of New York at Buffalo.

Thomas, F., & Johnston, O. (1995). *The illusion of life: Disney animation.* Hyperion.

KEY TERMS AND DEFINITIONS

Affective Characters: Characters that are capable of sensing, reasoning or expressing affective states in their interactions with other characters or players.

Agent Based Modelling: The generic procedure of conceptualizing processes (e.g. human social processes) and their underlying attributes for computer simulations emulating them.

Believability: The system's ability to convey the sense of real life to the user.

Character Authoring: The process of creating content and configuring a character's characteristics and attributes.

Companions: Characters used to provide assistance and actively follow (usually long-term) interactive experiences.

Emotion Modelling: The process of characterizing and integrating emotions' attributes and processes in typical non-player characters behaviours.

Intelligent Virtual Agents: Life-like characters that interact with other characters and users in modalities similar to those of humans.

Non-Player Character (NPC): Entities that embody a role in a game context that is usually performed by a person.

Social Intelligence: The ability to be sensitive, reason and react to a multitude of social concepts such as social relations, identity, power, culture, dependence, norms, etc.

ENDNOTES

1. From here on, we will refer to the agents as characters because it is this subset of agents that is the focus of this chapter.
2. http://gaips.inesc-id.pt/
3. http://gaips.inesc-id.pt/
4. http://fatima-modular.sourceforge.net/
5. http://en.wikipedia.org/wiki/Neverwinter_Nights
6. http://project-invite.eu/
7. http://ecute.eu/
8. http://sirenproject.eu
9. http://us.blizzard.com/en-us/games/sc/
10. Social sciences models are often highly descriptive, which makes it difficult (and in some cases, impossible) to create computational models from them.

Chapter 8
Individual Differences in the Enjoyment and Effectiveness of Serious Games

Dawn G. Blasko
Pennsylvania State University, USA

Heather C. Lum
Pennsylvania State University, USA

Matthew M. White
Pennsylvania State University, USA

Holly Blasko Drabik
University of Central Florida, USA

ABSTRACT

Individuals differ in a myriad of ways and the promise of using a digital game format to teach or train new knowledge and skills is that they may be designed to allow each user to take their own path through the game and therefore create a more person-centered experience. The current chapter explores the research on some of the many individual differences that may be important to the design, use, and success of a serious game. These include factors that influence motivation to play and learn and learner characteristics such as age, gender, and ethnicity. Cognitive characteristics such as working memory and spatial skills can influence the play environment and may actually be improved by regular gaming. Finally, one area that has been much less studied is individual differences in teachers and trainers who often are charged with the implementation of the serious games.

INTRODUCTION

At the heart of serious games are the learning objectives set forth by educators and researchers. Also called 'digital games for learning and training' serious games attempt to impart knowledge and skills using an entertaining game format. Serious games have been used as a means to engage learners in content learning and increase learner-centered control and motivation. In many cases, serious games have tackled difficult and complex topics, such as world hunger, political

DOI: 10.4018/978-1-4666-4773-2.ch008

Copyright © 2014, IGI Global. Copying or distributing in print or electronic forms without written permission of IGI Global is prohibited.

crises, and more. For example, in Darfur Is Dying (2009), developer mtvU attempted to use a serious game to raise awareness of the ongoing humanitarian crisis in Darfur, Western Sudan (Ruiz, York, Stein, Keating, & Santiago, 2009). Other games such as Amnesty the Game (2011) and Food Force (2005) have tackled similarly controversial issues.

Theories of effective learning suggest that to be successful, a serious game needs to be active, experiential, problem-based and provide immediate feedback (Boyle, Connolly & Hainey, 2011). Serious games must also be enjoyable and motivate individuals to play until they reach mastery. However, individual players differ in a variety of ways that may lead to a higher or lower level of engagement with the technology. One of the most attractive features of serious games, and educational technology more generally, is the possibility that the software can be tailored to assess the individual learner's skills and knowledge in real time as well as present new activities and concepts that are challenging but achievable at the learner's own pace. This idea of finding an optimal skill-to-challenge balance is often discussed in the context of Csikszentmihayli's concept of "flow" (Csikszentmihayli, 1997). One goal for serious games is to match a learner's skills with the right level of challenge in real-time.

The unifying focus of this chapter is to examine how individual differences are related to the enjoyment and effectiveness of serious games. As researchers, we strive to examine what makes us similar and, just as importantly, what makes us different. The study of these distinguishing characteristics is essential when considering the underlying mechanisms of serious game design. The current chapter explores how four classes of individual differences are important to consider in the design, use and assessment of serious games. The first class includes motivational factors such as learning self-efficacy, the second involves experiential factors such as gaming experience and video game self-efficacy, the

third involves demographic characteristics such as gender, socio-economic status, and age, and the fourth focuses on cognitive factors. We will briefly discuss the application of serious games for learners with individual differences in physical and cognitive deficits. Finally, it is important to consider individual differences in the teachers and trainers who are expected to implement the serious game. Their motivation, self-efficacy and attitudes towards the use of games for learning can be important to success. Although no one chapter can fully explore all of these factors, we hope to review some of the newer research in the field, present some interesting new data, identify some new areas for research and provide some helpful tips for serious game developers.

MAIN FOCUS OF THE ARTICLE

Learner Self-Efficacy and Motivational Factors

Bandura believed that the key to learning is a person's belief in his or her own abilities to succeed, that is their self-efficacy. His research showed that perceived self-efficacy is a significant factor in how much effort will be expended and how long the learner will persist in the face of obstacles and challenges (Bandura, 1997; 2011). Self-efficacy can occur on a number of levels. Learning self-efficacy occurs when the individual feels that he or she has the background and skills to master a new set of learning objectives. Carol Dweck (1986) has shown that training is much more effective if the learner has a "growth" mental model of intelligence than when they have a "fixed" model. Individuals with a fixed model believe that their intellectual ability is innate or fixed and have less confidence that intellectual change is possible. They will think: "I'm just bad at math so I can never learn calculus." Low self-efficacy can lead to an unhealthy pattern of less effort and avoidance of the topic so that less learning can occur, perpetuating the cycle of poor performance. On the other hand students with a "growth" mental model of intelligence believe that effort and practice lead to changes in the brain and improved performance. Such students are much more likely to benefit from training.

There is evidence to support the idea that short interventions can help shift students' models of intelligence. For example, Dweck & Masters (2008), using the metaphor of the brain as a muscle getting bigger and stronger with exercise and a short video depicting the process of neurons strengthening their connections, improved performance on both verbal and spatial tasks in comparison to a control group that did not see the video. In other areas of games research, White (2008) found a significant correlation between use of pRPGs and learning self-efficacy, while Locke & Latham (1990) found that high levels of mastery in game spaces led to confidence in other disciplines.

The motivation to play a game long enough to gain an educational benefit will be influenced by a player's feeling of self-efficacy. Behavior can be intrinsically or extrinsically motivated. Most models have emphasized intrinsic motivation, focusing on the motives to perform a task that are derived from the participation itself (Malone, 1981; Malone & Lepper, 1987). Malone (1981) proposed that the primary factors that make an activity intrinsically motivating are challenge, curiosity and fantasy and specifically applied this framework to the design of computer games. It has been shown that those with an intrinsic motivation to learn the material are more likely to "stay with it". Intrinsic motivation can be achieved by creating a more constructivist interaction with the game (Vos, van der Meijden, & Denessen, 2011). There were two game groups; one constructed their own memory "drag and drop" game, while the other played an existing "drag and drop" memory game. Analyses revealed a significant difference between the two conditions both on intrinsic motivation and deep strategy use in favor of the construction condition. The results suggest that constructing a game might be a better way to enhance student motivation and deep learning than playing an existing game. Therefore, developers of serious games must take into account that the success of their serious games may depend in part on the user's learning self-efficacy, their theories of intelligence and the motivations of the students.

Video Game Self-Efficacy and Experiential Factors

In recent years, exploration into the differential play habits of different gamer demographics has revealed that experience may have played a greater role in people's selection of, and playing of digital games than researchers had originally thought (White, 2012a). Video game self-efficacy is the level of confidence a player has that he or she can play any new video game successfully. One major issue in serious games is the lack of video game self-efficacy by people who are not typical 'gamers'. They may have less experience with technology and more difficultly learning how to use control systems and navigate games. Unlike gamers, non-gamers cannot transfer their knowledge of "how to play a game" from their experience with entertainment games. In group settings, this can reduce the self-efficacy of non-gamers making them less likely to want to master the game. Until the controls and navigation and structure of the game become automatized, the player is less likely to make progress on the learning goals.

Individuals who self-identify as 'gamers' have often spent literally thousands of hours building up expertise by playing numerous types of games. Games share similar characteristics and these games mechanics help to define how the play progresses, the events that occur in the game, and the winning or losing conditions for the game (Adams & Dormans, 2012). By mastering certain game mechanics, such as jumping, players who become adept at Super Mario Bros (1985) also become adept at other games employing similar mechanics. This experiential divide is then exploited by games producers releasing numerous sequels to the same game (White, 2009), such as Call of Duty: Black Ops (2010), and Call of Duty: Black Ops II (2010).

Expert players can rely on their pre-existing knowledge of the original game, as well as the genre of the game, in this case the first-person shooter, to perform at a high level of mastery. Novice players, however are left to contend with the games' insufficient or absent tutorial system, and are often frustrated by this experience, causing them to disengage (White, 2012a). Therefore game experience, perhaps more importantly than individual tastes or preferences, must be considered when designing serious games for learning and teaching environments.

While digital games for learning and training are not the same as commercial entertainment games, they embody many of the same characteristics. Both are designed using similar game mechanics and both seek to engage the player in an interactive system. While a game played for entertainment seeks only to 'teach' the player the mechanics, controls, and strategies necessary to master the game, serious games have a more daunting task. Not only must a serious game teach the player to attain play mastery, which is itself a difficult task, the game must then remain engaging while teaching an appropriate 'real-world' lesson of some kind.. Considering the general difficulty in teaching players to 'play' (White, 2012b), teaching them to play and to also motivate them to learn external content is doubly challenging.

In Persuasive Games, Bogost argues for a type of "procedural rhetoric" (Bogost, 2007), which introduces players to the 'lessons' being taught in a game via its mechanics, rather than in addition to them. Bogost mentions YOSHINOYA (2004), a game about a Japanese restaurant chain, in which players must act as the cook or server to maximize profits for the store. Implicit in the game are mechanics such as cleanliness, profit, and speed and the game is scored on these factors. The restaurant corporation also attempts to engender these values in its employees (Bogost, 2007). Consequently the mechanics of the game itself mirror the educational goals of the instructional designer. This kind of endogenous learning prevents the difficulties inherent in both teaching the player to play, as well as teaching them the lessons contained within the game itself.

This task-endogeneity is also demonstrated in the Alert Hockey (2007) serious game. Authors and developers Ciavarro, Dobson, and Goodman (2007) created a realistic hockey video game, similar to commercially available titles such as the NHL series by EA Games. In contrast with the commercial games however, the game included a subtle system that tracked aggressive behaviors in players, and penalized it by making the opponent AI increase in skill (etc.) for every excessively aggressive action. By contrasting the goals of the game with the desired behavioral outcome, the designers employed 'implicit learning' to teach players behaviorally that rewards in the form of game victory came when less aggressive play is used. Such implicit learning objectives are better received by users of serious games, as the pedagogical content and the game's outcomes are coherent, thus a cognitive dissonance between 'playing' and 'learning' is never produced.

Using techniques from the entertainment industry to create an exciting and enjoyable serious game that can motivate all learners to play until they master the intended concepts seems to solve this problem. However, entertainment games differ from serious games in an important way. They are freely chosen by the player based on factors such as interest in the content, recommendations from friends, advertising, current popularity and game type. Games developed for entertainment can be commercially successful and yet appeal only to a small section of the population, as demonstrated by games such as SUPER MEAT BOY (2010) or Minecraft (2011), which appeal to very particular tastes. Both games are relatively simple, low graphic online flash based games with the same objectives from level 1 to level 300, making the games either addictively fun or quickly boring depend on the player's personality. Serious games, on the other hand, are often mandatory in a school or training environment and therefore lose some of their attraction. For example, non-gamers who would not ordinarily choose to play, may feel frustrated at having to figure out how to play a game, they may feel less competent and this may lead to negative feelings and poor performance (Cardinu, Maas, Rosabianca, & Kiesner, 2005). This has been demonstrated even with very popular educational games, such as the Math Blaster (1991) series.

In order to create and foster higher video game self-efficacy, serious game designers should consider the intended audience for their game and design the game to be as intuitive as possible. Since learning is the main focus of serious games, the design of a game, both hardware and software should facilitate rather than hinder this. One way to achieve this may be to promote rapid interaction between player and non-player characters through speech recognition and natural language processing (Johnson, Vilhjalmsson, & Marsella, 2005, p. 308). When the learner is engaged in a conversation with a non-player character, there is a give and take between the characters. If the flow is constant, the interaction of action and reaction between the user's actions and the game's response will seem effortless and may lead to a higher level of self-efficacy. It may also be prudent to provide tutorial scaffolding while not interrupting the gameplay flow or learner performance.

The feedback structure that is developed in serious games is especially important to provide personalized support in games. In-game, this can be in the form of a skill bar, tasks completed box, or any verbal or visual information presented to the user. Effective feedback can provide immediate, meaningful information about the user's performance in order to improve their skills. Affordances should also be exploited to create a game that players of any skill level can play. Ac-

cording to Donald Norman, the term affordance "refers to the perceived and actual properties of the thing, primarily those fundamental properties that determine just how the thing could possibly be used." (Norman, 1988, p. 9). In the realm of games, "perceived affordances" should cue the user and guide their actions, both in the interface design and the actual controls used. Game designers should consider the ways to foster video game self-efficacy and increase experience naturally amongst non-players and players alike.

DEMOGRAPHIC CHARACTERISTICS

Gender Issues in Serious Games

Gender is one of the most widely studied but controversial aspects of individual differences. For many years psychologists, education scientists, and game researchers focused on the digital divide between genders. Boys had greater access to, interest in and use of computers and this led to boys showing better game playing skills and more video game self-efficacy than girls (Terlecki, Brown, Harner-Steciw, Irvin-Hannum, Marchetto-Ryan, Ruhl, & Wiggins, 2011). With boys having more exposure to technology and gender-role stereotypes supporting these interests, boys were also more interested in playing digital entertainment games than girls. Game developers tapped into this ready market, producing games that were in many cases stereotypically masculine, including sports games, war games, and action games that over the years became increasingly violent. According to a number of content analyses (Downs & Smith, 2010; Williams, Martins, Consalvo, & Ivory, 2009) in the most popular video games there were (and may still be) more male characters than female, more male roles available, and strongly sexualized physical attributes of both avatars and in game characters (Dickerman, Christensen, & Kerl-McClain, 2008).

Over time, some gender differences in the digital divide have appeared to decline. Recent data collected by the Pew Foundation found that game play in now ubiquitous among teens in the United States (Lenhardt, Kahne, Middaugh, Evans, & Vitek, 2008) with ninety-seven percent of teens reporting that they play some digital games. However, the data did show that strong gender differences are still evident in the patterns of play and game-playing habits. For example, the experience gap remains; boys played for more hours each week than girls and they also play a wider variety of games. Boys and girls also play different types of games, with girls playing more puzzle games and boys playing more action, sports and first-person shooter games (Lenhardt, et al, 2008; Terlecki, et al, 2011). Current work in the field of game studies has suggested that many gender differences can be attributed to an experiential gap (Jenson, Fisher, & De Castell, 2011; White, 2012a). Studies have shown that as female players gain efficacy and skill in play, they often move from a cooperative and helping dialog, to a more combative and competitive dialog (Jenson & De Castell, 2008; Jenson et al., 2011; White, 2012a). Therefore, the novice-expert divide might offer a better explanation of some of the factors that have been previously attributed to gender.

Therefore, the challenge for developers of digital games for education is to develop games that have high usability, and are interesting and enjoyable to both boy and girls despite differences in gender roles and experience. A point that is worth repeating is that although entertainment games are played by choice, serious games are often obligatory learning activities. They are assigned by teachers or trainers and expected to be played until some defined set of information or skills is mastered in-game while at the same time learning is expected to transfer beyond the game situation (Heeter, Lee, Magerko, Medler, 2011). This is certainly a high bar to reach. There were many suggestions about how to design serious games that were more engaging to girls and women. One

option has been to use more "feminine" environments; for example, designers put more emphasis on allowing players to choose their characters physical characteristics and clothing. They often create an environment with brighter colors and more pleasant audio elements, and include more social collaboration instead of competition in the play. In order to encourage girls to become interested in science, technology, engineering and math (STEM subjects) the National Science Foundation and other funders have provided support for the development of on-line environments and games designed with girls in mind (National Science Board, 2010). For example, Whyville.net is a girl friendly virtual town where citizens earn "clams" by playing educational games. For example, in one creative game, they can learn vector arithmetic while choreographing a dance routine.

The importance of understanding why individuals dislike a game is critical to effective design. For example, in a recent study (Blasko, Chadwick, & Bittner, in preparation) male and female college students were given a difficult math test that induced stress, and were then randomly assigned to play either a violent or nonviolent video game and then complete an evaluation of the game. The games were evaluated on three key dimensions: 1) the affective dimension which measured enjoyment, engagement and flow, 2) games mechanics including usability and 3) learning self-efficacy. Overall, students reported less stress after playing the game, but there were important gender and game genre differences that were not explained entirely by player experience. Consistent with previous work (Hamlen, 2001), many female students reported that they did not like the violent game. They reported that they felt capable of playing the game but simply did not enjoy it. Female students reported stronger feelings of personal challenge and flow in the nonviolent game while males reported more personal challenge in the violent game.

Creating interesting games that appeal to both males and females and motivate students to play often depends on clear relevance to an individual's life. For example, military simulations can be highly effective because they relate directly to actions and behaviors that players must internalize to succeed in the field. For example, as their final, pass/fail training exercise, NAVY cadets are complete a real world simulation of a disaster occurring on board a Navy Destroyer. To help prevent cadets from failing (and potentially being required to retake the entire basic training course) BNN and RETRO labs created a computer simulation which followed several key tasks the cadets would be asked to perform. To test the effectiveness of the simulation, a study was conducted comparing cadets who played the game for one hour with those who did not play the game. The cadets who played the game showed a large reduction in both communication errors and in critical or catastrophic safety errors that would have caused them to fail the final exam (Hussain, Bowers, Blasko-Drabik, & Blair, in press). One reason proposed for the dramatic improvement in the cadet's performance is that the game mimics the everyday communication and safety protocols that the cadets must learn. The cadets immediately can see the links between how well they perform in the game (via scores, completing objectives, and in game movie scenes) with what their instructors have been drilling into them during their other classes.

In the educational environment case studies are one way to it can be much more difficult establish relevance. It is possible to create a serious game that has some appeal to males and females, For example, research methods and statistics are the most intimidating areas for psychology majors and this is particularly the case for the women. In Courseware for Observational Research (COR) (Blasko, Kazmerski, & Torgerson, 2004), players took take the role of a psychologist asked to assess whether a 7 year old girl, who the teacher referred for aggressive behavior, should be removed from the classroom. Working in pairs to establish inter-rater reliability, players can interview parents and teachers, view actual behavior and are supported through the process of designing, carrying out and statistically analyzing the data from their observational study. Players then write a brief report and make a recommendation. Data from the evaluations of a two classes taught by the same instructor randomly assigned to either COR or traditional lecture training, found that both male and female students in the COR group showed greater learning and more enjoyment in comparison to the traditional teaching. Importantly the study also showed the students the relevance of research and statistics to their career discipline. Students' interpretations of the findings also encouraged critical thinking.

Although many of these efforts have been successful in increasing self-efficacy in girls and meeting their specific learning objectives, as a long term solution there are several problems with developing gender specific serious games. First they can increase the very stereotypes that they aim to reduce. By categorizing games as for either boys or girls, psychologically, individual differences within-group (e.g., all girls) are minimized and between-group differences (boys compared to girls) become maximized or exaggerated. Although most gender differences in the cognitive domains are very small and have high degrees of overlap, the perception of those differences remains strong as the popularity of books like "Men are from Mars and Women are from Venus" illustrates.

Race, Ethnicity and Socio-Economic Status

Often race, gender, and socio-economic status are intertwined and difficult to separate with regards to game use and acceptance as well as technology use in general. Jackson, Zhao, Kolenic, Fitzgerald, Harold, & Von Eye (2008) examined information technology use among African-American and Caucasian children. Their results indicated race and gender differences in the intensity of information technology use with African American males the least intense users of computers and the Internet, and African American females were the most intense users of the Internet. Males, regardless of race, were the most intense videogame players, and females, regardless of race, were the most intense cell phone users. IT use predicted children's academic performance. The length of time using computers and the Internet was a positive predictor of academic performance; whereas amount of time spent playing videogames was a negative predictor.

Non-gamers, whether male or female, are at a significant disadvantage when asked to play a serious game. However females and both males and females from minority groups (e,g, Latinos) and/or lower socio-economic status who have less access to technology are proportionally more likely to be non-gamers. Serious games are not effective for either gender unless players are motivated to play, feel that they can learn the game (video game self-efficacy), feel that they can learn the content (learning self-efficacy) and enjoy playing the game. For example in a large study with 330 undergraduates, Heeter, et al., (2011) examined three vulnerable groups of players: non-gamers, resistant players and females as they played four on-line games. Non-gamers showed poorer performance and displayed more negative affect than those with experience. Those who disliked the games performed worse than those who did not. As the authors put it, "serious games are a good way to reach gamers, and serious games are a potentially great way to reach players who enjoy the game." (Heeter, et al., 2011, p. 50).

Of course there were always girls who enjoy playing video games and show performance equivalent to most boys, just as there are boys who do not enjoy playing video games (Terlecki, et al., 2011) and show poorer performance. This has led some to claim that all the gender differences can be explained by this experience gap. This is an important point. As described above, experience does play an important role in predicting who

will benefit from a serious game. However sex and gender roles are based on complex cultural factors, including socio-economic status, family dynamics, social stigma, peer influences, and media influences to name just a few.

Serious Games and Older Adults

Although the majority of serious games have been developed for children or young adults, one of the most promising areas in the development of serious games is the potential to improve cognitive performance in older populations (Lustig, Shah, Seidler, & Reuter-Lorenz, 2009). Aging can cause declines in a variety of cognitive processes including processing speed, episodic memory, working memory, spatial orientation reasoning and dual task processing and these can lead to loss of independence and depression (Hertzog, Kramer, Wilson, & Lindenberger, 2009). At the same time, other cognitive processes are relatively spared such as simple short term memory, vocabulary, recognition memory, and procedural memory (Hertzog, et al., 2009). For those developing serious games for older adults it is important to understand which cognitive skills are being used at each level of the game. Older adults who are new to video games may experience difficulty in learning how to use the controller and/or control keys and this may lead them to give up on the game. Navigation in complex environments can also be a problem as spatial working memory may be more easily exceeded. Older adults may need more support in the way of hints and tutorials at the beginning of the game than younger adults. However once they have learned the basics, older adults often become highly skilled.

One major advantage of serious games is that they can be programmed to adapt to the learner's level of skill and present challenges that are tailored to the learner. There are now a variety of brain training games on the market: BRAIN AGE and BIG BRAIN ACADEMY are published by Nintendo Co. Ltd and Luminosity, is an on-line training program by Lumos Labs. A number of recent studies have shown that brain training video games can improve performance on some cognitive tasks among children (Miller & Robertson, 2011), young adults (Nouchi, et al., 2013) and older populations (Basak, Boot, Voss, & Kramer, 2008). A great deal of research will be needed to understand what will make a program effective both in the short term and over longer periods of time. One of the most important issues is whether improvements on the game will lead to transfer to other cognitive and performance domains.

Commercial game developers are well aware of the potential market in games for the expanding population of older adults. However there is a need for research to demonstrate the efficacy of such games outside of controlled situations. Home users are unlikely to be as motivated to play regularly given the multiple demands of everyday life, so whatever the positive impact that is found in the lab, it will undoubtedly be weaker in the field. Hertzog, Kramer, Wilson, and Lindenberg (2008) reviewed the efforts at cognitive enrichment in older adults and emphasized that improvements are most likely from programs that include cognitive (problem solving, critical thinking, working memory) social, and physical (aerobic) activities. However, they noted that a rapid return to a more negative developmental trajectory is possible when the training is discontinued. Longitudinal studies with remote data collection from actual users over long time spans that included demographics, user interest and enjoyment and questions about real-world performance (such as driving or budgeting) could help both developers and players to understanding how these games can best help. It is also important not to over-sell these games. Evidence of a performance increases does not mean that the brain is actually younger or that dementia will not occur, but incremental improvement may help individuals forestall the rate of age-related changes over time.

Cognitive Characteristics

Learning Styles and Principles

No discussion of individual differences in learning would be complete without a mention of learning styles (Honey, & Mumford, 1992). Both educators and parents have come to accept that there are different learning styles and supporters of learning-style assessment claim that instruction should be tailored to a person's unique preferred learning style (Ormrod, 2008). Felder's model includes several basic learning style dimensions: sensory/intuitive, visual/verbal, active/reflective, and sequential/global (Felder & Silverman, 1988). The implication of this theory is that teachers can reach more students by using a variety of instructional techniques. For instance, a visual learner might learn better from pictures and a verbal learner might learn better from lectures.

It should be noted however, that in a major review of the research, limited evidence was found to support the learning styles hypothesis that teaching via a student's preferred learning style was actually more effective than other styles (Pashler, McDaniel, Rohrer, & Bjork, 2008). This suggests that developing serious games that attempt to assess a person's learning style and then adapt instruction to that learning style may not be the best strategy to enhance learning. Instead, it might be best to use a variety of learning principles and modalities in any given game. Coffield, Moselely, Hall, and Eccelstone (2004) argue that it is more important to match the presentation of the material with the nature of the subject rather than attempting to match individual preferences. For example, games that are intended to teach geography would benefit from more high fidelity graphics and rich visual spatial information that allows exploration of the terrain, with verbal information playing the supporting role. In contrast, a language arts games will necessarily focus on verbal and semantic information with visual spatial information playing a supporting role in maintaining interest and attention.

Although individual differences in sensory abilities certainly do exist, what gives serious games the best chance to be successful for all learners is their ability to put the students in the center of the learning process and engage all of the senses in a challenging environment. Students are not just passive consumers of information. In good games, players feel that their actions and decisions are shaping the learning experience they are having. What the player does matters and each player, based on his or her own decisions and actions, takes a different trajectory through the game world (Gee, 2003). While it has always been the case that we learn by modeling our parents and others, as educators we have often focused only on the formal classroom setting but this is changing. We are recognizing the social and cultural components that make up active learning in an informal setting and that this is perhaps as important, or even more important than what we learn in school (Bransford, Brown & cocking, 2000). Serious games are one avenue in which we can be sensitive to the different learning needs of individuals while creating a deeper understanding of the material.

Spatial Skills

In additional to perceptual differences, there are a variety of cognitive skills that are relevant in considering the effectiveness of serious games including language skills, memory, and attention. The cognitive skill which has received most attention is with respect to games is spatial cognition. Males typically outperform females on dynamic spatial tasks such as mental rotation (Voyer, Voyer, & Bryden, 1995). Meta-analysis has shown this affect to be relatively robust in contrast to other spatial skills which have cognitive gender difference that have been shown to be small or nonexistent, such as spatial perception and spatial visualization (Voyer, et al., 1995). Spatial understanding and

performance is particularly important as games for entertainment and for learning increasingly use high fidelity graphics and audio tracks, as well as rich and complex virtual environments. It is a clear advantage to players to be able to quickly develop a mental map of the game environment, to be competent in navigation and way-finding and to have a well-developed spatial memory.

Moffat, Hampson and Hatzipantelis (1998) found that spatial ability and way-finding in virtual mazes were strongly correlated. Male players also out-performed female players on both spatial ability and the maze games. In a study of spatial activities (Terlecki & Newcombe, 2005) 1,300 undergraduate students were studied. On average, men had more spatial experience and also performed better on the mental rotation task. Computer experience was shown to mediate some of the gender difference that was found in performance on the mental rotation task.

Training spatial skills has been shown to improve performance and video games may be one way to improve a variety of spatial tasks. Only ten hours of training with an action video game has produced gains in both a spatial attention task (UFOV) and a mental rotation task (Feng, Spence & Pratt, 2007). In addition, in this study women benefited more than men from the video game training, thereby narrowing existing gender differences. Assessing and training spatial skills with virtual and hands on games has also been shown to improve spatial skills and to be correlated with higher course performance in first year engineering graphics courses (Blasko, Holliday-Darr, Mace, & Blasko-Drabik, 2004). Some evidence also suggests that assessing spatial skills early on and then providing a combination of computer games and workbook training can also help to reduce the college drop-out rates of women (Veurink et al., 2009).

Therefore, designers of serious games have to be very aware that highly complex virtual worlds, although challenging and exciting to some players, can provide barriers to learning for those with lower spatial skills. For example, when using a game developed to learn disaster prevention strategies, such as building on stilts and maintaining mangrove forests to prevent damage from a tsunami, those players with better spatial skills also learned more from the game (Blasko-Drabik, Blasko, & Lum, 2013).

For those players with less developed spatial skills, support systems such as tutorials, game maps, signposts and landmarks are particularly important in developing mental maps. Women tend to navigate more by landmarks and men by cardinal directions (Saucier, Bowman, & Elias, 2003); therefore designers should avoid using only one strategy, or else support the learning of both strategies. Non-gamers may particularly benefit from serious games that allow them the time to explore the environment at their own pace and form a mental map of the environment, before the more competitive elements of the game are introduced.

Working Memory

According to some theories, (Baddeley, Alan, & Hitch, 2011) working memory is central to most if not all cognitive processes. Working memory acts as a mental workbench that encodes and organizes new information before storage in long term memory and can retrieve relevant information from long term memory for the current task (Cantor & Engle, 1993; Duff & Logies, 2001. According to Baddeley, et al. (2011), the system also has three subsystems for different types of information, the phonological loop for language, the visuo-spatial sketchpad for spatial information and the episodic buffer for event-tagged personal memories. These buffers support the processing work of the central executive which also allocates resources. Theorists (e.g., Engle & Kane, 2004) have also suggested that the central executive of working memory may in fact be related to the control of attention.

Working memory capacity has been shown to predict performance in a large number of tasks which may be relevant in understanding the effectiveness of serious games. For example, working memory capacity influences reading comprehension and metaphor understanding (Kazmerski, Blasko & Dessalegn, 2003), problem solving (Barrett, Tugade, & Engle, 2004; Beilock & DeCaro, 2007; Ricks, Wiley, Turley, 2006), spatial reasoning, and visual search (Barrett, Tugade, & Engle, 2004; Klauer, Stgmaier, & Meiser, 1997; Toms, Morris, & Ward, 1993; Oh & Kim, 2004). Working memory is used throughout gameplay. In new situations and environments, players must remember how to play the game, figure out where to go and master the learning objectives of the serious game. Working memory is also critical to higher level executive functions such as inhibiting irrelevant information and actions and making decisions (Barrett, et al., 2004).

Despite a great deal of research on working memory capacity in psychology, there have been few high quality studies investigating how individual differences in working memory impact performance, motivation and enjoyment of serious games. Working memory capacity has been shown to affect comprehension and memory for computer-based hypertexts, with users having a higher working memory capacity able to recall more of a text than users with lower working memory capacity (Lee & Tedder, 2003). The concept of cognitive load is clearly related to working memory and when cognitive load is high and more attention is devoted to figuring out the game, then less can be devoted to learning (Mayer, 2005).

Those who frequently play video games tend to have better working memory (Colzato, van den Wildenberg, Zimgord, & Hommel, 2013; Garcia, Nussbaum, & Preiss, 2011). This finding has been taken to mean that playing video games improves working memory as well as other cognitive processes. But, this correlational finding does not necessarily rule out the possibility that those with better working memories are more likely to be successful at playing video games, perhaps because they find them easier to master, have a higher capacity for new information and more flexible control. Therefore, research is needed in the area to gain a better understanding of the relationships between cognitive skills and serious games.

Recent interest has focused on training working memory as a way to improve performance in a variety of areas. The results of this work are promising. Some studies suggest that working memory training can increase response inhibition, improve complex reasoning and reduce the symptoms of inattention and hyperactivity (Klingberg, et al., 2005). However, research still needs to be conducted to examine the extent of transfer effects to other domains and the degree of effectiveness over time. In one study, children with ADHD were randomly assigned to play a working memory game in either a game or non-game training format. In the game condition the training was enhanced with game elements that included a story line, animation, goals and rewards, competition and identification with a game character. Those in the game group showed greater motivation, more time training, better training performance and better working memory (Prins, Dovis, Ponsioen, Brink & van der Oord, 2011).

Working memory training may also be helpful for adults. Training on visuo-spatial and verbal working memory using a game-based working memory training program (Cogmed QM), has been shown in a randomized placebo controlled test-retest study to improve working memory and to have positive transfer effects, such as sustained attention, and self-reports of cognitive functioning. This was true for both younger adults ages 20-30 and older adults aged 60-70 (Brehmer, Westerberg, & Backman, 2012).

Solutions and Recommendations

We have argued throughout this chapter that users of serious games differ along a number of dimensions. Another difference between players concerns the sensory, intellectual and learning difficulties typical of those with mental and physical disabilities. This has been seen most recently with Title II of the Americans with Disabilities Act in the United States in which public funded agency websites must allow qualified individuals with disabilities equal access to their programs, services or activities. Many people with disabilities use assistive technology that enables them to use computers. Some assistive technologies involve separate computer programs or devices, such as screen readers, text enlargement software, and computer programs that enable people to control the computer with their voice. Other assistive technologies are built into computer operating systems. For example, basic accessibility features in computer operating systems enable some people with poor vision to see computer displays by simply adjusting color schemes, contrast settings, and font sizes. Operating systems enable people with limited manual dexterity to move the mouse pointer using key strokes instead of a standard mouse. Many other types of assistive technologies are available, and more are still being developed.

Poorly designed websites can create unnecessary barriers for people with disabilities, just as poorly designed buildings prevent some people with disabilities from entering. Access problems often occur because website designers mistakenly assume that everyone sees and accesses webpages in the same way. This mistaken assumption can frustrate assistive technologies and their users. Although this act focuses on websites, it is equally important for serious games designers to think about and implement products that are accessible for a wide range of users. One of the more rewarding areas of serious game development is creating games that do just that. Many groups may be helped by serious games, including those with visual difficulties (Carvelho, Allison, Irving, and Herriot, 2008), intellectual disabilities (Falk, Band, & McLaughlin, 2003), autism spectrum disorder (Baker, 2000) and learning difficulties such as dyslexia (Schneider, Roth, & Ennemoser, 2000). We have already discussed how working memory training can improve sustained attention and cognitive control in children diagnosed with ADHD (Klingberg, et al., 2005). Other games have been developed to improve reading speed and comprehension and phonological awareness in those with reading disabilities such as dyslexia (Kast, Meyer, Vogeli, Gross, & Jancke, 2007).

Serious games have several advantages in this arena. First many children with special needs are uneasy in normal classroom environments. Serious games and virtual reality can provide interactive ways to model and reinforce positive behaviors and to help players learn to interact with the world in a safer and more controlled environment where challenges can be gradually introduced (Standen & Brown, 2005). For example, Blum-Dimaya, Reeve, Reeve & Hoch, (2010) found that autistic children benefited from learning how to play the game Guitar Hero II (IITM). The children learned to follow the rules and manipulate the controls. They were able to maintain attentional focus to play the game. Importantly, learning of the repertoire of skills generalize beyond the game played in training (Blum-Dimaya, Reeve, Reeve & Hoch, 2010).

One of the newest areas of technology development focuses on mobile apps that can used anywhere. These are particularly useful to increase the independence of those with sensory impairments and intellectual disabilities such as Down's syndrome. Brown, Mchugh, Standen, Evett, Sohland and Bettersby (2010) discussed the development of a mobile android based app for learners with disabilities such as Down's syndrome, that uses games to teach players to plan a route in the city and later follow it. "Route Mate" uses GPS technologies, text to speech and other functions that are already available in the mobile phones operating system. Training games on mobile devices that can be accessed as needed help those with such disorders apply learning to a real world context (Brown, McHugh, Standen,

Evett, Shopland & Battersby, 2011). Games can give those with special needs a playful environment in which to practice skills (Lannen, Brown & Powell, 2002). Virtual environments also give users concrete situations with which to interact and experiment in which they do not have to worry about actually suffering the consequences of embarrassment of failure.

FUTURE RESEARCH DIRECTIONS

As we close this chapter, we would be remiss if we did not mention that the individual differences we have mentioned above also apply to the teachers and trainers tasked with using these applications. Although there is less research on this issue, teachers and trainers exert a very strong influence over their trainees' or students' attitudes and motivation. Too often the decision to use a serious game is made without much consideration of the teacher or the trainer who is simply expected to implement the program. If the teacher or trainer is resistant to the use of the technology or to the change in curriculum then the students or trainees will be less likely to see it as having value.

Age and cohort differences also play a role for both players and teachers. Many current teachers and trainers were raised before technology use and gaming were wide-spread, so some older teachers may be at a disadvantage when introducing new serious games to their students. According to the National Center for Educational Statistics in 2000, only 23 percent of teachers felt prepared to use computers in their teaching and an additional 10 percent of teachers felt very prepared. This leaves 66% unprepared. Newer teachers felt much more prepared than older teachers. In the classroom, if a teacher is less comfortable with the technology and less motivated to play, then it will be more difficult for those students with less experience or motivation to fully engage in the game. These data are more than a decade old and more people are comfortable using computers, but there are still large differences in the adult population. Many teachers have seen educational fads come and go so they are understandably skeptical of those with high expectations of the potential of serious games. This is complicated by the fact that serious games in school settings are often designed as a pedagogical 'tack-on' without clear educational goals. This simply adds one more thing that the teacher or trainer needs to fit into an already busy classroom.

In summary, developers of serious games must take into consideration individual differences in the skills, experience and acceptance of new learning tools among teachers and trainers as well as their students. Before implementation of a new serious game is attempted, teachers and trainers need to be convinced that the serious game is effective, meets the course learning objectives and fits well into the available instructional time. Before introduction of the serious game there should be sufficient time for training and practice so that the teacher or trainer can feel confident in their own ability to use the game. Self-efficacy is just as important for the teacher who will model positive attitudes as it is for the students.

CONCLUSION

Serious games attempt to impart knowledge and skills using an entertaining game format. Serious games have been used as a means of engaging learners in content learning and increase learner-centered control and motivation. One of the most attractive features of serious games and educational technology more generally is the possibility of personalization, that is that the game is programmed to assess the individual learner's skills and knowledge in real time and present new activities and concepts that are challenging but achievable at the learner's own pace and level. In commercial game design this is called "rubber-banding", where the player's score is used to unlock a new set of more difficult challenges

(usually several levels). If this technique was applied to serious games then the learner's skills or knowledge would be matched with the right level of gameplay challenge and the introduction of more complex knowledge. To be an effective learning tool, individuals must also be motivated to play until they reach mastery. This is mediated by player characteristics which will lead to a higher or lower level of engagement with the technology.

Using techniques from the entertainment industry to create an exciting and enjoyable serious game that can motivate learners to play until they master the intended concepts seems to solve this problem. However, in contrast with players of commercial entertainment games, there is often no typical player of a serious game; players come in many ages, with different backgrounds and experiences. Some will be eager to play a new game and master it quickly while others will be more resistant, either because of a lack of interest in the content or the technology, negative past experiences or low self-efficacy. Those who are resistant to playing games, may also have poorer cognitive skills such as language, spatial skills or working memory. Although these skills can be developed with time, it may be much more difficult for a player with poorer cognitive skills to learn to play the game and understand the game environment. The more attention such players need to devote to playing the game, the less capacity they will have for learning.

The prior knowledge of gamers, both of games generally and their experience with particular games, clearly gives them an advantage in their ability to achieve mastery in a given time period (White, 2012a). This is doubly true of serious games, with their dual approach to educative content. As a result, considerations must be made, often in the form of well-designed tutorial systems, to ensure that all players can access the lessons in serious game content.

Diversity of ethnicity and gender are areas that should be considered, but it is also important to remember that developing separate games for males and females or those of different ethnicities may also have the effect of exacerbating stereotypes and maintaining them for the next generation. It might be better to do the work necessary to develop games with rich context that appeal to a broader variety of players. From a developer standpoint, having more complexity in the storyline or options during game play makes sense because it allows the game to be more appealing to a wider audience as well as increase game replayability.

Game developers should also be aware of developments in the cognitive and learning sciences and take advantage of the recent work on brain plasticity. However, they should be careful not to abandon learning strategies that have been shown to be effective for new ideas that have not yet been proven. The initial excitement about learning styles among some in the educational and serious game community is a good example of expectations that might have been too high given the level of peer-reviewed research at the time. The enthusiasm to implement brain training strategies in serious games may be another development that may lead to significant advances in learning but that enthusiasm should be tempered by the findings of rigorous research.

Although other chapters will focus on assessment, it is important to note that serious games must be carefully evaluated to determine if their learning objectives have been met. Many of the studies on serious games and digital games for learning have poor experimental rigor and cannot establish a strong impact on learning. For example, Connolly, Boyle, MacArthur, Hainey, & Boyle (2012) conducted a systematic review of the literature on computer games and serious games and found that of 7392 papers identified, only 129 papers contained empirical results. Of those 129 papers, 90 were rated high quality and only 34 of them related to serious games or games for learning. Therefore, a great deal of research is needed and those studies need to address indi-

vidual differences whenever possible. Only rarely in research studies are the players' gender, gaming experience, gaming self-efficacy and cognitive profiles taken into account. In addition, there are a variety of personality and motivational factors that should also be considered.

Game developers typically focus on what functions are required to make a game work and which features can be incorporated to make it fun and enjoyable (Malone, 1981). They are usually less interested in what people are learning unless it relates to the skills needed to play the game. Educators and education researchers, on the other hand, are well grounded in cognitive and developmental theories and in methodologies of learning but typically know little about what gaming features would interest and motivate their students. So in order to create an effective serious game, a balance must be found between learning, usability, and enjoyment (Blasko-Drabik, Smoker, & Murphy, 2010). Researchers must be practical with what can be done in a given time with a given budget. However, the practice of including interdisciplinary teams before and during game development and conducting iterative evaluations with revisions based on different stages of evaluation will ultimately create better serious games.

Video games for entertainment have only been around for approximately 50 years and the serious games industry is even younger. Serious games show tremendous potential as a tool for learning but there is still much to discover about how to make them effective. Established educational principles and pedagogy that have served teachers has a long standing tradition and we can use this as a basis for creating effective serious games. It is important that we remember that the learning outcomes should forever be at the forefront of the game while incorporating theory, content, and game design principles as well. Technology through serious games may open the door to a richer, more engaging, and deeper level of learning.

REFERENCES

Adams, E., & Dormans, J. (2012). *Game mechanics: Advanced game design*. Berkeley, CA: New Riders Games.

Baddeley, A. D., Allen, R. J., & Hitch, G. J. (2011). Binding in visual working memory: The role of the episodic buffer. *Neuropsychologia*, *49*(6), 1393–1400. doi:10.1016/j.neuropsychologia.2010.12.042 PMID:21256143.

Baker, M. J. (2000). Incorporating the thematic ritualistic behaviors of children with autism into games: Increasing social play interactions with siblings. *Journal of Positive Behavior Interventions*, *2*, 66–84. doi:10.1177/109830070000200201.

Bandura, A. (1997). *Self-efficacy: The exercise of control*. New York: W.H. Freeman.

Bandura, A. (2011). Self-deception: A paradox revisited. *The Behavioral and Brain Sciences*, *34*(1), 16–17. doi:10.1017/S0140525X10002499.

Barrett, L. F., Tugade, M. M., & Engle, R. W. (2004). Individual differences in working memory capacity and dual-process theories of the mind. *Psychological Bulletin*, *130*(4), 553–573. doi:10.1037/0033-2909.130.4.553 PMID:15250813.

Basak, C., Boot, W. R., Voss, M. W., & Kramer, A. F. (2008). Can training in a real-time strategy video game attenuate cognitive decline in older adults? *Psychology and Aging*, *23*(4), 765–777. doi:10.1037/a0013494 PMID:19140648.

Beilock, S. L., & DeCaro, M. S. (2007). From poor performance to success under stress: Working memory. *Journal of Experimental Psychology. Learning, Memory, and Cognition*, *33*(6), 983–998. doi:10.1037/0278-7393.33.6.983 PMID:17983308.

Blasko, D., Chadwick, C., & Bittner, B. (2013). *Do games reduce math stress? The influence of gender and game genre*. Unpublished.

Blasko, D., Holliday-Darr, K., Mace, D., & Blasko-Drabik, H. (2004). VIZ: The visualization assessment and training website. *Behavior Research Methods, Instruments, & Computers*, *36*(2), 256–260. doi:10.3758/BF03195571 PMID:15354691.

Blasko, D., Kazmerski, V., & Torgerson, C. (2004). COR V2: Teaching observational research with multimedia courseware. *Behavior Research Methods, Instruments, & Computers*, *36*(2), 250–255. doi:10.3758/BF03195570 PMID:15354690.

Blasko Drabik, H., Blasko, D., & Lum, H. (2013). Investigating the impact of self-efficacy in learning disaster strategies in an on-line serious game. In *Proceedings of the Human Factors and Ergonomic Society*. San Diego, CA: IEEE.

Blasko-Drabik, H., Smoker, T., & Murphy, C. (2010). An adventure in usability: Discovering usability where it was not expected. In J. Canon-Bowers, & C. Bowers (Eds.), *Serious Game Design and Development: Technologies for Training and Learning*. Hershey, PA: IGI Global. doi:10.4018/978-1-61520-739-8.ch003.

Blum-Dimaya, A., Reeve, S. A., Reeve, K. F., & Hoch, H. (2010). Teaching children with autism to play a video game using activity schedules and game-embedded simultaneous video modeling. *Education & Treatment of Children*, *33*(3), 351–370. doi:10.1353/etc.0.0103.

Bogost, I. (2007). *Persuasive games: The expressive power of videogames*. Cambridge, MA: MIT Press. Retrieved from http://books.google.com/books?id=GC7MD17YvJEC

Boyle, E., Connolly, T. M., & Hainey, T. (2011). The role of psychology in understanding the impact of computer games. *Entertainment Computing*, *2*(2), 69–74. doi:10.1016/j.entcom.2010.12.002.

Bransford, J. D., Brown, A. L., & Cocking, R. R. (Eds.). (2000). *How people learn: Brain, mind, experience, and school*. Washington, DC: National Academy Press.

Brehmer, Y., Westerberg, H., & Bäckman, L. (2012). Working-memory training in younger and older adults: Training gains, transfer, and maintenance. *Frontiers in Human Neuroscience, 6*(63), 1–7. doi: doi:10.3389/fnhum.2012.00063 PMID:22279433.

Brown, D., McHugh, D., Standen, P., Evett, L., Shopland, N., & Battersby, S. (2011). Designing location-based learning experiences for people with intellectual disabilities and additional sensory impairments. *Computers & Education, 56*(1), 11–20. doi:10.1016/j.compedu.2010.04.014.

Cadinu, M., Maass, A., Rosabianca, A., & Kiesner, J. (2005). Why do women underperform under stereotype threat? *Psychological Science, 16*(7), 572–578. doi:10.1111/j.0956-7976.2005.01577.x PMID:16008792.

Cantor, J., & Engle, R. W. (1993). Working-memory capacity as long-term memory activation: An individual-differences approach. *Journal of Experimental Learning. Memory & Cognition, 19*(5), 1101–1114. doi:10.1037/0278-7393.19.5.1101.

Carvelho, T., Allison, R. S., Irving, E. L., & Herriot, C. (2008). *Computer gaming for vision therapy.* Washington, DC: IEEE.

Ciavarro, C., Dobson, M., & Goodman, D. (2007). Alert Hockey: An endogenous learning game. *Loading. The Journal of the Canadian Games Studies Association, 1*(1).

Coffield, F., Moseley, D., Hall, E., & Ecclestone, K. (2004). *Learning styles and pedagogy in post-16 learning: A systematic and critical review.* Retrieved on February 13, 2013 from http://www.lsrc.ac.uk/publications/index.asp

Colzato, L. S., van den Wildenberg, W., Zmigrod, S., & Hommel, B. (2013). Action video gaming and cognitive control: Playing first person shooter games is associated with improvement in working memory but not action inhibition. *Psychological Research, 77*, 234–239. doi:10.1007/s00426-012-0415-2 PMID:22270615.

Connolly, T. M., Boyle, E. A., MacArthur, E., Hainey, T., & Boyle, J. M. (2012). A systematic literature review of empirical evidence on computer games and serious games. *Computers & Education, 59*(2), 661–686. doi:10.1016/j.compedu.2012.03.004.

Csikszentmihalyi, M. (1997). Flow and education. *NAMTA Journal, 22*, 2–35.

Dickerman, C., Christensen, J., & Kerl-McClain, S. (2008). Big breasts and bad guys: Depictions of gender and race in video games. *Journal of Creativity in Mental Health, 3*(1), 20–29. doi:10.1080/15401380801995076.

Downs, E., & Smith, S. L. (2010). Keeping abreast of hypersexuality: A video game character content analysis. *Sex Roles, 62*, 721–733. doi:10.1007/s11199-009-9637-1.

Duff, S. C., & Logie, L. H. (2001). Processing and storage in working memory span. *The Quarterly Journal of Experimental Psychology. A, Human Experimental Psychology, 54*(1), 31–48. doi:10.1080/02724980042000011 PMID:11216320.

Dweck, C. S. (1986). Motivational processes affecting learning. *The American Psychologist, 41*(10), 1040–1048. doi:10.1037/0003-066X.41.10.1040.

Dweck, C. S., & Master, A. (2008). *Self-theories motivate self-regulated learning.* Mahwah, NJ: Lawrence Erlbaum Associates Publishers.

Engle, R. W., & Kane, M. J. (2004). Executive attention, working memory capacity, and a two-factor theory of cognitive control. In *The psychology of learning and motivation.* New York: Elsevier.

Falk, M., Band, M., & McLaughlin, T. F. (2003). The effects of reading racetracks and flashcards on sight word vocabulary of three third grade students with a specific learning disability: A further replication and analysis. *International Journal of Special Education, 18*(2), 51–57.

Felder, R. M., & Silverman, L. K. (1988). Learning and teaching styles in engineering education. *English Education*, 78(7), 674–681.

Feng, J., Spence, I., & Pratt, J. (2007). Playing an action video game reduces gender differences in spatial cognition. *Association for Psychological Science*, 18(10), 850–855. doi:10.1111/j.1467-9280.2007.01990.x PMID:17894600.

Garcia, L., Nussbaum, M., & Preiss, D. D. (2011). Is the use of information and communication technology related to performance in working memory tasks? Evidence from seventh-grade students. *Computers & Education*, 57(3), 2068–2076. doi:10.1016/j.compedu.2011.05.009.

Gee, J. P. (2003). *What video games have to teach us about learning and literacy*. New York: Palgrave/Macmillan. doi:10.1145/950566.950595.

Hamlen, K. R. (2001). Re-examining gender differences in video game play: Time spent and feelings of success. *Journal of Educational Computing Research*, 43(3), 293–308. doi:10.2190/EC.43.3.b.

Heeter, C., Lee, Y., Magerko, B., & Medler, B. (2011). Impacts of forced serious game play on vulnerable subgroups. *International Journal of Gaming and Computer-Mediated Simulations*, 3(3), 34–53. doi:10.4018/jgcms.2011070103.

Hertzog, C., Kramer, A. F., Wilson, R. S., & Lindenberger, U. (2008). Enrichment effects on adult cognitive development: Can the functional capacity of older adults be preserved and enhanced? *Psychological Science in the Public Interest*, 9(2), 1–65. doi: doi:10.1111/j.1539-6053.2009.01034.x.

Honey, P., & Mumford, A. (1992). *The manual of learning styles*. Berkshire, UK: Honey, Ardingly House.

Hussain, T. S., Bowers, C., Blasko-Drabik, H., & Blair, L. (2013). Validating cognitive readiness on team performance following individual game-based training. In H. F. O'Neil, R. S. Perez, & E. L. Baker (Eds.), *Teaching and measuring cognitive readiness*. New York: Springer.

Jackson, L. A., Zhao, Y., Kolenic, A., Fitzgerald, H. E., Harold, R., & Von Eye, A. (2008). Race, gender, and information technology use: The new digital divide. *Cyberpsychology & Behavior*, 11(4), 437–442. doi:10.1089/cpb.2007.0157 PMID:18721092.

Jenson, J., & De Castell, S. (2008). Theorizing gender and digital gameplay: Oversights, accidents and surprises. *Journal for Computer Game Culture*, 2(1), 15–25.

Jenson, J., Fisher, S., & De Castell, S. (2011). Disrupting the gender order: Leveling up and claiming space in an after-school video game club. *International Journal of Gender, Science and Technology, 3*(1).

Johnson, W. L., Vilhjalmsson, H., & Marsella, S. (2005). Serious games for language learning: How much game, how much AI? In C.-K. Looi, G. McCalla, B. Bredeweg, & J. Breuker (Eds.), *Artificial Intelligence in Education: Supporting Learning through Intelligent and Socially Informed Technology* (pp. 306–313). Amsterdam: IOS Press.

Kast, M., Meyer, M., Vogeli, C., Gross, M., & Jancke, L. (2007). Computer-based multisensory learning in children with developmental dyslexia. *Restorative Neurology and Neuroscience*, 25(3–4), 355–369. PMID:17943011.

Kazmerski, V., Blasko, D., & Dessalegn, B. (2003). ERP and behavioral evidence of individual differences in metaphor comprehension. *Memory & Cognition, 31*(5), 673–689. doi:10.3758/BF03196107 PMID:12956233.

Klauer, K. C., Stgmaier, R., & Meiser, T. (1997). Working memory involvement in propositional and spatial reasoning. *Thinking & Reasoning, 3*(1), 9–47. doi:10.1080/135467897394419.

Klingberg, T., Fernell, E., Olesen, P. J., Johnson, M., Gustafsson, P., & Dahlström, K. et al. (2005). Computerized training of working memory in children with ADHD--A randomized, controlled trial. *Journal of the American Academy of Child and Adolescent Psychiatry, 44*(2), 177–186. doi:10.1097/00004583-200502000-00010 PMID:15689731.

Lannen, T., Brown, D., & Powell, H. (2002). Control of virtual environments for young people with learning difficulties. *Disability and Rehabilitation, 24*(11-12), 578–578. doi:10.1080/09638280110111342 PMID:12182797.

Lee, M. J., & Tedder, M. C. (2003). The effects of three different computer texts on readers' recall: Based on working memory capacity. *Computers in Human Behavior, 19*(6), 767–783. doi:10.1016/S0747-5632(03)00008-6.

Lenhardt, A., Kahne, J., Middaugh, E., Macgill, A., Evans, C., & Vitak, J. (2008). Teens' gaming experiences are diverse and include significant social interaction and civic engagement. *Pew Internet & American Life Project*. Retrieved from: http://www.pewinternet.org/

Locke, E. A., & Latham, G. P. (1990). *A theory of goal setting & task performance*. Englewood Cliffs, NJ: Prentice-Hall, Inc.

Lustig, C., Shah, P., Seidler, R., & Reuter-Lorenz, P. (2009). Aging, training, and the brain: A review and future directions. *Neuropsychology Review, 19*(4), 504–522. doi:10.1007/s11065-009-9119-9 PMID:19876740.

Malone, T. W. (1981). What makes computer games fun? *Byte, 6*(12), 258–277.

Malone, T. W., & Lepper, M. R. (1987). Making learning fun: A taxonomy of intrinsic motivations for learning. In R. E. Snow & M. J. Farr (Eds.), Aptitude, learning, and instruction: Vol. 3: Conative and affective process analyses (pp. 223-253). Hillsdale, NJ: Lawrence Erlbaum.

Mayer, R. E. (Ed.). (2005). *Cambridge handbook of multimedia learning*. New York: Cambridge University Press. doi:10.1017/CBO9780511816819.

Miller, D. J., & Robertson, D. P. (2011). Educational benefits of using game consoles in a primary classroom: A randomised controlled trial. *British Journal of Educational Technology, 42*, 850–864. doi:10.1111/j.1467-8535.2010.01114.x.

Moffat, S., Hampson, S., & Hatzipantelis, M. (1998). Navigation in a virtual maze: Sex differences and correlation with psychometric measures of spatial ability in humans. *Evolution and Human Behavior, 19*(2), 73–87. doi:10.1016/S1090-5138(97)00104-9.

National Science Board. (2010). *Preparing the next generation of STEM innovators: Identifying and developing our nations' human capital*. Retrieved from http://www.nsf.gov/nsb/publications/2010/nsb1033.pdf

Norman, D. A. (1988). *The design of everyday things*. New York: Doubleday.

Norman, D. A. (1999). Affordances, conventions, and design. *Interaction, 6*(3), 38–41. doi:10.1145/301153.301168.

Nouchi, R., Taki, Y., Takeuchi, H., Hashizume, H., Nozawa, T., & Kambara, T. et al. (2013). Brain training game boosts executive functions, working memory and processing speed in the young adults: A randomized controlled trial. *PLoS ONE, 8*(2), 1–13. doi:10.1371/journal.pone.0055518 PMID:23405164.

Oh, S. H., & Kim, M. S. (2004). The role of spatial working memory in visual search efficiency. *Psychonomic Bulletin & Review, 11*(2), 275–281. doi:10.3758/BF03196570 PMID:15260193.

Ormrod, J. E. (2008). *Educational psychology: Developing learners* (6th ed.). Upper Saddle River, NJ: Pearson.

Pashler, H., McDaniel, M., Rohrer, D., & Bjork, R. (2008). Learning styles: Concepts and evidence. *Psychological Science in the Public Interest, 9*, 105–119. doi: doi:10.1111/j.1539-6053.2009.01038.x.

Prins, P. J. M., Dovis, S., Ponsioen, A., Brink, E. T., & van der Oord, S. (2011). Does a computerized working memory training with game elements enhance motivation and training performance in boys with ADHD? *Cyberpsychology. Behavior & Social Networking, 14*, 115–122. doi:10.1089/cyber.2009.0206.

Ricks, T. R., Turley-Ames, K. J., & Wiley, J. (2007). Effects of working memory capacity on mental set due to domain knowledge. *Memory & Cognition, 35*(6), 1456–1462. doi:10.3758/BF03193615 PMID:18035641.

Ruiz, S., York, A., Stein, M., Keating, N., & Santiago, K. (2009). *Darfur is dying*. Retrieved from http://www.darfurisdying.com/

Saucier, D., Bowman, M., & Elias, L. (2003). Sex differences in the effect of articulatory or spatial dual-task interference during navigation. *Brain and Cognition, 53*(2), 346–350. doi:10.1016/S0278-2626(03)00140-4 PMID:14607178.

Schneider, W., Roth, E., & Ennemoser, M. (2000). Training phonological skills and letter knowledge in children at risk for dyslexia: A comparison of three kindergarten intervention programs. *Journal of Educational Psychology, 92*, 284–295. doi:10.1037/0022-0663.92.2.284.

Standen, P., & Brown, D. (2005). Virtual reality in the rehabilitation of people with intellectual disabilities [Review]. *Cyberpsychology & Behavior, 8*(3), 272–282. doi:10.1089/cpb.2005.8.272 PMID:15971976.

Terlecki, M., Brown, J., Harner-Steciw, L., Irvin-Hannum, J., Marchetto-Ryan, N., Ruhl, L., & Wiggins, J. (2011). Sex differences and similarities in video game experience, preferences, and self-efficacy: Implications for the gaming industry. *Current Psychology (New Brunswick, N.J.), 30*(1), 22–33. doi:10.1007/s12144-010-9095-5.

Terlecki, M., & Newcombe, N. (2005). How important is the digital divide? The relation of computer and videogame usage to gender differences in mental rotation ability. *Sex Roles, 53*(5/6), 433–441. doi:10.1007/s11199-005-6765-0.

Toms, M., Morris, N., & Ward, D. (1993). Working memory and conditional reasoning. *The Quarterly Journal of Experimental Psychology Section A, 46*(4), 679–699. doi:10.1080/14640749308401033.

U.S. Department of Education, National Center for Education Statistics. (2000). *Internet access in U.S. public schools and classrooms: 1994–99*. Washington, DC: NCES.

Veurink, N. L., Hamlin, A. J., Kampe, J. C., Sorby, S. A., Blasko, D. G., & Holliday-Darr, K. A. et al. (2009). Enhancing visualization skills-improving options and success (EnViSIONS). *Engineering Design Graphics Journal, 73*(2), 1–17.

Vos, N., van Der Meijden, H., & Denessen, E. (2011). Effects of constructing versus playing an educational game on student motivation and deep learning strategy use. *Computers & Education, 56*(1), 127–137. doi:10.1016/j.compedu.2010.08.013.

Voyer, D., Voyer, S., & Bryden, M. P. (1995). Magnitude of sex differences in spatial abilities: A meta-analysis and consideration of critical variables. *Psychological Bulletin, 117*(3), 250–270. doi:10.1037/0033-2909.117.2.250 PMID:7724690.

White, M. (2008). *Level 10 human student: The effects of non-curricular role-playing game use on academic achievement and self-efficacy.* (Master's Thesis). University of New Brunswick, Fredericton, Canada.

White, M. (2009). The senescence of creativity: How market forces are killing digital games. *Loading, 3*(4), 1–20.

White, M. (2012a). *New tutorials for digital games: Game design meets instructional design.* (Ph.D. Dissertation). Memorial University of Newfoundland, St. John's, Canada.

White, M. (2012b). Designing tutorial modalities and strategies for digital games: Lessons from education. *International Journal of Game-Based Learning, 2*(2), 13–34. doi:10.4018/ijgbl.2012040102.

Williams, D., Martins, N., Consalvo, M., & Ivory, J. D. (2009). The virtual census: Representations of gender, race and age in video games. *New Media & Society, 11*(5), 815–834. doi:10.1177/1461444809105354.

ADDITIONAL READING

Akilli, G. (2007). Games and simulations: A new approach in education. In C. Aldrich, M. Prensky, & G. Gibson (Eds.), *Games and Simulations in Online Learning.* IGI Global. doi:10.4018/978-1-59904-941-0.ch078.

Becker, K. (2008). *The invention of good games: Understanding learning design in commercial video games.* (Ph.D. Dissertation). University of Calgary, Calgary, Alberta, Canada.

Bergstrom, K., Jenson, J., & De Castell, S. (2012). What's choice got to do with it?: avatar selection differences between novice and expert players of World of Warcraft and Rift. In *Proceedings of the International Conference on the Foundations of Digital Games, 97*–104. New York, NY, USA: ACM. doi:10.1145/2282338.2282360

Burton, J., Moore, D., & Magliaro, S. (1996). Behaviourism and instructional technology. In D. H. Jonassen (Ed.), *Handbook for research for educational communications and technology.* New York: Simon & Schuster MacMillan.

Graham, L. T., & Gosling, S. D. (2012). Impressions of World of Warcraft players' personalities based on their usernames: consensual but not accurate. *Journal of Research in Personality, 46,* 599–603. doi:10.1016/j.jrp.2012.05.002.

Graham, L. T., Sandy, C. J., & Gosling, S. D. (2011) Manifestations of personality in physical and virtual environments. In Chamorro-Premuzic T, Fumham A, von Stumm S, eds. Handbook of individual differences. Oxford: Whiley-Blackwell, pp. 773–800.

Ko, H., Roberts, M. S., & Cho, C. H. (2006). Cross-cultural differences in motivations and perceived interactivity: a comparative study of American and Korean Internet users. *Journal of Current Issues and Research in Advertising, 28,* 93–104. doi:10.1080/10641734.2006.10505201.

Lajoie, S. P. (2005). Extending the Scaffolding Metaphor. *Instructional Science, 33,* 541–557. doi:10.1007/s11251-005-1279-2.

Maltin, M. (1993). *The Psychology of Women.* Orlando, Fl: Holt, Rinehart & Winston, Inc.

Matthews, G., Davies, D. R., Westerman, S. J., & Stammers, R. B. (2000). Human Performance: Cognition, stress, and individual differences. Philadelphia, PA, Psychology Press, a Taylor & Francis Company.

McArthur, V., Peyton, T., Jenson, J., Taylor, N., & De Castell, S. (2012). Knowing, not doing: modalities of gameplay expertise in world of warcraft addons. In CHI '12 Extended Abstracts on Human Factors in Computing Systems (pp. 101–110). New York, NY, USA: ACM. doi: doi:10.1145/2212776.2212788.

Park, J., Song, Y., & Teng, C. I. (2011). Exploring the links between personality traits and motivations to play online games. *Cyberpsychology, Behavior, and Social Networks*, *14*, 747–751. doi:10.1089/cyber.2010.0502 PMID:21780935.

Ryan, R. M., & Deci, E. L. (2000). Intrinsic and extrinsic motivations: classic definitions and new directions. *Contemporary Educational Psychology*, *25*, 54–67. doi:10.1006/ceps.1999.1020 PMID:10620381.

Shelton, B. E., Satwicz, T., & Caswell, T. (2011). Historical Perspectives on Games and Education from the Learning Sciences. *International Journal of Game-Based Learning*, *1*, 83–106. doi:10.4018/ijgbl.2011070106.

Turner, M. L., & Engel, R. W. (1989). Is working memory capacity task dependent? *Journal of Memory and Language*, *28*, 127–154. doi:10.1016/0749-596X(89)90040-5.

White, M. M. (2011). Designing tutorial modalities and strategies for digital games: Lessons from education. *International Journal of Game-Based Learning*, *2*(2), 13–34. doi:10.4018/ijgbl.2012040102.

Whiton, N. (2011). Theories of Motivation for Adults Learning with Games. In *Improving Learning and Motivation through Educational Games: Multidisciplinary Approaches* (pp. 353–369). IGI Global. doi:10.4018/978-1-60960-495-0.ch017.

Yee, N. (2006). Motivations for play in online games. *Cyberpsychology & Behavior*, *9*, 772–775. doi:10.1089/cpb.2006.9.772 PMID:17201605.

Yee, N. The demographics, motivations, and derived experiences of users of massively-multiuser online graphical environments. *Presence (Cambridge, Mass.)*, *15*, 309–329. doi:10.1162/pres.15.3.309.

Yee, N., Ducheneaut, N., Nelson, L., & Likarish, P. (2011). Introverted elves and conscientious gnomes: the expression of personality in World of Warcraft. In *Proceedings of Conference on Human Factors in Computing Systems*, 753–762.

KEY TERMS AND DEFINITIONS

Extrinsic Motivation: The type of external motivation in which an individual is driven by outside reward to complete a task.

Individual Differences: The study of how individuals differ in their cognition, behavior, and actions.

Intrinsic Motivation: The type of internal motivation in which an individual is driven by pleasure or interest to complete a task.

Learner Self-Efficacy: The extent to which an individual feels that he or she has the background and skills to master a new set of learning objectives.

Spatial Ability: The ability to perceive the construction of an object.

Video Game Self-Efficacy: The extent to which an individual feels confident that they can play any video game successfully.

Working Memory: This is the component of short-term memory concerned with the temporary storage and manipulation of information necessary to complete a task.

Chapter 9
Rhetoric of Play:
Utilizing the Gamer Factor in Selecting and Training Employees

Ben Tran
Alliant International University, USA

ABSTRACT

Understanding the psychology of the gamer is important not just in studying video game players but also for understanding behaviors and characteristics of individuals who are non-players of video games. Currently, there is a gap in literature concerning the utilization of the gamer in selecting and training potential and current employees in organizational settings. The benefits of utilizing the gamer factor in selecting and training potential employees are: 1) identifying a qualified candidate who is a good fit to the organizational needs and 2) achieving and maintaining competitive advantage over competitors. Organizations are encouraged to utilize the Enneagram of Personality and Emotional Intelligence measures to identify gamers' other characteristics (O) and utilize the Tavistock method to assess gamers' factors. The Tavistock approach has been utilized in various formats including the Apprentice.

INTRODUCTION

Although player motivation is one of the main concerns of computer gaming, research so far has been able to identify only a limited set of motives, which are not founded on formal theories of human motivation. Human motivation is relevant in games because video games provide an extraordinary kind of intimacy with machines in interactive and rule-governed micro-worlds, where players enter into a virtual environment of infinite possibilities, experiencing altered states of consciousness and becoming absorbed in what is happening onscreen (Turkle, 1984).

These virtual environments, which are complex, emergent systems of uncertainty, information and conflict, are governed by the concept of play that refers to a range of activities accompanied by a state of pleasure and enjoyment. Sutton-Smith's (1997) seven rhetorics of play - progress, fate, power, identity, the imaginary, the self, and the frivolous - define the specific forms and uses of play embedded in our everyday lives.

A computer game can embody more than one rhetoric, but play as a form of conflict and contest (power), a means of expressing an identity and belonging to a group (identity), as imagination and creativity (the imaginary), and a means of relaxation and escape (the self), are the most

DOI: 10.4018/978-1-4666-4773-2.ch009

Copyright © 2014, IGI Global. Copying or distributing in print or electronic forms without written permission of IGI Global is prohibited.

common forms experienced in computer games. Regardless of the embedded play rhetoric, one of the primary concerns of industrial and organizational practitioners is the utilization of the gamer as a factor in selecting employees, and training employees in an organizational setting. Understanding the psychology of the gamer is important not just in studying video game players but also for understanding behaviors and characteristics of non-player characters (NPCs). As an industrial and organizational practitioner and researcher, it appears that currently there is still a gap in the literature concerning both the understanding of these psychological factors and the utilization of psychological factors of the gamer in selecting and training potential and current employees in organizational settings.

This gap in the literature is due to three reasons. First, in the field of psychology, the American Psychological Association (APA) has 56 divisions[1], but none of these addresses this topic and area of study. Second, this topic and area of study is not in the area of business (management or human resources), because both the research (academic) and the practice (practitioners) of business is not clinically-based. Third, more often than not, industrial and organizational (I/O) practitioners [for the business arena (also known as industrial and organizational psychologists for the non-business arena)] are the group of individuals who will, more likely than not, study and utilize this area in assessment. However, it does not mean that it is a common practice for I/O practitioners to adopt this methodology and I/O researchers to select this route of research.

Customarily, I/O practitioners are only able to make suggestions and recommendations to firms regarding best practices and most reliable implementations, but it does not mean that firms will accept or even utilize feedback from I/O practitioners. I/O psychologists on the other hand, frequently conduct (academic) research on topics and issues that are not only relevant, but the most current, in relation to concerns of society.

This is often reflected in doctoral research topics, academic research and publications, and tenure for faculty. On the other hand, there are video game and gaming magazines, newsgroups, blogs, and conventions, but not academic video gaming journals or gaming journals per se whose audiences are academic researchers or professional business practitioners. Due to these limitations and barriers, it often results in a lack of current research, as well as updated research data with regards to this topic and area of study in relation to selecting and training employees.

THE GAMER IN VIDEO GAMES

Concern about possible negative effects of violent video games has been accompanied by an increase in research, as is evident from meta-analyses identifying dozens of existing research reports, published over a period of more than twenty years, investigating the relationship between video games and aggression (Anderson, 2004; Anderson & Bushman, 2001; Bartholow & Anderson, 2002; Ivory & Kalyanaraman, 2007; Sherry, 2001). Some scholars claim that enough evidence exists to conclusively link violent video games to real-life aggression (Bushman & Anderson, 2002), but others maintain that there is not sufficient evidence to either support or to oppose this claim to establish a causal link between violent video game play and player aggression (Griffiths, 1999; Scott, 1995; Williams & Skoric, 2005). As such, one major issue frustrating reconciliation of the clouded body of research on violent video game play is the vast advancement in video game technology that has occurred over the years. Researchers agree that video games are advancing and changing rapidly[2] (Calvert & Tan, 1994; Sherry, 2001; Tamborini, Eastin, Skalski, Lachlan, Fediuk, & Brady, 2004) and that new games provide increasingly realistic play (Carnagey & Anderson, 2004; Gentile & Anderson, 2003). Scholars have also speculated that such advances in game technology may precipitate more dramatic negative effects[3].

The first explanation and the most frequently cited mechanism by which the games can result in aggressive behavior is social learning theory (Alman, 1992; Brusa, 1988; Chambers & Ascione, 1987; Graybill, Krisch, & Esselman, 1985; Hoffman, 1995; Irwin & Gross, 1995; Schutte, Malouff, Post-Gordon, & Rodasta, 1988; Silvern, Lang, & Williamson, 1987; Winkel, Novak, & Hopson, 1987). Social learning theory (SLT) posits that behavior is learned through imitation of attractive, rewarded models (Bandura, 1994). These behaviors can become a relatively enduring part of the learner's behavioral repertoire. Proponents of SLT for video games argue that video games should have particularly powerful effects due to the high attention levels of players and the active identification of players with characters on the screen. Some video game researchers also argue that game players are rewarded directly for enacting symbolic violence, and therefore may transfer the learned aggression to the outside world.

The second explanation offered for effects of violent video games is the general arousal model (Ballard & Wiest, 1995; Brusa, 1987; Calvert & Tan, 1994; Winkel, Novak, & Hopson, 1987). Tannenbaum and Zillmann's elementary arousal model (1975) holds that arousal is a heightened, nonspecific drive state. As such, the media and its methods of communication will heighten the already present response an individual has, emotional behaviors, and licit reaction of arousal. That is, "presented with a need or opportunity to respond in some manner to a particular environmental situation, the individual will do as he would ordinarily—but with increased energy and intensity due to the available residual arousal" (Tannenbaum & Zillmann, 1975: 161). Supporters of the arousal model for video games suggest that very violent video games provide the arousal that is necessary to heighten aggressive responses.

The third explanation is derived from several studies, which state that the neo-associative networks or priming effects mechanism, as an explanation of hypothesized effects of video games on aggression (Anderson & Ford, 1986; Anderson & Morrow, 1995; Hoffman, 1995). Berkowitz's priming effects theory of media influence posits that cues from violent content may lead to aggression or hostility due to the priming of semantically related informational nodes (Berkowitz & Rogers, 1986). In the case of video games, priming effects theory would suggest that exposure to violent games will prime a series of nodes associated with violence and aggression. The priming of these violence-related nodes presents the opportunity for transfer of aggressive thoughts into action (Jo & Berkowitz, 1994).

The fourth explanation proposed a mechanism that posits that violent-content video games will have a positive effect on users. Seven of the located studies have addressed the issue of the catharsis effects, in which violent content media are used as a safe outlet for aggressive thoughts and feelings (Calvert & Tan, 1994; Dominick, 1984; Graybill, Kirsch, & Esselman, 1985; Graybill, Strawniak, Hunter, & O'Leary, 1987; Kestenbaum & Weinstein, 1985; Silvern, Lang, & Williamson, 1987; Silvern & Williamson, 1987). This theory, originally proposed by Feshbach (1955), holds that individuals can discharge their aggressive feelings by watching a fictional portrayal of violence in the media. The authors argue that the interactive nature of the games allows players to act out aggression that is not allowed in the real world.

Detailed analysis of the conceptual components of player motivation focuses on matching each psychological need to common gaming situations in computer role-playing games (RPGs). Since this game genre provides interactive virtual environments capable of offering experience analogous to real life, it is highly relevant to motivational studies. The relationship between motivational factors and gaming situations is discussed with examples from recently released RPGs, which takes place in a fantasy world full of social issues and conflicts, where players usually find themselves in situations that require a choice between the lesser of two evils. This is not surprising given the Western cultural belief that people are responsible for their own behavior and that behavior is internally caused (Bartholow & Anderson, 2002; Dix, 1993).

Enjoyment for the Gamer

Enjoyment is defined as a complex construct with physiological, affective, and cognitive dimensions, and is the core of entertainment media (Vorderer, Klimmt, & Ritterfeld, 2004). Two important theories about individual motivations for using entertainment products for enjoyment are the mood management theory (Zillmann, 1988a, 1988b) and affective disposition theory (Zillmann, 1994, 1996). The hedonism hypothesis of the first theory assumes that people are more motivated toward experiences that maximize pleasant situations and moods. The second theory explains the process of emotional involvement and motivation of users in relation to the characters offered by such media.

Since both theories assume the user to be a passive witness of ongoing events, it is difficult to apply them to interactive and immersive forms of entertainment such as video game-playing. To understand the quality that differentiates computer games from other motivating experiences, it should be useful to examine the study of Pine and Gilmore (1999), who categorized different types of experiences on the basis of two dimensions: participation and connection. Participation is either active or passive. Connection, on the other hand, comes in two forms, absorption (attention direction) and immersion. Game players are not simply directing their attention but are physically or mentally becoming part of the gaming experience itself through active participation. Thus, according to this categorization, video games can be classified as escapist experiences where active participation and immersion play a central role.

Psychological Appeal for the Gamer

The psychological appeal of the escapist experiences derived from video games has been a popular subject for discussion among scholars, but most studies on player motivations so far either focus on the motivational aspects of games from an educational perspective (Gee, 2003, 2005; Loftus & Loftus, 1983; Prensky, 2001, 2002; Provenzo, 1991; Stewart, 1997) or are concerned with the negative effects of video games and violence in video games (Anderson, 2004; Anderson & Bushman, 2001; Anderson & Ford, 1986; Cooper & Mackie, 1996; Gentile, Lynch, Linder, & Walsh, 2004; Sherry, 2001). There have been attempts to define the underlying motives of players, but these studies identify motives that are not based on the fundamental components of human motivation. As such, two major studies that influenced researchers are the intrinsic motivations taxonomy of Malone and Lepper (1987) and the flow framework of Csikszentmihalyi (1990). Although their taxonomy was not specifically developed for computer games, Malone and Lepper analyzed intrinsic motivations for learning, and defined the individual and interpersonal components of motivation.

According to Malone and Lepper (Malone & Lepper, 1987), the elements to enhance intrinsic motivation are individually balanced between skills and challenges, goals whose attainment may be uncertain, and presenting surprises or attracting users' attention to stimulate their curiosity. Malone and Lepper, according to Medina (2005), also consider three rules to provide control for the learner: contingency, choice, and power. Finally, Malone and Lepper proposed to create fantasy situations to encourage learners to imagine themselves in imaginary contexts or events using vivid realistic images. Malone and Lepper defined an activity as being intrinsically motivating if people engage in it for its own sake, rather than in order to receive some external reward or avoid some external punishment (Malone & Lepper, 1987).

The studies of Malone and Lepper, which were done in 1980s, are deemed to be very influential studies in the field. The importance of Malone and Lepper's study is that it revealed and explained the four most important elements to create enjoyable computer games, and these four elements are of individual intrinsic motivation: challenge, curiosity, controls, and fantasy. Before Malone, very little was known, about how to provide enjoyment with technology (Kong, Ogata, Arnseth, Chan, Hirashima, Klett, Lee, Liu, Looi, Milrad, Mitrovic, Nakabayashi, Wong, & Yang, 2009). Csikszentmihalyi, on the other hand, studied states of optimal experience, focusing on deep enjoyment.

Csikszentmihalyi's investigation revealed that what makes experience genuinely satisfying is a state of consciousness called flow—a state of concentration so focused that it amounts to absolute absorption in an activity (Csikszentmihalyi, 1990). *Flow: The Psychology of Optimal Experience* described how this pleasurable state can be controlled, and not just left to chance, by setting ourselves challenges. Optimal experiences are reported to occur within sequences of activities that are goal-directed and bounded by rules - activities that require the investment of psychic energy and that could not be done without skills. For those who do not have the right skills, an activity is not challenging. Challenges of competition were found to be stimulating and enjoyable only when it is a means to perfect one's skills. *Flow* has five characteristics: clarity, centering, choice, commitment, and challenge.

Csikszentmihalyi's flow framework was applied to computer games by Sweetser and Wyeth (2005) who defined a model for evaluating player enjoyment. Another framework for positive and negative motivational factors in gameplay was defined by Kellar, Watters, and Duffy (2005), three essential motivational needs in video games were identified by Ryan, Rigby, and Przybylski (2006), and ten motivations for play in online games have been grouped into three factors by Yee (2006a).

The four gaming motivations (control, context, competency, and engagement)[4] defined by Kellar et al. (2005) and the three motivational factors (autonomy[5], competence, and relatedness) defined by Ryan et al. (2006) can be considered a subset of the union of variables identified by Malone and Lepper (1987) and Yee (2006a). Discussing the specifics of each variable defined by these studies is beyond the scope of this chapter, but it would be beneficial to compare the three studies (Malone & Lepper, 1987; Sweetser & Wyeth, 2005; Yee, 2006a) that are capable of identifying a relatively large number of variables for analyzing player behavior.[6]

A Comparison of Three Motivational Studies: Different approaches to motivational aspects of player behavior when applied to computer games with different structures and content should obviously represent different facets of player psychology. The taxonomy of Malone and Lepper (1987) was originally designed for analyzing learning situations, and the game flow model of Sweetser and Wyeth (2005) was founded on the flow framework of Csikszentmihalyi (1990), which attempted to identify the attractiveness of an activity that urges people to repeatedly engage in it. The motivation model of Yee (2006a) is based on the play styles of Bartle (2004), which have never been empirically tested to validate that the model's four player types are independent of each other. Hence it is also important to note that player motivations measured by subjective means such as questionnaires also depends on the content and structure of a game.

Fundamentals of Human (Player) Behavior: Human behavior is geared to effecting change in the environment, and changes in the environment are possible through the attainment of goals or disengagement from unattainable goals, which are facilitated by coordination of perceptions, skills, activities, and emotions (Heckhausen & Heckhausen, 2005). Motivation to reach a goal is influenced by both personal and situational factors. Personal factors are a person's needs, motives and goals and situational factors are opportunities and possible incentives provided by the environment. According to Murray (1938), goal-directed human behavior can be explained by continuous interactions between individuals and their environments. Interactions between personal and situational factors trigger actions. Outcomes are the results of actions, and reinforcers or punishers, are consequences that arise from outcomes. This basic structure of human behavior is also applicable to game players who experience different gaming situations with different incentives, within a virtual world, and then decide on an action based on their motives, needs, and goals.

Reinforcers are stimuli that select appropriate behaviors and teach us what to do and punishers are stimuli that select against appropriate behaviors and teach us what not to do (Skinner, 1938, 1953; Staddon & Simmelhag, 1971). Incentives are external stimuli that motivate or induce desired behaviors (Bolles, 1975; Logan & Wanger, 1965). A positive incentive motivates behavior and a negative incentive motivates avoidance behavior. The strength or appeal of an incentive, as well as the distance to the incentive, are also important factors that affect goal-directed behaviors.

Lewin (1936) described this phenomenon as a psychological force, which is dependent on both the valence (strength) of the incentive and the psychological distance to the incentive. In computer games, the valence of incentives is usually reflected in the rewards the player receives. Short-term goals have more immediately achievable rewards and long-term goals provide the overall reward structure of the game. As the player progresses, the positive valence of objects or activities, also increases accordingly. Psychological distance to incentives is reduced with the introduction of discrete transportation techniques such as teleporting, which enables the player to traverse long distances quickly.

Psychological Needs as a Source of Motivation: Need represents a state of disequilibrium (lack of something) in an organism and orients the organism towards certain goals that will reduce needs. Studies on needs started with McDougall (1908), who attempted to define all human behavior, in terms of motivational disposition. He defined instincts, some of which are assigned to corresponding emotions, to describe human behavior directed towards a specific goal. Maslow (1968) defined groups of needs in a hierarchical order, according to their relevance in personality development. However, it was Henry Murray (1938) who formalized the study of needs. Jackson (1974) translated Murray's needs into personality traits and Singer (1990) demonstrated how these needs can be conceived as life-goals. According to Allen (1994), such high-level uses guarantee that Murray's interaction-oriented needs will remain in the mainstream of personality and psychology research for an indefinite period of time.

According to Murray (1938), needs are a major source of human motivation, which arise from the person-environment interactions. The goals pursued to satisfy these needs determine human motivation. Murray defined two sets of needs: viscerogenic and psychohenic. Viscerogenic needs are physiological in nature and are characterized by periodic body changes. Psychogenic needs are psychological in nature, concerned with a person's mental and emotional states. Two important factors that affect needs are strength and periodicity (Murray, 1981). A need may be considered strong if it occurs regularly under certain conditions: if it occurs occasionally with great intensity or if it is persistent for a long period of time. Periodicity refers to the active and inactive cycles of a need. Viscerogenic needs are quite prone to periodicity and psychogenic needs show a tendency toward periodicity.

In his study, Murray (1938) identified 27 psychogenic needs that affect goal-directed human behavior. In his article, in terms of literature about psychogenic needs, these needs are grouped into six categories, three of which are major motivations in literature. Thus, 1) materialistic needs[7] are associated with inanimate objects (Furby, 1978;

James, 1890), 2) power needs[8] represent the will to arouse strong emotions in other people, to be in charge, and to be noticed (Anderson & Berdahl, 2002; Kipnis, 1976; Winter, 1988, 1992), 3) affiliation needs[9] represent the motive to establish, maintain, or restore positive social relationships with others (Fishman, 1966; Mehrabian, 1970), 4) achievement needs[10] stand for the desire to achieve success and to overcome obstacles (Atkinson, 1957; Heckhausen, 1974; Mehrabian, 1969), 5) information needs[11] symbolize the instinct to gather and analyze information (Cacioppo & Petty, 1982; Cohen, Stotland, & Wolfe, 1955), and 6) sensual needs[12] represent the tendency towards exciting or gratifying experiences that satisfy or are attractive to the senses (Zuckerman, 1994). Murray (1938) defined each need with appropriate desires and effects, related feelings and emotions, relevant character traits and attitudes, matching actions and their relationships with other needs.

The Gamer in Business Games

In the field of business, for practitioners more so than researchers, business is often perceived as a game, and like a game, it possesses its own special rules for playing. While players normally do not tolerate deceit, in the game of poker, bluffing is not only acceptable but is expected. Similarly, lies of omission, overstatements, puffery and bluffs are morally acceptable within business because, like a game, it has a special ethic which permits these normally immoral practices (Carr, 1968). Although critics of this reasoning have used deontological and utilitarian arguments (Bowie, 1993) to show that deceit in business is just as immoral as it is in any other realm of human practice, little attention has been paid to the fact that the argument is one of analogy. This oversight is unfortunate, given the strong intuitive appeal Carr's argument has to both business persons and to commerce students (Koehn, 1997). As such, Koehn (1997) identified nine traits in gamers and game playing. [13]: 1) A game is played to win, 2) In games, losers suffer

few consequences, 3) A game is constituted by certain rules, 4) The rules of the game are fixed, 5) The rules of the game are accepted by all who played the game, 6) Players act intermittently, 7) In games the scope for bluffing is quite narrow and well-understood, 8) Players in a game risk only what is theirs to risk, and 9) In a game, it is clear to whom any gain belongs.

But if business managers are allowed to engage in such maneuvers, there is no reason why, qua gamesters, they cannot execute these strategies in such a way as to maximize their own personal gains. The firm may have been driven into the ground under this business management. But if corporate ethics are those of the game, the manager is a good player who has played exceptionally well, availing himself of every legal opportunity to haul in the biggest pot. The problem, of course, is that firms will find it close to impossible to exist if management ceases to consider the larger corporate interest but ponders only how to increase its own income and wealth.

The Gamer Factor in Selecting and Training Employees in Organizational Settings

Most past studies have compared video-game players (VGPs) to novice video-game players (NVGPs) using tasks that measure reaction time (RTs) in order to draw conclusions about performance. Although usually not the primary focus of these studies, they invariably show that the VGPs are faster overall than those who do not play such games (Bialystok, 2006; Castel, Pratt, & Drummond, 2005; Clark, Lanphear & Riddick, 1987; Greenfield, deWinstanley, Kilpatrick, & Kaye, 1994). On the other hand, according to Matthew, Dye, Green, and Bavelier (2009), one area that has received considerable attention is the effect of action video games on visual cognition. Video-game players have been reported to show improved hand-eye coordination, increased visual processing in the periphery, enhanced mental-rotation skills, greater divided attention, and enhanced visuospatial memory. A series of studies has established that playing action video games enhances performance on tasks thought to measure different aspects of visual attention, including the ability to: 1) distribute attention across space, 2) efficiently perform dual tasks, 3) track several moving objects at once, and 4) process streams of briefly presented visual stimuli (Green & Bavelier, 2003, 2007). One such study focusing on visuospatial skills has suggested that action-game playing may provide a reliable training regimen to reduce gender differences in visuospatial cognition (Feng, Spence, & Pratt, 2007).

According to Yee (2006b), every day millions of users interact, collaborate, and form relationships with each other through avatars in online environments known as Massively Multi-User Online Role-Playing Games (MMORPGs). But beyond exploring how MMORPGs can shape the identities of individuals, these highly social and structured environments also allow one to explore whether certain valuable skills learned in an MMORPG, can transfer to the material world. Personal advancement in MMORPGs typically involves collaboration among groups of users in an attempt to achieve a challenging task. Thus, a prime candidate for acquired skills is leadership skills.

In emergent groups within the MMORPG environment, leaders deal with both administrative as well as higher-level strategy issues, most of which arise and have to be dealt with spontaneously. Administrative tasks include: role assignment, task delegation, crisis management, logistical planning and how rewards are to be shared among group members. Higher-level strategy tasks include: motivating group members, dealing with negative attitudes, dealing with group conflicts, as well as encouraging group loyalty and cohesion. These issues are even more salient in long-term social groups, such as guilds, which have formalized membership and rank assignments. In other words, MMORPGs provide many opportunities for short-term and long-term leadership experiences.

This sentiment is shared by many users. In the survey study (Yee, 2006c), 10% of users felt they had learned a lot about mediating group conflicts, motivating team members, persuading others, and becoming a better leader in general, while 40% of users felt that they had learned a little of the mentioned skills. This is striking given that these environments are not structured pedagogically to teach leadership. Acquisition of leadership skills in these environments is in fact an emergent phenomenon. But more importantly, these findings demonstrate that real-life skills can be acquired or improved upon in these environments. Certainly, self-reported assessments are not robust assessments, but these findings lay out the foundation for more controlled studies of the acquisition of complex social skills in these environments.

Massively Multi-User Online Role-Playing Games (MMORPGs) Defined

The study of MMORPGs is highly relevant to research on social interaction in Shared Virtual Environments and avatars at work and play in these environments. Although many of the theoretical implications of social interaction in virtual environments have been explored in the artificial confines of Virtual Reality research laboratories (Bailenson & Blascovich, 2002; Leigh, DeFanti, Johnson, Brown, & Sandin, 1997; Mania & Chalmers, 1998; Normand, Babski, Benford, Bullock, Carion, Farcet, Frécon, Kuijpers, Magnenat-thalmann, Raupp-Musse, Rodden, Slater, Smith, Steed, Thalmann, Usoh, Liempd, Harvey, & Kladias, 1999; Slate, Sadagic, Usoh, & Schroeder, 2000; Zhang & Furnas, 2002), MMORPGs are the only existing naturalistic setting where millions of users voluntarily immerse themselves in a graphical virtual environment and interact with each other through avatars on a daily basis.

History of Massively Multiplayer Online Role-Playing Game

MMORPGs are a new class of Multi-User Domains (MUDs), online environments where multiple users can interact with each other and achieve structured goals. The first MUD, an adventure game in a persistent world that allowed multiple users to log on at the same time, was created in 1979 by Roy Trubshaw and Richard Bartle (Bartle, 1990). While it is commonly thought that MUDs descended from table-top-role-playing games (RPGs) such as Dungeons and Dragons, the two genres emerged around the same time and co-evolved beginning in the early 1970s (Koster, 2002), becoming popular during the 1980s. Both games allow users to create characters based on numerical attributes and template roles with different strengths and weaknesses.

Literature on MMORPGs

The academic interest in MUDs was almost entirely driven by qualitative scholars. Turkle (1995) articulated how these environments revealed the fluid and decentralized nature of identities. Others, such as Nakamura, Rodman and Kolko (2000) have challenged the utopian visions of cyberspace, arguing that online communities do not foster racial equality for example but merely make racial minorities easier to suppress. The behavioral sciences have kept their distance from these online environments. With regards to video gaming in general, the field of psychology seems fixed on whether video games cause real-life aggression (Anderson, & Bushman, 1997, 2001; Anderson & Dill, 2000; Ballard & Lineberger, 1999; Bushman & Anderson, 2002; Ferguson, 2002; Funk & Buchman, 1996; Funk, Hagan, Schimming, Bullock, Buchman, & Myers, 2002; Griffiths, 1999; Scott, 1995).

Academic attention in MMORPGs has largely been driven by economic and legal scholars. Castronova (2002) calculated the Gross National Product of the World of EverQuest by aggregating e-Bay sales of virtual items and currency, and has also shown that male avatars sell far more than female avatars of exactly the same capabilities (2003). Legal scholars (Lastowka & Hunter, 2004) have examined the ownership of virtual property and whether avatars have enforceable legal rights. Griffiths (2003) has also aggregated online poll data at websites catering to EverQuest players to provide the basic demographics and preferences of EverQuest players.

Selecting and Training Employees Based on Gamers

Generally speaking, organizations have well-established approaches to selecting, and training employees. However, one problem with current approaches is the absence of formal, standardized selection methods (Tran, 2008). Another problem is that the decision is often based on the direct supervisor and the host location rather than whether the candidate is a good fit to the job (Halcrow, 1999). Together these are known as the "good ol' boys" network (Davidson & Cooper, 1992; Burke & McKeen, 1994; Fagenson, 1986; Henning & Jardim, 1977; Ibarra, 1993; Kanter, 1977; Linehan & Scullion, 2001; Smith & Hutchinson, 1995). Generally, when no formal or standardized selection method is used, the company relies on past results derived from existing personnel selection processes. The "personnel selection processes" are the methods organizations use to evaluate potential employees' knowledge, skills, and abilities in order to determine whether there is a good fit between an available position and a candidate. These are the commonly used sets of criteria that identify successful domestic candidates; these sets of criteria are well-known and have been used for a long time but again, primarily for domestic candidates.

Knowledge, skills, and abilities will be referred to as KSAs, while the criteria including "other" attributes will be referred to as KSAOs:

1. Knowledge is usually defined as the degree to which a candidate is required to know certain technical material.
2. Skill indicates adequate performance on tasks requiring the use of tools, equipment, machinery, etc.
3. Abilities are physical and mental capacities to perform tasks not requiring the use of tools, equipment, or machinery.
4. Other characteristics include personality, interest, or motivational attributes that indicate a candidate will learn certain tasks, rather than whether they can do those tasks (Schneider & Schmitt, 1992: 53).

RECOMMENDATION

According to Tran (2008), KSAs are applicable to domestic needs, and identified factors for the other characteristics (O) are based on international needs. The "O" factor, however, is applicable to domestic needs as well if effectively identified, assessed, and utilized. There are two methodologies which could be useful in effectively identifying, assessing, and then utilizing the "O" factor. The first is the Enneagram of Personality and the second is Emotional Intelligence (EI).

The Enneagram of Personality

The Enneagram of Personality is usually known simply as the Enneagram. The Enneagram system describes nine distinct personality types and their interrelationships, mapped around an ancient symbol of perpetual motion (Palmer, 1988). The term "enneagram" derives from two Greek words, ennea (nine) and grammi (line). The meaning of the symbol itself, together with the personality types organized around the nine points, convey a system of knowledge about nine distinct but interrelated personality types, or nine ways of seeing and experiencing the world (Wagele & Baron, 1994). The Enneagram of Personality is generally presented as a psycho-spiritual system for mapping and understanding these nine possible personality types (Maitri, 2001). Although mostly understood and taught as a typology (a model of personality types) (Riso & Hudson, 1996), the Enneagram of Personality is also taught in ways intended to develop higher states of being, essence and enlightenment (Naranjo, 1997). Each personality type associated with the Enneagram represents a map of traits that highlights patterns of thinking, feeling, and behaving.

By learning one's type and the patterns and habits associated with that type, one can use the Enneagram system as an effective tool for self-understanding and self-development (Daniels & Price, 2000). Adherents of the theory believe that each Enneagram personality type, or style, is based on a pattern of where attention goes. They believe that by learning about what kinds of things one habitually attends to and one habitually puts energy into, one can observe oneself more accurately and develop more self-awareness. In so doing an individual can enhance their self-awareness, exercise more choice about their functioning rather than engaging in patterns of thought, emotion, and behavior in an automatic, habitual, unconscious way (Palmer, 1988).

Development: Gurdjieff, Ichazo, and Naranjo: The Enneagram symbol was first brought to the attention of the modern world by G. I. Gurdjieff, the originator of a school of spiritual work near Paris in the 1920s. Although Gurdjieff used the Enneagram diagram to describe possibilities of human development, his concept of the diagram was related to the symbolic communication of ancient knowledge and the "self-work" process through which individuals can acquire insight rather than to the categorizing of personality styles (Maitri, 2001; Palmer, 1988). Oscar Ichazo, on the other hand, assigned "personalities" descriptions to each of the nine positions on the Enneagram diagram he called the Enneagram of Ego Fixations, which was the origination the Enneagram of Personality as we know it today. The popular use of the

Enneagram of personality began principally with Claudio Naranjo who had studied with Ichazo in Chile but was asked to leave before the intensive 1971 training had finished. Ichazo considers Naranjo's understanding of the Enneagram to be limited and incomplete, although Naranjo's Enneagram teachings, and those of other Enneagram teachers, have been more influential in popularizing familiarity of the Enneagram figure than any available works by Ichazo.

Claudio Naranjo, however, a Chilean-born, American-trained psychiatrist who had explored theories of personality extensively, studied with Ichazo and took Ichazo's teaching and further developed it, articulating the nine types in Western psychological terms. Naranjo then brought his understanding of the Enneagram system to Berkeley in the early 1970s, where he taught it to students in the context of his own program of self-development work (Riso & Hudson, 1999). Based on material first taught by Claudio Naranjo, Helen Palmer, Don Riso, Russ Hudson, Patrick O'Leary, Richard Rohr, Elizabeth Wagele and others published the first widely-read books on the Enneagram in the late 1980s and early 1990s.

The Nine Types: According to Enneagram of Personality theory, the points of the enneagram figure indicate a number of ways in which nine principal ego-archetypal forms or types of human personality ("Enneatypes") are psychologically connected (Daniels & Price, 2000). People of each Enneatype are usually referred to depending on the number of the point on the enneagram figure (Eights, Fours, Sixes, etc.) that indicates their particular psychological space and 'place' of connection to the other types. They are also often given names that suggest some of their more distinctive archetypal characteristics (Baron, 1998). The nine Enneatypes are as follows [One (the perfectionist), Two (the giver), Three (the performer), Four (the tragic romantic), Five (the observer), Six (the devil's advocate), Seven (the epicure), Eight (the boss), Nine (the mediator)].

The Three Centers of Intelligence: The nine Enneagram types are grouped into three groups of three, corresponding to the three Centers of Intelligence, through which information is processed (head, heart, and body) and the three core emotions (fear, grief, and anger). In the West, the head is commonly considered the only Center of Intelligence, but the Enneagram highlights the importance of the emotions and the body as equally important centers of functioning and interacting with the outside world. According to the Enneagram system, each of the nine types is limited by an imbalance involving one of the three Centers of Intelligence. The human faculty primarily involved with the Head Center is thinking, the faculty primarily involved with the Emotional Center is feeling, and the faculty primarily involved with the Body Center is will. Each of the head types has a different kind of imbalance involving thinking, each of the heart types a different kind of imbalance involving feeling, and each of the body types a different kind of imbalance involving will.

The three Centers of Intelligence also correspond to three core emotions that influence the character of the types. The head types (5, 6, and 7) are also the fear types, and their personality style is shaped by their relationship to fear. The heart types (2, 3, and 4) are also the grief or sadness types, and their personality style is fundamentally shaped by their relationship to grief. The body types (8, 9, and 1) are the anger types, and their personality is fundamentally shaped by their relationship to anger. The types on the inner triangle (3, 6, and 9) are also called the core points of each center's triad of types. Thus, type 3 is the core of the Heart Center types; type 6 is the core of the Head Center types; and type 9 is the core of the Body Center types (Riso & Hudson, 1999).

Emotional Intelligence (EI)

Emotional Intelligence (EI), often measured as an Emotional Intelligence Quotient (EQ), describes an ability, capacity, skill or (in the case of the trait EI model) a self-perceived ability, to identify, assess, and manage the emotions of one's self, of others, and of groups (Bradberry, Greaves, Lencioni, 2005). It is a relatively new area of psychological research. The definition of EI is constantly changing and there are many arguments about the definition of EI regarding both terminology and operationalization. One attempt toward a definition was made by Salovey and Mayer (1990) who defined EI as "the ability to monitor one's own and others' feelings and emotions, to discriminate among them and to use this information to guide one's thinking and actions". Despite this early definition, there has been confusion regarding the exact meaning of the construct. The definitions are so varied, and the field is growing so rapidly, that researchers are constantly amending even their own definitions of the construct (Dulewicz & Higgs, 2000).

Salovey and Mayer's conception strives to define EI within the confines of the standard criteria for new intelligence. Following continuing research, their initial definition of EI was revised to (1990): "The ability to perceive emotion, integrate emotion to facilitate thought, understand emotions and to regulate emotions to promote personal growth." The ability based model views emotions as useful sources of information that help one to make sense of and navigate the social environment (Salovey & Grewal, 2005). The model proposes that individuals vary in their ability to process information of an emotional nature and in their ability to relate emotional processing to wider cognition. This ability is seen to manifest itself in certain adaptive behaviors.

Origins of the Concept: The most distant roots of Emotional Intelligence can be traced back to Darwin's early work on the importance of emotional expression for survival and second adaptation (Bar-On, 2006). In the 1900s, even though traditional definitions of intelligence emphasized cognitive aspects such as memory and problem-solving, several influential researchers in the study of intelligence began to recognize the importance of the non-cognitive aspects. For instance, as early

as 1920, E. L. Thorndike used the term social intelligence to describe the skill of understanding and managing other people (Thorndike, 1920). Similarly, in 1940 David Wechsler described the influence of non-intellective factors on intelligent behavior, and further argued that our models of intelligence would not be complete until we could adequately describe these factors (Bar-On, 2006).

In 1983, Howard Gardner's *Frames of Mind: The Theory of Multiple Intelligences* (Gardner, 1983) introduced the idea of Multiple Intelligences which included both *Interpersonal intelligence* (the capacity to understand the intentions, motivations and desires of other people) and *Intrapersonal intelligence* (the capacity to understand oneself, to appreciate one's feelings, fears and motivations). In Gardner's view, traditional types of intelligence, such as IQ, fail to fully explain cognitive ability (Smith, 2002). Thus, even though the names given to the concept varied, there was a common belief that traditional definitions of intelligence are lacking in the ability to fully explain performance outcomes.

The first use of the term "Emotional Intelligence" is usually attributed to Wayne Payne's doctoral thesis, *A study of emotion: Developing emotional intelligence* from 1985 (Payne, 1985). However, prior to this, the term "emotional intelligence" had appeared in Leuner (1966). Greenspan (1989) also put forward an EI model, followed by Salovey and Mayer (1990), and Goleman (1995). As a result of the growing acknowledgement of professionals for the importance and relevance of emotions to work outcomes (Feldman-Barrett & Salovey, 2002), research on the topic continued to gain momentum, but it wasn't until the publication of Daniel Goleman's best seller *Emotional Intelligence: Why It Can Matter More Than IQ* that the term became widely popularized (Goleman, 1995). Nancy Gibbs' 1995 TIME magazine article highlighted Goleman's book and was the first in a string of mainstream media interest in EI (Gibbs, 1995). Thereafter, articles on EI began to appear with increasing frequency across a wide range of academic and popular outlets.

Assessing and Training the Gamer

The Tavistock method was derived from the Tavistock Institute, which was founded in 1946 by a group of key figures at the Tavistock Clinic including Elliott Jaques, Henry Dicks, Leonard Browne, Ronald Hargreaves, John Rawlings Rees, Mary Luff and Wilfred Bion, with Tommy Wilson as chairman, funded by a grant from the Rockefeller Foundation. The Tavistock method, also known as the group relations method, concentrates on the individual only insofar as he or she is manifesting something on behalf of the whole group. This method regards the group as a holistic entity that in some ways is greater than the sum of its part. The lens of Tavistock theory focuses not on the distinctions between individuals but rather brings into bold relief their commonality of task, function, and motivation. As a consequence, group-level phenomena that are usually invisible become clearer and more distinct. Despite its extraordinary power and theoretical richness, the Tavistock method is not well known or understood in the field of human relations training (Hayden & Molenkamp, 2002).

FUTURE RESEARCH

The basic premise of the Tavistock approach is that a cluster of persons becomes a group when interaction between members occurs, when members' awareness of their common relationship develops and when a common group task emerges. Various forces can operate to produce a group—an external threat, collective regressive behavior, or attempts to satisfy needs for security, safety, dependency, and affection. Other, more deliberate forces that result in the birth of a group are the conscious choices of individuals to band together to perform a task. Essential to the Tavistock approach is the belief that when a cololection of individuals becomes a group, the group behaves as a system - an entity or organism that is, in some respects, greater than the sum of its parts - and that the primary task of the group is *survival*. Although this primary task is frequently disguised or masked, *survival* as a group becomes the primary preoccupation and latent motivating force for all group members. This emphasis on *survival* provides the framework for the exploration of group behavior and all the overt and covert manifestations of the primary task (Hayden & Molenkamp, 2002).

The Tavistock approach has been capitalized by corporate America in various formats including reality television. For example the Apprentice is a simplified interpretation of the Tavistock approach. These simplified interpretations of the Tavistock approach are derived for two reasons: (a) reality made exciting for viewers based solely on ratings and for those who do not have a stake in the end result, and (b) a softer version of a scientific approach to assessing, analyzing, and resolving organizational dilemmas. The Apprentice has been adopted internationally (List 1), and the PC game version of The Apprentice was released on March 2005 by Legacy Interactive.

The Tavistock method provides the environmental setting within the game, where group tasks emerge and challenge both the individual and the group, allowing businesses to assess the individual's KSAOs in handling these tasks. Paramount components within the KSAOs may vary among businesses, for the right decisions, to some businesses are not desired, but possessing the necessary KSAOs to deriving the desired decisions are. Using the Tavistock method, businesses can utilize the Enneagram method to elicit and assess the desired KSAOs.

In the business arena the term "game" rhetorically has a negative connotation, often conjuring up questionable practices and ethical dilemmas. As such, in the business arena, the term "game" is not used as it is in the gaming industry, or in the research and academic (psychology) arena. In the business arena, under the usage and purpose of the gaming industry and the research and academic (psychology) arena, game is known as a "training" (or testing) methodology where firms utilize these methodological resources to assess their current and potential employees. Historically, businesses have been using these training methodologies as assessments, but have not been giving these methodological assessments the appropriate credit. For example, many businesses utilize this training for new employees' orientations and continuing education/certification (i.e. watch a video and successfully complete an online test) to demonstrate that the required knowledge, skills, and abilities have been acquired.

Furthermore, government and state jobs in the U.S. often assess interested candidates by utilizing these personality tests, but often via paper-and-pencil due to budget constraints in implementing assessments through games. This constraint yields a different aspect of validity, because when situations are presented via words on paper, decisions will be different compared with decisions made based on reactions to simulations in a game. It is the simulation within a game that captures gamers, just as it is the simulation of life-like situations via the Tavistock method within a game that elicit true personality, demeanors, behaviors, knowledge, skills, abilities and other characteristics (KSAOs) via the Enneagram method. Communication and collaboration take time. One important factor that will elevate this time factor is profit. The gaming industry can benefit from collaboration with academic psychologists and businesses to create and produce more games incorporating the Enneagram and the Tavistock methodologies if there is a profit to be made.

The Tavistock approach is a stealth assessment, a process of embedding assessments directly and invisibly into the learning or gaming environment (Shute & Kim, 2013; Shute & Ventura, 2013; Shute, Ventura, Small, & Goldberg, in press), and is often used as an assessment when traditional assessment formats are not optimal. The Tavistock approach, like a game, is an assessment where many games typically require a player to apply various competences to succeed in the game. The competences required to succeed in many games also happen to be the same ones that companies are looking for in today's highly competitive economy (Arum & Roska, 2011; Gee, Hull, & Lankshear, 1996). In addition to the arguments for using games as assessment devices, there is growing evidence of games supporting learning (Tobias & Fletcher, 2011; Wilson, Bedwell, Lazzara, Salas, Burke, Estock, Orvis, & Conkey, 2009).

Learning in games has historically been assessed indirectly and/or in a post hoc manner (Shute & Ke, 2012; Tobias, Fletcher, Dai, & Wind, 2011). In contrast the Tavistock approach, as a real-time assessment and learning game, is based on the dynamic of needs of players is the new genre of games. This is because the Tavistock approach, as a game, is a performance-based measure (Dede, 2005; DiCerbo & Behrens, 2012; Quellmalz, Timms, Silberglitt, & Buckley, 2012; Shute & Ke, 2012; Shute, Ventura, Kim, & Wang, in press; Ventura, Shute, & Zhao, 2012) crafted according to appropriate situations or problems to elicit a competency of interest.

According to Hayden and Molenkamp (2002), appreciating the group as a whole requires a *perceptual shift* on the part of the observer or consultant, a blurring of individuals' separateness, and a readiness to see the collective interactions generated by group members. When individuals become members of a group, behavior changes and a collective identity emerges: a task group or an organization—all become a new Gestalt in which the group is the focus and the individual members become the background. Membership becomes an exciting but ambiguous experience, one that invites individual members to join the task at hand and also triggers their fantasies and projections about belonging and their conflicts about leadership and authority in organizations. These characteristics are consistent with the "O" factor of gamers that needs to be identified, assessed, and utilized based on the Tavistock method.

In utilizing the gamer in selecting and training potential and current employees in organizational settings, organizations are strongly encouraged to utilize the Enneagram of Personality and the Emotional Intelligence methods to identify the gamers' other characteristics (O), and utilize the Tavistock method to assess the gamers' factors. The KSAs are potential employees' preexisting characteristics, or can be trained by the organization, but the O factor is more challenging even if it is trainable. It is useful to point out that neither the Enneagram of Personality nor emotional intelligence tests are commonly taught or researched in academic psychology but both are main-stream to organizational psychologists, industrial psychologists, and organizational developments (OD) practitioners in the U. S. As such, both personality tests are widely utilized in business contexts in the U. S. as a typology to gain insights into workplace dynamics, employees' behaviors and characteristics, and employees' knowledge, skills, abilities, and other characteristics (KSAOs). The popularity of these personality tests has also caught the attention of the Hollywood industry as in the Apprentice which utilizes the Tavistock method as a simulation to assess KSAOs via the Enneagram method.

CONCLUSION

A computer game can embody more than one rhetoric, but play as a form of conflict and contest (power), a means of expressing an identity and belonging to a group (identity), as imagination and creativity (the imaginary), and a means of relaxation and escape (the self), are the most common forms experienced in computer games. Regardless of the embedded play rhetoric, one of the primary concerns of industrial and organizational practitioners is the utilization of the gamer as a factor in selecting employees and training employees in an organizational setting so that the employee is a good fit to the organizational needs, to assist

the organization in achieving and maintaining competitive advantage over its rivals. Understanding the psychology of the gamer is important not just in studying video game players but also for understanding behaviors and characteristics of non-player characters (NPCs). Currently there is still a gap in literature concerning the utilization of the gamer in selecting and training potential and current employees in organizational settings. Organizations are strongly encouraged to utilize the Enneagram of Personality and the Emotional Intelligence methods to identify the gamers' other characteristics (O), and utilize the Tavistock method to assess the gamers' factors. The O factor is part of the knowledge, skills, and abilities factors, commonly known as KSAOs. The KSAs are potential employees' preexisting factors, or can be trained by the organization, but the O factor is more challenging even if it is trainable.

Many organizations are either attempting to assess, or are not aware of the fact that they are implementing either one, or both methods without knowing the terminologies of these methods. I/O practitioners, organizational behaviorists (OB), organizational psychologists (OP), and organizational development (OD) practitioners are not naïve to these methods, just as licensed marriage and family therapists (LMFT), psychologists, and clinical psychologists are not naïve to the Diagnostic and Statistical Manual of Mental Disorders (DSM). In fact, many organizations have been implementing an extremely simplified and watered-down version of these two methods, by asking candidates during interviews how they would react, handle, and address certain scenarios and situations. However, many interviewers are not trained or qualified to conduct interviews and implement assessment, but to decrease the possibility of errors and biases, invite and include various interviewers from various departments (i.e. invite one individual each from the accounting department, the information technology department, and the customer service department) to interview a wellness counselor.

More often than not, the human resource department is not part of the interview, but is only responsible for reviewing submitted resumes and forwarding the satisfactory resumes to the department that is in need of staffing. When the human resource department does participate in the interview, it is very common that the role of the representative from the human resources department is to witness and confirm that inappropriate, irrelevant, and illegal questions that do not pertain to the job duties, job requirements, and job responsibilities at hand are not asked. Another extremely simplified and watered-down version of these two methods that organizations are utilizing is, upon being hired, employees are placed on a probationary trial period (commonly 90 days). However, this method is time consuming, and a burden on resources. The benefits and competitive advantage of utilizing the gamer factor in selecting and training potential employees are: 1) identifying a qualified candidate who is a good fit to the organizational needs, and 2) assisting the organization to achieve and maintain competitive advantage over its rivals. This can be achieved by utilizing the Enneagram of Personality and the Emotional Intelligence methods.

REFERENCES

Allen, B. P. (1994). *Personality theories*. Boston, MA: Allyn and Bacon.

Alman, R. E. (1994). *Video games: Interaction vs. observation as sources of social learning*. (Unpublished master's thesis). Michigan State University, East Lansing, MI.

Anderson, C. A. (2004). An update on the effects of playing violent video games. *Journal of Adolescence*, *27*(1), 113–122. doi:10.1016/j.adolescence.2003.10.009 PMID:15013264.

Anderson, C. A., & Berdahl, J. L. (2002). The experience of power: Examining the effects of power on approach and inhibition tendencies. *The Journal of Social Psychology*, *83*(6), 1362–1377. PMID:12500818.

Anderson, C. A., & Bushman, B. J. (1997). External validity of trivial experiments: The case of laboratory aggression. *Review of General Psychology*, *1*(1), 19–41. doi:10.1037/1089-2680.1.1.19.

Anderson, C. A., & Bushman, B. J. (2001). Effects of violent video games on aggressive behavior, aggressive cognition, aggressive effect, physiological arousal, and prosocial behavior: A meta-analytic review of the scientific literature. *Psychological Science*, *12*(5), 353–359. doi:10.1111/1467-9280.00366 PMID:11554666.

Anderson, C. A., & Dill, K. E. (2000). Video games and aggressive thoughts, feelings, and behavior in the laboratory and in life. *Journal of Personality and Social Psychology*, *78*(4), 772–790. doi:10.1037/0022-3514.78.4.772 PMID:10794380.

Anderson, C. A., & Ford, C. M. (1986). Affect of the game player: Short-term effects of highly and mildly aggressive video games. *Personality and Social Psychology Bulletin*, *12*(4), 390–402. doi:10.1177/0146167286124002.

Arum, R., & Roska, J. (2011). *Academically adrift: Limited learning on college campuses*. Chicago, IL: The University of Chicago Press.

Atkinson, J. W. (1957). Motivational determinants of risk-taking behavior. *Psychological Review*, *64*(1-6), 359-372.

Bailenson, J. N., Beall, A. C., & Blascovich, J. (2002). Gaze and task performance in shared virtual environments. *Journal of Visualization and Computer Animation*, *13*(5), 313–320. doi:10.1002/vis.297.

Ballard, M. E., & Lineberger, R. (1999). Video game violence and confederate gender: Effects on reward and punishment given by college males. *Sex Roles*, *4*(7/8), 541–558. doi:10.1023/A:1018843304606.

Ballard, M. E., & Wiest, J. R. (1995). *Mortal Kombat: The effects on violent video technology on males' hostility and cardiovascular responding*. Paper presented at the biennial Meeting of the Society for Research in Child Development. Indianapolis, IN.

Bar-On, R. (2006). The bar-on model of emotional-social intelligence (esi). *Psicothema*, *18*, 13–25. PMID:17295953.

Baron, R. (1998). *What type am I: Discover who you really are*. New York, NY: Penguin Books.

Bartholow, B. D., & Anderson, C. A. (2002). Effects of violent video games on aggressive behavior: Potential sex differences. *Journal of Experimental Social Psychology*, *38*, 283–290. doi:10.1006/jesp.2001.1502.

Bartle, R. A. (1990). *Early MUD history*. Retrieved on December 23, 2012. Retrieved from http://www.mud.co.uk/richard/mudhist.htm

Bartle, R. A. (2004). *Designing virtual worlds*. New Riders Publishing.

Batholow, B. D., & Anderson, C. A. (2002). Effects of violent video games on aggressive behavior: Potential sex differences. *Journal of Experimental Social Psychology*, *38*(3), 283–290. doi:10.1006/jesp.2001.1502.

Berkowitz, L., & Rogers, K. II. (1986). A priming effect analysis of media influences. In J. Bryant, & D. Zillmann (Eds.), *Perspectives on media effects* (pp. 57–82). Hillsdale, NJ: Erlbaum.

Bialystok, E. (2006). Effect of bilingualism and computer video game experience on the Simon task. *Canadian Journal of Experimental Psychology*, *60*(1), 68–79. doi:10.1037/cjep2006008 PMID:16615719.

Bolles, R. C. (1973). *Theory of motivation*. New York: Harper & Row.

Bowie, N. E. (1993). Does it pay to bluff in business? In T. L. Beauchamp, & N. E. Bowie (Eds.), *Ethical theory and business* (pp. 443–448). Englewood Cliffs, NJ: Prentice Hall, Inc.

Bradberry, T., Greaves, J., & Lencioni, P. (2005). *The emotional intelligence quick book*. New York: Simon and Schuster.

Brusa, J. A. (1988). Effects of video game playing on children's social behavior. *Dissertation Abstracts International-B*, *48*(10), 3127.

Burke, R. J., & McKeen, C. A. (1994). Career development among managerial and professional women. In M. J. Davidson, & J. R. Burke (Eds.), *Women in Management: Current Research Issues* (pp. 65–79). London: Paul Chapman.

Bushman, B. J., & Anderson, C. A. (2002). Violent video games and hostile expectations: A test of the general aggression model. *Personality and Social Psychology Bulletin*, *28*(12), 1679–1686. doi:10.1177/014616702237649.

Cacioppo, J. T., & Petty, R. E. (1982). The need for cognition. *Journal of Personality and Social Psychology*, *42*(1), 116–131. doi:10.1037/0022-3514.42.1.116.

Calvert, S. L., & Tan, S. L. (1994). Impact of virtual reality on young adults' physiological arousal and aggressive thoughts: Interaction versus observation. *Journal of Applied Developmental Psychology*, *15*(1), 125–139. doi:10.1016/0193-3973(94)90009-4.

Carnagey, N. L., & Anderson, C. A. (2004). Violent video game exposure and aggression: A literature review. *Minerva Psichiatrica, 45*(1), 1–18.

Carr, A. Z. (1968). Is business bluffing ethical? In *Ethical theory and business* (pp. 143–153). Englewood Cliffs, NJ: Prentice Hall, Inc.

Castel, A. D., Pratt, J., & Drummond, E. (2005). The effects of action video game experience on the time course of inhibition of return and the efficiency of visual search. *Acta Psychologica, 119*(2), 217–230. doi:10.1016/j.actpsy.2005.02.004 PMID:15877981.

Castronova, E. (2002). *Virtual worlds: A first-hand account of market and society on the cyberian frontier*. Retrieved on December 23, 2012 from http://papers.ssrn.com/sol3/papers.cfm?abstract_id=294828

Castronova, E. (2003). *The price of man and woman: A hedonic pricing model of avatar attributes in a synthetic world*. Retrieved on December 23, 2012 from http://papers.ssrn.com/sol3/papers.cfm?abstract_id=415043

Chambers, J. H., & Ascione, F. R. (1987). The effects of prosocial and aggressive videogames on children's donating and helping. *The Journal of Genetic Psychology, 148*(4), 499–505. doi:10.1080/00221325.1987.10532488 PMID:3437274.

Clark, J. E., Lanphear, A. K., & Riddick, C. C. (1987). The effects of videogame playing on the response selection processing of elderly adults. *Journal of Gerontology, 42*(1), 82–85. doi:10.1093/geronj/42.1.82 PMID:3794204.

Cohen, A. R., Stotland, E., & Wolfe, D. M. (1955). An experimental investigation of need for cognition. *Journal of Abnormal and Social Psychology, 51*(2), 291–294. doi:10.1037/h0042761 PMID:13263045.

Cooper, J., & Mackie, D. (1986). Video games and aggression in children. *Journal of Applied Social Psychology, 16*(8), 726–744. doi:10.1111/j.1559-1816.1986.tb01755.x.

Csikszentmihalyi, M. (1990). *Flow: The psychology of optimal experience*. New York: Harper & Row.

Daniels, D., & Pice, V. (2000). *The essential enneagram: Test and self-discovery guide*. San Francisco, CA: Harper.

Davidson, M. J., & Cooper, C. L. (1992). *Shattering the glass ceiling: The women manager*. London: Paul Chapman.

Dede, C. (2005). Planning for neomillennial learning styles. *EDUCAUSE Quarterly, 28*(1), 7–12.

DiCerbo, K. E., & Behrens, J. T. (2012). Implications of the digital ocean on current and future assessment. In R. Lissitz, & H. Jiao (Eds.), *Computers and their impact on state assessment: Recent history and predictions for the future* (pp. 273–306). Charlotte, NC: Information Age Publishing.

Dix, T. (1993). Attributing dispositions to children: An interactional analysis of attribution in socialization. *Personality and Social Psychology Bulletin, 19*(5), 633–643. doi:10.1177/0146167293195014.

Dominick, J. R. (1984). Videogames, television violence, and aggression in teenagers. *The Journal of Communication, 34*(2), 136–147. doi:10.1111/j.1460-2466.1984.tb02165.x.

Dulewicz, V., & Higgs, M. (2000). Emotional intelligence – A review and evaluation study. *Journal of Managerial Psychology, 15*(4), 341–372. doi:10.1108/02683940010330993.

Fagenson, E. A. (1986). Women's work orientation: Something old, something new. *Group and Organization Studies, 11*(1), 75–100. doi:10.1177/105960118601100108.

Feldman-Barrett, L., & Salovey, P. (2002). *The wisdom in feeling: Psychological processes in emotional intelligence.* New York: Guilford Press.

Feng, J., Spence, I., & Pratt, J. (2007). Playing action video game reduces or eliminates gender differences in spatial cognition. *Psychological Science, 18*(10), 850–855. doi:10.1111/j.1467-9280.2007.01990.x PMID:17894600.

Ferguson, C. J. (2002). Media violence: Miscast causality. *The American Psychologist, 57*(6/7), 446–447. doi:10.1037/0003-066X.57.6-7.446b PMID:12094443.

Feshbach, S. (1955). The drive-reducing function of fantasy behavior. *Journal of Abnormal Psychology, 50*(1), 3–11. doi:10.1037/h0042214 PMID:13232919.

Fishman, D. B. (1966). Need and expectancy as determinants of affiliative behavior in small groups. *Journal of Personality and Social Psychology, 4*(2), 155–164. doi:10.1037/h0023565 PMID:5969140.

Funk, J. B., & Buchman, D. D. (1996). Playing violent video and computer games and adolescent self-concept. *The Journal of Communication, 46*(2), 19–32. doi:10.1111/j.1460-2466.1996.tb01472.x.

Funk, J. B., Hagan, J., Schimming, J., Bullock, W., Buchman, D. D., & Myers, M. (2002). Aggression and psychopathology in adolescents with a preference for violent electronic games. *Aggressive Behavior, 28*(2), 134–144. doi:10.1002/ab.90015.

Furby, L. (1978). Possession in humans: An exploratory study of its meaning and motivation. *Social Behavior and Personality, 6*(1), 49–65. doi:10.2224/sbp.1978.6.1.49.

Gardner, H. (1983). *Frames of mind.* New York: Basic Books.

Gee, J. P. (2003). *What video games have to teach us about learning and literacy.* New York: Palgrave MacMillan. doi:10.1145/950566.950595.

Gee, J. P., Hull, G. A., & Lankshear, C. (1996). *The new work order: Behind the language of the new capitalism.* Saint Leonards, Australia: Allen & Unwin.

Gentile, D. A., & Anderson, C. A. (2003). Violent video games: The Newest media violence hazard. In D. Gentile (Ed.), *Media violence and children* (pp. 205–226). Westport, CT: Praeger.

Gentile, D. A., Lynch, P. J., Linder, J. R., & Walsh, D. A. (2004). The effects of violent video game habits on adolescent aggressive attitudes and behaviors. *Journal of Adolescence, 27*(1), 5–22. doi:10.1016/j.adolescence.2003.10.002 PMID:15013257.

Gibbs, N. (1995). The eq factor. *Time Magazine.* Retrieved on December 25, 2012 from http://www.time.com/time/classroom/psych/unit5_article1.html

Goleman, D. (1995). *Emotional intelligence.* New York: Bantam Books.

Graybill, D., Kirsch, J., & Esselman, E. (1985). Effects of playing violent versus nonviolent video games on the aggressive ideation of aggressive and nonaggressive children. *Child Study Journal, 15*(3), 199–205.

Graybill, D., Strawniak, M., Hunter, T., & O'Leary, M. (1987). Effects of playing versus observing violent versus nonviolent video games on children's aggression. *Psychology: A Quarterly Journal of Human Behavior, 24*(3), 1-8.

Green, C. S., & Bavelier, D. (2003). Action video game modifies visual selection attention. *Nature, 29*(423), 534–537. doi:10.1038/nature01647.

Green, C. S., & Bavelier, D. (2007). Action video game experience alters the spatial resolution of attention. *Psychological Science, 18*(1), 88–94. doi:10.1111/j.1467-9280.2007.01853.x PMID:17362383.

Greenfield, P. M., deWinstanley, P., Kilpatrick, H., & Kaye, D. (1994). Action video games and informal education: Effects on strategies for diving visual attention. *Journal of Applied Developmental Psychology, 15*(1), 105–123. doi:10.1016/0193-3973(94)90008-6.

Greenspan, S. I. (1989). Emotional intelligence. In K. Field, B. J. Cohler, & G. Wool (Eds.), *Learning and education: Psychoanalytic perspective* (pp. 209–243). Madison, CT: International Universities Press.

Griffiths, M. D. (1999). Violent video games and aggression: A review of the literature. *Aggression and Violent Behavior, 4*(2), 203–212. doi:10.1016/S1359-1789(97)00055-4.

Griffiths, M. D. (2003). Breaking the stereotype: The case of on-line gaming. *Cyberpsychology & Behavior, 6*(1), 81–91. doi:10.1089/109493103321167992 PMID:12650566.

Hayden, C., & Molenkamp, R. J. (2002). *Tavistock primer II*. Jupiter, FL: The A. K. Rice Institute of the Study of Social Systems.

Heckhausen, H. (1974). *Leistung and chancengleichheit*. Gottingen, Germany: Hogrefe.

Heckhausen, J., & Heckhausen, H. (2005). *Motivation and action*. Cambridge, UK: Cambridge University Press.

Henning, M., & Jardim, A. (1977). *The managerial women*. London: Pan Books.

Hoffman, K. (1995). Effects of playing versus witnessing video game violence on attitudes towards aggression and acceptance of violence as a means of conflict resolution. *Dissertation Abstract International, 56*(3), 747.

Ibarra, H. (1993). Personal networks of women and minorities in management: A conceptual framework. *Academy of Management Review, 189*(1), 56–87.

Irwin, A. R., & Gross, A. M. (1995). Cognitive tempo, violent video games, and aggressive behavior in young boys. *Journal of Family Violence, 10*(3), 337–350. doi:10.1007/BF02110997.

Ivory, J. D., & Kalyanaraman, S. (2007). The effects of technological advancement and violent content in video games on players' feelings of presence, involvement, physiological arousal, and aggression. *The Journal of Communication, 57*(3), 532–555. doi:10.1111/j.1460-2466.2007.00356.x.

Jackson, D. N. (1974). *Personality research form manual*. Research Psychologists Press.

James, W. (1890). *Principles of psychology*. New York: MacMillan. doi:10.1037/11059-000.

Jo, E., & Berkowitz, L. (1994). A priming effect analysis of media influences: An update. In J. Bryant, & D. Zillmann (Eds.), *Media effects: Advances in theory and research* (pp. 43–60). Hillsdale, NJ: Erlbaum.

Kanter, R. M. (1977). Some effects of proportions of group life: Skewed sex ratios and responses to token women. *American Journal of Sociology, 82*(5), 965–990. doi:10.1086/226425.

Kellar, M., Watters, C., & Duffy, J. (2005). Motivational factors in game play in two user groups. In *Proceedings of the DiGRA 2005 Conference: Changing Views—Worlds in Play*. Vancouver, Canada: DiGRA.

Kestenbaum, G. I., & Weinstein, L. (1985). Personality, psychopathology and developmental issues in male adolescent video game use. *Journal of the American Academy of Child Psychiatry, 24*(3), 329–337. doi:10.1016/S0002-7138(09)61094-3 PMID:4008824.

Kipnis, D. (1976). *The powerholders*. Chicago, IL: University of Chicago Press.

Koehn, D. (1997). Business and game-playing: The false analogy. *Journal of Business Ethics, 16*(12/13), 1447–1452. doi:10.1023/A:1005724317399.

Kong, S. C., Pgata, H., Arnseth, H. C., Chan, C. K. K., Hirashima, T., & Klett, F. … Yang, S. J. H. (2009). Exploring variables affecting player's intrinsic motivation in educational games. In *Proceedings of the 17th International Conference on Computers in Education (CDROM)*. Hong Kong: Asia-Pacific Society for Computers in Education.

Koster, R. (2002). *Online world timeline*. Retrieved on December 23, 2012 from http://www.raphkoster.com/gaming/mudtimeline.shtml

Lastowka, G., & Hunter, D. (2004). *The laws of virtual worlds*. Retrieved on December 23, 2012 from http://papers.ssrn.com/sol3/papers.cfm?abstract_id=402860

Leigh, J., DeFanti, T. A., Johnson, A. E., Brown, M. D., & Sandi, D. J. (1997). Global tele-immersion: Better than being there. In *Proceedings of ICAT '97*. Tokyo, Japan: ICAT.

Leuner, B. (1966). Emotional intelligence and emancipation: A psychodynamic study on women. *Praxis der Kinderpsychologie und Kinderpsychiatrie, 15*(6), 196–203. PMID:5975008.

Lewin, K. (1936). *Principles of topological psychology* (F. Heider, & G. Heider, Trans.). New York: McGraw-Hill. doi:10.1037/10019-000.

Linehan, M., & Scullion, H. (2001). Challenges for female international managers: Evidence from Europe. *Journal of Managerial Psychology, 16*(3), 215–228. doi:10.1108/02683940110385767.

Loftus, G. R., & Loftus, E. F. (1983). *Mind at play: The psychology of video games*. New York: Basic Books.

Logan, F. A., & Wagner, A. R. (1965). *Reward and punishment*. Boston, MA: Allyn and Bacon.

Maitri, S. (2001). *The spiritual dimension of the enneagram: Nine faces of the soul*. Tarcher.

Malone, T. W., & Lepper, M. R. (1987). Making learning fun: A taxonomy of intrinsic motivations for learning. In R. E. Snow, & M. J. Farr (Eds.), *Aptitude, learning, and instruction: Conative and affective process analyses* (pp. 223–253). Hillsdale, NJ: Lawrence Erlbaum.

Mania, K., & Chalmers, A. (1998). A classification for user embodiment in collaborative virtual environments. In *Proceedings of the 4th International Conference on Virtual Systems and Multimedia*. Boca Raton, FL: IOS Press.

Maslow, A. H. (1968). *Towards a psychology of being* (2nd ed.). New York: Van Nostrand Reinhold.

Matthew, W. G., Dye, C., Green, S., & Bavelier, D. (2009). Increasing speed of processing with action video games. *Current Directions in Psychological Science, 18*(6), 321–326. doi:10.1111/j.1467-8721.2009.01660.x PMID:20485453.

McDougall, W. (1908). *An introduction to social psychology*. London: Dover Publications. doi:10.1037/12261-000.

Medina, E. (2005). Digital games: A motivational perspective. In *Proceedings of DiGRA 2005 Conference: Changing View—World in Play*. Vancouver, Canada: DiGRA.

Mehrabian, A. (1969). Measures of achievement tendency. *Educational and Psychological Measurement*, *29*(2), 445–451. doi:10.1177/001316446902900222.

Mehrabian, A. (1970). The development and validation of measures of affiliative tendency and sensitivity to rejection. *Educational and Psychological Measurement*, *309*(2), 417–428. doi:10.1177/001316447003000226.

Murray, H. A. (1938). *Explorations in personality*. Oxford, UK: Oxford University Press.

Murray, H. A. (1981). Proposals for a theory of personality. In E. S. Shneidman (Ed.), *Endeavors in psychology: Selections from the personology of Henry A. Murray* (pp. 125–203). New York: Harper and Row.

Nakamura, J., Rodman, G., & Kolko, B. (2000). *Race in cyberspace*. New York: Routledge.

Naranjo, C. (1997). *Transformation through insight: Enneatypes in life*. Hohm Press.

Normand, V., Babski, C., Benford, S., Bullock, A., Carion, S., & Farcet, N. et al. (1999). The COVEN project: Exploring applicative, technical, and usage dimensions of collaborative virtual environments. *Presence (Cambridge, Mass.)*, *8*(2), 218–236. doi:10.1162/105474699566189.

Palmer, H. (1988). *The enneagram: Understanding yourself and the others in your life*. New York: Haper & Row.

Payne, W. L. (1985). *A study of emotion: developing emotional intelligence, self integration, relating to fear, pain and desire*. (Doctoral dissertation). The Union for Experimenting Colleges and Universities.

Pine, B. J., & Gilmore, J. H. (1999). *The experience economy, work is theatre and every business a stage*. Boston, MA: Harvard Business School Press.

Prensky, M. (2001). *Digital game-based learning*. New York: McGraw-Hill.

Prensky, M. (2002). The motivation of gameplay: The real twenty-first century learning revolution. *Horizon*, *10*(1), 5–11. doi:10.1108/10748120210431349.

Provenzo, E. F. (1991). *Video kids: Making sense of Nintendo*. Cambridge, MA: Harvard Business Press.

Quellmalz, E. S., Timms, M. J., Silberglitt, M. D., & Buckley, B. C. (2012). Science assessments for all: Integrating science simulations into balanced state science assessment systems. *Journal of Research in Science Teaching*, *49*(3), 363–393. doi:10.1002/tea.21005.

Riso, D. R., & Hudson, R. (1996). *Personality types*. New York: Houghton Mifflin.

Ryan, R. M., Rigby, C. S., & Przybylski, A. (2006). The motivational pull of video games: A self-determination theory approach. *Motivation and Emotion*, *30*(4), 347–364. doi:10.1007/s11031-006-9051-8.

Salovey, P., & Grewal, D. (2005). The science of emotional intelligence. *Current Directions in Psychological Science*, *149*(16), 281–285. doi:10.1111/j.0963-7214.2005.00381.x.

Salovey, P., & Mayer, J. D. (1990). *Emotional intelligence*. Retrieved on December 24, 2012, available from http://www.unh.edu/emotional_intelligence/EIAssets/EmotionalIntelligenceProper/EI1990%20Emotional%20Intelligence.pdf

Schneider, B., & Schmitt, N. (1992). *Staffing organizations* (2nd ed.). Prospect Heights, IL: Waveland Press.

Schutte, N., Malouff, J., Post-Gordon, J., & Rodasta, A. (1988). Effects of playing video games on children's aggressive and other behaviors. *Journal of Applied Social Psychology*, *18*(5), 454–460. doi:10.1111/j.1559-1816.1988.tb00028.x.

Scott, D. (1995). The effect of violent games on feelings of aggression. *The Journal of Psychology*, *129*(2), 121–132. doi:10.1080/00223980.1995.9914952 PMID:7760289.

Sherry, J. L. (2001). The effects of violent video games on aggression. *Human Communication Research*, *27*(3), 409–431.

Shute, V. J., & Ke, F. (2012). Games, learning, and assessment. In D. Ifenthaler, D. Eseryel, & X. Ge (Eds.), *Assessment in game-based learning: Foundations, innovations, and perspectives* (pp. 43–58). New York, NY: Springer. doi:10.1007/978-1-4614-3546-4_4.

Shute, V. J., & Kim, Y. J. (2013). Formative and stealth assessment. In J. M. Spector, M. D. Merrill, J. Elen, & M. J. Bishop (Eds.), *Handbook of research on educational communications and technology* (4th ed.). New York, NY: Lawrence Erlbaum Associates, Taylor & Francis Group.

Shute, V. J., & Ventura, M. (2013). *Measuring and supporting learning in games: Stealth assessment*. Cambridge, MA: The MIT Press.

Shute, V. J., Ventura, M., Kim, Y. J., & Wang, L. (2013). Assessing learning in video games. In W. G. Tierney, Z. Corwin, T. Fullerton, & G. Ragusa (Eds.), *Postsecondary play: The role of games and social media in higher education*. Baltimore, MD: John Hopkins University Press.

Shute, V. J., Ventura, M., Small, M., & Goldberg, B. (2013). Modeling student competencies in video games using stealth assessment. In R. Sottilare, X. Hu, & A. Graesser (Eds.), *Design recommendations for adaptive intelligent tutoring systems: Learning modeling* (Vol. 1). Washington, DC: Army Research Laboratory.

Silvern, S. B., Lang, M. K., & Williamson, P. A. (1987). Social impact of video game play. In *Meaningful Play, Playful Meaning: Proceedings of the 11th Annual Meeting of the Association for the Anthropological Study of Play*. Champaign, IL: Human Kinetics.

Silvern, S. B., & Williamson, P. A. (1987). The effects of video game play on young children's aggression, fantasy, and prosocial behavior. *Journal of Developmental Psychology*, *8*(4), 453–462. doi:10.1016/0193-3973(87)90033-5.

Singer, J. A. (1990). Affective responses to autobiographical memories and their relationship to long-term goals. *Journal of Personality*, *58*(3), 535–563. doi:10.1111/j.1467-6494.1990.tb00242.x.

Skinner, B. F. (1938). *The behavior of organisms*. New York: Appleton Century Crofts.

Skinner, B. F. (1953). *Science and human behavior*. New York: MacMillan.

Slate, M., Sadagic, A., Usoh, M., & Schroeder, R. (2000). Small group behavior in a virtual and real environment: A comparative study. *Presence (Cambridge, Mass.)*, *9*(1), 37–51. doi:10.1162/105474600566600.

Smith, C. R., & Hutchinson, J. (1995). *Gender: A strategic management issue*. Sydney, Australia: Business & Professional Publishing.

Smith, M. K. (2002). *Howard Gardner and multiple intelligences, the encyclopedia of informal education*. Retrieved on December 25, 2009 from http://www.infed.org/thinkers/gardner.htm

Staddon, J. E. R., & Simmelhag, V. L. (1971). The superstition experiment: A reexamination of its implications for the principles of adaptive behavior. *Psychological Review*, *78*(1), 3–43. doi:10.1037/h0030305.

Stewart, K. M. (1997). Beyond entertainment: Using interactive games in web-based instruction. *Journal of Instruction Delivery Systems, 11*(2), 18–20.

Sutton-Smith, B. (1997). *The ambiguity of play.* Cambridge, MA: Harvard University Press.

Sweetser, P., & Wyeth, P. (2005). GameFlow: A model for evaluating player enjoyment in games. *Association for Computing Machinery Computers in Entertainment, 3*(3), 1–24.

Tamborini, R., Eastin, M. S., Skalski, P., Lachlan, K., Fediuk, T. A., & Brady, R. (2004). Violent virtual video games and hostile thoughts. *Journal of Broadcasting & Electronic Media, 48*(3), 335–358.

Tannenbaum, P. H., & Zillmann, D. (1975). *Emotional arousal in the facilitation of aggression through communication* (L. Berkowitz, Ed.). Advances in experimental social psychology New York, NY: Academic Press. doi:10.1016/S0065-2601(08)60250-6.

Thorndike, R. K. (1920). Intelligence and its uses. *Harper's Magazine, 140*, 227-335.

Tobias, S., & Fletcher, J. D. (2011). *Computer games and instructions.* Charlotte, NC: Information Age Publishers.

Tobias, S., Fletcher, J. D., Dai, D. Y., & Wind, A. P. (2011). Review of research on computer games. In S. Tobias, & J. D. Fletcher (Eds.), *Computer games and instruction* (pp. 127–222). Charlotte, NC: Information Age Publishers.

Tran, B. (2008). *Expatriate selection and retention.* (Doctoral dissertation). Alliant International University, San Francisco, CA.

Turkle, S. (1984). *The second self: Computers and the human spirit.* New York, NY: Simon & Schuster.

Turkle, S. (1995). *Life on the screen: Identity in the age of the internet.* New York: Simon and Schuster.

Ventura, M., Shute, V. J., & Zhao, W. (2013). The relationship between video game use and a performance-based measure of persistence. *Computers & Education, 60*, 52–58. doi:10.1016/j.compedu.2012.07.003.

Vorderer, P. Wulff, & Friedrichsen, M. (1996). Suspense: Conceptualizations, theoretical analyses, and empirical explorations. Mahwah, NJ: Routledge.

Vorderer, P., Klimmt, C., & Ritterfeld, U. (2004). Enjoyment: At the heart of media entertainment. *Communication Theory, 14*(4), 388–408. doi:10.1111/j.1468-2885.2004.tb00321.x.

Williams, D., & Skoric, M. (2005). Internet fantasy violence: A test of aggression in an online game. *Communication Monographs, 72*(2), 217–233. doi:10.1080/03637750500111781.

Wilson, K. A., Bedwell, W. L., Lazzara, E. H., Salas, E., Burke, C. S., & Estock, J. L. et al. (2009). Relationships between game attributes and learning outcomes: Reviews and research proposals. *Simulation & Gaming, 40*(2), 217–266. doi:10.1177/1046878108321866.

Winkel, M., Novak, D., & Hopson, H. (1987). Personality factors, subject gender and the effects of aggressive video games on aggression in adolescents. *Journal of Research in Personality, 2*(1), 211–223. doi:10.1016/0092-6566(87)90008-0.

Winter, D. G. (1988). The power motive in women—and men. *Journal of Personality and Social Psychology, 54*(3), 510–519. doi:10.1037/0022-3514.54.3.510.

Winter, D. G. (1992). Power motivation revisited. In C. P. Smith (Ed.), *Motivation and personality: Handbook of Thematic Content Analysis*. Cambridge, UK: Cambridge University Press. doi:10.1017/CBO9780511527937.022.

Yee, N. (2006a). Motivations of play in online games. *Cyberpsychology & Behavior*, 9(6), 772–775. doi:10.1089/cpb.2006.9.772 PMID:17201605.

Yee, N. (2006b). The psychology of massively multi-user online role-playing games: Motivations, emotional investment, relationships and problematic usage. In R. Schroeder, & A. Axelsson (Eds.), *Avatars at work and play: Collaboration and interaction in shared virtual environments* (pp. 187–207). London: Springer-Verlag. doi:10.1007/1-4020-3898-4_9.

Yee, N. (2006c). The demographics, motivations, and derived experiences of users of massively multi-user online graphical environments. *Presence (Cambridge, Mass.)*, 15(3), 309–329. doi:10.1162/pres.15.3.309.

Zhang, X., & Furnas, G. (2002). Social interactions in multiscale CVEs. In *Proceedings of 4ᵗʰ International ACM Conference on Collaborative Virtual Environments*. Bonn, Germany: ACM.

Zillmann, D. (1988a). Mood management through communication choices. *The American Behavioral Scientist*, 31(3), 327–340. doi:10.1177/000276488031003005.

Zillmann, D. (1988b). Mechanism of emotional involvement with drama. *Poetics*, 23(1/2), 33–51.

Zillmann, D. (1996). The psychology of suspense in dramatic expositions. In P. Vorderer, H. J. Wagele, & R. Baron (Eds.), *The enneagram made easy* (pp. 199–232). New York: HarperOne.

Zillmann, M. (1994). *Behavioral expressions and biosocial bases of sensation seeking*. Cambridge, UK: Cambridge University Press.

Zuckerman, M. (1994). *Behavioral expressions and biosocial bases of sensation seeking*. Cambridge, UK: Cambridge University Press.

ADDITIONAL READING

Astrachan, M. (1975). The Tavistock model of laboratory training. In K. D. Benne, L. P. Bradford, J. R. Gibb, & R. O. Lippitt (Eds.), *The laboratory method of changing and learning: Theory and application*. Palo Alto, CA: Science & Behavior Books.

Bailenson, J. N., Beall, A. C., & Blascovich, J. (2002). Mutual gaze and task performance in shared virtual environments. *Journal of Visualization and Computer Animation*, 13, 1–8. doi:10.1002/vis.297.

Banet, A. C., & Yang, Y. (1976). Perspectives on theories of group development. In J. W. Pfeiffer, & J. E. Jones (Eds.), *The 1976 annual handbook for group facilitators*. La Jolla, CA: University Associates.

Bargh, J., McKenna, K., & Fitzsimons, G. (2002). Can you see the real me? Activation and expression of the true self on the internet. *The Journal of Social Issues*, 58(1), 33–48. doi:10.1111/1540-4560.00247.

Benford, S., Bowers, J., Fahlen, L. E., Mariani, J., & Rodden, T. (1994). Supporting cooperative work in virtual environments. *The Computer Journal*, 37(8), 653–668. doi:10.1093/comjnl/37.8.653.

Bion, W. R. (1961). *Experiences groups*. New York: Basic Books. doi:10.4324/9780203359075.

Edery, D., & Mollick, E. (2009). *Goals and games: Designing your employees' goals like game designers design video game*. FT Press.

Fabrigar, L. R., Wegener, D. T., MacCallum, R. C., & Strahan, E. J. (1999). Evaluating the use of exploratory factor analysis in psychological research. *Psychological Methods*, *3*, 272–299. doi:10.1037/1082-989X.4.3.272.

Goleman, D. (2007). *Social intelligence: The new science of human relationships*. Bantam.

Goleman, D. (2011). *Leadership: The power of emotional intelligence*. More Than Sound.

Goleman, D., Boyatzis, R. E., & McKee, A. (2004). *Primal leadership: Learning to lead with emotional intelligence*. Harvard Business Review Press.

Kellerman, B. (2012). *The end of leadership*. HarperBusiness.

Kohler, A. T., Miller, J. C., & Klein, E. B. (1973). Some effects of intergroup experience on study group phenomena. *Human Relations*, *26*, 293–305. doi:10.1177/001872677302600302.

Leigh, J., & Johnson, A. E. (1996). Supporting transcontinental collaborative work in persistent virtual environments. *Institute of Electrical and Electronics Engineers (IEEE). Computer Graphics and Applications*, *16*(4), 47–51. doi:10.1109/38.511853.

Moreno, R., & Mayer, R. (2002). Learning science in virtual reality multimedia environments: Role of methods and media. *Journal of Educational Psychology*, *943*, 598–610. doi:10.1037/0022-0663.94.3.598.

Nolan, J. M., & Jones, J. M. (2012). *Games for training: Leveraging commercial off the shelf multiplayer gaming software for infantry squad collective training*. Amazon Digital Services, Inc.

Nunamaker, J. F. Jr. (1997). Future research in group support systems: Needs, some questions and possible directions. *International Journal of Human-Computer Studies*, *47*, 357–385. doi:10.1006/ijhc.1997.0142.

O'Connor, C. (1971). The Tavistock method of group study. *Science and Psychoanalysis*, *18*, 100–115.

Palm, H. (1991). *The enneagram: Understanding yourself and the others in your life*. HarperOne.

Rich, C., Waters, R. C., Schabes, Y., Freeman, W. T., Torrance, M. C., Golding, A. R., & Roth, M. (1994). An animated on-line community with artificial agents. *Institute of Electrical and Electronics Engineers (IEEE). Multimedia*, *1*(4), 32–42. doi:10.1109/93.338685.

Snyder, M., Tanke, E. D., & Berscheid, E. (1977). Social perception and interpersonal behavior: On the self-fulfilling nature of social stereotypes. *Journal of Personality and Social Psychology*, *35*(9), 656–666. doi:10.1037/0022-3514.35.9.656.

Taylor, R., & Berry, E. (1998). The use of a computer game to rehabilitate sensorimotor functional deficits following a subarachnoid hemorrhage. *Neuropsychological Rehabilitation*, *8*, 113–122. doi:10.1080/713755560.

Thomson, C., & Condon, T. (2001). *Enneagram applications: Personality styles in business, therapy, medicine, spirituality and daily life*. Changeworks.

Wagner, J. (2010). *Nine lenses on the world: The enneagram perspectives*. NineLens Press.

Williams, D., & Skoric, M. (2005). Internet fantasy violence: A test of aggression in an online game. *Communication Monographs*, *22*, 217–233. doi:10.1080/03637750500111781.

KEY TERMS AND DEFINITIONS

Abilities: Physical and mental capacities to perform tasks not requiring the use of tools, equipment, or machinery.

Aggression (Video Game Players): Video games should have particularly powerful effects due to the high attention levels of players and the active identification of players with characters on the screen where game players are rewarded directly for enacting symbolic violence, and therefore may transfer the learned aggression to the outside world.

Emotional Intelligence (EI): Often measured as an Emotional Intelligence Quotient (EQ), describes an ability, capacity, skill or (in the case of the trait EI model) a self-perceived ability, to identify, assess, and manage the emotions of one's self, of others, and of groups.

Enjoyment: Is defined as a complex construct with physiological, affective, and cognitive dimensions, and is the core of entertainment media.

Knowledge: The degree to which a candidate is required to know certain technical material.

Massively Multi-User Online Role-Playing Games (MMORPGs): A virtual world where millions of users interact, collaborate, and form relationships with each other through avatars in online environments.

Other Characteristics (O Factor): Personality, interest, or motivational attributes that indicate a candidate will learn certain tasks, rather than whether they can do those tasks.

Skills: Adequate performance on tasks requiring the use of tools, equipment, machinery.

Tavistock (Method): Also known as the group relations, concentrates on the individual only insofar as he or she is manifesting something on behalf of the whole group.

The Enneagram Personality: System describes nine distinct personality types and their interrelationships, mapped around an ancient symbol of perpetual motion.

ENDNOTES

[1] Please refer to the American Psychological Association's (APA) website for a complete list of the 56 divisions at http://www.apa.org/about/division/index.aspx

[2] In the industry of video games, video games are advancing and changing rapidly in the sense that not only are these games becoming more realistic (with better graphics and surround sound audio), but the design and operation of accessories (guns, arrows, etc.) to these games mirror actual weapons to the degree that U. S. law enforcement and community residents are unable to determine the authenticity of these instruments when individuals utilize these life-like instruments outside of gaming. The gaming industry is able to achieve this level of advancement due in parts to technology advancement, add-on accessories (Kinect), and the consultations from consultants (current law enforcement, retried law enforcement, seal team, etc.).

[3] Dramatic negative effects include the desensitizing and normalizing the action and the result of (causing, contributing, witnessing, and reception of) violence to the degree that the individual becomes detached from one's action, such that when the individual is committing the act, the individual feels that he/she is enacting a scene or a stage in the video game in one's mind. In so doing, the individual, at the moment in time, is detached from reality, due to the repeating scenario that the individual has lived through and experienced repeatedly because the individual has the ability to reload and restart such action. This is congruent to Csikszentmihalyi's Flow Framework.

[4] Kellar et al.'s context (2005) is similar to Malone and Lepper's fantasy (1987). Kellar and his colleagues defined engagement as personalization, rewards, role-playing, challenge, personal notes, collaboration, and communication, which is actually a combination of various factors defined in the framework of Malone and Lepper.

[5] Kellar et al. (2005) defined autonomy as the user's control of tasks.

6   Malone and Lepper's curiosity (1987) can be defined as an internal construct of challenge and fantasy, but it is an independent variable in the original study.

7   Materialistic Needs are: acquisition (nAcq), construction (nCons), order (nOrd), and retention (nRet).

8   Power Needs are: aggression (nAgg), blamavoidance (nBlam), counteraction (nCnt), defendance (nDfd), defence (nDef), Dominance (nDom).

9   Affiliation Needs are: abasement (nAba), affiliation (nAff), nurturance (nNur), rejection (nRej), and succorance (nSuc).

10 Achievement Needs are: achievement (nAch), autonomy (nAuto), harmavoidance (nHarm), infavoidance (nInf), recognition (nRec), and exhibition (nExh).

11 Information Needs are: cognizance (nCog), exposition (nExp), and understanding (nUnd).

12 Sensual Needs are: play (nPlay), sentience (nSen), Sex (nSex).

APPENDIX

The Apprentice

1. Original series – U.S.
2. International versions
    2.01 Africa
    2.02 Asia
    2.03 Australia
    2.04 South Africa
    2.05 Belgium
    2.06 Brazil
    2.07 Colombia
    2.08 Denmark
    2.09 Estonia
    2.10 Finland
    2.11 Germany
    2.12 Indonesia
    2.13 Ireland
    2.14 Italy
    2.15 Malaysia
    2.16 The Netherlands
    2.17 New Zealand
    2.18 Norway
    2.19 Pan-Arab
    2.20 Russia
    2.21 Spain
    2.22 Switzerland
    2.23 Turkey
    2.24 United Kingdom
3. Other Countries
4. The Games – Released on March of 2005 by Legacy Interactive

The Apprentice, adapted from Wikipedia, the free encyclopedia. Retrieved on May 28, 2013. Available at http://en.wikipedia.org/wiki/The_Apprentice_(TV_series)#The_Games

Chapter 10
Games and Social Networks

Yulia Bachvarova
Cyntelix, The Netherlands

Stefano Bocconi
Cyntelix, The Netherlands

ABSTRACT

Social media and social networks have gained an unprecedented role in connecting people, knowledge, and experiences. Game industry is using the power of social networks by creating Social Network Games, which can be even more engaging than traditional games. In this chapter, the main characteristics of Social Network Games and their potential are discussed. This potentiality can also be used for serious games (i.e. games with purposes beyond entertainment) and especially games related to learning and behavioural changes. This leads to introducing the emerging field of Serious Social Network Games and their unique characteristics that make them suitable for serious applications. Finally, the rising phenomenon of Social TV is discussed, which combines the power of TV and social media. Based on a project by the authors, preliminary findings on the most engaging techniques of Social TV Games are presented, together with initial suggestions on what constitutes good game mechanics for such games. The chapter concludes with future research directions for Social Network Games to become even more engaging and effective for purposes beyond pure entertainment.

INTRODUCTION

This chapter investigates several positive effects that potentially arise when combining games and social networks. A social network is "a set of people or groups each of which has connections of some kind to some or all of the others" (Rupnik, 2006). Social Network Games build upon these connections. Such games, often called just Social Games, can be defined - in the absence of a clear academic definition (Deterding et al., 2010) - as online games that use one's friendship ties for

play purposes while accommodating the players' daily routines (Järvinen, 2011). This can be, for example, in the form of notifying friends of one's achievements, or requesting friends to join in some game activity.

In this chapter we look not only at Social Network Games, but at Social TV games as well – games that lie in the intersection between social media and TV. Social media is 'a group of Internet-based applications that build on the ideological and technological foundations of Web 2.0, and that allow the creation and exchange of User Generated Content' (Kaplan & Haenlein,

DOI: 10.4018/978-1-4666-4773-2.ch010

Copyright © 2014, IGI Global. Copying or distributing in print or electronic forms without written permission of IGI Global is prohibited.

2010). Thus, to put it in a broader context, we examine in what ways the combinations of certain aspects of social networks and social media with games and TV media can create potentially more motivating and engaging environments. We focus particularly on games with purposes that go beyond pure entertainment, such as learning.

The power of the network is the ideology behind the Web 2.0 (Anderson, 2007). The combination of key Web 2.0 aspects and game principles led to the creation of new kinds of games, among which Social (Network) Games.

According to (Anderson, 2007) the key Web 2.0 principles are: (i) individual production and user generated content, (ii) harness the power of the crowd, (iii) data on an epic scale, (iv) architecture of participation, (v) network effects and (vi) openness.

Combining the second Web 2.0 principle (*harness the power of the crowd*) with certain game mechanisms defines a type of games called games with a purpose – "multiplayer online games where players generate useful data as a by-product of play" (Law & Von Ahn, 2011, p.81). The first game of this type is the ESP game (Von Ahn & Dabbish, 2004) where two players have to independently tag an image which the game presents to them. When the players annotate the image with the same tag they are awarded points. This turned out to be a hugely successful game and helped indexing enormous amounts of images that subsequently improve information retrieval on the Internet. The game mechanism which the ESP game employs is called 'output-agreement' where players get the same input and are rewarded if they reach an agreement on the output (Law & Von Ahn, 2011). The Web 2.0 principle incorporated in the game is employing the power of the crowd to do computational jobs that are difficult for computers.

Social Network Games, which are one of the focuses in this chapter, and which we already introduced earlier, are games which incorporate the *network effect principle* of Web 2.0 in their mechanics. The network effect principle states that

the value of a service increases when the number of its users increases. In Social Network Games the more people a player brings into the game, the more he/she progresses in the game. This chapter discusses in more detail the ways in which Social Network Games build on social networks and how to possibly leverage this aspect for the purposes of learning. In this discussion we put special attention on the relationship between social interaction and increased levels of communication.

An engaging environment where social interactions take place has the potential to increase the level of communication between players. Communication in a social environment, i.e. an environment where people feel a good connection to the other members, goes beyond casual exchange of friendly words (chatting) and can imply sharing of information and knowledge. Recent learning and knowledge management theories attribute a fundamental role to such social communications in processes related to learning.

Social Network Games can therefore be designed to fulfil purposes that go beyond pure entertainment and play a role in learning and, in a broader sense, in behavioural change. By utilizing social communication, Social Network Games can become an alternative to the prevailing classroom-based education for students. Also in adult learning, such as corporate training, Social Network Games can replace or supplement traditional learning forms.

The possibilities and the bottlenecks of these effects are discussed in this chapter. Social Network Games are quite young and literature, analysis and empirical research about them is scarce (Deterding et al., 2010). We present the existing information about these games in an attempt to start gaining some understanding about:

- What distinguishes this type of games from other existing games?
- What are the main game mechanics/principles pertinent to these games?
- Which further empirical or theoretical research is still needed?

We also examine the combination of Web 2.0 (more specifically social media) and games, in combination with TV and describe a prototype that was built to study the interdependencies between the three. The prototype that we implemented runs on top of a social network platform, but the main principles that we investigated hold for social media in general.

As Social Network Games are relatively new, an attempt to understand this field often leads to posing more questions than giving answers. All the questions though are potential avenues of further exploration of the possibilities of these games to become even more engaging and effective for purposes beyond entertainment.

SOCIAL NETWORK GAMES

Social Network Games are multiplayer games that utilize the social graph, i.e. the player's social connections (Chen, 2009). Social Network Games such as FarmVille[1] use social interactions in the gameplay, for example by notifying friends of what happens in the game and allowing them to influence the outcome of particular game activities. Facebook is the preferred social network platform on top of which these games are built, as it has the largest social base (Rossi, 2009).

Making use of the existing social networks happens in two main ways, leading to two different types of games: games in which the game mechanic does not require to enlarge one's social base and games for which involving more friends is a necessary condition to succeed in the game as well as is a rewarded game activity (Rossi, 2009). With respect to this distinction, Social Network Games, though a relatively new game genre, have been evolving from more simple games, where the main game principle is to bring into the game as many of one's social network friends as possible, into a second generation characterised by more challenging and more complex game dynamics (Rossi, 2009).

Collaborative play, characterized by game activities which are performed in collaboration with other players, creates shared experiences and is a key motivational factor for multiplayer games (Ducheneaut, Yee, Nickell, & Moore, 2005). This kind of play does not only lead to an increase in the number of game players but also to social interactions, which start within the game but can transcend the borders of the game into real life communication – some personal friendships that started as part of the World of Warcraft game turned into real life friendships.

Even though both types of games share the collaborative play aspect, Social Network Games are different from other online and MMO (massively multiplayer online) games and what happens within Social Network Games is not always comparable with what happens in MMO games (Rossi, 2009). The way Social Network Games differ is that they are built on top of an already existing social network infrastructure and they make use of this infrastructure in the gameplay, i.e. the gameplay happens through social interactions (De Andrade e Silva, 2012). In a multiplayer game it is very much the other way around – the social interaction happens within the existing game and the social connections are built as a result of playing the game and between game players. Rather than relying on already existing social networks, this type of games create their own network of game players (Rossi, 2009).

Main Principles

In this section we describe principles employed by Social Network Games that are specific to this type of games, i.e. they characterize Social Network Games and distinguish them from, for example, multiplayer games. We describe the principles of social interaction, casual gameplay, use of time and ambient awareness.

Social Interaction

Social Network Games are named social not only due to the collaborative play encouraged within the game, but also for the numerous social interactions that happen around (and are afforded by) them (Deterding et al., 2010). Social interactions trigger and, in turn, get enhanced by social emotions like competitiveness, affection, love, pride and envy. These social emotions are the basic building blocks of Social Network Games, and allow these games to create social experiences (Chen, 2009). For example, the need for social status is largely used in the design of Social Network Games (Chen 2009; Rossi 2009). The level of performance of the social game can influence the social status – this is a well used game mechanic that is also powerful in the social network context.

Most Social Network Games are played because of the social aspect related to them, that is the possibility to connect socially with other peers (De Andrade e Silva, 2012). Social Network Games make use of the existing social network as a strategic capital. By doing so, and as far as social communication is concerned, such games are engaging players in either bridging or bounding activities (Rossi, 2009). Bounding activities aim at strengthening the already existing relationships while bridging practices actually expand the network by creating new relationships.

A very important question is whether games indeed strengthen or expand relationships. Therefore, in multiplayer as well as in Social Network Games, an interesting aspect is whether the social interaction within the game leads to any real increase of the social capital, that is whether real friendships are established or 'friends' are just considered as resources that are needed to progress in the game. Social capital is broadly understood in terms of the resources accumulated through the relationships between people (Coleman, 2009).

Studies in the field of multiplayer games have been conducted to answer this question. The results of these studies reveal a very low level of social interaction with communication that is kept to the minimum. In World of Warcraft, this tendency has been observed at different levels:

- At the level of the whole game where players would see themselves as 'alone together'- surrounded by other players rather than actively communicating (Ducheneaut et al., 2005).
- At the level of "pick up groups" – a group formation of 5 to 25 players that is central for World of Warcraft because it allows the players to collaboratively overcome game challenges that would not be achievable singularly. In these groups the observed communication is almost non-existing, related to the gameplay only, and with frequent violations of social norms (for example leaving the group without notice or explanation, thus jeopardizing the overall group performance) (Eklund & Johansson, 2010).

The same tendency has been observed for Social Network Games, where the bridging activities do not really lead to increasing the social capital (Rossi 2009; Chen 2009). Players are actually more likely to add strangers for their 'friends' list to serve the game dynamic. Moreover, these 'friends' are handled in a different manner compared to the 'real' network (Rossi, 2009). On the other hand, Social Network Games can be beneficial for strengthening already existing relationships as they provide a new context for these relationships to evolve (Wohn, Lampe, Wash, Ellison, & Vitak, 2011). Little is known though what exactly the effect of Social Network Games is for maintaining existing relationships. In some cases, some 'friendships' initiated through the social network game extend into communication on topics outside the game and turn into real life friendships (Wohn et al., 2011). These reported cases indicate more a potential of Social Network Games rather than well understood and carefully crafted communication mechanisms within the game that are geared towards an increase of the social capital.

In conclusion, there is a predominant belief that social interaction in multiplayer games and in Social Network Games actually increases the social capital and leads to more socialization between the players. According to this belief, this would be particularly true in Social Network Games where using already existing social connections and establishing new ones is often brought to the level of main game mechanic. Even if this prevailing belief is confirmed in some situations for multiplayer games, the studies we presented above show actually just the opposite – the predominant social communication within the game is very limited and the collaborative spaces which these games create could be considered at times as antisocial. The same seems to be true for Social Network Games: by virtue of existing on top of social networks and employing the enlargement of social connections as a core game mechanic, these games are expected to increase the levels of socialization among players. In reality, Social Network Games do not always have this expected effect.

Casual Gameplay

Social Network Games are often casual, easy to play and can be played for short periods of time (De Andrade e Silva, 2012). They engage people in activities that do not require a lot of time and can be accomplished with a low level of attention (Rossi, 2009).

Social Network Games are often built around straightforward mechanics, give fast rewards and require simple controls (De Andrade e Silva, 2012). There are no sophisticated graphics and complicated gameplay. The main communication tools are direct messages, wall posts, group pages and chat systems that allow players to interact while they are playing (De Andrade e Silva, 2012).

Use of Time

There are two main aspects related to the use of time that distinguish Social Network Games from other games: (i) they support asynchronous play and (ii) they make a particular use of waiting time.

A big part of the success of Facebook games has been related to asynchronous play (Whitson & Dormann, 2011). The asynchronous play allows considerable freedom for players – they can log into the game at their own convenience, can play as much time as they feel and leave the game without coordinating with other players. Social interaction is maintained in an indirect manner, for example written messages, gift-giving, requests for favours (Chen, 2009). Asynchronous play is a typical game feature for Social Network Games and not that prominent for massive multiplayer online games where collaborative play happens simultaneously.

Social Network Games make use of the waiting time in a specific way, different from all other games. In social networks games the waiting time – this is time when players do not do anything - is actually time when the game evolves (Meurs, 2011). In FarmVille the player has to wait until the crops grow and are ready to be harvested, before being able to proceed with the game. The most similar corresponding use of time in all other games is called "dead time" – unchallenging and even boring gameplay, but needed for the advance of the play (Juul, 2004).

There are no available studies aimed at understanding what the effect of time in Social Network Games is (Meurs, 2011); whether asynchronous play and idle waiting time are actually enhancing any of the effects of gameplay and in what way.

Ambient Awareness

Ambient awareness is created by "a clutter of unfettered information" (Chen, 2009) – something that social websites provide, for example Facebook through its newsfeed. This is a lot of mundane information about a person's 'friends' for which any single piece of it might not have almost any value, but put together this information creates a general awareness of how and what the 'friends' are doing (Chen, 2009).

Social Network Games, by virtue of being built on top of social network platforms, utilize the same ambient awareness mechanisms and create similar type of awareness related to the game. Even starting to play a game is 'going public' on Facebook (Rossi, 2009). Furthermore, players would generally know the progress of their fellow players without searching for this information (Chen, 2009). In other words, gaming on Facebook is a semi-public activity (Rossi, 2009).

This specific feature for Social Network Games is supposedly beneficial for the game players but rather annoying for all the 'friends' who are not involved in playing the game. It is not known exactly in what ways ambient awareness is beneficial for games, which makes investigating this aspect a possible source for interesting insights.

SERIOUS SOCIAL NETWORK GAMES

In this section we investigate the potential of Social Network Serious Games, i.e. Social Network Games for purposes that go beyond pure entertainment.

In describing Social Network Games, we identified social interaction as one of the main principles that these games utilize. Researchers argue that the principles of social interaction and collaboration can support learning as they promote situated learning (De Andrade e Silva, 2012), as well as social learning (Reed et al., 2010). Situated learning is learning that takes place in the same context in which it is applied, as a social process whereby knowledge is co-constructed (Lave & Wenger, 1991). Social learning takes place in a social context and occurs through social interactions between participants in a social network (Reed et al., 2010). Because they shift the emphasis

from an individual context, which is promoted by video games and single player games, to a social context in a simulated environment, Social Network Games have the potential to support both situated and social learning.

However, in Social Network Games, as we discussed in the previous section, the social communication is minimal. We consider this a fundamental drawback for the successful utilization of Social Network Games for the purposes of learning, as learning is grounded in communication. A key aspect in the design of successful serious Social Network Games is therefore the understanding of how game design principles can enhance social communication. Social communication in turn can support processes like knowledge discovery, knowledge flow and the transfer and externalization of tacit knowledge.

Tacit knowledge is of particular importance in corporate training. One of the main characteristics of this type of knowledge is that it is difficult to verbalize and it can surface through social communication (Haldin-Herrgard, 2004). One metaphor that has been used to explain tacit knowledge is that of an iceberg; if all knowledge is thought of as an iceberg, the visible part of the iceberg is the explicit knowledge (easy to express, formalize and share), while the invisible part is the tacit knowledge (difficult to formulate and express) (Ancoria, Burethb, & Cohendet, 2000). While explicit knowledge is important for any job to be performed well, it is the mastering of the intangible tacit knowledge that allows people to excel (Brockmann & Anthony, 1998).

Social Network Games base their design principles on social emotions and this is an important aspect for the design of Social Networks Serious Games as well. Game design strategies which are related to social emotions, like sharing achievement (e.g. through posts on the Facebook wall), getting approval and encouragement from the others (e.g. the 'like' function), getting help from others, sharing as opposed to just viewing content, increase motivation and engagement (Chen, 2009) and have the potential to achieve better learning results. In our vision, successful Serious Social Network Games are games which design principles are weaved around and guided by the principles of social interaction (social emotions and social communication) and learning principles. For the latter, social learning and situated learning seem to be well-fitting paradigms.

Serious Social Network Games hold a significant promise for the field of corporate training as well. In that context learning is understood mainly in terms of knowledge flow and knowledge transfer happening within knowledge networks and through social communication.

Serious Social Network Games that extend the game world and the game action into the real world provide an interesting possibility for learning and behavioural change, since players can apply what they have learned in real life situations and learn from this experience as well. An example of such Social Networks Serious Games is the Trash Tycoon[2] game. In this game players collect the litter of a cluttered city and recycle it into environmental friendly products that they can later sale or exchange in the game. The actions in the game can be extended into participation in the recycling programmes of an existing company.

Social Change Games are another type of serious games. These games create social awareness of an issue, aim to change the attitude and behaviour of players and promote social engagement and political change (Whitson & Dormann, 2011). Social activism is very much grounded in debate and spread of information and ideas, all key aspects that social networks stimulate. Thus social activism constitutes a strong application domain for Serious Social Networks Games.

SOCIAL TV GAMES

Figure 1 represents the relationship between the three main themes we explore in this chapter: social networks, games and TV. In the previous sections we have been discussing some main ideas behind the attempt to bring the potential of

Figure 1. Intersection between Social Networks, Games and TV shows

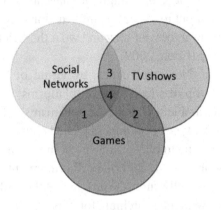

social networks to games. Referring to Figure 1, we have been looking at the intersection of social networks and games (area indicated with 1). Similarly, Social TV aims to bring the potential of social media and social networks to the TV experience (area indicated with 3 in Figure 1). And finally we describe a prototype of a social TV game which explores the interrelationship of games, social networks and TV (the area indicated with 4 in Figure 1).

The Social TV idea stems from the observation that, while watching TV programmes, people share their experiences and opinions related to these programmes through social media. This in turn can boost the TV ratings, as people get strongly influenced in their preferences by what their friends like.

The main question the field of Social TV tries to answer is how to bring together the social media communication channels and the more passive TV broadcasting into a more engaging experience. A format that has had more success in transforming passive viewers into active participants is represented by game shows. In this section we start by describing the current developments and tendencies in the field of Social TV. We then describe our project, "The Social Quiz Game", which lies at the intersection of social networks, games and TV shows, and discuss what makes an engaging Social TV format.

Social TV

Social TV conjugates the traditional broadcasting paradigm (one-to-many, mostly passive), with social interactions (active, many-to-many) in either the context of watching television, or related to TV content. As it is seen nowadays, Social TV lies in the intersection between social media, content industry and broadcasting. The main bottleneck for the wider spread of Social TV is the tension between the content industry (innovation-loving and available to experiment), and the broadcasters (usually more conservative and "gate-keepers").

Despite the intention to innovate, existing Social TV formats mostly consist of traditional TV show formats with a social layer on top. The traditional format and the social dimension coexist without any of them substantially changing under the influence of the other. This is the case of the talent show The Voice[3], where social media are only used as a way to poll the public mood. Other approaches transfer the social media paradigm on the television screen, by using the main principles of social networks to develop TV content around it. An example of this is The Audience ITV show[4]: 50 people walking behind a person and giving her help with daily problems.

TV content developers have difficulties getting out of the patterns of their thinking about TV show content. As mentioned before, a format that has had more success in transforming passive viewers into active participants is represented by game shows. In some Social TV games viewers can play on a second screen what is played on TV. An example of this is the UK Channel 4 Million Pound Drop quiz show[5], where viewers and TV show players play the same game at the same time. This is probably the most successful format and thought to be the most innovative, with 1.3 million active viewers (people who play along with the game) for 2 seasons of the game and a Bafta (the British Academy of Film & Television Arts) 2011 award in digital creativity category. Playing the same game along the TV show brings viewers closer

to experiencing the excitement of the show. One of the main drives related to watching TV is that people would associate with what is happening on the screen and experience certain emotions. *Doing* what is happening on the screen (playing together with the TV show contestants) turns the viewers into participants in the show and increases their levels of engagement. However, in the Million Pound Drop quiz viewers cannot interact with the TV show, they cannot influence the outcomes of the game. Also, they are not included in the game reward mechanic, which is a key aspect as far as the engagement levels are concerned.

Marie-José Montpetit, researcher at MIT's Research Lab of Electronic who pioneered the Social TV research, says that "The fact that you can interact to the level of impacting the actual events that are happening on the content, this is actually creating a new TV format' (interview in (Bulkeley, 2010)). Interacting with the TV content is a powerful engagement technique that has been successfully used by the Bravo Media production Top Chef[6], which also led to an increase of its viewers. The show introduced social media (Twitter and Facebook) to support its digital series Last Chance Kitchen. While the main Top Chef show was aired only on TV, the Last Chance Kitchen digital episodes were available "off" the TV airing time. In the digital series the contestants from the TV show, who had been eliminated, could compete again for the possibility to return to the main show. The audience could vote for the chef they wanted 'saved'. The highest rated episode of the Top Chef show was when the digital episode winner went back to the main show, that is when the offline experience and people's votes became meaningful by influencing the online (on TV) show. This is an example of two very important Social TV principles that were successfully employed. The first one is the understanding that social media or digital media can increase the viewing time by allowing access to content at any time. With that, viewers can get engaged beyond the TV time. Second is the interaction principle. The way to make the "off" air time meaningful and engaging is to connect it to the "on" air content via interaction techniques. These interaction techniques should allow the viewers to influence the TV content.

Main Principles

Our study of the existing Social TV formats and the reasons of their success can be summarised into the following main principles:

- Social TV is characterized by two distinctive and inherently different modes of delivering the content and engaging the users – *online* and *offline*. The online mode has to be understood in terms of 'on air', that is when the TV content is aired. The offline mode is when the content is not aired on TV but is accessible or happens via social media communication channels. The engagement techniques for the two different modes are different and there is a significant effort to keep the offline engagement active throughout all times (Wang, 2012).
- The interaction between the online and offline modes, in terms of content and user participation, is by itself one of the most powerful engagement mechanisms. The utilization of the offline mode, together with influencing the TV content as a result of the interaction mechanism, is what turns the passive TV viewers into active participants. The biggest hurdle for such interaction is the fact that often the TV content is pre-recorded and not possible to change.
- In the building of Social TV applications/ programmes, the starting point and the most important component is the content.

In conclusion, the formats that lead to increased audience are the ones that turn TV viewers into active participants. In order to increase the participation even further, users should be able to influence the outcomes of the TV show.

The Social Quiz Game

In this section we present a project that was done in cooperation with master students from the University of Aachen. The goal of the project was to design and develop a Social TV prototype that could allow a better understanding of the key design principles that can enhance the engagement of the Social TV formats.

We were aiming to understand whether increased interaction mechanisms connecting the two media can actually increase the engagement of the users with the content and which format can best support such interaction. Such understanding could eventually contribute to one of the main question the field of Social TV aims to address, namely in what ways social media can enhance the TV experience. In addition, as we developed a prototype that combines social networks, games and TV, we wanted to investigate the relationship between games and social networks, in this case in relation to a different medium.

In this chapter we describe the design and implementation of the prototype. At the time of writing there are no evaluation results yet towards the research issues the prototype addresses. This remains the goal for our future work.

Most of the Social TV formats follow a paradigm where the TV content is central, and social media support communication about this content (usually via Facebook or Twitter). In our project we aimed at creating a prototype that would shift from this paradigm and bring the two media closer, also on the content level. We assumed that thinking in terms of one unifying format, which distributes the content to the two media depending on the strengths of each, would provide a better position to understand how the combination of social media and TV could create a more engaging experience. More concretely, we chose a game as a unifying format. The game would be played via the TV and the social network. This approach required addressing the question of which mechanisms of combining the TV medium and Social Network Games would lead to more engaging experience.

Main Concept

The main idea behind the project was to extend the prevailing paradigm of considering TV content as central, and social media as a secondary communication channel, with no impact on the content. Our goal was to closely integrate the "social" and the "TV" aspects in order to understand which integration mechanisms led to more engagement. We were also aiming at verifying what we had observed in the field of Social TV, namely that interaction between the two media leads to an increased engagement with the delivered content.

The Rules of the Social Quiz Game

We designed a quiz game where players would play in teams against each other and against a team of experts during the TV show. During the online time (air time of the show), the team of experts would ask multiple choice questions, and each player would give an answer via a social network app (on Facebook). They would get rewarded for correct answers, either individually as well as a

team. Moreover, during the show air time, the team of experts would get open-ended questions proposed by each team. In case the experts would not be able to answer, the team that had proposed the question would get points. Those questions would be selected during the offline asynchronous time, by each team of players, with a mechanism of advancing candidate questions and voting by members of the team.

The game started with the players forming teams, by inviting their Facebook friends, or joining already existing teams (see Figure 2).

Team members would discuss and vote for the best quiz question they wanted to ask the expert team on TV (see Figure 3). The question which would get more votes would be selected to be sent to the TV game producers. The TV game producers would choose several, from all received questions, that would make it to the final show. Viewers would receive questions from the team of experts during air time on their second screens (see Figure 4). They would have limited time to answer before the session would close. Then the expert team in the TV studio would receive a question from the audience, and also have limited time to answer.

Figure 2. The user can join an existing team or create a new one

Figure 3. Voting for the best quiz question

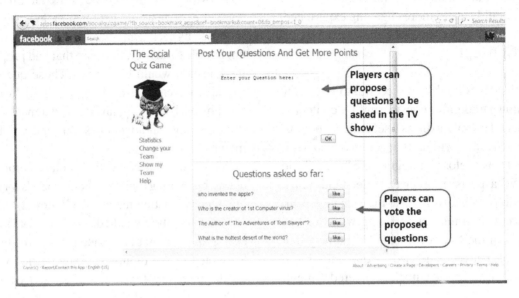

Figure 4. Multiple choice question from the experts to the public during the TV show

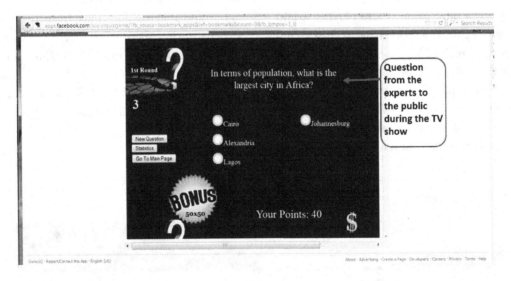

Points would be rewarded to each individual and to teams. At the level of individuals, points would be rewarded to each player when their team had proposed a question which the expert team would not be able to answer. Points would also be rewarded individually if a multiple choice question from the experts would be answered correctly. Thus the game would maintain two score (ranking) boards – one reflecting the performance of individuals (see Figure 5), the other one of the teams (see Figure 6).

At the level of a team, the team would receive points when winning against the expert team, by either posing a question the experts would not answer or by answering correctly a multiple choice question from them. In the latter case, the collective team answer would be determined based on which answer (from the multiple choice answers)

Figure 5. Ranking of individual players

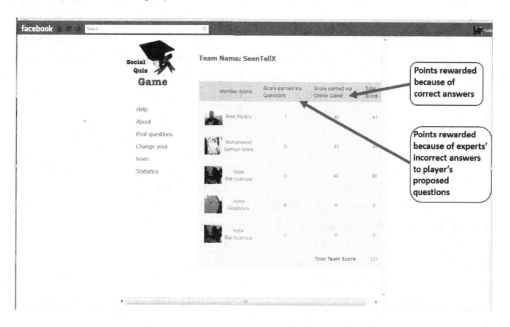

Figure 6. Ranking of teams

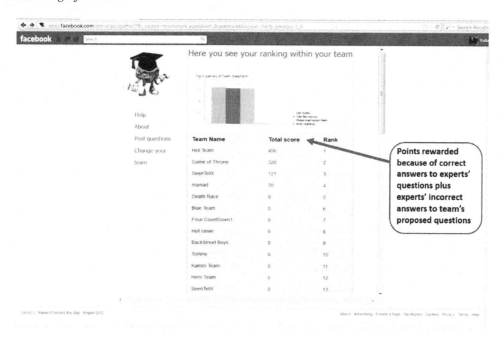

had been selected by the majority of gamers in a particular team.

The prototype was implemented as a client-server application, where the client was a Facebook application offering the functionality described above. The TV show was designed to be simulated by a Web broadcast.

Engagement Mechanics

In the design of the Social Quiz Game we were aiming at achieving high levels of interaction that go beyond the interaction between the online and the offline play. We therefore employed several engagement mechanics. Some of these mechanics are pertinent to the game when it is played in the TV studio (aired on TV), others are related to the social network game, and finally some belong to the interaction between the two.

An engagement mechanism belonging to the online part of the game was the interaction between the viewers and the game, while it was aired on TV. This translated in a game dynamic where the expert team would ask questions to all the viewers participating in the social network game, and questions from the viewers would be asked to the experts. An additional engagement mechanics we designed was that players who collected the highest score in the social network game would have the possibility to participate in the TV show. An engagement mechanism belonging to the offline part of the game was related to playing the social network game and specifically the formation of teams and the possibility to select the questions collaboratively. One of the strongest engagement mechanisms was making the viewers active participants in the game, being able to play against the expert team on TV and against competing teams, and participating in the reward system for the game. In this way we implemented a main principle of Social TV, namely that the audience is an active participant, and does not just watch the game.

FUTURE RESEARCH DIRECTIONS

In our future work we plan to perform more experiments with the Social Quiz Game prototype in order to understand the effect of the interaction levels in this game, and of passive viewers becoming active participants.

Furthermore, we are planning to address the research questions reported hereafter, which originate from the Social Network Game principles discussed so far. Such questions can lead to further exploration of the possibilities of these games to become even more engaging and effective for purposes beyond entertainment.

Can Social Network Games actually increase the social capital? As we discussed previously, Social Network Games use existing social connections or stimulate the creation of new ones. They do make use of the existing social capital but they seldom increase it. An interesting venue of investigation is to create game mechanics that can actually bring people together in the social space rather than just increase the number of their social connections.

Can time, as it is used by Social Network Games, bring added value to aspects that are paramount for learning and behavioural change? In depth analysis of time and the experience of time in Social Network Games is needed as this type of games uses time differently. Especially the asynchronous gameplay is different for Social Network Games compared to other multiplayer games. Moreover, Social Network Games make use of long periods of time when the players do not do anything, except waiting for some parts of the game to evolve. Some interesting aspects to investigate are:

- Does this specific use of time lead to more engagement?
- Does this specific use of time allow more flexibility and therefore is it able to attract dedicated as well as non-dedicated players, thus increasing the number of players?

- Is there any specific motivational aspect, related to idle waiting time, which can be utilized for serious purposes?

How can the power of Social TV and Social Network Games be utilized for serious purposes? The combination of the two media – TV and social media – and social networks and games can increase engagement, motivation and communication, thus creating more stimulating environments and mechanisms that can enhance learning or behavioural change. In this chapter we identified some of our initial insights in this direction, but much more empirical research is needed to unlock the mechanisms behind this envisioned potential.

Research results in answering (some of) these questions would increase the chance to have in the future Social Network Games applied for serious purposes.

CONCLUSION

Social Network Games hold potential beyond the entertaining purposes they are mostly designed for. High levels of engagement obtained by games and the social communication that takes place in social networks are characteristics that can be used to support serious purposes such as learning and behavioural changes. Unfortunately, the whole is not necessarily greater than the sum of its parts, as we discussed in this chapter. If Social Network Games seem to obtain good levels of engagement, the social communication can be very superficial and limited to achieving the goals set by the game. Such a "utilitarian" attitude is not necessarily an enabler for a type of communication where knowledge transfer and social learning takes place. Further research is required to understand what types of games and game mechanics can improve communication without sacrificing engagement.

The positive effect of games and social networks on engagement can also be extended to traditional formats such as TV shows. A key fac-

tor to exploit the strong points of each element is to think of the combination as a new format, and not, for example, as traditional TV shows with a social layer on top. There are two distinctive and inherently different modes of delivering the content, namely *online* (when the show is aired) and *offline* (when the show is not aired). This new format needs to incorporate both, as well as design an effective interaction between these modes, so that what happens during the online mode is influenced by the offline mode and vice versa.

The design of our Social Quiz Game takes into account all these requirements, making use of reward mechanisms and asynchronous (offline) as well as synchronous (online) dynamics.

ACKNOWLEDGMENT

The authors wish to thank Muhammad Salman Malik, Kateryna Iakubenko, Vaqar Hyder and Mohammad Ali Rostami for their contribution to the Social Quiz Game.

REFERENCES

Ancoria, B., Burethb, A., & Cohendet, P. (2000). The economics of knowledge: The debate about codification and tacit knowledge. *Industrial and Corporate Change*, 9(2).

Anderson, P. (2007). *What is web 2.0? Ideas, technologies and implications for education*. JISC Technology and Standards Watch.

Brockmann, E., & Anthony, W. (1998). The influence of tacit knowledge and collective mind on strategic planning. *Journal of Managerial Issues*, 10(2), 204–222.

Bulkeley, W. M. (2010). TR10: Social TV. *MIT Technology Review*. Retrieved from http://www2.technologyreview.com/article/418541/tr10-social-tv/

Chen, S. (2009). *The social network game boom.* Retrieved from http://www.gamasutra.com/view/feature/132400/the_social_network_game_boom.php

Coleman, J. (2009). Social capital in the creation of human capital. *The American Journal of Sociology, 94*(1988), S95–S120.

De Andrade e Silva, S. (2012). Click, share and learn! Social network games as serious play. In *Proceedings of the 6th European Conference on Games Based Learning.* ECGBL.

Deterding, S., Dreyer, S., Järvinen, A., Kirman, B., Kücklich, J., Paavilainen, J., et al. (2010). *Social game studies: A workshop report.* Retrieved from http://socialgamestudies.org/report

Ducheneaut, N., Yee, N., Nickell, E., & Moore, R. J. (2005). Alone together? Exploring the social dynamics of massively multiplayer online games. In R. Grinter, T. Rodden, P. Aoki, E. Cutrell, R. Jeffries, & G. Olson (Eds.), *Proceedings of the SIGCHI Conference on Human Factors in Computing Systems (CHI '06)* (pp. 407–416). ACM.

Eklund, L., & Johansson, M. (2010). Social play? A study of social interaction in temporary group formation (PUG) in World of Warcraft. In *Proceedings of DiGRA Nordic 2010: Experiencing Games: Games, Play, and Players.* DiGRA.

Haldin-Herrgard, T. (2004). Diving under the surface of tacit knowledge. In *Proceedings of OCLC 2004, The Fifth European Conference on Organizational Knowledge, Learning and Capabilities.* Vasa, Finland. Retrieved from http://www.coalescentknowledge.com/WP/diving.pdf

Järvinen, A. (2011). State of social in social games. *Casual Connect.* Retrieved from http://casualconnect.org/lectures/community-social/state-of-social-in-social-games/

Juul, J. (2004). An introduction to game time. In N. Wardrip-Fruin, & P. Harrigan (Eds.), *First Person: New Media as Story, Performance and Game* (pp. 131–141). Cambridge, MA: The MIT Press.

Kaplan, A. M., & Haenlein, M. (2010). Users of the world, unite! The challenges and opportunities of social media. *Business Horizons, 53*(1), 59–68. doi:10.1016/j.bushor.2009.09.003.

Lave, J., & Wenger, E. (1991). *Situated learning: Legitimate peripheral participation.* Cambridge, UK: Cambridge University Press. doi:10.1017/CBO9780511815355.

Law, E., & Von Ahn, L. (2011). Human Computation. *Synthesis Lectures on Artificial Intelligence and Machine Learning, 5*(3), 1–121. doi:10.2200/S00371ED1V01Y201107AIM013.

Reed, M. S., Evely, A. C., Cundill, G., Fazey, I., Glass, J., & Laing, A. (2010). What is social learning?. *Ecology and Society, 15*(4).

Rossi, L. (2009). Playing your network: Gaming in social network sites. In *Proceedings of DiGRA 2009: Breaking New Ground: Innovation in Games, Play, Practice and Theory.* DiGRA.

Rupnik, J. (2006). Finding community structure in social network analysis – Overview. *Journal of Mathematical Sociology.* Retrieved from http://eprints.pascal-network.org/archive/00003800/

van Meurs, R. (2011). Then you wait: The issue of dead time in social network games. In *Proceedings of DiGRA 2011 Conference* (Vol. 7). DiGRA.

Von Ahn, & Dabbish. (2004). Labeling images with a computer game. In *Proceedings of the SIGCHI Conference on Human Factors in Computing Systems* (pp. 319–326). Vienna, Austria: ACM.

Wang, T. (2012). *How must - see TV is now must - tweet TV.* Retrieved from http://www.youtube.com/watch?v=GCbhiBDsJDI&list=PL59D0CB455E1F5014&index=4

Whitson, J., & Dormann, C. (2011). Social gaming for change: Facebook unleashed. *First Monday*, *16*, 10–13. doi:10.5210/fm.v16i10.3578.

Wohn, D. Y., Lampe, C., Wash, R., Ellison, N., & Vitak, J. (2011). The S in social network games: Initiating, maintaining, and enhancing relationships. In *Proceedings of the 2011 44th Hawaii International Conference on System Sciences*. doi:10.1109/HICSS.2011.400

KEY TERMS AND DEFINITIONS

Offline Time: Time when a TV program is not aired, and activity is on social media.

Online Time: Time when a TV program is aired.

Serious Games: Games with a purpose beyond entertainment, such as learning or behavioural change.

Serious Social Network Games: Social network games with a purpose beyond entertainment.

Social Media: Websites that allow people to connect to each other and share content such as messages and status updates.

Social Networks: A network whose nodes are people and links exist between nodes if two persons are socially connected.

Social (Network) Games: Games that exploit the social connections among people.

Social TV: TV programs that use social media to reach the audience.

Social TV Games: TV programs that combine games and social media.

Social TV Serious Games: Social TV games with a purpose such as learning or behavioural change.

ENDNOTES

1   http://company.zynga.com/games/farmville
2   http://forum.trashtycoon.com/
3   http://www.nbc.com/the-voice/
4   http://www.thegardenproductions.tv/series.html
5   https://www.themillionpounddrop.com/
6   http://www.bravotv.com/top-chef

Section 2
Pedagogy and Assessment

Chapter 11
What is the "Learning" in Games–Based Learning?

Karen Orr
Queen's University Belfast, Northern Ireland

Carol McGuinness
Queen's University Belfast, Northern Ireland

ABSTRACT

This chapter explores the nature of "learning" in games-based learning and the cognitive and motivational processes that might underpin that learning by drawing on psychological theories and perspectives. Firstly, changing conceptions of learning over the last few decades are reviewed. This is described in relation to the changes in formal learning theories and connections made between learning theory and GBL. Secondly, the chapter reviews empirical research on the learning outcomes that have been identified for GBL, with specific focus on cognitive benefits, school attainment, collaborative working, and the motivational and engaging appeal of games. Finally, an overview of the dominant theoretical perspectives/findings mostly associated with GBL is presented in an attempt to broaden understanding of the potential for GBL in the classroom.

INTRODUCTION

One of the most debated changes in education in recent years has been the proposed use of computer games for learning purposes. Despite the great interest in the topic of games-based learning (GBL), the full potential of games for learning purposes is not often realised (Pivec, 2007). To appreciate the learning potential of games, it is important to understand how they fit within learning theory and the reported learning benefits documented in the research literature.

This chapter will adopt a psychological perspective on GBL. Firstly, the chapter will review changing conceptions of learning over the last few decades, noting the shift from passive and individual learning to active and collaborative learning. The associated developments in formal learning theory will also be reviewed and connections will be made between learning theory and new digital technologies, with specific reference to GBL.

Thereafter, existing research literature on the learning outcomes that have been identified for GBL will be reviewed. Specifically, the review

DOI: 10.4018/978-1-4666-4773-2.ch011

Copyright © 2014, IGI Global. Copying or distributing in print or electronic forms without written permission of IGI Global is prohibited.

will focus on evidence in the literature which addresses the following research questions:

- What value does GBL hold for general school attainment?
- What are the cognitive benefits of using GBL? For example, what are the specific benefits for cognitive functioning and higher-order thinking?
- How can GBL harness collaborative working?
- Is there evidence to support the motivational and engaging appeal of games?

LEARNING THEORY AND GBL

Over the past few decades, there have been several notable shifts in the conceptions of learning that are evident in learning theories – from a focus on passive learning to more active forms of learning and from an emphasis on individual learning to collaborative learning. These conceptual shifts are recognised in practice, for example, Garris et al., (2002) have noted the shift from 'learning-by-listening' approaches towards a more learner-centred, 'learning-by-doing' approach. Additionally, they are mirrored in changes in formal theories of learning, from learning behaviour and re-enforcement (behaviourism), to cognition and understanding (cognitivism, constructivism) to collaborative and socio-cultural learning (social-constructivism, learning communities).

It is widely recognised that digital technology has facilitated this more active and social view of learning, by transforming the role of learners from passive receivers to active constructors of knowledge (Fu, Su & Yu, 2009) and by affording more participatory experiences of learning and the co-construction of knowledge (Selwyn, 2008). Several writers have provided similar accounts of these shifts in learning theories and how they interact generally with e-learning (Holmes & Gardner, 2006) and more specifically with the

development of games for learning (Egenfeldt-Nielsen, 2006). Each learning theory will now be reviewed in the context of their origins, and in terms of how they relate to the practice of GBL.

Behaviourism

Behaviourism focuses on individual learning behaviour. Drawing on the theories of Pavlov, Thorndike and Skinner, it proposes that learning occurs through repetition of specific stimuli and specific behaviours coupled with reward and re-inforcement, associating learning with automation as opposed to active cognition.

Egenfeldt-Nielsen (2006) comments that many edutainment titles adhere (sometimes implicitly) to a behavioural learning approach, where the games offer a drill and practice style of learning, and where the focus is on the player learning to provide the correct response to a particular stimulus, with consequent rewards. He proposes that such edutainment titles rely more on extrinsic rather than intrinsic motivation, through the appeal to arbitrary rewards such as getting to the next level in the game. He offers the example of the game 'Math Missions: The Amazing Arcade Adventure', where money and playtime in an arcade are the rewards for the correct math answers provided. Egenfeldt–Neilsen (2006) points to the disadvantages of adapting such a learning approach to GBL, as he warns that such games can lead to the player focussing more on the goals of the game (rewards) as opposed to the goals of the learning experience.

Cognitive Constructivism

Unlike behaviourism, cognitive constructivism focuses on internal mental events such as cognitions and understandings. Building on theories such as Piaget and Bruner, and the cognitive revolution in psychology, the underlying assumption of this theory is that learners actively construct their own knowledge by building upon their current understanding. Through the processes of assimilation and accommodation (to use Piaget's terms), prior knowledge is refined and updated (through assimilation) and new knowledge and understanding are created (through accommodation of the new with the old). Although the focus is on the individual learner, constructivism does allow for social learning through the notion of scaffolding (Wood, Bruner and Ross, 1976), whereby the tutor embeds interventions within learning tasks that are suited to the learner's capabilities and offers a step up to the next learning stage. This aspect of social learning is developed more fully within the socio-constructivist perspective (see below).

Egenfeldt-Nilesen (2006) argues that edutainment titles embedded within a cognitive approach aim to encourage intrinsic motivation by combining the learning goals with the game experience, suggesting that such titles "stress the use of knowledge about how to organise material in terms of retrieval, encoding, chunking, modalities, and transfer problems" (p. 195). Egenfeldt-Nielsen (2006) provides an example of a game title adhering to this learning approach - Super Tangrams. Players have to manipulate geometric shapes in order for them to fit, and the goal of the game is integrated with the learning experience, so that play is motivated intrinsically by the game alone. He also notes that ideas from constructivism underpin microworlds such as the programming language LOGO. He argues that constructivist edutainment microworlds simulate "a part of the world allowing the player to explore this manifestation, resulting in strong learning experiences" (p. 198). He provides the example of 'My make believe castle' in which the player explores and constructs different elements of the castle, where the focus is not necessarily on content so much as general creativity, problem solving and memory skills.

Socio-Constructivism

The notion of requiring a facilitator or more knowledgeable tutor overlaps the previous approach with that of Socio-Constructivism, which suggests the requirement of a third party interacting between the learner and their environment. For example, Vygotsky focused on the learner's potential in terms of the difference between what the learner can currently do and what is just beyond their capability (without the help of a tutor or teacher). This is referred to as the zone of proximal development (ZPD). Vygotsky suggests a learner-centred process of bridging the gap whereby the tutor simply facilitates the process.

Socio-constructivism suggests learning that is "social, reflective, authentic, scaffolded, progressive and experiential" (Holmes & Gardner, 2006, p.84). The social aspect offered in this theory moves away from the individual learner and leads to the notion of 'learning communities' where people learn in collaboration with others in a wider social network (Holmes & Gardner, 2006).

When discussing socio-cultural perspectives of learning, Egenfeldt-Nielsen (2006) claims that this theoretical position provides the most holistic view of games for learning as it encompasses the learners, the game and the context. He argues that the area of GBL has yet to see the development of titles originating from this learning approach due to the fact that the theory focuses less on the actual game title and more on the context in which it is used. Despite this, many existing games are used in a manner consistent with socio-constructivist principles, where the learners construct their own knowledge and are guided by the teacher facilitating the learning experience within the context of an educational game, which is embedded in on-going lessons and class discussions.

Communal Constructivism

Holmes, Tangney, FitzGibbon, Savage and Meehan's (2001) original definition suggested that communal constructivism is:

an approach to learning in which students not only construct their own knowledge (constructivism) as a result of interacting with their environment (social constructivism), but are also actively engaged in the process of constructing knowledge for their learning community (p.3114).

With this theory the focus is not on the sole learner but on a community of learners, who are each constructing knowledge, not only for themselves, but for the benefit of others. Authors have recognised the importance of learning communities as they encourage the distribution of expertise (Brown & Campione, 1994), setting standards and practices for maintaining high quality learning (McGuinness, 2005).

Experiential Learning Theory and GBL

As well as the more general characterisations of learning and their relationship to GBL that have just been examined, another important influence comes from experiential learning theory. Several specific theories of GBL have been proposed that come from this tradition. They draw their initial inspiration from Kolb's (1984) experiential learning cycle. In the experiential learning cycle, learning begins with a concrete experience, which is followed by observation and reflection, which leads the learner to form conceptions, draw conclusions and form hypotheses to be tested in the next phase of the cycle, which leads to new concrete experiences, and so the cycle begins again. It is easy to see the attractions of the learning cycle as a model for the interactive experience of playing a computer game.

For example, Kiili (2005) advocated the use of experiential learning theory as "a fruitful basis for integration of game play and pedagogy" (p.17). As such, he proposed the 'Experiential Gaming Model', the purpose of which was to marry game play with experiential learning in order to encourage a 'flow' experience (more detail on 'flow' is provided later in the chapter). This

model is characterised by challenge, motivation, idea generation/ testing, and feedback.

Furthermore, in their Exploratory Learning Model (ELM), de Freitas and Neumann (2009) draw on Kolb's theory to present a learning model aimed at helping practitioners to create more effective exploratory/experiential learning environments. In their model, the authors place emphasis on: the role of an active learner; the 'exploratory' nature of the learning experience in a virtual environment; and on reflection and meta-reflection in the learning process, as this element facilitates the transfer of learning between the abstract, lived experience and the virtual dimensions. Additionally, it is also recognised that 'flow' may reinforce and maintain the learner's interest and motivation towards exploration. Figure 1 depicts the Exploratory Learning Model.

The 'Learning' in GBL: A Proposed Model

From this review of learning theory a general picture about the nature of learning in a GBL environment emerges; that is: learning has progressed from didactic to dynamic and collaborative experiences; learning is cyclical; learning is exploratory; learning is about constructing and testing ideas and meaning; learning benefits from feedback; learning is motivational; learning is self-regulatory and autonomous; and learning can give rise to feelings of flow in certain circumstances.

Linking Holmes and Gardner (2006) and Egenfeldt-Nielsen (2006), and drawing upon each of the learning theories reviewed, Table 1 highlights how games can facilitate different types of learning opportunities and learning outcomes.

This model summarises the various types of learning that can be demanded within a GBL application - beginning with the drill and practice type of learning that is evident within a behaviourist perspective, moving through to building learners' understanding and working with interactive games (cognitive constructivism), progressing

Figure 1. Exploratory learning model, (de Freitas & Neumann, 2009)

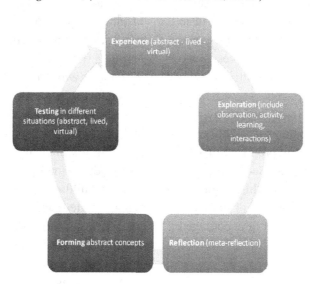

through games with the help of the teachers/tutors who facilitate classroom dialogue and meta-cognition (social constructivism), and finally establishing communities of learners, sharing knowledge and experience with co-learners (communal constructivism). As this progression takes place the context shifts from individual to social learning. The focus progresses from the game

Table 1. The 'learning' in GBL

Context	Learning Approach	Focus	Features of the Learning	Motivation
Individual ↑ ↓ Social	*Behaviourism* Drill and practice approach to learning, best suited to learning the mechanics of playing the game.	The game ↑	Repetition, feedback and reward.	Extrinsic ↑
	Cognitive Constructivism The learner works through simple to complex tasks within the games, building upon their understanding and knowledge and learns at a cognitive level.		The game affords opportunities to explore information and create/ test ideas. This forms a cyclical process as knowledge/ skill progresses and new information is explored and new ideas are created/ tested. Feedback and reward encourage progression.	
	Socio-Constructivism The teacher/ peers act as a facilitator guiding the learners through the learning process, also perhaps encouraging meta-cognition and thinking dialogue.		This learning approach progresses beyond the content/ features of the game. It focuses on the role of others as facilitators for learning. Despite facilitation, the expectation is that the learner will become self-directed.	
	Communal-Constructivism Through learning and gaming communities, learners share knowledge and experiences with a wider communal knowledge base to help both new learners and existing ones.	↓ The wider social context	Again, this learning approach extends beyond the contents/ features of the game. Here there is a strong focus on the agency of the learner. By sharing within a community of learners, individual learners further develop their own skills/knowledge as well as that of others. ·	↓ Intrinsic

alone to the game and the wider environment. Additionally, motivation develops from extrinsic motivation, e.g., earning coins/rewards in a game, to more intrinsic motivation, where success at the game and learning objectives motivates the learner.

It is recognised that certain games/ environments may offer further features or additions to this model. Despite this, it is proposed that by encompassing many of the key features established in this literature review, this particular model provides a holistic overview of the types of learning that might be evident or encouraged in a GBL environment.

BENEFITS TO LEARNING: EVIDENCE FROM EMPIRICAL STUDIES

Having established the developments in learning theory, and a proposed model representing the type of learning that is evident during GBL, this review will now focus on the evidence that discusses the educational benefits to be gained by employing GBL.

Before the educational benefits of game playing for learning purposes are discussed, it is necessary first to also recognise the benefits of computer game authoring. Although the empirical support for learning from *playing* games is much greater than that for learning by *designing* (Rieber, Smith & Noah, 1998), where the evidence can be quite anecdotal, the potential of computer game authoring is still worth noting. For example, reported benefits of computer game authoring include: encouraging meta-level reflection and the ability to think systematically (Salen, 2007); educational benefits brought about by encouraging students to learn by teaching others with their games (Keifer-Boyd, 2005); encouraging self-esteem (Robertson & Good, 2004); and providing a balance to the 'culture of consumption' (Peppler & Kafai, 2007, p. 7).

With regard to the more researched field of game playing for educational purposes, the potential of games to develop active and critical learning outcomes is widely recognised (Gee, 2003). However, the research evidence to support the claims is more mixed. This review focusses on studies that have used games (commercial and edutainment titles) for educational purposes, covering research in and out of the classroom, and studies employing adults, adolescents and younger children. The benefits found range from school-related achievements (e.g., literacy, numeracy, and concepts related to subject content) to learning gains in specific skills that are closely related to the game (e.g., spatial skills), to higher order reasoning skills and collaborative learning.

School Attainment

The research base assessing the value of games for general school attainment has studied a variety of different games, from programming languages, to games for leisure and edutainment products.

Programming Games: Studies demonstrating the educational benefits of games for learning curricular topics pre-date the technological advanced virtual environments seen in today's gaming applications. In particular, the use of microworlds, such as LOGO, pervaded the early GBL literature base. One example of an early study was reported by White (1984) that involved a game to help teach Newton's laws of motion. Prior to playing the game, White (1984) observed that, despite students' recent study of chapters relevant to this topic, they could not answer basic questions. However, having administered the game to some students, White found that these students improved their answering of relevant questions about the laws of motion in comparison to those who did not play the game.

Games for Leisure: Brain training games have been well researched in terms of their effectiveness. Miller and Robertson (2010) used Dr. Kawashima's Brain Training game for the Nintendo DS in a study involving 10/ 11 year olds. Using a small scale (n=71) controlled pre/ post-test design (one group used 'brain gym' techniques, and there was another no-treatment group) the authors found significant mathematical gains in the games console group in terms of accuracy and speed of calculations. Additionally, the games console group also demonstrated significant gains in terms of their global self-esteem. However, it is important to note that this paper has received criticism in relation to its statistics and methodology (see Logie and Della Sala, 2010). Nonetheless, Miller and Robertson (2011) have since replied to this criticism and have supported the findings of their paper.

Edutainment Game: Using pre- and post-test designs, numerous authors have also commented on the effectiveness of using edutainment games as an educational intervention. There is a strong evidence base around the topics of Maths and Science, at all levels of education. For example, Kebritchi, Hirumi, and Bai (2008) found that an educational math computer game had significant positive effects on mathematics achievement in an American public high school. Using a series of both single-player and multi-player maths computer games, the authors found that students who played the games scored significantly better on a post-test district wide mathematics bench mark exam in comparison with students who did not play the maths computer games.

More recent work by these same authors (Bai, Pan, Hirumi, and Kebritchi, 2012) reported the findings of a more robust evaluation (using a pre-/ post-test, cluster randomised controlled, quasi-experimental design (n=437)) of a maths game entitled Dimension M. Their results indicated that the game increased children's math knowledge in algebra, as well as maintaining motivation to learn. Additional work has also looked towards GBL for improving math ability with children with intellectual disabilities. For example, Brown, Ley, Evett, and Standen (2011), using a matched pairs design (8 students played the intervention fractions game, whilst 8 played control games)

compared pre- and post-measures of maths skill. Their results revealed that those who played games had a significant improvement in understanding of fractions, whereas those in the control group did not. However, it is important to interpret these results with caution, due to the small sample size (n=16).

Moving on to different curricular subjects, Papastergiou (2009) examined the learning effectiveness and motivational appeal of computer games for learning concepts related to computer science education. Using a pre- and post- test design (n=88) and comparing a gaming group of Greek high school students with a non-gaming group (content was the same, delivery, i.e., the game, was the only difference), Papastergiou found that the game was more effective at promoting computer science concepts and knowledge than the non-gaming equivalent. In addition, the game was considered to be more motivational. Researchers have also focussed their attention on younger students and science education. For example, Lim, Nonis, and Hedburg (2006) found a significant improvement in 10-11 year olds' performance in post-test scores, as well as improvements to their responses (i.e., more elaboration) after having used the 3D edutainment game Quest Atlantis in science classes.

There is also some evidence of effective GBL use in the geography curriculum. For example, Tuzun, Yilmaz-Soylu, Karakus, Inal, and Kizilkaya (2009) reported significantly higher post-test scores (compared to pre-test scores) in achievement tests, after 24 Turkish 4th and 5th graders had used a geography game. Additionally, Virvou, Katsionis, and Manos (2005) explored the educational effectiveness of an educational adventure game also aimed at geography education. This research points to the value of GBL especially for poor performing students. The authors compared the educational effectiveness of this game to alternative learning software with a simple conventional user interface, without any virtual reality game. Using 9/10 year old children (n=90), the pre- and post-test results revealed that the players of the game made fewer mistakes, and had an overall higher educational benefit in comparison to the non-gaming group. The groups were also categorised according to their previous geography marks, and results revealed that the subgroup of students who were previous poor performers, who had used the games, benefitted the most in comparison to all subgroups using the game (i.e., those with average and good performance).

Research has also been conducted in higher education settings. For example, recently, Kanthan and Senger (2011) reported the benefits of a specially designed game for improving pathology students' performance on exam scores, whilst also noting benefits to student satisfaction and engagement. Additionally, and with college aged students, Halpern, Millis, Graesser, Butler, Forsyth, and Cai (2012), reported the benefits of 'Operation ARA'. They found, using a pre- and post-test design, that ARA players had significantly higher learning gains, as measured by tests of knowledge regarding research methods and scientific reasoning, in comparison to the control group. However, Halpern et al., (2012) recognise that despite such encouraging results, without a more robust and controlled experimental design, they are unable to make strong claims regarding the benefits of this game.

There is clearly strong support for the potential of GBL for school learning, using different learning approaches. Despite the fact that sometimes the learning styles embedded are not always explicit/clear in the empirical evidence, there is some indication of different learning approaches throughout this work reported. There is evidence of constructivist learning styles in the early work of LOGO and the work by Halpern et al., (2012), as well as evidence of enquiry orientated learning, e.g., Lim, Nonis, and Hedberg, (2006). Social constructivism is also evident in some of the work. For example, Lim, Nonis, and Hedburg (2006) note the role of scaffolding and teacher

facilitation. Furthermore, Bai, Pan, Hirumi, and Kebritchi (2012) report the use of a maths game which was designed to use a variety of activities, such as team work and role setting, to help the children solve problems and encourage long-term learning.

In summary, it is clear from this review that the evidence supporting the use of GBL for school attainment is quite varied. The evidence comes from both educational and recreational games, and from the general population, as well as those with intellectual difficulty. Additionally, the evidence spans a variety of learning approaches, a wide age range, and numerous different school subjects. However, the bulk of the work tends to focus on the general population within a school setting, focussing on science-based subjects, that is, engineering, geography, computer science and maths. This points to the type of subject to which games might be more applicable, that is, subjects where specific skills and right or wrong answers, (and perhaps on occasion, drill and practice style learning) are more appropriate.

Cognitive Functioning and Specific Cognitive Skills

As well as focussing on general school attainment, research has also demonstrated the benefits of GBL on more specific aspects of cognitive processing and skills as demonstrated in laboratory-based tasks. For example, Pivec (2009) found that recreational adult game players scored on average 40% higher on cognitive tests than those who did not play computer games, and more so, those who played more frequently scored higher than less frequent players. Further research has also highlighted that interactive gaming technology can enhance a variety of specific cognitive skills. For example, early studies highlighted the benefits of computer games for children's (10-11 year old) spatial skills (Subrahmanyam & Greenfield, 1996) and visual/attention skills in older college aged participants (Greenfield, deWinstanley, Kilpatrick, & Kaye,

1996). More recent research has supported these findings. For example, Green and Bavelier (2003) reported that video game players (18-23 year olds) outperformed non-video game players in tests of visual attention capacity. Furthermore, this study establishes a causal effect of action video game playing on cognitive ability as the authors demonstrated the improvement made by non-game players after 10 days of training on an action game. This evidence was supported by a later similar study where Green, Pouget, and Bavelier (2010) found that action video game experience results in more efficient use of sensory evidence, as well as demonstrating a causal relationship between gaming experience (with action games) and skill improvement.

Despite these positive findings, it is important to question the extent to which these skills are transferred to different contexts beyond the game. Extensive research conducted on 'brain training games' highlights this cautionary point. For example, in a large scale study involving adults, Owen, Hampshire, Grahn, Stenton, Dajani, Burns, Howard and Ballard (2010) found that after six weeks of training on cognitive tasks aimed at improving a variety of cognitive skills, such as memory, attention, planning, reasoning and visuo-spatial skills, improvements were found. However, this was limited to the cognitive tasks that were trained, and no improvements were found of transfer effects to untrained tasks (despite cognitive similarities between some of the trained and untrained tasks). The issue of transfer was also raised by Pillay (2002). His study revealed that playing recreational games can positively influence performance on subsequent educational tasks, in terms of time efficiency and correct solutions offered, as significant differences were found between the control group and the experimental groups. However, negative transfer (i.e., inappropriate strategies transferred between a game and a subsequent educational task) was also reported, as Pillay (2002) found that the participants relied on the same strategies they employed during the

recreational game for the subsequent educational task, even when such strategies were inappropriate.

This is a complex picture and the implications for GBL are important. The goal of GBL is to encourage cognitive development, curricular knowledge, and a variety of skills that will enhance the pupils' repertoire of abilities, so that they can then select appropriate skills and strategies to match any learning context presented to them. These instances of poor transfer point to an important consideration for GBL, as it suggests a lack of critical engagement with the learning content. If pupils do not engage critically with games in the learning context, and are not able to transfer the skills learned beyond the digital world, then their value to education is limited. There are numerous potential solutions to encourage more critical engagement with the learning content, for example, as Halpern et al., (2012) suggest, it is important to ensure the game provides variability, as it is argued that this enhances transfer. Furthermore, it might also be beneficial to adopt a more social constructivist learning perspective, by using the teacher as a facilitator to guide, embed, and contextualise the learning gains available.

Higher-Order Thinking

Many authors have also supported the idea of using gaming technology for improving numerous different higher-order thinking skills, such as problem solving (Inkpen, Booth, Klawe, & Upitis, 1995; Sandford, Ulicsak, Facer & Rudd, 2006; Whitebread, 1997); logical thinking, reasoning skills (Higgins, 2000); and sequencing and reasoning ability (McFarlane, Sparrowhawk, & Heald, 2002).

The measurement of thinking skills lends itself to the analysis of dialogue and discourse. Therefore, with some of the literature focussing on higher-order thinking, a more socio-constructivist approach to learning becomes evident, where the presence of another person acts as a facilitator to the discourse, and subsequently the learning.

For example, using games designed specifically for educational purposes, Herrington and Oliver (1999) conducted a discourse analysis (coded according to Resnick's (1987) higher-order thinking categorization scheme) of pairs of student teachers working together on an interactive multimedia program. Their results demonstrated high levels of higher-order discourse/ thinking.

Using a different approach, VanDeventer and White (2002) assessed expert behaviours amongst children (10/11 year olds) who were observed teaching the popular Super Mario games to a less expert adult. This study found that more experienced video game players demonstrated expert characteristics (e.g., actively seeking new information, organizing, classifying and categorizing information, and considering input from multiple sources) more frequently than the less experienced or novice players. Additionally, and again using recreational games, and analysis of talk (qualitative verbal protocol analysis), Pillay, Brownlee, and Wilss (1999) found that while playing games, teenagers (14-18 year olds) engaged in complex cognitive processing. For example, the transcripts showed that the players were engaged in problem solving and inference making, that they used inductive reasoning to make associations between different pieces of information, as well as constantly monitoring their own thinking, revealing the use of meta-cognition.

Furthermore, work with younger children has also demonstrated the benefits of GBL for thinking. For example, Henderson, Klemes, and Eshet (2000) assessed the outcome of a game ('Message in a Fossil') which was designed for exploring plant/animal fossils, and used with 20 7 year old children. Although the authors claim that this game is based on a constructivist perspective, the way in which it was embedded into the classroom employed social constructivist principles. For example, there was teacher interaction and the students worked in pairs together at the computer. Using pre- and post- written and interview questionnaires, Henderson et al., (2000) found that

the children improved across a variety of thinking skills and strategies; e.g., they made inferences and classified information. Additionally, they provided more correct answers at post-test and their use of scientific language developed. Furthermore, the authors reported evidence of transfer in certain circumstances. For example, questions regarding items that would decay/become fossilised were answered extremely well (97% of correct answers at post-test, compared to 41% at pre-test), despite the fact that activities regarding what items would decay/ become fossilised were not used in the game. This finding demonstrates some internalization of the concepts of decay and preservation over time.

In summary, numerous benefits are noted in the GBL literature in terms of engaging learners in higher-order and more challenging kinds of thinking. Using a variety of different methodologies, such as protocol analyses, interview techniques and pre- and post-test designs, studies are highlighting the potential for games to encourage a variety of thinking skills, using both recreational and edutainment game products. However, despite the noted benefits on thinking and cognition in these studies, it should be remembered that the games were not designed to teach thinking *explicitly*. The thinking benefits reported in these studies were a by-product of the learners' interactions with the game and the curricular content. In a review of thinking skills and ICT technology, Wegerif (2002) concluded that there is little evidence that games can teach thinking skills on their own. Rather he points out that they can be used as a resource to support other teaching practices.

Finally, it should be noted that much of the research on the development of thinking skills involves the use of games from a socio-constructivist perspective, in that often there is the presence of an additional person, either students working in pairs, or interaction from the teacher. This learning approach allows for peer/teacher facilitation and can encourage dialogue, which in itself allows for the measurement of thinking (via talk), during GBL. Facilitation by the teacher can also contextualise the learning, and make it more visible in the classroom; this in turn could potentially encourage the transfer of learning from the digital to the real world.

Collaborative Learning

The potential gains from GBL extend beyond cognitive and school attainments; they also offer an opportunity for productive collaborative working, and therefore socio-constructivist/communal constructivist learning practices.

In general, the potential that collaborative working holds for educational benefits is well recognised (see, for example, Gokhale, 1995 and Howe, Tolmie, Thurston, Topping, Christie, Livingston, Jessiman, & Donaldson, 2007). Although early arguments in the computer game literature highlighted computer game playing as a solitary activity (see for example Selnow, 1984), many researchers are now studying their potential to encourage collaboration. In terms of educational games, it has been suggested that they foster collaboration (Tuzun, 2007) and enhance social skills (Sandford et al., 2006). For example, Tuzun (2007) found that although the tasks within the games used in his study did not specifically require collaboration, collaboration naturally emerged.

Some studies that have specifically examined the effects of collaborative work when using educational computer games have highlighted the benefits to be gained. For example, Inkpen et al. (1995) found that children playing together on one computer solved significantly more puzzles within an educationally relevant puzzle solving game than those who played alone. In addition, Klawe and Philips (1995) commented on the positive benefits from two students working together at a single computer while playing a maths game, commenting that it stimulated discourse, that the children found it more enjoyable, and that it encouraged the pupils to remain more connected to the learning environment, thus enhancing the

transfer from learning with the game to the wider curricular goals. Additionally, the research previously reviewed discusses the benefits of the social context whilst using games for learning (Herrington & Oliver, 1999; Henderson et al., 2000). However, less is known about how to maximise the social or communal aspect of GBL so as to fully realise learning potential.

Difficulty in Measuring Learning from Games and the Nature of the Evidence Provided

The studies reviewed in this chapter have employed a range of research designs to measure the learning outcomes achieved via GBL. However, when addressing the 'learning' in GBL it is important to consider the difficulty in measuring learning during game play as several different problems have been acknowledged. These include concerns about the *type* of learning achieved during game play (factual versus conceptual), *when* the learning should be evaluated (immediately or after time for consolidation), difficulties learners might have in *expressing the learning* (with or without opportunities for reflection), and the *type of tests* used to evaluate learning (knowledge versus transfer and application).

For example, Swaak and de Jong (1996) argued that the effects of GBL technology are not best evaluated by tests of knowledge; rather they should be measured by tests of application and transfer. Furthermore, Kiili and Lainema (2008) suggested that learning from games is conceptual as opposed to factual, and that students may find it more difficult to express gains in conceptual understanding. Plus, they suggested that the learning taking place during game play may take time to consolidate and so immediate measurement may not reliably measure learning outcomes. It is thought that learners might have difficulty in communicating learning through gaming as time might lapse before learning is consolidated (Lainema & Nurmi, 2006) as it is thought that learning takes place only after an opportunity for reflection (Garris et al., 2002). This 'delay' in learning in collaborative contexts is also recognised in the general literature on joint problem solving and collaborative working. For example, Howe, McWilliam and Cross (2005) make reference to the notion of 'incubation effects' (p. 67), in that the benefits of collaborative work may not be apparent until some time has passed. The measurement issues mentioned above are inevitably affecting confidence in the conclusions about the educational effectiveness and appropriateness of games in the classroom (Kearney, 2007; Williamson, 2009).

Another factor greatly impacting upon this confidence is the *amount* and *quality* of the data that are available. For example, Wideman, Owston, Brown, Kushniruk, Ho, and Pitts (2007) recognised that although numerous studies have supported the value of educational games, many of these studies do have methodological limitations, with an over reliance on self-report and impressionistic data. More recently, Hwang and Wu (2012) conducted a trend analysis on GBL research. They noted an increase in the number of publications in this area over the last 5/6 years. However, they also specified that the majority of the research focussed on motivation, perceptions, and attitudes, as opposed to focusing on learning outcomes. Additionally, O'Neil, Wainess, and Baker (2005) commented on the quality of the available evidence. They conducted a review of empirical research in the field of learning with games from 1990-2005. Their review was not on classroom learning specifically; the authors reviewed games used for training adults, and research specifying the use of multiplayer/ massively multiplayer games for training adults. But their findings are relevant more generally to GBL. The authors found that during this period several thousand papers had been published relating to games. However, only 19 were usable for the purposes of their study, that is, with either qualitative or quantitative data available. Overall, the authors concluded that "the evidence of potential is strik-

ing, but the empirical evidence for effectiveness of games as learning environments is scant" (p. 468).

The literature reviewed in this chapter also points to the potential of GBL for several different learning gains. However, they too must be interpreted with caution as often the research design employed or the sample sizes used cannot lead to substantive claims about the benefits of GBL for thinking, learning, or school attainment more generally. More rigorous impact evaluations are required, using robust, controlled, and randomised experimental designs, if GBL is to be seriously considered in education, where evidence-based practice is becoming much more common and indeed expected.

THE BENEFITS FOR MOTIVATION AND ENGAGEMENT

As well as cognitive, school and academic benefits, GBL holds great appeal for its motivational and engaging qualities. Motivation is a vital element in the learning process (Pintrich and Schunk, 1996). The general ICT literature has long recognised the beneficial and motivational effect that different forms of ICT have on pupils' learning (Cox, 1997; Denning, 1997; Passey, 1999; Reid, Burn, & Parker, 2002) and the great opportunities it offers for individualization of content (Cordova and Lepper, 1996). In terms of computer games in particular, it is proposed that games offer the opportunity for highly involved, intrinsically motivating experiences, free from real life constraints (Ritterfield & Weber, 2006). They, like other media forms, are enjoyable, fun and provide the opportunity to escape everyday reality (Sherry, 2004).

It is not just mainstream spare time computer games that are considered enjoyable. Studies employing games-based learning environments in an education setting have also noted the enjoyment that students experience during game play, as many authors have noted the motivational appeal that games and interactive multimedia can provide (Inal, & Cagiltay, 2007; Robertson & Good, 2004; Sedighian, 1997; Stoney & Oliver, 1999; Tuzun, 2007; Virvou et al., 2005).

Numerous theories have been suggested regarding the motivational appeal behind computer games, which highlights their appropriateness to education. For example, Malone and Lepper (1987) suggested that in order for an activity to be intrinsically motivating it should provide a mix of "challenge, curiosity, control and fantasy" (Malone and Lepper, 1987, p.230). These elements are evident in well-designed computer games and indeed edutainment products. Furthermore, Jayakanthan (2002) argued that games 'suck in' players, through "immersion, challenge, reward, …physical and mental engagement, and multisensory stimulation" (p. 99).

As well as encouraging motivation, the high levels of engagement often witnessed during computer game play cannot be overlooked; this is another factor that attracts educationalists to this popular medium (Connolly, Stansfield, & Hainey, 2007). It has been suggested that interactive multimedia can encourage cognitive engagement by attracting and maintaining learner focus (Stoney and Oliver, 1999) and by providing a level of immersion that few other mediums can provide. Authors have referred to this level of engagement as 'flow' (Csikszentmihalyi, 1990; Malone, 1980).

Flow describes a state of mind where individuals are so immersed in the activity at hand that they become oblivious to their external environment. Flow theory is based on a reciprocal, yet balanced relationship between skill and challenge (Shernoff, Csikszentmihalyi, Schneider, & Shernoff, 2003, p.160). It is a "self-contained activity, one that is done not with the expectation of some future benefit, but simply because the doing itself is the reward" (Csikszentmihalyi, 1990, p.67). Sweetser and Wyeth (2005) have adapted this theory to propose a set of game flow criteria to explain the elements within computer games that encourage flow. These are: concentration, challenge, skills,

control, clear goals, feedback, immersion, and social interaction (Sweetser & Wyeth, 2005).

When evident in educational gaming applications, such qualities hold the potential to encourage highly engaged learners. Indeed, Bulger, Mayer, Almeroth, and Blau (2008) reported that interactive game-like environments are more engaging than traditional teaching methods. Using American university students, they exposed some students to a simulation-based exercise, whilst a control group received no simulation; i.e., they received a traditional lecture format. Their results revealed that those students exposed to a no-simulation condition demonstrated lower engagement than those who were subject to the simulation condition, as measured by recording on- and off-task internet activity.

Additional research employing eye tracking while using educationally relevant computer games has indicated the potential for games to maintain learner focus and affect cognitive change. Using American university students, Alkan and Cagiltay (2007) measured fixation times of the students whilst engaged with an educationally relevant game. The results showed that the highest fixation time values of the participants were measured when they had to think of a solution, as opposed to the lowest fixation times that were evident during the menu function, where participants simply had to hit 'start'. This demonstrates the potential for games to maintain learner focus so long as the learners are being cognitively challenged.

Increased motivational appeal using GBL has also been evidenced in younger students. For example, the aforementioned study by Tuzun et al. (2009) compared motivation in a GBL class to motivation in the traditional school environment. Using a motivation scale aimed at measuring intrinsic and extrinsic motivations, the authors found that students demonstrated significantly higher intrinsic motivations and significantly lower extrinsic motivations in the GBL environment. This suggests that the challenges of the game itself were the motivational appeal in the GBL class, whereas extrinsic motivations were required or exhibited more in traditional classroom settings.

A Cautionary Word about Flow

Despite the motivational and engaging appeal of games, issues in the literature exist regarding the learning outcomes of such engagement, as well as debates surrounding the measurement of engagement/ flow. Firstly, it is not at all clear what learning outcomes are achieved as a result of high levels of engagement or flow-like experiences. Researchers have highlighted that perhaps the motivational energy invested in games is not entirely beneficial. For example, Okan (2003) posed the question that when learners are engaged with an interactive learning task, are they motivated to learn or to simply play with the computer?

Ko (2002) found that even when players performed poorly in a game, they enjoyed the activity. And Lim et al., (2006) also found that students became so immersed in the 3D world that they lost focus on their learning tasks. Additionally, Shin (2006) recognised that students' engagement with technology does not necessarily lead to learning; he suggested that the challenge for designers is to marry cognitive tasks with playfulness, so that students are enjoying the experience, yet learning at the same time. This notion is further supported by Egenfeldt-Neilsen (2006) who explained that sometimes players might be motivated more by the game's goals as opposed to the learning goals, and so may skip important text information etc., and sacrifice the learning outcomes.

Other authors have reported more positive effects of flow on learning outcomes, particularly in other non-traditional learning environments such as online environments (Herrington, Oliver, & Reeves, 2003). Ghani (1995), for example, has suggested that flow results in increased learning and creativity. Furthermore, Skadberg and Kim-

mel (2004) have supported this notion; in their study they evaluated visitors' experience while browsing a website. Amongst their results they found that when people are in a flow state, they have a tendency to learn more about the content presented in the website, concluding that flow had a positive impact on people's learning.

Secondly, as with the problematic measurement of the learning gains achieved while using games, so too is there difficulty in measuring flow, partly because of problems in defining the concept. Finneran and Zhang (2003 & 2005) recognised the discrepancies across the numerous flow models, suggesting that apart from challenge and skills, the constructs differ across all models. They pointed out that "inconsistent flow models pervade the literature" (p. 90).

Another measurement problem lies in the optimum time to measure flow. Webster, Trevino, and Ryan (1993) said that flow is best captured when measured during or immediately after an interaction. However, to measure the experience during an interaction there is a distinct risk of breaking the flow pattern; for example, to ask someone to complete an engagement survey during game play may then break the level of immersion an investigator wishes to measure. And to do so after the intervention will potentially fail to capture the extent of the immersion experienced during an interaction. This difficulty has been highlighted by Ijsselsteijn, de Kort, Poels, Jurgelionis, and Bellotti (2007) who recognised that to analyse the gaming experience whilst in the middle of it will 'break the spell' (p.1).

These questions and concerns about flow are not restricted to engagement during educational computer game use. However, they are likely to be particularly relevant to GBL in the classroom. Unless the high levels of engagement and flow witnessed during game play result in recognisable learning outcomes, then the uptake of GBL in the classroom is likely to be restricted.

CONCLUSION

This chapter has reviewed theoretical perspectives on GBL and empirical studies about the effects of GBL on learning. The review revealed that no single theoretical perspective is associated with GBL, although many writers draw on variations of experiential theory because it seems to capture aspects of the interactional and problem-solving experience that is typical of many games-based learning scenarios. Also, the concept of flow has emerged as important despite the cautionary opinions that have been expressed about the relationship between the experience of flow and desired curriculum-related learning outcomes.

General shifts in learning theories towards a social-constructivist perspective have also broadened the understanding of the types of learning and motivational experiences that might be associated with GBL and that would be beneficial for classroom learning – exploration, conceptual understanding, higher-order thinking, self-directed, and autonomous learning. Furthermore, a proposed model highlighting how games can facilitate different types of learning opportunities and learning outcomes is also presented.

With reference to the research questions posed at the beginning of the chapter, the research reviewed confirms the potential for GBL to improve cognitive functioning, for example, by improving spatial skills and visual attention skills, as well as by encouraging higher-order thinking skills, such as, problem solving and reasoning. The potential to improve school attainment is also confirmed, however, more so in science-based domains. The studies reviewed reflect constructivist perspectives about the nature of learning as well as placing an emphasis on the social nature of learning (teacher scaffolding, collaborative learning, dialogue etc.). Nevertheless, studies still continue to examine the effects of 'drill and practice' GBL. Additionally, there is support for the use of GBL to promote collaborative working, as well as support for the motivational and engaging appeal of GBL.

Certain areas where caution must be paid were also highlighted, that is, the issues of measurement (of both learning and flow), transfer, and the quality of the evidence provided. Firstly, with regard to learning measurement, there is debate as to how and when to measure the learning outcomes from GBL. Additionally, although the motivational appeal of games is the characteristic that is most strongly advocated, this too can be difficult to measure, especially in terms of its relationship with the intended learning outcomes in a classroom.

Secondly, the review highlights instances of both no transfer and negative transfer. This is an important consideration that must be monitored carefully when using gaming applications in the classroom, as it is vital that the learning promoted through a game is appropriately transferable to both the curriculum goals of the classroom and other real world contexts. In this regard, research on GBL is still in its infancy and the focus remains on research questions to see if it works, rather than on more refined questions about the reasons why it might work in one context and not in another, or whether transfer is more likely in one situation rather than another and so on.

Thirdly, the quality of the evidence provided in this review must be considered. Many of the studies reported could be critiqued methodologically, for example, for small sample sizes, or for their lack of robust designs. Although, the studies offered contribute greatly to the academic literature, the focus on evidence-based practice in education today suggests that if policy and classroom practice is to change, it is likely that more robust evaluations will be necessary.

Although not a cautionary note, it must also be acknowledged that the research reviewed in this chapter is largely representative of behavioural evaluation studies that have been researcher-led and conducted in relatively controlled settings, rather than embedded in the on-going activities of regular classrooms. However, an increasingly diverse range of research methodological approaches are contributing to this knowledge base. For example, there are some illuminating case study examples from the naturalistic classroom setting available in the literature. These case studies have reported on numerous benefits of GBL, such as: recognised skill development, e.g., problem solving, sequencing, reasoning, and memorisation skills (the Teem Report, McFarlane et al., 2002); improving academic performance in underperforming schools (de Freitas, 2006); and improvements in literacy and communication, especially amongst boys, using the game 'Myst' (a fantasy PC game) in conjunction with Tolkien's The Hobbit (Sandford & Williamson, 2005).

Additionally, neuroscience methods are now offering new ways to study the effects that computer games have on cognition, which can ultimately inform the measurement of learning. Bavelier, Green, and Dye (2010) in their recently published paper 'Children, Wired: For better and for worse' highlight the potential for using brain imaging techniques such as functional magnetic resonance imaging (fMRI), to study how new technologies are affecting cognitive development, in what they refer to as the more malleable developing brains of young people. For example, Granek, Gorbet, and Sergio (2009) examined the effect of video game play on hand eye coordination skills. Using fMRI scans, they showed additional prefrontal cortical activity in experienced video game players when planning for complex hand eye coordination tasks, suggesting that video game play may alter cortical networks. Bavelier et al. (2010) recognise the benefit of behavioural and neuroscientists working together in order to assess the neural processes that technology, such as computer games, demands in order to better understand behaviour and learning.

Finally, this review suggests that the next steps for GBL research are: interdisciplinary work, using robust methods, to strengthen the evidence around the use of GBL; insight into not just 'does GBL work', but in what contexts does it work best?; further exploration around the subjects that best suit GBL, and perhaps those that do not; practical guidance regarding selecting appropriate learning approaches and classroom practices suitable for games; further work addressing issues of measurement, both in terms of learning and motivation; and greater understanding of the role of transfer, specifically how to ensure it takes place between the digital and real world. Despite an abundance of work on games-based learning dating back to the 1970s, the role of games in the classroom is still relatively new. It is important that future GBL research focuses on these key factors in order to strengthen the available evidence, so as to inform and influence practice.

REFERENCES

Alkan, S., & Cagiltay, K. (2007). Studying computer game learning experience through eye tracking. *British Journal of Educational Technology*, *38*(3), 538–542. doi:10.1111/j.1467-8535.2007.00721.x.

Bai, H., Pan, W., Hirumi, A., & Kebritchi, M. (2012). Assessing the effectiveness of a 3-D instructional game on improving mathematics achievement and motivation of middle school students. *British Journal of Educational Technology*, *43*(6), 993–1003. doi:10.1111/j.1467-8535.2011.01269.x.

Bavelier, D., Green, S., & Dye, M. W. G. (2010). Children, wired: for better and for worse. *Neuron*, *67*, 692–701. doi:10.1016/j.neuron.2010.08.035 PMID:20826302.

Brown, A. L., & Campione, J. C. (1994). Guided discovery in a community of learners. In K. McGilly (Ed.), *Classroom lessons: Integrating cognitive theory and classroom practice* (pp. 229–270). Cambridge, MA: The MIT Press.

Brown, D. J., Ley, J., Evett, L., & Standen, P. J. (2011). Can participating in games based learning improve mathematic skills in students with intellectual disabilities? In *Proceedings of IEEE 1st International Conference on Serious Games and Applications for Health* (pp. 1-9). Braga, Portugal: IEEE.

Bulger, M. E., Mayer, R. E., Almeroth, K. C., & Blau, S. D. (2008). Measuring learner engagement in computer-equipped college classrooms. *Journal of Educational Multimedia and Hypermedia*, *17*(2), 129–143.

Connolly, T. M., Stansfield, M., & Hainey, T. (2007). An application of games-based learning within software engineering. *British Journal of Educational Technology*, *38*(3), 516–428. doi:10.1111/j.1467-8535.2007.00706.x.

Cordova, D. I., & Lepper, M. R. (1996). Intrinsic motivation and the process of learning: Beneficial effects of contextualization, personalization, and choice. *Journal of Educational Psychology*, *88*(4), 715–730. doi:10.1037/0022-0663.88.4.715.

Cox, M. J. (1997). *The effects of information technology on students' motivation: Final report*. London: King's College London.

Csikszentmihalyi, M. (1990). *Flow: The psychology of optimal experience*. New York: Harper and Row.

de Freitas, S. (2006). *Learning in immersive worlds: A review of games-based learning*. Bristol, UK: JISC. Retrieved from http://www.jisc.ac.uk/media/documents/programmes/elearninginnovation/gamingreport_v3.pdf

de Freitas, S., & Neumann, T. (2009). The use of 'exploratory learning' for supporting immersive learning in virtual environments. *Computers & Education*, *52*, 343–352. doi:10.1016/j.compedu.2008.09.010.

Denning, T. (1997). *IT and pupil motivation: A collaborative study of staff and pupil attitudes and experiences*. Keele, UK: Keele University.

Egenfeldt-Nielsen, S. (2006). Overview of research on the educational use of video games. *Digital Kompetanse*, *1*, 184–213.

Finneran, C. M., & Zhang, P. (2003). A person-artefact-task (PAT) model of flow antecedents in computer-mediated environments. *International Journal of Human-Computer Studies*, *59*, 475–496. doi:10.1016/S1071-5819(03)00112-5.

Finneran, C. M., & Zhang, P. (2005). Flow in computer-mediated environments: Promises and challenges. *Communications of the Association for Information Systems*, *15*, 82–101.

Fu, F., Su, R., & Yu, S. (2009). E game flow: A scale to measure learners' enjoyment of e-learning games. *Computers & Education*, *52*, 101–112. doi:10.1016/j.compedu.2008.07.004.

Garris, R., Ahlers, R., & Driskell, J. E. (2002). Games, motivation, and learning: A research and practice model. *Simulation & Gaming*, *33*, 441–467. doi:10.1177/1046878102238607.

Gee, J. P. (2003). *What video games have to teach us about learning and literacy*. New York: Palgrave Macmillan. doi:10.1145/950566.950595.

Ghani, J. A. (1995). Flow in human-computer interactions: Test of a model. In J. M. Carey (Ed.), *Human Factors in Information Systems: Emerging Theoretical Bases* (pp. 291–311). Norwood, NJ: Ablex Publishing Corporation.

Gokhale, A. A. (1995). Collaborative learning enhances critical thinking. *Journal of Technology Education*, *7*(1), 22–30.

Granek, J. A., Gorbet, D. J., & Sergio, L. E. (2009). Extensive video-game experience alters cortical networks for complex visuomotor transformations. *Cortex*, *46*, 1165–1177. doi:10.1016/j.cortex.2009.10.009 PMID:20060111.

Green, C. S., & Bavelier, D. (2003). Action video game modifies visual selective attention. *Nature, 423*, 534–537. doi:10.1038/nature01647 PMID:12774121.

Green, C. S., Pouget, A., & Bavelier, D. (2010). Improved probabilistic inference as a general learning mechanism with action video games. *Current Biology, 20*, 1573–1579. doi:10.1016/j.cub.2010.07.040 PMID:20833324.

Greenfield, P. M., deWinstanley, P., Kilpatrick, H., & Kaye, D. (1996). Action video games and informal education: Effects on strategies for dividing visual attention. In P. M. Greenfield, & R. R. Cocking (Eds.), *Interacting with video* (pp. 187–204). Norwood, NJ: Ablex Publishing Corporation.

Halpern, D. F., Millis, K., Graesser, A. C., Butler, H., Forsyth, C., & Cai, Z. (2012). Operation ARA: A computerized learning game that teaches critical thinking and scientific reasoning. *Thinking Skills and Creativity, 7*(2), 93–100. doi:10.1016/j.tsc.2012.03.006.

Henderson, L., Klemes, J., & Eshet, Y. (2000). Just playing a game? Educational simulation software and cognitive outcomes. *Journal of Educational Computing Research, 22*(1), 105–129. doi:10.2190/EPJT-AHYQ-1LAJ-U8WK.

Herrington, J., & Oliver, R. (1999). Using situated learning and multimedia to investigate higher-order learning. *Journal of Educational Multimedia and Hypermedia, 8*(4), 401–422.

Herrington, J., Oliver, R., & Reeves, T. C. (2003). Patterns of engagement in authentic online learning environments. *Australian Journal of Educational Technology, 19*(1), 59–71.

Higgins, S. (2000). The logical zoombinis. *Teaching Thinking, 1*(1).

Holmes, B., & Gardner, J. (2006). *e-Learning: Concepts and practice*. London. *Sage (Atlanta, Ga.)*.

Holmes, B., Tangney, B., FitzGibbon, A., Savage, T., & Meehan, S. (2001). *Communal constructivism: Students constructing learning for as well as with others*. Paper presented at the meeting of the 12th International Conference of the Society for Information Technology & Teacher Education (SITE). Charlottesville, VA: SITE.

Howe, C., McWilliam, D., & Cross, G. (2005). Chance favours only the prepared mind, incubation and the delayed effects of peer collaboration. *The British Journal of Psychology, 96*, 67–93. doi:10.1348/000712604X15527 PMID:15826325.

Howe, C., Tolmie, A., Thurston, A., Topping, K., Christie, D., & Livingston, K. et al. (2007). Group work in elementary science: Towards organizational principles for supporting pupil learning. *Learning and Instruction, 17*(1), 549–563. doi:10.1016/j.learninstruc.2007.09.004.

Hwang, G. J., & Wu, P. H. (2012). Advancements and trends in digital game-based learning research: A review of publications in selected journals from 2001 to 2010. *British Journal of Educational Technology, 43*(1), E6–E10. doi:10.1111/j.1467-8535.2011.01242.x.

Ijsselsteijn, W., de Kort, Y., Poels, K., Jurgelionis, A., & Bellotti, F. (2007). *Characterising and measuring user experiences in digital games*. Paper presented at the meeting of the ACE Conference 2007. Salzburg, Austria.

Inal, Y., & Cagiltay, K. (2007). Flow experiences of children in an interactive social game environment. *British Journal of Educational Technology, 38*(3), 455–464. doi:10.1111/j.1467-8535.2007.00709.x.

Inkpen, K., Booth, K. S., Klawe, M., & Upitis, R. (1995). *Playing together beats playing apart, especially for girls*. Paper presented at the meeting of Computer Support for Collaborative Learning (CSCL). Bloomington, IN.

Jayakanthan, R. (2002). Application of computer games in the field of education. *The Electronic Library*, *20*(2), 98–102. doi:10.1108/02640470210697471.

Kanthan, R., & Senger, J. L. (2011). The impact of specially designed digital games-based learning in undergraduate pathology and medical education. *Archives of Pathology & Laboratory Medicine*, *135*, 135–142. PMID:21204720.

Kearney, P. (2007). Cognitive assessment of game-based learning. *British Journal of Educational Technology*, *38*(3), 529–531. doi:10.1111/j.1467-8535.2007.00718.x.

Kebritchi, M., Hirumi, A., & Bai, H. (2008). *The effects of modern math computer games on learners' math achievement and math course motivation in a public high school setting* (Doctoral research brief). Retrieved from http://www.pearsonschool.com/live/images/custom/BasalEmails/dimension_m/media/UCFResearch_Brief.pdf

Keifer-Boyd, K. (2005). Children teaching children with their computer game creations. *Visual Arts Research*, *31*(60), 117–128.

Kiili, K. (2005). Digital game-based learning: Towards an experiential gaming model. *The Internet and Higher Education*, *8*, 13–24. doi:10.1016/j.iheduc.2004.12.001.

Kiili, K., & Lainema, T. (2008). Foundation for measuring engagement in educational games. *Journal of Interactive Learning Research*, *19*(3), 469–488.

Klawe, M. M., & Phillips, E. (1995). *A classroom study: Electronic games engage children as researchers*. Paper presented at the meeting of Computer Support for Collaborative Learning (CSCL). Bloomington, IN.

Ko, S. (2002). An empirical analysis of children's thinking and learning in a computer game context. *Educational Psychology*, *22*(2), 219–233. doi:10.1080/01443410120115274.

Kolb, D. A. (1984). *Experiential learning: Experience as the source of learning and development*. Englewood Cliffs, NJ: Prentice Hall.

Lainema, T., & Nurmi, S. (2006). Applying an authentic, dynamic learning environment in real world business. *Computers & Education*, *47*, 94–115. doi:10.1016/j.compedu.2004.10.002.

Lim, C. P., Nonis, D., & Hedberg, J. (2006). Gaming in a 3D multiuser virtual environment: Engaging students in science lessons. *British Journal of Educational Technology*, *37*(2), 211–231. doi:10.1111/j.1467-8535.2006.00531.x.

Logie, R. H., & Della Sala, S. (2010). Brain training in schools, where is the evidence? *British Journal of Educational Technology*, *41*(6), 127–128. doi:10.1111/j.1467-8535.2010.01101.x.

Malone, T. W. (1980). What makes things fun to learn? A study of intrinsically motivating computer games. *Dissertation Abstracts International*, *41*(5B), 1955.

Malone, T. W., & Lepper, M. R. (1987). Making learning fun: Taxonomy of intrinsic motivations for learning. In R. E. Snow, & M. J. Farr (Eds.), *Aptitude, learning and instruction III: Cognitive and affective process analysis* (pp. 223–253). Hoboken, NJ: Lawrence Erlbaum Associates.

McFarlane, A., Sparrowhawk, A., & Heald, Y. (2002). *Report on the educational use of games*. Retrieved from http://www.teem.org.uk/publications/teem_gamesined_full.pdf

McGuinness, C. (2005). Teaching thinking: Theory and practice. *BJEP Monograph series II, Number 3 – Pedagogy – Teaching for Learning, 1*(1), 107-126.

Miller, D. J., & Robertson, D. P. (2010). Using games consoles in the primary classroom: Effects of 'brain training' programme on computation and self-esteem. *British Journal of Educational Technology, 41*(2), 242–255. doi:10.1111/j.1467-8535.2008.00918.x.

Miller, D. J., & Robertson, D. P. (2011). Response to Logie and Della Sala: Brain training in schools, where is the evidence? *British Journal of Educational Technology, 42*(5), 101–102. doi:10.1111/j.1467-8535.2011.01205.x.

O'Neil, H. F., Wainess, R., & Baker, E. L. (2005). Classification of learning outcomes: Evidence from the computer games literature. *Curriculum Journal, 16*(4), 455–474. doi:10.1080/09585170500384529.

Okan, Z. (2003). Edutainment: Is learning at risk? *British Journal of Educational Technology, 34*(3), 255–264. doi:10.1111/1467-8535.00325.

Owen, A. M., Hampshire, A., Grahn, J. A., Stenton, R., Dajani, S., & Burns, A. S. et al. (2010). Putting brain training to the test. *Nature, 465*(7299), 775–778. doi:10.1038/nature09042 PMID:20407435.

Papastergiou, M. (2009). Digital game-based learning in high school computer science education: Impact on educational effectiveness and student motivation. *Computers & Education, 52*, 1–12. doi:10.1016/j.compedu.2008.06.004.

Passey, D. (1999). *Anytime, anywhere, learning project evaluation focus.* Lancaster, UK: Lancaster University/AAL.

Peppler, K. A., & Kafai, Y. (2007). *What videogame making can teach us about literacy and learning: Alternative pathways into participatory culture.* Paper presented at the 3rd International Conference of the Digital Games Research Association (DiGRA). Tokyo, Japan.

Pillay, H. (2002). An investigation of cognitive processes engaged in by recreational computer game players: Implications for skills of the future. *Journal of Research on Technology in Education, 34*(3), 336–350.

Pillay, S., Brownlee, J., & Wilss, L. (1999). Cognition and recreational computer games: Implications for educational technology. *The Journal of Research on Computing in Education, 32*(1), 203–216.

Pintrich, P. R., & Schunk, D. H. (1996). *Motivation in education: Theory, research and applications.* Englewood Cliffs, NJ: Prentice-Hall, Inc.

Pivec, M. (2007). Editorial: Play and learn: Potentials of game-based learning. *British Journal of Educational Technology, 38*(3), 387–393. doi:10.1111/j.1467-8535.2007.00722.x.

Pivec. (2009). *Game-based learning or game-based teaching.* Retrieved from http://emergingtechnologies.becta.org.uk/upload-dir/downloads/page_documents/research/emerging_technologies/game_based_learning.pdf

Reid, M., Burn, A., & Parker, D. (2002). *Evaluation report of the Becta digital video pilot project.* Retrieved from http://partners.becta.org.uk/pagedocuments/research/dvreport 241002.pdf

Resnick, L. (1987). *Education and learning to think.* Washington, DC: National Academy.

Rieber, L. P., Smith, L., & Noah, D. (1998). The value of serious play. *Educational Technology, 38*(6), 29–37.

Ritterfield, U., & Weber, R. (2006). Video games for entertainment and education. In P. Vorderer, & J. Bryant (Eds.), *Playing video games: Motives, responses, and consequences.* Hoboken, NJ: Lawrence Erlbaum Associates.

Robertson, J., & Good, J. (2004). *Children's narrative development through computer game authoring.* Paper presented at the Meeting of the 2004 Conference on Interaction Design and Children: Building a Community. Baltimore, MD.

Salen, K. (Ed.). (2007). *The ecology of games: Connecting youth, games, and learning.* Cambridge, MA: MIT Press.

Sandford, R., Ulicsak, M., Facer, K., & Rudd, T. (2006). *Teaching with games: Using commercial off-the-shelf computer games in formal education.* Retrieved from http://archive.futurelab.org.uk/resources/documents/project_reports/teaching_with_games/TWG_report.pdf

Sandford, R., & Williamson, B. (2005). *Games and learning: A handbook from Futurelab.* Retrieved from http://archive.futurelab.org.uk/resources/documents/handbooks/games_and_learning2.pdf

Sedighian, K. (1997). *Challenge-driven learning: A model for children's multimedia mathematics learning environments.* Paper presented at the meeting of ED-MEDIA 1997: World Conference on Educational Multimedia and Hypermedia. Calgary, Canada.

Selnow, G. W. (1984). Playing videogames: The electronic friend. *The Journal of Communication, 34*(2), 148–156. doi:10.1111/j.1460-2466.1984.tb02166.x.

Selwyn, N. (2008). *Education 2.0? Designing the web for teaching and learning: A commentary by the technology enhanced learning phase of the teaching and learning research programme.* Retrieved from http://www.tlrp.org/tel/files/2008/11/tel_comm_final.pdf

Shernoff, D. J., Csikszentmihalyi, M., Schneider, B., & Shernoff, E. S. (2003). Student engagement in high school classrooms from the perspective of flow theory. *School Psychology Quarterly, 18*(2), 158–176. doi:10.1521/scpq.18.2.158.21860.

Sherry, J. L. (2004). Flow and media enjoyment. *Communication Theory, 14*(4), 328–347. doi:10.1111/j.1468-2885.2004.tb00318.x.

Shin, N. (2006). Online learner's 'flow' experience: An empirical study. *British Journal of Educational Technology, 37*(5), 705–720. doi:10.1111/j.1467-8535.2006.00641.x.

Skadberg, Y. X., & Kimmel, J. R. (2004). Visitors' flow experience while browsing a website: Its measurement, contributing factors, and consequences. *Computers in Human Behavior, 20,* 403–422. doi:10.1016/S0747-5632(03)00050-5.

Stoney, S., & Oliver, R. (1999). Can higher order thinking and cognitive engagement be enhanced with multimedia?. *Interactive Multimedia Electronic Journal of Computer-Enhanced Learning, 1*(2).

Subrahmanyam, K., & Greenfield, P. M. (1996). Effect of video game practice on spatial skills in girls and boys. In P. M. Greenfield, & R. R. Cocking (Eds.), *Interacting with video* (pp. 95–114). Norwood, NJ: Ablex Publishing Corp.

Swaak, J., & de Jong, T. (1996). Measuring intuitive knowledge in science: The development of what-if test. *Studies in Educational Evaluation, 22*(4), 341–362. doi:10.1016/0191-491X(96)00019-3.

Sweetser, P., & Wyeth, P. (2005). GameFlow: A model for evaluating player enjoyment in games. *ACM Computers in Entertainment, 3*(3), 1. doi:10.1145/1077246.1077253.

Tuzun, H. (2007). Blending video games with learning: Issues and challenges with classroom implementations in the Turkish context. *British Journal of Educational Technology, 38*(3), 465–477. doi:10.1111/j.1467-8535.2007.00710.x.

Tuzun, H., Yilmaz-soylu, M., Karakus, T., Inal, Y., & Kizilkaya, G. (2009). The effects of computer games on primary school students' achievement and motivation in geography learning. *Computers & Education, 52*, 68–77. doi:10.1016/j.compedu.2008.06.008.

VanDeventer, S. S., & White, J. A. (2002). Expert behaviour in children's video game play. *Simulation & Gaming, 33*(1), 28–48. doi:10.1177/1046878102033001002.

Virvou, M., Katsionis, G., & Manos, K. (2005). Combining software games with education: Evaluation of its educational effectiveness. *Journal of Educational Technology & Society, 8*(2), 54–65.

Webster, J., Trevino, L. K., & Ryan, L. (1993). The dimensionality and correlates of flow in human-computer interactions. *Computers in Human Behavior, 9*, 411–426. doi:10.1016/0747-5632(93)90032-N.

Wegerif, R. (2002). *Literature review in thinking skills, technology and learning*. Retrieved from http://archive.futurelab.org.uk/resources/documents/lit_reviews/Thinking_Skills_Review.pdf

White, B. Y. (1984). Designing computer games to help physics students understand Newton's laws of motion. *Cognition and Instruction, 1*(1), 69–108. doi:10.1207/s1532690xci0101_4.

Whitebread, D. (1997). Developing children's problem-solving: The educational uses of adventure games. In A. Mc Farlane (Ed.), *Information technology and authentic learning: Realising the potential of computers in the primary classroom* (pp. 13–37). London: Routledge.

Wideman, H. H., Owston, R. D., Brown, C., Kushniruk, A., Ho, F., & Pitts, K. C. (2007). Unpacking the potential of educational gaming: a new tool for gaming research. *Simulation & Gaming, 38*(1), 10–30. doi:10.1177/1046878106297650.

Williamson, B. (2009). *Computer games, schools, and young people: A report for educators on using games for learning*. Retrieved from http://archive.futurelab.org.uk/resources/documents/project_reports/becta/Games_and_Learning_educators_report.pdf

Wood, D., Bruner, J. S., & Ross, G. (1976). The role of tutoring in problem solving. *Journal of Child Psychology and Psychiatry, and Allied Disciplines, 17*, 89–100. doi:10.1111/j.1469-7610.1976.tb00381.x PMID:932126.

KEY TERMS AND DEFINITIONS

Cognitive Skills: Skills relevant to different cognitive processes, e.g., attention and focus.

Collaborative Learning: Instances where multiple people work together for learning purposes.

Flow: High levels of immersion and engagement.

Games-Based Learning: The use of computer games for educational or learning purposes.

Higher-Order Thinking: Thinking processes that require greater cognitive effort.

Learning Theory: Conceptual frameworks used to explain learning processes.

Learning Outcomes: The learning established as a result of an activity/ lesson.

Motivation: The desire to do something.

Psychological Perspectives: Drawing on theories from the field of psychology.

Chapter 12
Games for and by Teachers and Learners

Peter van Rosmalen
Open University of The Netherlands, The Netherlands

Amanda Wilson
University of the West of Scotland, UK

Hans Hummel
Open University of The Netherlands, The Netherlands

ABSTRACT

With the advent of social media, it is widely accepted that teachers and learners are not only consumers but also may have an active role in contributing and co-creating lesson materials and content. Paradoxically, one strand of technology-enhanced learning (i.e. game-based learning) aligns only slightly to this development. Games, while there to experience, explore, and collaborate, are almost exclusively designed by professionals. Despite, or maybe because, games are the exclusive domain of professional developers, the general impression is that games require complex technologies and that games are difficult to organise and to embed in a curriculum. This chapter makes a case that games are not necessarily the exclusive domain of game professionals. Rather than enforcing teachers to get acquainted with and use complex, technically demanding games, the authors discuss approaches that teachers themselves can use to build games, make use of existing games, and even one step beyond use tools or games that can be used by learners to create their own designs (e.g. games or virtual worlds).

INTRODUCTION

With the advent of social media it is widely accepted that teachers and learners are not only consumers but also may have an active role in sharing and co-creating content, debate and share opinions (Silius et al., 2010). Social media such as social networks, online videos and wikis are not merely used to connect or entertain but also support informal learning (Sloep et al., 2011) by enabling learners to ask questions, to debate and to share opinions and materials with other learners. Online videos with a variety of learning content are widely shared and used by individuals and in the classroom. Wikis, essentially no more than a website with facilities for creating, editing, linking and navigating web pages, fit very well into the Web 2.0 paradigm of user involvement

DOI: 10.4018/978-1-4666-4773-2.ch012

Copyright © 2014, IGI Global. Copying or distributing in print or electronic forms without written permission of IGI Global is prohibited.

and user created content. They are, because of their ease of use and because they allow users to be actively involved, widely used in education for a variety of applications (see e.g. Ayers & Ortega, 2010; Riehle & Bruckman, 2009) such as notes sharing, collaborative writing, exchange of ideas, e-portfolios, shared learning tasks, getting used to ICT, and writing multi-media essays and project reports. Paradoxically, one strand of technology enhanced learning, i.e. game-based learning, aligns slightly with this development. Games, while there to experience, explore and collaborate, are almost exclusively designed by professionals, despite the fact that one of the first game-like learning environments, i.e. Turtle Logo (Fischer & Kling, 1974), was created to have learners explore their creativity by building their own mini-programmes. In most cases, games offer closed worlds or scenarios and teacher and learners can only act within the options given. Despite, or maybe because, games are the exclusive domain of professional developers, the general impression is that games require complex technologies and that games are difficult to organise and to embed in education curriculum. The latter is of importance since the use of ICT and games, in particular, only tends to be successful if it closely fits with the existing teaching practice (Vier in Balans Monitor, 2012, pp 45).

Although the domestic market of video entertainment games has been a fast-moving field over a number of years with annual growth rates well above 10% (PWC, 2010; National Gaming Survey, 2009), the use of games for educational purposes has remained quite limited (Ten Brummelhuis & Van Amerongen, 2010; Klopfer, Osterweil, & Salen, 2009). Barriers identified in the literature include teachers' lack of expertise, aspects of the school system, financial barriers and technical barriers (NFER, 2009). Only few data are available describing teachers' opinions on using games in their classrooms. In a survey (NFER, 2009) among 1632 UK primary and secondary school teachers, the majority of teachers (85%) were predominantly

positive about what could be learnt or developed as a result of playing computer games. The overall impression, however, is that many teachers are interested in game-based learning but experience severe barriers for using these in their classrooms (Van Rosmalen & Westera, 2012; Razak, Connolly & Hainey, 2011):

- **Expertise Barriers:** Williamson (2009) reports an urgent need for the training of teachers who wish to gain a better understanding of how to use games in their classrooms as well as understanding the implications of games as cultural forms of young people's lives.
- **Systemic Barriers:** Klopfer, Osterweil and Salen (2009) blame the school system for their reluctance of giving up text books or purchasing educational technologies that are not clearly linked to existing curriculum standards and the formal assessment standards. They notice that teachers find it difficult to integrate the play of a game within the fixed time structure of their schools Furthermore, within the school system teachers lack the time, incentives and support for this work. Role models that could demonstrate new modes of teaching are avoided. Finally, hardly any tools are available for teachers for adjusting existing game contents, for arranging subscriptions for their students, for setting up different game runs, for allocating different roles to different students, for monitoring the performances of their students, or guidelines how to provide guidance and support.
- **Financial Barriers:** The high price and lack of licensing agreements for games prohibit many schools from using these resources (Williamson, 2009). For teachers it is difficult to find game contents that match their needs. The education market displays limited sources of funding. Game companies and venture capitalists are un-

responsive to investing in risky products, particularly in educational technology markets that have proven to be rarely successful (FAS, 2006).

- **Technical Barriers:** Games as well as game development are inherently complex (Westera et al., 2008). For schools it is difficult to run their own games server or to arrange their own game development. Although increasingly online web-based games are coming available that conform to cross platform browser standards, there is a lack of dedicated equipment, in particular, up-to-date video/graphics cards, making it difficult for teachers to use games in their classrooms (De Freitas, 2006).

The objective of this chapter is to make a case and exemplify that games are not necessarily the exclusive domain of game professionals. Rather than forcing teachers to get acquainted with and use complex, technical demanding games, we will discuss approaches that teachers themselves can use to build games, make use of existing games and even one step beyond use tools or games that can be used by learners to create their own designs, e.g. games and virtual worlds.

In this chapter we will first provide a general overview of games for and by teachers and learners. We will discuss a variety of examples and their requirements and characteristics. Next, we will present three case studies. In case study one, we will discuss the use of wikis to build serious games. We will examine two examples; one in higher education and one in primary education, both aimed at the learning of a complex cognitive skill; i.e. argumentation and verb conjugation, respectively, and finally, it will be illustrated how teachers can make their own wiki-game. The second case study will discuss a game environment currently under development for scripting collaboration in games. It describes and reviews a first implementation of a mastership game for teachers-in-training and discusses how teachers

can flexibly adapt and extend the game play by adding their own structure and content to fit their needs. Finally, case three will discuss Scratch, an environment designed for learners to design and develop their own programs or games. The case will discuss an example in which Scratch (Wilson, Hainey & Connolly, 2012) was used as part of a curriculum in primary education to teach children programming concepts and programming. Lastly, the case will also review some other examples in the literature of how Scratch has been used. The chapter will conclude with a discussion and conclusions.

GAMES FOR AND BY TEACHERS AND LEARNERS: AN OVERVIEW

Although games nowadays are commonly associated with complex, immersive worlds featuring high quality graphics and smooth and fast interactions, this is not the only way to consider games. Games such as board games, with a relatively simple set of rules, have been popular for centuries. The main underlying game principles such as competition, individual challenge, collaboration, and recognition by others (Pernin, Michau, Mandran & Mariais, 2012) have shown to be motivating and successful. For teachers, there are many, simple tools for making such a serious game, e.g. by considering a wiki (Van Rosmalen, & Westera, 2012). Other more complex alternatives constitute of game engines with templates which teachers can modify within given constraints or to which they can add their own content (Hummel, Geerts, Slootmaker, Kuipers, & Westera, in press) or game engines with relatively simple editors which do not require specialised expertise (Torrente, Del Blanco, Marchiori, Moreno-Ger, & Fernández-Manjón, 2010; Overmars, 2004). Alternatively, following in the footsteps of Turtle Logo, teachers can position their learners in a designer role by making use of environments that enable the learners themselves to design or program examples (Maloney et al., 2008; Chou et al., 2011; Wilson, Hainey, & Connolly, 2012). In this section we will discuss a number of such examples going from simple general, yet promising tools through more advanced game environments that can be used by teachers to create games, to examples which are suited for learners.

Simple Tools for Games and Simple Games

As in regular games and in computer-based games there is a long tradition for simple games based on e.g. email (see for example Play by Email games http://www.pbm.com/~lindahl/pbm_list/) or, more recent, twitter (http://playgen.com/play/twitter-game/ or http://tweepi.com/blog/2011/07/4-most-addictive-twitter-games/). Though no literature could be found on their use in education, examples such as Artwiculate (@artwiculate), which intends to assist in learning a new word each day, or Twitbrain (@twitbrain) a game posting a math problem to be solved as quickly as possible, clearly have an educational potential. Similar there is a variety of online puzzles such as word games that, though designed for entertainment, may be used in education. Well known examples are mobile games such as Wordfeud (a scrabble-like game), Ruzzle (a word game to create as many words as possible with the letters of a 4*4 board in a given time) or Draw Something (a social drawing game to guess words). It should be relatively straightforward to use these games or comparable ones as part of a lesson plan for motivational aspects or for simple, well defined learning objectives.

There are many more options for making a simple, serious game by considering a wiki. A wiki, essentially, is no more than a website with facilities for creating, editing, linking and navigating web pages. Wikis have been around for over a decade and fit very well into the Web 2.0 paradigm of user involvement and user created content. Because of their ease of use and because they al-low users to be actively involved they are widely used in education for a variety of applications (see e.g. Ayers & Ortega, 2010; Riehle & Bruckman, 2009) such as notes sharing, collaborative writing, exchange of ideas, e-portfolios, shared learning tasks, getting used to ICT, and writing multi-media essays and project reports. Not surprisingly, wikis can also be used to build serious games. These games may be limited to relatively simple game mechanics but because of their sophisticated and easy to use tools, they still can be used to practice complex skills (Van Rosmalen & Westera, 2012; Bronk & Van Rosmalen, submitted). In section 3.1 we will review two examples of these so called wiki-games.

Game Engines for Teachers

Above we discussed examples of simple tools and games (see also Table 1) that teachers can use to either create a game or adopt one to be used within their lesson design. The strength of this approach is that it can be used by any teacher. However, the game elements that can be used are limited since the tools discussed do not easily allow the teacher to add any complex rules or immersive experiences. An alternative therefore is to use dedicated game design tools. Tools suitable for teachers vary in their flexibility and complexity (Table 1). They start with tools that are pre-designed around a specific setting or offer a limited set of templates. One example is a 'collaboration scripting' authoring environment (Hummel *et al.*, in press). It offers a set of adjustable parameters that are dedicated to guide and execute a collaboration script with varying structures and contents. It will be discussed in detail in section 3.2. A second example is ARLearn (Ternier, Klemke, Kalz, Van Ulzen & Specht, 2012). ARLearn is a location-based game engine that manages games and runs media items (e.g. multiple-choice questions, video objects and narrative items) and dependencies between these media items. The most interesting aspect of ARLearn is that it offers an immersive experience

Table 1. Overview of games for and by teachers and learners

	Teacher/ Learner	Complexity (1-3)	Description	Source	Supporting Materials
Twitter/ Email	T	1	Simple game	http://tweepi.com/blog/2011/07/4-most-addictive-twitter-games/ http://www.pbm.com/~lindahl/pbm_list/	n.a.
Wordfeud Ruzzle Draw something	T	1	Word game	http://wordfeud.com/ http://www.ruzzle-game.com/ http://drawsomethinggameonline.com/	n.a.
Wiki-games	T	1/2	Simple game	http://wiki-games-argument-sjabloon.wikispaces.com/	See source
Collaboration scripts	T	2	Collaboration scripts	Under development	n.a.
ARLearn	T	3	Location based game	Under development http://code.google.com/p/arlearn/	See source
eAdventure	T	2/3	3D/Video game	http://e-adventure.e-ucm.es	http://e-adventure.e-ucm.es/tutorial/
EMERGO	T	3+	Scenario game	http://www.emergo.cc	See source
Gamemaker	L/T	3	Game construction	http://www.yoyogames.com/	http://gmc.yoyogames.com/
Scratch	L	1/2	Game construction	http://scratch.mit.edu	http://scratched.media.mit.edu/resources
Lego Mindstorms	L	3	Construction game	http://mindstorms.lego.com	http://www.legoengineering.com/teaching-resources.html http://www.roberta-home.de/en
Minecraft	L	2	Construction game	http://www.minecraft.net	http://minecraftedu.com/

in an easy and affordable way. With an Android client, game play in the real world is possible; a StreetLearn client built on top of Google Street view offers game functionality in a virtual environment. ARLearn media items can be positioned on a map and can be made available as defined in the game logic. A video can be bound to a coordinate, but can also at a certain moment appear as a message in the player's inbox. The clients can be used independently or together; e.g. one player can take the role of an operator in StreetLearn, while other players take a different role with the smart phone client. Though the editing part of the environment is still under development, the first experiments indicate that it is relatively straight forward for teachers to design game scenarios.

eAdventure (http://e-adventure.e-ucm.es/), in contrast to ARLearn, designed from scratch to be used by teachers, is an authoring tool for the creation of point-and-click adventure video games for educational purposes. It uses a graphical interface for authoring and does not require programming skills. The games are standard (SCORM) compliant and, therefore, can be easily integrated into existing e-learning environments. An eAdventure game consists of one or more chapters with each chapter being a set of scenes and cut-scenes. In scenes the actions are designed, i.e. the players' interactions with objects and characters in the game. Cut-scenes are used to display slides or images (Slidescenes) or video (Videoscenes). eAdventure (Torrente et al., 2010) has been successfully applied in a variety of games (see http://www.ub.edu/euelearning/ProActive_GBL_Repository).

An essential element in designing a game in ARLearn, eAdventure and many other game toolkits is a narrative, script or didactic scenario. It is a fundamental element of the game design. It fosters the effective acquisition of more complex skills, since it gives the learners direction and guidance in exploring a more complex case problem to reach a professional solution. Without defining the problem to tackle, the role the student has to assume when solving this problem, the methodical steps to take in order to reach a professional solution, and the tools and sources to use en route, such game play would become aimless and coincidental.

Such narratives (or didactic scenarios) may take conflicts as starting points for learning, for discovering multiple aspects and perspectives of a problem. Conflicts can entail physical or mental obstacles, different perspectives, stakeholders and / or ethical dilemmas. For instance, when setting up a new business one partner can be made responsible to ensure that investments are sustainable and will not damage the natural environment, while another partner's main job is to guarantee that initial investments actually pay off. Besides entrepreneurial finance, such conflicts are often found in health care, governance and policy making, and other multi-disciplinary domains where experts from different disciplines have to work together to reach solutions and compromises, such as in water management. In one of our case studies, for instance, user conflicts when solving a water management problem have to be exchanged, reflected upon, and integrated by both taking an ecological and governmental perspective on the case.

Below a more concrete idea is described on how roles, perspectives, and collaboration to reach agreement could be elaborated in a didactic scenario. It describes the setup of the 'aquaculture' case (Hummel et al., 2011) developed with EMERGO. EMERGO (Nadolski et al., 2008) is a game engine to actively acquire complex cognitive skills. It is relatively easy to use. However, unlike eAdventure, it is not designed for teachers specifically. Its authoring interface is geared to professional users.

Didactic Scenario

Background: Aquaculture is a relatively new sector (in the Netherlands). Governmental and licensing institutions still struggle to find their way in dealing with entrepreneurs who want to start a new business in this sector, especially because aquaculture can become manifest in many ways and because current legislation can be contradictory and leaves room for subjective interpretation. Economic interests often do not coincide with the interest of (especially saline/marine) agriculture or recreation. Water management professionals have to deal with conflicts and dilemmas, and need to negotiate in order to reach agreement amongst various stakeholders involved in the development area. To assess the feasibility of new activity, professionals need extensive knowledge of water streams and water quality. The field of water management therefore is in need of professionals with a rather broad background who can approach these decisions from both an ecological (nature) and governance (policy) perspective.

Scenario: At the outset of the narrative of the "Aquaculture" game, the student is assigned the role of an externally hired advisor (working at a renowned foreign consultancy agency), and is asked to get to the Netherlands to investigate and draw up a feasibility report on what would be the most suitable location to start a new shellfish production site in a saline Volkerak Zoom Lake (VZL). After becoming sufficiently oriented on the task as a project leader, the student will be asked to deliver a first version of an elaborated and argued table of contents for the report, in which both perspectives (ecological and governance) have to be represented. By this point of time students will have discovered how complex this task is, which stakeholders have to be considered, and which dilemmas play a role.

The next step in the didactic scenario is the (virtual) collaboration script. The head of the consultancy agency now asks the student (still in the role of project leader) to make a choice: to continue elaborating the report from either an ecological or governance perspective. The head takes care to fly in a (virtual) colleague who will choose the other perspective and will collaborate with the student. When the student opts for the ecological perspective the focus will be on nutrient streams and flourishing of alga, ecological possibilities and the maximum exploitation of the area; user conflicts will be left out of scope. When the student opts for the governance perspective the focus will move to various stakeholders and their demands, policy and procedures for shellfish cultivation and the VZL area whereas suitable species, nursing methods and production numbers will be left out of scope. When the table of contents has been sufficiently worked out from the chosen perspective, an email with this *preliminary* (necessarily partial) elaboration of the report is sent to the (virtual) colleague for inspiration and reflection, and at the same time to the (real life) tutor of the course for assessment. In reality it will be the tutor who takes care that the student now receives the (also necessarily partial) elaboration from the colleague who took the other stance. Receipt is guaranteed within the next 24 hours (for an already running course, the tutor might pick a worked example from a growing stack of student works). Finally, the student has to reflect on and integrate both partial elaborations that will be confronting or contradictory, in the final advisory report to be sent and assessed as the individual learning outcome of this game.

Game Engines for Learners

Continuing on from games by teachers, it is only a very small step to start thinking about games by learners (Table 1). Most of the current generation of students are very familiar with games. Therefore it should fit very well with their interests to have students develop their own games and have them experience what it is to design and develop a game. To have students make their own computer applications is already a relatively old application. One of the first examples was Turtle LOGO, a programming environment for students. Gerard Fischer (Fischer & Kling, 1974) used Turtle LOGO to study the development of creativity in students in combination with the development of simple computer programs. A recent, much more advanced example is Lego Mindstorms (Chou et al., 2011). Lego Mindstorms is a Lego kit including motor, sensors and a programmer environment that allows students to build and program robots. Lego Mindstorms is used to give students a compelling introduction to contemporary technology. Students can design, build, program and test their own robot. It appeals to their creative and technical skills and gives an idea of how an "intelligent" robots works. For many years, there are also quite a number of other game environments, which unlike Lego Mindstorms, only require a computer, which are suitable or designed to be used by students. Overmars (2004) discusses various, still existing, tools including simple ones such as StageCast (www.stagecast.com) and Clickteam (www.clickteam.com) and, in detail, Gamemaker (http://www.yoyogames.com/) initially developed by himself. StageCast is a tool specifically for children, in which the user defines rules that link existing graphical situations to new situations, also Clickteam offers relatively simple to use tools to create games. Gamemaker is similar to eAdventure, a rapid-application development tool. It offers drag-and-drop techniques, so users can create games without real programming but it also includes a programming language. It is successfully in use for almost a decade and it is, in particular, popular to teach computer science and related topics.

A recent example is Scratch (Maloney et al., 2008). Scratch is a package that allows users develop interactive stories, games, animations and simulations. MIT developed a curriculum in 2012 of 20 lessons in which the students get to work with Scratch. The purpose behind the curriculum is to get students acquainted with creative computing (Brennan, Chung & Hawson, 2011). Many young people use the computer primarily as a consumer. When doing creative computing, students draw on their creativity and their computational skills to create something; i.e. they should select or create sound, pictures and devise a storyline and rely on their skills to combine this with the help of a formal computer program (e.g. use loops and conditions, and test and incrementally improve their program). The third example uses Minecraft (www.minecraft.net). Minecraft is an adventure game in which players make their tools and build or modify their environment using basic building blocks. Minecraft is not only for technical and mathematical subjects, but can also, for example, be used for communication and language learning (Schifter, 2012). Using Minecraft in education is still in development, but the advantage is that it makes use of an existing popular game. It should be clear from the above description that it will require effort to use and integrate the games discussed in the curriculum. The growing communities around these games do show it is possible and that with the growing amount of examples it will become stepwise more easy to adapt or make one's own examples. A detailed example of one of the environments, Scratch, will be discussed in section 4.

GAMES FOR AND BY TEACHERS

This section reviews two case studies of tools that can be used by teachers to design or adapt their own games. The first case study in this section discusses the use of an everyday tool, a wiki, to build serious games. As introduced in section 2, wikis are relatively powerful, yet easy and commonly used tools and fit very well into the Web 2.0 paradigm of user involvement and user created content. In our first case study we will see how wikis are used to create simple but motivating and useful games.

The second case study in this section describes an online collaboration game that facilitates teachers-in-training to deal with classroom management dilemmas. The script to support these students in collaborating on such practical tasks, independent of teacher intervention, as well as the content delivered by the players can be worked out in various online versions of a 'mastership' game. In section 3.2 we will further explain how the structure of the collaboration script can be adapted for every run, and how players will add their individual content to build unique runs. After assigning and discussing practical dilemmas during a small group play session, solutions are worked out individually in the form of small advisory reports, uploaded to the environment and assessed by both teachers and peers (co-players in the group).

Wiki-Games

The design and development of wiki-games started with the objective to challenge the serious games adoption barriers discussed in the introduction. The central research question of this challenge was to research to what extent it is possible to use commonly available and easy to use tools such as wikis to introduce serious games in education. More specific research questions were:

- Is it feasible at all to create appropriate and representative game scenarios in a wiki?
- Is there any learning and/or motivation effect?
- What are the teachers' and learners' experiences?

The research was done with the help of students of a Master Programme of Learning Sciences at the Open University of the Netherlands in two consecutive studies. For study 1 an argumentation game was designed. Argumentation is an important skill since it promotes the learner's ability to get into the details of a chosen topic; i.e. to find and connect information on a topic, to discuss and defend a topic from a given position, and to disprove counter-arguments raised by their opponent. Argumentation also fits very well within a wiki since wikis allow for creating, editing and linking to text. For study 2 some of the students designed their own wiki game for their learners. The topics chosen for their wiki-games ranged from how to spell verbs (primary education), radiology, freedom of speech to research methods (higher education). There was a variety of implementations ranging from minor modifications to new designs inspired by Argument. One of the resulting games, Werk!Woord!, a game on verb spelling, was also evaluated in the class room. The design and the results of the studies with Argument and Werk!Woord! are described below. Both studies followed a mainly qualitative research design.

Argument: The Argument game (Van Rosmalen & Westera, 2012) makes use of the collaborative nature of a wiki with (groups of) students producing argumentations either in favour or against preset propositions and mutually rate the quality of their argumentations. The teacher initiates a game by drawing up a proposition linked with a chosen domain of study. The Argument game (Figure 1) then uses four rounds:

- In round 1, the learners (in teams) write a short essay on the proposition either pro or contra.
- In round 2, the teams write five arguments in favour of their position. They may strengthen their arguments by adding a link to a reference. Moreover, in one of their arguments they may use a "cheat" argument (an argument that sounds valid but is not) which gives, if convincing enough to be accepted by the opposing team, additional points.
- In round 3, the teams challenge the arguments of their opponents.
- Finally, in round 4 the teams write a final, short essay summing up their arguments.

Figure 1. The home page of the wiki-game Argument with at the left its navigation panel

In each round a team can gain points for its contribution. A Hall of Fame is administered to show the scores. All details of the game are explained in the wiki including team compositions, position to defend or oppose, background resources, game rules, scores and scoring. Finally, each round is followed by a discussion either in a forum in the wiki or in the class room (the full details of the game including the manual are available in the game template – in Dutch – at: http://wiki-games-argument-sjabloon.wikispaces.com/).

Werk!Woord! (Bronk & Van Rosmalen, submitted) is a wiki-game that can be used to apply and to exercise with Dutch verb spelling algorithms. It aims to improve Dutch verb spelling skills and knowledge (in terms of correct use of given spelling algorithms). The algorithms used are part of the method "Taaljournaal" (Fourdraine et al., 2007). Before the start of the game the learners receive instruction on the algorithms in their classroom. The game should stimulate the learners to actually apply and therewith learn them. The game is played in teams of two learners who according to their level should be able to cooperate effectively. The teams can collect points in a number of tasks. The team that collects the most points will be the verb-spelling-champion. Each team receives the following assignment:

1. Think of and prepare six sentences with your team. Make one sentence with a misspelled verb. Your counter team will have to discover your mistake.

2. Discover the false sentence of another party given to you and explain why that sentence is wrong and the other sentences are right. You should use the Verb Algorithm Guide (a graphically depicted decision table that if followed and applied correctly gives the right spelling) for your explanations.

The game is played in three rounds. In each round, each team has the same assignment. At the end of each round, points are distributed:

- A team gets points if it did detect the wrong sentence of their counterpart.
- A team gets points if it can explain the sentences of their counterpart according to the Verb Algorithm Guide.
- A team gets points deducted if the team accidentally made an additional error in their sentences or if it did not make a wrong sentence.

A "Hall of Fame" shows the teams with the highest score. The winning team is the Werk!Woord! Champion and wins the Werk!Woord! 'trophy'.

The game is played in three rounds. This combines the requirement to fit it into the available time in the school's lesson plan and to have additional tension in the game; i.e. to compete for the highest overall position or to be the winner of a round. Support from the Verb Algorithm Guide is gradually reduced. Round 1 offers the complete Verb Algorithm Guide with all the decision steps whereas in round 3, the steps have to be entered by the learner themselves.

Methods

In study 1 (Argument), fifteen students participated. They volunteered following an open call for participation. The majority of these students, ranging in age from 24-54, have regular jobs as teachers in schools. Study 1 consisted of two separate experiments. In part 1, the participants evaluated an instantiation of Argument as a learner. In part 2, seven of the participants continued as a teacher and designed their instantiation of Argument. In part 1, the activities were planned in a three weeks period following a strict schedule (who, what and when). For part 2, the students were free in their planning. The following data was collected: (a) the contributions to a forum which included discussions on the use of and experience with Argument (part 1); (b) progress information as compared to the schedule (part 1); (c) a questionnaire on the background of the participants, their participation in and opinions of part 1 and part 2; (d) the designs created by the participants (part 2).

Study 2 (Werk!Woord!) took place in group 8 of a primary school, the final group of primary education. The number of learners was 12. Each week one round was played. The game was part of the learner's individual task assignments and accordingly they had to plan their work themselves. The game started with an explanation of the game in the class room. The experiment was set up as a pre-experimental study. It started with a pre-test, followed by a three week period in which Werk!Woord! was used and ended with a post-test. The experiment including the tests, scoring and observations was conducted by the first author. Additionally, at the end the learners received a questionnaire with questions on their background, and their experience with and appreciation of the game.

Results

The results demonstrate that a wiki is an appropriate tool for developing game-like activities that are motivating and fit well also for complex tasks. In more detail the outcomes are as follows.

- Is it feasible at all to create appropriate and representative game scenarios in a wiki?

Both Argument and Werk!Woord! do more or less follow all aspects as mentioned in commonly used definitions of serious games. Nadolski et al. (2006): "Multi-user online serious games are (mostly) competitive, situation-dependent, interactive digital (learning) environments based on a set of rules and / or an underlying model, which, subject to certain restrictions, under uncertainty, a challenging (learning) goal is being pursued for which cooperation is essential". The two games do follow game principles (Pernin, Michau, Mandran & Mariais, 2012) such as competition (between two teams and all teams), individual challenge (to

detect errors and to create not-easy-to-spot errors or to create or oppose arguments), collaboration (teams in which the members challenge each other to come up with the best not-easy-to spot-error or the best argument), recognition by others (by the opposing team and by all teams), and chance (players who are good in spelling have an advantage nevertheless 'winning' even for the best in spelling player or team is not guaranteed, the same applies for the best arguments). Nevertheless, when asked many of the users (Argument 54%, Werk!Woord! 50%) do not perceive them as a game. This is partly because the wiki-games do not meet the expectations raised by commonly used games (graphics and immersiveness) and partly as some of the Werk!Woord! users testify: "*since you learn something of it*" or "*because it is an assignment*". Overall, it can be concluded that wikis can be used to create game scenarios. Be it that wiki-games are probably best described by stating that they make use of game elements, in other words they more align with gamificiation (Raymer, 2011: http://en.wikipedia.org/wiki/Gamification: "Gamification is the use of game design techniques and mechanics to solve problems and engage audiences").

- Is there any learning and/or motivation effect?

Within the limitations of the set-up of both studies, the wiki-games were successful. For Argument the majority of the learners were neutral or negative about the motivational aspect. This was mainly due to the problems with the synchronisation of the activities due to the irregular availability of the co-learners. Nevertheless, they judged Argument as a good and instructive work format (70%) and they acknowledged that their involvement with Argument had a clear, positive effect on their knowledge of the topic discussed (70%). Werk!Woord! was both appreciated for its motivational and learning aspects. The learners liked to use Werk!Woord! because of the cooperation element (4 learners), the competition element (6 learners) or because you learn while you play (2 learners). Tutor observations of the learners playing the game showed that the learners were engaged in the game and collaborated well. The scores on a spelling test improved from 63% correct in a pre-test to 74% correct in a post-test. Even more interestingly, the explanations on how the spelling was performed also improved from 18% to 73% (or from 28% to 98% of the right answers).

- What are the teachers' and learners' experiences?

The final judgement of the participants on Argument, as a learner or as a teacher building their own wiki-game, was positive despite all the inherent limitations. A larger part of the participants indicated that Argument did inspire them to start using wikis and other (easy to use) ICT tools, as an introduction to using serious games, or use Argument or a variation of it directly. The students who built their own wiki-game confirmed that it was fairly easy not only to create a wiki-game but also to apply it in a useful manner to an educational learning context. Also Werk!Woord was experienced by most of the learners as a nice and challenging way to practice verb spelling. The observation that learners encouraged others to finish their work is not common practice. Nine out of the 12 pupils indicated that they liked Werk!Woord! and 10 out of 12 that it was instructive. Overall, there was only one drawback of using a wiki to build a game: checking the assignments and keeping the scores showed to be relatively labour intensive.

Mastership Games for Teachers-in-Training in Higher Education, Built with an Authoring Tool for Collaboration Scripts

Workplace learning, for instance for teachers during their classroom practice, is no longer restricted to acquiring or updating domain knowledge, but also has to deal with selecting and using this knowledge for certain problem situations in daily practice. Such learning is about acquiring competences such as information skills and media literacy, problem-solving, communication and collaboration skills, and above all critical reflection. Today's teaching professionals become lifelong learners who continuously have to face problem situations that are changing dynamically and rapidly. Serious collaboration games are considered to hold potential as more open, dynamic and flexible learning environments where such professional teaching skills could be acquired through self-determined learning with little or no direct teacher intervention. Collaboration scripts have been rarely implemented within educational games so far. They use the situated context (or authentic case) to have learners access tacit knowledge by sharing and co-creating new knowledge together (Bell, Kanar, & Kozlowski, 2008). Collaboration scripts (Kobbe et al., 2007) are an instructional method that structures the collaboration by guiding the interacting partners through a sequence of interaction phases with designated activities and roles. One of our most important research challenges is to look for flexible and effective ways to optimizing the type and amount of structured collaboration.

We developed both a card playing and online version of the 'Mastership game' that helps students, teachers-in-training in higher education, to find solutions to some of the most prevailing practical classroom management dilemmas in a playful way, to help them become better teachers. It can be assumed that collaborating on problems first will later increase their 'professional productivity' as teachers, simply because exchanging information and looking from various perspectives will increase the quality of the individual solutions, as shown by some CSCL studies (Gunawardena, Carabajal & Lowe, 2001; Jeong & Chi, 2000). The specific problems of the Mastership game that are under study here deal with (multiple perspectives on) classroom management dilemmas. What should a teacher do, for instance, when a pupil continues to disturb the lesson by insulting his peers? Should the problem be resolved during the lesson, even at the risk of losing valuable time to the expense of the majority of students who are not involved in the conflict? Or should the problem be resolved after the class has been dismissed, even at the risk that disturbances will continue during the lesson. Teaching can be considered to be an exciting game, as teachers will certainly have to face unexpected situations that demand finding solutions on the fly.

The Mastership game (Figure 2) can be played in small groups from two to six students and does not require any moderation or other intervention by teachers. After selecting their avatars, they start the group play both in the role of player (or problem owner) and of co-player (judging the way that players solve their problems). The game has a (basic, default) structure that consists of five consecutive phases, during which players discuss, elaborate and negotiate solutions to solve the problem. Communication is structured by various assignments and rules during these phases, but is possible by unstructured group chat as well. Dur-

Figure 2. Screens of the online version of the Mastership game: selecting three practical dilemmas in phase 1 (upper left hand), assigning and motivating themes in phase 3 (upper right hand), motivating and discussing declined themes in phase 4 (lower left hand), and peer assessment of elaborated assignments in phase 6 (lower right hand).

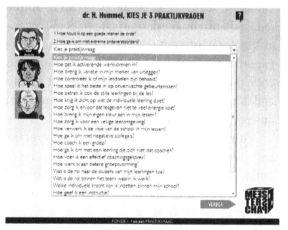
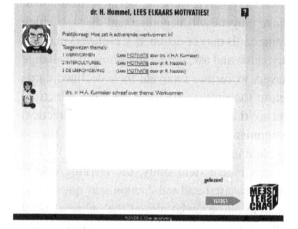
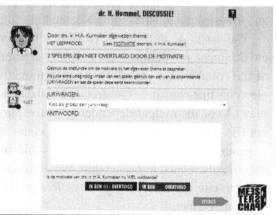

ing the *first phase* players select three practical dilemmas, either out of a pile of twenty-four, most prevailing practical classroom dilemmas (i.e., "How to maintain control in a good way", "How to deal with negative colleagues", or "How to deal with a pupil that does not want to get coached"), or by formulating one of their own. Then each player selects the problem that is considered most important. During the *second phase* players draw an exploratory assignment (e.g., "Provide an exemplary experience that shows why this problem is important for you"). The elaboration is judged by the co-players until the group is satisfied. During the *third phase* players take turns in drawing theme cards (e.g., "professional development", "dealing with losses", or "lesson preparation") that are placed at their co-players while motivating why this theme should be further explored in combination with the chosen dilemma, until every player has received three theme cards. In the *fourth phase* players will negotiate and discuss which theme cards may be declined. Co-players may use jury cards and ask further questions to challenge players to further motivate their declined cards before the group agrees on the final selection. During the *fifth phase* players select a practical assignment to further elaborate a solution for the problem in a short advisory report.

In a recent field study, the learning effects were measured and satisfaction was questioned for nine players who played the online version and ten players who played the face-to-face version of the Mastership game. All participants were third year teachers-in-training from various domains (like foreign language or science) following the game as part of a didactics course. The participants were randomly allocated to both conditions. Results have been controlled for the effects of domain, sex and age. Results showed that the collaboration of students on classroom dilemmas can indeed be successfully facilitated by this script, and that learning results do not differ for both versions. The latter holds potential for offering online and more flexible ways of workplace learning. Especially students playing the online version reported the need for simpler structures and clearer task instruction. Optimizing the level of structure in collaboration scripts therefore appears an issue for further study, and we will need flexible and user-friendly authoring environments to facilitate this. Collaborative learning online is not easy and depends on the richness and intensity of interactions (emergence of elaborated explanations, negotiation of meanings, mutual regulation of cognitive processes) as enabled by the collaboration structure. The holy grail of CSCL is to establish environments that (in)directly favour the emergence of rich interactions, which is commonly referred to as 'design for conversation' (e.g., Dillenbourg & Fischer, 2007).

Collaboration scripts seem to offer potential to be further adapted and examined in serious gaming research. The complexity can be further reduced and reusable design patterns could become available (Westera et al., 2008). The collaboration pattern (script) we described in this study produces code that can be instantiated in different settings and domains (where mutual regulation and various perspectives play a role).

This first study revealed that clear instruction and simple structure are especially important for online learning without direct teacher intervention. We therefore have continued our work with a comparative study differentiating high-structure (as in this version, but improved), medium-structure and low-structure in the online Mastership game.

The basis of defining a flexible authoring environment for defining the optimal structure of the collaboration script was to determine the elements that constitute the structure of the game play (A) or the mutual-dependency of the players (B). Preferably the nature of such elements is generic for all collaboration scripts and not specifically related to mastership. We decided to differentiate the following more or less generic structure elements:

- **A1:** The number of scenes in a phase (or round). Combining scenes signifies that players can move more freely within a phase, thus facing a lower structure.

- **A2:** The number of 'cards' that are to be drawn obligatory. If players are allowed to draw less than three or just one card in a phase obviously the structure becomes lower.

- **B1:** The order in which players proceed might be by taking turns or to work in parallel, with the later obviously being less dependent and facing a lower structure.

- **B2:** The way players may decide to move to a next scene or phase can be either by group consent or by individual choice, with the later obviously being less dependent and facing a lower structure.

- **B3:** The way players receive their 'cards' could be either by being drawn by others for them or by drawing the cards themselves, with the later obviously being less dependent and facing a lower structure.

We would like to stress that this is by no means the only or best differentiation imaginable, we could think of other elements as well. However, the approach to differentiate elements as 'handles' to be turned on/off in an authoring environment seems useful, and we provide our choices as an example. Based on these structure elements, we defined a high, medium and low level of structure (Table 2).

We have currently implemented these three levels of structure following this approach, have

Table 2. Structure table

	A1	A2	B1	B2	B3
High	True	3	True	True	True
Medium	False	1	False	True	True
Low	False	1	False	False	False

partially carried out a second field study comparing these versions of structure with actual students, and are in the process of completing the setup and data collection.

Besides looking into the effects of optimizing structure, and the role the authoring environment can play to facilitate this optimization by teachers themselves, we also intend to look how to generalize the findings. Dillenbourg & Hong (2008) propose *script families* as a higher level of abstraction that discriminate classes of scripts that use the same pattern, e.g., JigSaw (distributing knowledge among group members), ArgueGraph (raising a conflict pattern), or Reciprocal Teaching (using mutual regulation). The Mastership game belongs to the latter family, but it might be useful to explore others, as we have already successfully implemented and studied a conflict script in a game on water management (Hummel et al., 2011) whose narrative and collaboration script were described in the second section of this article. We also plan to implement Argument scripts (Van Rosmalen & Westera, 2012) in the collaboration scripting environment.

Finally, related to this and similar case studies that relate to collaboration on complex problems, structure is a highly important but not sole variable that should be adjustable in a flexible authoring environment for teachers. There are other variables in a serious game play that will have to be conceived, researched, and potentially included in the authoring environment we currently are working on, such as the following:

- **Problem Quality:** In the current studies we used 'cards' with a short description of a dilemma to be discussed and collaborated upon. Based on this description every player had to visualize and enrich this description by relating it to personal knowledge and experience. It might well be that personal experience is a stronger determinant for effective game play than the quality of the collaboration script and game play. It might be interesting to look into 'richer' case descriptions, for instance by using videos with teachers talking about dealing with classroom dilemmas, as available in the Didiclass video database (Geerts, Mitzschke & Van Laeken, 2009). Their usage and added value is planned to be studied in a subsequent study.

- **Modality:** In the current studies we used verbal information on cards. Students verbally exchanged information without receiving non-verbal cues about the conversation or cases. It might be useful to present audiovisual cases as suggested in the previous aspect (or even virtual worlds in which the cases are situated), or have audiovisual communication possibilities. For instance using technologies like biosensors to input information about co-players' stress level or language technologies to interpret communication automatically might increase the realism of the collaboration process.

- **Roles:** The differentiation of roles was relatively simple in the Mastership game, players were either player / problem owner or co-player / judge of others' problem elaboration. It might be interesting to look at collaboration scripts were players assume various roles or perspectives, as we described in the Aquaculture example in section 2.

- **Synchronicity:** In the current studies players to a large extent had to collaborate synchronously; only the individual elaboration of the assignment could be executed asynchronously. It appears complicated to synchronise the collaboration in a way without unwanted delay for some of the players because patterns of work differ. It might be interesting to further explore the optimal balance between synchronous and asynchronous parts of the collaboration scripts.

GAMES FOR AND BY LEARNERS

Continuing on from games by teachers, we will now discuss a case study of a tool, Scratch, which has been designed to be used by learners. As discussed above, to have students make their own computer applications is already a relatively old application. Moreover, since most of the current generation of students are very familiar with games, it should fit very well with their interests to have students develop their own games and have them experience what it is to design and develop a game.

Scratch

Logo (Papert, 1980) was the program that inspired Scratch. It is a visual-based tool and children are encouraged to create programs by simply snapping together the blocks provided to create their own program or script as it is known in Scratch. Figure 3 shows example screens shots of Scratch.

Scratch is primarily aimed at children aged around eight, however, statistics from the Scratch site show that the average age of users is 12 (MIT, 2011) and there is a wide age range of users for this tool. It was envisaged from the outset that while this project was to introduce computers to deprived areas eventually the informal educational benefits of it would be studied at a later date (Resnick, Kafai & Maeda, 2003). Although Scratch has been used in formal education (Malan & Leitner, 2007; Malan, 2010), there is currently little published research on whether Scratch can be used as a tool for teaching programming concepts in a primary classroom setting. Research has focused on the community around Scratch that has been built up since its introduction. Brennan, Resnick and Monroy-Hernández (2010) discuss how Scratch is used by the online Scratch community with participants ranging from socialisers through to creators of projects while Monroy-Hernández and Resnick (2008) discuss the collaborative nature of the community and

Figure 3. Example screenshots of scratch

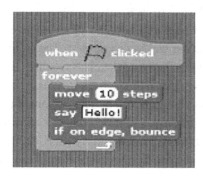

how groups of users are starting to set up their own "miniature companies" to produce games of high quality.

There is currently little published research on what learning takes place when constructing games with Scratch in a primary classroom setting (Hayes & Games 2008). Adams (2010) looked at the use of Scratch during a five day summer camp with 30 boys and 15 girls aged 13 and above. The children were given the chance to create either multimedia videos or games with Scratch and out of the 45 children who attended only 3 did not make games. The children all reported that they thoroughly enjoyed working with Scratch with the girls scoring the camp either very good or good on their opinions of their camp enjoyment. While Sivilotti and Laugel (2008) undertook out-of-school workshops with 13-14 year olds to gauge their opinions on Scratch, studies such as Maloney et al. focus on what blocks the children had used over an extended period of time in their Scratch projects during an after-school computer clubhouse.

Within educational establishments and during lesson time, projects such as those described by Wilson, Connolly, Hainey and Moffat (2011) show how Scratch can be used with young children aged 8-9 to learn programming concepts through the introduction of game making. Children were given 8 lessons to introduce them to programming and also to gauge how much they enjoyed working

with Scratch. Baytak and Land (2011) in their study focused on learning by design where 10 to 11 year old children planned and designed and then created their game with Scratch during a science project. At Harvard University Scratch has been used as an introduction to programming for new undergraduate students (Malan & Leitner, 2007; Malan, 2010). This entailed students developing Scratch projects as part of the introductory lessons to introduce programming concepts to help prepare them for using Java.

Scratch: Programming and Design in the ICT Curriculum

The Scottish Government has reviewed the Scottish curriculum over the past few years and, after much consultation, a new Curriculum for Excellence (CfE) has been implemented within Scottish schools (Scottish Executive, 2006). This reform of education is one of the biggest Scotland has seen and intends to give a coherent curriculum for children from 3 years through to 18 years (Scottish Executive, 2008). Teachers should also be taking the opportunities given in using Information and Communications Technology (ICT) for more interdisciplinary learning (HMIE, 2009). Within the CfE teachers are being encouraged to make more use of different styles of approaches to learning as well as interdisciplinary work, one of which is the use of ICT within learning. ICT as an approach to learning is being encouraged to develop children's digital literacy skills and some suggested means of implementing this are through the use of Glow – the Scottish schools' intranet system – or games-based learning (GBL) (LTS, 2011a), which is supported by the Consolarium (LTS, 2011b), an initiative set up by Education Scotland to support teachers in exploring the use of GBL in their class. This is further enhanced within the Technologies curricular area that looks for children to be making use of games through designing and creating their own games.

A pilot study of the use of Scratch was conducted within a Primary School in Glasgow. 60 children in 3 classes (27 girls and 33 boys) aged between 8 and 11 participated. The classes comprised of primary 4 that had 18 children; primary 5/6 that had 20 children and primary 6/7 that had 22 children. The children worked in the same pairs throughout the project: 7 pairs of boys, 5 pairs of girls, one group of 3 boys, one group of 2 boys and 1 girl and 16 boy/girl pairs.

The aim of the pilot study was to introduce Scratch into the primary ICT curriculum by way of eight lessons focusing introducing programming concepts though game construction. The games would then be evaluated at the end of the study to show what programming skills the children used within the games they created.

Over the course of eight weeks the children were given a one hour lesson with Scratch with the principle investigator leading the lessons alongside the class teacher. They were structured so that for the first few weeks the principal investigator spoke for the first 5 minutes of the lesson to explain the work and then the children worked in pairs on their computers on their games. Towards the end of the project the children were able to start lessons straight away on the computers to keep working on their games. During lessons when children were on the computer they were working in pairs, this was in part due to the limited resources of the school; however, collaborative work is actively encouraged within the CfE. The class teacher was also actively encouraged to help and become more involved in the work as the weeks progressed. Through this work it is envisaged that the class teachers themselves will then go on to teach future classes game construction with Scratch. The lessons were planned to introduce the basic concepts of programming to children as detailed by Rusk (2009a). Given the short timeframe a selection of the concepts were focused upon namely:

- Sequence,
- Iteration,
- Conditions,
- Coordination and Synchronisation.

As well as looking at the programming concepts children were going to be taught, it was important to match the lessons to CfE guidelines (LTS, 2009) in order for the class teachers to see how they are able to easily incorporate the use of game construction within their lessons. While the main focus was on "*Using appropriate software, I can work collaboratively to design an interesting and entertaining game which incorporates a form of control technology or interactive multimedia*" (LTS, 2009) the following outcomes were also used:

1. I can create, capture and manipulate sounds, text and images to communicate experiences, ideas and information in creative and engaging ways.
2. Having evaluated my work, I can adapt and improve, where appropriate, through trial and error or by using feedback.
3. Through discovery, natural curiosity and imagination, I explore ways to construct models or solve problems.
4. I explore software and use what I learn to solve problems and present my ideas, thoughts, or information.

Over the 8 lessons the children were first given an introduction to Scratch then shown how to make a simple maze game (see Figure 4) before finally creating their own game. Table 3 gives a breakdown of the lesson plan.

Concepts within Games

A coding scheme (see Table 4) was adapted from the scheme created by Denner, Werner and Ortiz (2012) and refined based on the programming

Figure 4. Simple maze game

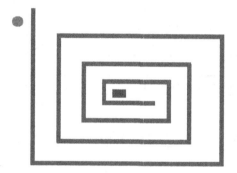

Table 3. Lessons given in class

	Lesson	Overview of Lesson(s)
Week 1	Introduction to Scratch using Scratch cards (Rusk, 2009b)	Children were given one of the twelve Scratch cards to work on. Once completed they were able to change cards and work their way through the set.
Weeks 2-4	Constructing a simple maze game (Brennan, 2009) with a timer	The children were given instructions in how to construct a basic maze game with one sprite and one background. They were shown how to control the sprite through the maze using the arrow keys. Finally, they were then shown how to add a timer and scoring to their game to increase the challenge.
Weeks 5-8	Constructing own game in Scratch	Children were able to continue their game construction either by making adaptations to the maze game they had been working on during the previous weeks or by constructing a new game by themselves.

concepts that could be learned with Scratch (Rusk, 2009a).

The 29 games that were constructed by the students varied in their complexity. Games ranged from adaptations of the maze game that included two player versions to original games like pair 17's two player game, which had player 1 being the fox and player 2 the box. The aim of this game was for player 1 to reach the bush on the other side while trying to get past player 2 and also before the time ran out (see Figure 5). This game scored well on originality although the pair had used a pre-made sprite instead of designing their own for the fox. However, this was the only element of the game not designed by the pair.

The only game from the 29 to use mouse control was one created by pair 7 in the Primary 4 class (Figure 6). The game was a join the dots game where the aim of the game was for the player to click on a dot then draw round the shape shown on screen.

This used functionality in Scratch that was influenced by Logo as the player can direct a pen to move up and down or, in this case, when the game starts the pen is put down and follows the mouse. Another game that did not use functionality through using keys to move the sprite was a game by pair 15 in the P5 class. This game used a series of questions asked to the player who would have to type the answer in (see Figure 7) and the sprite would progress across the screen if they got the correct answer. If they got a wrong answer a sound would play and they would be told "game over". This game was different from the other games as only one script was used for the whole game. The pair used nested if/else statements to control the questions (see Figure 8).

Throughout the project the children were actively encouraged to construct their own sprites and backgrounds for their games to demonstrate their creativity. This can be seen in games where the children have thought about their characters and drawn them out. Some children, though not

Table 4. Game coding categories and definitions

Programming Concepts Found in Scratch		Coding
1. Sequence	Are the blocks in a systematic order to execute the program correctly?	0/1
2. Iteration	Using forever and repeat to create iterations.	0-3
3. Variables	Variables can be created within Scratch and then be used within programs.	0-3
4. Conditional Statements	Using if, forever if and if-else to check for conditions.	0-3
5. Lists (arrays)	Allows for storing and accessing lists of strings and numbers.	0/1
6. Event handling	Responding to events triggered by either the user or another script.	0-2
7. Threads	Launching two independent scripts at the same time to execute in parallel.	0-2
8. Coordination and Synchronisation	Using blocks such as wait, broadcast and when I receive to coordinate the actions of multiple sprites.	0-3
9. Keyboard Input	Using blocks such as ask and wait prompts users to type in an answer.	0-2
10. Random Numbers	Pick Random is used to select random integers within any given range.	0/1
11. Boolean Logic	Using and, or, not.	0/1
12. Dynamic Interaction	Using mouse x or y and loudness can be used as dynamic input for interaction.	0/1
13. User Interface Design	Using when sprite clicked button can create an interactive user interface.	0/1
Code Organisation		
14. Extraneous blocks	Are there any blocks which are not initialised when the program is run?	-1/0
15. Sprite names (the default is overridden).	Are the default sprite names overridden?	0/1
16. Variable names	Are the variables given meaningful names when set up?	0/1
Designing for Usability		
17. Functionality	Does the game run when it is started (most games start when the green flag is clicked)?	0-3
18. Goal	Is there a clear defined goal to the game?	0-2
19. Sprite customisation	Is the sprite used a predefined sprite or has the sprite been customised and to what extent.	0-3
20. Stage customisation	Is the stage used a predefined stage or has the stage been customised and to what extent.	0-3
21. Instructions clear	Has the student defined how the game is supposed to run?	0-3
22. Game originality	Students were asked to create a maze game to give them the grounding in basic skills that were required. However when it came to creating their own game students were able to adapt the maze game or create a new game entirely.	0-3

many, chose to work with the sprites and backgrounds that Scratch is supplied with.

There are few prior studies that look at the learning of computing concepts though game construction. While previous research has shown that children are able to learn basic programming concepts through game making projects (Denner, Werner & Ortiz, 2012; Maloney et al., 2008) little is actually known within the primary classroom setting (Wilson, Connolly, Hainey & Moffat, 2011).

An important limitation within the study was the amount of time given to covering the programming concepts. The children only had a limited time with their introduction to Scratch, they also were working in groups which some children found difficult and some lessons were spent negotiating decisions on how their games were going to work, this is similar to the work of Denner, Werner and Ortiz (2012) who also found that games made may not have actually reflected what children were

Figure 5. Pair 17's two player original game

Figure 6. Shows start and end of pair 7's join the dots game

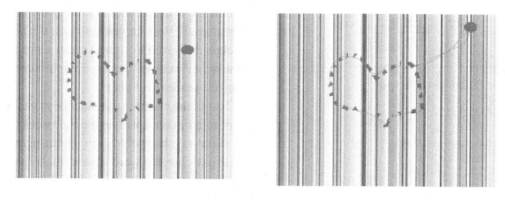

Figure 7. Pair 15's game

Figure 8. Script for pair 15's game

```
when  clicked
ask what is the capital of scotland and wait
if      answer = edinburgh
    move 90 steps
    ask what is 600 add on 972 = and wait
    if      answer = 1572
        move 90 steps
        ask what is smallest city in scotland and wait
        if      answer = stirling
            move 90 steps
            ask what is the tallest mountin in the uk and wait
            if      answer = ben nevis
                move 90 steps
                ask what is the capital of spain and wait
                if      answer = madrid
                    move 90 steps
                else
                    play sound BalloonScratch
                    say game over for 2 secs
            else
                play sound BalloonScratch
                say game over for 2 secs
        else
            play sound BalloonScratch until done
            say game over for 2 secs
    else
        say game over for 2 secs
        play sound BalloonScratch until done
else
    play sound BalloonScratch until done
    say game over for 2 secs
    stop script
```

capable of. The eight lessons covered the basics of game making with Scratch, given the timeframe and age of children this was a basic introduction. If more time had been available then the children would have been able to progress to making more complex games and learning more programming concepts. Most groups were successful in their attempts at creating their game whether it was a maze game or original creation. The primary 4 class did not make as many original games as the other two classes, however, they preferred to adapt the maze game that they had created and had the most amount of games that were functional or only with minor mistakes. Both primary 5/6 and primary 6/7 classes had equal amounts of original games, indeed 60% of each class made their own game. However the primary 5/6 class were more successful in implementing their games with more functionality than the primary 6/7 class.

The most used programming concepts by children in the project were similar to those found in Maloney et al. (2008), namely User Interaction (key handling), Loops (iteration) and Conditional Statements. While gender groupings did not have a significant effect on game scores, the primary 5/6 class did have the highest mean score as well as the most functional games. This class consisted of mixed gender groupings.

Overall the children did manage to gain some programming concepts over the eight week period. The study has shown that even within eight hours of lessons children were able to make progress with Scratch and their learning of programming. This was similar to the results of Baytak and Land (2011), who reported that children had completed games after 10 Scratch lessons or 6 for their experienced children, as well as being similar to the game construction work of Robertson and Howells (2008) with the Neverwinter Nights project.

Further research will entail expansion of the study to include further primary schools in the Glasgow region. This will involve inclusion of different age groups to attain further empirical results to produce more statistically significant evidence and assist in refining the instruments of evaluation through a series of pilot studies. The age groups targeted would be in the age range of eight to eleven at primary four, five, six and seven level. This will enable comparisons between the different primary school levels to ascertain the suitability of the computer game construction tool at different primary educational levels.

CONCLUSION

The objective of this chapter was to make a case and exemplify that the design and use of games in education is not necessarily the exclusive domain of game professionals or that it should be too complex to embed games in education. Starting from some very simple games that might be readily included in a lesson, we evolved to discuss game engines purposed on teachers and, finally, to games purposed on students themselves. We have only discussed a very limited sample of game tools available, nevertheless, we do think that the selection discussed is representative of what is available and have been used successfully.

The variety of the examples discussed, and in many cases the large and active communities around tools, show that serious games are within reach for teachers who are interested in using them in their lessons. Therefore we do hope this chapter will inspire teachers to build and use their own games. Hopefully, they will also realise that building a game already may be very rewarding. It is important to notice that the examples discussed clearly reveal that building games is not the exclusive domain of teachers in computer science or related domains but equally within reach for teachers in other domains. Finally, while we realise that while showing that games are within reach for teachers at the same level as social media, we have not shown how to design effective and motivating games. Therefore, we suggest teachers work together and take into account examples of best practice and (evolving) methods to design serious games.

REFERENCES

Adams, J. C. (2010). Scratching middle schoolers' creative itch. In *Proceedings of the 41st ACM Technical Symposium on Computer Science Education*. ACM.

Ayers, P., & Ortega, F. (Eds.). (2010). *Proceedings of the 6th international symposium on wikis and open collaboration 2010*. Gdansk, Poland: ACM.

Baytak, A., & Land, S. (2011). An investigation of the artifacts and process of constructing computers games about environmental science in a fifth grade classroom. *Educational Technology Research and Development*, *59*(7), 765–782. doi:10.1007/s11423-010-9184-z.

Bell, B. S., Kanar, A. M., & Kozlowski, S. W. J. (2008). Current issues and future directions in simulation-based training in North America. *International Journal of Human Resource Management*, *19*(8), 1416–1434. doi:10.1080/09585190802200173.

Brennan, K. (2009). *Maze game*. Retrieved September 5, 2011, from http://scratched.media.mit.edu/resources/lets-play

Brennan, K., Chung, M., & Hawson, J. (2011). *Scratch curriculum guide draft*. Retrieved January 2, 2013, from http://scratched.media.mit.edu/resources/scratch-curriculum-guide-draft

Brennan, K., Resnick, M., & Monroy-Hernández, A. (2010). Making projects, making friends: Online community as a catalyst for interactive media creation. *New Directions for Youth Development*, (128): 75–83. doi:10.1002/yd.377 PMID:21240955.

Bronk, S., & Van Rosmalen, P. (2013). *Learning Dutch verb spelling through a simple, yet powerful, wiki-game*. Unpublished.

Chou, L. D., Liu, T. C., Li, D. C., Chen, Y. S., Ieong, M. T., Lee, P. H., & Lin, Y. C. (2011). Development of a game-based learning system using toy robots. In *Proceedings of the 2011 IEEE 11th International Conference on Advanced Learning Technologies* (pp. 202-204). IEEE Computer Society.

De Freitas, S. (2006). *Learning in immersive worlds: A review of game-based learning.* London: JISC. Retrieved August, 24, 2012, from http://www.jisc.ac.uk/media/documents/programmes/elearninginnovation/gamingreport_v3.pdf

Denner, J., Werner, L., & Ortiz, E. (2012). Computer games created by middle school girls: Can they be used to measure understanding of computer science concepts? *Computers & Education, 58*(1), 240–249. doi:10.1016/j.compedu.2011.08.006.

Dillenbourg, P., & Fischer, F. (2007). Basics of computer-supported collaborative learning. *Zeitschrift für Berufs- und Wirtschaftspaedagogik, 21*, 111–130.

Dillenbourg, P., & Hong, F. (2008). The mechanics of CSCL macro scripts. *International Journal of Computer-Supported Collaborative Learning, 3*(1), 5–23. doi:10.1007/s11412-007-9033-1.

FAS. (2006). *Harnessing the power of video games for learning: Summit of educational games.* Washington, DC: Federation of American Scientists. Retrieved from http://www.fas.org/gamesummit/Resources/Summit%20on%20Educational%20Games.pdf

Fischer, G., & Kling, U. (1974). LOGO - Eine programmiersprache für schüler, inhaltliche und methodische aspekte ihrer anwendung. *Lecture Notes in Computer Science, 17*, 290–299. doi:10.1007/3-540-06907-0_87.

Fourdraine, A., Hotho, H., Janssen, D., Janssen, K., Maters, A., Munsterman, D., Pijl, J., Van der Veen, S., & Van der Vereijken-Jonkers, S.M. (2007). *Taaljournaal.* s-Hertogenbosch: Malmberg.

Geerts, W., Mitzsche, M., & Van Laeken, M. (Eds.). (2009). Wat zou je doen? Dilemma's in de onderwijspraktijk. Bussum: Coutinho.

Gunawardena, C. N., Carabajal, K., & Lowe, C. A. (2001). *Critical analysis of models and methods used to evaluate online learning networks.* Seattle, WA: AERA.

Hayes, E. R., & Games, I. A. (2008). Making computer games and design thinking: A review of current software and strategies. *Games and Culture, 3*(3–4), 309–332. doi:10.1177/1555412008317312.

HMIE. (2009). *Improving Scottish education.* HMIE.

Hummel, H. G. K., Geerts, W. M., Slootmaker, A., Kuipers, D., & Westera, W. (2013). Collaboration scripts for mastership skills: Online game about classroom dilemmas in teacher education. *Interactive Learning Environments.* doi:10.1080/10494820.2013.789063.

Hummel, H.G.K., Van Houcke, J., Nadolski, R.J., & Van der Hiele, T., Kurvers, & Löhr, A. (2011). Scripted collaboration in serious gaming for complex learning: Effects of multiple perspectives when acquiring water management skills. *British Journal of Educational Technology, 42*(6), 1029–1041. doi:10.1111/j.1467-8535.2010.01122.x.

Jeong, H., & Chi, M. T. H. (2000). *Does collaborative learning lead to the construction of common knowledge?* Retrieved July 9, 2004, from http://www.ircs.upenn.edu.edu/cogsci2000/PRCDNGS/SPRCDNGS/posters/jeo_chi.pdf

Klopfer, E., Osterweil, S., & Salen, K. (2009). *Moving learning games forward, obstacles opportunities & openness.* Cambridge, MA: MIT/The Education Arcade. Retrieved from http://education.mit.edu/papers/MovingLearningGamesForward_EdArcade.pdf

Kobbe, L., Weinberger, A., Dillenbourg, P., & Harrer, A., Hämäläinen, Häkkinen, P., & Fisher, F. (2007). Specifying computer-supported collaboration scripts. *Computer-Supported Collaborative Learning, 2*, 211–224. doi:10.1007/s11412-007-9014-4.

LTS. (2009). *Curriculum for excellence: Technologies experiences and outcomes.* LTS.

LTS. (2011a). *Approaches to learning*. Retrieved January 28, 2012, from http://www.ltscotland.org. uk/learningteachingandassessment/approaches/ index.asp

LTS. (2011b). *The consolarium*. Retrieved January 28, 2012, from http://www.ltscotland.org. uk/usingglowandict/gamesbasedlearning/consolarium.asp

Malan, D. J. (2010). Reinventing CS50. In *Proceedings of the 41st ACM Technical Symposium on Computer Science Education*. ACM.

Malan, D. J., & Leitner, H. H. (2007). Scratch for budding computer scientists. In *Proceedings of the 38th SIGCSE Technical Symposium on Computer Science Education*. ACM.

Maloney, J. H., Peppler, K., Kafai, Y. B., Resnick, M., & Rusk, N. (2008). Programming by choice: Urban youth learning programming with scratch. In *Proceedings of the 39th SIGCSE Technical Symposium on Computer Science Education*. ACM.

MIT. (2011). *Statistics on scratch users*. Retrieved May 5, 2011, from http://stats.scratch.mit.edu/

Monroy-Hernández, A., & Resnick, M. (2008). Empowering kids to create and share programmable media. *Interaction, 15*(2), 50–53. doi:10.1145/1340961.1340974.

Nadolski, R. J., Hummel, H. G. K., Van den Brink, H. J., Hoefakker, R., Slootmaker, A., Kurvers, H., & Storm, J. (2008). EMERGO: Methodology and toolkit for efficient development of serious games in higher education. *Simulation & Gaming, 39*(3), 338–352. doi:10.1177/1046878108319278.

Nadolski, R. J., Van der Hijden, P., Tattersall, C., & Slootmaker, A. (2006). *Multi-user online serious games: Beleid, ontwerp en gebruik* [Multi-user online serious game: Policy, design and use]. Utrecht, The Netherlands: Stichting Digitale Universiteit.

National Gaming Survey. (2009). *Detailed data of gaming in The Netherlands*. Retrieved February 24, 2012, from http://www.nationaalgamingonderzoek.nl

NFER. (2009). *Teacher voice omnibus survey*. Retrieved August 24, 2012, from http://www.nfer. ac.uk/nfer/what-we-offer/teacher-voice/PDFs/ futurelab.pdf

Overmars, M. (2004). Teaching computer science through game design. *Computer, 37*(4), 81–83. doi:10.1109/MC.2004.1297314.

Papert, S. (1980). *Mindstorms: Children, computers, and powerful ideas*. New York: Basic Books, Inc.

Pernin, J., Michau, F., Mandran, N., & Mariais, C. (2012). ScenLRPG, a board game for the collaborative design of Gbl scenarios: Qualitative analysis of an experiment. In *Proceedings of the 6th European Conference on Games Based Learning*. Cork, Ireland: IEEE.

PWC. (2010). *Global entertainment and media outlook: 2010-2014*. Retrieved from http://www. pwc.com/

Razak, A. A., Connolly, T. M., & Hainey, T. (2012). Teachers' views on the approach of digital games-based learning within the curriculum for excellence. *International Journal of Game-Based Learning, 2*(1), 33–51. doi:10.4018/ ijgbl.2012010103.

Resnick, M., Kafai, Y., & Maeda, J. (2003). *A networked, media-rich programming environment to enhance technological fluency at after-school centers in economically-disadvantage communities*. Academic Press.

Riehle, D., & Bruckman, A. (2009). *Proceedings of the 5th International Symposium on Wikis and open collaboration 2009*. Orlando, FL: ACM.

Robertson, J., & Howells, C. (2008). Computer game design: Opportunities for successful learning. *Computers & Education, 50*(2), 559–578. doi:10.1016/j.compedu.2007.09.020.

Rusk, N. (2009a). *Scratch programming concepts.* Retrieved September 5, 2011, from http://info.scratch.mit.edu/sites/infoscratch.media.mit.edu/files/file/ScratchProgrammingConcepts-v14.pdf

Rusk, N. (2009b). *Scratch cards.* Retrieved September 5, 2011, from http://scratched.media.mit.edu/resources/scratch-cards

Schifter, K. (2012). *Minecraft in an English class.* Paper presented at 6th European Conference on Games Based Learning. Cork, Ireland.

Silius, K., Miilumäki, T., Huhtamäki, J., Tebest, T., Meriläinen, J., & Pohjolainen, S. (2010). Students' motivations for social media enhanced studying and learning. *Knowledge Management & E-Learning: An International Journal, 2*(1), 51.

Sivilotti, P. A. G., & Laugel, S. A. (2008). Scratching the surface of advanced topics in software engineering: A workshop module for middle school students. *Learning*, 291-295.

Sloep, P. B., Van der Klink, M., Brouns, F., Van Bruggen, J., & Didderen, W. (Eds.). (2011). Leernetwerken, kennisdeling, kennisontwikkeling en de leerprocessen. Houten, The Nederland: Bohn, Stafleu, Van Loghum.

Ten Brummelhuis, A., & Van Amerongen, M. (2010). *Vier in balans monitor 2010: ICT in het onderwijs: de stand van zaken.* Kennisnet. Retrieved February 2, 2011, from http://onderzoek.kennisnet.nl/vierinbalansmonitor

Ternier, S., Klemke, R., Kalz, M., Van Ulzen, P., & Specht, M. (2012). ARLearn: Augmented reality meets augmented virtuality. *Journal of Universal Computer Science - Technology for Learning across Physical and Virtual Spaces.*

Torrente, J., Del Blanco, Á., Marchiori, E. J., Moreno-Ger, P., & Fernández-Manjón, B. (2010). e-Adventure: Introducing educational games in the learning process. In *Proceedings of the IEEE EDUCON 2010 Conference.* Madrid, Spain: IEEE.

Van Rosmalen, P., & Westera, W. (2012). Introducing serious games with wikis: Empowering the teacher with simple technologies. *Interactive Learning Environments.* doi:10.1080/10494820.2012.707128.

Vier in Balans Monitor. (2012). Retrieved December 5, 2012, from http://www.kennisnet.nl/fileadmin/contentelementen/kennisnet/Over.kennisnet/vier-in-balans-2012.pdf

Westera, W., Nadolski, R. J., Hummel, H. G. K., & Wopereis, I. (2008). Serious games for higher education: A framework for reducing design complexity. *Journal of Computer Assisted Learning, 24*(5), 420–432. doi:10.1111/j.1365-2729.2008.00279.x.

Williamson, B. (2009). *Computer games, schools, and young people: A report for educators on using games for learning.* Bristol, UK: Futurelab. Retrieved from http://archive.futurelab.org.uk/resources/documents/project_reports/becta/Games_and_Learning_educators_report.pdf

Wilson, A., Connolly, T. M., Hainey, T., & Moffat, D. (2011). Evaluation of introducing programming to younger school children using a computer game construction application. In *Proceedings of 5th European Conference on Games-based Learning.* Athens, Greece: IEEE.

Wilson, A., Hainey, T., & Connolly, T. (2012). Evaluation of computer games developed by primary school children to gauge understanding of programming concepts. In *Proceedings of the 6th European Conference on Games Based Learning.* Cork, Ireland: IEEE.

KEY TERMS AND DEFINITIONS

Collaboration Script: An instructional method that structures the collaboration by guiding the interacting partners through a sequence of interaction phases with designated activities and roles (Kobbe et al., 2007).

Design-Based Learning: A form learning in which students learn what they need to learn by actively trying to design something themselves. In the context of computers it is connected to creative computing. Most people use the computer primarily as a consumer. When doing creative computing, students draw on their creativity and their computational skills to create something; i.e. they should select or create sound, pictures and devise a storyline and rely on their skills to combine this with the help of a formal computer program (i.e. design, test and incrementally improve their program).

Game Principles: The underlying principles upon which (serious) games are built. They include among other things competition, individual challenge, collaboration, recognition by others, and chance (Pernin, Michau, Mandran & Mariais, 2012).

Location-Based Learning: Learning in the real world, it connects to real locations. Location based learning builds upon the location-based service of IP-capable mobile device and connects information and activities to a set of locations within the context of a pre-designed educational challenge.

Narrative: The narrative (or script or didactical scenario) is the underlying story element of a serious game. It is a fundamental element of the game design. It gives the learners direction and guidance by describing the context in which they operate, the role they have to assume, the challenge to be addressed and the tools and sources to use en route.

Serious Game: "Multi-user online serious games are (mostly) competitive, situation-dependent, interactive digital (learning) environments based on a set of rules and / or an underlying model, which, subject to certain restrictions, under uncertainty, a challenging (learning) goal is being pursued for which cooperation is essential" (Nadolski et al., 2006).

Wiki: A social writing platform with facilities to add text, images and hyperlinks to a set of webpages alone or with a group of people. Additionally, depending of the wiki, a wiki may include various other features such as for instance multi-media materials or assessment tools. Wiki's are available on modern browsers including access by tablet or phone.

Chapter 13

A Randomised Controlled Trial to Evaluate Learning Effectiveness Using an Adaptive Serious Game to Teach SQL at Higher Education Level

Thomas Hainey
University of the West of Scotland, UK

Mario Soflano
University of the West of Scotland, UK

Thomas M. Connolly
University of the West of Scotland, UK

ABSTRACT

The literature suggests that every learner has a particular Learning Style (LS) and it is beneficial for the teacher and the learning approach to adapt to and accommodate these differences. The traditional classroom fails to motivate some learners and to maintain their engagement level during learning, possibly because of lack of interactivity. Computer games on the other hand seem to be able to engage participants for prolonged periods of time and motivate them to replay the game repeatedly. Some educationalists consider games as a potential platform to support learning and the term Games-Based Learning (GBL) has been introduced into the curriculum to reflect this approach. While many GBL applications have been developed, there is still a lack of empirical evidence to support its validity. Furthermore, there are very few adaptive GBL applications developed and adaptive GBL frameworks proposed. Another issue with GBL is that games engage the learners differently compared to traditional teaching approaches or eLearning and learning styles may differ inside and outside of the game. For the purpose of this research, a game with three game modes was developed. The modes were 1) non-adaptivity mode, 2) a mode that customises the game according to the learner's LS identified by a LS questionnaire, and 3) a mode with an in-game adaptive system based on a newly developed framework that can automatically adapt content according to the learner's interactions with the game. GBL has been used to teach various disciplines;

DOI: 10.4018/978-1-4666-4773-2.ch013

Copyright © 2014, IGI Global. Copying or distributing in print or electronic forms without written permission of IGI Global is prohibited.

however, this research focuses on teaching Structured Query Language (SQL) at Higher Education (HE). A Randomised Controlled Trial (RCT) was conducted with 30 students for each of the above game modes and another 30 students in a control group who learned SQL using a traditional paper-based approach. The results show that the game developed, regardless of mode, produced better learning outcomes than those who learned from a textbook. Particularly for adaptive GBL, learning effectiveness was identified to be higher while the learning duration was shorter compared to the other modes of the game.

INTRODUCTION

It has been recognised by educationalists that each student has a different way of learning and processing information (Kolb, 1984; Felder & Brent, 2005). In the classroom, the benefits derived from delivering learning content in ways that match the learner's LS have also been identified (Smith & Renzulli, 1984; Price, 2004). As new modes of delivery of learning content such as computer-assisted learning systems (e.g. eLearning) have become increasingly popular, research into these has also identified the benefits of tailoring learning content to learning styles (Miller, 2005).

In terms of eLearning, Connolly and Stansfield (2006) have suggested, eLearning simply replicates the traditional education system (classroom style) and may be overly focussed on method of delivery, i.e. delivering materials over the web rather than on actual teaching and learning, and indeed motivating and engaging the learners in the learning process. In contrast, games, particularly video games, appear to be able to engage people over extensive periods of time and also motivate them to re-play the game repeatedly until they have mastered it (Kirriemuir & McFarlane, 2004). Therefore, some educationalists (for example, Prensky, 2006) have considered games to be a potential platform in supporting learning and have turned their attention to what is now called games-based learning (GBL).

While many GBL applications have been developed in the last two decades, there remains a lack of empirical evidence to support the use of GBL for learning purposes (Connolly *et al.*, 2012). Given that there appears to be genuine advantages for learning outcomes to be derived from the adaptation of teaching materials to learning styles in the classroom and remotely through eLearning, it may also be possible that GBL applications that are adapted to the individual's LS would improve learning outcomes. Kirriemuir and McFarlane (2004) have suggested that games, unlike classroom learning or eLearning, provide a different type of engagement as they demand constant interaction and generate a 'flow' that could assist in engaging learners. It is therefore possible for learners to adopt different leaning styles in GBL than they adopt in other learning settings.

In the next section, adaptivity is presented followed by a review of previous empirical work in adaptive GBL. Section 3 discusses the procedure for the Randomised Controlled Trial (RCT) including methodology, participants and marking scheme for SQL tests. Section 4 presents the results of the RCT with a particular emphasis on learning effectiveness in relation to learning styles, programme, gender, education level and completion time. Section 5 discusses the results and future research directions.

PREVIOUS RESEARCH

Definition of Adaptivity

In computing, there are two types of adaptation process: adaptability and adaptivity (Jameson, 2003). Adaptability refers to the ability of the learner to 'adapt' to the system by explicitly customising the system according to their preferences (Bontcheva, 2002). On the other hand, adaptivity, which is usually used in the context of a user-adaptive system, refers to the ability of the system to identify the learner's preferences or characteristics and customise the system accordingly; that is, the learner implicitly influences the adaptation process (Mulwa et al., 2010).

In modern computer systems, adaptability is usually implemented by providing customisation options that allow the student to customise the system according to their preferences. For example, in eLearning the learner can choose a font size and font style associated with the learning materials. Conversely, adaptivity does not explicitly require input from the learners and it is usually hidden from them. The learners simply see the result of the customisation process provided by the system. Although both types can exist in a computer system, each type has differences in terms of its usage. Nowadays, adaptability through learner customisation is widely used and exists in many computer systems. Whilst it is certainly useful in some circumstances, adaptability requires direct manipulation from the learner that can result in an increase in the learner's cognitive load, especially if there are many options that the learner needs to choose (Oppermann, Rashev & Kinshuk, 1997).

Conversely, adaptivity can capture the interactions between the learner and the learning system and the adaptivity analyses the historical interactions before making an automatic adjustment. Adaptivity is considered to be less intrusive compared to adaptability as it does not require the student to make any changes and, as a result, the interaction between the learner and the system can be maintained. This is useful especially in a system that has a considerable amount of elements that the learner would need to manipulate. In addition, adaptivity can be used for a behavioural pattern analysis of the learner's interaction with the system. Such an analysis may be used to create different learner experiences. The disadvantage of adaptivity is that the learner does not have direct control in customising the system.

For this particular research study, adaptivity is used to refer to the system's ability to automatically customise certain elements of the system based on a series of the learner's interactions with the system.

Adaptivity in GBL

Reflecting back to the benefits of accommodating learners' learning styles on the learning outcomes in classroom-style learning and in eLearning, the same benefits may also apply in GBL. However, not all elements of LS theory can be adopted in GBL. According to Becker (2007) one of the main characteristic of games, regardless of the genre, is their interactivity, which requires players to actively interact with the game, and indicates that the 'reflection' element of the Felder-Silverman LS may not be relevant to GBL. This statement is also supported by Boyle, Connolly and Hainey (2011) who indicated that games provided an active, experiential, situated and problem-based learning environment.

According to Charles et al. (2005) and Melis and Monthienvichienchai (2004) adaptation can be incorporated into games through:

1. **A Player's Character:** All actions undertaken by the character have implications; for example, if the character is wounded, the movement of the character is slower.
2. **Non-Player Character (NPC):** The player can access this feedback by 'talking' to the NPC. Besides providing feedback, the conversation itself may be used to alter the story based on the selections the player has made in the conversation.
3. **The Game Environment:** Adaptation through the game environment can be categorised into: customisation, contextualisation and personalisation (Melis & Monthienvichienchai, 2004). In the context of GBL, customisation is related to the functionalities of the learning system;

for example, when the student reaches a particular level, a new control will appear. Contextualisation means that the content that is going to be delivered is adaptable according to the student's performance, learning history or response to certain missions. Personalisation relates more to the student's preference, for example, the font size.

4. **Feedback/Scaffolding:** Can be used to inform the student about their status in the game and to help the student to achieve the game and educational objectives (Jackson, Krajcik & Soloway, 1998).

Adaptive GBL Applications-Empirical Evidence

A systematic literature search was conducted on electronic databases including: Association for Computing Machinery (ACM), Cambridge Journals Online, Institute of Electrical and Electronic Engineering (IEEE), Index to theses, IGI Global, Ingenta Connect, Science Direct, Springer Link, Wiley Online Library, Extended Academic ASAP, Simulation and Gaming and Emerald. The following search terms were used:

- Adaptive or adaptivity or personalisation or personalization or "learning style") and "serious games" OR "games-based learning."

The search returned 978 papers, however, after detailed analysis only 8 papers were identified as being relevant to adaptive GBL applications with empirical evidence and these are summarised in Table 1.

MathQuest was developed to teach maths (algebra) at secondary school level. Felicia and Pitt (2007, 2008, 2009) proposed a LS and personality traits concept based on the MBTI and the Big-5 model known as PLEASE (Personality, Learning styles, Emotions, Autonomy, Systematic approach and Evaluation). Using this model, Felicia and Pitt (2007) developed strategies that could be incorporated and implemented to the game design and game play. For example, for students with a high level of competitiveness, ranks and scores were displayed and for students with a high level of extraversion, frequent rewards were given. Felicia and Pitt (2009) conducted an experiment involving 80 secondary school students that investigated the effect of personality in learning through MathQuest. The experiment used a

Table 1. Existing empirical evidence in adaptive GBL

Authors	Area	Adaptivity
Felicia and Pitt (2007, 2008, 2009)	Maths	Learning style and personality traits (The Big-5 model).
Conati and Zhou (2002), Conati and Zhao (2004)	Maths	Cognitive theory of emotions (joy, distress, pride, shame, admiration and reproach).
Peirce, Conlan and Wade (2008)	Physics of optics	Number of interactions between the student and certain elements of the game.
Lynch, Steen, Pritchard, Buzzell and Pintauro (2008)	Food safety	Learning style based on Dunn and Dunn's theory.
Hwang, Sung, Hung, Huang and Tsai (2012)	Plantation	Felder-Silverman (sequential - global).
Lee and Ko (2011)	Logic programming	Successful rate of the code execution.
Yongyuth, Prada, Nakasone, Kawtrakul and Prendinger (2010)	Agriculture	Changes occurring in the environment caused by the student's actions.
Demmel, Kohler, Krusche and Schubert (2011)	Languages	Number of mistakes the student has made.

questionnaire on game preferences, an International Personality Item Pool (IPIP) personality questionnaire, pre-test and post-test of the subject matter and a questionnaire about the game. They found that adaptivity towards elements of the Big-5 such as neuroticism and conscientiousness did not have a significant impact in learning outcomes, whilst adaptivity towards agreeableness, openness and extraversion seemed to benefit the students. They concluded that although "not all students will benefit from a video game but that when settings and options match their preferences and learning style, improvements can be obtained" (Felicia & Pitt, 2009, p.151).

Prime Climb was developed to teach maths (factorisation) for grade 6 and 7 students (Conati & Zhao, 2004). To analyse the student's performance and actions with the game, two layers of dynamic Bayesian networks were developed. The first layer, the short-term student model, was used to capture changes in the student's behaviour from one interface action to the next whilst climbing a specific mountain. Conversely, the second layer was used to record the student's performance for each finished mountain. The game used cognitive theory of emotions (the OCC theory) as the basis for the student's profile (Conati & Zhou, 2002). The OCC theory consists of 22 emotion types and in Prime Climb the emotional types that were used were joy, distress, pride, shame, admiration and reproach. To evaluate the game, Conati and Zhao (2004) used a control group (who played the original game) and an experimental group (who play the game with adaptivity) with ten participants for each group. The results showed that the experimental group had significantly higher gain in learning effectiveness compared to the control group and the control group hardly improved without any external guidance. However, in terms of the correlation between agent hints and learning effectiveness, there was no conclusive evidence.

ELECTRA is an RPG game with micro-adaptivity implemented through feedback and hints. The game uses adaptivity logs that record the interaction between the student and the game. Peirce, Conlan and Wade (2008) investigated the effectiveness of the ELECTRA adaptivity procedure and its impact on the student's motivation. The experiment involved 49 participants split into four experimental groups (no hint, neutral hint, adaptive hint and counter-adaptive hint). The study conducted pre-tests and post-tests of the physics of optics to measure the participant's knowledge of the particular material. The post-test also included game evaluation to measure the gaming experience. The results showed that the learning outcomes and game experience for the game with adaptive hints was better than the other groups although the difference was not statistically significant.

Lynch et al. (2008) developed Ootle-U to teach aspects of food safety. The game is adapted to the learner's LS, based on Dunn and Dunn's theory: motivation/learning enjoyment (M); persistence towards task completion (P); sense of responsibility (R); structure (S); alone versus peer (AP); auditory (A); visual (V); tactile (T); and kinesthetic (K). The authors suggested that M, P, R and S were related to emotional preferences while A, V, T and K could be categorised as perceptual preferences. Their experiment involved 217 participants to measure the learning effectiveness of the game. The effectiveness was measured by comparing the pre-test and post-test scores. The experiment also assessed the impact of LS on learning effectiveness and the correlation between the learning achievement and the game. The results showed that the participants' knowledge in food safety was improved although the results indicated that the improvement was not significant because the students had prior knowledge of the subject matter. With respect to LS, the experiment indicated that a greater number of participants preferred to mix their learning methods rather than consistently use a single learning method. The authors suggested that perhaps the participants, who were considered as digital natives, interacted with various different media in their everyday life.

Hwang et al. (2012) developed an adaptive GBL application based on LS to teach about plantation. Their evaluation of the game involved 46 participants and they investigated whether learning in a game that could match the student's LS was better than a game without any consideration of the student's LS in terms of learning effectiveness and motivation. The experiment also evaluated the easiness and usefulness of the game. A pre-test/post-test experimental design was used with an equal number of participants in the control group (who played the game without any adaptivity) and the experimental group (who played the game with adaptivity based on the LS identified before the game). The LS adopted in this research was the 'sequential/global' element of the Felder-Silverman LS, identified using their LS questionnaire, while a test sheet was used in the pre-test and post-test to measure the knowledge of the participant on the subject matter. The results showed that the adaptive version had a significantly higher learning effectiveness.

Gidget is an autonomous agent in a GBL application developed by Lee and Ko (2011). The game itself teaches logic programming to novice programmers. Gidget has an adaptivity that is reflected in its expression based on the execution of the code (smile when the code is successful and look sad otherwise). The experiment involved 116 participants comprising 50 females and 66 males with an average age of 27.5 ranging from 18 to 59 years of age. The level of education of the participants were pre-high school (<1%), high school (13%), college (23%), associate degree (3%), bachelor degree (38%), master degree (14%) and doctoral degrees (6%). The experiment used two groups: a control group that played the game with non-adaptive feedback and an experimental group that played the game with adaptive feedback. The results indicated that Gidget with its expression had a positive effect on motivating the participants and the experimental group completed more levels compared to the control group in a similar completion time.

Agrivillage is a GBL application based on Second Life and its objective is to teach agriculture. The game itself was developed by Yongyuth et al. (2010) and it has an adaptivity implemented through NPCs based on changes that occur in the environment caused by the student's actions. The game was evaluated by 20 university students through the use of a questionnaire. While there was no pre-test and post-test of agriculture knowledge, the results suggested that the game had a positive impact on learning and raising awareness about the impact of agriculture on the environment.

Demmel et al. (2011) developed a collaborative and adaptive game called weMakeWords that teaches alphabetical words and symbols related to Chinese, German or English. The adaptivity is implemented through scaffolding based on the number of mistakes the student makes. Their preliminary research, involving children aged between 4 and 8 years of age, investigated the effectiveness of the adaptive game. The data gathered in this research was analysed by looking at how many characters the students could draw after the game. The results showed that children remembered on average four Chinese symbols and their meanings and some could draw the symbols after playing the game for 15 to 30 minutes.

From the empirical evidence generated from the adaptive GBL that has been discussed above, adaptivity has the potential for improving learning effectiveness in GBL. Moreover, it has also shown:

- The current trend in adaptive GBL research is the investigation of the effect of theories used as the basis for the adaptivity. Such theories may be personality theories as researched by Felicia and Pitt (2009) or learning styles as used by Lynch et al. (2008) and Hwang et al. (2012).
- The majority of research in adaptive GBL uses a pre-test/post-test experimental design. This is mostly used when measuring learning effectiveness as reflected in the differences between pre-test and post-test

either within or between control and experimental groups. The analysis methods adopted in the studies are mainly quantitative.

- The adaptive systems mostly use log files or a database to collect information about interactions between the games and the students.

Learning-Style-Based Adaptive GBL

For the purpose of this research, an adaptive GBL application based on LS was developed. The game was intended to teach the basics of the database programming language SQL (Structured Query Language) while the LS adopted in this game was the Felder-Silverman LS model (Felder & Silverman, 1988), particularly the presentation elements (picture-text). Felder-Silverman LS model has been widely used in eLearning and GBL and its reliability and validity have been tested. When compared to other LS model, Felder-Silverman model represents elements from most models which indicate the generalisability of the model. The selected genre of the game was role-playing games and it was developed by using NeverWinter Nights 2 engine.

In this study, there were three modes of the same game designed and developed:

- A non-adaptive mode of the game. This mode treats all students the same and takes no account of the student's LS.
- An out-of-game adaptive mode. The characteristics of a student are identified by means of the Felder-Silverman LS questionnaire completed in advance of playing the game and the game is then customised according to the student's LS.
- An in-game adaptive mode. In this mode, the student's characteristics are identified during the gameplay. As it is possible for the learner to change LS in the course of the game, the game has an adaptive system

that can automatically customise the game content in real-time according to the current LS.

The difference between the modes concerns the nature of the adaptive approach adopted while the rest of the game elements such as storyline, game environment, controls and game interface, are identical. The adaptive approach itself was implemented through the presentation of the learning materials presented by the conversation system of the game.

PROCEDURE

The main purpose of the Randomised Controlled Trial (RCT) is to evaluate whether the use of a game with adaptivity based on the student's in-game LS can improve the student's learning compared to the use of one without any use of adaptivity, or a game with adaptivity based on the student's LS as identified from a LS questionnaire and non-game/text-based learning. Thus, this experiment comprises four independent groups:

- A paper-based group that has the learning content presented in a textbook (control group).
- A 'non-adaptive game' group that played the game in non-adaptivity mode.
- An 'out-of-game adaptive game' group that had their LS identified by a learning-style questionnaire before playing the game and each participant in the group played the game that was customised to his/her previously identified LS.
- An 'in-game adaptivity game' group that played the game in the in-game-adaptivity mode. This mode allowed the game to automatically identify and adapt to the learner's LS based on his/her interaction with the learning content.

The learning content selected for the RCT was Structured Query Language (SQL). Teaching SQL has a few obstacles such as difficulties faced by the learners to construct and understand SQL statements, to memorise the database structure, to understand different forms of SQL and to understand the error feedback from the Database Management System (DBMS).

Methodology

In this experiment, a pre-test/post-test experimental design was selected to test learning outcomes using different variants of the game and paper-based material. The target participants were university students from different levels of study (undergraduate/postgraduate), from different programmes (computing/non-computing), different genders and different learning styles, all of whom had no knowledge of SQL. The postgraduate participants included PhD and masters students. The participants were recruited by visiting campuses, classes, libraries and student accommodation. The participants participated in the research on a voluntary basis. The participant was then randomly allocated to one of the four groups and they were told more details about the treatments according to their group. The participants had the option to withdraw from the experiment at any point.

To produce statistically significant results the number of participants for each group in this experiment was 30 to make the sample distribution approximately normal as suggested by Johnson (1988). The sample size intended for each group was approximately similar to the others to avoid potential errors in hypothesis testing.

In this experiment, pre-test and post-testing was used to investigate the effects on learning outcomes of learning through games and paper. At the beginning of the experiment, the participants were asked to answer questions relating to their knowledge of SQL. Only those who scored zero in the pre-test were selected to ensure that all participants shared the same level of knowledge of the subject before the experiment commenced. The

LS questionnaire was also completed before the experiment commenced to identify the LS of each participant. The Felder-Silverman learning-style questionnaire was used in this study because, it is widely used to identify LS for computer-assisted learning and its validity and reliability have been demonstrated in numerous studies (for example, Felder & Spurlin, 2005). As noted above, the target number for each group was 30 participants. Each participant was allocated randomly to one of the four groups in this experiment by rolling a die twice. The first roll determined whether the participant was to be included in the paper-based learning group or game-playing group (odd number: paper-based learning group, even number: games-based learning group). If an even number was rolled then the participant would roll the die again to determine which game group the participant would be allocated to.

The participants then carried out the experiment according to the group to which they have been allocated. At the end of the experiment, the participants were asked to answer a further set of questions on their knowledge of SQL similar to the questions in the pre-test. Participants of the experimental groups who play the game needed to answer a questionnaire to evaluate the game.

The experiments for the paper-based group and the game groups were similar in terms of sampling and pre-test and post-test except that in the former group, the participants, instead of playing a game, were given materials taken from a textbook and a selection of learning materials from the game. In both groups, participants were allowed to spend as much time as they wanted to read the materials through before attempting to answer the SQL post-test. The progress diagram of this study is shown in Figure 1.

This investigation also included a comparison of the completion times of the game groups. Furthermore, the relationship between programmes of study, LS, education level, and gender of the participants in each group and completion time and learning effectiveness was also investigated.

Figure 1. Experimental design for the RCT

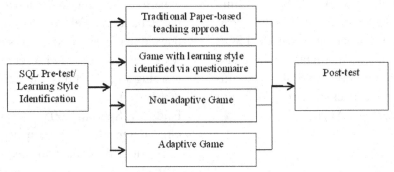

Participants

120 university students with no knowledge of SQL voluntarily participated in the study. Only the participants who scored 0 in the pre-test SQL test were selected for the study. The participants were 83 undergraduate students (69.2%) and 37 postgraduate students (30.8%) with 43 students from the University of the West of Scotland (35.8%), 46 students from Heriot-Watt University (38.3%), 19 students from Napier University (15.8%), 9 students from University of Edinburgh (7.5%), 2 students from Glasgow University (1.7%) and 1 student from Strathclyde University (0.8%). The participants were also selected from various programmes. There were 78 participants (65%) from a computing programme, 1 students from accounting (0.8%), 3 students from business (2.5%), 10 students from engineering (8.3%), 1 student from finance (0.8%), 3 students from languages (2.5%), 1 student from law (0.8%), 7 students from life science (5.8%), 9 students from management (7.5%), 2 students from mathematics (1.8%), 1 student from medicine (0.8%), 1 student from nursing (0.8%), 1 student from psychology (0.8%) and 2 students from social science programmes (1.8%). For the purposes of analysis, the participants were categorised into two groups, computing and non-computing students, because the number of participants in each of the non-computing programmes were too low

to be analysed individually. Each participant was allocated randomly to one of the four groups. In this chapter, the groups will be referred to as: the paper-based group, the non-adaptive game group, the out-of-game LS group and the in-game adaptive group. To maintain anonymity, the participants were be labelled with the numbers (1, 2, 3, etc).

Marking System SQL tests

The SQL tests were conducted twice: in both the pre-test and post-test. In the pre-test, the SQL test was used to identify the participants' knowledge of SQL. Those who had no knowledge of SQL were selected for the experiment. The SQL post-test was used to test the students' knowledge of SQL after learning SQL through the game. The SQL pre-test had similar questions to the post-test. Both had 11 questions in total.

The SQL taught in the game covered basic syntax and some functions for information retrieval. Each question was designed to evaluate the participants' knowledge of different forms of SQL syntax as described in Chapter 5. In the SQL test, each element was valued according to its existence and position. The evaluation rules were as follows:

- **Question 1:** 1 Mark (attribute names can be provided in place of '*').

- **Question 2:** 1 Mark (for restricting the SELECT clause to just those attributes required).
- **Question 3:** 1 Mark (for the WHERE clause).
- **Question 4:** 2.5 Marks (1 mark for each predicate and 0.5 marks for use of AND).
- **Question 5:** 4 Marks (0.5 marks for list of attributes in SELECT clause, 1 mark for each predicate and 0.5 marks for use of AND).
- **Question 6:** 1 Mark (for use of COUNT(*)).
- **Question 7:** 1 Mark (for use of MIN(price)).
- **Question 8:** 1 Mark (for use of MAX(price)).
- **Question 9:** 1 Mark (for use of AVG(price)).
- **Question 10:** 1 Mark (for use of DISTINCT).
- **Question 11:** 1.5 Marks (1 mark for ORDER BY clause and 0.5 marks for use of DESC).

The maximum points achievable for the SQL pre-test and post-test was 16. The analysis of the learning effectiveness to be conducted is a non-parametric test according to the Levene statistic = 8.280 ($p < 0.001$), while the analysis for the completion time is also a non-parametric test according to the Levene statistic = 3.879 ($p < 0.024$) (Kinnear & Gray, 2008). A Levene statistic with $p < 0.05$ means the homogeneity cannot be assumed. In this study, the confidence value used is 95% ($p < 0.05$).

RESULTS

Relationship between Learning Style and Student's Characteristics

This section investigates whether there is any relationship between LS (text/picture) and the characteristics of the student such as programme of study (computing/non-computing), gender (male/female) and level of education (undergraduate/postgraduate). The investigation aims to identify whether there is a dominant LS related to particular characteristic of the student.

In this experiment, there were 22 participants from non-computing programme identified to have text-based LS with 20 participants to have picture-based LS while 26 computing participants identified to have text-based LS with 52 participants to have picture-based LS. A chi-square test showed that although there are more female participants with a text-based LS, there is a clear relationship between level of education and LS for this group ($\chi^2(1) = 4.127$, $p < 0.053$).

Regarding the relationship between gender and LS, the result shows there were 16 female participants identified to have text-based LS with 12 participants to have picture-based LS while 32 male participants identified to have text-based LS with 60 participants to have picture-based LS. A chi-square test showed that there is clear relationship between LS and gender ($\chi^2(1) = 4.472$, $p < 0.047$).

Regarding the relationship between level of education and LS, the result shows there were 31 undergraduate participants identified to have text-based LS with 52 participants to have picture-based LS while 17 postgraduate participants identified to have text-based LS with 20 participants to have picture-based LS. A chi-square test showed that although there are more female participants with a text-based LS, there is no clear relationship between level of education and LS for this group ($\chi^2(1) = 0.788$, $p < 0.424$). The summary of the findings is presented in Table 1.

Learning Effectiveness

Before learning effectiveness can be measured, the reliability of the data must be tested by an independent rater. To analyse the reliability of the data analysis the Cronbach Alpha test (Kinnear & Gray, 2008) was used. The test showed that the Cronbach Alpha value of the data is 0.990,

Table 1. Relationship between learning style and student characteristics

Characteristic	Result
Learning style and programme of study	$\chi^2(1)= 4.127, p<0.053$
Learning style and gender	$\chi^2(1)= 4.472, p<0.047$
Learning style and level of education	$\chi^2(1)= 0.788, p<0.424$

which means the post-test scores marked by the experimenter were consistent with the scores marked by the independent rater.

The learning effectiveness of the paper-based SQL learning for 30 university students has a mean of 2.6 (SD=3.8065). The mean score of the learning effectiveness from the non-adaptivity game group, which consists of 30 university students, is 12.517 (SD = 4.690). The learning effectiveness of the out-of-game LS group, consisting of 30 university students, has a mean score of 12.35 (SD = 4.065). The learning effectiveness of the in-game adaptive group, which also consists of 30 university students, has a mean score of 14.042 (SD = 2.354).

When compared to any variant of the game, there is a significant difference in learning effectiveness between the groups. By using the Mann-Whitney U tests, the learning effectiveness for the non-adaptivity game group is significantly higher when compared to the paper-based learning group ($Z = -5.903$, $p<0.001$). The same results also apply when comparing the paper-based group and the out-of-game LS game group ($Z = -5.995$, $p<0.001$) and the in-game adaptive group ($Z = -6.495$, $p<0.001$).

However, the Mann-Whitney U test shows there is no significant difference between the non-adaptivity group and the out-of-game LS group ($Z = -0.872$, $p<0.389$). A similar result is found when comparing the learning effectiveness of the non-adaptivity group to the game with the in-game adaptivity ($Z = -0.378$, $p<0.711$) and between the

out-of game learning LS group and the in-game adaptive group ($Z = -1.546$, $p<0.124$).

So far, the tests have proven that the learning effectiveness for the variants of the game are significantly different than those for paper-based learning. A Kruskal-Wallis test was utilised to compare all these groups (paper-based, game without adaptivity, game with out-of-game LS and game with in-game adaptivity). The Kruskal-Wallis test is significant beyond the 0.01 level ($\chi^2 = 58.153$, $p<0.01$). A summary of the comparison analysis is presented in Table 2.

Differences in Learning Effectiveness between Learning Styles

This section investigates the differences in the learning effectiveness for those with different learning styles (picture/text) as reflected by the SQL post-test. In the paper-based group, there are 8 participants (27%), each have a text-based LS and the mean for learning effectiveness is 1.5 (SD = 2.7124), while 22 participants (73%) have a picture-based LS and the mean for their learning effectiveness is 3.0 (SD = 4.1144). In the non-

Table 2. Comparison of learning effectiveness

Groups	Learning Effectiveness
Paper-based Group and Non-adaptive Group	$Z = -5.903$, $p<0.001$ (Non-adaptive Group > Paper-based Group)
Paper-based Group and Out-of-game LS Group	$Z = -5.995$, $p<0.001$ (Out-of-game LS Group >Paper-based Group)
Paper-based Group and In-game Adaptive Group	$Z = -6.495$, $p<0.001$ (In-game Adaptive Group > Paper-based Group)
Non-adaptive Group and Out-of-game LS Group	$Z = -0.872$, $p<0.389$
Non-adaptive Group and In-game Adaptive Group	$Z = -0.378$, $p<0.711$
Out-of-game LS Group and In-game Adaptive Group	$Z = -1.546$, $p<0.124$
All Groups	$\chi^2 = 58.153$, $p<0.01$

adaptivity group, there are 13 participants (43%) with a text-based LS and the mean of the learning effectiveness is 13.481 (SD = 3.209), while 17 participants (57%) have a picture-based LS and the mean of their learning effectiveness is 11.779 (SD = 5.551). In the out-of-game LS group, there are 13 participants (43%) with a text-based LS and the mean for learning effectiveness is 10.788 (SD = 4.377), while 17 participants (57%) have picture-based LS and the mean of their learning effectiveness is 13.544 (SD = 3.477). In the in-game adaptive group, there are 14 participants (47%) with a text-based LS and the mean for the learning effectiveness is 13.411 (SD = 3.001), while 16 participants (53%) have a picture-based LS and the mean of their learning effectiveness is 14.594 (SD = 1.486).

When comparing the learning effectiveness of participants with different learning styles in the paper-based group, a Mann-Whitney U test indicated no difference in learning effectiveness between those participants who had a text-based LS and those who had a picture-based LS (Z = -1.016, p<0.323). The same result also applies to the non-adaptive game group (Z = -0.022, p<0.993) and the in-game adaptive group (Z = -0.697, p<0.498). However, for the out-of-game LS group, a Mann-Whitney U test showed that the learning effectiveness for learners with a picture-based LS is significantly higher than for those with a text-based LS (Z = -2.128, p<0.034).

When comparing the learning effectiveness of participants with different learning styles in all groups, a Mann-Whitney U test indicated no difference in learning effectiveness between those participants who had a text-based LS and those who had a picture-based LS (Z = -0.011, p<0.993). The same result is also found when comparing the learning effectiveness of participants with different learning styles across the game groups (Z = -1.477, p<0.142). The game groups in this case are the non-adaptive group, out-of-game LS group and in-game adaptive game group. A summary of the analysis is presented in Table 3.

Table 3. Differences in learning effectiveness between learning styles

Group Name	Differences in Learning Effectiveness between Learning Styles
Paper-based Group	Z = -1.016, p<0.323
Non-adaptive Group	Z = -0.022, p<0.993
Out-of-game LS Group	Z = -2.128, p<0.034 (picture-based > text-based)
In-game Adaptive Game Group	Z = -0.697, p<0.498
All Groups	Z = -0.011, p<0.993
All Game Groups	Z = -1.477, p<0.142

Differences in Learning Effectiveness between Programmes

This section investigates the differences in the learning effectiveness reflected by the SQL post-test for those on different programmes (computing/non-computing). In the paper-based group, there are 4 participants (13%) from a non-computing programme and the mean of learning effectiveness is 4.875 (SD = 1.7017), while there are 26 participants (87%) from the computing programme and the mean of their learning effectiveness is 2.250 (SD = 3.9376). In the non-adaptivity group, there are 6 participants (20%) from the non-computing programme and the mean of the learning effectiveness is 11.583 (SD = 4.104), while there are 24 participants (80%) from the computing programme and the mean for their learning effectiveness is 12.750 (SD = 4.877). In the out-of-game LS group, there are 19 participants (63%) from the non-computing programme and the mean for learning effectiveness is 11.382 (SD = 4.61), while there are 11 participants (37%) from the computing programme and the mean for their learning effectiveness is 14.203 (SD = 2.192). In the in-game adaptivity group, there are 13 participants (43%) from the non-computing programme and the mean of the learning effectiveness is 13.019 (SD = 2.803), while there are 17 participants (53%) from the computing programme and the mean for their learning effectiveness is 14.824 (SD = 1.627).

By comparing the learning effectiveness of participants from different programmes in the paper-based group, a Mann-Whitney U test shows that the learning effectiveness of the non-computing participants is significantly higher than for computing participants ($Z = -2.128$, $p<0.020$). On the other hand, a Mann-Whitney U test showed the learning effectiveness for the participants from the computing group was significantly higher than the learning effectiveness for those on non-computing programmes in the in-game adaptivity group ($Z = -1.979$, $p<0.049$). The opposite result applies when comparing the learning effectiveness of participants from different programmes in the non-adaptive game group ($Z = -0.964$, $p<0.353$) and those in the out-of game LS group ($Z = -1.538$, $p<0.129$) as it showed no differences in the learning effectiveness between computing and non-computing programmes.

When comparing the learning effectiveness of participants with different programmes in all groups, a Mann-Whitney U test indicated no difference in learning effectiveness between participants from non-computing programme and participants from computing programme ($Z = -0.274$, $p<0.787$). However, a Mann-Whitney U test indicated the learning effectiveness of participants from computing programme across the game groups was significantly higher than the learning effectiveness for those on non-computing programmes ($Z = -2.797$, $p<0.006$). A summary of the analysis is presented in Table 4.

Differences in Learning Effectiveness between Education Levels

This section investigates the differences in learning effectiveness, as reflected by the SQL post-test from different education levels (undergraduate/postgraduate). In the paper-based group, there are

Table 4. Differences in learning effectiveness between programmes

Group Name	Differences in Learning Effectiveness between Programmes
Paper-based Group (4 non-computing / 26 computing)	$Z = -2.128$, $p<0.020$ (non-computing > computing)
Non-adaptive Group (6 non-computing / 24 computing)	$Z = -0.964$, $p<0.353$
Out-of-game LS Group (19 non-computing / 11 computing)	$Z = -1.538$, $p<0.129$
In-game Adaptive Game Group (13 non-computing / 17 computing)	$Z = -1.979$, $p<0.049$ (computing > non-computing)
All Groups	$Z = -0.274$, $p<0.787$
All Game Groups	$Z = -2.797$, $p<0.006$ (computing > non-computing)

26 undergraduate participants (87%) and the mean for learning effectiveness is 1.942 (SD = 3.5618), while there are 4 postgraduate participants (13%) and the mean for their learning effectiveness is 6.875 (SD = 2.4958). In the non-adaptivity group, there are 19 undergraduate participants (63%) and the mean of learning effectiveness is 10.934 (SD = 5.281) while there are 11 postgraduate participants (37%) and the mean for their learning effectiveness is 15.250 (SD = 0.783). In the out-of-game LS group, there are 18 undergraduate participants (60%) and the mean for the learning effectiveness is 13.222 (SD = 3.659), while there are 12 postgraduate participants (40%) and the mean for their learning effectiveness is 11.042 (SD = 4.445). In the in-game adaptivity group, there are 20 undergraduate participants (67%) and the mean of the learning effectiveness is 13.925 (SD = 2.755) while there are 10 postgraduate participants (33%) and the mean of their learning effectiveness is 14.275 (SD = 1.315).

A Mann-Whitney test showed no significant difference in learning effectiveness between undergraduate participants and postgraduate participants in the out-of-game LS group ($Z = -1.556$, $p<0.124$) and the in-game adaptive group

(Z = -0.716, p<0.488). However, a Mann-Whitney *U* test shows that learning effectiveness for the postgraduate participants is significantly higher than for the undergraduate participants in the non-adaptive game group (Z = -2.090, p<0.037) and the paper-based group (Z = -2.676, p<0.005).

When comparing the learning effectiveness of participants with different education levels in all groups, a Mann-Whitney *U* test indicated that the learning effectiveness of postgraduate participants was significantly higher than undergraduate participants (Z = -2.138, p<0.033). However, a Mann-Whitney *U* test indicated there is no significant difference in learning effectiveness between undergraduate and postgraduate participants across the game groups (Z = -0.068, p<0.949). A summary of the analysis is presented in Table 5.

Differences in Learning Effectiveness between Genders

This section investigates the differences in learning effectiveness reflected by the SQL post-test according to gender (male/female). In the paper-based group, there are 5 female participants (17%) and the mean for learning effectiveness is 4.2 (SD = 4.0094), while there are 25 male participants (83%) and the mean for their learning effectiveness is 2.280 (SD = 3.7669). In the non-adaptivity group, there are 7 female participants (23%) and the mean for learning effectiveness is 12.857 (SD = 3.660) while there are 23 male participants (77%) and the mean for their learning effectiveness is 12.413 (SD = 5.029). In the out-of-game LS group, there are 8 female participants (27%) and the mean for learning effectiveness is 11.094 (SD = 4.698), while there are 22 male participants (73%) and the mean for their learning effectiveness is 12.807 (SD = 3.827). In the in-game adaptive group, there are 8 females participants (27%) and the mean for learning effectiveness is 12.875 (SD = 1.512), while there are 22 male participants (73%) and the mean for their learning effectiveness is 14.466 (SD = 2.486).

A Mann-Whitney *U* test shows no significant difference in learning effectiveness affecting the participants of different genders in the paper-based group (Z = -1.353, p<0.181), the non-adaptive game group (Z = -0.507, p<0.628) and the out-of game LS group (Z = -0.779, p<0.451). However, a Mann-Whitney test shows that the learning effectiveness of the male participants is significantly higher than for the female participants in the in-game adaptive group (Z = -2.598, p<0.009).

When comparing the learning effectiveness of participants from different genders, a Mann-Whitney *U* test indicated no difference in learning effectiveness between male and female participants (Z = -0.528, p<0.600). However, a Mann-Whitney *U* test indicated the learning effectiveness of male participants across the game groups was significantly higher than the learning effectiveness for female participants (Z = -2.115, p<0.035). A summary of the analysis is presented in Table 6.

Table 5. Differences in learning effectiveness between education levels

Group Name	Differences in Learning Effectiveness between Education Levels
Paper-based Group (26 undergraduate – 4 postgraduate)	Z = -2.676, p<0.005 (postgraduate > undergraduate)
Non-adaptive Group (19 undergraduate – 11 postgraduate)	Z = -2.090, p<0.037 (postgraduate > undergraduate)
Out-of-game LS Group (18 undergraduate – 12 postgraduate)	Z = -1.556, p<0.124
In-game Adaptive Game Group (20 undergraduate – 10 postgraduate)	Z = -0.716, p<0.488
All Groups	Z = -2.138, p<0.033 (postgraduate > undergraduate)
All Game Groups	Z = -0.068, p<0.949

Table 6. Differences in learning effectiveness between genders

Group Name	Differences in Learning Effectiveness between Genders
Paper-based Group (5 female / 25 male)	Z = -1.353, p<0.181
Non-adaptive Group (7 female / 23 male)	Z = -0.507, p<0.628
Out-of-game LS Group (8 female / 22 male)	Z = -0.779, p<0.451
In-game Adaptive Group (8 female / 22 male)	Z = -2.598, p<0.009 (male > female)
All Groups	Z = -0.528, p<0.600
All Game Groups	Z = -2.115, p<0.035 (male > female)

Completion Time

The completion time is the time required for the player to complete the game. This is measured for the purpose of comparison with the LS and the other characteristics associated with the player (gender, education level, programmes of study), as well as its correlation with the learning effectiveness. The mean completion time when learning through the game without adaptivity is 94.67 minutes (SD = 12.893), while the mean completion time for the out-of-game LS group is 90.67 minutes (SD = 14.284) and the mean completion time for the in-game adaptive group is 84.91 minutes (SD = 8.174). The summary of the completion time is presented in Table 7.

When comparing the completion time between the non-adaptive group and the out-of-game LS group, the Mann-Whitney *U* test shows no significant difference in completion time between these two variants (Z = -1.339, p<0.184). The same results also occur when comparing the completion time between the out-of-game LS group and the in-game adaptive group (Z = -0.955, p<0.345). However, the results show that the completion time for the in-game adaptive group

Table 7. Completion time

Groups	Completion Time
Non-adaptive Group	94.67 minutes (SD = 12.893)
Out-of-game LS Group	90.67 minutes (SD = 14.284)
In-game Adaptive Group	84.91 minutes (SD = 8.174)

Table 8. Comparison of completion times

Groups	Completion Time between Groups
Non-adaptive Group and Out-of-game LS Group	Z = -1.339, p<0.184
Non-adaptive Group and In-game Adaptive Group	Z = -2.814, p<0.005 (In-game Adaptive Group<Non-adaptive Group)
Out-of-game LS Group and In-game Adaptive Group	Z = -0.955, p<0.345
All Game Groups	$\chi^2 = 7.056$, p<0.03

is shorter than for the non-adaptive group (Z = -2.814, p<0.005).

To conduct an overall analysis between the groups, the completion time for all the groups was compared and analysed using a Kruskal-Wallis test. The test also showed that there is a significant difference in completion time between groups with the game with in-game adaptive is the shortest, followed by the out-of-game LS game, and the game without adaptivity ($\chi^2 = 7.056$, p<0.03). A summary of this analysis is presented in Table 8.

Correlation between Completion Time and Learning Effectiveness

The bivariate analysis using the Pearson correlation test (Kinnear & Gray, 2009) shows that the correlation between the completion times and learning effectiveness in the non-adaptive group is weak (*r(30)* = 0.349, p<0.059). The correlation is also weak in the out-of-game LS group (r(30) = 0.349, p<0.059). Similar to that shown for the previous groups, the correlation between learn-

Table 9. Correlation between completion time and learning effectiveness

Group Name	Completion Time and Learning Effectiveness
Non-adaptive Group	$r(30) = 0.349$, p<0.059
Out-of-game LS Group	$r(30) = 0.349$, p<0.059
In-game Adaptive Group	$r(30) = 0.182$, p<0.336

Table 10. Differences in completion times between programmes

Group Name	Completion Time between Programmes
Non-adaptive Group (non-computing: 98.67 (SD = 15.883); computing: 93.67 (SD = 12.229))	$Z = -0.104$, p<0.929
Out-of-game LS Group (non-computing: 93.11 (SD = 12.875); computing: 86.45 (SD = 16.201))	$Z = -1.509$, p<0.136
In-game Adaptive Group (non-computing: 84.62 (SD = 7.985); computing: 87.59 (SD = 7.977))	$Z = -0.154$, p<0.893

ing effectiveness and the completion time in the in-game adaptive group is weak ($r(30) = 0.182$, p<0.336). Overall, the results show completion time does not have any effect on learning effectiveness as shown on Table 9.

Differences in Completion Time Between Programmes

In the non-adaptivity group, the mean of the completion time for the participants from the non-computing programme is 98.67 (SD = 15.883), while from computing programme, the mean is 93.67 (SD = 12.229). In the out-of-game LS group, the mean of the completion time for the participants from the non-computing programme is 93.11 (SD = 12.875), while from the computing programme, the mean is 86.45 (SD = 16.201). In the in-game adaptive group, the mean of the completion time for the participants from the non-computing programme is 84.62 (SD = 7.985), while from the computing programme, the mean for the completion time is 87.59 (SD = 7.977). To investigate the differences in completion time between the different programmes for each group, a Mann-Whitney U test was used. This test showed that there is no significant difference in completion time for participants from the different programmes in the non-adaptive group ($Z = -0.104$, p<0.929), or in the out-of-game LS group ($Z = -1.509$, p<0.136) and in the in-game adaptive group ($Z = -0.154$, p<0.893). A summary of this analysis is presented in Table 10.

Differences in Completion Time between Education Levels

In the non-adaptivity group, the mean of the completion time for the undergraduate participants is 91.95 (SD = 11.345), while for the postgraduate participants, it is 99.36 (SD = 14.562). In the out-of-game LS group, the mean of the completion time for the undergraduate participants is 89.61 (SD = 13.682), while for the postgraduate participants it is 92.25 (SD = 15.621). In the in-game adaptive group, the mean of the completion time for the undergraduate participants is 84.30 (SD = 8.163), while for the postgraduate participants it is 90.30 (SD = 6.165). To investigate the difference in completion times on the basis of level of education for each group, a Mann-Whitney U test was used. This test showed no significant difference in completion time for participants of different education levels in the non-adaptive game group ($Z = -1.142$, p<0.263), in the out-of-game LS group level ($Z = -0.382$, p<0.715) and in the in-game adaptive group ($Z = -1.052$, p<0.311). A summary of the analysis is presented in Table 11.

Differences in Completion Time between Learning Styles

In the non-adaptivity group, the mean of the completion time for the participants with a

Table 11. Differences in completion times between education levels

Group Name	Completion Time between Education Levels
Non-adaptive Group (Undergraduate: 91.95 (SD=11.345); Postgraduate: 99.36 (SD=14.562))	Z = -1.142, p<0.263
Out-of-game LS Group (Undergraduate: 89.61 (SD=13.682); Postgraduate: 92.25 (SD=15.621))	Z = -0.382, p<0.715
In-game Adaptive Group (Undergraduate: 84.30 (SD=8.163); Postgraduate: 90.30 (SD=6.165))	Z = -1.052, p<0.311

Table 12. Differences in completion times between learning styles

Group Name	Completion Time between Learning Styles
Non-adaptive Group (picture-based learning: 94.06 (SD=14.289); text-based learning: 95.46 (SD = 11.326))	Z = -0.042, p<0.975
Out-of-game LS Group (picture-based learning: 91.12 (SD = 13.402); text-based learning: 90.08 (SD = 15.903))	Z = -0.231, p<0.829
In-game Adaptive Group (picture-based learning: 88.19 (SD = 8.534); text-based learning: 84.14 (SD = 6.982))	Z = -1.172, p<0.254

picture-based LS is 94.06 (SD = 14.289), while for those with a text-based LS, it is 95.46 (SD = 11.326). In the out-of-game LS group, the mean of the completion time for those participants with a picture-based LS is 91.12 (SD = 13.402), while for participants with a text-based LS it is 90.08 (SD = 15.903). In the in-game adaptive group, the mean of the completion time for the participants with a picture-based LS is 88.19 (SD = 8.534), while for those with a text-based LS, it is 84.14 (SD = 6.982).

To investigate the difference in completion times between learning styles for each group, a Mann-Whitney *U* test was used. This test showed no significant difference in completion time for those participants with different learning styles in the non-adaptive game group (Z = -0.042, p<0.975), in the out-of-game LS group (Z = -0.231, p<0.829), or in the in-game adaptive group (Z = -1.172, p<0.254). A summary of the analysis is presented in Table 12.

Differences in Completion Time between Genders

In the non-adaptivity group, the mean of the completion time for female participants is 95.00 (SD = 10.599), while for male participants, the mean is 94.57 (SD = 13.727). In the out-of-game LS group, the mean for the completion time of the

female participants is 93.12 (SD = 15.887), while for male participants, it is 89.77 (SD = 13.945). In the in-game adaptive group, the mean of the completion time of the female participants is 84.12 (SD = 7.039), while for male participants it is 87.09 (SD = 8.309).

To investigate the difference in completion time for each group according to gender, a Mann-Whitney *U* test was used. This test showed no significant difference in completion time for participants of different genders in the non-adaptive game group (Z = -0.025, p<0.991), in the out-of-game LS group (Z = -0.470, p<0.654) or in the in-game adaptive group (Z = -0.485, p<0.647). A summary of the analysis is presented in Table 13.

Table 13. Differences in completion times between genders

Group Name	Completion Time between Genders
Non-adaptive Group (Female: 95.00 (SD = 10.599); Male: 94.57 (SD = 13.727))	Z = -0.025, p<0.991
Out-of-game LS Group (Female: 93.12 (SD = 15.887); Male: 89.77 (SD = 13.945))	Z = -0.470, p<0.654
In-game Adaptive Group (Female: 84.12 (SD = 7.039); Male: 87.09 (SD = 8.309))	Z = -0.485, p<0.647

DISCUSSION

In terms of overall learning effectiveness, the participants in all three game intervention groups scored significantly higher than the paper-based group suggesting that games are an effective form of supplementary learning at Higher Education (HE) level for teaching SQL and similar subjects. The results indicate that there is clear relationship between programme of study and LS and also gender and LS, however there is no clear relationship between LS and level of education i.e. undergraduate/post-graduate. While the in-game adaptive group scored more highly than the out of game LS group and the non-adaptive game group, no game group significantly outperformed the others with regards to learning effectiveness.

With regards to the learning effectiveness in relation to different LSs, i.e. text-based or picture-based, there was no significant difference across all of the groups; however, there was a significant difference in the out-of game LS group where participants with a picture-based learning performed significantly better.

Computing students scored significantly better with regards to learning effectiveness across all of the game groups, however, there was no significant difference across all groups when the paper-based group is taken into consideration. It should be noted that there was an inordinately large amount of computing students in the paper-based group, which could have caused a bias. Mann-Whitney U tests indicated that computing students in the in-game adaptive group scored significantly higher than non-computing students, however, this is possibly due to the fact that computing students are more familiar with computer games. Postgraduate students scored significantly higher in terms of learning effectiveness across all of the groups. There were no significant differences in learning effectiveness with regards to gender when all four groups were brought into consideration. Males, however, performed significantly better when only the three game groups were brought into consideration.

In terms of completion times, the completion time for the in-game adaptive group was significantly shorter than for the non-adaptive group possibly suggesting that adaptivity in the game increased the efficiency of the assimilation of the material. However, completion time did not have any effect on learning effectiveness.

Very few RCTs were discovered in the literature that focused on comparing a serious games approach to traditional approaches of teaching and learning at HE level utilising learning styles. Hainey, Connolly, Stansfield and Boyle (2011a) conducted a systematic literature review that identified 24 papers discussing the use of serious games in computer science education. The results of this literature search have shown that the majority of the studies found in computer science education have no empirical evaluation evidence or have a small evaluation performed. Only a small number of these studies (3, 13%) used an appropriate form of control with larger samples and no longitudinal studies were discovered. Papastergiou (2009) evaluated a game called LearnMem2 to teach computer memory concepts. A RCT was utilised and the results suggested that serious games can be effective and motivational learning environments, regardless of gender, however, it should be noted that this was performed at secondary education level. Hainey, Connolly, Stansfield and Boyle (2011b) performed a RCT to evaluate whether a serious game could be effective at teaching requirements collection and analysis within computer science at tertiary education level. The results showed that a serious games approach can be used to teach software engineering concepts at a supplementary level in tertiary education. When comparing the empirical evidence collected in this chapter with other studies associated with the use of serious games in computer science education, the chapter has made a significant contribution by performing a RCT at HE level utilising three experimental groups and a control group with a sample large enough to provide statistically significant results.

With regards to comparing a traditional teaching approach to an adaptive serious game, only one paper was found to utilise a RCT and teach some aspect of computer science. Lee and Ko (2011) found that a personified programming tool increased participant motivation for programming, however the study was not specifically focussed at HE level. In summary the literature reviews have identified one study utilising a RCT in computing science education at secondary level, one RCT in computer science education at tertiary education level and one RCT utilising an adaptive serious game for computer science education at no particular level.

The overall results show that computer games can be used as an effective supplementary teaching approach at Higher Education (HE) to teach SQL. This study has provided valuable empirical evidence in games-based learning and adaptive games-based learning by presenting the results of a RCT experiment and comparing three different games approaches to a paper-based teaching approach. Future research directions will include adapting the games for another subject such as learning specific programming languages such as C++, C# of Java and collecting further empirical evidence in the area to attempt to produce generalisable results.

ACKNOWLEDGMENT

This work was partially supported by the Games and Learning Alliance (GaLA) - Network of Excellence for Serious Games under the European Community Seventh Framework Programme (FP7/2007 2013), Grant Agreement no. 258169.

REFERENCES

Becker, K. (2007). Digital game-based learning once removed: Teaching teachers. *British Journal of Educational Technology*, *38*(3), 478–488. doi:10.1111/j.1467-8535.2007.00711.x.

Bontcheva, K. (2002). Adaptivity, adaptability, and reading behaviour: Some results from the evaluation of a dynamic hypertext system. *Adaptive Hypermedia and Adaptive Web-Based Systems*, *2347*, 69–78. doi:10.1007/3-540-47952-X_9.

Boyle, E. A., Connolly, T. M., & Hainey, T. (2011). The role of psychology in understanding the impact of computer games. *Entertainment Computing*, *2*(2), 69–74. doi:10.1016/j.entcom.2010.12.002.

Charles, D., McNeill, M., McAlister, M., Black, M., Moore, A., Stringer, K., et al. (2005). Player-centred game design: Player modelling and adaptive digital games. In *Proceedings of DiGRA 2005 Conference: Changing Views – Worlds in Play*, (pp. 285-298). DiGRA.

Conati, C., & Zhao, X. (2004). Building and evaluating an intelligent pedagogical agent to improve the effectivenesss of an education game. In *Proceedings of IUI'04, International Conference on Intelligent User Interfaces*. Funchal, Portugal: IUI.

Conati, C., & Zhou, X. (2002). Modelling students' emotions from cognitive appraisal in educational games. In *Proceedings of the 6th International Conference on Intelligent Tutoring Systems*. London: Springer-Verlag, ACM.

Connolly, T. M., Boyle, E. A., MacArthur, E., Hainey, T., & Boyle, J. M. (2012). A systematic literature review of empirical evidence on computer games and serious games. *Computers & Education*, *59*, 661–686. doi:10.1016/j.compedu.2012.03.004.

Connolly, T. M., & Stansfield, M. H. (2006). Enhancing eLearning: Using computer games to teach requirements collection and analysis. In *Proceedings of Second Symposium of the WG HCI & UE of the Austrian Computer Society*. Vienna, Austria: WG.

Demmel, R. B., Kohler, B., Krusche, S., & Schubert, L. (2011). The serious game: Wemakewords. In *Proceedings of the 10th SIGPLAN Symposium on New Ideas, New Paradigms, and Reflections on Programming and Software*. New York: ACM.

Felder, R. M., & Brent, R. (2005). Understanding student differences. *Journal of Engineering Education*, *94*(1), 57–72. doi:10.1002/j.2168-9830.2005.tb00829.x.

Felder, R. M., & Silverman, L. K. (1988). Learning and teaching styles in engineering education. *English Education*, *78*(7), 674–681.

Felder, R. M., & Spurlin, J. (2005). Reliability and validity of the index of learning styles: A meta-analysis. *International Journal of Engineering Education*, *21*(1), 103–112.

Felicia, P., & Pitt, I. J. (2007). Evaluating the effect of personalities on the design of educational games. In *Proceedings of the ECGBL Conference*. Paisley, UK: ECGBL.

Felicia, P., & Pitt, I. J. (2008). Personalising educational games to students' learning styles. In *Proceedings of the International Technology in Education and Development Conference*. Valencia, Spain: IEEE.

Felicia, P., & Pitt, I. J. (2009). Profiling users in educational games. In T. M. Connolly, M. H. Stansfield, & E. Boyle (Eds.), *Games-based learning advancement for multisensory human computer interfaces: Techniques and effective practices*. Hershey, PA: Idea Group. doi:10.4018/978-1-60566-360-9.ch009.

Hainey, T., Connolly, T. M., Stansfield, M., & Boyle, E. A. (2011a). The use of computer games in education: A review of the literature. In P. Felicia (Ed.), *Handbook of Research on Improving Learning and Motivation through Educational Games: Multidisciplinary Approaches*. Hershey, PA: IGI Global. doi:10.4018/978-1-60960-495-0.ch002.

Hainey, T., Connolly, T. M., Stansfield, M. H., & Boyle, E. A. (2011b). Evaluation of a games to teach requirements collection and analysis in software engineering at tertiary education level. *Computers & Education*, *56*(1), 21–35. doi:10.1016/j.compedu.2010.09.008.

Hwang, G. J., Sung, H. Y., Hung, C. M., Huang, I., & Tsai, C. C. (2012). Development of a personalized educational computer game based on students' learning styles. *Personalized Learning*, *60*(4), 623–638.

Jackson, S. L., Krajcik, J., & Soloway, E. (1998). The design of learner-adaptable scaffolding in interactive learning environments. In *Proceedings of ACM CHI 1998 Conference on Human Factors in Computing Systems*. Los Angeles, CA: ACM.

Jameson, A. (2003). Adaptive interfaces and agents. In J. A. Jacko, & A. Sears (Eds.), *Human–Computer Interface Handbook*. Mahwah, NJ: Lawrence Erlbaum.

Johnson, R. (1988). *Elementary statistics* (5th ed.). Boston: PWS-Kent Publishing Company.

Kickmeier-Rust, M. D., & Albert, D. (2010). Micro adaptivity: Protecting immersion in didactically adaptive digital educational games. *Journal of Computer Assisted Learning, 7*, 95–105. doi:10.1111/j.1365-2729.2009.00332.x.

Kinnear, P. R., & Gray, C. D. (2008). *SPSS 16 made simple*. New York: Psychology Press.

Kirriemuir, J., & McFarlane, A. (2004). *Literature review in games and learning*. Bristol, UK: Furturelab.

Kolb, D. (1984). *Experiential learning*. Englewood Cliffs, NJ: Prentice-Hall Inc.

Lee, M. J., & Ko, A. J. (2011). Personifying programming tool feedback improves novice programmers' learning. In *Proceedings of the Conference on International Computing Education Research (ICER)*. Providence, RI: ACM.

Lynch, R. A., Steen, M. D., Pritchard, T. J., Buzzell, P. R., & Pintauro, S. J. (2008). Delivering food safety education to middle school students using a web-based, interactive, multimedia, computer program. *Journal of Food Science Education, 7*, 35–42. doi:10.1111/j.1541-4329.2007.00046.x.

Melis, E., & Monthienvichienchai, R. (2004). They call it learning style but it's so much more. In *Proceedings of World Conference on e-Learning in Corporate, Government, Healthcare, and Higher Education*. Chesapeake, VA: IEEE.

Miller, L. M. (2005). Using learning styles to evaluate computer-based instruction. *Computers in Human Behavior, 21*, 287–306. doi:10.1016/j.chb.2004.02.011.

Mulwa, C., Lawless, S., Sharp, M., Arnedillo-Sanchez, I., & Wade, V. (2010). Adaptive educational hypermedia systems in technology enhanced learning: A literature review. In *Proceedings of the 2010 ACM Conference on Information Technology Education*. Midland, MI: ACM.

Oppermann, R., Rashev, R., & Kinshuk. (1997). Adaptability and adaptivity in learning systems. In A. Behrooz (Eds.), *Knowledge Transfer* (2nd ed.). London: pAce, London.

Peirce, N., Conlan, O., & Wade, V. (2008). Adaptive educational games: Providing non-invasive personalised learning experiences. In *Proceedings of the Second IEEE International Conference on Digital Games and Intelligent Toys Based Education*. IEEE.

Prensky, M. (2006). *Don't bother me, mom, i'm learning! How computer and video games are preparing your kids for 21st century success and how you can help*. St. Paul, MN: Paragon House.

Price, L. (2004). Individual differences in learning: Cognitive control, cognitive style, and learning style. *Educational Psychology, 24*, 681–698. doi:10.1080/0144341042000262971.

Smith, L. H., & Renzulli, J. S. (1984). Learning style preferences: A practical approach for classroom teachers. *Theory into Practice, 23*, 44–50. doi:10.1080/00405848409543088.

Yongyuth, P., Prada, R., Nakasone, A., Kawtrakul, A., & Prendinger, H. (2010). AgriVillage: 3D multi-language internet game for fostering agriculture environmental awareness. In *Proceeding of the International Conference on Management of Emergent Digital Ecosystems*. New York: ACM.

KEY TERMS AND DEFINITIONS

Adaptability: The ability of the learner to 'adapt' to the system by explicitly customising the system according to their preferences.

Adaptivity: The ability of the system to identify the learner's preferences or characteristics and customise the system accordingly; that is, the learner implicitly influences the adaptation process.

Adaptive GBL: A games-based learning application where the system is able to identify the learner's preferences or characteristics and adjusts accordingly.

Learning Style: The strategy preferred by the learner to perceive, interact and respond to the learning environment.

Learning-Style-Based Adaptive GBL: A games-based learning application where the system is able to identify the learner's preferred learning style and adjusts accordingly.

Randomised Controlled Trial (RCT): A pre-test/post-test experimental/control group design where participants are randomly assigned to the experimental or control groups.

SQL: Structured Query Language (SQL) is an example of a transform-oriented language designed to use tables to transform inputs into outputs. SQL consists of a Data Definition Language (DDL) for defining database structure and controlling access to data and a Data Manipulation Language (DML) for retrieving and updating the data.

Chapter 14

The Quest for a Massively Multiplayer Online Game that Teaches Physics

Ricardo Javier Rademacher Mena
Futur-E-Scape, LLC, USA

ABSTRACT

The last 10 years have seen explosive growth in the fields of online gaming. The largest of these games are undoubtedly the Massively Multiplayer Online Games (MMOG), such as World of Warcraft or City of Heroes, which attract millions of users throughout the world every day. The last 20 years have also seen the growth of a new field of physics known as Physics Education Research (PER). This field consists of physicists dedicated to improving how we learn and teach the subject of physics. In this chapter, the author discusses his personal quest to combine PER with a MMOG and create an online virtual world dedicated to teaching Newtonian physics.

INTRODUCTION

The last 20 years have seen the growth of a new field of physics research known as Physics Education Research (PER). This field consists of physicists dedicated to improving how we learn and teach the subject of physics. The central problem confronting physicists is the difficulty in teaching the subject and the lack of retention seen in students after they leave the class (McDermott, 2001; OECE, 2008). The last 15 years have also seen an explosive growth in the field of online gaming. The largest of these games are undoubtedly the Massively Multiplayer Online Games (MMOG) such as *World of Warcraft* or *City of Heroes*, which attract millions of users

throughout the world every day. These games are known for their expansive environments and large virtual communities, with thousands of users interacting simultaneously, thus earning the "massively" prefix. These games are a subset of Virtual Worlds (VW's) which uses the Internet to provide a shared experience among users from geographically separated locations.

Against this background, this chapter will discuss 7 years in the author's quest to combine PER with a MMOG and create an online VW dedicated to teaching physics, in effect, to create a three-dimensional (3-D) VW to teach physics by virtue of the activities and measurements performed within it. In the years since the author sketched the first outlines of this idea (Figure 1),

DOI: 10.4018/978-1-4666-4773-2.ch014

Copyright © 2014, IGI Global. Copying or distributing in print or electronic forms without written permission of IGI Global is prohibited.

Figure 1. A physics experiment in a VW; concept sketch from 2002

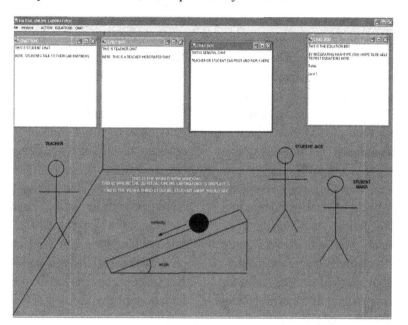

several applications best described as prototypes have been built. None of these applications are ready for commercial or academic use and yet each represents a significant step in developing the core idea, understanding of Game-Based Learning (GBL), and understanding of game development.

The primary purpose of this chapter is showcasing different implementations of the same idea: to create a 3-D virtual environment that teaches physics. The three implementations presented will also show three different avenues for GBL development ranging from the academic hallways to the corporate board room. All told this will show that even confined within one game genre and one educational subject there are several different ways to realize a game-based application. The secondary purpose is to demonstrate how educational concepts map into gameplay elements and vice versa. It is important to see how game elements can be leveraged for education and how the educational content can be mined for game elements. The reader should gain insight into how to transform their own educational concepts into games or game concepts into educational tools by seeing examples of how physics concepts were mapped into MMOG concepts in the three cases.

The first case will introduce the *Multiplayer Virtual Online Laboratory* (MVOL) and will define base-line proficiency with VW development. A mapping of VW elements to classroom elements, a theme which will be present throughout this chapter, will also be presented. The second case will introduce the *Massively Multi User Synchronous Collaborative Learning Environment* (MMUSCLE) system and will showcase initial steps in game-based development. The third and final case will be *Physics Adventures in Space and Time* (PAST) which is the most professional of all implementations. This last case delves into the business of VW development. Each case will begin with a prelude which sets the stage by describing projects, conferences, and other educational game related activities of the time. We will then proceed to introduce the cases and then describe its technical, educational, and entertainment aspects.

EDUCATION REVIEW

This review will focus on presenting some of the basic physics concepts that will be present in all three cases. This section starts with a broad outline of physics content, followed by a discussion of how that content is currently taught, and ends by introducing PER more thoroughly. This review is by no means comprehensive but presented as a background for the upcoming three cases.

Physics content can roughly be broken up into three different epochs: classical, modern, and current. The classical period comprises the work of Isaac Newton, James Maxwell, Thomas Joule and others to form the foundations of mechanics, thermodynamics, and electrodynamics. The modern period comprises the work of Albert Einstein, Niels Bohr, Edwin Hubble, and others in the fields of quantum mechanics, relativistic mechanics, particle physics, and solid-state. The current period is the result of the work of people like Roger Penrose, Stephen Hawking, Alan Guth and others pushing the boundaries of our understanding of the universe in the fields of cosmology, grand unified theories, exobiology, and more. All three cases presented in this manuscript will focus on the foundation of all physics, namely Newtonian Mechanics. Mechanics is further broken down into kinematics, which explains how things move, and dynamics, which explains why things move. Thus the three cases will present time, displacement, velocity, and acceleration as kinematic concepts and mass, force, momentum, and energy as dynamic concepts.

The way that physics is currently taught can be broadly categorized into three distinct areas. The traditional form of teaching is what most of us are familiar with comprising of a teacher using a blackboard to lecture and a desk upon which demos or experiments are presented. Often times the traditional model is supplemented with laboratories where students are given hands on experience with the physics. The traditional model relies heavily on standard textbooks (Serway et.

al, 2003; Halliday & Holzner, 2005; Hewitt, 2002) as well as catalogs of current lab experiments from providers such as *Pasco* or *Sargent-Welch*. Thanks to the findings of PER (Mazur, 1997; McDermott, 1996, Novak, 1999), the classrooms have become more interactive with the teacher becoming a facilitator and allowing students to guide their own instruction. This has led to several new technologies being introduced into the classroom (Clickers, 2009; Christian & Belloni, 2001) as well as new methodologies which encourage collaborative and interactive behavior in the classroom (Knight, 2002). The growth of the Internet has also led to the growth of pure online physics classes (Rademacher, 2009; 2010a) which substitute webpages for lectures and simulations for laboratory experiments (Wieman et. al., 2007). Finally, the rise of mobile technology has led to many apps being created for physics education including some created by the author[1].

The efficacy of these teaching models is a subject of great interest within the PER community. In fact, one of the strongest results from PER research is that the traditional lecture model of physics is the least effective in transference and retention of physics content. Thus the growth of collaboration and interactivity in the modern classroom is due to physics instructors trying to develop teaching methods that rely less on pure lecture. Since PER is research based, quantitative data must support any assertions made about the teaching efficacy of the different models. The most popular test of this efficacy is the Force Concept Inventory (FCI) (Hestenes et. al., 1992). The FCI consists of 30 multiple-choice questions regarding Newtonian mechanics. It emphasizes concepts, meaning that neither facts, procedures, nor metacognitive knowledge is being tested. The test is administered before the course begins as a pre-test and then again after the course ends as a post-test. By comparing a student pre- with their post- scores, a gain in physics knowledge is calculated symbolized by the letter "g". A traditional classroom was found to have approximately $g \sim .22$ (Hake, 1998); this meant that the class grade average goes up 22% as a result of attending traditional physics classes. By comparison, in a PER inspired interactive class g~.52; this is a 30% increase in the efficacy over a traditional model and is the strongest evidence we have for staying clear of the lecture model and embracing collaboration and interactivity. In terms of efficacy, the PER-based curriculum is considered to be the best way to teach physics; however in terms of popularity, the majority of schools still adopt a strictly offline traditional approach. Pure online classes are a distant third in popularity as the preferred means of teaching physics. Apart from showing greater educational gains in PER-based formats as opposed to the traditional format of teaching physics, the FCI can also serve as a model by which to evaluate the efficacy of an educational physics VW. The FCI has a large database of "g" values resulting from the test being administered to various different classrooms. By applying the FCI test within a VW and generating its own "g" values, one can compare the efficacy of an online environment to the off-line alternatives. We will see an example of how this test was integrated into a game environment in the third case.

ENTERTAINMENT REVIEW

While video games have been in the public consciousness since the late 1970's, it was not until the 1990's that dedicated and purposeful research into these games had been made. In this review some of the works in the field of games research that influenced the upcoming cases will be presented.

Game development books such as *Game Design and Development* (Adams & Rollings, 2007) and *Game Development Essentials* (Novak, 2005) where early inspirations in helping make the game portion of our educational game. As well, there was a seeming games renaissance with people constantly creating new ways of using games in novel ways. For example, Gee's (2007) ideas about

immersive gameplay, Salen and Zimmerman's (2004) *Rules of Play,* and Michael and Chen's (2006) *Serious Games: Games That Educate, Train, and Inform* all show how games have transcended from being mere entertainment into something more. As part of this Renaissance, in his seminal paper (Bartle, 1996) and book (Bartle, 2001), Bartle defined several motivations for why people play online games and came up with 4 to 8 player types. While based on his observations of text based Multi User Dungeons (MUD's) from the 80's and 90's, his ideas have been readily accepted and applied to the more graphical MMOGs. The initial four player types (the Socializer, the Explorer, the Achiever, and the Killer) form the foundation of many MMOGs designs. The cases presented herein are no exception; all cases have been designed with these player types in mind. For more information on how Bartle's taxonomy was used these cases, please refer to the authors other publications (Rademacher, 2010b; 2011).

As it will play a significant role in all three cases, it is important to discuss what a Role Playing Game (RPG) is and how it compares to other game genres. A RPG is a character-driven game experience where the human user plays a role within the game world and progresses through it by completing assignments and more often than not engaging in combat. The narrative is the main driving force behind the RPG and unraveling the storyline is often the main purpose of these games. Classic examples of the RPG genre span the history of video games starting with the pen and pencil *Dungeons and Dragons* and the quintessential text-based *Zork* moving on to the more graphical *Ultima* and *Bards Tale* series and culminating in their online versions with games such as *EverQuest, World of Warcraft*, or *Star Wars Galaxies*. These games stand in contrast to the Real Time Strategy (RTS) games in that a RTS is generally not played on an individual level but rather on a tactical or strategic level. Instead of playing one character as in a RPG, in games such as *Starcraft* and *Total Annihilation* the player takes command of an entire army and tens, if not hundreds of units. The First Person Shooter (FPS) requires the fastest reaction rate of all of the genres with games such as *Call of Duty* or *Modern Warfare*. Like a RPG, the FPS is in first person view but unlike it, there is no persistence of character from game session to game session.

To gain some perspective on technical specifications of the upcoming prototypes discussed in this chapter, consider the state-of-the-art in terms of MMORPG's, a blending of MMOG with RPG, during the development timeline. In 2002, one atypical MMORPG had a minimum system requirements of 512 MB of RAM, a 1.3 GHz Pentium 4 processor, and 56.6 kbps internet connection. By 2012, a new MMORPG would require 2 GB of RAM, a 2.0 GHz Duo IntelCore 2 processor, and broadband (2.0 Mbit) internet connection. And while there has been significant progression in the technical side of games, the game design of MMORPG's has remained fairly consistent in the last decade. Also, while new titles undoubtedly add new elements and refine on the original concept, one can still find many of the elements found in 2002's *Everquest* (such as quests, combat-based gameplay, experience and gold points) in 2012's *Guild Wars 2*.

CASE 1: MVOL (2002)

Prelude

By 2002, the MMORPG *Everquest* dominated the market with its then innovative networking and game style. There were few educational 3D virtual worlds known to the author aside from *Activeworld*[2], which used VRML technology to deliver educational web-based 3D worlds. Most of the online educational development and research up to this point had been focused on text-based environments (like MUDS), web-based projects (like *Activeworlds*), or stand-alone research projects (like *Supercharged*[3]). This year also marks

the beginning of the Serious Games movement with the Wilson Center's launching of the Serious Games Initiative[4].

Introduction

The *Multiplayer Virtual Online Laboratory* (MVOL) was completed at the end of 2002 and consists of a literal translation of physics concepts and procedures into a VW. It is the first attempt to meld a 3-D VW with physics pedagogy and was primarily used to learn the basics of VW development. It was quickly noted that academic programming skills (such as using supercomputers, programming for parallel processing, obscure programming languages, and numerical analysis) were not very applicable to the construction of a VW. But with the help of a Northern Kentucky University student that was hired as a freelancer and was more familiar with game development, programming began in August of 2002 and was completed in December of 2002. The size of the program did not exceed more than a few megabytes given that it had only basic networking and primitive graphics.

The MVOL consists of a virtual 3-D room into which students can log-in via their client applications and interact with other student via a chat interface (upper right of Figure 2) or directly via their in-game model (the cube-face in the middle left of Figure 2) as well as interact with objects within the room (the small ball in the middle right of Figure 2). While the world is rendered in 3-D, motion was constrained to the floor and thus we can only simulate 2-D motion. One purpose of the MVOL was to test the collaborative and interactive nature of a VW as applied to a physics lesson. The basic interaction in the world consisted of making a time or distance measurements on other players or objects. Any student that logged into the MVOL would see what every other student currently logged sees allowing the MVOL to be an adequate test of the collaborative nature of an online learning environment. The original intent was to create individual MVOL modules that would be used by teachers in a university classroom. These levels would be designed for non-major physics class students who would use these modules in the class (for example as a demo or part of lecture) or log in from their home (for example as homework or extra credit). Consistently throughout all cases, the target user will be a person aged 18 years or older who may or may not be taking physics class. This user will be known as the student or alternatively, the player.

Technology

The MVOL is based on the C++ code specified in the book *Multiplayer Game Programming* (Barron, 2001). This book was an excellent primer to networking and the basics of online game development at the time. The code included with the book is called *RPGQuest* and was freely available for modification as per its author's intent. This application consists of a single server that implements a modest online RPG. The robustness of this network was never tested beyond a handful of clients logged in simultaneously, making the MVOL unsuitable for classroom applications requiring 20 or 30 students to interact simultaneously.

The network was implemented via Microsoft's direct socket-based DirectX8 library and thus represents a low level of networking programming. There were no pre-built routines that would manage some of the common tasks of client to server connections; all of them had to be hardwired into the application itself. In addition, there were no routines dealing with physical movement within the environment. Instead, the physics had to be programmed directly into the simulation, a familiar topic thanks to previous work with partial step integrators in books like *Programming Gems* (Lake, 2011), *Physics for Game Programmers* (Palmer, 2005), and *Game Physics* (Eberly and Shoemake, 2004). The models used in this version of a VW were very primitive (our players were cubes) and there was no sound or music.

Building with the above, we implemented a virtual measuring tape (the line from bottom of the screen to the ball as seen in Figure 2) that went from the student's model to another model that they had selected. This line is also seen by all other students logged into the MVOL and therefore even though one student would be in effect performing the measurement, other students within the environment would be able to see the tape as well. Once a model is selected, a basic stopwatch and distance counter were displayed allowing the user to perform simple measurements within the environment. These displays can be seen in the upper right-hand corner of Figure 2. Also added was a rudimentary "Shout Chat" seen in the upper right corner of Figure 2 that would allow any student to textually communicate with any other student currently logged in.

Education

The MVOL and all subsequent cases are motivated by the observation that elements in a physics classroom can be mapped to elements within a MMOG. This section will examine these mapping in more detail. Figure 3 summarizes these mappings with the numbers representing the case in which a feature was first implemented.

In a MMOG there is the concept of a "Level" as a self-contained 3-D space that comprises part or all of a VW. This can range from open fields to enclosed dungeons, with initial levels being easy and getting progressively harder as the player advances through the game. In comparison, a traditional physics class also has a self-contained 3-D space that can range from vast auditorium-sized lecture halls to individual lab cubicles. Classes also increase in difficulty in the sense that an elementary school classroom will be much easier than a high school classroom. Thus the typical classroom is analogous to a game level. The MVOL implemented a level by skinning the inside of a 3-D digital box with the textures for ground, walls, and sky. Within the MMOG level

Figure 2. MVOL screenshot

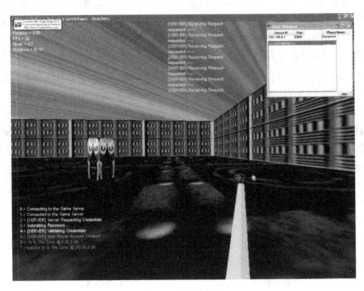

Figure 3. MMOG to Physics Classroom map

		Virtual World	...maps to...	Educational World
CASE				
1		Level	⟷	Classroom
1		Shout Chat	⟷	Public Q&A
1		Mobile Entities	⟷	Balls, Collision Carts
2	·	Player Character	⟷	Student
2		Player Statistics	⟷	Student Height, Weight
2		Player Equipment	⟷	Stopwatch, Meterstick
2		Graphical User Interface	⟷	Interactive Whiteboard
3		Non-Playing Character	⟷	Teacher
3		Group Quest	⟷	Lab
3		Solo Quest	⟷	Homework
3		Tell and Group Chat	⟷	Private Q&A
3		Static Entities	⟷	Air Track

there are various objects, some which move and some which do not. The former are called "Mobile Entities"; the latter "Static Entities". Likewise in the classroom there is non-moving equipment, such as an air track or a photogate timer, as well as moving equipment, such as collision carts and dropped balls. Continuing the comparison we see that communication within a VW is most often done through a textual chat system in which the written word serves as the primary means of communication within the world. The Shout Chat, which is global and everybody logged into the level can hear, has its counterpart in the classroom with a question and answer session between the students and a teacher or between the students themselves. The more private "Tell Chat" only allows communication between two students while the "Group Chat" has the extra restriction that the person you want to talk to has to be designated as in your group. These forms of communication can be evidenced in a classroom when a student talks to only one other student or the professor

(Tell Chat) or only with their lab group (Group Chat). Only a very basic Shout Chat interface was implemented in the MVOL with the private modes developed in later cases.

Using the above mappings as a guide, a typical lab experience was translated directly into a VW. The lab replicated with in the MVOL has the purpose of determining the speed of an object, a process which requires two measurements: one for time and another for distance covered. The distance covered is then divided by the time elapsed to obtain a speed. In the real world, a student would select a measuring device (stopwatch or ruler) and use it to perform the necessary measurement. The analogue in the MVOL is a student clicking on an object and a measuring tape deployed with the distance to the object listed or a stopwatch started which records time elapsed which combined can be used to calculate speed. As we shall see in the next section, this basic educational interaction of selecting an object and measuring its properties will also be used as a gameplay element.

Entertainment

As the MVOL is a direct mapping of traditional physics labs onto a VW, it does not have any game elements. As it was being developed, however, it was becoming clear that there might be benefits to introducing game elements into the VW. The game genre chosen for development was the RPG since the character development, narrative, and quest systems that normally serve as enough motivation for an entire game could also be used for educational purposes (as will be seen in the upcoming cases). The RTS game was not chosen since it is a top-down 2-D view and focus on combat did not seem appropriate to physics exploration. While the FPS seemed attractive since gameplay relies on projectile motion and an understanding of how things move, these games are defined by their fast-paced reactions and a "kill or be killed" attitude, two elements that are not conducive to reflection

on learning materials; thus, it was discarded as a genre upon which to develop the game.

An idea borrowed from RPGs that was implemented in the MVOL is that of complementary team roles. For example, in most RPG's a fighter can wield the sword but a magician cannot. On the other hand, the magician can cast a spell but a fighter cannot. And neither of them can heal, but a priest can. This means that in order to maximize effectiveness, an ideal team would have a priest, fighter, and magician so that they could deal with anything in the world. In the MVOL, this is mimicked in that a person could buy a measuring tape that allowed them to measure distance or they could buy a stopwatch to measure time but not buy both. Therefore, if a velocity or acceleration measurement was needed, a distance measuring and a time measuring student would need to pair up and share information in order to complete the assignment.

As the MMUSCLE system was developed, it was realized that more sophisticated game related concepts were needed. Rather than just a box for a room, a full-fledged game level would be required and rather than just cubes to represent the people, actual humanoid models would be required. In short, to motivate students to become players in the VW, what players have come to expect of MMOGs would need to be replicated.

Summary

While the MVOL is the earliest and most primitive of all the three prototypes, it served as an important primer to the basics of networking and game development. As well, its university background opened up the possibility of using the talents of students and teachers alike. As an example, using programmers from the computer science department or artists from the graphic design department, a university could in principle create their own GBL development team. This is what the author considers to be "Academic" game development in that the available resources of a university are leveraged towards the development of an educational world.

While it was never meant to be used as part of a study or in the classroom, the MVOL nonetheless served as a good foundation upon which to focus further research in the area of GBL. And while it was never released publically, it still managed to garner positive support within the university with the core ideas behind the MVOL easily abstracted to other fields of learning. For example, it is easy to conceive a MVOL for biology instead of physics: we can imagine that the level is comprised of the walls of an animal's cell with the player walking within the cell and performing PH measurements.

Another lesson learned during this phase was the difference between physics programming and game programming. In physics, there is little need for any type of graphics or sounds and it is only important to get numerical results. Programming simulations or crunching numbers for physics relies strictly on the raw CPU processing power of the computer. Game programming on the other hand is more holistic whereupon every part of the computer is relevant and a failure in any one component will affect the entire game experience. All of these issues really brought to bear that even if one has a solid programming background, there is still a lot to learn when creating a GBL application.

In the course of MVOL development, several things became clear. For one, a more dedicated software solution would be required for game development. Simply hacking together code from books was not going to accomplish what was needed. As well, better art and sound assets would be required to make the experience complete. To be comparable with commercial titles, more effort would need to be allocated to Audio-Visual (AV)

production. Meeting these needs is the motivation for case 2.

CASE 2: MMUSCLE (2003-2004)

Prelude

With the release of *Second Life* in 2003 and *World of Warcraft* in 2004, VW's started gathering national attention. The Serious Games Initiative led to dedicated conferences on the subject of games for more than entertainment in the form of the still ongoing Serious Games Conference (now known as the Serious Games Summit). At the same time, the Games Learning Society conference was independently tackling similar issues. At these conferences, several standout serious games are presented including the US Military's *America's Army* in the field of combat training, the United Nation's *Food Force* bringing focus to global food supply issues, Impact Game's *Peacemaker* in the field of conflict resolution, and Softonic's *Dimenxian* in the field of math. Note that none of these games are networked and thus do not provide a social experience to their players.

Introduction

The *Massively Multi User Synchronous Collaborative Learning Environment* (MMUSCLE) system is our second prototype, a direct successor to the MVOL, and the first version that is recognizably game-based. The MMUSCLE system consists of three levels, each corresponding to a different period in physics history. Each of these levels represents roughly a square kilometer of virtual space and allows for ample exploration by the player. The player is now represented within the world as a flying saucer model instead of the MVOL cube-headed model. MMUSCLE not only has better graphics and includes sound but also introduces several new interactions between players and environment. A key improvement in this version is that all models within MMUSCLE are completely physical and thus react to gravity, friction, and drag in 3-D. There was also a change in who would be using the application. By virtue of embracing a game-based learning model, MMUSCLE was meant to be deployed outside of the classroom as a commercial stand-alone gaming and educational experience. While it was still targeted at university students, the fact that it would be available online meant that it could also be used by a younger population interested in the subject of physics or independently by teachers who would access the VW and integrate it into their own curriculum.

The entire MMUSCLE code is roughly 100 MB and took about eight months of development to create. While the author was responsible for all the programming and initial art creation,

it became obvious that one person could not do everything and therefore the creation of art assets was outsourced. Upwards of 20 artists from South America, the USA, and Europe worked to create a large selection of assets. Due to budget and time constraints it became impossible to adequately populate the entire VW using only outsourcing and so commercially bought assets from sites such as *Turbosquid*[5] and *3DCafe*[6] were used. In doing research on how to improve MVOL development the concept of authorware was discovered and then implemented into MMUSCLE. Authorware is a generic term for a set of libraries or standalone applications dedicated to the creation of specific software; in this case, game software. The importance and adoption of authorware will be discussed in the next section.

Figure 4 is a MMUSCLE screenshot and a direct implementation of the 2002 conceptual sketch seen in Figure 1. In it, we see balls rolling down a wooden incline bench as an early physics test of the authorware's capabilities. In that screenshot, only the balls and incline are operational; everything

Figure 4. MMUSCLE screenshot of an incline bench physics test with placeholder GUI

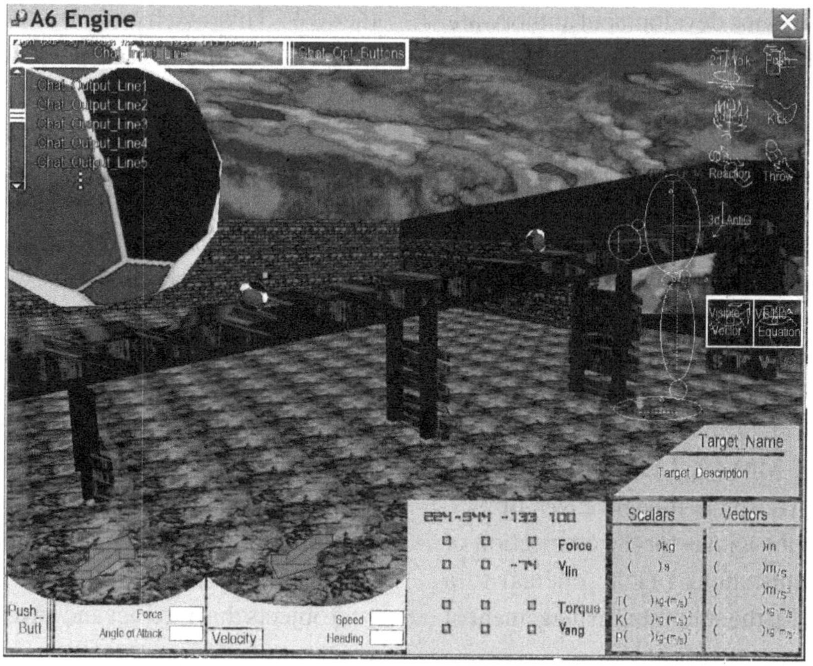

Figure 5. A projectile motion demonstration in MMUSCLE

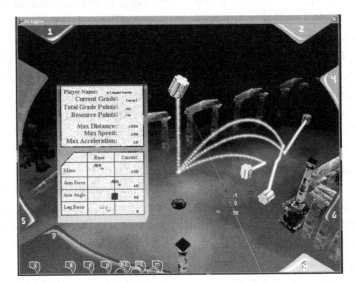

else seen is a non-operational mock-up. Figure 5 shows a screenshot from the final version of MMUSCLE with everything operational.

Technology

The use of authorware helped improve the overall quality of the MMUSCLE system as well as lowering its development time. There are many other competitive game development authorware products including *Unreal*, *Torque*, and *Unity* to name a few. Due to its low cost and lack of licensing restrictions, the MMUSCLE system was developed using *3-D Game Studio* (3DGS) by Conitec[7]. 3DGS has several distinct engines that a compiled application will use to deliver its content to the player. In this section, some of these engines will be examined as an overview of the technology that went into the MMUSCLE system.

The 3DGS network engine was originally based on Microsoft's *DirectPlay* network library and thus so is the MMUSCLE system. However it is now based on the more modern *ENet*[8] library. The network engine allows for the connection of several client applications (a.k.a.: clients) to a single server and for the automatic management of these clients once connected. Modifications to the functionality and any other engines within 3DGS are effected through its native language, *C-Script*. A problem that had to be dealt with in the earlier 3DGGS network engine was the enumeration of clients. As this was not done automatically by the earlier engine, complicated procedures had to be programmed, in C-Script to keep track of the clients so they could be referenced later within the VW. This machinery was cumbersome and perfecting it took a large portion of the total development time. With the switch to *ENet*, these functions are now handled automatically and thus every client is assigned a unique Client_ID by the server as soon as they join the network.

The 3DGS physics engine is originally based on the *ODE*[9] library and thus so is MMUSCLE; however it currently uses the more advanced *PhysX*[10] library. The physics engine is responsible for keeping track of all the various physical objects within the world and having them move according to the laws of physics, including collisions with air viscosity and ground friction taken into account. The physics engine works by having the program set an object with a "physical" flag. Any two objects that interact and have this flag set that will follow the laws of physics. The physics engine is quite robust and capable of simultaneously handling thousands of physical objects interacting simultaneously. Also, based on a models size, a default cubical "hull" is established around the model that forms its collision surface. Thus while an object may look like a ball in the VW, unless a sphere-specific hull size is set for that object, it will collide as if it were a box and not a sphere. Another challenge had to do with physics units. The 3DGS physics engine does not reference their units in standard physics units but rather in game relevant nomenclature. Thus instead of "meters" to measure distance, a "pixel" or a 3DGS "quant" becomes the measure of distance. In addition, where as in real physics there is only one time, in a game environment there may be many times including the main game process loop timer with units of "ticks" or an internal computer timer with units of "cycles" or more. Thus calculating something as simple as a speed means converting, in 3DGS, from "quants per tick" to "meters per second". This process often did not give consistent results due to timing differences between different computers. Thus while our objects behaved physically, performing a measurement using the correct units proved difficult.

As 3DGS has no native database engine, the MMUSCLE system uses a flat file storage system. This means that all the configuration and game time information was stored on text files on the same computer as the server. Given the amount of work that the server application has to do (including physics engine calculations, client management, and other logical procedures), reading and writing from the hard drive is very inefficient. As a result, we stored as little as possible outside the system and hardwired most of the world's configurations and parameters in order to enhance performance.

Education

The MMUSCLE system builds upon and re-uses the mappings first implemented in the MVOL as well as introducing several new educational concepts. Four concepts present in the MMUSCLE system that will be discussed here are: elements mapped from a traditional classroom, using physics history, using physics visualizations, and performing scientific measurements. These topics will be revisited in the next section to show how they have entertainment value as well.

Of central importance in any digital game is the Player Character (PC), which represents the embodiment of the human user within the game and the locus of their interaction. The PC is also generally the hero of the game narrative. Their educational counterpart in the classroom is clearly the student. This can be seen by realizing that the classroom experience is not for the teacher's or school's benefits but for the student; the hero of the educational narrative. It is for this reason that participants within an educational VW will sometimes be referred to as "students" and sometimes as "players", in recognition of the dual role they take within this world. While not implemented until the last prototype, it is worth noting that apart from PCs there are other characters, known as Non-Playing Characters (NPCs), that are completely under the control of the server. They serve many roles within the world such as vendors, quest givers, and more. Likewise, in the classroom there are "non-learning characters" such as the teacher, teaching assistant, lab managers, or other people within the institution who are not there to learn (as the student is) but rather to teach, administrate or fulfill any number of other roles. Finally, in a classroom a student will have various instruments with which to present information, record data, and keep notes such as notebooks and pencils as well as the whiteboard and projector. This corresponds to the Graphical User Interface (GUI) present in most digital games. The GUI is a of 2-D screen overlays on the player's screen that displays game-related information. Mini-maps, health bars, and targeting reticles are just a few examples of GUI elements. In MMUSCLE, the GUI is designed with physics education in mind and displays the student's kinematic and dynamic variables within the VW as a basis for physical experimentation and investigation.

Using interesting personalities and epochs from history allows for a convenient compartmentalization of the physics material to be covered. In any typical physics class, the material might be covered as follows: The first week is spent as an introduction to necessary mathematics and the basics of measurements, followed by a week discussing kinematics, and then perhaps two weeks dedicated to dynamics. The historical approach maps these three areas into three periods in physics history. We used the Grecian Isles as a background to Aristotle and his (albeit incorrect) "elemental" form of physics. This is also a natural background upon which to learn basic algebra, trigonometry, and perform tutorials on how to do things within the VW. In Italy, we encounter Galileo and the beginning of experimentation and science. This area serves as a convenient place to study kinematics and the "how" of motion. Finally in England, we meet Newton and are exposed to his three laws and therefore dynamics and the "why" of motion. The screenshots in Figure 5 shows a player currently in the Grecian level. This conversion of the history of physics into game levels is a technique that can be readily used in other subjects that can be organized chronologically and/or geographically.

Another educational tool within MMUSCLE is the use of unique visualizations to better understand physics concepts. One such visualization is called "Visible Vectors". Normally, a student is exposed to a vector as a purely numerical construct (such as 10 meters per second due west) or as an arrow in a 2-D textbook. Within the MMUSCLE system however, Visible Vectors are vector arrows embedded in the 3-D environment. This not only provides a full 3-D representation of where the arrow is pointing (i.e., the vector's direction) but

also by virtue of the length of the arrow we can visually see how much of that vector there is (i.e., its magnitude). Given the online nature of this environment, an arrow representing a physical vector would be seen by everybody logged in at the time and thus offers different perspectives of what the vector is. A vector can also be presented in a more conventional numerical form. This can be seen in the middle right of Figure 5 as a vector's three components (the X-direction, the Y-direction, and the Z-direction) are presented as a column of three numbers (-1, 0, 75). This allows students to think 3-D even when doing 2-D assignments. Another aspect of the Visible Vectors is an object trailing a line of particles behind them. This in essence replicates what in PER is known as a Motion Diagram[11] and leads to a clear view of the trajectory shapes. An example of objects leaving behind trails of particles is seen in Figure 5. There we see several objects being thrown at different angles. When thrown at less than 90°, they form the familiar parabolic shape of free-fall projectile motion. When thrown straight up, we see a straight line representing no horizontal motion. In addition, since the particles are emitted at a constant rate, the distance between respective particles relates information about the emitting object's velocity and acceleration as in a traditional motion diagram.

While a lab and a demo may use the same instrumentation, what sets a lab apart is that a student is expected to perform measurements. This paradigm is replicated in MMUSCLE through "Drag and Drop Measurements". Using a set of GUI elements seen in the lower left corner of Figure 5, a student can take measurements of any physical object in the VW. The student first left-clicks and then drags an icon representing a unique variable (such as "X" for position or "T" for time) until it is on top of an in-game model and then upon dropping it (i.e., releasing the left mouse button), a continuous readout begin of the selected object's position or time value. Using this method a player can not only take real world measurements, such as distance and time, but also measurements that cannot be directly taken in the real world such as kinetic energy or momentum. Gravity, drag, and any other physics constants can also be modified within the VW. Thus a student can throw an object in Earth's gravity and plot its trajectory using the Visible Vectors and then modify the environment to Moon gravity, throw the object again, and compare trajectories. Thanks to the aforementioned Visible Vectors, the trajectory of the Earth and Moon gravity throws would be clearly distinct and can serve as objects of study in by the student. These measurements are automatically stored within the server and accessible to player and teacher alike. The data generated from the readout can itself be "Drag and Dropped" onto answer slots in order to complete assignments within the world. This process allows a student player to complete any assignment without having to leave the virtual environment. Thus students never need type an answer as they always get the answer from their experiences within the VW.

Entertainment

With the adoption of 3DGS, it was finally possible to enact entertainment ideas that were impractical in the MVOL. First and foremost, the graphics were drastically improved. As can be seen in Figures 4 and 5 in comparison with Figure 2, the quality and quantity of digital assets were greatly expanded. Also, the addition of sound and better mouse and keyboard controls gave the player a more up-to-date game experience. This was beneficial in not only helping convey physics information but also presenting the world's narrative.

With the MMUSCLE system we started to incorporate distinct RPG elements. As such, a pressing need was that of a narrative to propel the student through the game content. Given the aim of experiencing physics through different time periods, the story of an inter-dimensional

being caught in our dimension by accident was chosen. As such, they have no knowledge of our physics and they would have to learn from scratch how our world works. Being from another dimension, space and time have little meaning and thus it can start its journey wherever and whenever it wants. With players taking the roles of these inter-dimensional beings, they will travel from Grecian temples to Victorians cities with each place focusing on a specific physics lesson. This narrative is necessary to not only tie in different physics content as discussed previously, but also to provides something beyond pure education to entertainment student in world.

Unlike the MVOL, the MMUSCLE system has a fully developed GUI. The borders in Figure 5 are a set of numbered panels, each representing a different piece of information. One sheet that is open in Figure 5 displays the "Player Statistics". This is the embodiment of the player within the world. Like a traditional MMOG, the player has several numerical values that define them. However given the educational nature of this game, a mapping was chosen with education in mind and thus we have "current grade points" instead of "experience points" or "maximum acceleration" instead of "maximum armor class". On the bottom of the Character Sheet we can see an interactive slider that allows the user to modify the angle and force with which their player will throw an object. While this has obvious educational ramifications in terms of understanding what effect force and angle would have on the range and trajectory of an object, from a gameplay perspective it replicates popular trajectory-based games such as *Scorched 3-D* (Jurcevic, 2008) or *Angry Birds*[12].

Another aspect of a RPG that has been translated to the MMUSCLE system is that of player equipment. In a traditional RPG, equipment would allow a player to make themselves stronger, faster, tougher, etc. In the MMUSCLE system, equipment has a physical effect. For example, if a player wears an item that masses 5 kg, their physical interaction with the world will be as if they had five more kilograms of inertia. As well, shoe selection would affect the friction that a player would have with the ground while a wide assortment of capes can be bought to modify a player's drag coefficient. While the equipment can lead to realistic changes within the character, we also created fantasy equipment. For example, the player can also buy a rocket pack which would allow them to increase their maximum speed or a magic crystal which would lower their inertia without losing any mass.

The entertainment components within the MMUSCLE system are closely related to their educational components. We shall now look at the same three areas previously presented for education but now expose their entertainment value. The first area explored was that of the history of physics. Besides providing scaffolding upon which to present the traditional physics content, each area has a unique visual look. In addition, the challenges that a student player would engage in each area would be distinct. For example, in Aristotle's time a student might be given the quest to find an object of each of the four elements (fire, water, air, earth). However, during Isaac Newton's time the student player might be asked to document objects with different potential energy. Finding the four elements may require little more than a scavenger hunt around the VW while finding different potential energy items requires the student to realize that potential energy depends on mass and height . In addition to the personalities that the player will meet on their journey, they will also be immersed in that period. So in Italy for example, the player will get the opportunity to drop objects from the tower of Pisa or in England, the player will find Newton and play a game of snookers with him.

Two other educational features discussed previously, visualizations and in-game measurements, work together to create the central gameplay dynamic within the MMUSCLE system in what can best be described as a "measurement scavenger hunt". A student is asked to find a particular measurement or physical phenomena within the world, something related to projectile motion for example. While traveling in the world, the student comes upon another player shooting arrows. The trajectories seen in Figure 5 could easily correspond to the trajectories of these arrows. At the same time one player is shooting arrows, another student could be taking measurements of that same trajectory in order to complete their assignments. This student then submits these measurements for review and if it's the correct measurement, they successfully complete the assignment. If it is not the correct measurement, they may need to redo the experiment (i.e., shooting the arrow) or find it elsewhere in the world.

Summary

MMUSCLE development represents the author's first foray into true game development. With the use of 3DGS, it was possible to make a single-server multi-client application that showcased several of the features we considered important in creating an immersive educational experience for the student.

Through this prototype, we can better illustrate the educational flow that is intended. A student would log into the world not knowing any physics. There would be other people already within the world who know physics and who might help this new person take their first steps in the world. Even if this new person would rather not interact with others, there are plenty of activities within the world which the student would complete on their own schedule in order to not only progress through the narrative content but also the physics content. And within the world, there would also be teachers passing as students who could interact with new and old students to make their gameplay and educational experience better.

We can imagine how the MMUSCLE system might be abstracted to other fields of education. Continuing the example first presented in case 1, in order to make a biology MMUSCLE, a teacher would identify the visual elements from their field and imagine how they might be implemented in a virtual world. For example, cellular biology could be taught with the entirety of the cell being a level and the various proteins being the equipment a player collects. The player could then take the role of a miniaturized doctor on a mission to save a life, one cell at a time, by interacting with the environment directly or modifying the local chemical balances.

At the end of its development, MMSUCLE was a collection of different interactive elements but not a standalone game. While this produced the basics of a game, more AV assets, a better architecture, and a generally more professional approach was required. In contrast to the "Academic" development environment of the MVOL, the MMUSCLE system was created under what we termed a "Solo" environment since one person was in charge of all aspects of development and project management. While this development strategy achieved a lot, it became obvious that a larger and more organized game development structure was needed and this sets the stage for case 3.

CASE 3: PAST (2005-2008)

Prelude

By 2005, MMORPGs are in full swing with dozens of titles released and dozens on the way. Second Life has expanded and now has a dedicated section for education. There is also an explosion of educational games conferences with the continuation of the Serious Games Summit and Games Learning Society summit and the inclusion of Futureplay, ITSEC's Serious Games Showcase, and others. This is also when we start seeing dedicated projects exploring MMORPG's and education in projects like Georgia Tech's *Mermaids*[13] and the University of Central Florida *Lunar Quest*[14] (in which the author was a creative consultant and subject matter expert).

Introduction

Physics Adventures in Space and Time (PAST) is the latest and most complete example of a physics education VW. PAST has a hard drive footprint of around 1GB and a development timeframe of roughly two and a half years, starting in January of 2006 and ending in July 2008. During this time, the author exclusively assumed a managerial and design role. Employees ranged from two to five programmers and upwards of twenty international freelance artists remotely creating AV assets.

With the completion of MMUSCLE, we had something with a lot of potential but none of the structure or depth required for use in the classroom or sold to the public. To further our mission, Futur-E-Scape (FES) was created as a Limited Liability Corporation. This new corporate nature of development defined two phases to PAST development.

The first phase of development started in 2005 and lasted roughly a year. This is when the company was formed and initial revisions to the MMSUCLE system were created to make it a more robust platform upon which to fulfill the VW's entertainment and educational needs. During this phase, the plan was to create a toolkit that would allow people to piece together an MMORPG's with ease. We would create in effect authorware specific to MMOG's. To fund and complement this venture, we also opened up an AV asset e-commerce shop, called *MyMMOG*[15]. The AV assets created for e-commerce and profit, would also be used in our own game development. During this process, over 400 AV assets were created for FES ranging from character models to full musical compositions. This plan was eventually dropped but there are many MMOG authorware platforms available today such as *BigWorld* or *HeroEngine*.

The second phase started in 2006. Further development of AV assets for *MyMMOG* had halted and the plan focused on developing a modest VW which could be sold to private schools. To accomplish this goal, the company moved into a business incubator known as the *EZone*[16]. Within this incubator, we had access to office space, printing and secretarial services, meeting rooms with teleconferencing and electronic whiteboard, and more. We immediately began the process of hiring programmers for the office with AV asset creation completely outsourced. During this time we won several awards from the state of Kentucky. Since these funds could not go into the construction of the software itself, the money was used to hire several consultants and create a new website[17]. In order to fund the actual development of the software other sources of capital had to be pursued, like angel investors and venture capitalists. Unfortunately, they almost always demanded an exit strategy that had the company going public or being sold to a larger company, options that took creative and educational control away from us. Therefore, game development was entirely privately funded by the author and his family. The target audience shifted once again given the commercial nature of FES. We kept the target user of our software as a university student aged 18 years or older. Professional analysts were contracted to review our demographics and it was decided to try to make a target a hybrid demographic inspired by the previous prototypes. Creating an open world into which anyone could sign-up for and enter created the problem of sustaining a revenue based on an educational title… while creating applications for learning institutional use brought with it the difficulty of selling products to universities and public school districts. Based on this, the private school sector was chosen as a viable compromise between our two previous demographics. This is because decisions to buy new educational applications are less bureaucratic in a private school thus making it easier to infiltrate that market and once infiltrated, the private school sector would provide a steadier revenue stream.

Lacking sustained capital with which to develop the VW and compounded by the economic conditions of the time, PAST development ended in the middle of 2008. Compared to the MVOL (which was developed in an Academic environment), and the MMUSCLE system (which was developed in a Solo environment), the PAST development structure can best be described as "Indie", short for Independent. This is because while we used many of the procedures and organizational structures of large game companies, our source of funding was strictly private and did not use any external investment, such as from venture capitalists or going public. The presentation of case 3 that follows references the 2008 version of PAST developed at the *EZone*.

Technology

PAST is built using the same 3DGS authorware as MMUSCLE but with many additions reflecting our growing understanding of authorware and game development. The two major changes are the inclusion of a SQL server and an architecture redesign.

A major addition in PAST was integrating a *MySQL*[18] server as the database. This is an open-source standalone database server that is responsible for handling all the non-logic information within the world. This server uses a relational database so that massive amounts of information can be stored and retrieved quickly. This meant that all the game's textual and configuration information (such as characters names, login information, gold, and experience points) could be managed by the MySQL database. As a standalone application MySQL could be deployed on a separate computer and accessed by any or all other clients and servers within the network.

The many processes required to run a MMOG (such as clients joining, running physics calculations, or managing quests) overwhelmed the single server used in the MVOL and MMUSCLE. The architecture therefore had to be modified to something that was more robust and stable under large client loads. Also, since PAST was meant to handle a large number of clients, we wished to separate any business transactions a user might need to undertake to enter our world from the actual game processes required to play the game. In this way if the business operations crashed for any reason, the game world would in principle be insulated and vice-versa. We therefore split the entire user experience over two networks.

The first network a user encounters is the Business Network (BNET), responsible for handling registration and authorization protocols. The BNET consists of four applications: the "Presentation Client", which is what the user uses to access the network, the "Administration Server", which manages all the client connections, a "Business Server", which handles all transactions, and finally the previously mentioned MySQL server, responsible for storing user accounts.

Only when a user has created an account and logged in through the BNET with their proper credentials will they be allowed to progress into the second network, the Game Network (GNET). The GNET is where the actual game is played. The GNET shares the same application structure as the BNET but with additional logic applications. As such there is a "Physics Logic Server" responsible for handling all the physics calculations, a "Detection Logic Sever" responsible for keeping track of where all the clients are relative to each other, a "Chat Logic Server" responsible for all inter-player communication, and more.

When we put the BNET and GNET together, we have effectively broken up the functionality present in the single server of the MMUSCLE systems over roughly a dozen independent applications. Since each of these applications can run on a separate computer, load-balancing was achieved and we could have hundreds of concurrent users. Figure 6 enumerates these applications both client and server-side.

Education

The educational mission in PAST is unchanged from MMUSCLE. Apart from implementing several new features, several of the systems implemented in MMUSCLE were either modified or

directly implemented in PAST such as the Visible Vectors, player statistics, and ability to modify global parameters like drag and friction

The measurement system was one feature that was revised. Instead of being a direct mapping to a laboratory experiment (where the data is taken, analyzed, graphed, and conclusions made) the new measurement procedure was simplified. Measurements are still done but they rely less on repetitive procedures while making things more automatic for the student. Previously in the MMUSCLE system, to complete a lab a student would take several measurements and choose one or all of those data points to answer lab questions. Within the PAST system, this process is now self-contained and automatic. For example, when a student goes out on a quest they will be asked to take three measurements of three different velocities. Upon completing these three measurements, that is the end of the quest; there is no choosing which data to use and no follow-up. If they obtain the correct three values, the system will automatically use it to answer whatever assignment is being done. PAST also expands on MMUSCLE assignments by allowing conventional multiple-choice assignments (as seen in Figure 7) that require the student to perform experiments or interact with other students to generate the right answer. Thus, a question will not ask a student to submit what the final velocity of a projectile might be but would rather present multiple-choices on what the correct velocity might be and the student must perform experiments on their own within the VW to determine the right answer.

The biggest educational addition to PAST is the implementation of a Quest system. A player approaches a NPC known as the "Quest Giver" and receives an assignment (i.e., receives a quest). As shown in Figure 7, the Quest Giver asks a question based on a diagram that is found within the VW. The player must then explore or ask for directions to where this particular diagram is located. Having found the diagram, the student might immediately know the answer or he/she

Figure 6. PAST's server- and client-side applications

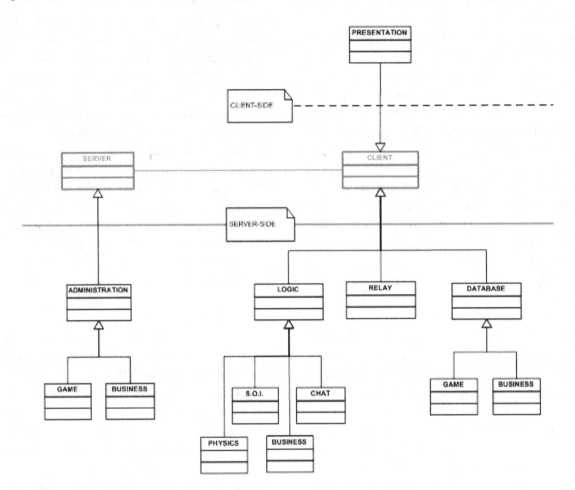

Figure 7. Interaction between player and quest giver in PAST

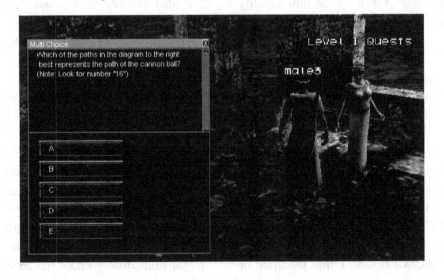

may need to perform actions in the world (such as throwing objects or making measurements) to produce the right insight and answer. If the chosen answer is correct, that particular assignment is checked off and the player receives rewards in the forms of experience points, gold, or other unique abilities. If the choice is incorrect, the player has the opportunity to examine the question again (i.e., redo the quest). While there are many "Solo Quests" that require only one person to complete (and maps to the concept of homework) there are equally many "Group Quests" that require two or more people working together to make observations and measurements towards a common goal (and maps to the concept of group-based labs). We have already seen one such Group Quest in the MVOL: obtaining a speed from one student performing a distance measurements and another student performing a time measurement. In PAST, this same scenario is implemented in that each student would see the two measurement requirements in their quest sheet but they could only contribute to one item in the quest, either a distance or a time. If this quest had three slots, then three different players would have to participate in the quest to complete it successfully. This type of collaborative learning is based on the findings of PER (Gütl et. al., 2012) stating the importance of collaboration for physics retention.

With the addition of Quests, there is a complete mapping of the physics classroom to the VW. In a traditional course, a student would enter the classroom, a teacher would present them with an assignment, the student would then perform a lab alone or with lab partners, and then turn in a write-up. Within PAST, a player would be able to enter the VW, a quest-giver would present them with a quest, and they would then complete the quest by interacting with other players and returning with an answer or required object. As well, with the addition of quests it was finally possible to implement ideas from PER and educational theory. For example several of the quests are pulled directly from the FCI test. Thus what was a multiple-choice

question on the FCI test becomes a Solo Quest with the same diagram, the same narrative asking the same question, and the same answers in the same order. In fact, figure 7 is just such a question. This direct virtual mapping of the FCI was intended to generate data which researchers and teachers could use to measure the effectiveness of PAST at teaching physics. However, it could also be used to as a way for students to proactively guide their education, by performing educational activities in areas where they test weakest.

Entertainment

Much like its educational components, PAST uses and expands upon several entertainment elements from MMUSCLE as well as introduces new elements to make the players experience more immersive and enjoyable. The graphical improvements can be seen in Figures 7 and 8.

In order to support the collaborative quests, two new forms of chat were introduced. One was "Tell Chat", which represents private communication between two players. This is useful when a player does not want anyone but one individual to know what they say. The other is "Group Chat", which represents communication among a selection of players, namely those players in your group. This is useful if there are many groups in the same area or if a player wants to keep their results private from other individuals but not the players in their quest. These private chat channels along with the global "Shout Chat" complete the basic forms of textual communication within a VW.

The narrative was changed and expanded upon. Instead of just a loose set of inter-dimensional ideas, consultants were brought in to help in creating a professional story that was entertaining and fit to teach physics. The idea of literal historical time travel was discarded and instead a fantasy world was created. The threefold breakdown of physics content (with Greece corresponding to mathematics, Italy corresponding to kinematics, and England corresponding to dynamics) was

Figure 8. Satellite view of a PAST level

kept but modified to fit this new fantasy motif. Therefore now we had an Earth-like planet that took on the role of ancient Greece and is home to the "Humes", a less-dense planet that took the role of Italy and is home of the "Elvs", and a denser planet that took the role of England and is home to the "Dwarvs". There is now an over-arching plot associated with the breakdown of the magical system and the need to restore it. The narrative that included magic is a convenient entertainment device but also serves an educational purpose as it was based on Aristotle's original four elements and thus magic was used as examples of "wrong" physics. All of these narrative elements came together with the overall theme of the world as a quest to re-discover physics. Thus the player engages in traditional fantasy gameplay but at the same time is encouraged to learn physics as a means to progress through the game.

The amount of interaction available to a player in the world was also expanded. Apart from changing the angle and force of a thrown ball as in previous versions, the player could also pick up objects and carry them around, kick them, or change their physical characteristics such as mass or drag coefficient. In addition, as was discussed in the above education section, a quest system was

set up that was based on physics. However, not every quest need be a physics exercise and thus there is plenty of room for quests that are merely entertaining. These quests could be scavenger hunts in which the player must explore the world in order to find certain items or they could require the player having to interact with other players or NPCs within the world to uncover more of the storyline. Note that PAST, like previous prototypes, is non-violent. While shooting guns and killing enemies is an attractive and visceral gameplay element, we believe it sends the wrong message in terms of what science can do for the world. Therefore a "Grief" system was implemented so that whenever a player was attacked and took damage, they incurred grief and became sadder. In this way, rather than dying, the player merely becomes despondent and unable to take any actions until they feel better after a period of time. Thus even if a player was struck by an object falling off a cliff, there would be no bloodshed and no death.

Another addition to PAST were mini-games scattered throughout the world. We built these mini-games using elements within the VW already created: the mobile entities in the forms of balls and the player interaction in terms of kicking and throwing. Further, we created new static entities that served as goals, targets, and scoreboards. Using these components, several games inspired by real sports were created that are not only entertaining but could also be used as the basis for physics investigations. These mini-games harken back to the ideas of the MVOL in that they are direct mappings of the physics experiments only in game format. For example, the projectile motion experiment [19] has been modified into archery contests against inanimate but mobile targets. This game relies on the accuracy of the throw via a set angle and force to hit a target. Thus knowledge of how much force to use, what the optimum angle is, and what the range is are integral to success in this mini-game. The traditional 2-D air track upon which objects behave as if on a frictionless surface has been reimagined as a football pitch that can have variable friction and drag. The lessons usually conveyed in an air track such as conservation of energy and momentum in 2-D collisions can easily be replicated within this pitch in a dynamic and entertaining way. Moreover, allowing the ball to go up and down allows players to do something that is rarely able to be done in a laboratory and that is explore full motion in all three dimensions at once. While these games can be completed purely as entertainment, knowledge of physics can help improve the performance of a player in this game and thus it would be actively sought by players who want to achieve greater status within this world.

Summary

PAST represents the most professional of all our attempts to create a VW to teach physics. Its development represented the effort of many years, thousands of dollars, and dozens of people. It succeeded in bringing together all the elements of previous prototypes such as visible vectors, measurements as gameplay, and a pseudo-historical

perspective while introducing new elements like quests and mini-games.

During this time, many consultants were hired to give business and game advice. The advice from the consultants, far from defining the path the game took, modified and strengthened it into something that was more fun and educational than it would have been without them. An ongoing lesson from all three cases is the importance of realizing what your own personal strengths and weaknesses are such that you may outsource the weaknesses and build on your strengths.

Two major technical challenges limited the applicability of PAST. The most pressing one has to do with 3DGS's network engine's inability for servers to communicate amongst each other. The network structure was strictly one server, multi-client and did not allow a true server farm. To circumvent this requirement, we connected several clients server-side and only ran a specific GNET logical function, such as physics or chat, on each of them. This structure can be seen in Figure 7 where we see some client application client-side and some client applications server-side. Thus if you imagine a tree, we had several clients at the roots which mimicked a server farm, the true server as the trunk which connected these roots with the leaves, which represent the clients run by the user. A disproportionate amount of time was spent in making this arrangement work and it became worse the more applications we had running simultaneously. Another major challenge was in transitioning from a local area network to a wide area net. The game runs stable and with hundreds of interacting playing and non-playing characters within the walls of our office. However, it proved very difficult for clients to connect from outside through the Internet cloud and into our offices. This inability for our game to go fully online prevented us from showcasing it at several events and convincing investors of the potential for this product.

However, what was achieved is still an accomplishment. Even if only within the walls of the office, an entire physics world had been created in which a player can throw and kick things around, perform measurements, go on quests, buy equipment, interact with other players and all in the name of science. In effect, we have created a world in which a player does not need to learn science to have fun... but it helps.

CHAPTER SUMMARY

In this chapter, three different applications created between 2002 and 2008 are presented as examples of how a VW can be used to teach physics. The MVOL was the first environment created and was little more than a set of walls with objects moving

about it. It did, however, provide the foundation for understanding game development and finding out about authorware. The choice of 3DGS then led directly to the creation of the MMUSCLE system, which represented a more interactive experience within a VW. It is also the first recognizably game-based world that the author created. Finally, PAST represents our latest effort in professional game development. By creating a company and a server farm powerful enough to handle our clients, a true MMOG experience has been replicated with clear entertainment and educational features. It contains all the elements for a complete game experience whether accessed at home or in the classroom. It is hoped that other teachers and game developers can draw inspiration from the lessons contained in this chapter and build on our successes in creating their own educational VW experience (see Table 1.)

Table 1. Overview of the three prototypes discussed in this chapter

Project Name	Years	Educational Elements	Entertainment Elements	Technology Elements
MVOL Multiuser Virtual Online Lab	2002	Single measurement on single object.	none	Game development book C++ codebase.
MMUSCLE *Massively MultiUser Synchronous Collaborative Learning Environment*	2003-2004	Multiple measurements with variable environment and objects.	Throw, kick, carry and shout. Amateur narrative.	3DGS authorware. Amateur AV assets
PAST *Physics Adventures in Space-Time*	2005-2008	As MMUSCLE but with student assessment via quests.	As MMUSCLE with sound, music, equipment, quests, and a professional narrative.	3DGS with MySQL functionality. Professional AV assets.

REFERENCES

Adams, E., & Rollings, A. (2007). *Fundamentals of game design*. Upper Saddle River, NJ: Pearson Prentice Hall.

Barron, T. (2001). *Multiplayer game programming*. Roseville, CA: Prima Tech.

Bartle, R. A. (1996). *Hearts, clubs, diamonds, spades: Players who suit muds*. Retrieved April 14, 2009, from http://www.mud.co.uk/richard/hcds.htm

Bartle, R. A. (2003). *Designing virtual worlds*. Bloomington, IN: New Riders Publishing.

Christian, W., & Belloni, M. (2001). *Physlets*. Englewood Cliffs, NJ: Prentice Hall.

Clickers. (2009). Retrieved from http://telr.osu.edu/clickers.

Eberly, D. H., & Shoemake, K. (2004). *Game physics*. Amsterdam: Elsevier/Morgan Kaufmann.

Gee, J. (2007). *What video games have to teach us about learning and literacy*. Basingstoke, UK: Palgrave Macmillan.

Gütl, C., Scheucher, T., Bailey, P. H., Belcher, J., Ricardo dos Santos, F., & Berger, S. (2012). Towards an immersive virtual environment for physics experiments supporting collaborative settings in higher education. In A. Azad, M. Auer, & V. Harward (Eds.), *Internet Accessible Remote Laboratories: Scalable E-Learning Tools for Engineering and Science Disciplines*. Hershey, PA: IGI Global.

Hake, R. R. (1998). Interactive engagement vs. traditional engagement: A six thousand student survey of mechanics test data for introductory physics courses. *American Journal of Physics*, *66*, 64–74. doi:10.1119/1.18809.

Halliday, D., Resnick, R., & Walker, J. (2005). *Fundamentals of physics*. Chichester, UK: John Wiley & Sons.

Hestenes, D., Wells, M., & Swackhamer, G. (1992). Force concept inventory. *The Physics Teacher*, *30*, 141–158. doi:10.1119/1.2343497.

Hewitt, P. (2002). *Conceptual physics*. Harlow, UK: Addison Wesley.

Jurcevic, J. S. (2008). Learning projectile motion with the computer game scorched 3D. *The Physics Teacher*, 46.

Knight, R. (2002). *Five easy lessons*. Harlow, UK: Addison Wesley.

Lake, A. (2011). *Game programming gems 8*. Boston, MA: Course Technology.

Mazur, E. (1997). *Peer instruction*. Englewood Cliffs, NJ: Prentice Hall.

McDermott, L. (2001). Oersted medal lecture 2001: Physics education research – The key to student learning. *American Journal of Physics*, *69*(11). doi:10.1119/1.1389280.

McDermott, L. C. (1996). *Physics by inquiry*. London: J. Wiley.

Michael, D. R., & Chen, S. (2006). *Serious games that educate, train, and inform*. Boston, MA: Thomson Course Technology PTR.

Novak, G. (1999). *Just-in-time teaching*. Englewood Cliffs, NJ: Prentice Hall.

Novak, J. (2005). *Game development essentials: An introduction*. Clifton Park, NY: Thomson/Delmar Learning.

OECE. (2008). *Encouraging student interest in science and technology studies*. Paris: OECD Publishing.

Palmer, G. (2005). *Physics for game programmers*. Berkeley, CA: Apress.

Rademacher, R. (2010b). A proposed framework for studying educational virtual worlds. In P. Zemliansky (Ed.), *Design and Implementation of Educational Games*. Hershey, PA: IGI Global.

Rademacher, R. (2011). Assessing serious games using the EE grid. In *Computer games education review*. Rotterdam, The Netherlands: Sense Publishers.

Rademacher, R. J. (2009). *An assessment of current pure online physics courses*. Paper presented at the American Association of Physics Teachers Winter Meeting. Chicago, IL.

Rademacher, R. J. (2010a). Best practices in teaching and designing a pure online science classroom. In Y. Katz (Ed.), *Learning Management Systems Technologies and Software Solutions for Online Teaching: Tools and Applications*. Hershey, PA: IGI Global.

Salen, K., & Zimmerman, E. (2004). *Rules of play*. Cambridge, MA: MIT Press.

Serway, R., Faughn, J., & Moses, C. (2003). *College physics*. Sydney, Australia: Thomson-Brooks/Cole.

Wieman, C., Perkins, K. K., & Adams, W. K. (2007). Interactive simulations for teaching physics: What works, what doesn't, and why. *American Journal of Physics*, 76(4-5).

KEY TERMS AND DEFINITIONS

Authorware: Software designed specifically for fast development of video games.

Client-Server: A name given to a computer architecture that has minimal information on the software the user uses (the client) while most of the information and processing is done on a separate computer (the server) usually housed many miles away from the client.

MMOG (Massively Multiplayer Online Game): A subset of VW, this refers to online games that have thousands of users (or players) simultaneously active.

MMORPG (Massively Multiplayer Online Role Playing Game): A subset of MMOG, these games have the user (or player) take on the role of a personage within the VW with most popular genres for these types of game include fantasy and science fiction.

Newtonian Physics: The study of nature as modeled by Isaac Newton. It consists of describing all motion much slower than the speed of light in terms of mass, time, and position.

PER (Physics Education Research): A name given to research on how we learn and teach physics.

VW (Virtual World): A name given to any computer and network (online) aided environment that replicates the real world.

ENDNOTES

[1] These apps are available for free download by searching for "Futur-e-scape" in the Google play market.
[2] http://www.activeworlds.com
[3] http://educationarcade.org/supercharged
[4] http://www.wilsoncenter.org/publication-series/serious-games
[5] http://www.turbosquid.com
[6] http://www.3dcafe.com
[7] http://www.3dgamestudio.com
[8] http://enet.bespin.org
[9] http://www.ode.org
[10] http://www.geforce.com/Hardware/Technologies/physx
[11] http://webphysics.davidson.edu/physlet_resources/western_kentucky/MotionDiagrams
[12] http://www.angrybirds.com
[13] http://egg.lmc.gatech.edu/?cat=8
[14] http://ucfretrolab.org/2011/08/17/lunar-quest/
[15] http://www.futur-e-scape.com
[16] http://www.madisone-zone.com
[17] http://TheVniversity.com
[18] http://mysql.com
[19] http://phet.colorado.edu/en/simulation/projectile-motion

Chapter 15
Assessment Integration in Serious Games

Thomas Hainey
University of the West of Scotland, UK

Thomas M. Connolly
University of the West of Scotland, UK

Yaëlle Chaudy
University of the West of Scotland, UK

Elizabeth Boyle
University of the West of Scotland, UK

Richard Beeby
University of the West of Scotland, UK

Mario Soflano
University of the West of Scotland, UK

ABSTRACT

Serious Games (SG) are developing a reputation with some educationalists as a useful supplementary approach for teaching and learning. Two important issues for SG application developers and educationalists are how the learning is assessed and how assessment is integrated into a SG application. This chapter presents the results of a systematic literature review on assessment integration in SG and highlights the state of the literature in this area by outlining important papers to act as a guide for educationalists tackling this important issue. This chapter defines assessment and discusses formative and summative assessment and embedded and external assessment. A discussion of traditional assessment approaches and assessment approaches in SG are presented along with a discussion of existing frameworks for the integration of assessment into a SG application. The chapter presents a number of examples of assessment in serious games.

INTRODUCTION

Serious Games (SG) have gained interest from educationalists and have been used in some of the following areas to motivate and engage: Maths (Habgood, 2007; Ke, 2006), Languages (Johnson and Wu, 2008; Rankin, Gold and Gooch, 2006) Technologies (Sheng et al., 2007) Sciences (Squire, Barnett, Grant and Higginbotham, 2004; Dede, Clarke, Ketelhut, Nelson and Bowman, 2005), Health and Wellbeing (Lennon 2006; Beale, Kato, Marin-Bowling, Guthrie and Cole, 2007), Social Studies (Piper, O'Brien, Morris and Winograd, 2002; Paul, Messina and Hollis, 2006), Expressive Arts (Wagner, Schmalstieg and Billinghurst, 2006; Robertson and Oberlander, 2002) and Religious and Moral Education (Paiva et al., 2005). SG developers and educationalists have to

DOI: 10.4018/978-1-4666-4773-2.ch015

Copyright © 2014, IGI Global. Copying or distributing in print or electronic forms without written permission of IGI Global is prohibited.

address various issues surrounding assessment when developing or utilising serious games for learning and teaching. One issue is related to the type of assessment to be adopted with the serious game, for example, formative and/or summative assessment. Another issue is whether the assessment should be embedded in the serious game or external to it. A third issue is what particular form should this assessment take, for example, selection of a course of action, multiple choice questions, solving puzzles, performing particular tasks in the correct sequence or fully integrated and identified as a natural part of the gameplay. A further issue would be whether there are any recognised models and/or standards that could be used for the integration of assessment into the game. Additional issues around assessment include the wide range of potential outcomes, the difficulty in measuring abstract skills such as teamwork and leadership and identifying cheating (BinSubaih, Maddock and Romano, 2009). Each of these issues presents particular problems. This chapter will discuss the various types of assessment and will then present the findings of a systematic literature review to find studies that have addressed these problems.

LEARNING OUTCOMES AND ASSESSMENT

Learning Outcomes

According to the European Qualifications Framework (EQF) (Education and Culture DG, 2008) learning outcomes means statements of what a learner knows, understands, and is able to do on completion of a learning process. They are defined in terms of knowledge, skills and competence:

- **Knowledge:** Means the outcome of the assimilation of information through learning. Knowledge is the body of facts, principles, theories and practices that are related to a

field of work or study. In EQF, knowledge is described as theoretical and/or factual;
- **Skill:** Means the ability to apply knowledge and use know-how to complete tasks and solve problems. In EQF, skills are described as cognitive (involving the use of logical, intuitive or creative thinking) or practical (involving manual dexterity and the use of methods, materials, tools or instruments);
- **Competence:** Means the proven ability to use knowledge, skills and personal, social and/or methodological abilities, in work or study situations and in professional and personal development. In EQF, competence is described in terms of responsibility and autonomy.

Assessment

Good assessment serves multiple objectives and benefits a number of stakeholders. Kellough and Kellough (1999) identified seven purposes of assessment:

1. Improve student learning.
2. Identify students' strengths and weaknesses.
3. Review, assess and improve the effectiveness of different teaching strategies.
4. Review, assess and improve the effectiveness of curricular programs.
5. Improve teaching effectiveness.
6. Provide useful administrative data that will expedite decision making.
7. Communicate with stakeholders.

Traditional forms of assessment include some of the following approaches: written exams, presentations, demonstrations, multiple choice tests, practical course works (individual or group based), quizzes, aural examinations, oral examinations and dissertations. Weng et al. (2011) state that "traditional assessments are usually conducted at the end of a learning unit in a summative manner that makes pronouncements about the student's learning achievements." Mislevy et al. (2003) define assessment as a "machine for reasoning about what students know, can do, or have accomplished, based on a handful of things they say, do, or make in a particular setting." The UK Assessment Reform Group (1999) identifies five principles of assessment for learning:

1. Effective feedback to students.
2. Active involvement of students in their own learning.
3. Adjusting teaching to address the results of assessment.
4. Recognising the significant influence assessment has on students' motivation and self-esteem.
5. Need for students to be able to assess themselves and understand how to improve.

Reeves (2000) suggests that new forms of assessment need to be developed to align them with new learning outcomes desired and expected from online learning. It is necessary to highlight that the term 'assessment' is sometimes used synonymously with the term 'evaluation' leading to ambiguity. Gavin (2008) defines evaluation as: "Research involving systematic appraisal of organisations, processes or programmes leading to feedback on improvement or performance". Gikandi, Morrow and Davis (2011) recognise that both assessment and evaluation have a component of measurement but make the following distinction between them and consider evaluation to be "… operations associated with measuring worthiness/value of non-person entities (such as curricula, programmes, courses, instructional strategies among others) in relation to identified goals" whereas the term assessment is used "… to refer to operations associated with measuring achievements of persons in relation to desirable outcomes". We agree with this distinction and in this chapter we use the term 'assessment' to refer to the measurement of an individual's

learning achievements and 'evaluation' to refer to the measurement of non-person entities such as a serious game.

Formative and Summative Assessment

Similar to the categorisation of assessment given by Conole and Warburton (2005), Black and Wiliam (1998) view assessment as activities undertaken by teachers (and students in assessing themselves) that provide feedback to modify teaching and learning activities and state that assessment "…becomes formative assessment when the evidence is actually used to adapt the teaching to meet student needs". It is recognised that there are varying degrees of formative assessment, for example, Nyquist (2003) developed the following typology for formative assessment:

*   **Weaker Feedback Only:** Students are provided only with their own score or grade.
*   **Feedback Only:** Students are given their own score or grade, together with either clear goals to work towards, or feedback on the correct answers to the questions they attempt, often described as 'knowledge of correct results'.
*   **Weak Formative Assessment:** Students are given information about the correct results, together with some explanation.
*   **Moderate Formative Assessment:** Students are given information about the correct results, some explanation, and some specific suggestions for improvement.
*   **Strong Formative Assessment:** Students are given information about the correct results, some explanation, and specific activities to undertake in order to improve.

Wiliam and Thompson (2008) show that formative assessment is not only just between the instructor and students but student peers are involved in the process as well. Formative assessment is intended to inform and guide adjustments to learning on an on-going basis and should allow the instructor to use the serious game as a motivational tool for learning and teaching (Weng et al., 2011). Weng et al. (2011) state that formative assessment adds a considerable weight to an instructor's workload as it can be difficult to implement and intensive in terms of time and labour.

Summative assessment is intended to monitor progress and evaluate the overall success of both students and instructional programmes on a long-term basis. Summative assessment is defined by the QAA (2006) as "used to indicate the extent of a learner's success in meeting the assessment criteria used to gauge the intended learning outcomes of a module or programme". Hargreaves (2008) states that summative assessment "measures what students have learned at the end of an instructional unit, end of a course, or after some defined period". Gikandi, Morrow and Davis (2011) highlight that the primary disadvantage of summative assessment is that it encourages surface learning and in most cases only assesses basic application and declarative knowledge with no evidence of deep reflection (see Table 1)

In general serious games developers and educationalists have to address whether they want the serious game to result in surface learning or deep reflective learning. This may result in a combination of both types of assessment being integrated into a serious game.

Embedded (Internal) and External Assessment

Underwood, Kruse and Jakl (2010) define embedded assessmentembedded assessment as: "the process of measuring knowledge and ability as part of a learning activity rather than after the fact, when it is only an approximation of learner behaviour" and suggest that "... student actions can be evaluated within context while carrying out tasks, or otherwise interacting in a gaming environment". Shute, Ventura, Bauer and Zapata-Rivera (2009) state that the term 'embedded' refers to assessments with a formative purpose of obtaining accurate information about the learner inserted into the game or curriculum in an unobtrusive manner on which the students, instructional environment or teacher can act. Eseryl, Ifenthaler and Ge (2011) point out that embedded assessment is a part of the serious game, should not interrupt the game flow and should optimally be integrated into the tasks or actions. Underwood, Kruse and Jakl (2010) identify the following challenges for embedded assessment in serious games: adapting the environment for the learner, assessing the processes and skills and not just the content, embed assessments into the fabric of the game, maintaining flow while collecting in-game data and analysing the data with appropriate techniques.

Eseryl, Ifenthaler and Ge (2011) state that "external assessment is not part of the game-based

Table 1. Issues to be considered in terms of integration

Formative Assessment	Summative Assessment
Whether the assessment is going to be embedded in the game or external	Whether the assessment is going to be embedded into the game or external
Degree of formative assessment that is going to be integrated into the game	What particular form the summative assessment take (e.g. a paper-based examination a multiple choice test within the game)
How this formative assessment is going to be provided (e.g. from the game itself or other players in the game or an instructor/facilitator)	Whether any existing assessment framework and/or assessment standards can be used to integrate the assessment into the game
How the assessment is going to be implemented (e.g. making decisions, playing puzzles, undertaking tests)	
Whether any existing assessment framework and/or assessment standards can be used to integrate the assessment into the game	

environment it will interrupt playing the game, which is not desirable." An example of external assessment is a paper-based exam that can take place after the game is finished.

LITERATURE REVIEW

Search Terms and Criteria

A literature review was performed to identify different approaches to integrating assessment into serious games. The literature review was performed using the following search terms which included terms in conjunction with computer games and terms for assessment and feedback:

- ("serious games" OR "game based learning" OR "educational games") AND (assessment OR feedback.)

Relevant papers were identified using the following three pieces of criteria: papers discussing the different types of assessment used in serious games; papers discussing any assessment frameworks for serious games and papers from 2004 onwards. Where possible the search was based on abstracts, titles and keywords to focus on relevant papers.

Databases Searched

The electronic databases searched in this review included those identified as relevant to education, information technology and social science: ACM (Association for Computing Machinery), ASSIA (Applied Social Sciences Index and Abstracts), BioMed Central, Cambridge Journals Online, ChildData, Index to Theses, Oxford University Press (journals), Science Direct, EBSCO (consisting of Psychology and Behavioural Science, PsycINFO, SocINDEX, Library, Information Science and Technology Abstracts, CINAHL), ERIC (Education Resources Information Center),

IngentaConnect, Infotrac (Expanded Academic ASAP), Emerald, Springer and IEEE (Institute of Electrical and Electronics Engineers) Computer Society Digital Library (CSDL).

Results

The search returned 2036 studies, which were then reduced in an analysis to 27 relevant papers after our three pieces of criteria were applied. We added, afterwards, 4 articles found in the references. Out of the 31 relevant papers, only 5 presented empirical evidence of the assessment system. The studies discovered in the literature review presented in Table 2 have the following main approaches to integrating assessment into serious games:

- Monitoring of states-completion assessment, process assessment and teacher evaluation.
- Quests types.
- Use of an assessment model or profile.
- Micro-adaptive non-invasive assessment of competencies.
- Quizzes.
- Peer assessment.

Assessments

1. A qualitative experiment was conducted; every teacher and pupil has been interviewed individually following the trial. Two sets of questions (one for the teachers, one for the pupils) have been used as basis for the semi-structured interview. The majority of answers reflected a clear preference for the assessment in the game against a paper-based one. Students found it more "fair".

2. Conducted an experiment, comparing their diagnostic tool with an online questionnaire for a given game. The students' average for the questionnaire was 1.56 and the in-game assessment diagnosed 1.55. With a p-value at

Table 2. Papers found from search on assessment integration

Study	Description	Empirical Evidence of Assessment
Monitoring of States- Completion Assessment, Process Assessment and Teacher Evaluation		
Chen and Michael (2005)	Discusses three different methods of integrating assessment into a serious game in terms of: a) completion assessment (did the player complete the lesson or pass the test?); b) process assessment (how did the player choose his or her actions? did he or she change her mind and, if so, at what point?); c) teacher evaluation (based on the observation of the student, does the teacher think that the student now knows/understands the material).	No
Torrente, Moreno-Ger, Fernández-Manjón and Sierra (2008)	Describes a Visual Editor for <e-Adventure> giving the instructor the ability to enter three kinds of assessment: a) associating a final grade to end states (completion assessment); b) association of partial increments when states are reached (process assessment); c) the association of time counters between states, which could be potentially used for teacher evaluation. Default <e-Adventure> outputs include: whether the game has been completed or not, a numerical assessment of the student's performance, the time from the beginning to the end of the game and real-play time excluding times when the player is not interacting with the game.	No
Westera, Nadolski, Hummel and Wopereis (2008)	Assessment is achieved by the monitoring and updating of states (completion and process assessment) in the game world; for example, learning tasks started/not started completed/not completed.	No
Sliney, Murphy and O'Mullane (2009) and Sliney and Murphy (2011)	Primary and secondary information are extracted from the game-play session of the learner and can be assessed either by him/herself (comparing his/her log file to the correct procedure), or by a senior doctor. The game also adapts, selecting test patients according to the learner performances and introducing helpful non-player characters into the game.	No
Torrente, Lavín-Mera, Moreno-Ger and Fernández-Manjón (2008); Moreno-Ger, Burgos, Martínez-Ortiz, Sierra and Fernández-Manjón (2008)	Presents the <e-Adventure> platform, which produces games that can be packaged as an LO (Learning Object) and bundled with standard metadata using the IEEE LOM, integrated with LMSs through game exportation following SCORM 1.2 and 2004 and IMS Content Packaging, and can be integrated with the content repository Agrega. The platform provides a common API for assessment and tracking purposes. The API uses SCORM's communication specifications to act as a middleware between the games and a SCORM-compliant LMS. The API gathers the results of the game, produces a detailed assessment report with partial or final grade according to a set of assessment rules defined by the instructor and sends the report to the LMS to be attached to the student's profile.	No
Quest types		
Chang and Kinshuk (2010)	Provides formative and summative feedback using a game to teach Java programming skills utilising the five following different quest types: greeting, delivery, multiple-choice/true or false, fill in the blank and coding.	No
Connolly, Stansfield and Hainey (2011)	Describes an Alternate Reality Game (ARG) that provides informal peer assessment to solve problems in language learning and also uses the concepts of rewards, progression and leadership boards for formative and summative assessment. Webquests are used to motivate and engage the students.	No
McAlpine, van der Zanden and Harris (2010)	Covers formative and summative assessment. Uses serious game for formal assessment within the Scottish Credit and Qualifications Framework (SCQF) for Level 5 Retail and Level 4 for Health Sector using Thinking Worlds. The assessment was primarily integrated using selection (selecting the correct answer), matching (matching the correct answer to a description) and locating (locating particular items or NPCs in the game). The game produces a report that is passed to a human marker to verify the game and provide summative assessment.	Yes (1)
Morsi, Richards and Rizvi (2010)	Formative and summative assessment was used in BINX, a game to teach Engineering Education, specifically number systems and arithmetic operations in Digital Logic Design. The game provides practise and overall feedback for the player. The game integrates fill in the blank assessment for completing the correct answer.	No
Tang, Chen, Ku, Chao, Shih and Weng (2009)	Provides basic assessment content authoring such as multiple choice, multiple choices or short-answer question. They are embedded in the game map as special quest types. A non-player character can give hints if needed.	No

continued on following page

Table 2. Continued

Study	Description	Empirical Evidence of Assessment
Monitoring of States- Completion Assessment, Process Assessment and Teacher Evaluation		
Use of an Assessment Model or Profile		
Raybourn (2006)	Formative and summative assessment is described in serious game-based adaptive training systems. Presents the Simulation Experience Design Method with in-game assessment, feedback and AAR (After Action Review). In-game assessment is implemented by allowing players to quantitatively and qualitatively analyse the performance of other individuals and groups while the game is in progress. The advantages of incorporating feedback and assessment into the games as part of training tasks enhance and build metacognitive skills.	No
Zielke *et al.* (2009)	Summative assessment utilising a 3D Asymmetric Domain Analysis and Training (ADAT) model for analysis of cultural behaviour such as positive and negative actions.	No
Zaibon and Shiratuddin (2010)	Presents a framework for mobile serious games development based on learning theories. Assessment is described in relation to the assess performance category in Gagne's nine events of instruction (Gagné, 1965).	No
McAlpine, van der Zanden and Harris (2010)	Covers formative and summative assessment. The assessment model utilised in this study was Gagne's nine events of instruction (Gagné, 1965).	Yes (1)
Wouters, van der Spek and van Oostendorp (2011)	Proposes a list of guidelines for the use of structural assessment within serious games.	No
del Blanco, Torrente, Moreno-Ger and Fernández-Manjón (2009)	Provides a middleware architecture model between a Virtual Learning Environment and games with an Abstract Adaptation and Assessment Model. Summative assessment is provided as the instructor uses the data to generate an assessment report.	No
del Blanco, Torrente, Moreno-Ger and Fernández-Manjón (2010)	Formative and summative assessment for <e-Adventure> using an assessment profile. The game is customisable in the sense that it can construct pedagogically relevant scenarios and feedback to the student and the instructor.	No
Serrano, Marchiori, del Blanco, Torrente and Fernández-Manjón (2012)	Authoring assessment tool implemented in the new version of <e-Adventure> enables real time feedback and relies on learning analytics (analysis of relevant interaction data) and semantic rules created for each game to transform the events captured into meaningful data.	No
Augustin, Hockemeyer, Kickmeier-Rust and Albert (2011)	Presents a mathematical framework that draws probabilistic conclusions about the learner's knowledge from the monitoring of his behaviour during the game.	No
Del Blanco, Torrente, Marchiori, Martínez-Ortiz, Moreno-Ger and Fernández-Manjón (2010)	Presents the integration of games created with <e-Adventure> into LAMS (Learning Activity Management System) so that the author of a game has access to all information gathered during a game-play session for formative and summative assessment.	No
Torrente, Lavín-Mera, Moreno-Ger and Fernández-Manjón (2008); Moreno-Ger, Burgos, Martínez-Ortiz, Sierra and Fernández-Manjón (2008)	Presents the <e-Adventure> platform, which produces games that can be packaged as an LO (Learning Object) and bundled with standard metadata using the IEEE LOM, integrated with LMSs through game exportation following SCORM 1.2 and 2004 and IMS Content Packaging, and can be integrated with the content repository Agrega. The platform provides a common API for assessment and tracking purposes. The API uses SCORM's communication specifications to act as a middleware between the games and a SCORM-compliant LMS. The API gathers the results of the game, produces a detailed assessment report with partial or final grade according to a set of assessment rules defined by the instructor and sends the report to the LMS to be attached to the student's profile.	No

continued on following page

Table 2. Continued

Study	Description	Empirical Evidence of Assessment
Monitoring of States- Completion Assessment, Process Assessment and Teacher Evaluation		
Micro-Adaptive Non-Invasive Assessment of Competencies		
Kickmeier-Rust, Hockemeyer, Albert and Augustin (2008)	Proposes micro-adaptive non-invasive assessment of competencies and knowledge based on a player's solution to a particular overall problem taking into account the player's interactions with objects in the learning situation without compromising the game.	No
Thomas, Labat, Muratet and Yessad (2012)	Provides an automated tool for monitoring and analyzing the actions performed by the learners. It uses petri nets extracted from the expert behaviour in the game and compares the learner interactions to it using several diagnosis indicators (right action, too early, too late, sub-optimal, erroneous and missing).	Yes (2)
Shute, Masduki, Donmez (2010)	Presents a stealth assessment based on an evidence centred design composed of three models. The competency model represents the object of the assessment (knowledge, skills...), the evidence model links these variables with a behaviour or performance that demonstrates them and the task model lists the situations and tasks that would draw out such behaviours or performances. It uses system thinking and Bayesian networks.	No
Thomas and Young (2010)	Proposes an integration of learning goals within the core mechanics of the game based on plan-based knowledge representation. It determines whether the student is in difficulties or if the task is too easy for him. It uses a five-valued scale to infer where the learner stands regarding a certain skill: "Highly Likely, Likely, Neutral, Unlikely, Highly Unlikely".	Yes (3)
Csapó, Lörincz and Molnár (2012)	Provides an empirical study to prove that the Online Diagnostic Assessment System is helpful in the learning process. Formative assessment using a monitoring of head movement and facial expression through video recording.	Yes (4)
Shute and Spector (2008)	Presents an adaptive training system based on pervasive monitoring of the learner. Using Bayesian networks and probabilistic inference the system infers the user competencies and allows formative assessment as well as micro and macro adaptation of the content.	No
Kickmeier-Rust, Mattheiss, Steiner and Albert (2011)	Learning skills and motivation are assessed using a probabilistic approach updated after each action performed by the user. The game is adaptive, triggering various types of interventions suitable for the learner to help him/her and/or increase his/her motivation.	Yes (5)
Quizzes		
Chang and Kinshuk (2010)	Provides formative and summative feedback using a game to teach Java programming skills utilising the five following different quest types: greeting, delivery, multiple-choice/true or false, fill in the blank and coding.	No
Weng et al. (2011)	Formative assessment is integrated into a personalised QuizMASter game by using adaptive feedback. A pre-test is utilised to determine player proficiency and then an algorithm is utilised to determine group proficiency and questions are selected based on this. The player is assessed on his/her ability to answer questions correctly before opponents. Feedback is provided to the learners and instructors.	No
Healy, Connolly and Dickie (2008)	Formative and summative assessment is provided by the use of quizzes in each of the games at various stages.	No
Zaibon and Shiratuddin (2010)	Formative assessment in the form of a quiz throughout mobile SG culture game.	No
Schmitz, Czauderna and Specht (2011)	Presents a browser-based game for the acquisition of IT knowledge. The game is partially based on the Open ICOPER Content Space (OICS). In the OICS, *learning outcome definitions* capture the key characteristics of a learning outcome. Learning content is held as SCORM units stored in the OICS content repository. The OICS associates *assessments* with learning outcomes, which allows generating personal achievements, and are stored in the IMS Question & Test Interoperability (QTI) format. In the OICS, *personal achievement profiles* allow learners to organize their achieved learning outcomes. Evidence records are stored in the PALO data format and assessment results delivered from the QTI engine are stored into the profile repository using the PALO format.	No

continued on following page

Table 2. Continued

Study	Description	Empirical Evidence of Assessment
Monitoring of States- Completion Assessment, Process Assessment and Teacher Evaluation		
Morillo Arroyo *et al.* (2010)	Presents the implementation of an assessment engine for the 3D virtual world Open Wonderland using the QTI specification.	No
Peer Assessment– Assessment Received from Other Players During the Course of the Game		
Connolly, Stansfield and Hainey (2007)	Peer assessment is provided in the subject of requirements collection and analysis as the player must collect a requirements wish list and assessment is provided by the project manager who either rejects or accepts the requirements wish list.	No
Connolly, Stansfield and Hainey (2011)	Provides informal peer assessment using an Alternate Reality Game (ARG) to solve problems in language learning.	No

0.69, the assessment tool can be considered accurate.

3. Conducted an experimental evaluation of the assessment tool, comparing the results found by "Annie", their system, with the conclusions of a human observer regarding a prediction of answers to a questionnaire given to the student at the end of the game. On average Annie predicted correctly 76% of the learner answers and the human expert 75% with a student-by-student correlation of 0.89. The in-game assessment behaviour is close to the human expert one.

4. Conducted a 4 weeks pilot study with 6-8 years old to provide empirical evidence that the teaching game with Online Diagnostic Assessment System helps compensate students' learning difficulties. The pupils with performance significantly lower than 50% were part of the experimental group and the others were part of the control group. The results of the study showed a significant diminution in the difference of means between the two groups for the pre-test (41.7% difference) and post-test (27.6% difference).

5. In this study, a variable was introduced called "approach to solution" (ATS) that takes into account if the learner actions are closer to final solution, further from that or without effect. Then, an experiment was conducted

providing learners with a game that gave no intervention / adaptive intervention / inappropriate intervention / neutral intervention and compared the ATS value from all four groups. The results show that the average ATS (relative to no intervention) is at its best for adaptive interventions, neutral intervention appears to be useful even if 5 times lower, inappropriate intervention, on the other hand seems to confuse the learner rather than help him.

EXAMPLES OF ASSESSMENT IN SERIOUS GAMES

In this section, the different categories highlighted in the literature review will be explained and illustrated with concrete examples of serious games. A rapid introduction of the serious games will be given along with the presentation of their assessment integration.

Monitoring of States

Monitoring the states of a game-play allows the system to perform both summative and formative assessment. States can be as general as 'level completed', 'task completed' or 'answer given' but they can also show a more detailed knowledge of the game-play with 'location visited', 'task started', 'NPC met' or 'content accessed'.

Junior Doctor

JDoc (Sliney, Murphy and O'Mullane 2009; Sliney and Murphy 2011) is a serious game with an assessment system based on the monitoring of states. The purpose of the game is to train junior doctors, providing them with a virtual hospital and various ill patients. The learner has to give a diagnosis and a prescription to each patient. He/she has the possibility of running different types of tests such as x-rays. The diagnosis and the prescription are the primary information needed for assessment; the learner could gain feedback only with those two answers. The system also collects secondary information for more formative assessment. The assessment system records every meaningful action the junior doctor undertakes in the virtual hospital. The whole process of how the learner arrived at the final diagnosis is registered along with the time he/she took for each step. The system has, then, two different setups for assessment:

1. The record can be shown to the learner along with an annotation for each state, for example "No peripheral nervous exam should have been done, time wasted", for him/her to do a self-assessment.

2. The record can also be sent directly to an external assessor, a senior doctor (see Figure 1).

Quests Types

The assessment of learning can also be part of the game as a particular quest type. Each quest, when completed, can be then assessed. A non-player character, or puppetmaster as in the first example presented below, can give hints if the task is too complicated. The assessment quests can be, for instance, 'search the Internet', 'create content' or 'match description'.

Tower of Babel ARG

ARGs, sometimes referred to as 'immersive gaming', are a form of online interactive narrative and puzzle solving (Connolly et al., 2009) often

Figure 1. Example of the report of a game play

```
Scenario: ST Elevation
Date: 23/11/10

Dr. Murphy started the simulator. He then went to call the hospital
(1.12)After ring the hospital Dr. Murphy thought the patient could have been suffering from peptic ulcer disease
(2.15)He talked to Dr Smith but Dr Murphy left before the doctor finished talking
(4.43)He talked to nurse Carla
(5.02)He walked into patient's room
(5.30)He asked him did he have shortness of breath.
(5.55)He asked his patient was he feeling sick. He asked for the bloods. He looked at the end of bed notes.
+++ He began to examine the patient +++

(6.25)He spent 12 minutes at a peripheral nervous exam
          No peripheral nervous exam should have been done, time wasted
(18.32)45 seconds were used on auscultation of the respiratory system.
(19.05)He did a 20-second auscultation of the cardiovascular system.
+++ Dr Murphy finished examining the patient +++

When the Medical reg asked "What's wrong with the patient and what's your reasoning behind your answer?"
Dr. Murphy replied: "ST Elevation, ECG showed it."
When asked "What treatment would you like to start while the medical reg is on his way?" Dr. Murphy replied:
"Give him Panadol".
```

involving multiple media and game elements to tell a story that may be affected by the actions and/ or ideas of the players. The narrative is gradually revealed to the participants through a series of media that can include websites, instant messenger (IM) conversations, text messages, emails, as well as TV and newspaper adverts and telephone calls. A central role in the development and running of an ARG is played by the puppetmaster who steers players in different directions as the game's story unfolds. Collaboration among players forms a key role as players must work together in solving quests or puzzles and ultimately successfully completing the game, which is why as well as being a form of computer game, ARGs are also viewed as being heavily built around social networking. The puppetmaster can adopt the role of an adversary to the players by placing obstacles in their path to solving a quest, or an ally by providing deliberate clues that enable players to find resources to overcoming obstacles.

Although ARGs have previously been developed and implemented as promotional and marketing tools for entertainment related products, ARGs can provide a useful educational context and platform through their collaborative nature and opportunities for students to explore ideas and views with each other, search for relevant information and engage in problem-solving tasks related to learning modern languages. The Tower of Babel ARG (arg.uws.ac.uk) was developed to encourage European secondary school students to learn a second language.

The scenario for the development of the ARG was based on a set of characters who collectively plan to build a contemporary Tower of Babel, which refers to notions and values well established in European civilisation. The characters, along with the game participants, discover through the game how to build the foundations of the tower, which are based on the principles and values of Europe including democracy, tolerance and respect, freedom and the rule of law, and access to education. The gameplay for the ARG centred around promoting pluri-lingualism in which the storyline is based around taking students to a future world in order to save languages that are under threat and can only be saved if students collaborate with each other and with ARG characters to bring people from different parts of Europe together by learning more about each others' histories, traditions and daily lives. Through building the foundations and the tower step-by-step, the aim was for students to gain an understanding of other languages and cultures. The tower was designed as an ever growing wiki where students could add their own building blocks, which could be narrative, videos, quests, blogs, emails, as well as text. As part of the gameplay, students had to send information about languages and cultures to a futuristic world where both have vanished to save the earth from the same fate. Communication in different languages from the future is sent by a secret rebel society, which arrives with the players through email and through a special game portal. Members of the secret society ask players to solve a series of quests to help the world of the future remember what culture and languages are. If players find the right answer then they can add blocks to their virtual Tower of Babel.

In order to find answers to some quests, students had to conduct research and were encouraged to use search engines and other resources. Some of the quests required a correct answer – using multiple choice – whilst other quests involved more open-end questions that required students to upload text, sound and image files that were representative of themselves and their cultures. Most of the quests involved students searching for the information and working collaboratively with other students who were speakers of different languages – for example, Bulgarian learners of English would have to identify Spanish learners of English or French learners of Spanish in order to find out information relating to a particular quest. As well as student-student interaction, the ARG was also designed to provide students and teachers with opportunities to interact, i.e. teacher-student, teacher-teacher interaction. The initial multilingual pilot of the ARG was designed to support English, French, Spanish, German, Dutch and Bulgarian languages.

Figure 2 provides some examples of quests in the game and an example of a student response. The multi-lingual game was piloted in 2009 with 328 14-16 year old school students and 95 language teachers spread across 17 European countries. In general, student attitudes towards the ARG were very positive with evidence suggesting that the ARG managed to deliver the motivational experience expected by the students. The majority of students either agreed or strongly agreed that they would be willing to play the game over a prolonged period of time as part of a foreign language course. In addition, through using the ARG, students believed that they obtained skills relating to cooperation, collaboration and teamwork (Connolly, Stansfield and Hainey, 2011).

StartUp

StartUp (startup-eu.net) is a European project designed to motivate secondary school students by replicating the excitement and creative innovation of a new startup company. The project is running a competition across Europe in 2013 for school teams (3-4 students per team) to come up with a company startup for a new technology innovation. A set of educational mini-games have been developed that allows students to practice and enhance their entrepreneurial skills as they develop their own business ideas collaboratively and autonomously across Europe. Mini-games have been created to support a number of challenges including:

- Sparking creativity.
- Building your company team.
- Understanding your clients.
- Marketing your product.
- How to develop your IT product.

Assessment in each mini-game is through the use of quests and how well an individual or team performs determines their final score. Mini-games can be played more than once to increase a player's score (that is, increase their learning). For example, in the mini-game 'Understanding

Figure 2. Example set of quests/quizzes from the Tower of Babel ARG

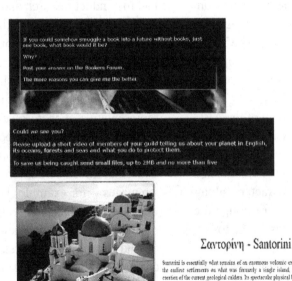

your clients' the player plays the role of a salesman who sells a number of products. By driving a car through part of a city, the player has to find potential clients and match them to a suitable product. On finding a client, the player is allowed to ask a number of questions to help select the most appropriate product. Figure 3 provides an illustration of this mini-game.

As a second example, in the mini-game 'Marketing your product', the player is given a marketing budget and has to identify characteristics of his clients that may indicate how the budget should be spent. For example, one client may travel by train and watch TV, while another might travel by train and use the Internet frequently. Given

that two clients travel by train, this might suggest that some of the marketing budget should be allocated to train advertising with a lower spend on TV adverts and Internet adverts. Figure 4 provides an illustration of two screens for this game, one where the player is identifying characteristics of a client and the second screen showing an example of how the marketing budget is being allocated.

Use of Assessment Model or Profile

Some of the papers found used an assessment modelassessment model or profile to assess the player. In this section, we provide an example of

Figure 3. StartUp mini-game "Understanding your clients"

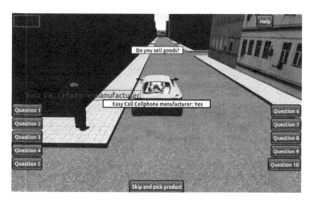

Figure 4. StartUp mini-game 'Marketing your product': (a) finding out about the clients; (b) allocating the marketing budget

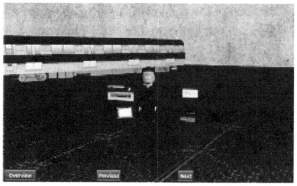

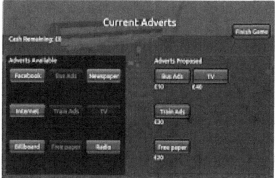

(a)　　　　　　　　　　　　　　(b)

a serious game that uses an in-game assessment model based on the Felder-Silverman learning style (1988). Soflano (2013) has created an adaptive serious game to teach the database query language SQL (Structured Query Language) using the Aurora toolset from NeverWinter Nights 2. Three variants of the game were created:

- The game with non-adaptivity. This variant only monitors the student's learning style during the game.
- The game with out-of-game learning style adaptivity. This variant has the learning content customised according to the student's learning style identified by using the Felder-Silverman learning style questionnaire before playing the game. This variant only takes into consideration the learning style identified prior to the game and does not provide any options to enable the student to change their learning style during game play.
- The game with in-game adaptivity. This variant monitors the student's learning style in real-time when the student interacts with the learning content and dynamically adapts the content to suit the student's current in-game learning style.

In the game, the student assumes the role of a criminal investigator who undertakes quests for information to arrest criminal masterminds, using warrants the student gains based on the evidence and information collected. During the course of the game, the student is also required to collect data and evidence by talking to NPCs before a warrant to arrest the criminals can be issued. The game is designed to require the student to retrieve the required data and evidence from a fictional database by using appropriate SQL statements, in order to get the warrant. The game structures learning by increasing the level of complexity of the SQL statements that the student must construct as the game progresses. In total, the game contains three main missions and a number of

side missions. For each mission, the student learns different forms of SELECT statements. To help the student complete the tasks, there are instructions specific to each task and the student can choose how these instructions are presented to reflect their Felder-Silverman learning style. By completing these tasks, the student can learn how to create and use SELECT statements by entering the appropriate statement into a textbox to solve a given task. Once the student has successfully created SQL queries in response to the task requirements, the warrant to arrest the key criminals is issued, which allows the student to arrest these criminals. When the key criminal on a mission is arrested, the student receives a reward and positive feedback from NPCs, and then the game story proceeds to the next mission.

The storyline is designed in such a way that the student can easily find out what to do by using the 'Journal', which provides details of the missions including the relevant locations for the missions, and where to go by using a map that pinpoints important characters and locations. To gather data and evidence, the student is required to travel between game areas. The game contains four principal outside areas: City Core, Dock, Forest and Central Plain. At the beginning of the game, the student will appear in the headquarters (Figure 5) that is located in the City Core.

To determine learning effectiveness, a controlled experiment with a control group that used paper-based materials and experimental groups for each of the game variants with 30 university students per group was established. Based on a post-test questionnaire with a maximum score of 16, the learning effectiveness of the paper-based group had a mean score of 2.6 (SD=3.8065), for the non-adaptivity group the mean score was 12.517 (SD = 4.690), for the out-of-game learning style group the mean score of 12.35 (SD = 4.065) and for the in-game adaptivity group the mean score was 14.042 (SD = 2.354). When compared to any variant of the game, there was a significant difference in learning effectiveness between the groups. By using Mann-Whitney U

Figure 5. Screenshot of the headquarters

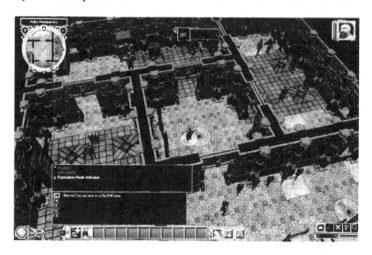

tests, the learning effectiveness for the non-adaptivity game group was found to be significantly higher compared to the paper-based group ($Z = -5.903$, p<0.001). The same results were also found when comparing the paper-based group and the out-of-game learning style group ($Z = -5.995$, p<0.001) and the in-game adaptivity group ($Z = -6.495$, p<0.001). However, a Mann-Whitney U test showed there was no significant difference between the non-adaptivity group and the out-of-game learning style group ($Z = -0.872$, p<0.389). A similar result was found when comparing the learning effectiveness of the non-adaptivity group to the game with the in-game adaptivity ($Z = -0.378$, p<0.711) and between the out-of game learning style group and the in-game adaptivity group ($Z = -1.546$, p<0.124). A Kruskal-Wallis test comparing all groups (paper-based, game without adaptivity, game with out-of-game learning style and game with in-game adaptivity) was significant ($?2 = 58.153$, p<0.01).

Micro-Adaptive, Non-Invasive Assessment of Competencies

This form of assessment may seem more difficult to develop but the possibilities it offers are interesting. It allows assessment to be undertaken without the stress that can be inherent with assessment, as the student is unaware assessment is taking place. Many of the systems found in the literature search also adapt the game according to the student performances, triggering an intervention from a non-player character for instance, or selecting the next mission from a set of possibilities. The pervasive assessment can be performed using, for example, Bayesian networks, reverse engineering, Petri nets and learning analytics.

Taiga Park

Taiga park (Shute, Masduki and Donmez 2010; Shute and Spector 2008) is a virtual park with a river. Three main groups of people are settled in the park and use the river; the Mulu farmers, the Build-Rite Timber Company and the K-Fly Fishing tour Company. The fish population of the Taiga park river is declining and the learner's goal is to find out the reason and propose a solution to the dying-fish problem. Students will conduct surveys within the park, talking to various non-playing characters and collecting opinions about what is causing the fish to die. At the end of the first phase, the player has to formulate a hypothesis about the problem.

In the second phase, students go to three different places on the river to collect samples for analyzing the water quality. Depending on the results, they submit an interpretation and determine which of the three stakeholders causes the problem. In a third phase, they are asked to produce a preliminary scientific conclusion. Using a time machine, the learner is able to see the park two years into the future and fulfil his/her forth mission. The stakeholder identified previously has been ejected from the park but the dying-fish problem remains; the player has to explain why. The final phase gives the player an opportunity to re-think his/her first hypothesis, taking into account a more complex system.

The assessment system, based on Evidence Centred Design and Bayesian networks, is able to infer how much of a certain knowledge or skill a student possesses according to his/her action. Everything the learner does in the game is propagated through the nodes of the Bayesian network, thus updating the estimating value.

Quizzes

Some of the serious games described in the papers used an assessment modelassessment model based on integrating quizzes at various stages of the game. The quizzes could be of various types, for example, multiple choice, multiple response, true/false, and fill in the blanks.

CHERMUG Quantitative Game

The CHERMUG Quantitative Game was created as part of the CHERMUG (Continuing Higher Education Research Methods Using Games) project and aims to support the teaching of an introductory research methods and statistics module. The purpose of the game is to get the players to investigate a selected research question; for example: what is the relationship between gender and food reward selected? The game begins with a narrative to outline the research area context, which for the current prototype game is food preferences and obesity. The player must then select the appropriate statistical analysis technique from a variety of options including: independent sample t-test, Mann-Whitney U test, repeated measures t-test and chi-squared. The player must also use a drag and drop facility to produce a number of hypotheses to progress in the game. The requirements for the CHERMUG research and statistics game were formulated from a Cognitive Task Analysis (CTA) performed by Boyle et al., (2012). Figure 6 shows the CHERMUG Quantitative Game during play giving an example of formative quiz-based/multiple choice assessment.

Figure 6. The CHERMUG Quantitative Game

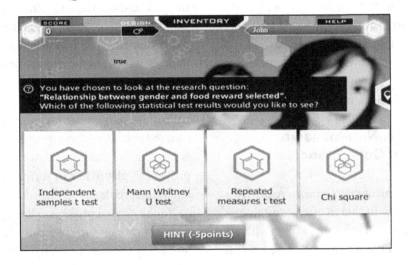

E-CLIL (European Content and Language Integrated Learning)

E-CLIL (e-clil.uws.ac.uk) was an EU-funded project to develop and build a resource centre for the use of Content Language Integrated Learning (CLIL). The project focused on language learning, learning strategies, multilingualism and multi-culturalism. CLIL is dual-focused instructional approach during which language is taught at the same time as content from a different school subject. It has already been established as a valuable approach to both teaching foreign languages and specific subjects. As part of this project, a games engine was developed that allows CLIL teachers to develop their own multi-lingual content. To make the content more engaging, the engine provides a scoring system based on how the students perform in their assessments and, as the students' scores increase, they are given access to an expanding range of short web-based games. The platform also maintains a range of high scores (overall score, per game, per subject) and students can compete against other students to gain the highest score. To assess learning, the engine currently supports the following question types:

- Multiple Choice.
- Multiple Response.
- Drag-and-Drop.
- Point-and-Click.
- Sorting.
- A range of maths-related games.

Between April 2012 and July 2012, a number of CLIL teachers were invited to use the platform. The teachers who volunteered were using CLIL to teach English and German to French students and English to German students. 18 teachers evaluated the engine: 11 participants (61%) were female and 5 participants (39%) were male. The teachers were asked to rate the general usefulness of the tool on a Likert scale from 1 to 5 (1 being the highest and 5 being the lowest). The results were extremely

positive and the participants gave a mean rating of 1.06 (SD = 0.24). All teachers rated the engine easy to use and gave the multilingual capability of the platform a mean rating of 1.06 (SD = 0.24) and the graphics as 1.39 (SD = 0.5). The teachers asked 82 of their students to answer a questionnaire on the platform: 47 participants (57%) were male and 35 participants (43%) were female with a mean age of 9.38 years (SD = 1.37) with a range of 6 to 12 years. Participants were asked to rate the games platform overall on a Likert scale ranging from 1 to 5, 1 being the highest and 5 being the lowest. The results were very positive where 78 participants (95%) gave a rating of 1 and the rest of the participants (4, 5%) gave a rating of 2. Participants were asked to rate the following aspects of the games engine tool on a 5 point Likert scale (1 being the highest and 5 being the lowest): ease of use (mean 1.01, SD = 0.11); graphics (mean 1.02, SD = 0.16); mini-games (mean 1.07, SD = 0.26); and the high score system (mean 1.27, SD = 0.50). Figures 7 and 8 show examples of games that were created by teachers during the piloting.

Peer Assessment

The last way of assessing knowledge in serious games found in the papers was through peer assessment. This includes informal peer assessment in a forum, for instance, or given a special status for some of the players enabling them to provide the others with feedback.

Requirements Collection and Analysis Game (RCAG)

The RCAG (Hainey, Connolly, Boyle and Stansfield, 2011) is a serious game to simulate the software development process. The basic idea of the RCAG is for a team (comprising of one or more players) to manage and deliver a number of software development projects. Each player has a specific role, such as project manager, systems analyst, systems designer or team leader. A bank

Figure 7. Example of Multiple-choice game created by teacher using E-CLIL engine

Figure 8. Example of Doodle God game created by teacher using E-CLIL engine

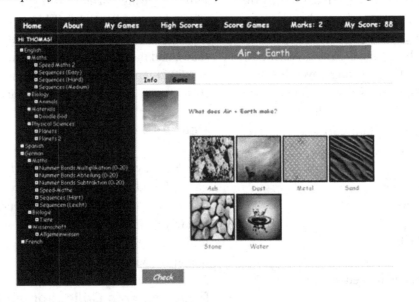

of scenarios have been created based on case studies the authors have been using for many years in teaching and learning; for example, the DreamHome Estate Agency, the StayHome Online DVD Rentals company and the PerfectPets Veterinary Clinic, the Blackwood Library and the Fair Winds Marina. The player(s) assigned to the system analyst role has to identify the requirements

for the project. To do this, the player must move through the game and 'talk' to the non-player characters (NPCs) in the game, as illustrated in Figure 9. In addition, there are objects in the game that can also convey relevant information when found (for example, a filing cabinet may convey requirements). Each NPC's dialogue contains some general background details and a number of

Figure 9. RCAG during requirements collection

requirements and the analyst has to distinguish the requirements from the general details). Visiting the same NPC may generate the same speech or a new speech. Each speech generates a transcript that the analyst can visit at any point in the game. The transcript is presented as a numbered list of requirements. During the play, the analyst can use the transcripts to produce an initial 'wishlist' of requirements, which can be refined until such time as the analyst believes all requirements have been identified, at which point the analyst can send the completed requirements to the project manager. The project manager now has two choices: send the requirements to the designer to produce an outline high-level design or consider the requirements to be incorrect and ask the analyst to rework the requirements. The RCAG is an example of peer assessment as other players assess each other i.e. the project manager assessing the requirements specification wish list of the systems analyst.

DISCUSSION/CONCLUSION

This chapter has explored and defined the different types of assessment that can be integrated into a serious game. The chapter has highlighted the difference between assessment and evaluation and presented some of the issues that should be addressed when integrating assessment into a serious game. These issues can include: whether the overall assessment strategy utilised is summative and/or formative; the extent that formative assessment will be utilised; how formative and summative assessment should be implemented and when in the game cycle it should be implemented; whether assessment should be embedded in the game or external to the game.

The literature review performed in this study has shown that there is a dearth of empirical evidence associated with the integration of assessment into serious games and very few relevant studies were found. A preliminary analysis of the literature search has highlighted 31 relevant studies and showed that assessment could be integrated and implemented in some of the following ways: integration of different quest types, utilisation of adaptation and assessment models in middleware, micro-adaptive non-invasive assessment of competencies, quizzes, after action reviews and the monitoring and upgrading of states.

Future work will entail the development of an assessment integration model and framework to allow developers and researchers to address how the assessment is actually going to be implemented into the serious game. The assessment integration model and framework will be utilised to design and implement a generalised assessment engine that can be use within serious games.

ACKNOWLEDGMENT

This work has been co-funded by the EU under the FP7, in the Games and Learning Alliance (GaLA) Network of Excellence, Grant Agreement nr. 258169 and the EU Lifelong Learning Programme under contract 518060-LLP-I-2011-1-UK-COMENIUS-CMP (StartUp_EU - Be a High Tech Entrepreneur).

REFERENCES

Augustin, T., Hockemeyer, C., Kickmeier-Rust, M. D., & Albert, D. (2011). Individualized Skill Assessment in Digital Learning Games: Basic Definitions and Mathematical Formalism. In IEEE Transactions on Learning Technologies, 4(2).

Beale, I. L., Kato, P. M., Marin-Bowling, V. M., Guthrie, N., & Cole, S. W. (2007). Improvement in cancer-related knowledge following use of a psycho educational video game for adolescents and young adults with cancer. *The Journal of Adolescent Health*, *41*, 263–270. doi:10.1016/j.jadohealth.2007.04.006 PMID:17707296.

BinSubaih. A., Maddock, S., & Romano, D. (2009). Serious Games for the Police: Opportunities and Challenges, Special Reports & Studies Series at the Research & Studies Center (Dubai Police Academy).

Black, P. J., & Wiliam, D. (1998). Inside the black box: Raising standards through classroom assessment. *Phi Delta Kappan*, *80*(2), 139–148.

Boyle, E., van Rosmalen, P., MacArthur, E., Connolly, T. M., Hainey, T., Johnston, B., et al. (2012). Cognitive Task Analysis (CTA) in the Continuing/ Higher Education Methods Using Games (CHERMUG) Project. In *Proceedings of 6th European Conference on Games-based Learning (ECGBL)*. 4 – 5 October 2012, Cork, Ireland.

Chang, M., & Kinshuk, (2010). Web-based Multiplayer Online Role Playing Game (MORPG) for Assessing Students' Java Programming Knowledge and Skills. In *Proceedings of 2010 IEEE International Conference on Digital Game and Intelligent Toy Enhanced Learning*.

Chen, S., & Michael, D. (2005). *Proof of learning: Assessment in serious games*. Gamasutra.

Connolly, T. M. Stansfield, M., Hainey, T., Cousins, I., Josephson, J., O'Donovan, A., Rodriguez Ortiz, C., Tsvetkova, N., Stoimenova, B., & Tsvetanova, S. (2009). ARGuing for multilingual motivation in Web 2.0: a games-based learning platform for language learning, In *Proceedings of 3rd European Conference on Games-based Learning (ECGBL)*, 12-13 October 2009, Graz, Austria

Connolly, T. M., Stansfield, M. H., & Hainey, T. (2007). An application of games-based learning within software engineering. *British Journal of Educational Technology*, *38*(3), 416–428. doi:10.1111/j.1467-8535.2007.00706.x.

Connolly, T. M., Stansfield, M. H., & Hainey, T. (2011). An alternate reality game for language learning: ARGuing for multilingual motivation. *Computers & Education*, *57*, 1389–1415. doi:10.1016/j.compedu.2011.01.009.

Conole, G., & Warburton, B. (2005). A review of computer-assisted assessment. *ALT-J. Research in Learning Technology*, *13*(1), 17–31. doi:10.3402/rlt.v13i1.10970.

Csapó, B., Lörincz, A., & Molnár, G. (2012). Innovative Assessment Technologies in Educational Games Designed for Young Students. In Assessment in Game-Based Learning, 235-254.

Dede, C., Clarke, J., Ketelhut, D. J., Nelson, B., & Bowman, C. (2005). Students' motivation and learning of science in a multi-user virtual environment. Paper presented at the meeting of the *American Educational Research Association*, Montréal, Quebec.

Del Blanco, Á. Torrente, J., Moreno-Ger, P., & Fernández-Manjón, B. (2010). Towards the Generalization of Games-based Learning: Integrating Educational Video Games in LAMS. In *Proceedings of 10th IEEE Conference on Advanced Learning Technologies.*

Del Blanco, Á., Torrente, J., Marchiori, E. J., Martínez-Ortiz, I., Moreno-Ger, P., & Fernández-Manjón, B. (2010). Easing Assessment of Game-based Learning with <e-Adventure> and LAMS. In *Proceedings of the second ACM International Workshop on Multimedia Technologies for Distance Learning.*

Del Blanco, Á., Torrente, J., Moreno-Ger, P., & Fernández-Manjón, B. (2009). A General Architecture for the Integration of Educational Videogames in Standards-compliant Virtual Learning Environments. In *Proceedings of 9th IEEE International Conference on Advanced Learning Technologies.*

Eseryel, D., Ifenthaler, D., & Ge, X. (2011). Alternative Assessment Strategies for Complex Problem Solving in Game-Based Learning Environments. In Proceedings of Multiple Perspectives on Problem Solving and Learning in Digital Age, 159–178.

Felder, R. M., & Silverman, L. K. (1988). Learning and Teaching Styles in Engineering Education. *English Education, 78*(7), 674–681.

Gagné, R. M. (1965). *The conditions of learning and theory of instruction.* New York, NY: Holt, Rinehart & Winston.

Garris, R., Ahlers, R., & Driskell, J. E. (2002). Games, motivation, and learning: A research and practice model. *Simulation & Gaming, 33*(4), 441–467. doi:10.1177/1046878102238607.

Gavin, H. (2008). Understanding Research Methods and Statistics in Psychology. In Sage Publications Lyd.

Gikandi, J. W., Morrow, D., & Davis, N. E. (2011). Online formative assessment in Higher Education: A review of the literature. *Computers & Education, 57*, 2333–2351. doi:10.1016/j.compedu.2011.06.004.

Habgood, M. P. J. (2007). *The Effective Integration of Digital Games and Learning Content.* Thesis submitted to the University of Nottingham. Retrieved 4th April, 2012 from http://zombiedivision.co.uk/.

Hainey, T., Connolly, T. M., Baxter, G. J., Boyle, L., & Beeby, R. (2012). Assessment Integration in Games-based Learning: A Preliminary Review of the Literature, In *Proceedings of 6th European Conference on Games Based Learning*, Cork, Ireland, 4-5 October 2012.

Hainey, T., Connolly, T. M., Stansfield, M. H., & Boyle, E. A. (2011). Evaluation of a Games to Teach Requirements Collection and Analysis in Software Engineering at Tertiary Education Level. *Computers & Education, 56*(1), 21–35. doi:10.1016/j.compedu.2010.09.008.

Hargreaves, E. (2008). Assessment. In G. McCulloch and D. Crook (Eds.), The Routledge international encyclopedia of education, 37–38. New York: Routledge.

Healy, A., Connolly, T. M., & Dickie, A. (2008). ThinknDrinkn?: An Evaluation of the use of Games Based Learning (GBL) for Alcohol Awareness, In *Proceedings of 2nd* European Conference on Games-based Learning (ECGBL), 16-17 October 2008, Barcelona, Spain.

Johnson, W. L., & Wu, S. (2008). Assessing aptitude for learning with a serious game for foreign language and culture. In *Proceedings of 9th International Conference on Intelligent Tutoring Systems*, Montreal, April 2008.

Ke, F. (2006). Classroom goal structures for educational math game application. In *Proceedings of the 7th International Conference on Learning Sciences ICLS '06*, Publisher: International Society of Learning Sciences.

Kellough, R. D., & Kellough, N. G. (1999). *Secondary school teaching: A guide to methods and resources; planning for competence.* Upper Saddle River, New Jersey: Prentice Hall.

Kickmeier-Rust, M. D., Hockemeyer, C., Albert, D., & Augustin, T. (2008). Micro Adaptive, Non-Invasive Knowledge Assessment in Educational Games. In *Proceedings of Second IEEE International Conference on Digital Games and Intelligent Toys Based Education Game and Intelligent Toy Enhanced Learning.*

Kickmeier-Rust, M. D., Mattheiss, E., Steiner, C. M., & Albert, D. (2011). A Psycho-Pedagogical Framework for Multi-Adaptive educational games. *International Journal of Game-Based Learning, 1*, 45–58. doi:10.4018/ijgbl.2011010104.

Knight, P. T. (2001). A briefing on key concepts: Formative and summative, criterion and norm-referenced assessment. York: Learning and Teaching Support Network (LTSN) Generic Centre ASS007.

Lennon, J. L. (2006). Debriefings of web-based malaria games. *Simulation & Gaming, 37*(3), 350–356. doi:10.1177/1046878106291661.

McAlpine, M., van der Zanden, L., & Harris, V. (2010). Using Games Based Technology in Formal Assessment of Learning. In *Proceedings of the 4th European Conference on Games-Based Learning.*

Mills, C., & Dalgarno, B. (2007). A Conceptual Model for Game Based Intelligent Tutoring Systems. In Ascilite conference 2007.

Mislevy, R. J., Steinberg, L. S., & Almond, R. G. (2003). On the structure of educational assessments. *Measurement: Interdisciplinary Research and Perspectives, 1*, 3–67. doi:10.1207/S15366359MEA0101_02.

Moreno-Ger, P., Burgos, D., Martínez-Ortiz, I., Sierra, J. L., & Fernández-Manjón, B. (2008). Educational game design for online education. *Computers in Human Behavior, 24*(6), 2530–2540. doi:10.1016/j.chb.2008.03.012.

Morillo Arroyo, D., Santos Rodríguez, P., Pérez Calle, D., Delgado Kloos, C., Ibáñez Espiga, M. B., & Hernández-Leo, D. (2010). Assessment in 3D Virtual Worlds: QTI in Wonderland, In Congreso Iberoamericano de Informática Educativa, 410-417.

Morsi, R., Richards, C., & Rizvi, M. (2010). Work In Progress - BINX: A 3D XNA Educational Game for Engineering Education. In *Proceedings of 40th ASEE/IEEE Frontiers in Education Conference, S1E-1.*

Nyquist, J. B. (2003). *The benefits of reconstructing feedback as a larger system of formative assessment: A meta-analysis.* Unpublished Master of Science thesis, Vanderbilt University.

Paiva, A., Dias, J., Sobral, D., Aylett, R., Woods, S., Hall, L., & Zoll, C. (2005). Learning by Feeling: Evoking Empathy with Synthetic Characters. *Applied Artificial Intelligence, 19*, 35–266. doi:10.1080/08839510590910165.

Paul, S. T., Messina, J. A., & Hollis, A. M. (2006). A Technology Classroom Review Tool for General Psychology. *Teaching of Psychology, 33*(4). *Aut, 2006*, 276–279.

Piper, A. M. (2002, December). O'Brien, E. Morris, M.R., & Winograd, T. (2002). SIDES: A Cooperative Tabletop Computer Game for Social Skills Development. *Simulation & Gaming, 33*(4), 526–532.

QAA (2006). Section 6: Assessment of students, Code of practice for the assurance of academic quality and standards in higher education. Retrieved May 8 2013 from http://www.qaa.ac.uk/.

Rankin, Y., Gold, R., & Gooch, B. (2006). Gaming as a Language Learning Tool. *Proceedings of the ACM SIGGRAPH Educators Program*, 2006.

Raybourn, E. M. (2006). Applying Simulation Experience Design Methods to Creating Serious Game-based Adaptive Training Systems. *Interacting with Computers*.

Reeves, T. C. (2000). Alternative Assessment Approaches for Online Learning Environments in Higher Education. *Journal of Educational Computing Research, 21*(1).

Robertson, J., & Oberlander, J. (2002). Ghostwriter: Educational Drama and Presence in a Virtual Environment. *Journal of Computer-Mediated Communication, 8*(1), October 2002.

Schmitz, B., Czauderna, A., & Specht, M. (2011). Game Based Learning for Computer Science Education, In Proceedings of the Computer Science Education Research Conference CSERC'11

Serrano, A., Marchiori, E. J., del Blanco, Á., Torrente, J., & Fernández-Manjón, B. (2012). A Framework to Improve Evaluation in Educational Games. In *Global Engineering Education Conference (EDUCON)*.

Sheng, S., Magnien, B., Kumaragurg, P., Acquisiti, A., Cranor, L. F., Hong, J., & Nunge, E. (2007). Anti-Phishing Phil: The Design and Evaluation of a Game That Teaches People Not to Fall for Phish. In *Proceedings of the 3rd symposium on Usable privacy and security SOUPS '07*, Publisher: ACM Press.

Shute, V. J., Masduki, I., & Donmez, O. (2010). Conceptual Framework for Modeling, Assessing and Supporting Competencies within Game Environments. In Tech., Inst., Cognition and Learning, 8, 137–161.

Shute, V. J., & Spector, J. M. (2008). SCORM 2.0 White Paper: Stealth Assessment in Virtual Worlds. In *Learning*.

Shute, V. J., Ventura, M., Bauer, M. I., & Zapata-Rivera, D. (2009). Melding the power of serious games and embedded assessment to monitor and foster learning: Flow and grow. In U. Ritterfeld, M. Cody, & P. Vorderer (Eds.), *Serious games: Mechanisms and effects* (pp. 295–321). Mahwah, NJ: Routledge, Taylor and Francis.

Sliney, A., & Murphy, D. (2011). Using Serious Games for Assessment. In Serious Games and Edutainment Applications, 225-243.

Sliney, A., Murphy, D., & O'Mullane, J. (2009). Secondary Assessment Data within Serious Games. In Serious Games on the Move, 225-233.

Soflano, M. (2013). *Adaptivity and Personalisation in Games-based Learning*. PhD thesis, University of the West of Scotland.

Squire, K., Barnett, B., Grant, J. M., & Higginbotham, T. (2004). Electromagnetism Supercharged! Learning physics with digital simulation games. In *Proceedings of the international conference on Learning sciences, 6*, 513–520.

Tang, J.-Y., Chen, J.-H., Ku, D. T., Chao, L. R., Shih, T. K., & Weng, M. M. (2009). Constructing the 2D Adventure Game-Based Assessment System. In Lecture Notes in Computer Science, 2009, Volume 5686, Advances in Web Based Learning – ICWL.

Thomas, J. M., & Young, R. M. (2010). Annie: Automated Generation of Adaptive Learner Guidance For Fun Serious Games. In IEEE Transactions on Learning Technologies, 3(4).

Thomas, P., Labat, J.-M., Muratet, M., & Yessad, A. (2012). How to Evaluate Competencies in Game-Based Learning Systems Automatically? In Lecture Notes in Computer Science, 7315, Intelligent Tutoring System.

Torrente, J., & Lavín-Mera, P. Moreno-Ger, P., & Fernandez-Manjon, B. (2008). Coordinating Heterogeneous Game-based Learning Approaches in Online Learning Environments. *In Proceedings of Sixth International Game Design and Technology Workshop and Conference (GDTW2008)*, 27-36, Liverpool, UK.

Torrente, J., Moreno-Ger, P., Fernandez-Manjon, B., & Sierra, J. L. (2008). Instructor-oriented Authoring Tools for Educational Videogames. In *Proceedings of 8th International Conference on Advanced Learning Technologies*.

UK Assessment Reform Group. (1999). *Assessment for learning: beyond the black box*. Cambridge: University of Cambridge School of Education.

Underwood, J. S., Kruse, S., & Jakl, P. (2010). Moving to the Next Level: Designing Embedded Assessments into Educational Games. In P. Zemliansky, & D. Wilcox (Eds.), *Design and Implementation of Educational Games: Theoretical and Practical Perspectives*. doi:10.4018/978-1-61520-781-7.ch009.

Wagner, D. Schmalstieg, D., & Billinghurst, M. (2006). Handheld AR for Collaborative Edutainment. *Advances in Artificial Reality and Tele-Existence*. Lecture Notes in Computer Science Springer Berlin / Heidelberg.

Weng, M. M., Fakinlede, I., Lin, F., Shih, T. K., & Chang, M. (2011). A Conceptual Design of Multi-Agent based Personalised Quiz Game. In *Proceedings of 11th IEEE International Conference on Advanced Technologies*.

Westera, W., Nadolski, R. J., Hummel, H. G. K., & Wopereis, I. G. J. H. (2008). Serious games for higher education: a framework for reducing design complexity. *Journal of Computer Assisted Learning, 24*, 420–432. doi:10.1111/j.1365-2729.2008.00279.x.

Wiliam, D., & Thompson, M. (2008). Integrating assessment with instruction: What will it take to make it work? In C. A. Dwyer (Ed.), *The future of assessment: Shaping teaching and learning* (pp. 53–82). Mahwah, NJ: Lawrence Erlbaum Associates.

Wouters, P., van der Spek, E. D., & van Oostendorp, H. (2011). Measuring Learning in Serious Games; A Case Study with Structural Assessment. *Educational Technology Research and Development, 59*(6), 741–763. doi:10.1007/s11423-010-9183-0.

Zaibon, S. B., & Shiratuddin, N. (2010). Adapting Learning Theories in Mobile Game-Based Learning Development. In *Proceedings of IEEE International Conference on Digital Game and Intelligent Toy Enhanced Learning*.

Zielke, M. A., Evans, M. J., Dufour, F., Christopher, T. V., Donahue, J. K., Johnson, P., et al. (2009). Serious Games for Immersive Cultural Training. In *Proceedings of IEEE Computer Graphics and Applications*.

KEY TERMS AND DEFINITIONS

Assessment: The measurement of an individual's learning achievements.

Assessment Integration: A mechanism or mechanisms used to incorporate assessment process into a serious game.

Assessment Model/Profile: Assessment achieved through the use of a particular model or assessment profile e.g. Gagne's nine events of instruction. This model can either be theoretical or technological i.e. middleware.

Embedded Assessment: Assessment with a formative purpose of obtaining accurate information about the learner inserted into the game or curriculum in an unobtrusive manner on which the students, instructional environment or teacher can act.

External Assessment: Assessment that is not part of the serious game.

Formative Assessment: Assessment intended to inform and guide adjustments to learning on an on-going basis and should allow the instructor to use the serious game as a motivational tool for learning and teaching.

Learning Outcomes: Statements of what a learner knows, understands, and is able to do on completion of a learning process.

Micro-Adaptive Non-Invasive Assessment of Competencies: Assessment achieved through a non-invasive automated tool for monitoring and analysing the actions performed by the learners.

Monitoring of States: Assessment achieved by the monitoring and updating of states in the game world; for example, learning tasks started/not started completed/not completed.

Peer Assessment: Assessment received from other players during the course of the game.

Quest Types: Assessment achieved through the allocation and completion of quests in a serious game.

Quizzes: Assessment achieved through the use of questions in the form of multiple choice/true or false, fill in the blank etc.

Summative Assessment: Assessment is intended to monitor progress and evaluate the overall success of both students and instructional programmes on a long-term basis.

Chapter 16

A Case for Integration:
Assessment and Games

Alex Moseley
University of Leicester, UK

ABSTRACT

There is growing interest in assessment of student learning within education, not least because assessment practice within some sectors (the UK higher education sector for example) is stagnant: many courses designed independently to the assessment method and assessed through a small number of traditional methods. Games-based learning has shown little deviation from this pattern – games themselves often removed from assessment of the skills they are designed to teach, and in the worst cases from the intended learning outcomes: gamification being a particularly formulaic example. This chapter makes the case for an integrated approach to assessment within learning games and the wider curriculum, drawing on elements within game design that provide natural opportunity for such integration. To demonstrate and evaluate such an approach, integrated assessment case studies (including a full study from the University of Leicester) are presented and discussed.

INTRODUCTION

Assessment and games share a number of features, both in their design and in their tendency to stick to tried and tested methods. In this chapter, these similarities will be discussed in light of the current interest in both assessment and games for learning.

Written from a standpoint within UK Higher Education (HE), the chapter opens with an overview of assessment within this context, and within game design itself, including the recent interest in gamification approaches.

There are various design features within games that provide good models for assessing student progress and learning, and these will be considered in detail and developed into a range of internal and external models for assessment in learning games. The most integrated of these, *implicit assessment*, was used by the author in an undergraduate History games-based course, and this will be used as a case study in applying the models to a real world example.

It is hoped that this chapter will question existing approaches to assessment within learning games, and encourage the reader to see the advantage in using game elements to integrate assessment deeply within both games-based, and non-games-based learning activities.

DOI: 10.4018/978-1-4666-4773-2.ch016

Copyright © 2014, IGI Global. Copying or distributing in print or electronic forms without written permission of IGI Global is prohibited.

BACKGROUND: A LENS ON ASSESSMENT

The recent interest in academic assessment (and its close partner feedback) has developed as governments, institutions and parents focus on the quality of programmes and - in particular – student outcomes. In Higher Education in the UK, the annual National Student Survey (NSS, 2011) has, over the past five years, revealed assessment and feedback as the area students are most dissatisfied with across the sector (in 2009 and 2010 they produced the lowest average score for all areas of student satisfaction: 65 and 67% satisfaction respectively). In UK secondary education, OFSTED reported as far back as 1996 that marking *"fails to offer guidance on how work can be improved"* and *"reinforced under-achievement and under-expectation by being too generous or unfocussed"* (cited by Black, Harrison, and Lee in their 2004 review of existing practice, that revealed similar concerns across the sector).

What is assessment in a learning context? The question/subject is too broad to cover in detail here, but within the author's own context, UK Higher Education, the Quality Assurance Agency for UK Higher Education (QAA), in its 2012 Quality Code, defines assessment as fulfilling four roles: promoting learning through feedback; evaluating knowledge, understanding, abilities or skills; establishing student performance/progress via a mark or grade; and publically acknowledging a level of achievement (QAA, 2011, p1).

Rowntree (1987, pp117-162) identifies a number of opposing aspects of assessment, that help to give a sense of both the length and breadth of the topic. These are:

- **Formal vs. Informal:** Also to be thought of as obtrusive vs. unobtrusive, formal assessments are those developed by the instructor specifically with the aim of assessing (such as an examination); whereas informal assessment occurs naturally as students work/study/practice/perform.

- **Formative vs. Summative:** Linked closely with the role of feedback, formative assessment is that whose main aim is to help the student learn and develop; whereas those assessments that serve to grade, categorise or assess against formal criteria are summative. The two types can be merged in one assessment.

- **Continuous vs. Terminal:** Assessments are continual if they take place throughout the course; they are terminal if they only take place at the end (where they tend to be both formal and summative).

- **Course Work vs. Examinations:** Course work is produced as the student works through the course, yet may be submitted and marked either continuously or terminally; examinations assess the students' knowledge at a particular point of time on a particular topic.

- **Process vs. Product:** Assessments often result in a tangible *product*: a report, essay, painting, website, mathematical solution, etc. Instructors can assess this product, or the process the student goes through to create it (where much of their development occurs).

- **Internal vs. External:** The assessor who also teaches, tutors or assists the students on their course is *internal*; assessors who are divorced from the day to day learning, and simply assess the product or process are *external*.

- **Convergent vs. Divergent:** Assessments can elicit or reward *convergent* thinking (ie. thinking that arrives at a single well defined answer) or *divergent* thinking (that which uses creativity or imagination to develop several answers to a problem).

- **Idiographic vs. Nomothetic:** Idiographic assessments are those that consider the individual student by themselves, whereas nomothetic assessments consider the student in relation to other students, other cohorts, or other external markers. These broadly map onto formative and summative modes: formative assessment tends to tell students how they are performing in relation to their own previous work; whereas summative assessment usually uses nomothetic approaches such as grade schemes derived from external standards, awarding levels based on the relative performance of other students, etc.

This wide view of assessment is not shared by many practitioners within institutions, however. MacLellan (2001) found, in a study of 80 lecturers and 130 undergraduates, that both groups predominantly saw assessment as a means to grade or rank (83% staff, 82% students) and that essays and case notes were the dominant assessment forms. Other sectors have more variety, incorporating forms of continuous or portfolio-based assessment, but as Brown, Bull & Pendlebury (1997) note, assessment tends to have a dramatic effect on much of the learning students partake in, and so development of assessment approaches should be foremost in the minds of most educators, regardless of sector.

The role of assessment within an overall programme has also been scrutinised in the last quarter century with the increasing role of the *instructional design* movement in tertiary education (strong in the USA and Australasia, and becoming more prevalent now in Europe). *Constructive alignment* describes a closely linked three-part system that sees learning outcomes, teaching methods and assessment all parts of an integrated system (Biggs, 1999). Change one, and another must change too to keep in line. Historically, as Price, Carroll, O'Donovan and Rust (2010, p480) noted in their critique of current assessment practice, "*in practice one aspect of the model – that is teaching methods – is habitually privileged over the other two*"; increasingly though, the situation is being improved through benchmarking and audits - the QAA Quality Code referred to above will require constructive alignment across programmes by the time audits begin later this decade.

In the light of heightened interest in assessment, there has been a re-awakening of interest in assessment and feedback design, with practices developing more widely across the aspects Rowntree described. This is evidenced in approaches such as feed-forward or ipsative assessment (which both use feedback to encourage tailored individual development of students) and a wide range of other creative approaches that can be broadly grouped into cognitive assessment (assessing higher-order learning), performance assessment (measuring process or activity rather than an end result) and portfolio assessment (long-term collection and review of work to look at both the process and product) (Reeves, 2000). These new or reawakened forms are also being augmented by technological advances, either to improve administration, clarity and speed, or to utilise new media or approaches. In the UK, the Re-engineering Assessment Practices in Scottish Higher Education (REAP) project is collecting and documenting many of these for HE (JISC, 2011).

All of this converges to a current status in education, that sees the sector open to creative, well designed forms of assessment; and as the rest of this chapter aims to demonstrate, this provides a fertile platform on which to build some creative games-based approaches to learning and assessment.

Assessment in Games

In some ways games (as playful experiences) are polar opposites of more formal forms of assessment: one of the strengths of games is allowing students to make mistakes, learn from them, and try a different approach - without fear of being monitored or assessed as they play. However, almost all games already provide forms of both assessment and feedback; in fact that 'make mistakes, learn and improve' cycle is often encouraged and scaffolded by clever in-game feedback, helping the player to first learn how to play and then develop their skill as they move through the game.

Artefacts familiar in an assessment context are core to many games; points, levels and scoreboards / leader boards all have parallels in education. In games though, these are obvious, continuous (they are always there, always visible: *continuous* and *process* assessment from Rowntree's definitions), and help both the player and the game monitor progress or growing ability. In some cases this may be personal advancement; levels, in particular, are used as personal 'rewards' for performing various tasks or achieving certain points totals; rising in levels helps the player track their personal performance irrespective of any other players or opponents (a form of *idiographic* assessment). Whereas in others they may have a social or *nomothetic* element – comparisons of point scores on leader boards, for example. They tend to have a direct or indirect effect on success in the game (players need to either reach a particular score or level, or achieve a certain point in the game that will see the player generate a score or level as a side effect).

Levels and leader boards are interesting elements in themselves. There is much rhetoric, but little evidence, for the motivational value of such elements: although their more general role as indicators of reward was shown to provide external, rather than internal, motivation by Deci, Koestner & Ryan (2001); Whitton (2010a, p146) supports this view from her own work, adding that competitive elements alone may not be motivating for all, yet when communal aspects are included motivation to engage may be more widespread. The author's own work in this area (some of which is detailed in the case study later in this paper) suggests that leader boards used within an assessment context provide motivation to a majority of students - and don't appear to demotivate in this context.

Feedback too plays a large part in successful games; for example, Schell (2008, p230) notes that players get *"judgement, reward, instruction, encouragement and challenge"* from game feedback. Games tend to set up a balanced *feedback loop*,

combining both *positive* and *negative feedback*. Salen and Zimmerman (2004, p215) liken these processes to cybernetic systems: negative feedback circuits *"bringing the system to a steady state"* and positive feedback *"encourages the system to exhibit more and more extreme behaviour"*. Chris Hazard, a designer for Hazardous Software Ltd, gives a good example of negative feedback in a game:

Think of the racing games you may have played. If you've noticed that the computer players tend to perform better when you're winning, this is a typical example of negative feedback. This particular scenario is often referred to as the 'elastic band'; imagine a rubber band keeping the computer players with a certain distance of the lead. When negative feedback is done right, the player doesn't really notice and the game remains engaging and competitive.(Hazard, 2010).

Positive feedback, conversely, is when a particular effect is amplified (whether good or bad); for example, collecting five coins in a maze gives the player a special ability; or bumping into a wall the first three times causes minor injuries, but the fourth time breaks an arm. The two combine in many scenarios – think about that bridge which cannot be jumped across, or the 'boss' at the end of the level who cannot be defeated. Repeated plays (and deaths) give clues about how to approach it next time round, and each time gets a little bit easier or provides better and better rewards (keeping the player motivated to have 'just one more go: this time'). Feedback as a whole therefore helps to guide players through a game, learn its rules, and keep them engaged by matching the game to their own developing level of ability.

Contextual and Open

In-game assessment differentiates from formal assessment in education in two key areas: almost all of it is *contextual* and *open*. Points are awarded for completing particular actions vital to the gameplay (such as defeating enemies, collecting jewels, or reaching the end of levels) and are awarded instantaneously and obviously (players will see their score appear as soon as they complete the action, and be able to see its point value); they will receive immediate feedback if they approach a task incorrectly. Levels in role-playing style games are even more interesting: players gain *experience* through various in-character tasks to progress through levels, and as they do so they become more versed with the skills and attributes needed to be successful as that character. Experience points and levels therefore represent a true reflection of player development in the game role they have chosen.

These notions of *contextual* (always relating to the player's skills or activities in the game) and *open* (you see how much you score, when you score it) are important concepts when considering effective assessment in learning games. They link closely to the *formative, continuous, process* and *idiographic* aspects of assessment and feedback in education.

Gamification

Coined in 2003 by Nick Pelling for his consultancy firm Conundra, but gaining widespread interest by 2010 with mobile applications such as *Foursquare* (which provides points and badges for visiting and 'checking in' at certain locations) and a number of Facebook 'games' (like *Farmville*), *gamification* describes the "integration of *Game Mechanics* and game-thinking in *non-game* environments to boost *Engagement, Loyalty* and Fun!" (gamification.org).

However, as discussed above, an important aspect of points and scoring in games is their close relation to the gameplay, or *context* of the game; just taking the idea of points and scoring out of a game, and adding them to something that does not have similar gameplay elements (like mundane tasks or chores) might only transfer the limited

(and contested) inherent motivation of points and leader boards, and not the other powerful elements that, when combined, make them into a highly engaging game. Robertson (2010), a game designer with Hide & Seek, notes: "Points and badges have no closer a relationship to games than they do to websites and fitness apps and loyalty cards. They are great tools for communicating progress and acknowledging effort, but neither points nor badges in any way constitute a game". But she goes on to say "It's crucial that we stop conflating points and games. Firstly, because it devalues points. Points are great. So are badges... Game designers resort to them... so often because they're fantastic tools, and as with all tools there is real art and science behind deploying them well. They deserve to be studied, refined and adapted on their own terms, with their own vocabulary" (Robertson, 2010). She coined the term *pointsification* to better describe this use.

On this basis points in themselves have some useful applications within assessment in education. A growing number of applications built for or within education use pointsification to provide leader boards and badges for non-gaming activity. *750words.com* is a site that encourages writing, giving points every time you write something in a day, more points if you write 750 words, and bonuses/badges if you do this over many consecutive days – a simple reward system that is, effectively, assessing the quantity you write. The *Lemon Tree* project at the University of Huddersfield (Walsh, 2012) adds points and badge rewards for borrowing and reviewing books and other library resources, and has seen high levels of take-up and interest across the institution.

The University of Brighton introduced a novel way to engage students with the barrage of information they need as first year entrants (such as local town information, how much the printing costs, what a lecture is like). Packaging these snippets of information as online multiple choice questions, adding leader boards to keep track of students' scores, and (most effectively) adding grouping levels to the leader boards, resulted in high student engagement: divided into their houses, students played the game regularly to raise their group scores and beat rival houses. The *Never-Ending Uni Quiz* is unashamedly points-based (rather than games-based) but enjoys high levels of take-up (1,500 users after a year) and raises engagement amongst students. Moseley, Culver, Piatt, and Whitton (2009, p6) note:

Initial analysis of players' behaviour, and feedback, shows bursts of intense activity - often playing for over an hour in a session until a target (e.g. top of the leader board for their team) is achieved. The model of attaching a leader board to a 'standard' activity, such as an online multiple choice quiz, does seem to transform the activity into something substantially more motivating to players than without.

In his popular book Game Frame, Dignan (2011) proposes a theoretical framework that moves beyond pointsification, and aims to incorporate more gaming elements in other contexts (business training or informal child learning, for example) through the design of 'behavioural games', that follow a 10-step design process not dissimilar to game development. Although the case he makes is not yet grounded on any real success, the examples he takes from games and applies to real-world situations show potential and suggest that there may be a place for more considered gamification in wider contexts, including education.

The application of the game-derived ideas of points, leader boards and similarly engaging features therefore clearly has a role to play in education, and should not be discounted. But their use alone, without the *contextual* aspect that points have in games (although the examples above utilize the *open* aspect to good effect) does not make a game – and as such the levels of engagement and integration of game-with-subject are less than might be possible with a higher level of game-based input.

Game Based Learning and Assessment

In an education context, *game-based learning and assessment* could refer to several different things; focussing in, there are two distinct uses: (a) assessment of and within game-based learning activities, and (b) the use of games themselves as assessment tools. Whitton (2010) usefully categorised this range of use (see Table 1).

The matrix in Table 1 shows, for simplicity, two teaching methods: game-based and traditional (i.e. lectures, tutorials, seminars, etc.) and two assessment methods: in-game and external to the game. In-game refers to the built-in features of the game, such as scoring or levelling-up, that could be used to assess progress; external to the game refers to a variety of assessment methods that can potentially be integrated into or around a game-based learning scenario (such as a reflective discussion or written report after playing the game). In practice, courses may mix and match different teaching and assessment methods.

The discussion of assessment present within games (including pointsification) in the previous section all fits within the bottom row on the matrix; in an educational context, these features would provide in-game assessment. Whilst it can offer pedagogic advantages and certain benefits in administration and consistency of marking, game-based assessment is typically very poor at fostering reflection or meta-cognition around

Table 1. Forms of game based learning and assessment (Whitton, 2010)

		Teaching Method	
		Game-Based	**Traditional**
Assessment Method	External	Game-based learning and traditional assessment	Traditional learning and assessment
	In-game	Game-based learning and assessment	Traditional learning and game-based assessment

347

the learning process (there are no natural pauses or gaps, or accompanying instruction, in which such practice can be encouraged in traditional assessment). There may also be factors outside of the subject learning that affect game-based assessment (the students' engagement with the game, their skill or experience with some of the game mechanics, usability issues, etc.).

In-game assessment has been recognised as a useful tool, and has already been embedded within some existing learning games. Delacruz (2011) notes that *"one defining characteristic of games is that they evaluate the player"* and Michael & Chen (2005) discuss the use of analytics within games to determine the progress/learning choices of the student. They use PIXELearning, based in Coventry, UK, as an example: PIXELearning regularly incorporate in-game assessment of student performance within their games, including adjustments in the game and feedback to the student as they play. GlassLab, a non-profit organisation, are working with commerical game companies and educators to develop *SimCityEDU* which builds on the existing popular SimCity simulation game to provide specific assessed challenges in-game for students of STEM (Science, Technology, Engineering and Maths) subjects (Schwartz 2013).

In-game assessment of this type is often called *stealth assessment* (Shute, 2011): computer-based analytics and assessments that are built invisibly within the fabric of the game, and track the player's performance without them knowing. Although useful for contributing to *formal* and *summative* assessments, such 'secret' assessments are hidden entirely from the student, hence denying the student the *formative continuous* assessment and feedback they would need to help them improve as they play.

Traditional forms of assessment, in contrast to in-game forms, are equipped to capture a wide range of outputs, including reflection and critical thinking as well as knowledge-checking. When used most effectively, they allow a wider view of assessment as part of the learning process – building in feedback and development over a number of assessment points, and enabling application to other contexts. Core to this is the human factor: skilled tutors setting, marking and feeding back to individual students, enabling individually-structured development and support. There is therefore good reason to keep this predominant form of assessment in mind when designing assessments around learning games.

A COMBINED APPROACH

As discussed earlier, there is current bad practice in both game-based and traditional assessment: most students will have experienced poorly designed or lazy traditional assessment and feedback; and many may have experienced educational games that provide a meaningless score at the end of a learning task (or no feedback on performance at all). Equally, there is good practice in both of these areas, some examples of which were given above. There is potential, therefore, to utilise the best parts of both game-based and traditional assessment to create something better for students and tutors.

Key to any successful assessment strategy is careful design. From that basis, there are two ways in which game-based and traditional approaches can be combined to offer effective assessment. The first is to use a combination of in-game game-based assessment (quantitative, lower order tests utilising *formative*, *continuous* and *process* types) with external traditional assessment (adding higher order, qualitative elements, widening to other contexts, and covering the whole range of assessment types).

The second approach is to use what can be termed *implicit* assessment: assessment that is designed so closely with the game design, learning outcomes and wider course, that the lines are blurred between in-game and external. In this way the whole range of assessment methods can be utilised, with no apparent break or in-game/external split to the student. This approach is detailed later.

Designing External (Traditional) Assessment

Outside of the game, and often wrapped around the game (as a pre- or post- test activity), external assessment can draw from a wide range of traditional assessment types. For example:

- A questionnaire or group discussion before the game, to investigate existing subject knowledge or opinions.
- Reports on actions taken and decisions made in the game, with critical analysis of the consequences of decisions, or personal reflection on them.
- Creation of artefacts based on and extending the action in the game (e.g. posters, digital video, audio, graphics).
- Narratives associated with the action in the game (e.g. characterizations, back stories, future scenarios).
- Portfolios detailing the use of the game, decisions made, artefacts created, consequences and learning.

Developing in-Game Assessment

Assessment within games can map game elements directly to assessment techniques used in education. This is in contrast to the application of a layer or element over the top of the game itself (pointsification), although may include the use of in-game analytics. Developing such assessment is not as difficult as it might sound: most assessment systems within formal education allocate marks (out of 10, 100, or other nominal scales) to rate a student's performance in particular learning outcomes on a scale. There is little difference between this and awarding points for completing a particular action in a game, particularly as many games give more points for better efforts or higher achievements. The idea of progression too, where academic assessment gradually raises the bar to improve students' performance over the longer term (e.g. harder, or more critical, or more reflective, skills are required as the course or academic level progresses) has an almost direct parallel in certain games using levels or stages of increasing difficulty, where players are tested, and rewarded, at a higher level, as they progress through the game.

As discussed above, however, this is where the parallels tend to diverge. Points in games are awarded in real time, as players complete a task, and in direct relation to that task; feedback on the task is instantaneous; and new levels or stages are awarded as soon as the player achieves the required level - the notions of *contextual* and *open* that were introduced earlier. In contrast, formal assessment in education tends to be at certain fixed points within the course (usually at the end of a long period of learning), tends to assess many aspects of work within one assessment mark (such as content, style, grammar, understanding, critical awareness, reflection) and the majority of students progress to the next year or level of study together, at the same time.

There is no reason, though, why some of the *contextual* and *open* aspects of game scoring and feedback couldn't be utilised, and moulded to fit an educational context. In particular:

- **Contextual Assessment:** Designing assessment to match the subject or skills the students are learning. For example, on a business studies course, assess students' ability to produce reports or present to shareholders.
- **Open Assessment:** Marking students on particular activities *as they do them*, and on broken down scales (e.g. separate marks for content, style, etc. *or* a clear matching of the mark to a particular level of expertise, through a rubric or similar). This will provide immediate feedback on a particular activity and gives the option of opening up marks to a group and using leader boards or similar devices.

- **Negative Feedback:** Giving students gradually harder or easier tasks depending on their performance in the previous one (always pushing or scaffolding them a little more) - this would move beyond something like ipsative assessment (or feed-forward) by amending the assessments themselves in relation to the student. Difficult to achieve in formal assessment, although a proportion of an overall mark could be allocated to individualised targets provided each student's task has a similar level of difficulty in relation to their starting point.
- **Positive Feedback:** Already built in to many assessment schemes in a simplistic way (high scores in a number of courses result in a higher overall mark); this could be more creative and engaging: for example, learning several different skills or topics, or finding and analysing particular resources, gains a special mark, award or useful resource.

Some of these elements have already been used in educational environments (contextual assessment in particular, particularly in professionally-linked programmes: producing a business report in a Business Studies course, or a case history within a Medicine degree), but the redesign of assessment for a whole course by Lee Sheldon at Indiana University utilises several of them (Sheldon, 2011). Sheldon had the advantage that his course was *Multiplayer game design:* an easy subject to introduce contextual games approaches to, which would reduce the need to persuade staff and students of its academic suitability but nevertheless his approach (now in its fourth year of use) provides a working case study for the use of game concepts as assessment.

Instead of grades, Sheldon assigns *experience points* to his students for their academic work (experience points being the equivalent of gaining experience in the academic and practical sides of the subject); when students amass a certain number of experience points, they rise in *levels*. Well before the end of the course, students can see which level they are on (and what they need to do to rise in level), and so have far greater visibility of their progress (see Table 2). Extending the concept, Sheldon uses guilds rather than group work, and a variety of other games-based terms for course activities.

Sheldon's assessment design is interesting in the way that individual grades or experience are far less important than the gradually increasing levels – that help to show students that essays and other assessment points are just elements (or *side quests*) within the greater aim (or *campaign*) of development as experts in the subject.

Sheldon's use of game features pervades throughout the course, beyond assessment and into the day-to-day learning activities themselves, and so evaluation of the effectiveness of his approach is difficult to separate into distinct parts. In the first two iterations of his approach at Indiana University and Rensselaer Polytechnic Institute (RPI), both in the United States, average grades for the course rose from a C (before the approach was applied) to a B; and at RPI from a B to an A- (Sheldon 2011, p125), although Sheldon provides no detailed

Table 2. Assessment grades based on experience points (Sheldon 2011)

Level	Experience Points	Grade
12	1860	A
11	1800	A-
10	1740	B+
9	1664	B
8	1600	B-
7	1540	C+
6	1460	C
5	1400	C-
4	1340	D+
3	1260	D
2	1200	D-
1	0	F

analysis of the affect the assessment alone had on his classes. Other institutions who adopted *only* the assessment approach also found a small increase in grade score following its introduction: Valencia Community College History department saw a rise from an average grade of 59.9% to 66.7% (Sheldon 2011, p179); and Marked Tree High School Biology department saw the percentage of high-scoring students increase markedly: a rise from 62% to 98% of students passing with a grade D or higher, with 36% scoring A to B - up from 10% previously (Sheldon 2011, p55-56). None of these studies are yet detailed enough to identify particular elements of success or prove the approach beyond doubt, but there clearly seems to be some benefit to adopting game-like elements within an assessment structure across a number of disciplines.

Implicit Assessment

The use of game concepts as a way to rethink assessment design and make it more relevant and useful for students is a compelling one, moving on from simple pointsification and approaching what might be termed *implicit assessment*: assessment that is woven into the subject and students' activities so closely that it becomes a natural part of the activity (differing from stealth assessment in that the assessment is not hidden: it is embedded so deeply as to become part of the learning game).

Full *implicit assessment* can be obtained when games-based approaches are applied to the course as a whole, assessment included. More than a combination of game-based learning and traditional assessment, this approach uses game concepts alongside traditional learning and teaching concepts during the course design phase, so that the resulting teaching, learning and assessment are invisibly entwined.

The author undertook this implicit design process for a course designed four years ago at the University of Leicester, the *Great History Conundrum*, or GHC: a module that teaches critical research skills to 200 History undergraduates. Puzzles that introduce students to real-life research problems are solved for points, and further points are obtained by discussing the puzzles and research issues within a group discussion board. Gradually, the students collect knowledge and techniques and build them into a shared Wiki, that they can use as a reference in their continuing studies.

Assessment design played a key part in the development of this course and, most crucially, was designed at the beginning along with the gameplay. The following key principles were used when considering the assessment methods:

- Students should be assessed on real and identifiable activity and should know what is required of them for a particular score.
- Students should receive immediate or close-to-immediate feedback on their activity.
- Students should be able to select a level and type of activity comfortable to them at the start of the course and be able to choose an appropriate development path through it; this should be supported, not hindered, by assessment.
- Students should know at all times what their current achievement level is and what they need to attain for success.
- The assessment types should accommodate different learning styles, using Kolb's (2004) converger, diverger, assimilator and accommodator as models.

Notice that many of these draw from the four game concepts outlined above (*contextual* and *open* assessment, and *positive* and *negative* feedback).

From these principles, the following assessment design was produced, using a simple approach: think about scoring systems used in games, think about the skills and activity to be assessed, and then think of the most direct way to link these together.

351

Assessment is linked directly to the three main areas of the activity, and marks are awarded continuously as it progresses:

- Each puzzle carries a points total indicative of its level of difficulty (1–10): when successfully solved, these points are immediately added to a student's *puzzle score*, which is their assessed mark for this aspect of the course. This direct link between assessment score and higher points for higher difficulty, that comes directly from games, means that students immediately see both the difficulty *and* value of the puzzle to their overall assessment/development. It also means the students can self-select their difficulty level - they may choose to start with 1 or 2 point puzzles, but will realise that to achieve a pass mark of 40% they will need to attempt some 4, 5, 6+ point puzzles before too long. When they attempt the higher levels, and how many puzzles they attempt, is up to the individual student (which provides flexibility for different learning styles). In a post-course survey 56% of students liked the open, continuous aspects of the assessment, with 25% wanting all marks on the course to be delivered in this same way (see Figure 1).

- Once they have solved a puzzle (or if they are stuck on one), students are encouraged to post hints, resources, or requests for help within a group discussion forum. Each forum post is marked with brief feedback by a postgraduate moderator within 24 hours of posting, based on a visible rubric that awards higher marks for increasing depth of understanding and critical thinking. These marks are added to the student's *discussion score*, that is their assessed mark for this aspect of the course. The visible rubric, swift marking and supportive feedback by the moderators, means that students are always aware of what they

Figure 1. Student views on the continuous and open assessment within the GHC (n=45)

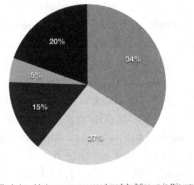

- I really like being able to see my assessed mark building up in this way
- It didn't go far enough: I would have liked my Wiki marks up front as well
- It wasn't clear how my scores were linked to my final mark, so was confusing
- I prefer a single assessed mark at end of course, rather than continuous assessment
- No response

need to do to be successful in the subject and how to develop to the higher levels. Like the puzzle marks, they are also being marked directly, and openly, on a specific contextual activity.

- Each student's current puzzle score and discussion score are visible at all times on the student's GHC home page (instantly updated) and also on an overall leader board, where they can see where they lie alongside friends and peers in the cohort. The top three students in puzzle and discussion scores at the end of the course receive prizes. This open leader board is designed to provide competitive and potentially motivating elements to the course (from game design principles). In practice, this was found to be somewhat true: students voted this the fourth most motivating aspect of the course behind open assessment, puzzle solving and collaboration, and above the grand prizes and forum activity (see Table 3), and each year sees a big rise in activity on the final 2-3 days as students try to raise their place on the leader board above friends and peers (see Figure 2: the other smaller peaks relate to a weekly newsletter

Table 3. Student responses on the most motivating aspects of the GHC. A score of 1 is the most motivating; 5 is the least (n=106).

Aspect of the GHC	Motivation Score
Assessment score/passing the module	1.49
Getting and solving new puzzles	2.81
Working with other students on problems	2.93
Checking my position on the leader boards	3.18
Checking the forums regularly	3.42
Aiming for the grand prizes	4.62

that is sent each Friday containing the latest leader boards and hints and tips). The leader board has a secondary advantage: it shows a combined average for the puzzle and discussion scores, that gives the student a current aggregate score for the whole course. In this way, students get an obvious indication that they can specialise in either puzzles or discussion (as befits their learning style) and yet arrive at the same final mark as a friend who specialised the other way round.

• The group-produced Wikis form the final portion of assessment. These are marked by teaching staff within the department,

to a visible rubric, and a group mark and feedback provided to all students who contributed to the Wiki. This assessment is more traditional, in that it marks a final product and is awarded around a week after the students submit. In many ways the inclusion of this alongside the other open/immediate assessment helped to give the course a 'trustworthy' academic grounding in the department, although it also fits well alongside the initial principles, as the activity and method of assessment models a 'research group output', namely the production and assessment of a final resource.

In this way the course, game and assessment were all designed as a single entity: making the assessment *implicit* to the gameplay.

The course has now run for five years, adjusted in response to student feedback each year, and in the last four years (see Table 4) at least 98% of students have successfully passed the course, with an average of 75% achieving grades over 60%: dramatic increases in the grade averages from years before the GHC was introduced (undocumented, but an idea can be obtained by comparing to 2008 figures that represent a hybrid approach from the old course to the new). What is most revealing is the average puzzle mark in the years 2010-2012:

Figure 2. Student activity over the four week course

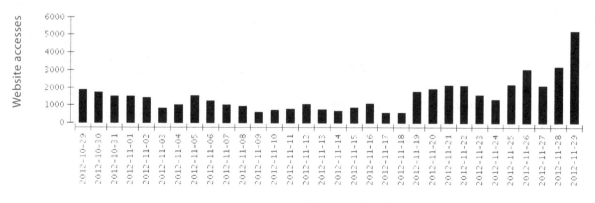

Table 4. Student performance on the GHC, 2008-2012

Year	2008%	2009%	2010%	2011%	2012%
Average mark (puzzles)	80	91	108	127	105
Average mark (discussion)	52	70	79	74	85
Average mark (Wiki)	58	61	62	58	59
Average overall mark	55	68	74	70	68
% passed (40%+)	86	99	98	98	98
% passed at over 60%	36	70	82	76	74

the average student is solving more puzzles than are needed to obtain a full 100% of this element; in other words, they are engaged enough to continue playing even when they know they are not receiving credit for their actions.

Based on the evidence to date, this *implicit* approach to assessment within a learning game, from design through to year-on-year evaluation and development, is providing students with a useful, engaging approach: the open and continuous aspects are preferred to more traditional methods by a majority of students, and some of the game design elements (feedback through open assessment and the leader boards) show high levels of engagement.

FUTURE RESEARCH DIRECTIONS

Although the case study presented describes one successful application of this approach, more work is needed before the implicit assessment design approach can be shown to work across different contexts. In particular, more research is needed into the effect of leader boards, points and other game design elements on engagement and motivation

within educational contexts: whether as part of a game or as separate, applied elements.

The novelty value of new forms of assessment and learning experiences should not be underestimated. Although the case studies presented in this chapter all show aspects of increased engagement amongst students, none take place over more than a single course: would similar levels of engagement and satisfaction occur if students were to experience games-based forms of assessment throughout a whole year, or whole programme? On a more realistic level, research into the use of games-based assessment within two or more courses for the same students on the same programme, noting changes in performance and engagement, would be of value.

CONCLUSION

When using games within a learning environment where there is also a need to assess performance in that environment, a range of different assessment strategies can be adopted: *in-game*, *external* to the game, and fully integrated between the game and the overarching course or programme (*implicit*).

This chapter has discussed the options and methods for each of these assessment modes. In each case, four approaches drawn from game design principles can be used alone or in combination to make assessment as effective and engaging as scoring or levelling up in a well-designed game: *contextual* and *open* assessment, and *negative* and *positive* feedback.

The discussion and case study demonstrate that there is no reason to approach assessment in games for learning any differently to assessment on traditional academic programmes: by thinking about the learner context, learning outcomes, the course, the game(s) and assessment together, games become fully integrated into the learning experience - to the benefit of the learner. Additionally, the use of game design features in an integrated way can lead to increased student engagement.

More work is, however, needed in this area. Does an implicit approach to assessment work in all learning contexts, or are there limitations? The need to understand more about the motivational aspects of game design elements such as leader boards, points and levels also remains.

REFERENCES

Biggs, J. (1996). Enhancing teaching through constructive alignment. *Higher Education, 32*, 1–18. doi:10.1007/BF00138871.

Biggs, J. (1999). *Teaching for quality learning at university*. Buckingham, UK: SRHE and Open University Press.

Black, P., Harrison, C., & Lee, C. (2003). *Assessment for learning: putting it into practice*. New York: Open University Press.

Brown, G., Bull, J., & Pendlebury, M. (1997). *Assessing student learning in higher education*. London: Routledge.

Deci, E., Koestner, R., & Ryan, R. (2001). Extrinsic rewards and intrinsic motivations in education: Reconsidered once again. *Review of Educational Research, 71*(1), 1–27. doi:10.3102/00346543071001001.

Dignan, A. (2011). *Game frame: Using games as a strategy for success*. New York: Simon & Schuster.

Hazard, C. (2010). *Feedback in games design*. [Blog post]. Retrieved January 20, 2013 from http://blog.wolfire.com/2010/04/Feedback-In-Game-Design

JISC. (2011). *Re-engineering assessment practices in Scottish higher education (REAP)*. Retrieved January 20, 2013 from http://www.jisc.ac.uk/whatwedo/programmes/elearningsfc/reap.aspx

Kolb, D. A. (1984). *Experiential learning: Experience as the source of learning and development*. Englewood Cliffs, NJ: Prentice-Hall.

MacLellan, E. (2001). Assessment for learning: The differing perceptions of tutors and students. *Assessment & Evaluation in Higher Education, 26*(4), 307–318. doi:10.1080/02602930120063466.

Michael, D., & Chen, S. (2005). *Proof of learning: Assessment in serious games*. [Blog post]. Retrieved April 14th, 2013 from http://www.gamasutra.com/view/feature/2433/proof_of_learning_assessment_in_.php

Moseley, A., Culver, J., Piatt, K., & Whitton, N. (2009). *Motivation in alternate reality gaming environments and implications for learning*. Paper presented at the 3rd European Conference on Games Based Learning. Graz, Austria.

NSS. (2011). *NSS 2010 shows continued high levels of satisfaction among higher education undergraduate students*. Retrieved January 20, 2013 from http://www.hefce.ac.uk/news/hefce/2010/nssresult.htm

Price, M., Carroll, J., O'Donovan, B., & Rust, C. (2011). If I was going there I wouldn't start from here: A critical commentary on current assessment practice. *Assessment & Evaluation in Higher Education, 36*(4), 479–492. doi:10.1080/02602930903512883.

QAA. (2011). *Chapter B6: Assessment of students and accreditation of prior learning*. Gloucester, UK: The UK Quality Code for Higher Education.

Reeves, T. C. (2000). Alternative approaches for online learning environments in higher education. *Journal of Educational Computing Research, 23*(1), 101–111. doi:10.2190/GYMQ-78FA-WMTX-J06C.

Robertson, M. (2010). *Can't play, won't play*. [Blog post]. Retrieved January 20, 2013 from http://www.hideandseek.net/2010/10/06/cant-play-wont-play/

Rowntree, D. (1987). *Assessing students: How shall we know them?* New York: Taylor & Francis.

Salen, K., & Zimmerman, E. (2004). *Rules of play: Game design fundamentals.* Cambridge, MA: MIT Press.

Schell, J. (2008). *The art of game design: A book of lenses.* San Francisco, CA: Morgan Kaufmann.

Schwartz, K. (2013). *SimCityEDU: Using games for formative assessment.* [Blog post]. Retrieved April 4, 2013 from http://blogs.kqed.org/mindshift/2013/03/video-games-as-assessment-tools-game-changer/

Sheldon, L. (2011). *Gaming the classroom: Syllabus.* Retrieved January 20, 2013 from http://gamingtheclassroom.wordpress.com/syllabus/

Shute, V. J. (2011). Stealth assessment in computer-based games to support learning. In S. Tobias, & J. D. Fletcher (Eds.), *Computer games and instruction* (pp. 503–524). Charlotte, NC: Information Age.

Walsh, A. (2012). *Final report on lemon tree, May 2012.* Retrieved April 4, 2013 from http://www.hud.ac.uk/tali/projects/tl_projects_11/lemon_tree/

Whitton, N. (2010a). *Assessment of game-based learning.* Retrieved January 24, 2013 from http://www.transformingassessment.com/events_27_october_2010.php

Whitton, N. (2010b). *Learning with digital games: A practical guide to engaging students in higher education. New York, NY.* Abingdon: Routledge.

KEY TERMS AND DEFINITIONS

Continuous Assessment: Small assessments that occur at regular, or numerous, points within a process.

Contextual Assessment: Assessment linked directly to the context of the subject or students being assessed.

Idiographic Assessment: Assessments that consider the individual student, by themselves.

Implicit Assessment: Assessment designed so closely with the game design, learning outcomes and wider course, that the lines are blurred between in-game and external.

Gamification: The use of Game Mechanics and game-thinking in non-game environments.

Nomothetic Assessment: Assessments that consider the student in relation to other students, other cohorts, or other external markers.

Open Assessment: Assessment which is visible to students; usually linked to continuous assessment.

Process Assessment: Assessment that considers the work done towards a final product, rather than the final product.

Chapter 17
A Brief Methodology for Researching and Evaluating Serious Games and Game-Based Learning

Igor Mayer
Delft University of Technology, The Netherlands

Geertje Bekebrede
Delft University of Technology, The Netherlands

Harald Warmelink
Delft University of Technology, The Netherlands

Qiqi Zhou
Delft University of Technology, The Netherlands

ABSTRACT

In this chapter, the authors present a methodology for researching and evaluating Serious Games (SG) and digital (or other forms of) Game-Based Learning (GBL). The methodology consists of the following elements: 1) frame-reflective analysis; 2) a methodology explicating the rationale behind a conceptual-research model; 3) research designs and data-gathering procedures; 4) validated research instruments and tools; 5) a body of knowledge that provides operationalised models and hypotheses; and 6) professional ethics. The methodology is intended to resolve the dilemma between the "generality" and "standardisation" required for comparative, theory-based research and the "specificity" and "flexibility" needed for evaluating specific cases.

DOI: 10.4018/978-1-4666-4773-2.ch017

Copyright © 2014, IGI Global. Copying or distributing in print or electronic forms without written permission of IGI Global is prohibited.

INTRODUCTION

The growing interest in digital and other forms of game-based learning (GBL), serious games and simulation gaming (both abbreviated as SG) is accompanied by an increasing need to know the effects of what we are doing and promoting (Mayer, Bekebrede et al., 2013; Mayer, Warmelink, & Bekebrede, 2012). Meeting this need requires proper methods, tools and principles that can be agreed upon, validated and applied by the fragmented GBL and SG communities. In other words, we must move towards a 'science of game-based learning' (Sanchez, Cannon-Bowers, & Bowers, 2010). Considerable efforts and resources are currently being devoted to researching and evaluating SG and GBL, thereby increasing both the number and the quality of such evaluations (see discussion below). Considerable weaknesses remain, however, including the following:

- A lack of comprehensive, multipurpose frameworks for comparative, longitudinal evaluation (Blunt, 2006; Meyer, 2010; Mortagy & Boghikian-Whitby, 2010; Vartiainen, 2000.)
- Few theories with which to formulate and test hypotheses (Mayer, 2005; Noy, Raban, & Ravid, 2006.)
- Few operationalised models with which to examine 'causal' relations (e.g. in structural equation models) (Connolly, Stansfield, & Hainey, 2009; Hainey, 2011; Hainey & Connolly, 2010.)
- Few validated questionnaires, constructs or scales, whether from other fields (e.g. psychology) or constructed especially for SG and GBL (Boyle, Connolly, & Hainey, 2011; Brockmyer et al., 2009; Mayes & Cotton, 2001.)
- A lack of proper research designs that can be used in dynamic, professional learning contexts other than that of the less preferable randomised controlled trials

(RCT), which are impractical, unethical and uncommon in almost every domain except medicine, therapy and related fields (Connolly, Boyle, MacArthur, Hainey, & Boyle, 2012; Kato, Cole, Bradlyn, & Pollock, 2008; Knight et al., 2010; Szturm, Betker, Moussavi, Desai, & Goodman, 2011; van der Spek, Wouters, & Van Oostendorp, 2011; van der Spek, 2011.)
- The absence of generic tools for unobtrusive ('stealth') data-gathering and assessment in and around SG (Kickmeier-Rust, Steiner, & Albert, 2009; Shute, Masduki, & Donmez, 2010; Shute, Ventura, Bauer, & Zapata-Rivera, 2009; Shute, 2011.)

In short, despite a promising increase in publications, methods, tools and findings, we continue to lack an overarching methodology for SG research. The fragmented SG and GBL community faces the enormous challenge of aligning itself in order to evaluate and research gaming for learning in a comparative, systematic fashion using procedures, frameworks and methods that can be validated, checked and reproduced. It is valuable to identify the effects of playing games through randomised, controlled trials (RCT), many of which involve students in laboratories. Nevertheless, it is also essential to identify the effects of GBL and SG in uncontrolled circumstances and within the context of objectives that truly matter for real-life performance (e.g. emergency management, leadership), as is usually the case in professional learning and training. The challenge is to gather data on the quality, application and outcomes of a broad range of SG on different topics and with different objectives, within and for different institutional contexts, at different times and under uncontrolled conditions.

Research Objective

The objective of this chapter is to present a condensed methodology for researching and evaluating SG and GBL. The methodology comprises a framework, conceptual models, research designs, data-gathering techniques, hypothesis formulation, directions for developing and using evaluation constructs and scales, and procedures for testing structural equation models. The methodology is derived from the results of a long-term research project (2005-2013) involving the systematic, uniform and quantitative evaluation of several hundred SG sessions with 12 SG, aimed at creating a dataset containing information on 2 500 respondents in higher education or work organisations. Our ambition is to resolve the dilemma between the generality and standardisation required for comparative, longitudinal, theory-based research and the specificity and flexibility needed for evaluating singular cases.

IN SEARCH OF A METHODOLOGY

A social scientific discipline of SG research should comprise the following elements (see Figure 1):

- **Frame-Reflective Analysis:** The multiple, often conflicting ways in which we perceive and discuss SG and GBL (Chong & Druckman, 2007; Shaffer, 2006; Squire, 2001.)
- **Methodology:** The rationale and principles upon which a conceptual model for SG and GBL research is founded (Lawson & Lawson, 2010; Mackenzie & Knipe, 2006.)
- **Research Designs and Data-Gathering Procedures:** What works, why and when? (De Vaus, 2001; Schneider, 2005.)
- **Validated Research Instruments and Tools:** Questionnaires, surveys and instruments for logging and tracking SG and GBL, including their validation, for SG and GBL (Boyle et al., 2011; Brockmyer et al., 2009; Chertoff, Goldiez, & LaViola,

2010; Egenfeldt-Nielsen, 2006a; Mayes & Cotton, 2001; Wright, 2009.)
- **A dynamic body of knowledge** identifying the state of the art and knowledge gaps leading to research questions, operationalised models, hypotheses for testing (Janssen & Klievink, 2010; Ma, Williams, Prejean, & Richard, 2007; Raphael, Bachen, Lynn, Baldwin-Philippi, & McKee, 2009; Young et al., 2012.)
- **Professional ethics** for SG researchers, professionals and users (Babbie, 2007; Chandler & Torbert, 2003; Kimmel, 1988.)

There is a great need for such a discipline, for the following reasons:

- **Accountability:** 'Users' (clients, players, learners) are increasingly becoming exposed to and familiar with SG. They have the right to know what they are actually buying, using or playing, and they are entitled to insight into the reasons for and the effects or consequences of the application of SG and gamification. We also expect that users will become more demanding, critical and sceptical.
- **Responsibility:** This is the opposite of accountability. A discipline that advocates the use of SG and gamification to repair a broken reality (McGonigal, 2011), especially in contexts involving vulnerable groups in society (e.g. children, patients, immigrants), has a great responsibility to engage in critical reflection on the short-term and long-term value and structural consequences of the gamification tools that they are developing, promoting and using.

In this chapter, we discuss the design of the methodology with regard to the aforementioned six blocks of methodology (see Figure 1.)

Figure 1. Building blocks for a science of SG and GBL

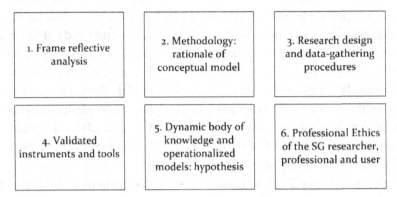

FRAME-REFLECTIVE ANALYSIS

For any emerging science or methodology, it is necessary to provide a clear specification of the locus and focus of its research. One way to accomplish this is to provide clear definitions and/or develop classifications and taxonomies (Göbel, 2010; Jantke, 2010; Krathwohl, Bloom, & Betram, 1973; Maier & Grössler, 2000; Sawyer, 2008). Words can have different meanings, depending upon the disciplinary backgrounds in which they are used, the interests upon which they are based and other aspects. 'Learning', 'serious games', 'effectiveness', 'evaluation', 'research' and similar concepts can easily become a source of confusion or disagreement for different sub-communities. Definitions or taxonomies are generally problematic, however, especially in newly emerging and highly interdisciplinary research disciplines like SG, for the following reasons:

- 'Anti-essentialists' have argued that 'games' cannot be defined (Rockwell & Kee, 2011; Wittgenstein, 1953.)
- Definitions and taxonomies of SG and GBL are '*political*'. They have a tendency to exclude diverging views from access to resources (e.g. funding and publication).
- Definitions and taxonomies kill innovation. By definition, new combinations (Schumpeter's *neue combinationen*) do not fit into any of the boxes of taxonomy.
- Definitions and taxonomies *reify*. They focus on games as things and not on experiences. Reification does not promote a critical discourse about the underlying worldviews and assumptions.

In our view, *framing theory* (Benford & Snow, 2000; Fisher, 1997; Giddens, 1988; Scheufele, Iyengar, Kenski, Hall, & Eds, 2002) and frame-reflective (discourse) analysis (Adams & Goffman, 1979; Hart, 2008) can provide some necessary foundations for an emerging scientific discipline of SGs research. As noted above, words can take on different meanings when used in different contexts, possibly generating confusion or disagreement within research communities. Framing is the act of attributing meaning to events and phenomena. It is a way in which to create order out of chaos by providing critical analysis of the multiple, often conflicting ways in which we perceive and discuss particular topics, including the utility of games in society, business and politics. In addition to definitions and taxonomies, it is important to develop a better understanding of the frames that people construct and use when addressing and answering the following questions:

- Does frequent playing of digital games affect leadership styles, preferences for team collaboration, motor skills and other characteristics?
- Are games effective as interventions designed for change or learning (e.g. at school, work or in therapy, healthcare or the military)?
- How is innovation achieved in the game industry, and what can other businesses learn from these practices (Kim & Kim, 2011)?
- Can games promote (sell) products and services or influence ideas and beliefs?
- Can the use of game principles or game technology help societal and political communities and institutions to organise themselves or improve their self-organisation (Zichermann & Linder, 2010)?

Frame Analysis

A frame is "an instrument for defining reality", as opposed to "an instrument for describing reality" (Donati 1992 in Fisher, 1997: 5.4). Frames are neither mutually exclusive nor easily suited to specific individuals. They exist in parallel, and many researchers (including the authors) implicitly or explicitly switch frames or adopt several frames simultaneously. Other constructs closely resemble frames, including 'lenses' and 'belief systems'. In sociology, frame analysis (FA) originates in Goffman's (1974) sociological theory and studies on the organisation of experiences:

I assume that definitions of a situation are built up in accordance with principles of organization which govern events – at least social ones – and our subjective involvement in them; [...] that is my definition of a frame. [...] frame analysis is a slogan to refer to the examination of the organization of experience (Goffman, 1974:11).

In other words, frame analysis is a reflection on "how people understand an issue, and to track

the way in which this understanding changes over time" (Fisher, 1997, 6.2).

One appropriate question therefore concerns the dominant frames through which researchers currently view and discuss the utility of games for society, business and politics. Another question concerns how framing lays the foundation for a methodology of SG research. In the following subsections, we discuss:

- Frames on SG.
- Frames on learning.
- Frames on research.

Frames on SG

Any science of SG and any methodology for SG research should reflect upon the assumptions underlying its ontology (being) and epistemology (knowing). A detailed discussion of the philosophy of science would obviously exceed the scope of this chapter. For our purposes, we need only define two 'drivers' with which to construct four frames on the utility of games (see Table 1.)

1. Whether the world as we know it is more likely to be real (ontological realism) or constructed (ontological idealism): If the world is real, we are more likely to be able to observe it, measure it and come as close as possible to understanding it as it really is. If it is rooted in our ideas (mind), we

Table 1. Four frames

	Interventionism - Decisionism	Evolutionism - Determinism
Realism; Empiricism	I. SG = Tool, therapy, drug Example: Healseeker	II. SG = Creative innovation Example: Ford Virtual factor
Idealism; Phenomenology	III. SG = Persuasion Example: PING, Wikileaks	IV. SG = Self-organization. Example: Foldit

can only explore and try to understand our relationship to the world as we think it is, expanding our understanding through interaction with others who may think differently (phenomenology).

2. How we consider change in the world (and in 'ourselves' within it): If we assume that the subject ('I'/'we') can exercise some degree of control in changing its environment, we acknowledge 'interventionism'. We then assume that we can 'decide' (build, construct, repair, steer) parts of the world in which we live as we see fit. If we assume that actual change is less the creation of one or several individuals than it is the emergent result of

various intentional and unintentional forces within a system, we accept a type of 'evolutionism' or 'determinism'. The system is assumed to influence the subjects to a much greater extent than the subject can influence the system.

We thus construct a two-dimensional space in which we place four frames on the utility of games or SG (see Table 2). We discuss these frames in the sections below.

- **SG as Tool, Therapy:** This frame reflects the majority and most frequently cited examples of SG for a wide range of purposes

Table 2. Frame-reflective discourse analysis

	Interventionism - Decisionism	Evolutionism - Determinism
Realism; **Empiricism**	**I. SG = Tool, therapy, drug**	**II. SG = Creative innovation**
	Positive claims: Effectiveness	Positive claims: Effectiveness, innovation (€)
	Gaming is a more effective, better means of learning, training and supporting decisions.	global economic race;
	Likely criticism: Lack of Proof	Gaming = Innovation in economic sectors
	Show me the evidence.	Likely criticism:
	Are we teaching the right things?	Disturbance, over-optimism, side effects;
	Possible negative effects (e.g. aggression, addiction)?	risks to industrial policy (subsidies, protection)
Idealism; **Phenomenology**	**III. SG = Persuasion**	**IV. SG = Self-organization.**
	Positive claims: Persuasion	Positive claims: Playfulness
	Games are rhetorical; they can convince or change the ideas and beliefs of players, consumers and citizens.	Ludification/gamification of society, organisation, politics, leadership, management
	Likely criticism: Manipulation	Likely criticism: Inequality, social-economic exclusion
	Risk of manipulation, abuse of power, hidden agendas and ideologies	What are the consequences for society and power
	Battle of Ideologies	gap between generations, rich/poor, nations?

(e.g. therapy, education, health, decision-making, training). Through this frame, we see a 'thing' that can be measured, indexed and taxonomised. In other words, we see a 'tool' that might or might not work (De Caluwé, Hofstede & Peters, 2008). The language in this frame is pervaded with words like 'effectiveness', 'efficacy', randomised controlled trials (RCTs) and 'evidence-based'. The tool itself is measured in terms of 'metrics' and its effects in terms of 'analytics'. Especially within the context of health, it is treated as a new type of therapy, the effectiveness of which must be assessed in clinical trials (Fernández-Aranda et al., 2012). Research revolves around the question of whether games offer a more effective tool for learning, education, health and training. Proponents do their best to prove it and understand how that works. Opponents might argue that game-play does not work, that there is inconclusive evidence or even that it has countervailing effects, like addiction (see Table 3). Watching the healseeker game (Healseeker|Yulius Academie, n.d.) and reading its documentation, it is interesting to note how the words used by the designers, researchers and sponsors reflect a medical frame (Kato et al., 2008), directed towards the search for scientific evidence that patients (in this case, young children with ADHD) might improve by playing the game.

- **SG as Creative Innovation:** From this frame, we see SGs as a part of evolutionary change, and especially as a significant factor in the competitive race among nations, regions, companies and even individuals. The argument in this frame is that the phenomenon of digital games is built upon highly competitive business models that might be more suitable for Society 2.0 and that the games are surrounded by tech-

nological innovation, creativity and other processes that could generate a competitive advantage in design, production and organisation (Nieborg, 2011; Schrage, 2000). Failure to use game technology, game principles or related resources comes close to stepping out of the race. The arguments of a great many policymakers and business leaders are derived from within this frame, promoting SG as 'a way to the future' or 'a chance for innovation'. Watching and reading the case of the FORD virtual reality factory (Virtual Reality at Ford Motor Company, n.d.), it is interesting to note that it is presented as an almost unavoidable and self-evident innovation. If the company does not go virtual, others will, and the company will lose its competitive advantage. Whereas games like Healseeker are aimed at curing and repairing that which is broken, games within this frame aim to build a new future. Many examples from national or EU policy documents (e.g. on the creative industries or innovation policy) can illustrate how this frame colours the ways in which policymakers interpret SG. Obvious criticisms concern the relative novelty, validity and uniqueness of this view on games as 'creative innovation' or 'competitive advantage'. Research issues revolve around understanding the principles of creativity and innovation in and around games (and the game industry) and finding ways to utilise it. Counterarguments might assert that the political-economic support for the creative-game industry promotes incumbent winners while eliminating true innovators and entrepreneurs.

- **SG as Persuasion:** From this frame, we see the world as engaged in a power struggle of beliefs and ideas. Games are a powerful new means of communication, and an even more powerful means of persuasion and rhetoric (Bogost, 2007a). This can be used for selling products or services (e.g. advergames, many forms of gamification, games for branding), as well as for effecting change in social behaviour (e.g. bullying prevention) or political ideas. Examples of such SG are numerous. Some of these SG, like September 12 (Frasca, 2007), are well-known and have put a mark on the debate about SG. Many others (e.g. the Wikileaks examples) are known only within small communities. The vast majority have simple, non-engaging game-play, although their procedural rhetoric remains very clear and strong (Bogost, 2007). The development of relatively complicated games has been driven by a few large institutions and companies, including America's Army (AA; Nieborg, 2004) and €conomia (€conomia, n.d.). In our view, the case of PING (Poverty Is Not A Game (PING), n.d.) falls somewhere between Frame I and Frame III. In its presentation, however, it contains much of the rhetoric of intervened social change (i.e. making children aware of poverty). Although researchers have investigated the types of ideas that are expressed through games, most studies focus primarily on how discourses in society respond to such games and ideas, on whether and how they influence the discourse in society or certain communities, and on how this works.

- **SG as Self-Organisation:** Through this frame, we see games as part of an evolution in society and cultures at large. Adherents argue that we are witnessing the ludification (Raessens, 2006, 2009) of cultures, due to the growing pervasiveness of digital games, especially amongst the younger generation. Ludification (or gamification) affects the ways in which people organise and interact in everyday life (e.g. in social-political-cultural life or at work). For many, this cultural change might be subtle, slow

and unnoticed. It might also become submerged in self-organising communities on the web or in our efforts to gamify science by using games to organise crowd sourcing or political participation. One of the best examples of SG as self-organisation is Foldit (Cooper et al., 2010). Although some researchers attempt to explain ludification within this frame, most try to find and exploit game principles for self-organisation as part of gamification (A World without Oil, McGonigal, 2011). Critics might argue that ludification and gamification could potentially create a new divide based upon access to and literacy in digital games. Furthermore, a wide range of ethical questions exists with regard to the use of games for self-organisation (e.g. in the work place.)

Frames on Learning

There are numerous frames (theories, models) for learning. Although space limitations prevent us from reconstructing them in this chapter, SG research reflects a strong bias towards 'individual', 'educational' learning. We would like to draw attention to the fact that games are connected to other forms of learning (not restricted to education), including the various forms of learning systems.

System change can be brought about by uncontrollable, external factors (e.g. disasters, crises) or as the result of internal, intentional processes (i.e. learning) that are intended to improve control over the system's environment. The first type of change can trigger the second; failure to learn can cause the first.

Systems and system boundaries can obviously be established in different ways and at different levels (e.g. individual, group, organisation, society). In other words, individuals are not the only parties that learn; groups, organisations and societies learn as well. Many theories have been developed on group, organisational and system learning (Argyris & Schön, 1974; Argyris, 1977; Meadows, 1999; Senge, Roberts, & Ross, 1994; Senge, 1990; Sweeney & Meadows, 2001).

Individuals (e.g. students) are thus not the only parties that can learn from playing games; systems and organisations can also learn through playing and gaming (Schrage, 2000). For this reason, SG can be used as deliberate interventions to change the performance of groups, organisations or systems (Duke & Geurts, 2004; Mayer & Veeneman, 2002). They can also be used to foster public awareness and critical discourse concerning particular issues (Bogost, 2007; Rebolledo-Mendez, Avramides, & de Freitas, 2009.)

The emerging discipline of GBL is roughly segregated into 'SG for education' and 'simulation games for societal and organisational change'. Relationships between the individual and system levels of GBL and SG are insufficiently understood (Argyris, 1977, 1982, 1995; Berends, Boersma, & Weggeman, 2003; Simon, 1991.)

Gaming and associated forms of playful experimentation (e.g. simulations, policy exercises) can be viewed as built-in mechanisms with which systems can prepare for or cope with change. They offer a way for individuals/systems to determine whether change is needed, whether this would be a time to change, what would happen if the change were to take place and whether they are capable of changing when necessary.

For systems, gaming is adaptation, although this adaptation has no intrinsic morality. Whether the adaptation should be regarded as 'good' or 'bad' depends upon the individual's value framework. A person can 'learn' to be an effective serial killer; the state can 'learn' to become an effective dictatorship. Institutionalised norms and values obviously do indicate the value of learning (e.g. through self-actualisation, progress, achievement, commercial success.)

Although SG is commonly associated with 'education', education is a changing system in itself. It is a subsystem institutionalised within societies in order to manage change in learning. The effectiveness of SG and GBL (an issue in Frame I) can be considered in different ways:

1. GBL at the individual level, group, organisational, network or system level.
2. GBL in formal education, as well as outside formal education (e.g. professional or post-academic training), as with on-the-job training, learning within the context of management, decision-making, planning or politics.
3. GBL by different actors in and around the game (e.g. the actual player, the spectator, the designer, the analyst): GBL is not restricted or limited to those who actually play the game.

GBL is thus much wider and richer than the dominant frame is: GBL = games in/for education (Wu, Hsiao, Wu, Lin, & Huang, 2011) (see Table 3.)

Table 3. Evaluation and learning at three levels

	Analytical: Learning from a Game	Learning: Learning during a Game	Instrumental: Development, Training through a Game
System	(*Ex ante*) validation, assessment of a complex system	Enhancement of learning systems, organisations	Development of concrete strategy, decision, policy
Network, chain	(*Ex ante*) validation, assessment of network, chain	Enhancement of learning network or chain	Development of governance, co-ordination or other processes
Actor/group	(*Ex ante*) validation, assessment of individuals, teams	Situational awareness, sense making, team learning	SOPs: Job-oriented training (JOT), skills and competencies

Frames of SG Research

Like 'learning', the notion of 'game' can take on different meanings within contexts of 'research' or 'science'. The following are several frames on the use of 'game' within the context of research:

- **Research Theory:** Game theory as used in economics, political science and similar fields (Leyton-Brown & Shoham, 2008; Ordeshook, 1986; Shubik, 1999; Varoufakis, 2008.)
- **Research Concept:** Organisation, management, decision-making as a strategic or political game (Firestone, 1989; Scharpf, 1997; Steunenberg, Schmidtchen, & Koboldt, 1999.)
- **Research Object:** Studying game cultures, game economics, game politics and similar aspects (Castronova, Williams, Ratan, & Keegan, 2009; Castronova, 2005; Ermi & Mäyrä, 2003; Salomon & Soudoplatoff, 2010; Shaw, 2010.)
- **Design Artefact:** Game as a socio-technical design, as an artefact or as another object (Annetta, 2006; Björk & Holopainen, 2005; Harteveld, 2011; Kankaanranta & Neittaanmki, 2008; van der Spek, 2011).
- **Research Method:** Game as a research method comparable to simulation or experimentation (Barnaud, Promburom, Trebuil, & Bousquet, 2007; Ducrot, 2009; Lempert & Schwabe, 1993; Mayer, Carton, Jong, Leijten, & Dammers, 2004; Meijer, 2009; Meijer, Mayer, van Luipen, & Weitenberg, 2011; Taylor, 1971; Tykhonov, Jonker, & Meijer, 2008.)
- **Intervention Method:** Game as therapy or as a method for education, learning, change or decision support (Geurts, Duke, & Vermeulen, 2007; Preschl, Wagner, Forstmeier, & Maercker, 2011; Wenzler,

2008; Whitlock, McLaughlin, & Allaire, 2012.)
- **Data-Gathering Method:** Game as an environment for observation, group interview or data modelling (Cooper et al., 2010; Good & Su, 2011; Khatib et al., 2011; Wood, Griffiths, & Eatough, 2004.)

Similarly, the concepts of 'research', 'evaluation' and 'assessment' can also have different meanings in different contexts. Table 4 provides an overview of several frames on research, evaluation and assessment.

Types of Evaluation Research

There are several different types of SG research and evaluation:

1. **Constructivist vs. Objectivist Evaluation:** Constructivists emphasise that evaluation is an interactive, interpretative process among stakeholders; objectivists emphasise that the characteristics of evaluation should include factuality, distantiality, impartiality and neutrality (Guba & Lincoln, 1989.)
2. **Theory-Based vs. Explorative Evaluation:** Theory-based evaluation emphasises that hypotheses should be derived in advance from previous scientific research and theory; explorative evaluation emphasises that explanatory theories and hypotheses can be derived from the 'ground up' (Weiss, 1997.)
3. **Summative vs. Formative Type of Evaluation:** Summative evaluation focuses on ex post goal achievement; formative evaluation focuses on adaptation purposes (Bloom, Hastings, & Madaus, 1972.)
4. **Learning vs. Accountability Type of Evaluation:** The learning type of evaluation emphasises lessons for the future; the accountability type of evaluation emphasises

Table 4. Research, evaluation and assessment of SG

Research	Social scientific research	To understand or explain something without a specific predefined, societal purpose, using scientific methods
		Action research: scientific research approach that assumes that research and change are and should be intertwined
	Applied research (e.g. contract research, policy analysis, consultancy)	To improve or change, primarily with a predefined societal purpose and often for a problem owner, client, issue or stakeholder group, using methods that derive their legitimacy and credibility from scientific criteria
		Evaluation = a specific type of applied research
Evaluation	Applied research with the specific intention of determining the 'value' of something or someone in the light of past, present or future objectives, tasks, function or other aspects	Evaluator = person who is evaluating.
		Evaluans = the object/person being evaluated
		Output/outcome evaluation = to evaluate something or someone primarily according to outputs or outcomes, regardless of how they have been achieved
		Process evaluation = to evaluate something or someone according to internal processes, regardless of their outputs or outcomes
		Evaluation of learning = to establish the value of a learning process and/or output
		Learning type of evaluation: evaluation primarily intended to learn from the past, with the goal of improving something or someone in the future
		Performance evaluation of process, output, outcome, person (i.e. assessment)
Assessment	Evaluation with the specific intention to establish/judge the performance, suitability and/or cost-effectiveness of something or someone in the light of past, present or future objectives, tasks, function or other aspects	Assessor = person who is assessing
		Assessans = object/person being assessed
		Assessment = the process of assessing or being assessed

'responsibility for the past' (Edelenbos & Van Buuren, 2005.)

5. **Broad vs. Narrow Evaluation:** Broad evaluation considers many different perspectives, aspects, dimensions and disciplines; narrow evaluation focuses on one or only a few specific details.

6. **Rigorous vs. Generic Evaluation:** Rigorous evaluation emphasises depth and rigour at the expense of resources; generic evaluation emphasises resources at the expense of depth.

The dimensions described above are obviously not restrictive. They are nevertheless important for demonstrating that the issue of evaluation research on SG can be placed within a much wider methodological context. This is not a plea for doing haphazard research; it is simply a reminder of the various epistemological and ontological perspectives that have been developed throughout the history of science and that should not be ignored in a science of SG and GBL.

Our frame analysis clearly indicates that our methodology for SG research fits within Frame I and that it is of the evaluation type (primarily objectivist, theory based, summative). Methodologies for Type II (e.g. economics of innovation), Type III (e.g. political science, sociology), and Type IV (e.g. cultural and organisational studies) have yet to be developed.

METHODOLOGY: RATIONALE AND CONCEPTUAL MODEL

Literature Overview

A great many PhD theses have now been published on the effects of game-based learning and/or SG experiments (Becker, 2008; Bekebrede, 2010; Blunt, 2006; Bremson, 2012; Calleja, 2007; Copier, 2007; Djaouti, 2011; Egenfeldt-Nielsen, 2005; Gasnier, 2007; Hainey, 2010; Harteveld, 2012; Houtkamp, 2012; Hussaan, 2012; Kuit, 2002; Leemkuil, 2006; Meijer, 2009; Squire, 2004; Steinkuehler, 2005; van der Spek, 2011; van Houten, 2007; van Staalduinen, 2012). Several review articles on game-based learning have also been published, and such articles are now appearing with increasing frequency (Adams, 2010; Barlett, Anderson, & Swing, 2008; Beyer & Larkin, 1978; Boyle, Connolly, Hainey, & Boyle, 2012; Connolly et al., 2012; Coulthard, 2009; Egenfeldt-Nielsen, 2006b; Girard, Ecalle, & Magnan, 2012; Gosen & Washbush, 2004; Graafland, Schraagen, & Schijven, 2012; Greenblat, 1973; Hays, 2005; Jenson & de Castell, 2010; Ke, 2009; Lee, 1999; Leemkuil, Jong, & Ootes, 2000; Mayer, 2009; Papastergiou, 2009; Randel, Morris, Wetzelf, & Whitehill, 1992).

Few of these publications provide high-quality evaluation frameworks regarding what should be measured in a comparative fashion and how to do so, taking into account the real-life and dynamic setting of the project (De Freitas & Oliver, 2006). Hainey and colleagues have recently published a useful overview of 11 evaluation frameworks (Connolly et al., 2009; Hainey & Connolly, 2010). The frameworks reviewed include the four-dimensional evaluation framework proposed by De Freitas and colleagues (2010). Other models that can be considered include the framework for theory-based evaluation developed by Kriz and Hense (Bekebrede, 2010; Kriz & Hense, 2004, 2006). In general, few publications present evaluation frameworks for game-based learning in higher education, let alone within the context of professional, in-company training or group and organisational learning.

Limitations of Existing Models

Most of the existing models and frameworks are high-level models. They specify a limited number of generic concepts that can or should be considered when evaluating SG. These models and frameworks nevertheless offer:

1. Few indications for how to use the models, for what purpose, with what scope and under which conditions.
2. Few procedures for validating the conceptual research/evaluation model.
3. Few research hypotheses and research designs.
4. Few definitions of or relationships and interrelationships between the concepts in the model.
5. Few operationalisations and validations of constructs.

Furthermore, the application of the models is characterised by:

- The dominance of single case-studies, single games, single contexts of application.
- A lack of information on the questionnaires used.
- A focus on the GBL of children in formal education, with little attention to advanced–professional learning outside of education.
- A focus on the learning of individuals in formal training or the educational context, with little attention to the learning of teams, groups, organisations, networks or systems within policy or organisational contexts.

Requirements

One important question therefore concerns the requirements for a good evaluation framework for SG evaluation research. A generic evaluation framework (and corresponding procedures) for GBL and SG research should ideally have the following characteristics:

1. **Broad Scope:** It should consider the broad range of educational contexts, games, learning objectives and topics.
2. **Comparative:** It should allow the use of particular data from different games for comparison.
3. **Standardised:** The use of pre-/quasi-experimental research designs requires the standardisation of materials and procedures.
4. **Specific:** It should measure data precisely by pinpointing variables.
5. **Flexible:** Given that game play cannot be always predicted, data gathering should be flexible for measurement, while meeting all other requirements (e.g. standardisation, specificity.)
6. **Triangulated:** It should use a mixed-method approach with qualitative and quantitative data.
7. **Multi-Level:** It should consider the individual, game, team, organisation and system levels.
8. **Validated:** It should use validated research methods (e.g. research method and game design.)
9. **Expandable:** It should offer the possibility of measurement on new variables.
10. **Unobtrusive:** The use of gaming for systematic and extensive data gathering (e.g. research, comparative or theory-based evaluation) should be unobtrusive.
11. **Fast and Non-Time Consuming:** The use of real-world cases for data gathering implies that tools and methods should be fast and non-time-consuming, given that real-world projects do not allow much time and resources to be devoted to research.
12. **Multi-Purpose:** It should persuade stakeholders to extend their data-gathering efforts beyond the obvious and the minimal.

An evaluation of GBL or SG should be broad in scope but light in operation. It should address both the formative and the summative purposes of evaluation (Bloom et al., 1972), as well as the evaluation interests of the designers, players, financers and other stakeholders. At the other end of the spectrum, the data should be suitable for deeper analysis, in order to understand what happens and why.

Comparative, Theory-Based Evaluation

The establishment of learning effectiveness and contributing factors requires an evaluation framework that allows:

1. The operationalisation of independent, dependent and mediating/context variables, including 'engagement' (in this case, independent), 'learning effectiveness' (in this case, dependent) and age (or age-mediating)/ psychological safety (context.)
2. A systematic, unobtrusive process for data gathering and data analysis.
3. The formulation of research questions and hypotheses based on a conceptual research model.

Conceptual Framework

A generic model for social scientific research, evaluation and assessment regarding SG in real-world contexts should provide:

- A flexible and generally applicable research model from which we can derive:
- A set of research questions and hypotheses.
- A research design for applying the model.
- A suite of research tools and instruments.
- Guidelines, practices and rules for applying, falsifying, validating and improving the elements specified.
- Empirical testing of the robustness of the model.

The core of the model portrayed in Figure 2 is a deconstruction of GBL into the following elements:

- **The pre-game condition** (the subject's attitudes, knowledge, skills and behaviour relevant to GBL and SG and/or the case at hand before playing the game): We measure a variety of items and constructs, including attitudes towards GBL and organisational commitment (see 3.1–3.4 in Figure 2.)
- **The quality of the GBL intervention:** subdivided into the quality of the actual game design, game-play, interaction with the facilitator/instructor and interaction with the digital game environment (see 4.1–4.2 in Figure 2.)
- **The post-game condition:** the subject's attitudes, knowledge, skills and behaviour relevant to the GBL and related matters (see 5.1–5.4 in Figure 2.)

Background Variables

Socio-demographic variables (e.g. age, sex, nationality) (see 1.1 in Figure 2.)

Professional and student characteristics (e.g. position, work experience, level of education) (see 2.1 in Figure 2.)

Mediating Variables

- Individual as a participant (e.g. personality characteristics; Big 5, Hexaco) (see 1.2 in Figure 2.)
- Individual as a learner (e.g. learning styles) (see 1.3 in Figure 2.)
- Individual as a gamer (e.g. game skill, game experience, game attitudes, game-play style) (see 1.4 in Figure 2.)
- Professional/student as a serious gamer (e.g. previous experience with SG in a professional context) (see 2.4 in Figure 2.)
- Professional/student as a participant (e.g. intrinsic/extrinsic motivation) (Ainley & Armatas, 2006.)
- **Context Variables:** Organisational/institutional climate in which the GBL/SG takes place (e.g. commitment to the organisation, identification with leader or organisation, psychological safety) (see 6.1 in Figure 2.)
- **First-Order Learning:** Direct influence of playing the game on the individual, small-group attitudes, knowledge, skills or behaviour (see 7 in Figure 2.)
- **Second-Order Learning:** Direct/indirect, short or long-term influence of the game as a whole (incl. design process, sessions, discussions, publications, other interventions and other factors) at the group, network, organisational and system levels (see 8 in Figure 2.)

QUASI-EXPERIMENTAL RESEARCH DESIGN

The model can now be translated into a *quasi-experimental design*. In other words, it can be translated from the simple 'post-test only' design into a 'pre-test/post-test' design involving 'randomisation (R)', 'control group (C)' and 'repeated measurement' (Campbell & Stanley, 1963; Cook

Figure 2. Conceptual framework

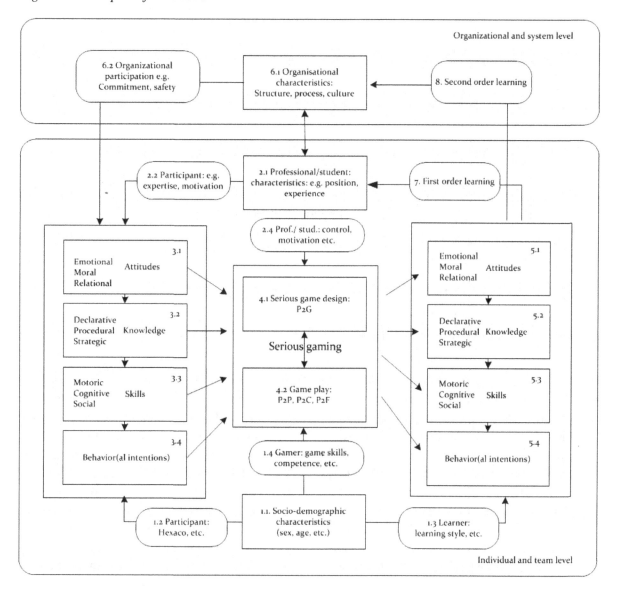

& Campbell, 1979; Creswell, 2002). Figure 3 illustrates the basic translation of the conceptual model into a quasi-experimental design (R and C not included in Figure 3.)

DATA-GATHERING

One of the special features that SG can offer for advanced learning is that the games provide excellent environments for mixed-method data gathering (i.e. triangulation), including crowd sourcing, panel discussions, surveys and observations (including video observations). Figure 4 provides a visual impression of the methods that can be mixed with SG.

The following are a few examples of different forms of data gathering:

Figure 3. Generic quasi-experimental design for GBL and SG

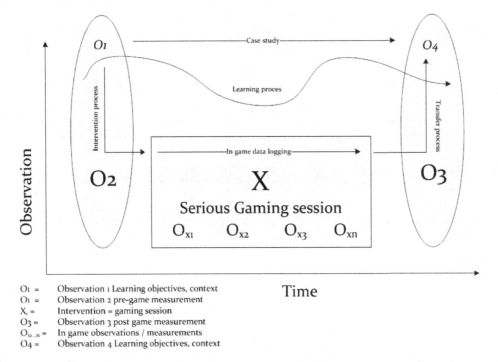

O₁ = Observation 1 Learning objectives, context
O₁ = Observation 2 pre-game measurement
X₁ = Intervention = gaming session
O₃ = Observation 3 post game measurement
O_{x1...n} = In game observations / measurements
O₄ = Observation 4 Learning objectives, context

- **MSP Challenge 2011:** We used a group of 70 international players as an expert panel in a survey assessing the state of marine spatial planning (MSP) in the 13 countries in which the players worked (Mayer, Zhou, et al., 2012, 2013.)
- **XVR Training Simulators:** We used video observations and network analysis of 8 sessions with 100 first responders to analyse team communication patterns and effectiveness (Ruijven, n.d.)
- **Levee Patroller (Deltares Deltabrain, n.d.):** We conducted pre-game, in-game and post-game knowledge tests to measure the increase in knowledge of geo-mechanical levee failures as a result of playing eight exercises in the 3D SG Levee Patroller (Harteveld, 2012.)
- **Servant-Leadership Game:** We used validated pre-game and in-game questionnaires on relevant psychological constructs, including servant-leadership and commitment to change (Kortmann et al., 2012.)

- **TeamUp:** We performed in-game logging and tracking on hundreds of events and results, including distances, paths, play time and avoidable mistakes, in combination with questionnaires (Bezuijen, 2012.)
- **SimPort–MV2 (TU Delft, Tygron Serious Gaming, & Port of Rotterdam, n.d.):** We used pre-game and post-game questionnaires on such aspects as learning satisfaction, game play and motivation, in combination with maps and strategic decisions on the second Maasvlakte port area (Bekebrede, 2010.)

Evaluation data are gathered through mixed methods, in most cases combining pre-game and post-game surveys amongst the players with live or video observations, transcripts of after-action reviews and game results. In a few cases, methods are applied more rigorously through in-game knowledge tests or network and communication analyses from video observations. Table 5 provides an overview of how to mix the various methods in the pre-game, in-game and post-game stages.

Figure 4. SG and data-gathering methods

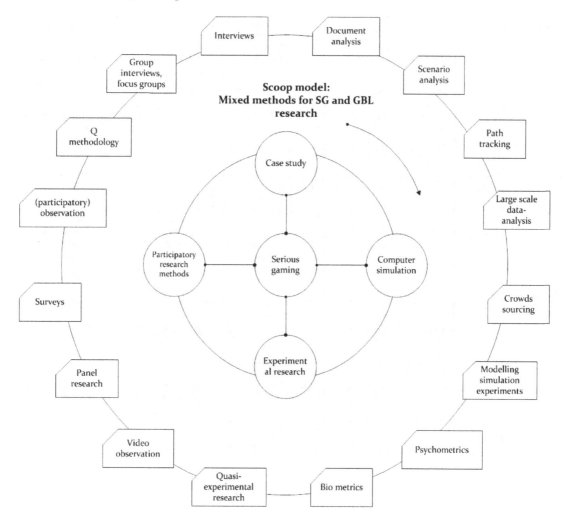

VALIDATED INSTRUMENTS AND TOOLS

In our comparative research, we gradually built a set of validated and reusable questions for the following constructs and items:

Pre-Game

- **Socio-demographic factors** (e.g. sex, age, nationality and culture) (Bekebrede, Warmelink, & Mayer, 2011; Boyle & Connolly, 2008; Brown, Ley, Evett, & Standen, 2011; Brown, Hall, Holtzer, Brown, & Brown, 1997; Erfani et al., 2010;

Hofstede, 1986; Jenson & de Castell, 2010; Kinzie & Joseph, 2008; Pfister, 2011.)

- **Previous experiences/skills** (e.g. with computers, games and virtual learning environments) (Erfani et al., 2010; Harper et al., 2007; Mortagy & Boghikian-Whitby, 2010.)

- **Attitudes** (e.g. change, conflicts, intrinsic and extrinsic motivation, learning styles) (Ashton & Lee, 2009; Garris, Ahlers, & Driskell, 2002; Guay, Vallerand, & Blanchard, 2000; Huang, 2011; K. Lee & Ashton, 2004; Malone & Lepper, 1987a, 1987b.)

Table 5. What to measure, how and when?

How		What?	Pre-Game	In Game	Post-Game
Self-reported	Qual.	Personality, player experiences, context etc.	Interviews, focus group, logbook	Logbook, interviews or small assignments as part of the game	Interviews focus group, after-action review
	Quant	Soc-dem., opinions, motivations, attitudes, engagement, game-quality learning, power, influence, reputation, network centrality, learning satisfaction etc.	Survey, questionnaires, individual or expert panel	In-game questionnaires	Survey, questionnaires, individual or expert panel
Tested	Qual.	Behaviour, skills etc.	Actor role-play, case-analysis, assessment, mental models etc.	Game-based behavioural assessment	Game-based behavioural assessment
	Quant	Values, knowledge, attitudes, skills, personality, power	Psychometric, socio-metric tests (e.g. personality, leadership, team roles, IQ)	Game-based behavioural performance analysis	Game-based behavioural performance analysis
Observed	Qual.	Behavioural performance of student, professionals, player and/or facilitator, others; decisions, strategies, policies, emotions, conflicts etc.	Participatory observation, ethnographic methods	Video, audio personal observation, ethnography, maps, figures, drawings, pictures etc.	Participatory observation, ethnographic methods
	Quant	Biophysical–psychological responses, including stress (heart rate, perspiration)	Participatory observation, network analysis, biophysical–psychological observation	In-game tracking and logging; network analysis, data mining, biometric observation	In-game log file analysis, network analysis

- **Skills:** personal competence (e.g. with games, learning, particular professional skills) (Brown et al., 2011; Enochsson et al., 2004; Holsbrink-Engels, 1998; Verdaasdonk et al., 2009; Wolfe & Box, 1988.)
- **Behaviours** (behavioural intentions.)
- **Group, team, organisational characteristics** (e.g. team/group conflict, psychological safety, psychological collectivism, team and organisational commitment) (Brockner & Higgins, 2001; Carmeli, Brueller, & Dutton, 2009; Edmondson, 1999; Ferris, 2005; Jackson, Colquitt, Wesson, & Zapata-Phelan, 2006.)

In-Game

- **Game performance:** based upon in-game scores (e.g. time, avoidable mistakes) (Baba, 1993; Blumberg, 2000; Oslin, Mitchell, & Griffin, 1998; Tallir, Lenoir, Valcke, & Musch, 2007; Trepte & Reinecke, 2011.)
- **Game-play** (e.g. effort; dominance, influence, power.)
- **Game experience** (e.g. flow, immersion, presence) (Admiraal, Huizenga, Akkerman, & Ten Dam, 2011; Csikszentmihalyi, 1991; Martin & Jackson, 2008.)

Post-Game

- **Game experience** (e.g. engagement, fun while playing the game) (Boyle et al., 2012; Mayes & Cotton, 2001; Schuurink, Houtkamp, & Toet, 2008.)
- **Player satisfaction with:** the game (e.g. clarity, realism); user interaction (e.g. attractiveness, ease of use, computer malfunctions, support); the quality of the facilitator (e.g. supportive, player identification with facilitator); interaction with other students (e.g. player efforts, motivation); identification of players with role; team engagement (Olsen, Procci, & Bowers, 2011; Reichlin et al., 2011) (See also Table 3 and the discussion)
  - **First-order learning** (short-term, individual, participants):
    - **Player learning satisfaction**, self-reported, self-perceived learning (e.g. broad range of items.)
    - **Measured changes** in knowledge, attitudes, skills and behaviours (behavioural intentions.)
  - **Second-order learning** (medium-term, long-term, collective, participants and non-participants):
    - **Self-reported, case-based, reconstructive:** asking clients, participants or other parties how the results of the GBL have been implemented.
    - **Measured changes in team, group or organisational characteristics** (e.g. safety, commitment, performance.)

Tooling for Stealth Assessment and Evaluation

One of the advantages of using digital SG instead of analogue simulation games for training and assessment is that digital SG allow data to gathered, logged, saved and analysed unobtrusively, for purposes of debriefing, assessment or research. Stealth assessment (i.e. non-invasive, unobtrusive assessment) could potentially increase the learning efficacy of SG, given that much of the learning in SG now remains relatively 'implicit' and 'subjective' (e.g. as noted in personal debriefings).

In the assessment of both players and trainers, it continues to be relatively difficult to monitor and keep track of what happens, to objectify the observations and to compare them to other sessions, as well as to provide authoritative feedback on the information in order to enhance learning or support a judgement. Stealth assessment in SG can therefore serve several functions (Kickmeier-Rust et al., 2009; Petersen & Bedek, 2012; Seitlinger, Bedek, Kopeinik, & Albert, 2012; Shute & Kim, 2010; Shute et al., 2010, 2009; Shute, 2011; Zapata-Rivera, VanWinkle, Doyle, Buteux, & Bauer, 2009):

- **Mirroring:** providing a better factual account of what exactly happened during the game (e.g. in terms of decisions, actions, arousal, network centrality) and in which sequence.
- **Sense making:** providing improved support for the facilitator, trainer or instructor in the interpretation of behaviour and performance, as with the visual-dynamic portrayal of what happened (e.g. moving graphs, stills) or with comparison to other player (groups); objectification of player performance (e.g. top or bottom 10% of all teams that played this game.)

- **Adaptation:** ensuring improved adaptation of the game to the level of the players, or improved game design.
- **Research:** storing data to construct and/or validate underlying scientific theories, either domain-oriented or method-oriented.
- **Data mining, crowd sourcing:** similar to (4), but explorative and at a larger scale.

As part of the research methodology discussed here, we are therefore developing tools for mixed-method research. The objectives include the following:

1. To develop a conceptual model for the stealth assessment of individual and team behaviour and performance in and around digital SG.
2. To incorporate stealth assessment into SG.
3. To construct feedback dashboards for immediate-action review and game-based learning.
4. To evaluate the results of stealth in-game data with validated psychometric constructs and tests.
5. To use the patterns of game behaviour and performance to improve the game, the after-action review and learning efficacy.
6. To validate the efficacy of stealth assessment for training, assessment and research, and to provide guidelines and recommendations.

Figure 5 presents an impression of a digital tool that provides guidance and structure to data collection and that can connect observed, reported and logged data in and around game sessions. The tool has been titled Q.E.D., which stands for Quasi-Experimental Design as well as for Quod Erat Demonstrandum.

OPERATIONALISATION OF THE RESEARCH MODEL AND HYPOTHESES

The operationalisation of the generic conceptual model (Figure 2) within the context of a dynamic, multi-stakeholder project can pose a true challenge. A great variety of games, players and learning contexts, and trade-offs must be made with regard to time, resources and the focus of the evaluation (see above).

Given that not everything can be included in an evaluation, and given the possibility of conflict between different evaluation objectives, it is important to identify the exact purpose of the evaluation in order to define the proper type of questions, which should subsequently be translated into an operationalised model and hypotheses for testing.

We classify the types of research questions and research hypotheses that can guide GBL and SG research into the following categories:

Figure 5. Q.E.D. tool

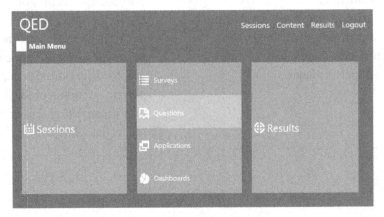

- **Design-oriented research (artefact):** 'making it (better).'
  - The validation of specific and generic game-based artefacts and events.
  - The development and validation of design theories, methods and tools.
- **Intervention-oriented research (e.g. learning, change, policymaking, management):** 'making it work.'
  - The learning effectiveness/impact of game-based interventions.
  - The transfer of game-based interventions to the real world.
- **Domain-oriented research (e.g. healthcare, military, energy):** 'making it matter.'
  - The effectiveness of using SG to understand complexity, dynamics in specific domains.
- **Disciplinary research (e.g. methodology, ethics, explanatory and interpretative theories):** 'making it understandable.'
  - The sociological, economic, political, cultural and other frames on SG.
  - Theory construction on GBL and SG.
  - Methodology: design and validation of research methods and tools.
  - Reflection and ethics.

Operationalising the Evaluation Instrument

Depending upon the case at hand, it is now possible to define and construct pre-game, in-game and post-game instruments for measuring or observing relevant variables. This is accomplished by selecting the constructs and items that are necessary and relevant for the specific configuration of game/client/setting/players/purpose.

Operationalising the Research Model

The operationalisation of constructs and items should proceed parallel to the preliminary operationalisation of the research model that will be tested later. Operationalisation of the model implies selecting and filtering from the conceptual model (Figure 1). The elements and parts that are relevant can and should be included. Figure 6 presents a basic example of an operationalised conceptual model.

Testing the Model

First-order learning effects (see Figure 2) can be established as changes between pre- and post-game measurements, with or without a control group.

Second-order effects (see Figure 2; i.e. transfer of learning to performance of the system) is much more difficult to assess. Empirical data of the first order are supportive, and they provide direction. Learning transfer at the individual or small-group level could possibly be assessed by using the same or similar research tools after some time. Learning transfer at the chain, network, organisational or system level is most likely to be performed through reconstructive case studies with triangulated data gathering (e.g. KPIs, interviews). To our knowledge, very few research publications address the impact of serious gaming on organisations and systems.

In a few situations, measurements of change and learning can be performed in the form of objective 'tests'. Self-constructed items or constructs for measuring attitude, knowledge, skills and behaviours cannot always be 'tested' or 'validated' in advance. Self-reporting or self-assessment of change and learning is common; it is often necessary in addition to other data and, in many cases, it is sufficient. A thorough mixed-method evaluation study of the game Levee Patroller by (Harteveld, 2012) revealed high and significant correlations between observed, measured and self-reported learning effects.

Even when based upon self-reporting, however, high-quality questionnaires that include items, constructs and scales for comparative and longitudinal measurements are not commonly available. In due course, the number and quality of validated

Figure 6. Operationalised model (example)

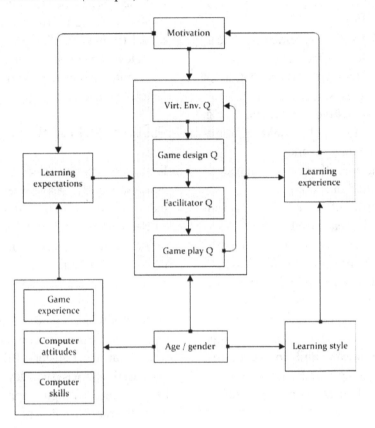

constructs for SG will increase. Psychometric measurement from behavioural sciences (e.g. psychology, management) is largely unexplored territory for SG research.

Data Reduction and Analysis

A final and important concern involves the reduction and analysis of data. As indicated above, we frequently use the same scales or constructs to measure 'game design quality' and 'player satisfaction' through such constructs as clarity, realism, facilitator quality and user interaction. Over the years, we have varied and adapted items, questions and constructs. Data reduction through factor analysis and the reliability analysis of scales are increasingly allowing us to select the influential and distinguishing items and construct scales.

Our present dataset now contains 960 variables concerning 12 games (Mayer, 2012; Mayer, Bekebrede, et al., 2013).

The ultimate goal of comparative research is to construct and test the efficacy of GBL and SG through structural models (including structural equation models), using validated or newly constructed psychometric scales and constructs for the broad range of constructs listed above. Although we are progressing, we are still far from achieving this ambition. Figure 7 presents an example of a structural model that has recently been published (Mayer, Warmelink, et al., 2012).

Figure 7. Example of a structural model (Mayer, Warmelink, et al., 2012)
Source: Mayer, Warmelink, et al., 2012

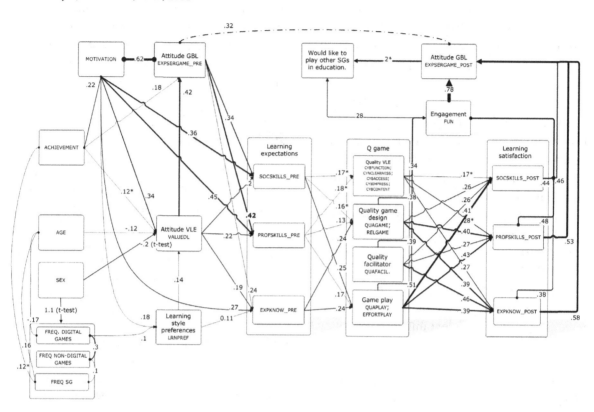

RESEARCH AND PROFESSIONAL ETHICS

This section contains a final word about ethics within the context of SG. The relationship between ethics and games is viewed in terms of the following:

1. The ethics involved in making, disseminating or playing games (e.g. of a violent or controversial nature.)
2. Using SG to allow players to adopt particular codes of conduct or to reflect upon ethical dilemmas (GATE, 2011.)

Very little attention has been paid to the social-ethical role of SG designers, SG researchers, SG professionals or SG users. When games are utilised in society for purposes of therapy,

innovation, persuasion or self-organisation, they are inherently based upon specific value systems, and they subtly exert power.

First, SG can be very coercive. It is a common mistake to believe that SG participation is always voluntary, with high intrinsic motivation due to the supposedly engaging nature of the games. In many cases, teachers or managers request or demand that players participate in SG. Refusal might result in failing a course or losing a promotion. An organisation might expect employees to fulfil job-related training requirements through an online game, possibly assessing them according to their performance.

Second, SG might not be as pleasurable as many might assume; they might cause pain and frustration. Participants might fail in front of their colleagues. A great deal of attention is currently being paid to the pleasurable aspects of SG (e.g. engagement, fun, immersion, flow), while very little attention is being paid to emotions that accompany deep learning and change (e.g. 'frustration' and 'pain'). Good SG should not only be 'engaging'; they should also be painful (i.e. 'hard fun').

Third, SG might be used for manipulation or questionable political purposes. A government department recently asked us to design and run a simulation game to improve stakeholder coordination within the governmental immigration chain. The key performance indicator was to be an increase in the number of immigrants sent back (after final judicial denial of a permit to stay) to their countries of origin after the gaming sessions (Frame I). We obviously refused. The root of the problem was not inefficiency in the immigration chain, but internal and external stakeholder disagreement with government immigration policy (Frame III).

Fourth, many SG are designed and used for vulnerable target groups (e.g. young children with ADHD, people with mental disorders or cancer, unemployed people, immigrants). Additional reflection upon the ethics and potentially harmful effects of the game-based intervention model is needed, as is additional 'informed consent' when doing game experiments with such participant-players.

CONCLUSION

In this chapter, we formulate frames, requirements and a conceptual research model that can be translated into quasi-experimental research designs and operationalised into a model for evaluating specific cases and contexts of GBL. We are aware of the many assumptions we needed to make. We are also aware of our inability to mention all popular SG and cite additional important references. Given the purpose of this book, we restricted our focus to types of research associated with Frame I (i.e. SG as a tool for learning). As stated previously,

research methodologies associated with Frames II, III and IV are largely in need of elaboration within the emerging science of SG, as are the network, organisational and system levels of learning with games and second- order effects. We wish to assure the reader that we have only begun.

REFERENCES

Adams, E. M., & Goffman, E. (1979). Frame analysis: An essay on the organization of experience. *Philosophy and Phenomenological Research, 39*(4), 601. doi:10.2307/2106908.

Adams, S. A. (2010). Use of serious health games in health care: A review. *Studies in Health Technology and Informatics, 157*, 160–166. PMID:20543383.

Admiraal, W., Huizenga, J., Akkerman, S., & Dam, G. T. (2011). The concept of flow in collaborative game-based learning. *Computers in Human Behavior, 27*(3), 1185–1194. doi:10.1016/j.chb.2010.12.013.

Ainley, M., & Armatas, C. (2006). Motivational perspectives on students ' responses to learning in virtual learning environments. In J. Weiss, J. Nolan, J. Hunsinger, & P. Trifonas (Eds.), *The international handbook of virtual learning environments* (pp. 365–394). Dordrecht, The Netherlands: Springer. doi:10.1007/978-1-4020-3803-7_15.

Annetta, L. A. (2006). Serious games: Incorporating video games in the classroom - Games designed using sound pedagogy actively engage the net generation in learning. *EDUCAUSE, 29*(3).

Argyris, C. (1977). Double loop learning in organizations. *Harvard Business Review, 55*(5), 115–125.

Argyris, C. (1982). The executive mind and double-loop learning. *Organizational Dynamics, 11*(2), 5–22. doi:10.1016/0090-2616(82)90002-X PMID:10256769.

Argyris, C. (1995). Action science and organizational learning. *Journal of Managerial Psychology*, *10*(6), 20–26. doi:10.1108/02683949510093849.

Argyris, C., & Schön, D. A. (1974). *Theory in practice: Increasing professional effectiveness*. San Francsico, CA: Jossey-Bass Publishers.

Ashton, M. C., & Lee, K. (2009). An investigation of personality types within the HEXACO personality framework. *Journal of Individual Differences*, *30*(4), 181–187. doi:10.1027/1614-0001.30.4.181.

Baba, D. M. (1993). Determinants of video game performance. *Advances in Psychology*, *102*, 57–74. doi:10.1016/S0166-4115(08)61465-X.

Babbie, E. (2007). The ethics and politics of social research. In E. Babbie (Ed.), *The practice of social research* (pp. 60–83). London: Thomson Wadsworth.

Barlett, C. P., Anderson, C. A., & Swing, E. L. (2008). Video game effects—Confirmed, suspected, and speculative: A review of the evidence. *Simulation & Gaming*, *40*(3), 377–403. doi:10.1177/1046878108327539.

Barnaud, C., Promburom, T., Trebuil, G., & Bousquet, F. (2007). An evolving simulation/gaming process to facilitate adaptive watershed management in northern mountainous Thailand. *Simulation & Gaming*, *38*(3), 398–420. doi:10.1177/1046878107300670.

Becker, K. (2008). *The invention of good games: Understanding learning design in commercial video games*. Calgary, Canada: University of Calgary.

Bekebrede, G. (2010). *Experiencing complexity: A gaming approach for understanding infrastructure systems*. TU Delft. Retrieved May 3, 2013, from http://www.narcis.nl/publication/RecordID/oai:tudelft. nl:uuid:dae75f36-4fb6-4a53-8711-8aab42378878

Bekebrede, G., Warmelink, H. J. G., & Mayer, I. S. (2011). Reviewing the need for gaming in education to accommodate the net generation. *Computers & Education*, *57*(2), 1521–1529. doi:10.1016/j.compedu.2011.02.010.

Benford, R. D., & Snow, D. A. (2000). Framing processes and social movements: An overview and assessment. *Annual Review of Sociology*, *26*(1), 611–639. doi:10.1146/annurev.soc.26.1.611.

Berends, H., Boersma, K., & Weggeman, M. (2003). The structuration of organizational learning. *Human Relations*, *56*(9), 1035–1056. doi:10.1177/0018726703569001.

Beyer, J. L., & Larkin, R. P. (1978). Simulation review: A review of instructional simulations for human geography. *Simulation & Gaming*, *9*(3), 339–352. doi:10.1177/104687817800900306.

Bezuijen, A. (2012). *Teamplay the further development of TeamUp, a teamwork focused serious game*. Delft, The Netherlands: TU Delft.

Björk, S., & Holopainen, J. (2005). *Patterns in game design*. Boston: Charles River Media.

Bloom, B. S., Hastings, T. J., & Madaus, G. F. (1972). Handbook on formative and summative evaluation of student learning. *Studies in Art Education*, *14*(1), 68–72. doi:10.2307/1319918.

Blumberg, F. C. (2000). The effects of children's goals for learning on video game performance. *Journal of Applied Developmental Psychology*, *21*(6), 641–653. doi:10.1016/S0193-3973(00)00058-7.

Blunt, R. D. (2006). *A causal-comparative exploration of the relationship between game-based learning and academic achievement: Teaching management with video games*. Minneapolis, MN: Walden University.

Bogost, I. (2007). *Persuasive games: The expressive power of videogames*. Cambridge, MA: MIT Press.

Boyle, E. A., & Connolly, T. M. (2008). Games for learning: Does gender make a difference? In *Proceedings of 2nd European Conference on Games Based Learning*, 69–76.

Boyle, E. A., Connolly, T. M., & Hainey, T. (2011). The role of psychology in understanding the impact of computer games. *Entertainment Computing*, 2(2), 69–74. doi:10.1016/j.entcom.2010.12.002.

Boyle, E. A., Connolly, T. M., Hainey, T., & Boyle, J. M. (2012). Engagement in digital entertainment games: A systematic review. *Computers in Human Behavior*, 28(3), 771–780. doi:10.1016/j.chb.2011.11.020.

Bremson, J. (2012). *Using gaming simulation to explore long range fuel and vehicle transitions*. University of California. Retrieved May 3, 2013, from http://steps.ucdavis.edu/its_publications/dissertations/Bremson_Joel.pdf

Brockmyer, J. H., Fox, C. M., Curtiss, K., Mc-Broom, E., Burkhart, K. M., & Pidruzny, J. N. (2009). The development of the game engagement questionnaire: A measure of engagement in video game-playing. *Journal of Experimental Social Psychology*, 45(4), 624–634. doi:10.1016/j.jesp.2009.02.016.

Brockner, J., & Higgins, E. T. (2001). Regulatory focus theory: Implications for the study of emotions at work. *Organizational Behavior and Human Decision Processes*, 86(1), 35–66. doi:10.1006/obhd.2001.2972.

Brown, D. J., Ley, J., Evett, L., & Standen, P. (2011). Can participating in games based learning improve mathematic skills in students with intellectual disabilities? In *Proceedings of 2011 IEEE 1st International Conference on Serious Games and Applications for Health SeGAH* (pp. 1–9). IEEE. doi:10.1109/SeGAH.2011.6165461

Brown, M., Hall, L. R., Holtzer, R., Brown, S., & Brown, N. (1997). Gender and video game performance. *Seks Roles*, 36(11), 793–812. doi:10.1023/A:1025631307585.

Calleja, G. (2007). *Digital games as designed experience: Reframing the concept of immersion*. Wellington, New Zealand: Victoria University of Wellington.

Campbell, D. T., & Stanley, J. C. (1963). Experimental and quasi-experimental designs for research on teaching. In N. L. Gage (Ed.), *Handbook of research on teaching* (pp. 171–246). Chicago: Rand McNally.

Carmeli, A., Brueller, D., & Dutton, J. E. (2009). Learning behaviours in the workplace? The role of high quality interpersonal relationships and psychological safety. *Systems Research and Behavioral Science*, 26, 81–98. doi:10.1002/sres.932.

Castronova, E. (2005). *Synthetic worlds: The business and culture of online games*. Chicago: University of Chicago Press.

Castronova, E., Williams, D., Ratan, R., & Keegan, B. (2009). As real as real? Macroeconomic behavior in a large-scale virtual world. *New Media & Society*, 11(5), 685–707. doi:10.1177/1461444809105346.

Chandler, D., & Torbert, B. (2003). Condescending ethics and action research. *Action Research*, 1(2), 37–47.

Chertoff, D. B., Goldiez, B., & LaViola, J. J. (2010). Virtual experience test: A virtual environment evaluation questionnaire. In *Proceedings of 2010 IEEE Virtual Reality Conference VR* (pp. 103–110). IEEE. doi:10.1109/VR.2010.5444804

Chong, D., & Druckman, J. N. (2007). Framing theory. *Annual Review of Political Science*, 10(1), 103–126. doi:10.1146/annurev.polisci.10.072805.103054.

Connolly, T. M., Boyle, E. A., MacArthur, E., Hainey, T., & Boyle, J. M. (2012). A systematic literature review of empirical evidence on computer games and serious games. *Computers & Education*, 59(2), 661–686. doi:10.1016/j.compedu.2012.03.004.

Connolly, T. M., Stansfield, M., & Hainey, T. (2009). *Towards the development of a games-based learning evaluation framework: Games-based learning advancements for multisensory human computer interfaces: techniques and effective pratices*. Academic Press. doi:10.4018/978-1-60566-360-9.

€conomia. (n.d.). *Serious game about EU financial policy*. European Central bank (ECB). Retrieved from http://www.ecb.int/ecb/educational/economia/html/index.en.html

Cook, T. D., & Campbell, D. T. (1979). *Quasi-experimentation: Design and analysis issues for field settings*. Boston: Houghlin Mifflin Company.

Cooper, S., Khatib, F., Treuille, A., Barbero, J., Lee, J., & Beenen, M. et al. (2010). Predicting protein structures with a multiplayer online game. *Nature*, *466*(7307), 756–760. doi:10.1038/nature09304 PMID:20686574.

Copier, M. (2007). *Beyond the magic circle: A network perspective on role-play in online games*. Utrecht University. Retrieved from http://igitur-archive.library.uu.nl/dissertations/2007-0710-214621/index.htm

Coulthard, G. J. (2009). *A review of the educational use and learning effectiveness of simulations and games*. Retrieved May 3, 2013, from http://www.coulthard.com/library/paper-simulation.html

Creswell, J. W. (2002). Research design: Qualitative, quantitative, and mixed methods approaches. *Organizational Research Methods*, *6*, 246.

Csikszentmihalyi, M. (1991). *Flow: The psychology of optimal experience*. New York: Harper-Perennial.

De Caluwe, L., Hofstede, G. J., & Peters, V. A. M. (2008). *Why do games work: In search of the active substance*. Retrieved from http://www.narcis.nl/publication/RecordID/oai:library.wur.nl:wurpubs/368664

De Freitas, S., & Oliver, M. (2006). How can exploratory learning with games and simulations within the curriculum be most effectively evaluated? *Computers & Education*, *46*(3), 249–264. doi:10.1016/j.compedu.2005.11.007.

De Freitas, S., Rebolledo-Mendez, G., Liarokapis, F., Magoulas, G., & Poulovassilis, A. (2010). Learning as immersive experiences: Using the four-dimensional framework for designing and evaluating immersive learning experiences in a virtual world. *British Journal of Educational Technology*, *41*(1), 69–85. doi:10.1111/j.1467-8535.2009.01024.x.

De Vaus, D. (2001). Research design in social research. *British Educational Research Journal*, *28*, 296.

Delft, T. U. Tygron Serious Gaming, & Port of Rotterdam. (n.d.). *SimPort MV2 serious game*. Retrieved May 3, 2013, from http://www.simport.eu/

Deltares Deltabrain. (n.d.). *Levee patroller*. Delft, The Netherlands. *Deltares*.

Djaouti, D. (2011). *Serious game design - Considérations théoriques et techniques sur la création de jeux vidéo à vocation utilitaire*. (Thèse de doctorat en informatique). Université de Toulouse III, Toulouse, France.

Ducrot, R. (2009). Gaming across scale in peri-urban water management: Contribution from two experiences in Bolivia and Brazil. *International Journal of Sustainable Development World Ecology*, *16*(4), 240–252. doi:10.1080/13504500903017260.

Duke, R. D., & Geurts, J. L. A. (2004). *Policy games for strategic management: Pathways into the unknown*. Amsterdam: Dutch University Press.

Edelenbos, J., & Van Buuren, A. (2005). The learning evaluation: A theoretical and empirical exploration. *Evaluation Review*, *29*(6), 591–612. doi:10.1177/0193841X05276126 PMID:16244054.

Edmondson, A. C. (1999). Psychological safety and learning behavior in work teams. *Administrative Science Quarterly, 44*(2), 350. doi:10.2307/2666999.

Egenfeldt-Nielsen, S. (2005). *Beyond edutainment: Exploring the educational potential of computer games.* Retrieved May 3, 2013, from http://www.seriousgames.dk/downloads/egenfeldt.pdf

Egenfeldt-Nielsen, S. (2006). Overview of research on the educational use of video games. *Digital Kompetanse, 1*, 184–213.

Egenfeldt-Nielsen, S. (2006a). Can education and psychology join forces: The clash of benign and malign learning from computer games. *Nordicom Review, 26*(2), 103–107.

Enochsson, L., Isaksson, B., Tour, R., Kjellin, A., Hedman, L., & Wredmark, T. et al. (2004). Visuospatial skills and computer game experience influence the performance of virtual endoscopy. *Journal of Gastrointestinal Surgery Official Journal of the Society for Surgery of the Alimentary Tract, 8*(7), 876–882. doi:10.1016/j.gassur.2004.06.015 PMID:15531242.

Ermi, L., & Mäyrä, F. (2003). *Power and control of games: Children as the actors of game cultures.* Retrieved May 3, 2013, from http://www.uta.fi/~tlilma/Ermi_Mayra_Power_and_Control_of_Games.pdf

Fernández-Aranda, F., Jiménez-Murcia, S., Santamaría, J. J., Gunnard, K., Soto, A., & Kalapanidas, E. et al. (2012). Video games as a complementary therapy tool in mental disorders: PlayMancer, a European multicentre study. *Journal of Mental Health (Abingdon, England), 21*(4), 364–374. doi:10.3109/09638237.2012.664302 PMID:22548300.

Ferris, G. R. (2005). Development and validation of the political skill inventory. *Journal of Management, 31*(1), 126–152. doi:10.1177/0149206304271386.

Firestone, W. A. (1989). Educational policy as an ecology of games. *Educational Researcher, 18*(7), 18–24. doi: doi:10.3102/0013189X018007018.

Fisher, K. (1997). Locating frames in the discursive universe. *Sociological Research Online, 2*(3), 1–41. Retrieved from http://www.socresonline.org.uk/2/3/4.html doi:10.5153/sro.78.

Frasca, G. (2007). *12th September.* Retrieved from http://www.newsgaming.com/newsgames.htm

Garris, R., Ahlers, R., & Driskell, J. E. (2002). Games, motivation, and learning: A research and practice model. *Simulation & Gaming, 33*(4), 441–467. doi:10.1177/1046878102238607.

Gasnier, A. (2007). *The patenting paradox: A game-based approach to patent management.* Delft, The Netherlands: Eburon.

GATE. (2011). *Help! Over de ontwikkeling van een serious game als oefenmiddel voor burgemeesters om zich voor te bereiden op een incident.* Utrecht, The Netherlands: Game Research for Training and Entertainment.

Geurts, J. L. A., Duke, R. D., & Vermeulen, P. A. M. (2007). Policy gaming for strategy and change. *Long Range Planning, 40*(6), 535–558. doi:10.1016/j.lrp.2007.07.004.

Giddens, A. (1988). Goffman as a systematic social theorist. In P. Drew, & A. Wootton (Eds.), *Erving Goffman Exploring the interaction order* (pp. 250–279). New York: Polity Press.

Girard, C., Ecalle, J., & Magnan, A. (2012). Serious games as new educational tools: How effective are they? A meta-analysis of recent studies. *Journal of Computer Assisted Learning, 19*(3), 207–219. doi: doi:10.1111/j.1365-2729.2012.00489.x.

Göbel, S. (2010). Definition serious games term – Approach – Examples – Conclusion serious games – Motivation, der mensch ist nur da ganz mensch wo er spielt. *Technology (Elmsford, N.Y.), 12*.

Goffman, E. (1974). *Frame analysis: An essay on the organization of experience*. New York: Harper & Row.

Good, B. M., & Su, A. I. (2011). Games with a scientific purpose. *Genome Biology, 12*(12), 135. doi:10.1186/ gb-2011-12-12-135

Gosen, J., & Washbush, J. (2004). A review of scholarship on assessing experiential learning effectiveness. *Simulation & Gaming, 35*(2), 270–293. doi:10.1177/1046878104263544.

Graafland, M., Schraagen, J. M., & Schijven, M. P. (2012). Systematic review of serious games for medical education and surgical skills training. *British Journal of Surgery, 99*(10), 1322–1330. doi:10.1002/bjs.8819 PMID:22961509.

Greenblat, C. S. (1973). Teaching with simulation games: A review of claims and evidence. *Teaching Sociology, 1*(1), 62–83. doi:10.2307/1317334.

Guay, F., Vallerand, R. J., & Blanchard, C. (2000). On the assessment of situational intrinsic and extrinsic motivation: The situational motivation scale (SIMS). *Motivation and Emotion, 24*(3), 175–213. doi:10.1023/A:1005614228250.

Guba, E. G., & Lincoln, Y. S. (1989). *Fourth generation evaluation*. Thousand Oaks, CA: Sage Publications.

Hainey, T. (2010). *Using games-based learning to teach requirements collection and analysis at tertiary education level*. Retrieved May 3, 2013, from http://scholar. google.com/scholar ?hl=en&btnG=Search&q=intitle:Using+Gam es-Based+Learning+to+Teach+ Requirements +Collection+and+Analysis+at+Tertiary+Educ ation+Level#1

Hainey, T., & Connolly, T. M. (2010). Evaluating games-based learning. *International Journal of Virtual and Personal Learning Environments, 1*(1), 57–71. doi:10.4018/jvple.2010091705.

Harper, J. D., Kaiser, S., Ebrahimi, K., Lamberton, G. R., Hadley, H. R., Ruckle, H. C., et al. (2007). Prior video game exposure does not enhance robotic surgical performance. *Journal of Endourology / Endourological Society, 21*(10), 1207–1210. doi:10.1089/end.2007.9905

Hart, C. (2008). Critical discourse analysis and metaphor: Toward a theoretical framework. *Critical Discourse Studies, 5*(2), 91–106. doi:10.1080/17405900801990058.

Harteveld, C. (2011). *Triadic game design*. London: Springer. doi:10.1007/978-1-84996-157-8.

Harteveld, C. (2012). *Making sense of virtual risks, a quasi experimental investigation into game-based training*. Delft, The Netherlands: IOS Press.

Hays, R. T. (2005). *The effectiveness of instructional games: a literature review and discussion*. Orlando, FL: Naval War Center: Training Systems Division.

Healseeker. (n.d.). *Yulius academie*. Retrieved April 11, 2013, from http://www.yuliusacademie. nl/nl/healseeker

Hofstede, G. (1986). Cultural differences in teaching and learning. *International Journal of Intercultural Relations, 10*(3), 301–320. doi:10.1016/0147-1767(86)90015-5.

Hofstede, G. J., De Caluwe, L., & Peters, V. A. M. (2010). Why simulation games work-in search of the active substance: A synthesis. *Simulation & Gaming, 41*(6), 824–843. doi:10.1177/104687811037 5596

Holsbrink-Engels, G. A. (1998). *Computer-based role playing for interpersonal skills training*. Enschede, The Netherlands: Universiteit Twente.

Houtkamp, J. (2012). *Affective appraisal of virtual environments*. Retrieved from http://igitur-archive. library.uu.nl/dissertations/2012-0620-200449/ UUindex.html

Huang, W.-H. (2011). Evaluating learners' motivational and cognitive processing in an online game-based learning environment. *Computers in Human Behavior*, *27*(2), 694–704. doi:10.1016/j.chb.2010.07.021.

Hussaan, A. M. (2012). *Generation of adaptive pedagogical scenarios in serious games*. Lyon, France: University of Lyon.

Jackson, C. L., Colquitt, J., Wesson, M. J., & Zapata-Phelan, C. P. (2006). Psychological collectivism: A measurement validation and linkage to group member performance. *The Journal of Applied Psychology*, *91*(4), 884–899. doi:10.1037/0021-9010.91.4.884 PMID:16834512.

Janssen, M., & Klievink, B. (2010). Gaming and simulation for transforming and reengineering government: Towards a research agenda. *Transforming Government People Process and Policy*, *4*(2), 132–137. doi:10.1108/17506161011047361.

Jantke, K. P. (2010). Toward a taxonomy of game based learning. In *Proceedings of IEEE International Conference on Progress in Informatics and Computing*, (pp. 858–862). IEEE. doi:10.1109/PIC.2010.5687903

Jenson, J., & De Castell, S. (2010). Gender, simulation, and gaming: Research review and redirections. *Simulation & Gaming*, *41*(1), 51–71. doi:10.1177/1046878109353473.

Kankaanranta, M., & Neittaanmki, P. (2008). Design and use of serious games. *Engineering*, *37*, 208. doi: doi:10.1007/978-1-4020-9496-5.

Kato, P. M., Cole, S. W., Bradlyn, A. S., & Pollock, B. H. (2008). A video game improves behavioral outcomes in adolescents and young adults with cancer: A randomized trial. *Pediatrics*, *122*(2), e305–e317. doi:10.1542/peds.2007-3134 PMID:18676516.

Ke, F. (2009). *A qualitative meta-analysis of computer games as learning tools*. Hershey, PA: IGI Global.

Khatib, F., Cooper, S., Tyka, M. D., Xu, K., Makedon, I., & Popovic, Z. et al. (2011). Algorithm discovery by protein folding game players. *Proceedings of the National Academy of Sciences of the United States of America*, *108*(47), 1–5. doi:10.1073/pnas.1115898108 PMID:22065763.

Kickmeier-Rust, M. D., Steiner, C. M., & Albert, D. (2009). Non-invasive assessment and adaptive interventions in learning games. In *Proceedings of Intelligent Networking and Collaborative Systems 2009 INCOS 09 International Conference* (pp. 301–305). IEEE. doi:10.1109/INCOS.2009.30

Kim, R. B., & Kim, J. P. (2011). Creative economy in Korea: A case of online game industry. *Actual Problems of Economics*, *124*(10), 435–442.

Kimmel, A. J. (1988). Ethics and values in applied social research. *Methods (San Diego, Calif.)*, *12*, 160. doi: doi:10.4135/9781412984096.

Kinzie, M. B., & Joseph, D. R. D. (2008). Gender differences in game activity preferences of middle school children: Implications for educational game design. *Educational Technology Research and Development*, *56*(5–6), 643–663. doi:10.1007/s11423-007-9076-z.

Knight, J. F., Carley, S., Tregunna, B., Jarvis, S., Smithies, R., & De Freitas, S. et al. (2010). Serious gaming technology in major incident triage training: A pragmatic controlled trial. *Resuscitation*, *81*(9), 1175–1179. doi:10.1016/j.resuscitation.2010.03.042 PMID:20732609.

Kortmann, R., Bekebrede, G., Van Daalen, C. E., Harteveld, C., Mayer, I. S., & Van Dierendonck, D. (2012). Veerkracht—A game for servant-leadership development. In *Proceedings of the 43rd Annual Conference of the International Simulation and Gaming Association*. ISGA.

Krathwohl, D. R., Bloom, B. S., & Betram, B. M. (1973). *Taxonomy of educational objectives, the classification of educational goals: Handbook II: Affective domain.* New York: David McKay Co., Inc.

Kriz, W. C., & Hense, J. U. (2004). Evaluation of the EU-project simgame in business education. In W. C. Kriz, & T. Eberle (Eds.), *Bridging the gap: Transforming knowledge into action through gaming and simulation* (pp. 352–363). Munchen, Germany: Sagsaga.

Kriz, W. C., & Hense, J. U. (2006). Theory-oriented evaluation for the design of and research in gaming and simulation. *Simulation & Gaming, 37*(2), 268–283. doi:10.1177/1046878106287950.

Kuit, M. (2002). *Strategic behavior and regulatory styles in The Netherlands energy industry.* Retrieved May 3, 2013, from http://www.narcis.nl/publication/RecordID/oai:tudelft.nl:uuid:f940a515-f967-4cf3-9a96-07cb69a61ae5

Lawson, L. L., & Lawson, C. L. (2010). Video game-based methodology for business research. *Simulation & Gaming, 41*(3), 360–373. doi:10.1177/1046878109334038.

Lee, J. (1999). Effectiveness of computer-based instructional simulation: A meta analysis. *International Journal of Instructional Media, 26*(1), 71–85. Retrieved May 3, 2013, from http://www.questia.com/googleScholar.qst?docId=5001238108

Lee, K., & Ashton, M. C. (2004). Psychometric properties of the HEXACO personality inventory. *Multivariate Behavioral Research, 39*(2), 329–358. doi:10.1207/s15327906mbr3902_8.

Leemkuil, H. (2006). *Is it all in the game? Learner support in an educational knowledge management simulation game.* Enschede, The Netherlands: University of Twente. Retrieved May 3, 2013, from http://users.gw.utwente.nl/leemkuil/PhDThesisLeemkuil2006.pdf

Leemkuil, H., de Jong, T., & Ootes, S. (2000). *Review of educational use of games and simulations.* Retrieved from http://kits.edte.utwente.nl/documents/D1.pdf

Lempert, R. J., & Schwabe, W. (1993). *Transition to sustainable waste management, a simulation gaming approach.* Santa Monica, CA: Rand Corporation.

Leyton-Brown, K., & Shoham, Y. (2008). Essentials of game theory. In R. J. Brachman, & T. Dietterich (Eds.), *Political science.* San Francisco, CA: Morgan & Claypool Publishers.

Ma, Y., Williams, D., Prejean, L., & Richard, C. (2007). A research agenda for developing and implementing educational computer games: Colloquium. *British Journal of Educational Technology, 38*(3), 513–518. doi:10.1111/j.1467-8535.2007.00714.x.

Mackenzie, N., & Knipe, S. (2006). Research dilemmas: Paradigms, methods and methodology. *Issues in Educational Research, 16*(2), 193–205.

Maier, F. H., & Grössler, A. (2000). What are we talking about? A taxonomy of computer simulations to support learning. *System Dynamics Review, 16*(2), 135–148. doi:10.1002/1099-1727(200022)16:2<135::AID-SDR193>3.0.CO;2-P.

Malone, T. W., & Lepper, M. (1987a). Intrinsic motivation and instructional effectiveness in computer-based education. In R. E. Snow, & M. J. Farr (Eds.), *Aptitude learning and instruction.* London: Lawrence Erlbaum Associates Publishers.

Malone, T. W., & Lepper, M. (1987b). Making learning fun: A taxonomy of intrinsic motivation for learning. In R. E. Snow, & M. J. Farr (Eds.), *Aptitude, learning, and instruction: III: Cognitive and affective process analysis* (pp. 223–225). Hillsdale, NJ: Lawrence Erlbaum Associates Publishers.

Martin, A. J., & Jackson, S. (2008). Brief approaches to assessing task absorption and enhanced subjective experience: Examining short and core flow in diverse performance domains. *Motivation and Emotion, 32*(3), 141–157. doi:10.1007/s11031-008-9094-0.

Mayer, I. S. (2009). The gaming of policy and the politics of gaming: A review. *Simulation & Gaming, 40*(6), 825–862. doi:10.1177/1046878109346456.

Mayer, I. S. (2012). Towards a comprehensive methodology for the research and evaluation of serious games. In *Proceedings VS-Games 2012* (Vol. 15, pp. 1–15). Genoa, Italy: Procedia Computer Science. doi:10.1016/j.procs.2012.10.075

Mayer, I. S., Bekebrede, G., Harteveld, C., Warmelink, H. J. G., Zhou, Q., & Lo, J. et al. (2013). The research and evaluation of serious games: Towards a comprehensive methodology. *British Journal of Educational Technology.* doi:10.1111/bjet.12067.

Mayer, I. S., Carton, L., De Jong, M., Leijten, M., & Dammers, E. (2004). Gaming the future of an urban network. *Futures, 36*(3), 311–333. doi:10.1016/S0016-3287(03)00159-9.

Mayer, I. S., & Veeneman, W. (Eds.). (2003). *Games in a world of infrastructures: Gaming simulation for research, learning and intervention.* Eburon Publishers.

Mayer, I. S., Warmelink, H. J. G., & Bekebrede, G. (2013). Learning in a game-based virtual environment: A comparative evaluation in higher education. *European Journal of Engineering Education, 38*(1), 85–106. doi:10.1080/03043797.2012.742872.

Mayer, I. S., Zhou, Q., Lo, J., Abspoel, L., Keijser, X., Olsen, E., et al. (2012). Integrated, ecosystem-based marine spatial planning? First results from international simulation-game experiment. In *Proceedings of Third International Engineering Systems Symposium.* Delft, The Netherlands: IEEE.

Mayer, I. S., Zhou, Q., Lo, J., Abspoel, L., Keijser, X., Olsen, E., et al. (2013). Integrated, ecosystem-based marine spatial planning: Design and results of a game-based quasi-experiment. *Ocean and Coastal Management, 82,* 7–26. doi:dx.doi.org/10.1016/j.ocecoaman.2013.04.006

Mayer, R. E. (2005). Cognitive theory of multimedia learning. In R. E. Mayer (Ed.), *The Cambridge handbook of multimedia learning* (pp. 31–48). Cambridge, MA: Cambridge University Press. doi:10.1017/CBO9780511816819.004.

Mayes, D. K., & Cotton, J. E. (2001). Measuring engagement in video games: A questionnaire. In *Proceedings of the Human Factors and Ergonomics Society 45th Annual Meeting* (pp. 692–696). Retrieved May 3, 2013, from http://www.scopus.com/inward/record.url?eid=2-s2.0-0442310948&partnerID=40&md5=b56e3e59c17f58d4d21a35d7755b9f6a

McGonigal, J. E. (2011). *Reality is broken: Why games make us better and how they can change the world. New York.* The Penguin Press.

Meadows, D. L. (1999). Learning to be simple: My odyssey with games. *Simulation & Gaming, 30*(3), 342–351. doi:10.1177/104687819903000310.

Meijer, S. A. (2009). *The organisation of transactions: Studying supply networkd using gaming simulation.* Retrieved from http://www.narcis.nl/publication/RecordID/oai:library.wur.nl:wurpubs/376893

Meijer, S. A., Mayer, I. S., Van Luipen, J., & Weitenberg, N. (2011). Gaming rail cargo management: Exploring and validating alternative modes of organization. *Simulation & Gaming, 43*(1), 85–101. doi:10.1177/1046878110382161.

Meyer, B. (2010). Comparative studies in game-based language learning: A discussion of methodology. In *Proceedings of the 9th European Conference on Elearning,* (pp. 362–369). IEEE.

Mortagy, Y., & Boghikian-Whitby, S. (2010). A longitudinal comparative study of student perceptions in online education. *Interdisciplinary Journal of Elearning and Learning Objects, 6,* 23–44.

Nieborg, D. B. (2004). America's army: More than a game. [Munich, Germany: SAGA.]. *Proceedings of ISAGA, 2004,* 883–891.

Nieborg, D. B. (2011). *Triple-A the political economy of the blockbuster video game.* Amsterdam: Universiteit van Amsterdam.

Noy, A., Raban, D. R., & Ravid, G. (2006). Testing social theories in computer-mediated communication through gaming and simulation. *Simulation & Gaming, 37*(2), 174–194. doi:10.1177/1046878105286184.

Nygaard, C., Courtney, N., & Leigh, E. (Eds.). (2012). *Simulations, games and role play in university education.* Fringdon Oxfordshire, UK: Libri Publishing.

Olsen, T., Procci, K., & Bowers, C. (2011). Serious games usability testing: How to ensure proper usability, playability, and effectiveness. In A. Marcus (Ed.), *Design User Experience and Usability Theory Methods Tools and Practice Proceedings First International Conference DUXU 2011.* doi:10.1007/978-3-642-21708-1

Ordeshook, P. C. (1986). *Game theory and political theory: An introduction.* Retrieved from http://books.google.com/books?id=faytzOKtquMC&pgis=1

Oslin, J. L., Mitchell, S. A., & Griffin, L. L. (1998). The game performance assessment instrument (GPAI), some concerns and solutions for further development. *Journal of Teaching in Physical Education, 17*(2), 220–240.

Papastergiou, M. (2009). Digital game-based learning in high school computer science education: Impact on educational effectiveness and student motivation. *Computers & Education, 52*(1), 1–12. doi:10.1016/j.compedu.2008.06.004.

Petersen, S. A., & Bedek, M. A. (2012). Challenges and opportunities in evaluating learning in serious games: A look at behavioural aspects. In M. Ma, M. Fradinho, J. B. Hauge, H. Duin, & K.-D. Thoben (Eds.), *Serious Games Development and Applications - Third International Conference, SGDA 2012* (LNCS), (vol. 7528). Berlin: Springer.

Pfister, R. (2011). Gender effects in gaming research: A case for regression residuals? *Cyberpsychology Behavior and Social Networking, 14*(10), 603–607. doi:10.1089/cyber.2010.0547 PMID:21486141.

Poverty Is Not, A. Game (PING). (n.d.). *Serious game on poverty awareness.* Retrieved from http://www.povertyisnotagame.com/?lang=en

Preschl, B., Wagner, B., Forstmeier, S., & Maercker, A. (2011). E-health interventions for depression, anxiety disorder, dementia, and other disorders in older adults: A review. *CyberTherapy and Rehabilitation, 4*(3), 371–385.

Raessens, J. (2006). Playful identities, or the ludification of culture. *Games and Culture, 1*(1), 52–57. doi:10.1177/1555412005281779.

Raessens, J. (2009). Homo ludens 2.0. *Metropolis M,* (5), 64–69, 85–88.

Randel, J. M., Morris, B. A., Wetzelf, C. D., & Whitehill, B. V. (1992). The effectiveness of games for educational purposes: A review of the research. *Simulation & Gaming, 25,* 261–276. doi:10.1177/1046878192233001.

Raphael, C., Bachen, C., Lynn, K. M., Baldwin-Philippi, J., & McKee, K. A. (2009). Games for civic learning: A conceptual framework and agenda for research and design. *Games and Culture*, 5(2), 199–235. doi:10.1177/1555412009354728.

Rebolledo-Mendez, G., Avramides, K., & De Freitas, S. (2009). Societal impact of a serious game on raising public awareness: The case of FloodSim. *Methodology*, *148*(2), 15–22. doi: doi:10.1145/1581073.1581076.

Reichlin, L., Mani, N., McArthur, K., Harris, A. M., Rajan, N., & Dacso, C. C. (2011). Assessing the acceptability and usability of an interactive serious game in aiding treatment decisions for patients with localized prostate cancer. *Journal of Medical Internet Research*, *13*(1), e4. doi:10.2196/jmir.1519 PMID:21239374.

Ritterfeld, U., Cody, M. J., & Vorderer, P. (2009). *Serious games: Mechanisms and effects*. Retrieved from http://books.google.com/books?id=GwPf7tbO5mgC&pgis=1

Rockwell, G. M., & Kee, K. (2011). The leisure of serious games: A dialogue. *Game Studies, 11*(2).

Salomon, M., & Soudoplatoff, S. (2010). Why virtual-world economies matter. *Journal of Virtual Worlds Research*, *2*(4), 14.

Sanchez, A., Cannon-Bowers, J., & Bowers, C. (2010). Establishing a science of game based learning. In J. A. Cannon-Bowers, & C. Bowers (Eds.), *Serious game design and development: Technologies for training and learning* (pp. 290–304). Hershey, PA: IGI Global. doi:10.4018/978-1-61520-739-8.ch016.

Sawyer, B. (2008). *Serious games taxonomy*. Sawyer, Ben Smith, Peter.

Scharpf, F. W. (1997). Games real actors play? Actor-centered institutionalism in policy research. In P. Sabatier (Ed.), *Theoretical lenses on public policy*. Boulder, CO: Westview Press.

Scheufele, D. A., Iyengar, S., Kenski, K., Hall, K., & Eds, J. (2002). The state of framing research: A call for new directions. In K. Kenski, & K. H. Jamieson (Eds.), *The Oxford handbook of political communication theories* (pp. 1–27). Oxford, UK: Oxford, University Press.

Schneider, D. K. (2005). *Research design for educational technologists*. Geneva: AACE.

Schrage, M. (2000). *Serious play: How the world's best companies simulate to innovate*. Boston: Harvard Business School Press.

Schuurink, E., Houtkamp, J., & Toet, A. (2008). Engagement and EMG in serious gaming: experimenting with sound and dynamics in the levee patroller training game. In P. Markopoulos, B. de Ruyter, W. Ijsselsteijn, & D. Rowland (Eds.), *Fun and games: Second international conference*, (pp. 139-149). Eindhoven, The Netherlands: Springer Verlag. doi:10.1007/978-3-540- 88322-7_14

Seitlinger, P., Bedek, M. A., Kopeinik, S., & Albert, D. (2012). Evaluating the validity of a non-invasive assessment procedure. In M. Ma, M. Fradinho, J. B. Hauge, H. Duin, & K.-D. Thoben (Eds.), *Serious games development*. Retrieved from http://www.springerlink.com/index/K66751M360805G62.pdf

Senge, P. M. (1990). *The fifth discipline, the art and practice of the learning organization*. New York: Doubleday.

Senge, P. M., Roberts, C., & Ross, R. B. (1994). *The fifth discipline fieldbook, strategies and tools for building a learning organization*. Garden City, NJ: Doubleday.

Shaffer, D. W. (2006). Epistemic frames for epistemic games. *Computers & Education*, *46*(3), 223–234. doi:10.1016/j.compedu.2005.11.003.

Shaw, A. (2010). What is video game culture? Cultural studies and game studies. *Games and Culture*, 5(4), 403–424. doi:10.1177/1555412009360414.

Shubik, M. (1999). *Political economy, oligopoly and experimental games: The selected essays of Martin Shubik volume one.* Cheltenham, UK: Elgar.

Shute, V. J. (2011). Stealth assessment in computer-based games to support learning. In S. Tobias, & J. D. Fletcher (Eds.), *Computer games and instruction* (pp. 503–524). Charlotte, NC: Information Age Publishers.

Shute, V. J., & Kim, Y. J. (2010). Formative assessment: Opportunities and challenges. *Journal of Language Teaching and Research, 1*(6), 838–841. doi: doi:10.4304/jltr.1.6.838-841.

Shute, V. J., Masduki, I., & Donmez, O. (2010). Conceptual framework for modeling, assessing and supporting competencies within game environments. *Cognition and Learning, 8*(2), 137–161.

Shute, V. J., Ventura, M., Bauer, M., & Zapata-Rivera, D. (2009). Melding the power of serious games and embedded assessment to monitor and foster learning? Flow and grow. *Serious Games Mechanisms and Effects, 1*(1), 1–33.

Simon, H. A. (1991). Bounded rationality and organizational learning. *Organization Science, 2*(1), 125–134. doi:10.1287/orsc.2.1.125.

Squire, K. (2002). Cultural framing of computer/video games. *The International Journal of Computer Game Research, 2*(1).

Squire, K. (2004). *Replaying history: Learning world history through playing civilization III.* Bloomington, IN: Indiana University.

Steinkuehler, C. A. (2005). *Cognition & learning in massively multiplayer online games: A critical approach.* Madison, WI: University of Wisconsin-Madison.

Steunenberg, B., Schmidtchen, D., & Koboldt, C. (1999). Strategic power in the European Union: Evaluating the distribution of power in policy games. *Journal of Theoretical Politics, 11*(3), 339–366. doi:10.1177/0951692899011003005.

Sweeney, L. B., & Meadows, D. L. (2001). *The systems thinking playbook.* Durham, NC: Pegasus Communication.

Szturm, T., Betker, A. L., Moussavi, Z., Desai, A., & Goodman, V. (2011). Effects of an interactive computer game exercise regimen on balance impairment in frail community-dwelling older adults: A randomized controlled trial. *Physical Therapy, 91*(10), 1449–1462. doi:10.2522/ptj.20090205 PMID:21799138.

Tallir, I. B., Lenoir, M., Valcke, M., & Musch, E. (2007). Do alternative instructional approaches result in different game performance learning outcomes? Authentic assessment in varying game conditions. *International Journal of Sport Psychology, 38*(3), 263–282.

Taylor, J. L. (1971). *Instructional planning systems, a gaming-simulation approach to urban problems.* London: Cambridge University Press. doi:10.1017/CBO9780511720789.

Trepte, S., & Reinecke, L. (2011). The pleasures of success: Game-related efficacy experiences as a mediator between player performance and game enjoyment. *Cyberpsychology Behavior and Social Networking, 14*(9), 555–557. doi:10.1089/cyber.2010.0358 PMID:21342012.

Tykhonov, D., Jonker, C., & Meijer, S. A. (2008). *Agent-based simulation of the trust and tracing game for supply chains and networks, & social simulation.* Retrieved May 3, 2013, from http://jasss.soc.surrey.ac.uk/11/3/1.html

Van der Spek, E. D. (2011). (n.d.). *Experiments in serious game design: A cognitive approach*. Retrieved May 3, 2013, from http://www.narcis.nl/publication/RecordID/oai:dspace. library.uu.nl:1874/211480

Van der Spek, E. D., Wouters, P., & Van Oostendorp, H. (2011). Code red: Triage or cognition-based design rules enhancing decisionmaking training in a game environment. *British Journal of Educational Technology*, *42*(3), 441–455. doi:10.1111/j.1467-8535.2009.01021.x.

Van Houten, S. P. A. (2007, November 6). *A suite for developing and using business games: Supporting supply chain business games in a distributed context*. Retrieved from http://www.narcis.nl/publication/RecordID/oai:tudelft. nl:uuid:006a4dfd-8aba-47e5-8a15-c481eace87e1

van Ruijven, T. (n.d.). *Virtual emergency management training*. Delft, The Netherlands: Delft University of Technology.

Van Staalduinen, J. P. (2012). *Gamers on games and gaming: Implications for Educational game design*. Delft, The Netherlands: TU Delft.

Varoufakis, Y. (2008). Game theory: Can it unify the social sciences? *Organization Studies*, *29*(8-9), 1255–1277. doi:10.1177/0170840608094779.

Vartiainen, P. (2000). *Evaluation methods and comparative study*. Retrieved May 3, 2013, from http://cjpe.ca/distribution/20001012_vartiainen_pirkko.pdf

Verdaasdonk, E. G. G., Dankelman, J., Schijven, M. P., Lange, J. F., Wentink, M., & Stassen, L. P. S. (2009). Serious gaming and voluntary laparoscopic skills training: Amulti-center study. *Official Journal of the Society for Minimally Invasive Therapy*, *18*(4), 232–238. doi:10.1080/13645700903054046.

Virtual Reality at Ford Motor Company. (n.d.). Retrieved April 11, 2013, from http://www.youtube.com/watch?v=zmeR-u-DioE

Weiss, C. H. (1997). Theory-based evaluation: Past, present, and future. *New Directions for Evaluation*, (76): 41–55. doi:10.1002/ev.1086.

Wenzler, I. (2008). The ten commandments for translating simulation results into real-life performance. *Simulation & Gaming*, *40*(1), 98–109. doi:10.1177/1046878107308077.

Whitlock, L. A., McLaughlin, A. C., & Allaire, J. C. (2012). Individual differences in response to cognitive training: Using a multi-modal, attentionally demanding game-based intervention for older adults. *Computers in Human Behavior*, *28*, 1091–1096. doi:10.1016/j.chb.2012.01.012.

Wittgenstein, L. (1953). *Philosophical investigations*. Malden, MA: Blackwell.

Wolfe, J., & Box, T. M. (1988). Team cohesion effects on business game performance. *Simulation & Gaming*, *19*(1), 82–98. doi:10.1177/003755008801900105.

Wood, R. T. A., Griffiths, M. D., & Eatough, V. (2004). Online data collection from video game players: Methodological issues. *Cyberpsychology & Behavior*, *7*(5), 511–518. doi: doi:10.1089/cpb.2004.7.511 PMID:15667045.

Wright, J. D., & Marsden, P. V. (Eds.). (2010). *Handbook of survey research* (2nd ed.). Bingley, UK: Emerald Group Publishing.

Wu, W.-H., Hsiao, H.-C., Wu, P.-L., Lin, C.-H., & Huang, S.-H. (2011). Investigating the learning-theory foundations of game-based learning: A meta-analysis. *Journal of Computer Assisted Learning*, *28*. doi: doi:10.1111/j.1365-2729.2011.00437.x.

Young, M. F., Slota, S., Cutter, A. B., Jalette, G., Mullin, G., & Lai, B. et al. (2012). Our princess is in another castle: A review of trends in serious gaming for education. *Review of Educational Research*, *82*(1), 61–89. doi:10.3102/0034654312436980.

Zapata-Rivera, D., VanWinkle, W., Doyle, B., Buteux, A., & Bauer, M. (2009). Combining learning and assessment in assessment-based gaming environments: A case study from a New York City school. *Interactive Technology and Smart Education*, *6*(3), 173–188. doi:10.1108/17415650911005384.

Zichermann, G., & Linder, J. (2010). *Game-based marketing: Inspire customer loyalty through rewards, challenges, and contests*. Hoboken, NJ: Wiley.

KEY TERMS AND DEFINITIONS

Assessment: Evaluation with the specific intention to establish / judge the performance, suitability and / or cost-effectiveness of something or someone in the light of past, present or future objectives, tasks, function or other properties.

Evaluation: Applied research with the specific intention of determining the 'value' of something or someone in the light of past, present or future objectives, tasks, function or other properties.

Frame: An instrument for defining reality rather than describing reality.

Frame Analysis: How people understand an issue, and to track the way in which this understanding changes over time.

Learning: Adaptive changes of a system in response to internal incommensurability and/or external pressure.

Method: Means, manner or procedure for systematic inquiry or action.

Methodology: The rationale and principles upon which systematic inquiry is founded.

Quasi Experimental Design: Form of experimental research where because of practical, functional and/or ethical reasons some requirements for experimental control, like randomization, control group or lab conditions, cannot / should not be met.

Research Design: Description of the setup of systematic inquiry, including study type, research questions, hypotheses, operationalization, data collection and analysis.

Serious Game: Non-definable but common reference to the many different forms in which (principles, technology, elements of) games are utilized for society, business, politics.

Chapter 18
Study Design and Data Gathering Guide for Serious Games' Evaluation

Jannicke Baalsrud Hauge
*Bremer Institut für Produktion und Logistik
(BIBA), Germany*

Johann C. K. H. Riedel
Nottingham University, UK

Elizabeth Boyle
University of the West of Scotland, UK

Pablo Moreno-Ger
Universidad Complutense de Madrid

Igor Mayer
Delft University of Technology, The Netherlands

Francesco Bellotti
Università degli Studi di Genova, Italy

Rob Nadolski
*Open University of The Netherlands, The
Netherlands*

Theodore Lim
Heriot-Watt University, UK

James Ritchie
Heriot-Watt University, UK

ABSTRACT

The objective of this chapter is to provide an overview of the different methods that can be used to evaluate the learning outcomes of serious games. These include Randomised Control Trials (RCT), quasi-experimental designs, and surveys. Case studies of a selection of serious games developed for use in higher education are then presented along with evaluations of these games. The evaluations illustrate the different evaluation methods, along with an assessment of how well the evaluation method performed. Finally, the chapter discusses the lessons learned and compares the experiences with the evaluation methods and their transferability to other games.

DOI: 10.4018/978-1-4666-4773-2.ch018

Copyright © 2014, IGI Global. Copying or distributing in print or electronic forms without written permission of IGI Global is prohibited.

INTRODUCTION

In the last decade higher education has taken a digital turn in the use of games and simulations for learning and training. The long and well-established tradition of using teacher-led, no-technology or low-technology simulation games in higher education is 'under the spell' of online simulations, 3-D virtual worlds and digital Serious Games (SGs). So, what have we gained and/or possibly lost with this digital turn to Game-based Learning (GBL)? To answer this question we need to have ways of evaluating the learning impact of games. This chapter sets out to review and provide examples of the different evaluation methods that can be applied to serious games.

Considerable efforts and resources are now being put into the evaluation and assessment of game-based learning. As a result, both the number and the quality of evaluations of games for learning are increasing (see for a recent overview Connolly et al., 2012). However, there are still considerable weaknesses, for example, the absence of tools for unobtrusive, 'stealth' data gathering and assessment, and good research designs other than randomized controlled trials. Here, we wish to make a contribution by looking at how different evaluation methods have been applied to some serious games and to see what has been measured and how.

This chapter will present several case studies of serious games and their evaluation methodologies. It will identify the differences in the evaluation methods, and also discuss what this means for the transferability of the evaluation methods to other types of games.

EVALUATION METHODS FOR SG LEARNING OUTCOMES

The evaluation of games is complex and multidimensional since it involves evaluation not just of whether there is an improvement in performance on the targeted learning outcomes, but also evaluation of the user acceptance of, engagement with, and satisfaction with the game. The introduction of a serious game into the curriculum raises similar issues to any other educational intervention, since the aim of a game is to improve performance on a specific learning outcome. Woolfson (2011) proposes a hierarchy of evidence for evaluating educational interventions:

1. Meta-analyses.
2. Randomised controlled trials (RCT).
3. Quasi-experimental designs.
4. Single case experimental designs–pre & post test.
5. Non experimental designs–surveys, correlational, qualitative.

Meta-Analyses: At the top of the hierarchy of evidence for the effectiveness of interventions are meta-analyses. Meta-analysis combines the results from previous studies to identify patterns in research findings, especially with respect to whether games are effective methods in learning. Meta-analysis requires a reasonable number of empirical studies as input to compare – in serious games we still have a way to go to produce the needed studies, hence it has not been included in this chapter.

Randomised Control Trials (RCT): The Randomised Control Trial (RCT) is considered to be the gold standard for evaluating educational interventions. In a RCT participants are randomly allocated to an experimental (game) group or a control (non-game) group and their performance on the target skill/behaviour before and after the game intervention is tested. Ideally pre-testing should confirm no existing difference between the groups, while post-testing should show whether the experimental group performs better than the control group. Improvements in the target skill/behaviour for the experimental compared with the control group in a follow-up study would allow further confirmation that the intervention was successful.

Papastergiou (2009) developed a game to teach computer memory concepts and carried out a classic RCT, comparing the performance of a games group with a control group on tests of knowledge of computer memory concepts before and after the serious game intervention. She found that students in the gaming group performed better and also liked the game based approach better than students in the control condition. This provides evidence to support the view that educational computer games can be exploited as effective and motivating learning environments. This study raised an interesting methodological point which is true for many educational studies. In a true RCT each participant is randomly assigned to a gaming or non-gaming condition, but in this case participants were randomly assigned by intact classes to gaming or non-gaming groups.

Beale, Kato, Marin-Bowling, Guthrie and Cole (2007) carried out a RCT to investigate whether a video game, Re-Mission, could actively involve young people with cancer in their own treatment and increase self-care and cancer illness knowledge. A test on cancer-related knowledge was given prior to game play (baseline) and again after 1 and 3 months. Knowledge test scores for both control and experimental groups improved significantly over the follow-up periods, but the significant group by time interaction showed that the scores of the experimental Re-Mission game group improved significantly more than the control group($F(1,302)= 4.07, p= .04, f=.013$).

Quasi-Experimental Designs: While a RCT requires the random assignment of participants to experimental or control groups, in educational interventions this is not always possible. In that case a quasi-experimental design would have to be used (Field and Hole, 2003). This kind of design is also used to refer to a one group post-test design where participants' behaviours are measured following an intervention and to a one group pre-test/post-test design where participants' performance is measured before and after the intervention. In group comparison designs, the performance of two

(or more) groups is measured after the intervention. These designs are all of lower quality than a RCT, but for pragmatic reasons may have to be used in real world research. An example of a study that compared four different groups but only after the intervention was Cameron and Dwyer (2005) who compared the impact of four different instructional conditions on knowledge acquisition in learning about the operation of the human heart: the digitised instructional unit with (a) no game plus questions, (b) game plus questions, (c) game plus questions plus knowledge of accuracy of response to questions, and (d) game plus questions plus elaborative feedback which provided the answer to the question and reasons why that was correct. The results showed that there was no difference in performance in the no-game condition (a) and the game condition (b), suggesting that the competitive structure of the game was not sufficient to increase knowledge retention. However, there were significant advantages on two outcome measures when response feedback was introduced and on all the performance measures when elaborative feedback was included, indicating that feedback to players about the accuracy of their responses was more important than the competitive structure of the game. While not an RCT, this kind of study can clearly provide detailed information about how different kinds of game mechanics provide support for learning in a game.

Surveys: Survey research typically uses a questionnaire methodology to ask many respondents about their attitudes to, perceptions of, or use of games generally, or of a specific game. The results are typically reported in terms of descriptive statistics reporting for example what percentage of people play games, intend to play games, enjoyed a game or felt that the game had helped them achieve the intended skills. Some studies, such as Connolly et al (2007) and Karakus et al (2008) examined game playing generally, while others, such as Lindh et al (2008), studied students' use of a specific game. Surveys can also be used as part of a formative evaluation or user requirements analysis to assess whether potential players of a game would perceive a particular kind of game as useful.

Connolly et al (2007) surveyed Scottish students about their game playing habits, their motives for playing both entertainment and educational games and their acceptance of educational games in Higher Education. Findings confirmed the popularity of playing entertainment games as a leisure time activity for students, especially male students. There was also a high level of acceptance amongst students that games could be used for learning in Higher Education. Fewer female students played games and those who did play played less and played a less varied selection of games than males, suggesting that there may still be some way to go in persuading female students of the value of computer games in learning.

Rather than just reporting descriptive data, it is possible to carry out more sophisticated analysis with survey data, looking at links between variables and this would typically be done where a theoretical model is being tested. Weibel et al (2008) for example used regression analysis to examine the relationship between engagement variables, presence, flow and enjoyment, in an online game. They found that flow mediated the relationship between presence and enjoyment.

Structural equation modelling has also been used and again this kind of analysis would typically test a theoretical model. The Technology Acceptance Model (TAM) proposes that the perceived ease of use and perceived usefulness of a software application determines how much it will be used. Hsu & Lu (2004) tested an extended version of the TAM model and found that social norms (i. e. players' perceptions of other people's views of the technology), critical mass (the number of people using the technology) and flow were more important in predicting time spent playing entertainment games than the traditional TAM variables.

Qualitative Research: In terms of the hierarchy of evidence, qualitative research is regarded as lower quality than quantitative research. Qualitative research is more subjective than quantitative since it is more interpretative, but it can provide a much broader brush approach to examining the skills that playing games can support.

Steinkuehler and Duncan (2008) reported a high quality qualitative analysis of the scientific reasoning skills displayed by players in their contributions to the online discussion boards while they played the popular online game, World of Warcraft (WoW). Steinkuehler and Duncan developed a rigorous coding system for players' contributions based on the benchmarks of the American Association for the Advancement of Sciences (AAAS, 1993) for scientific reasoning, Chinn and Malhotra's (2002) theoretical framework for evaluating enquiry tasks and Kuhn's (1962) framework for categorising epistemological stances in argumentation. They found that WoW players demonstrated an impressive variety of higher order scientific reasoning skills in these fora, such as using data and argument, building on others' ideas and using system based reasoning. Players' contributions to discussion boards provided evidence of the higher level evaluative thinking demonstrated in discussion, knowledge sharing and debate and 86% of players' contributions to the fora were examples of this kind.

The following table summarises the types of evaluation methods that can be used and when they can be used for evaluating serious games. It is followed by examples of studies using some of the methods.

Evaluation data can be gathered through mixed methods, mostly combining pre-game and post-game questionnaires of the players, live or video observations, transcripts of after-action reviews and game results. In a few cases, methods are applied more rigorously with in-game knowledge tests or network and communication analyses from logging tools or video observations. Table 1 gives an overview of how to mix the various methods in pre-game, in-game and post-game stages.

Table 1. What to measure, how and when

How		What?	Pre-Game	In Game	Post-Game
Self-reported	Qual.	Personality, player experiences, context, etc.	Interviews, focus group, logbook.	Logbook, interviews or small assignments as part of the game.	Interviews focus group, after-action review.
	Quant.	Social/demographic, opinions, motivations, attitudes, engagement, game-quality learning, power, influence, reputation, network centrality, learning satisfaction, etc.	Survey, questionnaire, individual or expert panel.	In-game questionnaires.	Survey, questionnaire, individual or expert panel.
Tested	Qual.	Behaviour, skills, etc.	E.g. actor role-play, case-analysis, assessment, mental models.	Game-based behavioural assessment.	Game-based behavioural assessment.
	Quant.	Values, knowledge, attitudes, skills, personality, power.	Psychometric, socio-metric tests: e.g. personality, leadership, team roles, IQ.	Game-based behavioural performance analysis.	Game-based behavioural performance analysis.
Observed	Qual.	Behavioural performance of student, professionals, player and/or facilitator, others; decisions, strategies, policies, emotions, conflicts, etc.	Participatory observation, ethnographic methods.	Video, audio personal observation, ethnography, Maps, text, figures, drawings, pictures, etc.	Participatory observation, ethnographic methods.
	Quant.	Biophysical–psychological responses, like stress (heart rate, perspiration).	Participant observation, network analysis, Biophysical–psychological observation.	In-game tracking and logging, network analysis, data mining, biometric observation.	In-game log file analysis, network analysis.

In the previous chapter, Mayer et al. discussed the need for proper methods, tools and principles for the evaluation of serious games and game based learning was discussed. Mayer also stated that there is a "lack of comprehensive, multipurpose frameworks for comparative and longitudinal evaluation". While RCT is the gold standard for evaluating educational interventions, very often it cannot be applied in practice due to the difficulties in having randomly selected control groups, and the arising ethical issues and practical concerns. So there is a need for other kinds of evaluation. Furthermore, an upcoming issue is the need for seamless, or "stealth" data-gathering and assessment in SGs (Bellotti et al, 2013a) as well as for performance based evaluation (Bellotti et.al

2013b). These are all activities under development, and thus not yet deployed on a large scale. However, every teacher being interested in using serious games in his /her classes, has, at the end, to deliver a proof of effectiveness and to show how the game supported the learning objectives of the course as well as the individual learning outcomes.

This section has reviewed the different study designs that can and have been applied to evaluating the learning effectiveness of computer games. The next section presents case studies of several of these methods.

CASE STUDIES

The objective in this section is to show different approaches for the evaluation of the learning outcomes of serious games and to discuss the advantages and disadvantages of the methods used. This discussion is based on seven case studies reporting the authors' own experiences in using games in their own courses. In this chapter we present the evaluation of these serious games. (see Table 2)

The serious games we have looked at here are used in different settings in higher education and vocational training. Most of them are facilitated and used in a blended learning approach, only one case study reports on a game which is not facilitated. There is a mixture of individual and team-based games. The topics addressed by the games are varied, ranging from aquaculture to supply chain management.

Table 2. Overview of the case studies and the evaluation methods

Game	Authors	Application Domain	Evaluation Method	Outcomes Measured	Individual/ Team Game
Supply Net Game	Baalsrud-Hauge et al (2007) Delhoum (2009)	Supply Chain and Inventory management	RCT	Marginal inventory costs.	Team
Hemocrit (HCT)	Moreno-Ger et al. (2010)	Health	Quasi-experimental; comparison of game group and control group	Rating of difficulty in understanding and performing procedure and in using equipment; variance in performance.	Individual
Beware	Baalsrud Hauge et al. (2008)	Supply Chain Management Risks	Formative; Quasi-experimental: pre, during & post questionnaire	Assessment of knowledge risk management procedures and methods, PKI on users' performance in the game (time, quality, costs, collaboration (no. of interaction with the other players)), scores on final report.	Team
SimVenture	Bellotti et al. (2012); Bellotti et al. (2013c)	Enterpreneurship Management	Quasi-experimental: pre & post tests	Assessment of knowledge of entrepreneurship-related topics; user acceptance of the serious games and of the overall course based on them.	Individual game played by teams
Emergo	Hummel et al. (2011)	Aquaculture	Quasi-experimental: pre & post-tests	Scores on preliminary and final feasibility reports.	Individual
Cosiga	Riedel, Pawar, & Barson (2001)	New product development	Survey. In process/ during game tests	Questionnaire on subjective situational awareness administered at regular intervals during game play.	Team
Shortfall	Corriere (2003)	Inventory Management	Surveys: usability survey and player perceptions survey	System Usability Scale (SUS) questionnaire; 10 question post-test survey on player perceptions of game.	Team

Supply Net Game: Case Study Using RCT

Description

This case study describes the use of a serious game for system analysis – the Supply Net Game. The game is simulation based and uses the system dynamics methodology (Coyle, 1977). The simulation of a production network was produced using the VensimDSS software (Scholz-Reiter and Delhoum, 2007). Vensim is simulation software usable for modelling dynamic systems (http://vensim.com/vensim-software/) in a realistic way. It is a cooperative game with four participants, each of them being responsible for the inventory and the replenishment in one of four factories, thus the players have to place orders in each simulation period. They also have to control the cash-flow as well as make sure that they do not run out of stock. Each player has an overview of their costs. The aim of the players is the minimisation of the inventory costs. The GUI delivers enough information for taking decisions and comprises: work in progress, back logs, etc. The interface of the game offers the participants feedback so that they can decide on the level of their orders.

Learning Objective

The aim of the game is to support systems thinking in a dynamic environment. The participants are required to learn about inventory management, back logs and the bullwhip effect (Arnold et al, 2002), as well as experience how important communication is. The target for the participants during the game is to minimize their costs, while still being able to deliver. Marginal inventory costs are the key performance measure of the game (Baalsrud Hauge et al., 2007).

Evaluation Method

The game was evaluated using a Randomised Control Trial (RCT) with 106 students, 78 in the experimental group and 28 in the control group at the University of Bremen. There were two groups, one group (the experimental group) only playing the game, and one group (the control group) first getting an introduction to the left-hand elicitation (Delhoum, 2009) method before playing the game. The game included a systems-thinking intervention with a method for mental model elicitation. For the pre and post-tests, we used questionnaires. Ten of the questions were objective, while two of them were judgmental. The same questionnaire was used twice, before and after the main phase of testing to the participants to identify learning effects after running the simulation game for the control group, or after experiencing the left-hand column elicitation method and playing the serious game for the experimental group. Learning was measured by (i) the responses of the students and decision makers to a questionnaire that tests systems-thinking skills and (ii) total inventory costs achieved by a team during the serious game.

Experimental Setup

The game was embedded in a five-step workshop based on Kolb's learning cycle. The participants were divided into two groups. The first group was the control group with 28 participants and met twice. Due to organisational constraints the experimental group had 78 participants. The experimental group was also introduced to elicitation and mental models before they played the game. On an organisational level, two principal characteristics were retained. First, the distribution of the students' pool to the teams was random in the first round. Second, the same teams were built and maintained in both rounds whether this was for the control or experimental group.

Results

The students had lower costs in the second part of the lab, so it was expected that the level of detail and the complexity of the answers given in the questionnaire should have improved. However this could not be verified since the students in the control group scored equally in the pre-test, while the experimental group answered marginally better in the pre-test than in the post-test.

Evaluation of the Evaluation Method

While this study used a RCT, there were pragmatic difficulties in actually implementing a RCT in a regular course at a university. The curriculum specifies how teaching should be delivered, and there was little room for change or innovation. For example for practical reasons it was necessary to include 78 students in the experimental condition but only 28 in the control condition when ideally there would be equal numbers in each. Secondly, if we could produce the evidence that a specific method (in this case the elicitation method) would bring the student a specific advantage, it would not be ethical to randomly exclude students from the same opportunity. In addition, including a control group increases the workload, and thus it is not always possible when running courses.

Validation of the Learning Goals

The learning goals for the supply net game were to understand how inventory control works in a dynamic environment as well as to get a better understanding of system dynamics. Even though the results showed a decrease in costs in the second round of the game, the results do not show significantly higher achievements on the learning objective when comparing the experimental and control groups. The absence of a significant effect is disappointing but has to be viewed in the context of students appearing to enjoy the game and learning how complex any decision in a dynamic environment is.

EMERGO: A Game on Aquaculture Management Game

Aquaculture deals with the development of flora (plants) and fauna (animals) in water. To assess the influence of the new use on the system and other purposes, professionals working in the domain of water management have to both possess natural science knowledge and have a keen eye for the context of policy-making that is involved. Aquaculture is a relatively new sector. Governmental and licensing institutions still struggle to find their way in dealing with entrepreneurs that want to start new businesses in this sector.

Learning Objective

The serious game on aquaculture is the practical part of the aquaculture course that most students follow during their third year of the Bachelor of Water Management programme at OUNL. The main learning objective is to deal with conflicts and dilemmas and to negotiate. The student is assigned the role of an externally hired project leader and is asked to investigate and draw up a feasibility report on what would be the most suitable location to start a new shellfish production site.

Evaluation Method

We compared the quality of advisory reports that students in the domain of water management had to draw up for an authentic case problem, both before and after collaborating on the problem with (virtual) peer students in the game. Peers studied the case from either an ecological or governance perspective, and during collaboration both perspectives had to be confronted and reflected upon. Twelve water management students of the HZ University of Applied Science in the Netherlands participated in this case study. The average age of the participants was 22 years, with a range from 19-26. Seven were male and five were female.

Experimental Setup

For research purposes, the course tutor allocated one of the two perspectives to each student and they had one month to deliver the final report. Virtual collaboration on average took place after about 75% of the period. The same (real life) tutor collected, scored and compared both the preliminary (before virtual collaboration) and final (after virtual collaboration) reports, in close cooperation with another tutor, using a learning effect correction model. Although we did not explicitly measure the inter-subjective reliability of the correction model, both tutors assessed the reports and agreed upon the scores to be given on the various items of the model. Partial elaborations (preliminary reports) before collaboration were assessed as pre-test results, and integrative elaborations (final reports) after collaboration were assessed as post-test results. Appreciation of the serious game was measured by online questionnaires that students had to fill in at the start and at the end (i. e. after sending in their final reports).

Results

A paired t-test (two-tailed) confirmed that the mean scores following the collaborative intervention (M = 54.00, SD = 6.28) were significantly higher than the scores before the intervention (M = 19.92; SD = 8.47), (t = -14.53; p < 0.001). The most important hypothesis therefore can be confirmed: virtual collaboration indeed improves learning effectiveness. We controlled for the influence of perspective on this learning effect (i. e. on the increase of scores), which appears to be missing (F (1, 11) = 0.72, MSE = 46.67, p = 0.42, $\eta p2$ = 0.07).

While assessing the quality of the reports, tutors observed a number of more qualitative results that also provide evidence for the contribution of collaboration. Increases between preliminary and final reports were to the largest degree attributable by gains in scores on the integration items of the correction model. For instances, an integrated map was distilled from information from both perspectives, information about known cultivation methods (ecological perspectives) was linked to existing legislation (governance perspective), and confrontation of perspectives led to better rethinking the selection of most suitable shellfish species. Overall, it is the opinion of both tutors, that the conclusions could not be reached based on one perspective, or learning trajectory alone.

Evaluation of the Evaluation Method

The evaluation method used in this study was a pre and post-test. There was good agreement between the tutors' assessments, showing the reliability of the scoring method. It was planned to compare these results from a brand new course with the results from the previous ones that might have been working as a control group. The issue with a control group is that this is a brand new course on Aquaculture, so there was not an existing course which could have been used for a control group. It was decided that there was no real control group possible, mainly as the only alternative for the game might have been face-to-face (f2f) or virtual working groups with high tutor load. Such working groups were practically not feasible because of tutors' limited availability due to other working obligations. Students were dispersed through the region (Province of Zeeland), which made it practically infeasible for them to work together in f2f working groups, so virtual working groups might have been the best alternative. However, the issue with limited tutor availability would still have been the case and considerable costs for setting up a virtual working groups course environment was beyond project budget for game development and testing.

Validation of the Learning Goals

Results from this case study using the educational (serious) game 'Aquaculture' have shown that scripted collaboration significantly improved the quality of learning output. Furthermore, students indicated that the game helped them gain more insight into the various perspectives that play a part in their professional development. According to the questionnaire results, participants preferred real life collaboration over virtual collaboration, although they see that online education does increase the flexibility of study. It therefore could not be concluded that students prefer these kinds of virtual learning environments over more traditional face-to-face settings of collaboration.

Beware: A Game on Supply Chain Risk Management

This game was developed for use in a blended learning environment as part of a course for masters students at the University of Bremen. It is a multi-user, role based game. It has been in use since 2006, and is continuously improved. It is process driven and comprises two levels. The game is facilitated and played in a distributed environment. The facilitator has a monitoring tool, which allows him/her to monitor the game without taking an active part in the game. It also offers the possibility of actively controlling the game by setting events. The facilitator can also communicate with the players via a chat function; she/he can set events and reset processes.

Learning Objective

The objectives of the Beware game are to increase the understanding and awareness of risks in enterprise networks, to improve the players' skills in risk management in a supply network as well as to apply common risk management methods to gain some experience in a risk free environment. Thus, the knowledge on methods and procedure

on risk management was measured. In addition it was assessed how well the students were able to apply the methods and to apply the methods. During the game we measure the interaction among the players, the costs, net –margin, logistics costs, performance, delivery on time etc is measured and compared in each round.

Evaluation Method

In this game two forms of evaluation were used. The first is formative - the facilitator monitors the gaming process, collects information on how the different players are playing and on the communication and collaboration between them. Also a set of indicators is continuously collected. These can also be used by the players to evaluate how they play during the game play. This information is used in the debriefing stage in order to analyse and evaluate what happened in the game and thus to construct new knowledge.

The second part of the evaluation is the use of pre, mid-term and post-game questionnaires completed by the players to find if the players have gained knowledge from playing the game. It is only on reconstructable knowledge, so it does not deliver enough information concerning if the player has improved his/her skills on resilience. The outcome of the evaluations is used for improving the game.

Experimental Setup

The Beware game concept foresees that the teacher can introduce the theory to students in advance. Even though the game is process driven, the levels are scenario based. Normally, the students complete two levels. The playing time is 3.5-4 hours, followed by a debriefing and reflection phase. In order to internalise the knowledge acquired during the class, students meet one week after to explain the tasks and the analysis they need to carry out during the two gaming sessions. The observation of how the other participants solved their tasks and applied the methods leads to a reflection on the method and thereby to improving the understanding among the participants. Finally, the last step for the participants is to prepare a report in which they reflect on the problems experienced and to assess the strategies they developed at the beginning to reduce the occurring risks (Baalsrud Hauge et al. 2008).

Results

The evaluation of the learning outcome on risk awareness and management showed that the students were able to identify risks, apply risk assessment and management methods, as well as reporting that the game helped them to apply their theoretical knowledge and develop strategies. Applying risk management successfully requires that the participants know the steps of the process. The tests show that the players are able to apply the theory and to use different methods. It also shows that the longer they play, the better they get at identifying and assessing the different types of risks at an early stage. However, if we compare the mid test with the final test, the results show that the level increases more after the game than after the introduction. The participants mentioned two main challenges (provoked by the game); first, they lost the overview and did not manage to deal with the user interface and what was happening. Secondly, they found it difficult to identify hidden risks. We see an example of the outcome of the post test in Figure 1.

The performance in each game is dependent on the players and on the communication level. At the beginning, before the facilitator's tool was in use, it was sometimes the case that the game hardly worked well. The facilitator's tool offers the possibility to track the communication flow against the performance in the game. The communication carried out by using the chat function is stored in the database, and the facilitator can monitor the communication throughout the game

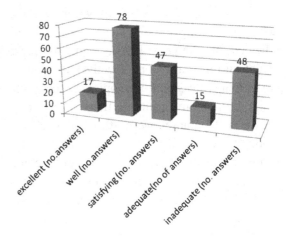

Figure 1. Results of the question: Please list as many main steps in a risk management process as you know and put them in the order you will carry them out.

play. Debriefing is a central part of the two stage game, and time is set aside to analyse the communication and collaboration problems identified during the game in this phase. The trend in these discussions supports the impression of the author/facilitator, that the communication level has an important impact both on the key performance indicators (KPI) as well as the risks the participants need to deal with.

Evaluation of the Evaluation Method

Tracking the communication as well as all the actions taken by the participants is very helpful, but requires a lot of experience of the facilitator. This information also helps in the debriefing sessions.

Using pre, mid and post questionnaires as well as collecting communication data and using inbuilt performance measures is time consuming. The experiments shows, that the students are motivated and reach the learning goals. However, the evaluation process is complex (especially the part based on interaction and communication), gives good results, but is time consuming and does not support immediate feedback.

Validation of the Learning Goals

The results show that for students without any, or with a little knowledge of risk management, it is important to make their task more visible in the first game level. Furthermore, it was seen that the process of playing one game, debriefing it and then playing another game level helps to increase the performance on the second game because of the transfer of knowledge from one game to another through debriefing. The participants identified the risks, as well as developed strategies for reducing the collaboration risks to a much higher degree. The continuous evaluation of the learning effect demonstrates that the time required to transfer information into knowledge not only depends on the essential debriefing phase but also relies on the experience that the participant already has. This needs to be taken into consideration at an early stage of the experimental set up so that the students can be supplied with the necessary information on methods and approaches in advance.

Cosiga: Evaluating a Team-Based Multiplayer Serious Game

Cosiga is a multimedia computer based simulation game of new product development for the education of European engineers, designers, managers and students.

Learning Goals

Cosiga was designed as a complement to engineering and manufacturing courses to give an experience of what the new product development process is like. The game aims to realistically simulate the collaborative and co-operative process of the new product development process inherent in a concurrent engineering approach (Riedel et al, 2001). It is a role playing game with five participants which requires participants to work collaboratively together, using communication tools to specify, design, and produce the final product which is a type of truck. The final product's conformance to specification, development time and costs are used to calculate the team's score.

Evaluation Method

In this study situational awareness (SA) was used to measure the performance of participants during the Cosiga simulation game. The aim was to compare the performance of collocated teams and virtual teams. SA is conceptualised as the current knowledge about what is actually happening in a given situation, what it means and what to do about it. It is a mental model of the dynamic context in which one is operating, including its status and dynamics, with which one evaluates current and possible future situations in terms of one's goals, thereby optimising decision-making and performance. "*SA is the perception of the elements in the environment within a volume of time and space, the comprehension of their meaning, and the projection of their status in the near future*" (Endsley, 1995). In our study questionnaires which measure subjective situational awareness were used (while subjective SA has its limitations compared to objective SA, nevertheless if participants do not subjectively feel they have good awareness – whether or not it matches the reality of the situation – they are likely to make mistakes (Endsley 1998).

Experimental Setup

A controlled empirical study was conducted using engineering personnel from the UK aerospace and defence company BAE Systems. Two conditions were set up – a collocated game with all five participants located in the same room and a virtual condition with the five participants located in different rooms, see Table 3.

Typically a game run takes one working day, starting with participants' briefing, game practice session, gaming session, and debriefing. Once the five participants had gathered in the room, they

Table 3. Overview of the Cosiga experimental design

Condition 1: Virtual Game	**Condition 2: Collocated Game**
All players in separate rooms with only telephone and text messaging for communication. No face-to-face contact during gaming session.	All players in one room with text messaging for communication. Face-to-face contact at participants' discretion.

were allocated with their role in the game. For the situation awareness evaluation, in-game questionnaires were issued at four intervals – starting after one hour of gaming and roughly one hour apart. The data was analysed using analysis of variance – ANOVA. The main aim was to look at the effect of the virtual/collocated condition on the situational awareness of the players over the duration of the game. The data were pooled for all roles to give a sample size of 10 (5 roles and 2 conditions).

Results

For brevity only the results for two items of the situation awareness questionnaire are presented here – as the results for most of the SA items were similar. The first item is Question 1: Would you say that you have observed all events and information that are relevant to your role in the production of the truck? The second item is Question 2: Would you say that you have a good sense of the future course of events and likely outcomes with regard to the production of the truck? (See Figure 2.)

The interaction between condition and time was significant (Two-way interaction condition by time $F_{(3,15)}=3.32$, $p=0.0488$). Analysis suggests that there is a significant difference between collocated and dispersed teams at time intervals 3 and 4. It would appear that the difference between groups became apparent only after a prolonged period of time (2 hours) was spent working on the game. The data suggests that this finding is a result of the virtual team's understanding becoming worse with time and the collocated team's understanding improving with time (see Figure 3.)

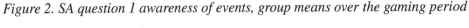

Figure 2. SA question 1 awareness of events, group means over the gaming period

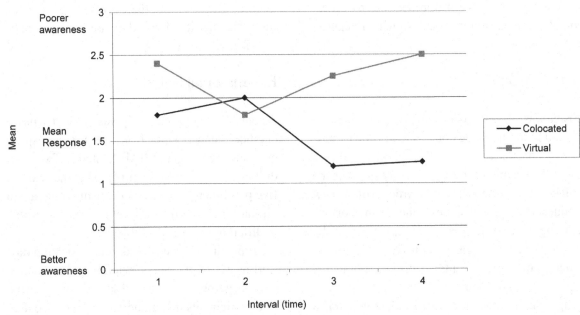

Figure 3. SA question 3 sense of the future course of events, group means over the gaming period

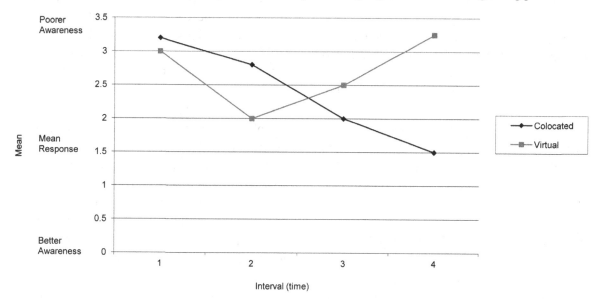

There is again a significant interaction between condition and time (two way interaction $F(3,15)=4.08$, $p=0.0265$). Post hoc tests showed that measures of situation awareness are different between collocated and virtual teams at interval 4 and that situation awareness is better (smaller values) at intervals 3 and 4 from interval 1 for the collocated team. The data suggest that the collocated team was building up an understanding of the future course of events as time elapsed during the game, whereas the virtual team was unable to develop an understanding of the future course of events. In addition the situation awareness in the collocated team was better at the end of the game (interval 4) than in the virtual team.

The results have highlighted statistically significant differences between the two conditions with virtual teams having less situation awareness. There were significant differences between the collocated and virtual teams at the third and fourth measurement points. The collocated team was much more aware of what was going on than the virtual team. In terms of understanding – that is, how easy it was to make sense of the information being provided – the results were not significant,

but there was a clear trend indicating that the collocated team found it easier and increasingly easier to make sense of the task as the game progressed. This was not so evident for the virtual team.

Evaluation of the Evaluation Method

The use of situation awareness for evaluating the process and performance of team role play games was successful and produced interesting results. The situation awareness questionnaire used covered only subjective (participants' evaluations) SA. Nevertheless, it was short – 8 questions, took only two to three minutes to complete and was easily completed at regular intervals during the game. This enables its use to monitor the progress of players during the game – which can even be shown to them graphically afterwards during the debriefing to get them to reflect upon the result. This evaluation method is suitable to see how players' awareness developed during the game. However, it is not so suitable for identifying what the players had learnt, which is something that needs to be done with objective pre and post-tests.

Validation of the Learning Goals

The evaluation of Cosiga indicated that measuring situation awareness was a valuable method to understand what was happening during the gameplay. It showed that as the game progressed the collocated players improved their understanding of what was going on, whereas the virtual team did not. Analysis of the data from the experiment shows that progression requires the involvement of different disciplines and continuous information sharing, which is the crux of team work.

The Hematocrit (HCT) Game

The HCT game was designed to facilitate the activities of medical students in laboratory sessions (Moreno-Ger et al., 2010). The game simulates the steps of performing an experiment to determine the Hematocrit (HCT) of a blood sample through centrifugation, allowing the students to fail in different steps, providing feedback on what went wrong and allowing the students to repeat the exercise until the highest possible score is obtained. The game simulates the actual workstations at the laboratory, allowing the students to interact with the different objects (Figure 4). The game also exaggerates the negative outcomes, often humorously, balancing interest and providing feedback in a way that students can relate to (Figure 4).

The evaluation process for the game did not focus on knowledge gain, but on other (often overlooked) aspects including student confidence in handling the equipment, anxiety during the laboratory sessions and reliability of the results.

Learning Objective

The exercise of determining Hematocrit in a blood sample is performed in a laboratory, using blood samples from laboratory animals. As such, the students are only allowed to rehearse it once per year during the course and (sometimes) as part of their practical exam. However, the practical exercise can hardly be replaced, even with the most realistic game: handling the actual blood, touching the instruments and even sometimes receiving a spoiled blood sample are parts of the experience that cannot be substituted with current technology. Therefore, the main objective in this game was not to learn how to process the blood sample, but to allow the students to rehearse the procedure before going into the lab, thus taking full advantage of their limited time in the laboratory.

Evaluation Method

Unlike many studies, the evaluation did not focus on knowledge gain, but on whether the game was successful in improving the learning experience in the posterior practical session. The evaluation assessed the following aspects:

Figure 4. Screenshots from the game showing the work station and a (badly) spoiled centrifuge

- Perceived difficulty of the experiment.
- Performance in handling the equipment.
- Reliability of the results.

After the laboratory session, all students were given access to the game so that they could rehearse before the practical exam.

Experimental Setup

The students were assigned to an Experimental Group (n=66) or a Control Group (n=77) according to their laboratory groups, which are designated alphabetically (and therefore practically random). Students in the Experimental Group were invited to play the game during a class which took place one week before attending the laboratory session, while the control group did not receive any intervention, and went to the laboratory after receiving the usual lecture on dealing with blood samples.

After the laboratory session, the students answered a very brief questionnaire with one 5-point Likert item for each research question:

Q1: Please rate the difficulty you experienced to understand and perform this procedure.

Q2: Please rate the difficulty you experienced to use the required equipment for this procedure.

Q3: Please indicate the HCT value you have obtained.

The answers to questions Q1 & Q2 were compared through an unpaired Students' t-Test as well as Mann-Whitney U tests, to identify differences in perceived difficulty (it was assumed that the results were parametric, but the U test was used for verification). In turn, Q3 was analyzed by comparing the Standard Deviation for each group. Since each group worked with blood from different animals, the results were normalized and an F test was used to statistically compare the variances.

Results

The results for Q1 indicated a mean perceived difficulty of 3.52 (SD 0.28) for the experimental group and 4.39 (SD 0.16) for the control group, a 0.86 difference considered significant after a Mann-Whitney U test ($P = .016$). Regarding the perceived difficulty in using the equipment (Q2) the result for the experimental group was 3.41 (SD 0.40) and 4.02 (SD 0.20) for the control group. The difference was lower (0.31) and not significant ($P = .47$).

As described above, the obtained values for Q3 were normalized and studied in terms of variance, as this would give an estimate of how reliably the students were obtaining the required values. Higher variance would mean less precise results. Comparing the normalized responses of the students, a much lower variability was observed in the results of the experimental group (3.10 vs 26.94 SD for experimental group and control group groups, respectively). An F test showed that variances between the two groups were significantly different ($P(68.19) < .001$; F: 75.25).

Evaluation of the Evaluation Method

The evaluation method compared the perceived difficulty for the experimental group which played the game with that of a control group who did not. The design paid attention to balancing the students and keeping the groups random. The study was limited to a single class, so that all students would have been taking classes from the same instructors, and the assignment to the groups was almost random: for logistic reasons the laboratory groups were used, but the groups were assigned alphabetically and can be considered random in practice.

The evaluation was successful in measuring its initial objectives, even though no gains were evidenced in one of the research questions. The most difficult item to assess was the reliability of the group, which required normalization processes before the statistical analysis.

Validation of the Learning Goals

The learning goals for the HCT game were not the standard "knowledge gain", but more abstract measures such as confidence, perceived difficulty and skill-based achievements (in the form of lower error rates). The game was successful in allowing the students to focus more on the exercise and less on the steps and proper handling of the materials, resulting in a lower perceived difficulty and, most significantly, in a higher reliability in the results. In turn, the game did not make it easier for the students to use the actual equipment, a conclusion that reinforces the importance of the actual physical practice session.

SimVenture: A Game on Entrepreneurship and Managerial Skills

SimVenture is a single player business simulation game which aims to teach the basis of company management (www.simventure.com). The player is an entrepreneur who manages a small computer assembly and selling company.

Learning Objective

The player's managerial/ entrepreneurial skills are solicited and put to the test in this simulated environment. The simulation is quite detailed and the options and parameters to be managed are numerous. The player is exposed to a number of factors concerning business development in the four functional areas of: sales and marketing, organisation, operations (design and production) and finance.

This complexity allows for the division of responsibilities within a single company team (e.g., director of marketing, director of purchases, financial director, etc.) and also allows experiment-

ing with several different strategies and situations. This is very positive since a player can explore and play for a long time without repeating or getting bored. However, the simulation algorithms are completely opaque, and thus the outcomes of the simulation are not easy to understand and interpret by the players, who have difficulty in learning from their own experience and mistakes. After every simulated month, SimVenture supplies a detailed report, with graphs providing a very detailed break-down of the player's activity and company status (profit and loss, cash-flow, production, employee satisfaction, etc.).

The simulation game provides pre-defined scenarios (e.g., start-up, company growth management, cash-flow crisis), that put the player in different problematic situations, that need to be addressed in different ways. The scenarios vary also in terms of complexity (number of available modules and of parameters modifiable by the player) and difficulty (e. g. initial availability of money).

Experimental Set Up

SimVenture has been used in a short course (20 hours) on entrepreneurship at the University of Genoa within the Stimulating Entrepreneurship in Higher Education through Serious Games (eSG) project (www.esg-project.eu). The course was attended by around 40 volunteer BSc (2nd year), MSc (2nd year) and PhD students. The process of collection of requirements for the course, the game selection process and the structure of the course are described in detail in (Bellotti et al., 2012 and in Bellotti et al., 2013c).

Evaluation Method

Here we focus on the user assessment, which involved several aspects, as reported in the following (and synthesised in Figure 5):

Figure 5. Assessment steps in the Entrepreneurship course

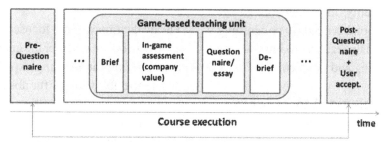

- A questionnaire about knowledge on entrepreneurship-related topics was administered before and after the course, in order to assess the students' improvement. Quantitative results are still being processed, but they are positive both for the open and closed questions. The post-questionnaire also involved questions about user acceptance of the serious games as a tool to support learning.
- The students - divided in teams of three participants each - played 6 matches, of increasing levels of simulation complexity and difficulty, also exploiting SimVenture's pre-defined scenarios. Before every game the teacher gave a briefing to introduce the simulation match. After the match the score was assigned by the teacher on the basis of the SimVenture simulation's reports. In particular, the main assessment parameters considered by the teacher in defining the teams' scores were the company's profit and cash-flow levels.
- A questionnaire was also administered after every game session, where the teams could provide free comments and were asked questions about the game's usability and, overall, economic and management topics covered in the simulation. The questionnaire was evaluated with a score which was added (with similar weights) to those coming from the match (previous bul-

let) and from the debriefing session (next bullet).
- During the de-briefing session held in class after each game competition (which was done at home) each team was asked to discuss their performance and the strategies they employed in the game. Also the de-briefing sessions were assessed with a score assigned to each team by the facilitator.

Evaluation of the Evaluation Method-

This assessment is complex and involves several steps. However, we believe that it was necessary in order to consider all the different aspects. On the one hand, games are very interesting for competitive people. But it is important to combine extrinsic motivation, which should be aroused through games, and intrinsic motivation, which is the fundamental element, in the long-term. On the other hand, the complexity of reality (in particular the world of entrepreneurship and innovation) cannot be fully captured in a game/simulation.

Validation of the Learning Goals

Some teams tended to over-fit the game mechanics (once they had discovered them) and developed some misconceptions, also because of some possible software bugs. Overall, these motivations strengthen the need for the presence of the teacher as a competent expert that introduces the young generations to the reality. In conclusion, games are a new, powerful tool that needs to be carefully studied and employed by teachers to improve the students' understanding and practice.

Shortfall: A Supplement to Teaching Manufacturing Principles

The Shortfall game (Corriere, 2003) was designed to facilitate learning the principles for creating and managing a sustainable manufacturing enterprise. The game centres on raising awareness of the environmental impact in the supply chain as a result of decisions made. The goal of game play is to minimise environmental impacts while maximising profits. The context of Shortfall used in this case study pertains to supplementing taught modules on engineering manufacturing at Heriot-Watt University, across two campuses; UK and Dubai. The aim was to provide students with an alternative approach to classical teaching about the principles of manufacturing enterprises and the technologies employed therein. From the academic perspective, it was about how Shortfall could be used as an abstraction layer to broaden their knowledge and implementation strategy of manufacturing concepts and as a platform for team work.

Learning Objectives and Outcomes

Successful manufacturing requires the integration of the latest manufacturing methodologies, techniques, and innovative technologies. Energy conservation and environmental impact are part and parcel of 21st century manufacturing. Students on completion of the course should have acquired a detailed understanding of the product development process as well as appreciate the impact of sustainability at each stage of the process on the business and organisation with respect to information dependence and manufacturing processes employed.

Evaluation Method

The evaluation was not focused purely on knowledge gain but on whether the game was successful in improving the learning experience and if students were able to apply the abstractness provided by the game with that of the taught material and its implementation.

The evaluation follows a usability study and compares the following aspects:

- Perceived usefulness of the game.
- Knowledge of manufacturing practices.
- Tandem use of game with class lectures.
- Reliability of the results.

The focus of this course is the application of knowledge and the development of decision making skills. Teaching is through a combination of core lectures and supported by coursework, in this case a 12-week case study on sustainable manufacturing for which Shortfall was used as a supplement. The assessment is a combination of exam and coursework. After the introductory session to the course and case study, all students were given access to the game.

Experimental Setup

The students formed teams of three and are tasked to play three rounds of the game. A total of 17 groups of three were formed in the UK while a total of 8 groups of three were formed in Dubai. The UK students were largely un-facilitated while the Dubai students were facilitated. This difference was due mainly to the cultural difference and also because the student cohort was smaller. It should be noted here, that unlike standard practice of control groups, each location could be considered its own control group.

A total of 3 rounds were played by each team during the 12-week case study. After each round was played, the team spends two weeks reflecting on how they performed, their strategy, how the lecture material compares to real world scenarios, and how it contextualises with the game. Each team was expected to keep a log book in the form of a wiki. Reflective questions such as "How can manufacturers use existing technologies in new ways?" and "What innovations are in store for users (in materials, equipment, software, systems, and/or design)?" were asked during the reflection surgery classes to encourage students to probe the philosophical conundrums. The lectures were scheduled such that the knowledge accrued would increase the relevance of game play.

After the 12-week case-study, each team gives a short presentation on how they conducted their game rounds; the time spent in making the choices, the reasoning of the choices made, the consequences of those choices and any other pertinent information with regards the strategy the team chose, etc. It is important that each team member demonstrates their understanding of manufacturing methods and the use of technologies thereof.

Students are then asked to complete a System Usability Scale (SUS) questionnaire, which is a well established tool used in usability engineering (Brooke, 1996). An open question in the exam was used to gauge if the game had influenced their understanding to create and manage a benign manufacturing system/enterprise. The question raised issues on technology causality both on the game side and that of the real world, and how it might influence supply chain strategies and decision making processes. Rather than issuing a questionnaire, the exam probes how elements in the game enable students to identify and link the knowledge and information accrued from the taught material to implement these concepts within the manufacturing domain.

Results

It is important to note that the SUS scores for individual items are not meaningful on their own. The scoring of SUS requires a composite measure of the overall usability. The SUS average score

for the UK was 81.6 and for Dubai it was 78.3. This suggests that as a supplement to core material playing Shortfall was deemed by the students to be beneficial.

An additional 10 question post-test survey (Gennett, 2010) was also adopted for this course and used to evaluate student perceptions regarding the effect that the game play had on their knowledge and ability for a variety of areas such as supply chain management and strategies, manufacturing practices, working as a team and individually. The average score for the UK was 65.2 and for Dubai it was 65.8.

Results Analysis

From the perspective of conducting an RCT, the study was limited due to the fact that different staff were involved due to the different campus locations. While every effort was made to ensure consistent teaching and grading of coursework, there will inevitably be some discrepancies. This is due to having different instructors, students' academic level and engagement, and the fact that culturally there is a vastly different approach required for the two student populations. It was perceived that facilitation would be required for the Dubai campus. On the other hand, this would be an advantage in the sense that it would enable the usability of Shortfall to be assessed - the hypothesis being that if the game was designed well, it could be operated with or without facilitation.

The score averages indicate that Shortfall was indeed useful as a supplement to the learning of sustainable manufacturing. The post-test SUS reveals that Shortfall can be conducted either fully facilitated or not at all; i.e. 65.2 and 65.8 respectively. To validate the post test, the exam averages were compared across both campuses. The UK average was 68% (A/B grades) and Dubai average was 66% (A/B grades) for the course. To further establish if Shortfall as a supplement had an effect, results over two preceding years were compared indicating an improvement in top level grades of 12.7%.

Mean scores for the post test questions on enjoyment of the game were 3.21 and 3.34 respectively, suggesting that the students enjoy the game and found it a useful supplement to the taught material. Students have however indicated that they would prefer a game with more realism.

Validation of the Learning Goals

The learning goals for Shortfall were not simply focused on knowledge acquisition. The fact that the game abstracts the values and paradigms of a manufacturing enterprise allowed the students to contextualise with the real world which classical methods could not. Playing the game allowed students to learn and understand new technologies, linking that to new knowledge while expanding on how to best adapt and integrate existing technologies. The team play also enriches communication and collaboration. Shortfall was successful in allowing the students to focus on the application of knowledge and the causality of strategy selection and decision making.

DISCUSSION AND CONCLUSION

In the previous chapter Mayer et al. provided a comprehensive methodology for evaluating Serious Games and Games Based Learning. The current chapter complements Mayer's by providing an overview of the different study designs that can be used to evaluate the learning outcomes of serious games, along with specific examples of these from the literature on serious games. Seven case studies of games were then presented with details of evaluations that have been carried out on these games. The games described in the case studies were all developed for use in higher education to support teaching across a range of disciplines including business, health and engineering manufacturing. The games had varied, and usually complex,

learning objectives. The case studies illustrate some of the pragmatic and ethical issues which arise for researchers and teachers in developing and using games in education.

With respect to research design, only one of the case studies, Supply Net, reported using an RCT to evaluate students' performance. Despite optimism that Supply Net would improve systems thinking, the evaluation showed that students in the experimental group performed no better than those in the control group and they actually performed worse in the post-test than the pre-test. While the RCT is the design of choice in evaluating games, this study highlights an interesting dilemma for teachers in utilising the results of the evaluation. How much weight should they attach to the RCT results compared to subjective feedback from several years of using the game for teaching which suggests that students like it!

The other case studies used the less rigorous quasi-experimental design in evaluation. The evaluations of the Emergo, Beware and SimVenture studies all used a pre-test/ post-test design where a performance measure was administered before and after participants played the game. Use of the game improved students' performance in writing feasibility reports on water management (Emergo), knowledge of risk assessment (Beware) and knowledge of entrepreneurship (SimVenture) respectively. While we can conclude that the game did help students to achieve better performance on the specified outcome measures, the absence of a control group in these studies constrains our conclusion about the effectiveness of the game compared to traditional teaching methods.

The HCT study also used a quasi-experimental design. In this case a between groups design was used, with around half of the students assigned to the game group and the other half to a control group which received the traditional teaching only. Care was taken to randomly allocate students to the experimental or control conditions, although, as is frequently the case in educational studies, this was at the level of lab groups rather than individuals. The evaluation of Cosiga also compared two groups. This was not exactly an RCT, as a pre-test/post-test was not used, but it was rigorous in looking at changes in several variables over time.

Ideally researchers will use objective tests of performance on the specified learning outcomes to assess whether the use of a game leads to better performance than traditional methods of learning. This requires a very clear specification of what the required learning outcome for the game are. Most of the games described in the case studies present players with complex problems which require them to integrate several different dimensions of the problem where opposing views might be presented. Objective measures of performance used in the case studies included knowledge of systems thinking (Supply Net), knowledge of risk management (Beware) and entrepreneurial knowledge (SimVenture). Knowledge was typically assessed by multiple choice questions, although in the case of Emergo was assessed by a written report about an authentic problem case, which was part of the students' coursework. This example illustrates how it is possible to weave the use of a game into the achievement of curricular objectives.

Subjective assessments of performance can be used instead of objective assessments, but these have less validity. HCT game focused on preparing medical students for subsequent work in the laboratory and the evaluation compared students' self-assessments of the perceived difficulty of the task rather than their actual performance on the task. The Cosiga study also used a subjective measure, collecting data on players' situational awareness. This is the players' self-evaluation of their abstract understanding of the current state of the complexity of the problem. While these subjective perceptions provided evidence about players' experiences of the impact of the game, ideally they would be supplemented by objective measures.

Evaluation of the Shortfall game used a survey method looking at players' perceptions of the game and its usability. Surveys are typically used early on in the evaluation to establish that players perceive that the game is fit for purpose. This study had a further objective which was to compare whether the game had a similar impact on students on both campuses, UK and Dubai, of the university. This was important not just to identify possible cultural differences but because different tutors delivered the course on the two campuses. The evaluation confirmed that students on both campuses benefited equally from the game.

The case studies discussed in the current chapter help to illustrate some of practical and ethical issues in evaluating games in the classroom. An important practical consideration is the recognition that it is asking a lot of tutors to take up their limited teaching time to pilot the use of a game which has not yet been shown to produce effective learning outcomes. University lecturers are accountable for the delivery and quality of their modules. They want students to learn and they want to include activities which will help them to learn. Teachers typically have a limited amount of class contact time and, although they might be keen to use the game, they might not be happy about the amount of time it takes away from class time with no guaranteed outcome.

Lack of time was the main difficulty mentioned in the Emergo study as a reason for not setting up a suitable control group. Tutors would have had to mark pre and post intervention assessments for this group. This would have placed an unacceptable load on staff both in terms of their time and the expense. In addition the "traditional teaching" experience might have been of limited value to students.

To provide an objective assessment of the value of a game the evaluation should be carried out by an independent evaluator. However, very often the evaluation of the game is carried out by the people who are developing it.

A number of ethical issues are evident in evaluating games. Games are frequently introduced into modules where students' performance is going to be assessed. Students who are assigned to the control group of an RCT may feel disadvantaged if other students (in the experimental group) are perceived to be given an advantage, even although playing the game has not yet been shown to provide an advantage in learning. In medical RCTs participants typically do not know whether they are in the experimental group or the control group, whereas with RCTs of games it is clear to both staff and students who is in which group. This may be less obvious if the random assignment is done at the level of classes, although there are still possible confounding variables with this solution, such as different groups having different tutors.

Assigning students randomly to treatment groups, as required in an RCT, is also problematic for the reason that many universities specify that students should be treated equally. A possible solution to the problem of equity is to carry out the evaluation at the beginning of a module and then release the game to everyone later in the semester, to ensure that there are not issues with unfairness before the exams.

In the previous chapter Mayer et al. suggested that the participation of students in evaluating a game should be voluntary. Frequently however, students will feel under pressure to participate in the piloting of the game, if the tutor recommends this as part of their learning experience.

Education policy is following medicine in its demand for evidence based practice. Games developers and researchers are well aware of the need to provide evidence that serious games and games based learning supports students in learning. Although RCTs provide the best evidence about the effectiveness of learning in a game, the use of quasi-experimental evaluation methods can also provide useful information. However as Mayer's evaluation model in the previous chapter shows, comprehensive evaluation of a game goes beyond an RCT based on performance to include

very many different aspects of games, players and contexts and changes in these over time. Each of the case studies considers only a small subset of these different facets.

The breadth of factors that need to be taken into account in evaluation raises a further difficult question for teachers and researchers: "Which factors are most important?". We have already considered the case of a game which was not shown to be more effective than traditional teaching but which students liked. What if a game did result in better performance on an RCT but the players didn't actually like it? Should we take on board Mayer's suggestion that hard learning is not all about having fun and insist the students play the game?

There are many areas to develop in our understanding of the evaluation of games and the implications of evaluation for classroom teachers. An interesting area for future development, especially with respect to making evaluation less time consuming, is stealth assessment, assessment of in-game behaviours of players as they play games looking for example at decisions they have made which reflect their level of understanding.

ACKNOWLEDGMENT

The research reported in this paper has been partially supported by the European Union, particularly through the projects: GaLA - The European Network of Excellence on Serious Games (FP7-ICT-2009.4.2-258169) www.galanoe.eu; Cosiga (MM1003). The work in the Stimulating Entrepreneurship in Higher Education through Serious Games (eSG) project (www.esg-project. eu) was partially funded by the EACEA under the Lifelong Learning Programme, contract number: 518742-LLP-1-2011-1-IT-ERASMUS-FEXI. The study on Shortfall was partially funded by EPSRC-IMRC (EP/F02553X/1) under the theme Serious Games for Computer Aided Engineering

REFERENCES

American Association for the Advancement of Science (AAAS). (1993). *Project 2061: Benchmarks for science literacy.* New York: Oxford University Press.

Arnold, D., Isermann, H., Kuhn, A., & Tempelmeier, H. (2002). *Handbuch der logistik.* Berlin: Springer.

Baalsrud Hauge, J., Delhoum, S., Thoben, K.-D., & Scholz-Reiter, B. (2007). The evaluation of learning the task of inventory control with a learning lab. In *Proceeding Learning with Games 2007.* Learning with Games.

Baalsrud Hauge, J., Duin, H., & Thoben, K.-D. (2008). Increasing the resiliency of global supply network by using games. In *Proceedings of ISL 2008, Centre for Concurrent Enterprise.* Nottingham, UK: Nottingham University Business School.

Baalsrud Hauge, J., & Riedel, J. C. K. H. (2012). Evaluation of simulation games for teaching engineering and manufacturing. In *Proceedings of the 4th International Conference on Games and Virtual Worlds for Serious Applications (VS-GAMES'12),* (vol. 15, pp. 210-220). London: Elsevier Procedia Computer Science.

Beale, I. L., Kato, P. M., Marin-Bowling, V. M., Guthrie, N., & Cole, S. W. (2007). Improvement in cancer-related knowledge following use of a psycho-educational video game for adolescents and young adults with cancer. *The Journal of Adolescent Health, 41,* 263–270. doi:10.1016/j.jadohealth.2007.04.006 PMID:17707296.

Bellotti, F., Berta, R., De Gloria, A., Lavagnino, E., Dagnino, F., Ott, M., et al. (2012). Designing a course for stimulating entrepreneurship in higher education through serious games. In *Proceedings of the 4th International Conference on Games and Virtual Worlds for Serious Applications (VS-GAMES'12).* Elsevier Procedia Computer Science.

Bellotti, F., Kapralos, B., Lee, K., & Moreno-Ger, P. (2013a). *User assessment in serious games and technology-enhanced learning.* Hindawi Advances in Human-Computer Interaction. doi:10.1155/2013/120791.

Bellotti, F., Kapralos, B., Lee, K., Moreno-Ger, P., & Berta, R. (2013b). *Assessment in and of serious games: An overview.* Hindawi Advances in Human-Computer Interaction. doi:10.1155/2013/136864.

Bellotti, F., Berta, R., De Gloria, A., Lavagnino, E., Antonaci, E., Dagnino, F., & Ott, M. (2013c). A gamified short course for promoting entrepreneurship among ICT engineering students. In *Proceedings of IEEE International Conference on Advanced Learning Technologies (ICALT).* Bejing, China: IEEE.

Brooke, J. (1996). *SUS—A quick and dirty usability scale.* Reading, UK: Redhatch Consulting Ltd.

Cameron, B., & Dwyer, F. (2005). The effect of online gaming, cognition and feedback type in facilitating delayed achievement of different learning objectives. *Journal of Interactive Learning Research, 16*(3), 243–258.

Chinn, C. A., & Malhotra, B. A. (2002). Epistemologically authentic inquiry in schools: A theoretical framework for evaluating inquiry tasks. *Science Education, 86*(2), 175–218. doi:10.1002/sce.10001.

Connolly, T. C., Boyle, E. A., Hainey, T., McArthur, E., & Boyle, J. M. (2012). A systematic literature review of empirical evidence on computer games and serious games. *Computers & Education, 59,* 661–686. doi:10.1016/j.compedu.2012.03.004.

Connolly, T. M., Boyle, E., & Hainey, T. (2007). A survey of students' motivations for playing computer games: A comparative analysis. In *Proceedings of the 1st European Conference on Games-Based Learning* (ECGBL). Paisley, UK: ECGBL.

Corriere, J. D. (2003). *Shortfall: An educational game on environmental issues in supply chain management*. (M.S. Thesis). Northeastern University, Boston, MA.

Coyle, R. G. (1977). *Management system dynamics*. London: John Wiley & Sons.

Delhoum, S. (2009). *Evaluation of the impact of learning labs on inventory control: An experimental approach with a collaborative simulation game of a production network*. Berlin: Gito-Verlag.

Endsley, M. R. (1995). Towards a theory of situation awareness in dynamic systems. *Human Factors*, *37*(1), 32–64. doi:10.1518/001872095779049543.

Endsley, M. R. (1998). A comparative analysis of SAGAT and SART for evaluations of situation awareness. In *Proceedings of the Human Factors and Ergonomics Society 42nd Annual Meeting* (pp. 82–86). Santa Monica, CA: The Human Factors and Ergonomics Society.

Field, A., & Hole, G. (2003). *How to design and report experiments*. London: Sage Publications.

Gennett, Z. (2010). *Shortfall online: The development of an educational computer game for teaching sustainable engineering to millennial generation students*. (MS Thesis). Deptartment of Mechanical and Industrial Engineering, Northeastern University, Boston, MA.

Hsu, C.-L., & Lu, H.-P. (2004). Why do people play on-line games? An extended TAM with social influences and flow experience. *Information & Management*, *41*, 853–868. doi:10.1016/j.im.2003.08.014.

Hummel, H. G. K., van Houcke, J., Nadolski, R. J., van der Hiele, T., Kurvers, H., & Lahr, A. (2011). Scripted collaboration in serious gaming for complex learning: Effects of multiple perspectives when acquiring water management skills. *British Journal of Educational Technology*, *42*(6), 1029–1041. doi:10.1111/j.1467-8535.2010.01122.x.

Karakus, T., Inal, Y., & Cagiltay, K. (2008). A descriptive study of Turkish high school students' game-playing characteristics and their considerations concerning the effects of games. *Computers in Human Behavior*, *24*(6), 2520–2529. doi:10.1016/j.chb.2008.03.011.

Kuhn, T. S. (1962). *The structure of scientific revolutions*. Chicago: University of Chicago Press.

Lindh, J., Hrastinski, S., Bruhn, C., & Mozgira, L. (2008). Computer-based business simulation games as tools for learning: A comparative study of student and teacher perceptions. In *Proceedings of the 2nd European Conference on Games-Based Learning (ECGBL)*. Barcelona, Spain: ECGBL.

Mayer, I. S. (2012). Towards a comprehensive methodology for the research and evaluation of serious games. In *Proceedings VS-Games 2012* (Vol. 15, pp. 1–15). Genoa, Italy: Elsevier Procedia Computer Science. doi:10.1016/j.procs.2012.10.075

Mayer, I. S., Bekebrede, G., Harteveld, C., Warmelink, H. J. G., Zhou, Q., & Lo, J. et al. (2013). The research and evaluation of serious games: Towards a comprehensive methodology. *British Journal of Educational Technology*. doi:10.1111/bjet.12067.

Moreno-Ger, P., Torrente, J., Bustamante, J., Fernández-Galaz, C., Fernández-Manjón, B., & Comas-Rengifo, M. D. (2010). Application of a low-cost web-based simulation to improve students' practical skills in medical education. *International Journal of Medical Informatics*, *79*(6), 459–467. doi:10.1016/j.ijmedinf.2010.01.017 PMID:20347383.

Papastergiou, M. (2009). Digital game-based learning in high school computer science education. *Computers & Education*, *52*(1), 1–12. doi:10.1016/j.compedu.2008.06.004.

Riedel, J. C. K. H., Pawar, K. S., & Barson, R. (2001). Academic & industrial user needs of a concurrent engineering computer simulation game. *Concurrent Engineering: Research & Applications*, *9*(3), 223–237. doi:10.1177/1063293X0100900304.

Scholz-Reiter, B., & Delhoum, S. (2007). The effect of enhanced collaboration on the performance of subjects for the task of inventory control. In K. D. Thoben, J. Baalsrud Hauge, R. Smeds, & J. O. Riis (Eds.), *Multidisciplinary research on new methods for learning and innovation in enterprise networks*. Verlagsgruppe Mainz GmbH Aachen.

Steinkuehler, C., & Duncan, S. (2008). Scientific habits of mind in virtual worlds. *Journal of Science Education and Technology*, *17*, 530–543. doi:10.1007/s10956-008-9120-8.

Weibel, D., Wissmath, B., Habegger, S., Steiner, Y., & Groner, R. (2008). Playing online games against computer- vs. human-controlled opponents: Effects on presence, flow, and enjoyment. *Computers in Human Behavior*, *24*(5), 2274–2291. doi:10.1016/j.chb.2007.11.002.

Woolfson, L. M. (2011). *Educational psychology: The impact of psychological research on education*. London: Prentice Hall, Pearson Education.

KEY TERMS AND DEFINITIONS

Case Study: An investigation of a phenomenon (in this case a game) in its real life context.

Evaluation: Judgement of the value or the strengths and weaknesses of an intervention using established procedures.

Game Based Learning: Learning methods which use games to deliver educational outcomes.

Learning Outcomes: The skills, knowledge or understanding that a student should have as a result of completing specified learning tasks or activities.

Quasi-Experiment: An experimental method where participants are not randomly allocated to conditions or where the experimenter does not have control over the manipulation of the independent variable.

Randomised Control Trial (RCT): An experimental method of evaluating an intervention where participants are randomly allocated to an experimental group or a control group and their performance on the target skill/behaviour before and after the intervention is tested. Ideally pre-testing should confirm no existing difference between the groups, while post-testing should show whether the experimental group performs better than the control group.

Serious Games: Games designed with a different purpose than pure entertainment.

Compilation of References

€conomia. (n.d.). *Serious game about EU financial policy*. European Central bank (ECB). Retrieved from http://www.ecb.int/ecb/educational/economia/html/index.en.html

Ackerman, P. L., Beier, M. E., & Boyle, M. O. (2005). Working memory and intelligence: The same or different constructs? *Psychological Bulletin, 131*(1), 30–60. doi:10.1037/0033-2909.131.1.30 PMID:15631550.

Adams, J. C. (2010). Scratching middle schoolers' creative itch. In *Proceedings of the 41st ACM Technical Symposium on Computer Science Education*. ACM.

Adams, E. M., & Goffman, E. (1979). Frame analysis: An essay on the organization of experience. *Philosophy and Phenomenological Research, 39*(4), 601. doi:10.2307/2106908.

Adams, E., & Dormans, J. (2012). *Game mechanics: Advanced game design*. Berkeley, CA: New Riders Games..

Adams, E., & Rollings, A. (2007). *Fundamentals of game design*. Upper Saddle River, NJ: Pearson Prentice Hall..

Adams, S. A. (2010). Use of serious health games in health care: A review. *Studies in Health Technology and Informatics, 157*, 160–166. PMID:20543383.

Adelabu, D. H. (2007). Time perspective and school membership as correlates to academic achievement among African American adolescents. *Adolescence, 42*(167), 525–538. PMID:18047236.

Admiraal, W., Huizenga, J., Akkerman, S., & ten Dama, G. (2011). The concept of flow in collaborative game-based learning. *Computers in Human Behavior, 27*, 1185–1194. doi:10.1016/j.chb.2010.12.013.

Ainley, M., & Armatas, C. (2006). Motivational perspectives on students' responses to learning in virtual learning environments. In J. Weiss, J. Nolan, J. Hunsinger, & P. Trifonas (Eds.), *The international handbook of virtual learning environments* (pp. 365–394). Dordrecht, The Netherlands: Springer. doi:10.1007/978-1-4020-3803-7_15.

Ajzen, I. (1991). The theory of planned behavior. *Organizational Behavior and Human Decision Processes, 50*(2), 179–211. doi:10.1016/0749-5978(91)90020-T.

Alkan, S., & Cagiltay, K. (2007). Studying computer game learning experience through eye tracking. *British Journal of Educational Technology, 38*(3), 538–542. doi:10.1111/j.1467-8535.2007.00721.x.

Allen, B. P. (1994). *Personality theories*. Boston, MA: Allyn and Bacon..

Alloway, T. P. (2012). Can interactive working memory training improve learning? *Journal of Interactive Learning Research, 23*(3), 197–207.

Alloway, T. P., Bibile, V., & Lau, G. (2013). Computerized working memory training: Can it lead to gains in cognitive skills in students? *Computers in Human Behavior, 29*, 632–638. doi:10.1016/j.chb.2012.10.023.

Alman, R. E. (1994). *Video games: Interaction vs. observation as sources of social learning*. (Unpublished master's thesis). Michigan State University, East Lansing, MI.

American Association for the Advancement of Science (AAAS). (1993). *Project 2061: Benchmarks for science literacy*. New York: Oxford University Press..

American Association for the Advancement of Science. (1993). *Benchmarks for science literacy*. New York: Oxford University Press..

Ancoria, B., Burethb, A., & Cohendet, P. (2000). The economics of knowledge: The debate about codification and tacit knowledge. *Industrial and Corporate Change, 9*(2).

Anderson, C. A. (2004). An update on the effects of playing violent video games. *Journal of Adolescence, 27*(1), 113–122. doi:10.1016/j.adolescence.2003.10.009 PMID:15013264.

Anderson, C. A., & Berdahl, J. L. (2002). The experience of power: Examining the effects of power on approach and inhibition tendencies. *The Journal of Social Psychology, 83*(6), 1362–1377. PMID:12500818.

Anderson, C. A., & Bushman, B. J. (1997). External validity of trivial experiments: The case of laboratory aggression. *Review of General Psychology, 1*(1), 19–41. doi:10.1037/1089-2680.1.1.19.

Anderson, C. A., & Bushman, B. J. (2001). Effects of violent video games on aggressive behavior, aggressive cognition, aggressive affect, physiological arousal, and prosocial behavior: a meta-analytic review of the scientific literature. *Psychological Science, 12*, 353–359. doi:10.1111/1467-9280.00366 PMID:11554666.

Anderson, C. A., & Dill, K. E. (2000). Video games and aggressive thoughts, feelings, and behavior in the laboratory and in life. *Journal of Personality and Social Psychology, 78*(4), 772–790. doi:10.1037/0022-3514.78.4.772 PMID:10794380.

Anderson, C. A., & Ford, C. M. (1986). Affect of the game player: Short-term effects of highly and mildly aggressive video games. *Personality and Social Psychology Bulletin, 12*(4), 390–402. doi:10.1177/0146167286124002.

Anderson, P. (2007). *What is web 2.0? Ideas, technologies and implications for education.* JISC Technology and Standards Watch..

Anderson, P. J. (2002). Assessment and development of executive function (EF) during childhood. *Child Neuropsychology, 8*(2), 71–82. doi:10.1076/chin.8.2.71.8724 PMID:12638061.

Andersson, U. (2008). Working memory as a predictor of written arithmetical skills in children: The importance of central executive functions. *The British Journal of Educational Psychology, 78*, 181–203. doi:10.1348/000709907X209854 PMID:17535520.

Ang, C. S., Zaphiris, P., & Mahmood, S. (2007). A model of cognitive loads in massively multiplayer online role playing games. *Interacting with Computers, 19*(2), 167–179. doi:10.1016/j.intcom.2006.08.006.

Angelakis, E., Stathopoulou, S., Frymiare, J. L., Green, D. L., Lubar, J. F., & Kounios, J. (2007). EEG neurofeedback: A brief overview and an example of peak alpha frequency training for cognitive enhancement in the elderly. *The Clinical Neuropsychologist, 21*(1), 110–129. doi:10.1080/13854040600744839 PMID:17366280.

Annetta, L. A. (2006). Serious games: Incorporating video games in the classroom - Games designed using sound pedagogy actively engage the net generation in learning. *EDUCAUSE, 29*(3).

Apostolidis, T., & Fieulaine, N. (2004). Validation française de l'e'chelle de temporalité' the zimbardo time perspective inventory. *European Review of Applied Psychology, 54*, 207–217. doi:10.1016/j.erap.2004.03.001.

Argyris, C. (1977). Double loop learning in organizations. *Harvard Business Review, 55*(5), 115–125.

Argyris, C. (1982). The executive mind and double-loop learning. *Organizational Dynamics, 11*(2), 5–22. doi:10.1016/0090-2616(82)90002-X PMID:10256769.

Argyris, C. (1995). Action science and organizational learning. *Journal of Managerial Psychology, 10*(6), 20–26. doi:10.1108/02683949510093849.

Argyris, C., & Schön, D. A. (1974). *Theory in practice: Increasing professional effectiveness.* San Francsico, CA: Jossey-Bass Publishers..

Ariely, D. (2009). *Predictably irrational: The hidden forces that shape our decisions.* New York: Harper..

Arnold, D., Isermann, H., Kuhn, A., & Tempelmeier, H. (2002). *Handbuch der logistik.* Berlin: Springer..

Arum, R., & Roska, J. (2011). *Academically adrift: Limited learning on college campuses.* Chicago, IL: The University of Chicago Press..

Asbell-Clarke, J., Edwards, T., Rowe, E., Larsen, J., Sylvan, E., & Hewitt, J. (2012). Martian boneyards: Scientific inquiry in an MMO game. *International Journal of Game-Based Learning, 2*(1), 52–76. doi:10.4018/ijgbl.2012010104.

Ashton, M. C., & Lee, K. (2009). An investigation of personality types within the HEXACO personality framework. *Journal of Individual Differences, 30*(4), 181–187. doi:10.1027/1614-0001.30.4.181.

Atkinson, J. W. (1957). Motivational determinants of risk-taking behavior. *Psychological Review, 64*(1-6), 359-372.

Augustin, T., Hockemeyer, C., Kickmeier-Rust, M. D., & Albert, D. (2011). Individualized Skill Assessment in Digital Learning Games: Basic Definitions and Mathematical Formalism. In IEEE Transactions on Learning Technologies, 4(2)..

Averill, J. (1979). Anger. In H. Howe & R. Dienstbier (Eds.), *Nebraska Symposium on Motivation* (pp. 1–80). Lincoln, NE: University of Nebraska Press.

Ayaz, H., Shewokis, P. A., Bunce, S., & Onaral, B. (2011). An optical brain computer interface for environmental control. In Proceedings - IEEE Engineering in Medicine and Biology Society (pp. 6327–6330). IEEE..

Ayers, P., & Ortega, F. (Eds.). (2010). *Proceedings of the 6th international symposium on wikis and open collaboration 2010.* Gdansk, Poland: ACM.

Aylett, R., Paiva, A., Dias, J., Hall, L., & Woods, S. (2009). Affective agents for education against bullying. In *Affective Information Processing* (pp. 75–90). London: Springer. Retrieved from http://link.springer.com/chapter/10.1007/978-1-84800-306-4_5

Baalsrud Hauge, J., & Riedel, J. C. K. H. (2012). Evaluation of simulation games for teaching engineering and manufacturing. In *Proceedings of the 4th International Conference on Games and Virtual Worlds for Serious Applications (VS-GAMES'12),* (vol. 15, pp. 210-220). London: Elsevier Procedia Computer Science.

Baalsrud Hauge, J., Duin, H., & Thoben, K.-D. (2008). Increasing the resiliency of global supply network by using games. In *Proceedings of ISL 2008, Centre for Concurrent Enterprise.* Nottingham, UK: Nottingham University Business School.

Baalsrud Hauge, J., Delhoum, S., Thoben, K.-D., & Scholz-Reiter, B. (2007). The evaluation of learning the task of inventory control with a learning lab. In *Proceeding Learning with Games 2007.* Learning with Games..

Baba, D. M. (1993). Determinants of video game performance. *Advances in Psychology, 102,* 57–74. doi:10.1016/S0166-4115(08)61465-X.

Babbie, E. (2007). The ethics and politics of social research. In E. Babbie (Ed.), *The practice of social research* (pp. 60–83). London: Thomson Wadsworth..

Baddeley, A. (1998). *Human memory.* Boston: Allyn and Bacon..

Baddeley, A. (1998). The central executive: A concept and some misconceptions. *Journal of the International Neuropsychological Society, 4,* 523–526. doi:10.1017/S135561779800513X PMID:9745242.

Baddeley, A. D., Allen, R. J., & Hitch, G. J. (2011). Binding in visual working memory: The role of the episodic buffer. *Neuropsychologia, 49*(6), 1393–1400. doi:10.1016/j.neuropsychologia.2010.12.042 PMID:21256143.

Baddeley, A. D., & Hitch, G. (1974). Working memory. In G. H. Bower (Ed.), *The psychology of learning and motivation: Advances in research and theory* (Vol. 8, pp. 47–89). New York: Academic Press..

Baddeley, A., & Della Sala, S. (1996). Working memory and executive control. *Philosophical Transactions of the Royal Society of London. Series B, Biological Sciences, 351,* 1397–1404. doi:10.1098/rstb.1996.0123 PMID:8941951.

Bai, H., Pan, W., Hirumi, A., & Kebritchi, M. (2012). Assessing the effectiveness of a 3-D instructional game on improving mathematics achievement and motivation of middle school students. *British Journal of Educational Technology, 43*(6), 993–1003. doi:10.1111/j.1467-8535.2011.01269.x.

Bailenson, J. N., Beall, A. C., & Blascovich, J. (2002). Gaze and task performance in shared virtual environments. *Journal of Visualization and Computer Animation, 13*(5), 313–320. doi:10.1002/vis.297.

Baker, M. J. (2000). Incorporating the thematic ritualistic behaviors of children with autism into games: Increasing social play interactions with siblings. *Journal of Positive Behavior Interventions, 2,* 66–84. doi:10.1177/109830070000200201.

Baldaro, B., Tuozzi, G., Codispoti, M., Montebarocci, O., Barbagli, F., Trombini, E., & Rossi, N. (2004). Aggressive and non-violent videogames: Short-term psychological and cardiovascular effects on habitual players. *Stress and Health, 20*(4), 203–208. doi:10.1002/smi.1015.

Ballard, M. E., & Wiest, J. R. (1995). *Mortal Kombat: The effects on violent video technology on males' hostility and cardiovascular responding*. Paper presented at the biennial Meeting of the Society for Research in Child Development. Indianapolis, IN.

Ballard, M. E., & Lineberger, R. (1999). Video game violence and confederate gender: Effects on reward and punishment given by college males. *Sex Roles, 4*(7/8), 541–558. doi:10.1023/A:1018843304606.

Bandura, A. (1997). *Self-efficacy: The exercise of control*. New York: W.H. Freeman..

Bandura, A. (2011). Self-deception: A paradox revisited. *The Behavioral and Brain Sciences, 34*(1), 16–17. doi:10.1017/S0140525X10002499.

Barab, S., & Dede, C. (2007). Games and immersive participatory simulations for science education: An emerging type of curricula. *Journal of Science Education and Technology, 16*(1), 1–3. doi:10.1007/s10956-007-9043-9.

Barbera, E., Gros, B., & Kirschner, P. (2012). Temporal issues in e-learning research: A literature review. *British Journal of Educational Technology, 43*(2), 53–55. doi:10.1111/j.1467-8535.2011.01255.x.

Barlett, C. P., Anderson, C. A., & Swing, E. L. (2008). Video game effects—Confirmed, suspected, and speculative: A review of the evidence. *Simulation & Gaming, 40*(3), 377–403. doi:10.1177/1046878108327539.

Barlett, C. P., Vowels, C. L., Shanteau, J., Crow, J., & Miller, T. (2009). The effect of violent and non-violent computer games on cognitive performance. *Computers in Human Behavior, 21*(1), 96–102. doi:10.1016/j.chb.2008.07.008.

Barnaud, C., Promburom, T., Trebuil, G., & Bousquet, F. (2007). An evolving simulation/gaming process to facilitate adaptive watershed management in northern mountainous Thailand. *Simulation & Gaming, 38*(3), 398–420. doi:10.1177/1046878107300670.

Baron, R. (1998). *What type am I: Discover who you really are*. New York, NY: Penguin Books..

Bar-On, R. (2006). The bar-on model of emotional-social intelligence (esi). *Psicothema, 18*, 13–25. PMID:17295953.

Barrett, L. F., Tugade, M. M., & Engle, R. W. (2004). Individual differences in working memory capacity and dual-process theories of the mind. *Psychological Bulletin, 130*(4), 553–573. doi:10.1037/0033-2909.130.4.553 PMID:15250813.

Barron, T. (2001). *Multiplayer game programming*. Roseville, CA: Prima Tech..

Bartholow, B. D., & Anderson, C. A. (2002). Effects of violent video games on aggressive behavior: Potential sex differences. *Journal of Experimental Social Psychology, 38*, 283–290. doi:10.1006/jesp.2001.1502.

Bartle, R. A. (1990). *Early MUD history*. Retrieved on December 23, 2012. Retrieved from http://www.mud.co.uk/richard/mudhist.htm

Bartle, R. (1996). Hearts, clubs, diamonds, spades: Players who suit muds. *Journal of MUD Research, 1*(1), 1–24.

Bartle, R. A. (2004). *Designing virtual worlds*. New Riders Publishing..

Basak, C., Boot, W. R., Voss, M. W., & Kramer, A. F. (2008). Can training in a real-time strategy video game attenuate cognitive decline in older adults? *Psychology and Aging, 23*(4), 765–777. doi:10.1037/a0013494 PMID:19140648.

Bates, J., Loyall, A. B., & Reilly, W. S. (1994). An architecture for action, emotion, and social behavior. In *Selected papers from the 4th European Workshop on on Modelling Autonomous Agents in a Multi-Agent World, Artificial Social Systems* (pp. 55–68). London: Springer-Verlag. Retrieved from http://dl.acm.org/citation.cfm?id=646907.710645

Bates, J. (1992). Virtual reality, art, and entertainment. *Presence: The Journal of Teleoperators and Virtual Environments, 1*(1), 133–138.

Bateson, G. (1972). *Steps to an ecology of mind*. New York: Ballantine Books..

Bavelier, D., Green, S., & Dye, M. W. G. (2010). Children, wired: for better and for worse. *Neuron, 67*, 692–701. doi:10.1016/j.neuron.2010.08.035 PMID:20826302.

Baytak, A., & Land, S. (2011). An investigation of the artifacts and process of constructing computers games about environmental science in a fifth grade classroom. *Educational Technology Research and Development, 59*(7), 765–782. doi:10.1007/s11423-010-9184-z.

Beale, I. L., Kato, P. M., Marin-Bowling, V. M., Guthrie, N., & Cole, S. W. (2007). Improvement in cancer-related knowledge following use of a psycho educational video game for adolescents and young adults with cancer. *The Journal of Adolescent Health, 41*, 263–270. doi:10.1016/j.jadohealth.2007.04.006 PMID:17707296.

Becker, K. (2007). Digital game-based learning once removed: Teaching teachers. *British Journal of Educational Technology, 38*(3), 478–488. doi:10.1111/j.1467-8535.2007.00711.x.

Becker, K. (2008). *The invention of good games: Understanding learning design in commercial video games*. Calgary, Canada: University of Calgary..

Becker, M. W., Alzahabi, R., & Hopwood, C. J. (2013). Media multitasking is associated with symptoms of depression and social anxiety. *Cyberpsychology, Behavior, and Social Networking, 16*(2), 132–135. doi:10.1089/cyber.2012.0291 PMID:23126438.

Beck, J. (2005). The impact of video gaming on decision-making and team-working skills. *Campus-Wide Information Systems, 22*(5), 320–326. doi:10.1108/10650740510632226.

Beeli, G., Casutt, G., Baumgartner, T., & Jäncke, L. (2008). Modulating presence and impulsiveness by external stimulation of the brain. *Behavioral and Brain Functions, 4*(33), 1–7. PMID:18173840.

Beier, G. (2004). *Kontrollüberzeugungen im umgang mit technik: Ein persönlichkeitsmerkmal mit relevanz für die gestaltung technischer systeme*. Retrieved from http://www.dissertation.de

Beilock, S. L., & DeCaro, M. S. (2007). From poor performance to success under stress: Working memory. *Journal of Experimental Psychology. Learning, Memory, and Cognition, 33*(6), 983–998. doi:10.1037/0278-7393.33.6.983 PMID:17983308.

Bekebrede, G. (2010). *Experiencing complexity: A gaming approach for understanding infrastructure systems*. TU Delft. Retrieved May 3, 2013, from http://www.narcis.nl/publication/RecordID/oai:tudelft.nl:uuid:dae75f36-4fb6-4a53-8711-8aab42378878

Bekebrede, G., Warmelink, H. J. G., & Mayer, I. S. (2011). Reviewing the need for gaming in education to accommodate the net generation. *Computers & Education, 57*(2), 1521–1529. doi:10.1016/j.compedu.2011.02.010.

Bekoff, M. (2002). *Minding animals: Awareness, emotions, and heart*. Oxford, UK: Oxford University Press..

Belbin, M. (1981). *Management teams*. London: Heinemann..

Bell, B. S., Kanar, A. M., & Kozlowski, S. W. J. (2008). Current issues and future directions in simulation-based training in North America. *International Journal of Human Resource Management, 19*(8), 1416–1434. doi:10.1080/09585190802200173.

Bellotti, F., Berta, R., De Gloria, A., Lavagnino, E., Antonaci, E., Dagnino, F., & Ott, M. (2013c). A gamified short course for promoting entrepreneurship among ICT engineering students. In *Proceedings of IEEE International Conference on Advanced Learning Technologies (ICALT)*. Bejing, China: IEEE.

Bellotti, F., Berta, R., De Gloria, A., Lavagnino, E., Dagnino, F., Ott, M., et al. (2012). Designing a course for stimulating entrepreneurship in higher education through serious games. In *Proceedings of the 4th International Conference on Games and Virtual Worlds for Serious Applications (VS-GAMES'12)*. Elsevier Procedia Computer Science.

Bellotti, F., Kapralos, B., Lee, K., & Moreno-Ger, P. (2013a). *User assessment in serious games and technology-enhanced learning*. Hindawi Advances in Human-Computer Interaction. doi:10.1155/2013/120791.

Bellotti, F., Kapralos, B., Lee, K., Moreno-Ger, P., & Berta, R. (2013b). *Assessment in and of serious games: An overview*. Hindawi Advances in Human-Computer Interaction. doi:10.1155/2013/136864.

Benford, R. D., & Snow, D. A. (2000). Framing processes and social movements: An overview and assessment. *Annual Review of Sociology*, *26*(1), 611–639. doi:10.1146/annurev.soc.26.1.611.

Berends, H., Boersma, K., & Weggeman, M. (2003). The structuration of organizational learning. *Human Relations*, *56*(9), 1035–1056. doi:10.1177/0018726703569001.

Berkowitz, B. D., & Goodman, A. E. (1989). *Strategic intelligence for American national security*. Princeton, NJ: Princeton University Press..

Berkowitz, L., & Rogers, K. H. (1986). A priming effect analysis of media influences. In J. Bryant, & D. Zillmann (Eds.), *Perspectives on media effects* (pp. 57–82). Hillsdale, NJ: Erlbaum..

Berliner, D. C. (1990). What's all the fuss about instructional time? In M. Ben-Peretz, & R. Bromme (Eds.), *The nature of time in schools* (pp. 3–35). New York: Teachers College Press..

Bernard, C. (1974). *Lectures on the phenomena of life common to animals and plants*. Thomas. Retrieved from http://books.google.pt/books?id=zMhqAAAAMAAJ

Beyer, J. L., & Larkin, R. P. (1978). Simulation review: A review of instructional simulations for human geography. *Simulation & Gaming*, *9*(3), 339–352. doi:10.1177/104687817800900306.

Bezuijen, A. (2012). *Teamplay the further development of TeamUp, a teamwork focused serious game*. Delft, The Netherlands: TU Delft..

Bialystok, E. (2006). Effect of bilingualism and computer video game experience on the Simon task. *Canadian Journal of Experimental Psychology*, *60*(1), 68–79. doi:10.1037/cjep2006008 PMID:16615719.

Biggs, J. (1996). Enhancing teaching through constructive alignment. *Higher Education*, *32*, 1–18. doi:10.1007/BF00138871.

Biggs, J. (1999). *Teaching for quality learning at university*. Buckingham, UK: SRHE and Open University Press..

BinSubaih. A., Maddock, S., & Romano, D. (2009). Serious Games for the Police: Opportunities and Challenges, Special Reports & Studies Series at the Research & Studies Center (Dubai Police Academy).

Birbaumer, N., Elbert, T., Canavan, A., & Rockstroh, B. (1990). Slow potentials of the cerebral cortex and behavior. *Physiological Reviews*, *70*(1), 1–28. PMID:2404287.

Birbaumer, N., Ghanayim, N., Hinterberger, T., Iversen, I., Kotchoubey, B., & Kübler, A. et al. (1999). A spelling device for the paralysed. *Nature*, *398*(6725), 297–298. doi:10.1038/18581 PMID:10192330.

Birbaumer, N., & Schmidt, R. (2006). *Biologische psychologie* (6th ed.). Heidelberg, Germany: Springer-Verlag..

Björk, S., & Holopainen, J. (2005). *Patterns in game design*. Boston: Charles River Media..

Black, P. J., & Wiliam, D. (1998). Inside the black box: Raising standards through classroom assessment. *Phi Delta Kappan*, *80*(2), 139–148.

Black, P., Harrison, C., & Lee, C. (2003). *Assessment for learning: putting it into practice*. New York: Open University Press..

Blakemore, S. J., & Choudhury, S. (2006). Development of the adolescent brain: implications for executive function and social cognition. *Journal of Child Psychology and Psychiatry, and Allied Disciplines*, *47*(3-4), 296–312. doi:10.1111/j.1469-7610.2006.01611.x PMID:16492261.

Blankertz, B., Sannelli, C., Halder, S., Hammer, E. M., Kübler, A., & Müller, K.-R. et al. (2010). Neurophysiological predictor of SMR-based BCI performance. *NeuroImage*, *51*(4), 1303–1309. doi:10.1016/j.neuroimage.2010.03.022 PMID:20303409.

Blasko Drabik, H., Blasko, D., & Lum, H. (2013). Investigating the impact of self-efficacy in learning disaster strategies in an on-line serious game. In *Proceedings of the Human Factors and Ergonomic Society*. San Diego, CA: IEEE.

Blasko, D., Chadwick, C., & Bittner, B. (2013). *Do games reduce math stress? The influence of gender and game genre*. Unpublished.

Blasko, D., Holliday-Darr, K., Mace, D., & Blasko-Drabik, H. (2004). VIZ: The visualization assessment and training website. *Behavior Research Methods, Instruments, & Computers*, 36(2), 256–260. doi:10.3758/BF03195571 PMID:15354691.

Blasko, D., Kazmerski, V., & Torgerson, C. (2004). COR V2: Teaching observational research with multimedia courseware. *Behavior Research Methods, Instruments, & Computers*, 36(2), 250–255. doi:10.3758/BF03195570 PMID:15354690.

Blasko-Drabik, H., Smoker, T., & Murphy, C. (2010). An adventure in usability: Discovering usability where it was not expected. In J. Canon-Bowers, & C. Bowers (Eds.), *Serious Game Design and Development: Technologies for Training and Learning*. Hershey, PA: IGI Global. doi:10.4018/978-1-61520-739-8.ch003.

Bloom, B. S., Hastings, T. J., & Madaus, G. F. (1972). Handbook on formative and summative evaluation of student learning. *Studies in Art Education*, 14(1), 68–72. doi:10.2307/1319918.

Blumberg, F. C. (2000). The effects of children's goals for learning on video game performance. *Journal of Applied Developmental Psychology*, 21(6), 641–653. doi:10.1016/S0193-3973(00)00058-7.

Blumberg, F. C., Rosenthal, S. F., & Randall, J. D. (2008). Impasse-driven learning in the context of video games. *Computers in Human Behavior*, 24(4), 1530–1541. doi:10.1016/j.chb.2007.05.010.

Blum-Dimaya, A., Reeve, S. A., Reeve, K. F., & Hoch, H. (2010). Teaching children with autism to play a video game using activity schedules and game-embedded simultaneous video modeling. *Education & Treatment of Children*, 33(3), 351–370. doi:10.1353/etc.0.0103.

Blunt, R. D. (2006). *A causal-comparative exploration of the relationship between game-based learning and academic achievement: Teaching management with video games*. Minneapolis, MN: Walden University..

Bogost, I. (2007). *Persuasive games: The expressive power of videogames*. Cambridge, MA: MIT Press. Retrieved from http://books.google.com/books?id=GC7MD17YvJEC

Bolles, R. C. (1973). *Theory of motivation*. New York: Harper & Row..

Bontcheva, K. (2002). Adaptivity, adaptability, and reading behaviour: Some results from the evaluation of a dynamic hypertext system. *Adaptive Hypermedia and Adaptive Web-Based Systems*, 2347, 69–78. doi:10.1007/3-540-47952-X_9.

Booth, J. N., Boyle, J. M., & Kelly, S. W. (2010). Do tasks make a difference? Accounting for heterogeneity of performance of children with reading difficulties on tasks of executive function: Findings from a meta-analysis. *The British Journal of Developmental Psychology*, 28(1), 133–176. doi:10.1348/026151009X485432 PMID:20306629.

Boot, W. R., Blakely, D. P., & Simons, D. J. (2011). Do action video games improve perception and cognition? *Frontiers in Psychology*, 2. PMID:21738514.

Boot, W. R., Kramer, A. F., Simons, D. J., Fabiani, M., & Gratton, G. (2008). The effects of video game playing on attention, memory, and executive control. *Acta Psychologica*, 129(3), 387–398. doi:10.1016/j.actpsy.2008.09.005 PMID:18929349.

Bottino, R. M., Ott, M., & Tavella, M. (2008). The impact of mind game playing on children's reasoning abilities: Reflections from an experience. In *Proceedings of the 2nd European Conference on Games-Based Learning (ECGBL)*. Barcelona, Spain: ECGBL.

Bottino, R. M., Ferlino, L., Ott, M., & Tavella, M. (2007). Developing strategic and reasoning abilities with computer games at primary school level. *Computers & Education*, 49, 1272–1286. doi:10.1016/j.compedu.2006.02.003.

Bowie, N. E. (1993). Does it pay to bluff in business? In T. L. Beauchamp, & N. E. Bowie (Eds.), *Ethical theory and business* (pp. 443–448). Englewood Cliffs, NJ: Prentice Hall, Inc.

Boyd, J., & Zimbardo, P. (2005). Time perspective, health, and risk taking. In Strathman & Joireman (Eds.), Understanding behavior in the context of time: Theory, research, and application. Mahwah, NJ: Lawrence Erlbaum Associates..

Boyle, E. A., & Connolly, T. M. (2008). Games for learning: Does gender make a difference? In *Proceedings of 2nd European Conference on Games Based Learning*, 69–76.

Boyle, E., van Rosmalen, P., MacArthur, E., Connolly, T. M., Hainey, T., Johnston, B., et al. (2012). Cognitive Task Analysis (CTA) in the Continuing/ Higher Education Methods Using Games (CHERMUG) Project. In *Proceedings of 6ᵗʰ European Conference on Games-based Learning (ECGBL)*. 4 – 5 October 2012, Cork, Ireland.

Boyle, E. A., Connolly, T. M., & Hainey, T. (2011). The role of psychology in understanding the impact of computer games. *Entertainment Computing*, 2, 69–74. doi:10.1016/j.entcom.2010.12.002.

Boyle, E. A., Connolly, T. M., Hainey, T., & Boyle, J. M. (2012). Engagement in digital entertainment games: A systematic review. *Computers in Human Behavior*, 28(3), 771–780. doi:10.1016/j.chb.2011.11.020.

Bradberry, T., Greaves, J., & Lencioni, P. (2005). *The emotional intelligence quick book*. New York: Simon and Schuster..

Bransford, J. D., Brown, A. L., & Cocking, R. R. (Eds.). (2000). *How people learn: Brain, mind, experience, and school*. Washington, DC: National Academy Press..

Brehmer, Y., Westerberg, H., & Bäckman, L. (2012). Working-memory training in younger and older adults: Training gains, transfer, and maintenance. *Frontiers in Human Neuroscience*, 6(63), 1–7. doi: doi:10.3389/fnhum.2012.00063 PMID:22279433.

Bremson, J. (2012). *Using gaming simulation to explore long range fuel and vehicle transitions*. University of California. Retrieved May 3, 2013, from http://steps.ucdavis.edu/its_publications/ dissertations/Bremson_Joel.pdf

Brennan, K. (2009). *Maze game*. Retrieved September 5, 2011, from http://scratched.media.mit.edu/resources/lets-play

Brennan, K., Chung, M., & Hawson, J. (2011). *Scratch curriculum guide draft*. Retrieved January 2, 2013, from http://scratched.media.mit.edu/resources/scratch-curriculum-guide-draft

Brennan, K., Resnick, M., & Monroy-Hernández, A. (2010). Making projects, making friends: Online community as a catalyst for interactive media creation. *New Directions for Youth Development*, (128): 75–83. doi:10.1002/yd.377 PMID:21240955.

Breuer, J., & Bente, G. (2010). Why so serious? On the relation of serious games and learning. *Journal for Computer Game Culture*, 4(1), 7–24.

Brockmann, E., & Anthony, W. (1998). The influence of tacit knowledge and collective mind on strategic planning. *Journal of Managerial Issues*, 10(2), 204–222.

Brockmyer, J. H., Fox, C. M., Curtiss, K. A., McBroom, E., & Burkhart, K. M. (2009). The development of the game engagement questionnaire: a measure of engagement in video game-playing. *Journal of Experimental Social Psychology*, 45, 624–634. doi:10.1016/j.jesp.2009.02.016.

Brockner, J., & Higgins, E. T. (2001). Regulatory focus theory: Implications for the study of emotions at work. *Organizational Behavior and Human Decision Processes*, 86(1), 35–66. doi:10.1006/obhd.2001.2972.

Bronk, S., & Van Rosmalen, P. (2013). *Learning Dutch verb spelling through a simple, yet powerful, wiki-game*. Unpublished.

Brooke, J. (1996). *SUS—A quick and dirty usability scale*. Reading, UK: Redhatch Consulting Ltd.

Brookfield, S. (2006). *The skillful teacher: On technique, trust, and responsiveness in the classroom*. San Francisco, CA: Jossey-Bass..

Brown, D. J., Ley, J., Evett, L., & Standen, P. J. (2011). Can participating in games based learning improve mathematic skills in students with intellectual disabilities? In *Proceedings of IEEE 1st International Conference on Serious Games and Applications for Health* (pp. 1-9). Braga, Portugal: IEEE.

Brown, A. L., & Campione, J. C. (1994). Guided discovery in a community of learners. In K. McGilly (Ed.), *Classroom lessons: Integrating cognitive theory and classroom practice* (pp. 229–270). Cambridge, MA: The MIT Press..

Brown, A., & Bartram, D. (2005). *Relationships between OPQ and enneagram types*. Thames Ditton..

Brown, D., McHugh, D., Standen, P., Evett, L., Shopland, N., & Battersby, S. (2011). Designing location-based learning experiences for people with intellectual disabilities and additional sensory impairments. *Computers & Education*, 56(1), 11–20. doi:10.1016/j.compedu.2010.04.014.

Brown, G., Bull, J., & Pendlebury, M. (1997). *Assessing student learning in higher education.* London: Routledge..

Brown, M., Hall, L. R., Holtzer, R., Brown, S., & Brown, N. (1997). Gender and video game performance. *Seks Roles, 36*(11), 793–812. doi:10.1023/A:1025631307585.

Brünken, R., Steinbacher, S., Plass, J. L., & Leutner, D. (2002). Assessment of cognitive load theory in multimedia learning using dual-task methodology. *Experimental Psychology, 49*(2), 109–119. doi:10.1027//1618-3169.49.2.109 PMID:12053529.

Brusa, J. A. (1988). Effects of video game playing on children's social behavior. *Dissertation Abstracts International-B, 48*(10), 3127.

Budzynski, T., Budzynski Kogan, H., Evans, J., & Abarbanel, A. (2009). Introduction to quantitative EEG and neurofeedback. *The Journal of Head Trauma Rehabilitation.*

Bulger, M. E., Mayer, R. E., Almeroth, K. C., & Blau, S. D. (2008). Measuring learner engagement in computer-equipped college classrooms. *Journal of Educational Multimedia and Hypermedia, 17*(2), 129–143.

Bulkeley, W. M. (2010). TR10: Social TV. *MIT Technology Review.* Retrieved from http://www2.technologyreview.com/article/418541/tr10-social-tv/

Bull, R., Espy, K. A., & Senn, T. E. (2004). A comparison of performance on the Towers of London and Hanoi in young children. *Journal of Child Psychology and Psychiatry, and Allied Disciplines, 45*(4), 743–754. doi:10.1111/j.1469-7610.2004.00268.x PMID:15056306.

Burde, W., & Blankertz, B. (2006). Is the locus of control of reinforcement a predictor of brain-computer interface performance. In *Proceedings of the 3rd International Braincomputer Inferface Workshop and Training Course 2006* (pp. 76–77). IEEE.

Burke, J., Prewett, M., Gray, A., Yang, L., Stilson, F., Coovert, M., et al. (2006). Comparing the effects of visual-auditory and visual-tactile feedback on user performance: A meta-analysis. In *Proceedings of the 8th International Conference on Multimodal Interfaces* (pp. 108–117). IEEE.

Burke, R. J., & McKeen, C. A. (1994). Career development among managerial and professional women. In M. J. Davidson, & J. R. Burke (Eds.), *Women in Management: Current Research Issues* (pp. 65–79). London: Paul Chapman..

Burt, C. (1954). The differentiation of intellectual ability. *The British Journal of Educational Psychology, 24*(2), 76–90. doi:10.1111/j.2044-8279.1954.tb02882.x.

Bushman, B. J., & Anderson, C. A. (2002). Violent video games and hostile expectations: A test of the general aggression model. *Personality and Social Psychology Bulletin, 28*(12), 1679–1686. doi:10.1177/014616702237649.

Buzsáki, G. (2006). *Rhythms of the brain.* New York: Oxford University Press. doi:10.1093/acprof:oso/9780195301069.001.0001.

Cacioppo, J. T., & Petty, R. E. (1982). The need for cognition. *Journal of Personality and Social Psychology, 42*(1), 116–131. doi:10.1037/0022-3514.42.1.116.

Cadinu, M., Maass, A., Rosabianca, A., & Kiesner, J. (2005). Why do women underperform under stereotype threat? *Psychological Science, 16*(7), 572–578. doi:10.1111/j.0956-7976.2005.01577.x PMID:16008792.

Caillois, R. (1961). *Man, play, and games.* New York: Free Press..

Caird-Daley, A., & Harris, D. (2007). *Training decision making using serious games.* Human Factors Integration Defence Technology Centre..

Caldwell, J. H., Huitt, W. G., & Graeber, A. O. (1982). Time spent in learning: Implications from research. *The Elementary School Journal, 82,* 471–480. doi:10.1086/461282.

Calleja, G. (2007). *Digital games as designed experience: Reframing the concept of immersion.* Wellington, New Zealand: Victoria University of Wellington..

Calvert, S. L., & Tan, S. L. (1994). Impact of virtual reality on young adults' physiological arousal and aggressive thoughts: Interaction versus observation. *Journal of Applied Developmental Psychology, 15*(1), 125–139. doi:10.1016/0193-3973(94)90009-4.

Cameirao, M. S., Bermudez i Badia, S., & Verschure, P. F. M. J. (2008). Virtual reality based upper extremity rehabilitation following stroke: A review. *Journal of CyberTherapy & Rehabilitation, 1*(1), 63–73.

Camerer, C. (2003). *Behavioral game theory: Experiments in strategic interaction*. Princeton, NJ: Princeton University Press..

Cameron, B., & Dwyer, F. (2005). The effect of online gaming, cognition and feedback type in facilitating delayed achievement of different learning objectives. *Journal of Interactive Learning Research, 16*(3), 243–258.

Campbell, D. T., & Stanley, J. C. (1963). Experimental and quasi-experimental designs for research on teaching. In N. L. Gage (Ed.), *Handbook of research on teaching* (pp. 171–246). Chicago: Rand McNally..

Campos, J., Martinho, C., & Paiva, A. (2013). Conflict inside out: A theoretically-based approach to conflict from an agent's point of view. In *Proceedings of the 12th International Conference on Autonomous Agents and Multiagent Systems (AAMAS 2013)*. AAMAS.

Campos, J., Martinho, C., Ingram, G., Vasalou, A., & Paiva, A. (2013). My dream theatre: Putting conflict in center stage. In *Proceedings of 8th International Conference on the Foundations of Digital Games (FDG 2013)*. Foundations of Digital Games.

Cantor, J., & Engle, R. W. (1993). Working-memory capacity as long-term memory activation: An individual-differences approach. *Journal of Experimental Learning. Memory & Cognition, 19*(5), 1101–1114. doi:10.1037/0278-7393.19.5.1101.

Carmeli, A., Brueller, D., & Dutton, J. E. (2009). Learning behaviours in the workplace? The role of high quality interpersonal relationships and psychological safety. *Systems Research and Behavioral Science, 26*, 81–98. doi:10.1002/sres.932.

Carnagey, N. L., & Anderson, C. A. (2004). Violent video game exposure and aggression: A literature review. *Minerva Psichiatrica, 45*(1), 1–18.

Carr, A. Z. (1968). Is business bluffing ethical? In *Ethical theory and business* (pp. 143–153). Englewood Cliffs, NJ: Prentice Hall, Inc.

Carroll, J. B. (1963). A model of school learning. *Teachers'. College Record, 64*, 723–733.

Carvalho, A., Brisson, A., & Paiva, A. (2012). Laugh to me! Implementing emotional escalation on autonomous agents for creating a comic sketch. In *Proceedings of the 5th Joint International Conference on Interactive Digital Storytelling: Interactive Storytelling*. Berlin: Springer-Verlag.

Carvelho, T., Allison, R. S., Irving, E. L., & Herriot, C. (2008). *Computer gaming for vision therapy*. Washington, DC: IEEE..

Casasanto, D., & Boroditsky, L. (2008). Time in the mind: Using space to think about time. *Cognition, 106*, 579–593. doi:10.1016/j.cognition.2007.03.004 PMID:17509553.

Cassell, J., Bickmore, T., Billinghurst, M., Campbell, L., Chang, K., Vilhjálmsson, H., & Yan, H. (1999). Embodiment in conversational interfaces: Rea. In *Proceedings of the SIGCHI Conference on Human Factors in Computing Systems: The CHI is the Limit* (pp. 520–527). New York, NY: ACM. doi:10.1145/302979.303150

Castel, A. D., Pratt, J., & Drummond, E. (2005). The effects of action video game experience on the time course of inhibition of return and the efficiency of visual search. *Acta Psychologica, 119*(2), 217–230. doi:10.1016/j.actpsy.2005.02.004 PMID:15877981.

Castronova, E. (2002). *Virtual worlds: A first-hand account of market and society on the cyberian frontier*. Retrieved on December 23, 2012 from http://papers.ssrn.com/sol3/papers.cfm?abstract_id=294828

Castronova, E. (2003). *The price of man and woman: A hedonic pricing model of avatar attributes in a synthetic world*. Retrieved on December 23, 2012 from http://papers.ssrn.com/sol3/papers.cfm?abstract_id=415043

Castronova, E. (2005). *Synthetic worlds: The business and culture of online games*. Chicago: University of Chicago Press..

Castronova, E., Williams, D., Ratan, R., & Keegan, B. (2009). As real as real? Macroeconomic behavior in a large-scale virtual world. *New Media & Society, 11*(5), 685–707. doi:10.1177/1461444809105346.

Cavazza, M., Charles, F., & Mead, S. J. (2001). Character-driven story generation in interactive storytelling. In *Proceedings 7th International Conference in Virtual Systems and Multimedia* (pp. 609–615). IEEE.

Cavazza, M., Charles, F., & Mead, S. J. (2003). Generation of humorous situations in cartoons through plan-based formalisations. In *Proceedings of CHI-2003 Workshop: Humor Modeling in the Interface*. ACM.

Chambers, J. H., & Ascione, F. R. (1987). The effects of prosocial and aggressive videogames on children's donating and helping. *The Journal of Genetic Psychology*, *148*(4), 499–505. doi:10.1080/00221325.1987.105 32488 PMID:3437274.

Chandler, D., & Torbert, B. (2003). Condescending ethics and action research. *Action Research*, *1*(2), 37–47.

Chang, M., & Kinshuk, (2010). Web-based Multiplayer Online Role Playing Game (MORPG) for Assessing Students' Java Programming Knowledge and Skills. In *Proceedings of 2010 IEEE International Conference on Digital Game and Intelligent Toy Enhanced Learning*.

Charles, D., McNeill, M., McAlister, M., Black, M., Moore, A., Stringer, K., et al. (2005). Player-centred game design: Player modelling and adaptive digital games. In *Proceedings of DiGRA 2005 Conference: Changing Views – Worlds in Play*, (pp. 285-298). DiGRA.

Chase, W. G., & Simon, H. A. (1973). The mind's eye in chess. In W. G. Chase (Ed.), *Visual Information Processing*. New York: Academic Press..

Chellapilla, K., & Fogel, D. B. (1999). Evolution, neural networks, games, and intelligence. *Proceedings of the IEEE*, *87*(9), 1471–1496. doi:10.1109/5.784222.

Chen, S. (2009). *The social network game boom*. Retrieved from http://www.gamasutra.com/view/feature/132400/the_social_network_game_boom.php

Chen, S., & Michael, D. (2005). *Proof of learning: Assessment in serious games*. Gamasutra..

Chertoff, D. B., Goldiez, B., & LaViola, J. J. (2010). Virtual experience test: A virtual environment evaluation questionnaire. In *Proceedings of 2010 IEEE Virtual Reality Conference VR* (pp. 103–110). IEEE. doi:10.1109/VR.2010.5444804

Chiang, T., Shih, R., Liu, E. Z., & Lee, A. J. (2011). Using game-based learning and interactive peer assessment to improve career goals and objectives for college students edutainment technologies. *Lecture Notes in Computer Science*, *6872*, 507–511. doi:10.1007/978-3-642-23456-9_91.

Chiappe, D., Conger, M., Liao, J., Caldwell, J. L., & Vu, K. P. L. (2013). Improving multi-tasking ability through action videogames. *Applied Ergonomics*, *44*(2), 278–284. doi:10.1016/j.apergo.2012.08.002 PMID:22981314.

Chi, M. T. H. (1997). Quantifying qualitative analyses of verbal data: A practical guide. *Journal of the Learning Sciences*, *6*(3), 271–315. doi:10.1207/s15327809jls0603_1.

Chinn, C. A., & Malhotra, B. (2002). Epistemologically authentic inquiry in schools: A theoretical framework for evaluating inquiry tasks. *Science Education*, *86*(2), 175–218. doi:10.1002/sce.10001.

Cho, B.-H., Kim, S., Shin, D. I., Lee, J. H., Lee, S. M., Kim, I. Y., & Kim, S. I. (2004). Neurofeedback training with virtual reality for inattention and impulsiveness. *Cyberpsychology & Behavior: The Impact of the Internet. Multimedia and Virtual Reality on Behavior and Society*, *7*(5), 519–527.

Cho, B.-H., Ku, J., Jang, D. P., Kim, S., Lee, Y. H., & Kim, I. Y. et al. (2002). The effect of virtual reality cognitive training for attention enhancement. *Cyberpsychology & Behavior: The Impact of the Internet. Multimedia and Virtual Reality on Behavior and Society*, *5*(2), 129–137.

Chong, D., & Druckman, J. N. (2007). Framing theory. *Annual Review of Political Science*, *10*(1), 103–126. doi:10.1146/annurev.polisci.10.072805.103054.

Chou, L. D., Liu, T. C., Li, D. C., Chen, Y. S., Ieong, M. T., Lee, P. H., & Lin, Y. C. (2011). Development of a game-based learning system using toy robots. In *Proceedings of the 2011 IEEE 11th International Conference on Advanced Learning Technologies* (pp. 202-204). IEEE Computer Society.

Christian, W., & Belloni, M. (2001). *Physlets*. Englewood Cliffs, NJ: Prentice Hall..

Christou, C., Jones, K., Mousoulides, N., & Pittalis, M. (2006). Developing the 3DMath dynamic geometry software: Theoretical perspectives on design. *The International Journal for Technology in Mathematics Education, 13*(4), 168–174.

Ciavarro, C., Dobson, M., & Goodman, D. (2007). Alert Hockey: An endogenous learning game. *Loading. The Journal of the Canadian Games Studies Association, 1*(1).

Cicchetti, D. (2002). The impact of social experience on neurobiological systems: Illustration from a constructivist view of child maltreatment. *Cognitive Development, 17*, 1407–1428. doi:10.1016/S0885-2014(02)00121-1.

Clark, J. E., Lanphear, A. K., & Riddick, C. C. (1987). The effects of videogame playing on the response selection processing of elderly adults. *Journal of Gerontology, 42*(1), 82–85. doi:10.1093/geronj/42.1.82 PMID:3794204.

Clickers. (2009). Retrieved from http://telr.osu.edu/clickers.

Coben, R., & Evans, J. (2010). *Neurofeedback and neuromodulation techniques and applications*. London: Elsevier Academic Press..

Coffield, F., Moseley, D., Hall, E., & Ecclestone, K. (2004). *Learning styles and pedagogy in post-16 learning: A systematic and critical review*. Retrieved on February 13, 2013 from http://www.lsrc.ac.uk/publications/index.asp

Cogmed. (2013). *Cogmed working memory training*. Retrieved from http://www.cogmed.com/program

Cohen, A. R., Stotland, E., & Wolfe, D. M. (1955). An experimental investigation of need for cognition. *Journal of Abnormal and Social Psychology, 51*(2), 291–294. doi:10.1037/h0042761 PMID:13263045.

Coleman, J. (2009). Social capital in the creation of human capital. *The American Journal of Sociology, 94*(1988), S95–S120.

Colwell, J. (2007). Needs met through computer game play among adolescents. *Personality and Individual Differences, 43*, 2072–2082. doi:10.1016/j.paid.2007.06.021.

Colzato, L. S., van den Wildenberg, W., Zmigrod, S., & Hommel, B. (2013). Action video gaming and cognitive control: Playing first person shooter games is associated with improvement in working memory but not action inhibition. *Psychological Research, 77*, 234–239. doi:10.1007/s00426-012-0415-2 PMID:22270615.

Colzato, L. S., van Leeuwen, P. J., van den Wildenberg, W. P., & Hommel, B. (2010). DOOM'd to switch: Superior cognitive flexibility in players of first person shooter games. *Frontiers in Psychology, 1*, 8. doi:10.3389/fpsyg.2010.00008 PMID:21833191.

Conati, C., & Zhao, X. (2004). Building and evaluating an intelligent pedagogical agent to improve the effectivenesss of an education game. In *Proceedings of IUI'04, International Conference on Intelligent User Interfaces*. Funchal, Portugal: IUI.

Conati, C., & Zhou, X. (2002). Modelling students' emotions from cognitive appraisal in educational games. In *Proceedings of the 6th International Conference on Intelligent Tutoring Systems*. London: Springer-Verlag, ACM.

Connolly, T. M. Stansfield, M., Hainey, T., Cousins, I., Josephson, J., O'Donovan, A., Rodriguez Ortiz, C., Tsvetkova, N., Stoimenova, B., & Tsvetanova, S. (2009). ARGuing for multilingual motivation in Web 2.0: a games-based learning platform for language learning, In *Proceedings of 3rd European Conference on Games-based Learning (ECGBL)*, 12-13 October 2009, Graz, Austria

Connolly, T. M., & Stansfield, M. H. (2006). Enhancing eLearning: Using computer games to teach requirements collection and analysis. In *Proceedings of Second Symposium of the WG HCI & UE of the Austrian Computer Society*. Vienna, Austria: WG.

Connolly, T. M., Boyle, E., & Hainey, T. (2007). A survey of students' motivations for playing computer games: A comparative analysis. In *Proceedings of the 1st European Conference on Games-Based Learning* (ECGBL). Paisley, UK: ECGBL.

Connolly, T. C., Boyle, E. A., Hainey, T., McArthur, E., & Boyle, J. M. (2012). A systematic literature review of empirical evidence on computer games and serious games. *Computers & Education, 59*, 661–686. doi:10.1016/j.compedu.2012.03.004.

Connolly, T. M., Stansfield, M. H., & Hainey, T. (2011). An alternate reality game for language learning: ARGuing for multilingual motivation. *Computers & Education, 57*, 1389–1415. doi:10.1016/j.compedu.2011.01.009.

Connolly, T. M., Stansfield, M., & Hainey, T. (2007). An application of games-based learning within software engineering. *British Journal of Educational Technology, 38*(3), 416–428. doi:10.1111/j.1467-8535.2007.00706.x.

Connolly, T. M., Stansfield, M., & Hainey, T. (2009). *Towards the development of a games-based learning evaluation framework: Games-based learning advancements for multisensory human computer interfaces: techniques and effective pratices.* Academic Press. doi:10.4018/978-1-60566-360-9.

Conole, G., & Warburton, B. (2005). A review of computer-assisted assessment. *ALT-J. Research in Learning Technology, 13*(1), 17–31. doi:10.3402/rlt.v13i1.10970.

Cook, T. D., & Campbell, D. T. (1979). *Quasi-experimentation: Design and analysis issues for field settings.* Boston: Houghlin Mifflin Company..

Cooley, W. W., & Lohnes, P. R. (1976). *Evaluation research in education.* New York: Irvington publishers..

Cooper, J., & Mackie, D. (1986). Video games and aggression in children. *Journal of Applied Social Psychology, 16*(8), 726–744. doi:10.1111/j.1559-1816.1986.tb01755.x.

Cooper, S., Khatib, F., Treuille, A., Barbero, J., Lee, J., & Beenen, M. et al. (2010). Predicting protein structures with a multiplayer online game. *Nature, 466*(7307), 756–760. doi:10.1038/nature09304 PMID:20686574.

Copier, M. (2007). *Beyond the magic circle: A network perspective on role-play in online games.* Utrecht University. Retrieved from http://igitur-archive.library.uu.nl/dissertations/2007-0710-214621/index.htm

Cordova, D. I., & Lepper, M. R. (1996). Intrinsic motivation and the process of learning: Beneficial effects of contextualization, personalization, and choice. *Journal of Educational Psychology, 88*(4), 715–730. doi:10.1037/0022-0663.88.4.715.

Corriere, J. D. (2003). *Shortfall: An educational game on environmental issues in supply chain management.* (M.S. Thesis). Northeastern University, Boston, MA.

Costa, P. T. Jr, & McCrae, R. R. (1992). *Revised NEO personality inventory (NEO-PI-R) and NEO five-factor inventory (NEO-FFI) manual.* Odessa, FL: Psychological Assessment Resources..

Coulthard, G. J. (2009). *A review of the educational use and learning effectiveness of simulations and games.* Retrieved May 3, 2013, from http://www.coulthard.com/library/paper-simulation.html

Cournot, A. A. (1838). *Recherches sur les principes mathématiques de la théorie des richesses.* L. Hachette..

Cowley, B., Charles, D., Black, M., & Hickey, R. (2008). Towards an understanding of flow in video games. *ACM Computers in Entertainment, 6*(2), 1–27. doi:10.1145/1371216.1371223.

Cox, M. J. (1997). *The effects of information technology on students' motivation: Final report.* London: King's College London..

Coyle, R. G. (1977). *Management system dynamics.* London: John Wiley & Sons..

Coyle, S. M., Ward, T. E., & Markham, C. M. (2007). Brain-computer interface using a simplified functional near-infrared spectroscopy system. *Journal of Neural Engineering, 4*(3), 219–226. doi:10.1088/1741-2560/4/3/007 PMID:17873424.

Craig, A. D. (2002). How do you feel? Interoception: The sense of the physiological condition of the body. *Nature Reviews. Neuroscience, 3*(8), 655–666. PMID:12154366.

Crawford, C. (1984). *The art of computer game design.* New York, NY: McGraw-Hill..

Creswell, J. W. (2002). Research design: Qualitative, quantitative, and mixed methods approaches. *Organizational Research Methods, 6*, 246.

Csapó, B., Lörincz, A., & Molnár, G. (2012). Innovative Assessment Technologies in Educational Games Designed for Young Students. In Assessment in Game-Based Learning, 235-254..

Csíkszentmihályi, M. (1990). *Flow: The psychology of optimal experience*. New York: Harper and Row..

Csikszentmihalyi, M. (1997). Flow and education. *NAMTA Journal, 22*, 2–35.

Cui, X., Bray, S., & Reiss, A. L. (2010). Speeded near infrared spectroscopy (NIRS) response detection. *PLoS ONE, 5*(11), e15474. doi:10.1371/journal.pone.0015474 PMID:21085607.

Cutrona, C. E., Suhr, J. A., & MacFarlane, R. (1990). Interpersonal transactions and the psychological sense of support. *Personal Relationships and Social Support*, 30–45.

Damasio, A. (2011). *Self comes to mind: Constructing the conscious brain*. New York: Random House. Retrieved from http://books.google.pt/books?id=2ILun_SB4NIC

Damasio, A. (2005). *Descartes' error: Emotion, reason, and the human brain*. New York: Penguin Books..

Daniels, D., & Pice, V. (2000). *The essential enneagram: Test and self-discovery guide*. San Francisco, CA: Harper..

Danielsson, H., Henry, L., Messer, D., & Rönnberg, J. (2012). Strengths and weaknesses in executive functioning in children with intellectual disability. *Research in Developmental Disabilities, 33*(2), 600–607. doi:10.1016/j.ridd.2011.11.004 PMID:22155533.

Daum, I., Rockstroh, B., Birbaumer, N., Elbert, T., Canavan, A., & Lutzenberger, W. (1993). Behavioural treatment of slow cortical potentials in intractable epilepsy: Neuropsychological predictors of outcome. *Journal of Neurology, Neurosurgery, and Psychiatry, 56*(1), 94–97. doi:10.1136/jnnp.56.1.94 PMID:8429329.

Dautenhahn, K. (1999). *Computation for metaphors, analogy, and agents*. Berlin: Springer-Verlag. Retrieved from http://dl.acm.org/citation.cfm?id=1830925.1830936

Davidson, M. C., Amso, D., Anderson, L. C., & Diamond, A. (2006). Development of cognitive control and executive functions from 4 to 13 years: Evidence from manipulations of memory, inhibition, and task switching. *Neuropsychologia, 44*(11), 2037–2078. doi:10.1016/j.neuropsychologia.2006.02.006 PMID:16580701.

Davidson, M. J., & Cooper, C. L. (1992). *Shattering the glass ceiling: The women manager*. London: Paul Chapman..

Davis, F. D. (1989). Perceived usefulness, perceived ease of use, and user acceptance of information technology. *Management Information Systems Quarterly, 13*, 319–339. doi:10.2307/249008.

De Andrade e Silva, S. (2012). Click, share and learn! Social network games as serious play. In *Proceedings of the 6th European Conference on Games Based Learning*. ECGBL.

De Caluwe, L., Hofstede, G. J., & Peters, V. A. M. (2008). *Why do games work: In search of the active substance*. Retrieved from http://www.narcis.nl/publication/RecordID/oai:library.wur.nl:wurpubs/368664

de Freitas, S. (2006). *Learning in immersive worlds: A review of games-based learning*. Bristol, UK: JISC. Retrieved from http://www.jisc.ac.uk/media/documents/programmes/elearninginnovation/gamingreport_v3.pdf

de Freitas, S., & Neumann, T. (2009). The use of 'exploratory learning' for supporting immersive learning in virtual environments. *Computers & Education, 52*, 343–352. doi:10.1016/j.compedu.2008.09.010.

De Freitas, S., & Oliver, M. (2006). How can exploratory learning with games and simulations within the curriculum be most effectively evaluated? *Computers & Education, 46*(3), 249–264. doi:10.1016/j.compedu.2005.11.007.

De Freitas, S., Rebolledo-Mendez, G., Liarokapis, F., Magoulas, G., & Poulovassilis, A. (2010). Learning as immersive experiences: Using the four-dimensional framework for designing and evaluating immersive learning experiences in a virtual world. *British Journal of Educational Technology, 41*(1), 69–85. doi:10.1111/j.1467-8535.2009.01024.x.

De Vaus, D. (2001). Research design in social research. *British Educational Research Journal, 28*, 296.

deCharms, R. C., Maeda, F., Glover, G. H., Ludlow, D., Pauly, J. M., & Soneji, D. et al. (2005). Control over brain activation and pain learned by using real-time functional MRI. *Proceedings of the National Academy of Sciences of the United States of America, 102*(51), 18626–18631. doi:10.1073/pnas.0505210102 PMID:16352728.

Deci, E. L., & Ryan, R. M. (1985). *Intrinsic motivation and self-determination in human behaviour*. New York: Plenum. doi:10.1007/978-1-4899-2271-7.

Deci, E., Koestner, R., & Ryan, R. (2001). Extrinsic rewards and intrinsic motivations in education: Reconsidered once again. *Review of Educational Research, 71*(1), 1–27. doi:10.3102/00346543071001001.

Deci, E., & Ryan, R. (Eds.). (2002). *Handbook of self-determination research*. Rochester, NY: University of Rochester Press..

Dede, C., Clarke, J., Ketelhut, D. J., Nelson, B., & Bowman, C. (2005). Students' motivation and learning of science in a multi-user virtual environment. Paper presented at the meeting of the *American Educational Research Association*, Montréal, Quebec.

Dede, C. (2000). A new century demands new ways of learning: An excerpt from the digital classroom. In D. T. E. Gordon (Ed.), *The Digital Classroom*. Cambridge, MA: Harvard Education Letter..

Dede, C. (2005). Planning for neomillennial learning styles. *EDUCAUSE Quarterly, 28*(1), 7–12.

Del Blanco, Á. Torrente, J., Moreno-Ger, P., & Fernández-Manjón, B. (2010). Towards the Generalization of Games-based Learning: Integrating Educational Video Games in LAMS. In *Proceedings of 10ᵗʰ IEEE Conference on Advanced Learning Technologies*.

Del Blanco, Á., Torrente, J., Marchiori, E. J., Martínez-Ortiz, I., Moreno-Ger, P., & Fernández-Manjón, B. (2010). Easing Assessment of Game-based Learning with <e-Adventure> and LAMS. In *Proceedings of the second ACM International Workshop on Multimedia Technologies for Distance Learning*.

Del Blanco, Á., Torrente, J., Moreno-Ger, P., & Fernández-Manjón, B. (2009). A General Architecture for the Integration of Educational Videogames in Standards-compliant Virtual Learning Environments. In *Proceedings of 9ᵗʰ IEEE International Conference on Advanced Learning Technologies*.

Delft, T. U. Tygron Serious Gaming, & Port of Rotterdam. (n.d.). *SimPort MV2 serious game*. Retrieved May 3, 2013, from http://www.simport.eu/

Delhoum, S. (2009). *Evaluation of the impact of learning labs on inventory control: An experimental approach with a collaborative simulation game of a production network*. Berlin: Gito-Verlag..

Deltares Deltabrain. (n.d.). *Levee patroller*. Delft, The Netherlands. *Deltares*..

Demmel, R. B., Kohler, B., Krusche, S., & Schubert, L. (2011). The serious game: Wemakewords. In *Proceedings of the 10ᵗʰ SIGPLAN Symposium on New Ideas, New Paradigms, and Reflections on Programming and Software*. New York: ACM.

Dempsey, J. V., Haynes, L. L., Lucassen, B. A., & Casey, M. S. (2002). Forty simple computer games and what they could mean to educators. *Simulation & Gaming, 33*(2), 157–168. doi:10.1177/1046878102332003.

Demsetz, H. (1967). Towards a theory of property rights. *The American Economic Review, 57*(2), 347–359.

Denner, J., Werner, L., & Ortiz, E. (2012). Computer games created by middle school girls: Can they be used to measure understanding of computer science concepts? *Computers & Education, 58*(1), 240–249. doi:10.1016/j.compedu.2011.08.006.

Denning, T. (1997). *IT and pupil motivation: A collaborative study of staff and pupil attitudes and experiences*. Keele, UK: Keele University..

Deterding, S., Dreyer, S., Järvinen, A., Kirman, B., Kücklich, J., Paavilainen, J., et al. (2010). *Social game studies: A workshop report*. Retrieved from http://socialgamestudies.org/report

Diamond, A. (2013). Executive functions. *Annual Review of Psychology, 64*. PMID:23020641.

Dias, J., & Paiva, A. (2005). Feeling and reasoning: A computational model for emotional characters. In C. Bento, A. Cardoso, & G. Dias (Eds.), *Progress in Artificial Intelligence* (pp. 127–140). Berlin: Springer. Retrieved from http://link.springer.com/chapter/10.1007/11595014_13

Dias, J., & Paiva, A. (2013). I want to be your friend: Establishing relations with emotionally intelligent agents. In *Proceedings of the 12th International Conference on Autonomous Agents and Multiagent Systems (AAMAS 2013)*. AAMAS.

Dias, J., Mascarenhas, S., & Paiva, A. (2011). *Fatima modular: Towards an agent architecture with a generic appraisal framework*. Paper presented at the Workshop in Standards in Emotion Modeling. Leiden, The Netherlands.

Díaz-Morales, J. F. (2006). Estructura factorial y fiabilidad del inventario de perspectiva temporal de zimbardo. *Psicothema*, *18*(3), 565–571. PMID:17296088.

DiCerbo, K. E., & Behrens, J. T. (2012). Implications of the digital ocean on current and future assessment. In R. Lissitz, & H. Jiao (Eds.), *Computers and their impact on state assessment: Recent history and predictions for the future* (pp. 273–306). Charlotte, NC: Information Age Publishing..

Dickerman, C., Christensen, J., & Kerl-McClain, S. (2008). Big breasts and bad guys: Depictions of gender and race in video games. *Journal of Creativity in Mental Health*, *3*(1), 20–29. doi:10.1080/15401380801995076.

Dietz, T. L. (1998). An examination of violence and gender role portrayals in video games: Implications for gender socialization and aggressive behavior. *Sex Roles*, *38*, 5–6, 425–442. doi:10.1023/A:1018709905920.

Dignan, A. (2011). *Game frame: Using games as a strategy for success*. New York: Simon & Schuster..

Dillenbourg, P., & Fischer, F. (2007). Basics of computer-supported collaborative learning. *Zeitschrift für Berufs- und Wirtschaftspaedagogik*, *21*, 111–130.

Dillenbourg, P., & Hong, F. (2008). The mechanics of CSCL macro scripts. *International Journal of Computer-Supported Collaborative Learning*, *3*(1), 5–23. doi:10.1007/s11412-007-9033-1.

Dimas, J., & Prada, R. (2013). You are who you hang out with: Agents with dynamic identity. In *Proceedings of the 12th International Conference on Autonomous Agents and Multiagent Systems (AAMAS 2013)*. AAMAS.

Dixit, A. K. (1990). *Optimization in economic theory*. Oxford, UK: Oxford University Press..

Dix, T. (1993). Attributing dispositions to children: An interactional analysis of attribution in socialization. *Personality and Social Psychology Bulletin*, *19*(5), 633–643. doi:10.1177/0146167293195014.

Djaouti, D. (2011). *Serious game design - Considérations théoriques et techniques sur la création de jeux vidéo à vocation utilitaire*. (Thèse de doctorat en informatique). Université de Toulouse III, Toulouse, France.

Dominick, J. R. (1984). Videogames, television violence, and aggression in teenagers. *The Journal of Communication*, *34*(2), 136–147. doi:10.1111/j.1460-2466.1984.tb02165.x.

Dondlinger, M. J. (2007). Educational video games design: A review of the literature. *Journal of Applied Educational Technology*, *4*(1), 21–31.

Donohue, S. E., James, B., Eslick, A. N., & Mitroff, S. R. (2012). Cognitive pitfall! Videogame players are not immune to dual-task costs. *Attention, Perception & Psychophysics*, *74*(5), 803–809. doi:10.3758/s13414-012-0323-y PMID:22669792.

Doud, A. J., Lucas, J. P., Pisansky, M. T., & He, B. (2011). Continuous three-dimensional control of a virtual helicopter using a motor imagery based brain-computer interface. *PLoS ONE*, *6*(10), e26322. doi:10.1371/journal.pone.0026322 PMID:22046274.

Downs, E., & Smith, S. L. (2010). Keeping abreast of hypersexuality: A video game character content analysis. *Sex Roles*, *62*, 721–733. doi:10.1007/s11199-009-9637-1.

Driver, J., & Spence, C. (1998). Cross modal links in spatial attention. *Proceedings. Biological Sciences*, *353*, 1–13.

Ducheneaut, N., Yee, N., Nickell, E., & Moore, R. J. (2005). Alone together? Exploring the social dynamics of massively multiplayer online games. In R. Grinter, T. Rodden, P. Aoki, E. Cutrell, R. Jeffries, & G. Olson (Eds.), *Proceedings of the SIGCHI Conference on Human Factors in Computing Systems (CHI '06)* (pp. 407–416). ACM.

Ducheneaut, N., & Moore, R. J. (2005). More than just XP: Learning social skills in massively multiplayer online games. *Interactive Technology and Smart Education*, *2*(2), 89–100. doi:10.1108/17415650580000035.

Ducrot, R. (2009). Gaming across scale in peri-urban water management: Contribution from two experiences in Bolivia and Brazil. *International Journal of Sustainable Development World Ecology*, *16*(4), 240–252. doi:10.1080/13504500903017260.

Duff, S. C., & Logie, L. H. (2001). Processing and storage in working memory span. *The Quarterly Journal of Experimental Psychology. A, Human Experimental Psychology, 54*(1), 31–48. doi:10.1080/02724980042000011 PMID:11216320.

Duke, R. D., & Geurts, J. L. A. (2004). *Policy games for strategic management: Pathways into the unknown.* Amsterdam: Dutch University Press..

Dulewicz, V., & Higgs, M. (2000). Emotional intelligence – A review and evaluation study. *Journal of Managerial Psychology, 15*(4), 341–372. doi:10.1108/02683940010330993.

Dweck, C. S. (1986). Motivational processes affecting learning. *The American Psychologist, 41*(10), 1040–1048. doi:10.1037/0003-066X.41.10.1040.

Dweck, C. S., & Master, A. (2008). *Self-theories motivate self-regulated learning.* Mahwah, NJ: Lawrence Erlbaum Associates Publishers..

Dye, M. W. G., Green, C. S., & Bavelier, D. (2009). Increasing speed of processing with action video games. *Current Directions in Psychological Science, 18,* 321–326. doi:10.1111/j.1467-8721.2009.01660.x PMID:20485453.

Eatwell, J., Milgate, M., & Newman, P. (Eds.). (1989). *The new palgrave: Game theory.* New York: Macmillan Reference Books..

Eberly, D. H., & Shoemake, K. (2004). *Game physics.* Amsterdam: Elsevier/Morgan Kaufmann..

Edelenbos, J., & Van Buuren, A. (2005). The learning evaluation: A theoretical and empirical exploration. *Evaluation Review, 29*(6), 591–612. doi:10.1177/0193841X05276126 PMID:16244054.

Edmondson, A. C. (1999). Psychological safety and learning behavior in work teams. *Administrative Science Quarterly, 44*(2), 350. doi:10.2307/2666999.

Egenfeldt-Nielsen, S. (2005). *Beyond edutainment: Exploring the educational potential of computer games.* Retrieved May 3, 2013, from http://www.seriousgames.dk/downloads/egenfeldt.pdf

Egenfeldt-Nielsen, S. (2006). Overview of research on the educational use of video games. *Digital Kompetanse, 1,* 184–213.

Egenfeldt-Nielsen, S. (2006a). Can education and psychology join forces: The clash of benign and malign learning from computer games. *Nordicom Review, 26*(2), 103–107.

Egner, T., & Gruzelier, J. H. (2001). Learned self-regulation of EEG frequency components affects attention and event-related brain potentials in humans. *Neuroreport, 12*(18), 4155–4159. doi:10.1097/00001756-200112210-00058 PMID:11742256.

Egner, T., & Gruzelier, J. H. (2004). EEG biofeedback of low beta band components: Frequency-specific effects on variables of attention and event-related brain potentials. *Clinical Neurophysiology, 115*(1), 131–139. doi:10.1016/S1388-2457(03)00353-5 PMID:14706480.

Eklund, L., & Johansson, M. (2010). Social play? A study of social interaction in temporary group formation (PUG) in World of Warcraft. In *Proceedings of DiGRA Nordic 2010: Experiencing Games: Games, Play, and Players.* DiGRA.

Ellis Weismer, S., Evans, J., & Hesketh, L. J. (1999). An examination of verbal working memory capacity in children with specific language impairment. *Journal of Speech, Language, and Hearing Research: JSLHR, 42*(5), 1249–1260. PMID:10515519.

Endsley, M. R. (1998). A comparative analysis of SAGAT and SART for evaluations of situation awareness. In *Proceedings of the Human Factors and Ergonomics Society 42nd Annual Meeting* (pp. 82–86). Santa Monica, CA: The Human Factors and Ergonomics Society.

Endsley, M. R. (1995). Towards a theory of situation awareness in dynamic systems. *Human Factors, 37*(1), 32–64. doi:10.1518/001872095779049543.

Engle, R. W., & Kane, M. J. (2004). Executive attention, working memory capacity, and a two-factor theory of cognitive control. In *The psychology of learning and motivation.* New York: Elsevier..

Ennis, R. H. (1987). A taxonomy of critical thinking dispositions and abilities. In J. B. Baron, & R. J. Sternberg (Eds.), *Teaching thinking skills: Theory and practice* (pp. 9–26). New York: Freeman..

Enochsson, L., Isaksson, B., Tour, R., Kjellin, A., Hedman, L., & Wredmark, T. et al. (2004). Visuospatial skills and computer game experience influence the performance of virtual endoscopy. *Journal of Gastrointestinal Surgery Official Journal of the Society for Surgery of the Alimentary Tract, 8*(7), 876–882. doi:10.1016/j.gassur.2004.06.015 PMID:15531242.

Ericsson, K. A., Charness, N., Feltovich, P. J., & Hoffman, R. R. (Eds.). (2006). *The Cambridge handbook of expertise and expertise performance.* Cambridge, UK: Cambridge University Press. doi:10.1017/CBO9780511816796.

Ermi, L., & Mäyrä, F. (2003). *Power and control of games: Children as the actors of game cultures.* Retrieved May 3, 2013, from http://www.uta.fi/~tlilma/Ermi_Mayra_Power_and_Control_of_Games.pdf

Eseryel, D., Ifenthaler, D., & Ge, X. (2011). Alternative Assessment Strategies for Complex Problem Solving in Game-Based Learning Environments. In Proceedings of Multiple Perspectives on Problem Solving and Learning in Digital Age, 159–178..

European Commission. (2008). *The European qualifications framework for lifelong learning (EQF).* Luxembourg: Office for Official Publications of the European Communities..

Eysenck, M. W., & Keane, M. T. (2010). *Cognitive psychology: A student's handbook* (6th ed.). New York: Psychology Press..

Fagenson, E. A. (1986). Women's work orientation: Something old, something new. *Group and Organization Studies, 11*(1), 75–100. doi:10.1177/105960118601100108.

Falk, M., Band, M., & McLaughlin, T. F. (2003). The effects of reading racetracks and flashcards on sight word vocabulary of three third grade students with a specific learning disability: A further replication and analysis. *International Journal of Special Education, 18*(2), 51–57.

FAS. (2006). *Harnessing the power of video games for learning: Summit of educational games.* Washington, DC: Federation of American Scientists. Retrieved from http://www.fas.org/gamesummit/Resources/Summit%20on%20Educational%20Games.pdf

Fehr, E., & Schmidt, K. (2005). *The economics of fairness, reciprocity and altruism: Experimental evidence and new theories.* Retrieved 17 April, 2013, from http://epub.ub.uni-muenchen.de/726/1/Fehr-Schmidt_Handbook(2005-Munichecon).pdf

Felder, R. M., & Brent, R. (2005). Understanding student differences. *Journal of Engineering Education, 94*(1), 57–72. doi:10.1002/j.2168-9830.2005.tb00829.x.

Felder, R. M., & Silverman, L. K. (1988). Learning and Teaching Styles in Engineering Education. *English Education, 78*(7), 674–681.

Felder, R. M., & Spurlin, J. (2005). Reliability and validity of the index of learning styles: A meta-analysis. *International Journal of Engineering Education, 21*(1), 103–112.

Feldman-Barrett, L., & Salovey, P. (2002). *The wisdom in feeling: Psychological processes in emotional intelligence.* New York: Guilford Press..

Felicia, P., & Pitt, I. J. (2007). Evaluating the effect of personalities on the design of educational games. In *Proceedings of the ECGBL Conference.* Paisley, UK: ECGBL.

Felicia, P., & Pitt, I. J. (2008). Personalising educational games to students' learning styles. In *Proceedings of the International Technology in Education and Development Conference.* Valencia, Spain: IEEE.

Felicia, P. (2009). *Digital games in schools: A handbook for teachers.* Brussels, Belgium: European Schoolnet..

Felicia, P., & Pitt, I. J. (2009). Profiling users in educational games. In T. M. Connolly, M. H. Stansfield, & E. Boyle (Eds.), *Games-based learning advancement for multisensory human computer interfaces: Techniques and effective practices.* Hershey, PA: Idea Group. doi:10.4018/978-1-60566-360-9.ch009.

Fell, J., Axmacher, N., & Haupt, S. (2010). From alpha to gamma: Electrophysiological correlates of meditation-related states of consciousness. *Medical Hypotheses, 75*(2), 218–224. doi:10.1016/j.mehy.2010.02.025 PMID:20227193.

Fell, J., Staresina, B., Do Lam, A., Widman, G., Helmstaedter, C., Elger, C., & Axmacher, N. (2012). Memory modulation by weak synchronous deep brain stimulation: A pilot study. *Brain Stimulation.* PMID:22939277.

Feng, J., Spence, I., & Pratt, J. (2007). Playing an action video game reduces gender differences in spatial cognition. *Psychological Science*, *18*(10), 850–855. doi:10.1111/j.1467-9280.2007.01990.x PMID:17894600.

Ferguson, C. J. (2002). Media violence: Miscast causality. *The American Psychologist*, *57*(6/7), 446–447. doi:10.1037/0003-066X.57.6-7.446b PMID:12094443.

Fernández-Aranda, F., Jiménez-Murcia, S., Santamaría, J. J., Gunnard, K., Soto, A., & Kalapanidas, E. et al. (2012). Video games as a complementary therapy tool in mental disorders: PlayMancer, a European multicentre study. *Journal of Mental Health (Abingdon, England)*, *21*(4), 364–374. doi:10.3109/09638237.2012.664302 PMID:22548300.

Ferrara, J. (2012). *Playful design: Creating game experiences in everyday interfaces*. New York: Louis Rosenfeld..

Ferris, G. R. (2005). Development and validation of the political skill inventory. *Journal of Management*, *31*(1), 126–152. doi:10.1177/0149206304271386.

Feshbach, S. (1955). The drive-reducing function of fantasy behavior. *Journal of Abnormal Psychology*, *50*(1), 3–11. doi:10.1037/h0042214 PMID:13232919.

Field, A., & Hole, G. (2003). *How to design and report experiments*. London: Sage Publications..

Finneran, C. M., & Zhang, P. (2003). A person-artefact-task (PAT) model of flow antecedents in computer-mediated environments. *International Journal of Human-Computer Studies*, *59*, 475–496. doi:10.1016/S1071-5819(03)00112-5.

Finneran, C. M., & Zhang, P. (2005). Flow in computer-mediated environments: Promises and challenges. *Communications of the Association for Information Systems*, *15*, 82–101.

Firestone, W. A. (1989). Educational policy as an ecology of games. *Educational Researcher*, *18*(7), 18–24. doi:doi:10.3102/0013189X018007018.

Fischer, G., & Kling, U. (1974). LOGO - Eine programmiersprache für schüler, inhaltliche und methodische aspekte ihrer anwendung. *Lecture Notes in Computer Science*, *17*, 290–299. doi:10.1007/3-540-06907-0_87.

Fisher, C., Berliner, D., Filby, N., Marliave, R., Cahen, L., & Dishaw, M. (1980). Teaching behaviors, academic learning time, and student achievement: An overview. In C. Denham, & A. Lieberman (Eds.), *Time to learn*. Washington, DC: National Institute of Education..

Fisher, K. (1997). Locating frames in the discursive universe. *Sociological Research Online*, *2*(3), 1–41. Retrieved from http://www.socresonline.org.uk/2/3/4.html doi:10.5153/sro.78.

Fishman, D. B. (1966). Need and expectancy as determinants of affiliative behavior in small groups. *Journal of Personality and Social Psychology*, *4*(2), 155–164. doi:10.1037/h0023565 PMID:5969140.

Forsyth, R., Whitton, N., & Whitton, P. (2011). Accreditation! The responsive curriculum game. In D. Gouscos & M. Meimaris (Eds.), *Proceedings of the 5th European Conference on Games Based Learning* (pp. 176–182). Reading, MA: Academic Publishing Limited.

Fourdraine, A., Hotho, H., Janssen, D., Janssen, K., Maters, A., Munsterman, D., Pijl, J., Van der Veen, S., & Van der Vereijken-Jonkers, S.M. (2007). *Taaljournaal*. s-Hertogenbosch: Malmberg.

Frasca, G. (2007). *12th September*. Retrieved from http://www.newsgaming.com/newsgames.htm

Frederick, S. (2005). Cognitive reflection and decision making. *The Journal of Economic Perspectives*, *19*(4), 25–42. doi:10.1257/089533005775196732.

French, J. R. P. Jr., & Raven, B. (1959). The bases of social power. In Studies in social power (pp. 150–167). Oxford, UK: University of Michigan..

Fu, F., Su, R., & Yu, S. (2009). E game flow: A scale to measure learners' enjoyment of e-learning games. *Computers & Education*, *52*, 101–112. doi:10.1016/j.compedu.2008.07.004.

Funk, J. B., & Buchman, D. D. (1996). Playing violent video and computer games and adolescent self-concept. *The Journal of Communication*, *46*(2), 19–32. doi:10.1111/j.1460-2466.1996.tb01472.x.

Funk, J. B., Hagan, J., Schimming, J., Bullock, W., Buchman, D. D., & Myers, M. (2002). Aggression and psychopathology in adolescents with a preference for violent electronic games. *Aggressive Behavior*, *28*(2), 134–144. doi:10.1002/ab.90015.

Furby, L. (1978). Possession in humans: An exploratory study of its meaning and motivation. *Social Behavior and Personality*, *6*(1), 49–65. doi:10.2224/sbp.1978.6.1.49.

Gagné, R. M. (1965). *The conditions of learning and theory of instruction*. New York, NY: Holt, Rinehart & Winston..

Garcia, L., Nussbaum, M., & Preiss, D. D. (2011). Is the use of information and communication technology related to performance in working memory tasks? Evidence from seventh-grade students. *Computers & Education*, *57*(3), 2068–2076. doi:10.1016/j.compedu.2011.05.009.

Gardner, H. (1983). *Frames of mind*. New York: Basic Books..

Gardner, H. (1999). *Intelligence reframed: Multiple intelligence for the 21st century*. New York: Basic Book..

Garris, R., & Driskell, J. E. (2002). Games, motivation, and learning: A research and practice model. *Practice*, 1–17.

Gasnier, A. (2007). *The patenting paradox: A game-based approach to patent management*. Delft, The Netherlands: Eburon..

GATE. (2011). *Help! Over de ontwikkeling van een serious game als oefenmiddel voor burgemeesters om zich voor te bereiden op een incident*. Utrecht, The Netherlands: Game Research for Training and Entertainment..

Gathercole, S. E., & Pickering, S. J. (2000). Working memory deficits in children with low achievements in the national curriculum at 7 years of age. *The British Journal of Educational Psychology*, *70*, 177–194. doi:10.1348/000709900158047 PMID:10900777.

Gavin, H. (2008). Understanding Research Methods and Statistics in Psychology. In Sage Publications Lyd..

Gee, J. P. (2003). *What video games have to teach us about learning and literacy*. New York: Palgrave Macmillan. doi:10.1145/950566.950595.

Gee, J. P. (2005). Learning by design: Good video games as learning machines. *E-learning*, *2*(1), 5–16. doi:10.2304/elea.2005.2.1.5.

Gee, J. P. (2009). Video games, learning, and content. In C. Miller (Ed.), *Games: Purpose and potential in education*. Boston, MA: Springer. doi:10.1007/978-0-387-09775-6_3.

Gee, J. P., Hull, G. A., & Lankshear, C. (1996). *The new work order: Behind the language of the new capitalism*. Saint Leonards, Australia: Allen & Unwin..

Geerts, W., Mitzsche, M., & Van Laeken, M. (Eds.). (2009). Wat zou je doen? Dilemma's in de onderwijspraktijk. Bussum: Coutinho..

Gennett, Z. (2010). *Shortfall online: The development of an educational computer game for teaching sustainable engineering to millennial generation students*. (MS Thesis). Deptartment of Mechanical and Industrial Engineering, Northeastern University, Boston, MA.

Gentile, D. A., & Anderson, C. A. (2003). Violent video games: The Newest media violence hazard. In D. Gentile (Ed.), *Media violence and children* (pp. 205–226). Westport, CT: Praeger..

Gentile, D. A., & Gentile, J. R. (2007). Violent video games as exemplary teachers: A conceptual analysis. *Journal of Youth and Adolescence*, *37*(2), 127–141. doi:10.1007/s10964-007-9206-2.

Gentile, D. A., Lynch, P. J., Linder, J. R., & Walsh, D. A. (2004). The effects of violent video game habits on adolescent aggressive attitudes and behaviors. *Journal of Adolescence*, *27*(1), 5–22. doi:10.1016/j.adolescence.2003.10.002 PMID:15013257.

Geurts, J. L. A., Duke, R. D., & Vermeulen, P. A. M. (2007). Policy gaming for strategy and change. *Long Range Planning*, *40*(6), 535–558. doi:10.1016/j.lrp.2007.07.004.

Gevensleben, H., Holl, B., Albrecht, B., Schlamp, D., Kratz, O., & Studer, P. et al. (2010). Neurofeedback training in children with ADHD: 6-month follow-up of a randomised controlled trial. *European Child & Adolescent Psychiatry*, *19*(9), 715–724. doi:10.1007/s00787-010-0109-5 PMID:20499120.

Ghani, J. A. (1995). Flow in human-computer interactions: Test of a model. In J. M. Carey (Ed.), *Human Factors in Information Systems: Emerging Theoretical Bases* (pp. 291–311). Norwood, NJ: Ablex Publishing Corporation..

Gibbs, N. (1995). The eq factor. *Time Magazine*. Retrieved on December 25, 2012 from http://www.time.com/time/classroom/psych/unit5_article1.html

Gibson, D., Aldrich, C., & Prensky, M. (2007). *Games and simulations in online learning: Research and development frameworks*. Information Science Publishing..

Giddens, A. (1988). Goffman as a systematic social theorist. In P. Drew, & A. Wootton (Eds.), *Erving Goffman Exploring the interaction order* (pp. 250–279). New York: Polity Press..

Gikandi, J. W., Morrow, D., & Davis, N. E. (2011). Online formative assessment in Higher Education: A review of the literature. *Computers & Education, 57*, 2333–2351. doi:10.1016/j.compedu.2011.06.004.

Gilbert, D. (2006). *Stumbling on happiness*. New York: Vintage..

Gilboa, I. (2010). *Making better decisions: Decision theory in practice*. Oxford, UK: Wiley-Blackwell..

Girard, C., Ecalle, J., & Magnan, A. (2012). Serious games as new educational tools: How effective are they? A meta-analysis of recent studies. *Journal of Computer Assisted Learning, 19*(3), 207–219. doi: doi:10.1111/j.1365-2729.2012.00489.x.

Göbel, S. (2010). Definition serious games term – Approach – Examples – Conclusion serious games – Motivation, der mensch ist nur da ganz mensch wo er spielt. *Technology (Elmsford, N.Y.), 12*.

Goebel, R., Sorger, B., Kaiser, J., Birbaumer, N., & Weiskopf, N. (2004). BOLD brain pong: Self regulation of local brain activity during synchronously scanned, interacting subjects. In *Proceedings of 34th Annual Meeting of the Society for Neuroscience*. IEEE.

Goffman, E. (1959). *The presentation of self in everyday life*. New York: Doubleday..

Goffman, E. (1974). *Frame analysis: An essay on the organization of experience*. New York: Harper & Row..

Gokhale, A. A. (1995). Collaborative learning enhances critical thinking. *Journal of Technology Education, 7*(1), 22–30.

Goleman, D. (1995). *Emotional intelligence*. New York: Bantam Books..

Goleman, D. (1996). *Emotional intelligence, why it can matter more than IQ*. London: Bloomsbury..

Good, B. M., & Su, A. I. (2011). Games with a scientific purpose. *Genome Biology, 12*(12), 135. doi:10.1186/gb-2011-12-12-135

Gosen, J., & Washbush, J. (2004). A review of scholarship on assessing experiential learning effectiveness. *Simulation & Gaming, 35*(2), 270–293. doi:10.1177/1046878104263544.

Graafland, M., Schraagen, J. M., & Schijven, M. P. (2012). Systematic review of serious games for medical education and surgical skills training. *British Journal of Surgery, 99*(10), 1322–1330. doi:10.1002/bjs.8819 PMID:22961509.

Granek, J. A., Gorbet, D. J., & Sergio, L. E. (2009). Extensive video-game experience alters cortical networks for complex visuomotor transformations. *Cortex, 46*, 1165–1177. doi:10.1016/j.cortex.2009.10.009 PMID:20060111.

Gratch, J., Rickel, J., Andre, E., Cassell, J., Petajan, E., & Badler, N. (2002). Creating interactive virtual humans: Some assembly required. *IEEE Intelligent Systems, 17*(4), 54–63. doi:10.1109/MIS.2002.1024753.

Graybill, D., Strawniak, M., Hunter, T., & O'Leary, M. (1987). Effects of playing versus observing violent versus nonviolent video games on children's aggression. *Psychology: A Quarterly Journal of Human Behavior, 24*(3), 1-8.

Graybill, D., Kirsch, J., & Esselman, E. (1985). Effects of playing violent versus nonviolent video games on the aggressive ideation of aggressive and nonaggressive children. *Child Study Journal, 15*(3), 199–205.

Greenblat, C. S. (1973). Teaching with simulation games: A review of claims and evidence. *Teaching Sociology, 1*(1), 62–83. doi:10.2307/1317334.

Green, C. S., & Bavelier, D. (2003). Action video game modifies visual selective attention. *Nature, 423*, 534–537. doi:10.1038/nature01647 PMID:12774121.

Green, C. S., & Bavelier, D. (2006a). Effect of action video game playing on the spatial distribution of visual selective attention. *Journal of Experimental Psychology*, *32*, 1465–1478. PMID:17154785.

Green, C. S., & Bavelier, D. (2006b). Enumeration versus multiple object tracking: The case of action video game players. *Cognition*, *101*, 217–245. doi:10.1016/j.cognition.2005.10.004 PMID:16359652.

Green, C. S., & Bavelier, D. (2007). Action video game experience alters the spatial resolution of attention. *Psychological Science*, *18*(1), 88–94. doi:10.1111/j.1467-9280.2007.01853.x PMID:17362383.

Green, C. S., & Bavelier, D. (2012). Learning, attentional control, and action video games. *Current Biology*, *22*, 197–206. doi:10.1016/j.cub.2012.02.012 PMID:22226749.

Green, C. S., Pouget, A., & Bavelier, D. (2010). Improved probabilistic inference as a general learning mechanism with action video games. *Current Biology*, *20*(17), 1573–1579. doi:10.1016/j.cub.2010.07.040 PMID:20833324.

Green, C. S., Sugarman, M. A., Medford, K., Klobusicky, E., & Bavelier, D. (2012). The effect of action video game experience on task-switching. *Computers in Human Behavior*, *28*, 984–994. doi:10.1016/j.chb.2011.12.020 PMID:22393270.

Greenfield, P. M., deWinstanley, P., Kilpatrick, H., & Kaye, D. (1994). Action video games and informal education: Effects on strategies for diving visual attention. *Journal of Applied Developmental Psychology*, *15*(1), 105–123. doi:10.1016/0193-3973(94)90008-6.

Greenfield, P. M., deWinstanley, P., Kilpatrick, H., & Kaye, D. (1996). Action video games and informal education: Effects on strategies for dividing visual attention. In P. M. Greenfield, & R. R. Cocking (Eds.), *Interacting with video* (pp. 187–204). Norwood, NJ: Ablex Publishing Corporation..

Green, R., & Turner, G. (2010). Growing evidence for the influence of meditation on brain and behaviour. *Neuropsychological Rehabilitation*, *20*(2), 306–311. doi:10.1080/09602010903172239 PMID:20204915.

Greenspan, S. I. (1989). Emotional intelligence. In K. Field, B. J. Cohler, & G. Wool (Eds.), *Learning and education: Psychoanalytic perspective* (pp. 209–243). Madison, CT: International Universities Press..

Grendler, M. E. (1996). Educational games and simulations, a technology in search of a research paradigm. In D. H. Jonassen (Ed.), *Handbook of research for educational communications and technology*. New York: Simon & Schuster Macmillan..

Griffiths, M. D. (1999). Violent video games and aggression: A review of the literature. *Aggression and Violent Behavior*, *4*(2), 203–212. doi:10.1016/S1359-1789(97)00055-4.

Griffiths, M. D. (2003). Breaking the stereotype: The case of on-line gaming. *Cyberpsychology & Behavior*, *6*(1), 81–91. doi:10.1089/109493103321167992 PMID:12650566.

Griffiths, M. D., & Davies, M. N. O. (2002). Excessive online computer gaming: implications for education. *Journal of Computer Assisted Learning*, *18*, 379–380. doi:10.1046/j.0266-4909.2002.00248.x.

Gross, J. J., & Thompson, R. A. (2007). Emotion regulation: Conceptual foundations. In J. J. Gross (Ed.), *Handbook of emotion regulation*. New York: Guilford Press..

Gruber, M. J., Watrous, A. J., Ekstrom, A. D., Ranganath, C., & Otten, L. J. (2013). Expected reward modulates encoding-related theta activity before an event. *NeuroImage*, *64*, 68–74. doi:10.1016/j.neuroimage.2012.07.064 PMID:22917987.

Gruzelier, J., & Egner, T. (2005). Critical validation studies of neurofeedback. *Child and Adolescent Psychiatric Clinics of North America*, *14*(1), 83–104. doi:10.1016/j.chc.2004.07.002 PMID:15564053.

Gruzelier, J., Egner, T., & Vernon, D. (2006). Validating the efficacy of neurofeedback for optimising performance. *Progress in Brain Research*, *159*, 421–431. doi:10.1016/S0079-6123(06)59027-2 PMID:17071246.

Gruzelier, J., Inoue, A., Smart, R., Steed, A., & Steffert, T. (2010). Acting performance and flow state enhanced with sensory-motor rhythm neurofeedback comparing ecologically valid immersive VR and training screen scenarios. *Neuroscience Letters*, *480*(2), 112–116. doi:10.1016/j.neulet.2010.06.019 PMID:20542087.

Guay, F., Vallerand, R. J., & Blanchard, C. (2000). On the assessment of situational intrinsic and extrinsic motivation: The situational motivation scale (SIMS). *Motivation and Emotion*, *24*(3), 175–213. doi:10.1023/A:1005614228250.

Guba, E. G., & Lincoln, Y. S. (1989). *Fourth generation evaluation*. Thousand Oaks, CA: Sage Publications..

Guger, C., Edlinger, G., Harkam, W., Niedermeyer, I., & Pfurtscheller, G. (2003). How many people are able to operate an EEG-based brain-computer interface (BCI)? *IEEE Transactions on Neural Systems and Rehabilitation Engineering*, *11*(2), 145–147. doi:10.1109/TNSRE.2003.814481 PMID:12899258.

Gunawardena, C. N., Carabajal, K., & Lowe, C. A. (2001). *Critical analysis of models and methods used to evaluate online learning networks*. Seattle, WA: AERA..

Güth, W., Schmittberger, R., & Schwarze, B. (1982). An experimental analysis of ultimatum bargaining. *Journal of Economic Behavior & Organization*, *3*(4), 367–388. doi:10.1016/0167-2681(82)90011-7.

Gütl, C., Scheucher, T., Bailey, P. H., Belcher, J., Ricardo dos Santos, F., & Berger, S. (2012). Towards an immersive virtual environment for physics experiments supporting collaborative settings in higher education. In A. Azad, M. Auer, & V. Harward (Eds.), *Internet Accessible Remote Laboratories: Scalable E-Learning Tools for Engineering and Science Disciplines*. Hershey, PA: IGI Global..

Habgood, M. P. J. (2007). *The Effective Integration of Digital Games and Learning Content*. Thesis submitted to the University of Nottingham. Retrieved 4th April, 2012 from http://zombiedivision.co.uk/.

Habgood, M. P. J., & Ainsworth, S. E. (2011). Motivating children to learn effectively: Exploring the value of intrinsic integration in educational games. *Journal of the Learning Sciences*, *20*, 169–206. doi:10.1080/10508406.2010.508029.

Habgood, M. P. J., Ainsworth, S. E., & Benford, S. (2005). Endogenous fantasy and learning in digital games. *Simulation & Gaming*, *36*(4), 483–498. doi:10.1177/1046878105282276.

Hainey, T. (2010). *Using games-based learning to teach requirements collection and analysis at tertiary education level*. Retrieved May 3, 2013, from http://scholar. google. com/scholar?hl=en&btnG=Search&q=intitle:Using+Games-Based+Learning+to+Teach+Requirements+Collection+and+Analysis+at+Tertiary+Education+Level#1

Hainey, T., Connolly, T. M., Baxter, G. J., Boyle, L., & Beeby, R. (2012). Assessment Integration in Games-based Learning: A Preliminary Review of the Literature, In *Proceedings of 6th European Conference on Games Based Learning*, Cork, Ireland, 4-5 October 2012.

Hainey, T., & Connolly, T. M. (2010). Evaluating games-based learning. *International Journal of Virtual and Personal Learning Environments*, *1*(1), 57–71. doi:10.4018/jvple.2010091705.

Hainey, T., Connolly, T. M., Stansfield, M. H., & Boyle, E. A. (2011b). Evaluation of a games to teach requirements collection and analysis in software engineering at tertiary education level. *Computers & Education*, *56*(1), 21–35. doi:10.1016/j.compedu.2010.09.008.

Hainey, T., Connolly, T. M., Stansfield, M., & Boyle, E. A. (2011a). The use of computer games in education: A review of the literature. In P. Felicia (Ed.), *Handbook of Research on Improving Learning and Motivation through Educational Games: Multidisciplinary Approaches*. Hershey, PA: IGI Global. doi:10.4018/978-1-60960-495-0.ch002.

Hake, R. R. (1998). Interactive engagement vs. traditional engagement: A six thousand student survey of mechanics test data for introductory physics courses. *American Journal of Physics*, *66*, 64–74. doi:10.1119/1.18809.

Haldin-Herrgard, T. (2004). Diving under the surface of tacit knowledge. In *Proceedings of OCLC 2004, The Fifth European Conference on Organizational Knowledge, Learning and Capabilities*. Vasa, Finland. Retrieved from http://www.coalescentknowledge.com/WP/diving.pdf

Hall, E. T., & Hall, M. R. (1987). *Hidden differences: Doing business with the Japanese*. Garden City, NJ: Anchor Books Doubleday..

Halliday, D., Resnick, R., & Walker, J. (2005). *Fundamentals of physics*. Chichester, UK: John Wiley & Sons..

Halpern, D. F., Millis, K., Graesser, A. C., Butler, H., Forsyth, C., & Cai, Z. (2012). Operation ARA: A computerized learning game that teaches critical thinking and scientific reasoning. *Thinking Skills and Creativity, 7*(2), 73–100. doi:10.1016/j.tsc.2012.03.006.

Hamlen, K. R. (2001). Re-examining gender differences in video game play: Time spent and feelings of success. *Journal of Educational Computing Research, 43*(3), 293–308. doi:10.2190/EC.43.3.b.

Hammer, E. M., Halder, S., Blankertz, B., Sannelli, C., Dickhaus, T., & Kleih, S. et al. (2012). Psychological predictors of SMR-BCI performance. *Biological Psychology, 89*(1), 80–86. doi:10.1016/j.biopsycho.2011.09.006 PMID:21964375.

Hanneforth, D., & Mutschke, A. (1991). *Ärger-spiele: Varianten und verschärfungen von mensch-ärgere-dich-nicht bis malefiz*. Reinbek: Rororo..

Hardin, G. (1968). The tragedy of the commons. *Science, 162*, 1243–1248. doi:10.1126/science.162.3859.1243 PMID:5699198.

Hargreaves, E. (2008). Assessment. In G. McCulloch and D. Crook (Eds.), The Routledge international encyclopedia of education, 37–38. New York: Routledge..

Harnischfeger, A., & Wiley, D. E. (1985). Origins of active learning time. In C. W. Fisher, & D. C. Berliner (Eds.), *Perspectives on instructional time* (pp. 133–156). New York: Longman..

Harper, J. D., Kaiser, S., Ebrahimi, K., Lamberton, G. R., Hadley, H. R., Ruckle, H. C., et al. (2007). Prior video game exposure does not enhance robotic surgical performance. *Journal of Endourology / Endourological Society, 21*(10), 1207–1210. doi:10.1089/end.2007.9905

Hart, C. (2008). Critical discourse analysis and metaphor: Toward a theoretical framework. *Critical Discourse Studies, 5*(2), 91–106. doi:10.1080/17405900801990058.

Harteveld, C. (2011). *Triadic game design*. London: Springer. doi:10.1007/978-1-84996-157-8.

Harteveld, C. (2012). *Making sense of virtual risks, a quasi experimental investigation into game-based training*. Delft, The Netherlands: IOS Press..

Harviainen, J. T. (2012). Ritualistic games, boundary control, and information uncertainty. *Simulation & Gaming, 43*(4), 506–527. doi:10.1177/1046878111435395.

Hayden, C., & Molenkamp, R. J. (2002). *Tavistock primer II*. Jupiter, FL: The A. K. Rice Institute of the Study of Social Systems..

Hayes, E. R., & Games, I. A. (2008). Making computer games and design thinking: A review of current software and strategies. *Games and Culture, 3*(3–4), 309–332. doi:10.1177/1555412008317312.

Hays, R. T. (2005). *The effectiveness of instructional games: a literature review and discussion*. Orlando, FL: Naval War Center: Training Systems Division..

Hazard, C. (2010). *Feedback in games design*. [Blog post]. Retrieved January 20, 2013 from http://blog.wolfire.com/2010/04/Feedback-In-Game-Design

Healseeker. (n.d.). *Yulius academie*. Retrieved April 11, 2013, from http://www.yuliusacademie.nl/nl/healseeker

Healy, A., Connolly, T. M., & Dickie, A. (2008). ThinknDrinkn?: An Evaluation of the use of Games Based Learning (GBL) for Alcohol Awareness, In *Proceedings of 2nd* European Conference on Games-based Learning (ECGBL), 16-17 October 2008, Barcelona, Spain.

Heckhausen, H. (1964). Entwurf einer psychologie des spielens. *Psychologische Forschung, 27*, 225–243. doi:10.1007/BF00424560 PMID:14114184.

Heckhausen, H. (1974). *Leistung und chancengleichheit*. Gottingen, Germany: Hogrefe..

Heckhausen, J., & Heckhausen, H. (2005). *Motivation and action*. Cambridge, UK: Cambridge University Press..

Heeter, C., Lee, Y., Magerko, B., & Medler, B. (2011). Impacts of forced serious game play on vulnerable subgroups. *International Journal of Gaming and Computer-Mediated Simulations, 3*(3), 34–53. doi:10.4018/jgcms.2011070103.

Henderson, L., Klemes, J., & Eshet, Y. (2000). Just playing a game? Educational simulation software and cognitive outcomes. *Journal of Educational Computing Research*, 22(1), 105–129. doi:10.2190/EPJT-AHYQ-1LAJ-U8WK.

Henning, M., & Jardim, A. (1977). *The managerial women*. London: Pan Books..

Herrington, J., & Oliver, R. (1999). Using situated learning and multimedia to investigate higher-order learning. *Journal of Educational Multimedia and Hypermedia*, 8(4), 401–422.

Herrington, J., Oliver, R., & Reeves, T. C. (2003). Patterns of engagement in authentic online learning environments. *Australian Journal of Educational Technology*, 19(1), 59–71.

Hertzog, C., Kramer, A. F., Wilson, R. S., & Lindenberger, U. (2008). Enrichment effects on adult cognitive development: Can the functional capacity of older adults be preserved and enhanced? *Psychological Science in the Public Interest*, 9(2), 1–65. doi: doi:10.1111/j.1539-6053.2009.01034.x.

Herz, J. C. (1997). *Joystick nation*. New York: Little, Brown and Company..

Hestenes, D., Wells, M., & Swackhamer, G. (1992). Force concept inventory. *The Physics Teacher*, 30, 141–158. doi:10.1119/1.2343497.

Heuer, R. J. Jr. (1999). *Psychology of intelligence analysis*. Washington, DC: US Government Printing Office..

Hewitt, P. (2002). *Conceptual physics*. Harlow, UK: Addison Wesley..

Higgins, S. (2000). The logical zoombinis. *Teaching Thinking, 1*(1).

HMIE. (2009). *Improving Scottish education*. HMIE..

Hoedlmoser, K., Pecherstorfer, T., Gruber, G., Anderer, P., Doppelmayr, M., Klimesch, W., & Schabus, M. (2008). Instrumental conditioning of human sensorimotor rhythm (12-15 Hz) and its impact on sleep as well as declarative learning. *Sleep*, 31(10), 1401–1408. PMID:18853937.

Hoffman, K. (1995). Effects of playing versus witnessing video game violence on attitudes towards aggression and acceptance of violence as a means of conflict resolution. *Dissertation Abstract International, 56*(3), 747.

Hofstede, G. J., De Caluwe, L., & Peters, V. A. M. (2010). Why simulation games work-in search of the active substance: A synthesis. *Simulation & Gaming, 41*(6), 824–843. doi:10.1177/104687811037 5596

Hofstede, G. (1986). Cultural differences in teaching and learning. *International Journal of Intercultural Relations, 10*(3), 301–320. doi:10.1016/0147-1767(86)90015-5.

Hofstede, G., Hofstede, G. J., & Minkov, M. (2010). *Cultures and organizations: Software for the mind* (3rd ed.). New York: McGraw-Hill..

Hogg, M. A. (2003). Social Identity. In M. R. Leary, & J. P. Tangney (Eds.), *Handbook of Self and Identity*. London: Guilford Press..

Holbrook, J., & Rannikmae, M. (2009). The meaning of scientific literacy. *International Journal of Environmental and Science Education, 4*(3), 275–288.

Holmes, B., Tangney, B., FitzGibbon, A., Savage, T., & Meehan, S. (2001). *Communal constructivism: Students constructing learning for as well as with others*. Paper presented at the meeting of the 12th International Conference of the Society for Information Technology & Teacher Education (SITE). Charlottesville, VA: SITE.

Holmes, B., & Gardner, J. (2006). *e-Learning: Concepts and practice*. London. Sage (Atlanta, Ga.).

Holsbrink-Engels, G. A. (1998). *Computer-based role playing for interpersonal skills training*. Enschede, The Netherlands: Universiteit Twente..

Holzapfel, S., Strehl, U., Kotchoubey, B., & Birbaumer, N. (1998). Behavioral psychophysiological intervention in a mentally retarded epileptic patient with brain lesion. *Applied Psychophysiology and Biofeedback, 23*(2), 189–202. doi:10.1023/A:1022299422116 PMID:10384250.

Homann, K., & Lütge, C. (2005). *Einführung in die wirtschaftsethik*. Münster: LIT-Verl..

Honey, P., & Mumford, A. (1992). *The manual of learning styles*. Berkshire, UK: Honey, Ardingly House..

Houtkamp, J. (2012). *Affective appraisal of virtual environments*. Retrieved from http://igitur-archive.library.uu.nl/dissertations/2012-0620-200449/UUindex.html

Howard-Jones, P., Demetriou, S., Bogacz, R., & Yoo, J. H. (2011). Toward a science of learning games. *Mind, Brain, and Education, 5*(1), 33–41. doi:10.1111/j.1751-228X.2011.01108.x.

Howe, C., McWilliam, D., & Cross, G. (2005). Chance favours only the prepared mind, incubation and the delayed effects of peer collaboration. *The British Journal of Psychology, 96*, 67–93. doi:10.1348/000712604X15527 PMID:15826325.

Howe, C., Tolmie, A., Thurston, A., Topping, K., Christie, D., & Livingston, K. et al. (2007). Group work in elementary science: Towards organizational principles for supporting pupil learning. *Learning and Instruction, 17*(1), 549–563. doi:10.1016/j.learninstruc.2007.09.004.

Hsu, C.-L., & Lu, H.-P. (2004). Why do people play online games? An extended TAM with social influences and flow experience. *Information & Management, 41*, 853–868. doi:10.1016/j.im.2003.08.014.

Huang, O. W. S., Cheng, H. N. H., & Chan, T. (2007). Number jigsaw puzzle: A mathematical puzzle game for facilitating players' problem-solving strategies. In T. W. Chan, A. Paiva, & D. W. Shaffer (Eds.), *Proceedings of the First IEEE International Workshop on Digital Game and Intelligent Toy Enhanced Learning* (pp. 130-134). Los Alamitos, CA: IEEE Computer Society.

Huang, H.-W. (2011). Evaluating learners' motivational and cognitive processing in an online game-based learning environment. *Computers in Human Behavior, 27*, 694–704. doi:10.1016/j.chb.2010.07.021.

Huang, H.-W., & Johnson, T. (2008). Instructional game design using cognitive load theory. In R. Ferdig (Ed.), *Handbook of Research on Effective Electronic Gaming in Education* (pp. 1143–1165). Hershey, PA: IGI Global. doi:10.4018/978-1-59904-808-6.ch066.

Huettel, S. A., Song, A. W., & McCarthy, G. (2009). *Functional magnetic resonance imaging* (2nd ed.). Boston: Sinauer Associates, Inc.

Hughes, C., Roman, G., Hart, M. J., & Ensor, R. (2013). Does maternal depression predict young children's executive function? A 4-year longitudinal study. *Journal of Child Psychology and Psychiatry, and Allied Disciplines, 54*(2), 169–177. doi:10.1111/jcpp.12014 PMID:23171379.

Huizenga, J., Admiraal, W., Akkerman, S., & Dam, G. T. (2009). Mobile game-based learning in secondary education: Engagement, motivation and learning in a mobile city game. *Journal of Computer Assisted Learning, 25*(4), 332–344. doi:10.1111/j.1365-2729.2009.00316.x.

Huizinga, J. (1955). *Homo ludens: A study of the play element in culture*. Boston: Beacon Press..

Hummel, H. G. K., Geerts, W. M., Slootmaker, A., Kuipers, D., & Westera, W. (2013). Collaboration scripts for mastership skills: Online game about classroom dilemmas in teacher education. *Interactive Learning Environments*. doi:10.1080/10494820.2013.789063.

Hummel, H.G.K., Van Houcke, J., Nadolski, R.J., & Van der Hiele, T., Kurvers, & Löhr, A. (2011). Scripted collaboration in serious gaming for complex learning: Effects of multiple perspectives when acquiring water management skills. *British Journal of Educational Technology, 42*(6), 1029–1041. doi:10.1111/j.1467-8535.2010.01122.x.

Hung, P.-H., Hwang, G.-J., Lee, Y.-H., & Su, I.-H. (2012). A cognitive component analysis approach for developing game-based spatial learning tools. *Computers & Education, 59*, 762–773. doi:10.1016/j.compedu.2012.03.018.

Huppert, T. J., Hoge, R. D., Diamond, S. G., Franceschini, M. A., & Boas, D. A. (2006). A temporal comparison of BOLD, ASL, and NIRS hemodynamic responses to motor stimuli in adult humans. *NeuroImage, 29*(2), 368–382. doi:10.1016/j.neuroimage.2005.08.065 PMID:16303317.

Hussaan, A. M. (2012). *Generation of adaptive pedagogical scenarios in serious games*. Lyon, France: University of Lyon..

Hussain, T. S., Bowers, C., Blasko-Drabik, H., & Blair, L. (2013). Validating cognitive readiness on team performance following individual game-based training. In H. F. O'Neil, R. S. Perez, & E. L. Baker (Eds.), *Teaching and measuring cognitive readiness*. New York: Springer..

Hwang, G. J., Sung, H. Y., Hung, C. M., Huang, I., & Tsai, C. C. (2012). Development of a personalized educational computer game based on students' learning styles. *Personalized Learning, 60*(4), 623–638.

Hwang, G. J., & Wu, P. H. (2012). Advancements and trends in digital game-based learning research: A review of publications in selected journals from 2001 to 2010. *British Journal of Educational Technology, 43*(1), E6–E10. doi:10.1111/j.1467-8535.2011.01242.x.

Ibarra, H. (1993). Personal networks of women and minorities in management: A conceptual framework. *Academy of Management Review, 189*(1), 56–87.

Ijsselsteijn, W., de Kort, Y., Poels, K., Jurgelionis, A., & Bellotti, F. (2007). *Characterising and measuring user experiences in digital games*. Paper presented at the meeting of the ACE Conference 2007. Salzburg, Austria.

Inal, Y., & Cagiltay, K. (2007). Flow experiences of children in an interactive social game environment. *British Journal of Educational Technology, 38*(3), 455–464. doi:10.1111/j.1467-8535.2007.00709.x.

Inkpen, K., Booth, K. S., Klawe, M., & Upitis, R. (1995). *Playing together beats playing apart, especially for girls*. Paper presented at the meeting of Computer Support for Collaborative Learning (CSCL). Bloomington, IN.

Irwin, A. R., & Gross, A. M. (1995). Cognitive tempo, violent video games, and aggressive behavior in young boys. *Journal of Family Violence, 10*(3), 337–350. doi:10.1007/BF02110997.

Issacs, R. (1955). *Differential games: A mathematical theory with applications to warfare and pursuit, control and optimization*. Academic Press..

Ivory, J. D., & Kalyanaraman, S. (2007). The effects of technological advancement and violent content in video games on players' feelings of presence, involvement, physiological arousal, and aggression. *The Journal of Communication, 57*, 532–555. doi:10.1111/j.1460-2466.2007.00356.x.

Jackson, S. L., Krajcik, J., & Soloway, E. (1998). The design of learner-adaptable scaffolding in interactive learning environments. In *Proceedings of ACM CHI 1998 Conference on Human Factors in Computing Systems*. Los Angeles, CA: ACM.

Jackson, C. L., Colquitt, J., Wesson, M. J., & Zapata-Phelan, C. P. (2006). Psychological collectivism: A measurement validation and linkage to group member performance. *The Journal of Applied Psychology, 91*(4), 884–899. doi:10.1037/0021-9010.91.4.884 PMID:16834512.

Jackson, D. N. (1974). *Personality research form manual*. Research Psychologists Press..

Jackson, L. A., Zhao, Y., Kolenic, A., Fitzgerald, H. E., Harold, R., & Von Eye, A. (2008). Race, gender, and information technology use: The new digital divide. *Cyberpsychology & Behavior, 11*(4), 437–442. doi:10.1089/cpb.2007.0157 PMID:18721092.

Jameson, A. (2003). Adaptive interfaces and agents. In J. A. Jacko, & A. Sears (Eds.), *Human–Computer Interface Handbook*. Mahwah, NJ: Lawrence Erlbaum..

James, W. (1890). *Principles of psychology*. New York: MacMillan. doi:10.1037/11059-000.

Janssen, M., & Klievink, B. (2010). Gaming and simulation for transforming and reengineering government: Towards a research agenda. *Transforming Government People Process and Policy, 4*(2), 132–137. doi:10.1108/17506161011047361.

Jantke, K. P. (2010). Toward a taxonomy of game based learning. In *Proceedings of IEEE International Conference on Progress in Informatics and Computing*, (pp. 858–862). IEEE. doi:10.1109/PIC.2010.5687903

Järvinen, A. (2011). State of social in social games. *Casual Connect*. Retrieved from http://casualconnect.org/lectures/community-social/state-of-social-in-social-games/

Jayakanthan, R. (2002). Application of computer games in the field of education. *The Electronic Library, 20*(2), 98–102. doi:10.1108/02640470210697471.

Jennett, C., Cox, A. L., Cairns, P., Dhoparee, S., Epps, A., Tijs, T., & Walton, A. (2008). Measuring and defining the experience of immersion in games. *International Journal of Human-Computer Studies, 66*(9), 641–661. doi:10.1016/j.ijhcs.2008.04.004.

Jenson, J., Fisher, S., & De Castell, S. (2011). Disrupting the gender order: Leveling up and claiming space in an after-school video game club. *International Journal of Gender, Science and Technology, 3*(1).

Jenson, J., & De Castell, S. (2008). Theorizing gender and digital gameplay: Oversights, accidents and surprises. *Journal for Computer Game Culture*, *2*(1), 15–25.

Jenson, J., & De Castell, S. (2010). Gender, simulation, and gaming: Research review and redirections. *Simulation & Gaming*, *41*(1), 51–71. doi:10.1177/1046878109353473.

Jeong, H., & Chi, M. T. H. (2000). *Does collaborative learning lead to the construction of common knowledge?* Retrieved July 9, 2004, from http://www.ircs.upenn.edu.edu/cogsci2000/PRCDNGS/SPRCDNGS/posters/jeo_chi.pdf

Jerman, O., & Swanson, H. L. (2005). Working memory and reading disabilities: A selective meta-analysis of the literature. In T. E. Scruggs & Mastropieri (Eds.), Advances in Learning and Behavioural Disabilities, Cognition and Learning in Diverse Settings (Vol. 18, pp. 1-31). Oxford, UK: Elsevier..

JISC. (2011). *Re-engineering assessment practices in Scottish higher education (REAP)*. Retrieved January 20, 2013 from http://www.jisc.ac.uk/whatwedo/programmes/elearningsfc/reap.aspx

Jo, E., & Berkowitz, L. (1994). A priming effect analysis of media influences: An update. In J. Bryant, & D. Zillmann (Eds.), *Media effects: Advances in theory and research* (pp. 43–60). Hillsdale, NJ: Erlbaum..

Johnson, L., Smith, R., Willis, H., Levine, A., & Haywood, K. (2011). *The 2011 horizon report*. Austin, TX: The New Media Consortium. Retrieved from http://net.educause.edu/ir/library/pdf/HR2011.pdf

Johnson, W. L., & Wu, S. (2008). Assessing aptitude for learning with a serious game for foreign language and culture. In *Proceedings of 9th International Conference on Intelligent Tutoring Systems*, Montreal, April 2008.

Johnson, D. W., & Johnson, R. T. (1996). Conflict resolution and peer mediation programs in elementary and secondary schools: A review of the research. *Review of Educational Research*, *66*(4), 459–506. doi:10.3102/00346543066004459.

Johnson, L., Smith, R., Willis, H., Levine, A., & Haywood, K. (2011). *The 2011 horizon report*. Austin, TX: The New Media Consortium..

Johnson, R. (1988). *Elementary statistics* (5th ed.). Boston: PWS-Kent Publishing Company..

Johnson, W. L., Vilhjalmsson, H., & Marsella, S. (2005). Serious games for language learning: How much game, how much AI? In C.-K. Looi, G. McCalla, B. Bredeweg, & J. Breuker (Eds.), *Artificial Intelligence in Education: Supporting Learning through Intelligent and Socially Informed Technology* (pp. 306–313). Amsterdam: IOS Press..

Jonassen, D. H. (1997). Instructional design model for well-structured and ill-structured problem-solving learning outcomes. *Educational Technology Research and Development*, *45*(1), 65–95. doi:10.1007/BF02299613.

Jonassen, D. H. (2004). *Learning to solve problems, an instructional design guide*. San Francisco, CA: Pfeiffer..

Jones, L. A. (1988). Motor illusions: What do they reveal about proprioception? *Psychological Bulletin*, *103*(1), 72–86. doi:10.1037/0033-2909.103.1.72 PMID:3279446.

Jones, T. S. (2004). Conflict resolution education: The field, the findings, and the future. *Conflict Resolution Quarterly*, *22*(1-2), 233–267. doi:10.1002/crq.100.

Jurcevic, J. S. (2008). Learning projectile motion with the computer game scorched 3D. *The Physics Teacher*, 46.

Juul, J. (2003). The game, the player, the world: Looking for a heart of gameness. In M. Copier, & J. Raessens (Eds.), *Proceedings of level-up: Digital games research conference*. Utrecht, The Netherlands: University of Utrecht..

Juul, J. (2004). An introduction to game time. In N. Wardrip-Fruin, & P. Harrigan (Eds.), *First Person: New Media as Story, Performance and Game* (pp. 131–141). Cambridge, MA: The MIT Press..

Kahneman, D. (2011). *Thinking, fast and slow*. New York: Farrar, Straus and Giroux..

Kahneman, D., & Tversky, A. (1979). Prospect theory: An analysis of decisions under risk. *Econometrica*, *47*(2), 263–291. doi:10.2307/1914185.

Kalyuga, S., & Plass, J. (2009). Evaluating and managing cognitive load in games. In R. E. Ferdig (Ed.), *Handbook of Research on Effective Electronic Gaming in Education* (pp. 719–737). Hershey, PA: IGI Global..

Kane, M. J., & Engle, R. W. (2002). The role of prefrontal cortex in working memory capacity, executive attention and general fluid intelligence: An individual-differences perspective. *Psychonomic Bulletin & Review, 9*, 637–671. doi:10.3758/BF03196323 PMID:12613671.

Kankaanranta, M., & Neittaanmki, P. (2008). Design and use of serious games. *Engineering, 37*, 208. doi: doi:10.1007/978-1-4020-9496-5.

Kanter, R. M. (1977). Some effects of proportions of group life: Skewed sex ratios and responses to token women. *American Journal of Sociology, 82*(5), 965–990. doi:10.1086/226425.

Kanthan, R., & Senger, J. L. (2011). The impact of specially designed digital games-based learning in undergraduate pathology and medical education. *Archives of Pathology & Laboratory Medicine, 135*, 135–142. PMID:21204720.

Kantrowitz, T. M. (2005). *Development and construct validation of a measure of soft skills performance.* (Ph. D. Dissertation). Georgia Institute of Technology, Atlanta, GA.

Kaplan, A. M., & Haenlein, M. (2010). Users of the world, unite! The challenges and opportunities of social media. *Business Horizons, 53*(1), 59–68. doi:10.1016/j.bushor.2009.09.003.

Kaplan, R. M., & Saccuzzo, D. P. (2009). Standardized tests in education, civil service, and the military. In *Psychological testing: Principles, applications, and issues.* Belmont, CA: Wadsworth..

Karakus, T., Inal, Y., & Cagiltay, K. (2008). A descriptive study of Turkish high school students' game-playing characteristics and their considerations concerning the effects of games. *Computers in Human Behavior, 24*(6), 2520–2529. doi:10.1016/j.chb.2008.03.011.

Karle, J. W., Watter, S., & Shedden, J. M. (2010). Task switching in video game players: Benefits of selective attention but not resistance to proactive interference. *Acta Psychologica, 134*(1), 70–78. doi:10.1016/j.actpsy.2009.12.007 PMID:20064634.

Kast, M., Meyer, M., Vogeli, C., Gross, M., & Jancke, L. (2007). Computer-based multisensory learning in children with developmental dyslexia. *Restorative Neurology and Neuroscience, 25*(3–4), 355–369. PMID:17943011.

Kato, P. M., Cole, S. W., Bradlyn, A. S., & Pollock, B. H. (2008). A video game improves behavioral outcomes in adolescents and young adults with cancer: A randomized trial. *Pediatrics, 122*(2), e305–e317. doi:10.1542/peds.2007-3134 PMID:18676516.

Kaufman-Scarborough, C., & Lindquist, J. D. (1999). Time management and polychronicity: Comparisons, contrasts, and insights for the workplace. *Journal of Managerial Psychology*, 288–312. doi:10.1108/02683949910263819.

Kazmerski, V., Blasko, D., & Dessalegn, B. (2003). ERP and behavioral evidence of individual differences in metaphor comprehension. *Memory & Cognition, 31*(5), 673–689. doi:10.3758/BF03196107 PMID:12956233.

Ke, F. (2006). Classroom goal structures for educational math game application. In *Proceedings of the 7th International Conference on Learning Sciences ICLS '06*, Publisher: International Society of Learning Sciences.

Kearney, P. (2007). Cognitive assessment of game-based learning. *British Journal of Educational Technology, 38*(3), 529–531. doi:10.1111/j.1467-8535.2007.00718.x.

Kebritchi, M., Hirumi, A., & Bai, H. (2008). *The effects of modern math computer games on learners' math achievement and math course motivation in a public high school setting* (Doctoral research brief). Retrieved from http://www.pearsonschool.com/live/images/custom/BasalEmails/dimension_m/media/UCFResearch_Brief.pdf

Kebritchi, M., & Hiruni, H. (2008). Examining the pedagogical foundations of modern educational computer games. *Computers & Education, 51*, 1729–1743. doi:10.1016/j.compedu.2008.05.004.

Ke, F. (2009). *A qualitative meta-analysis of computer games as learning tools.* Hershey, PA: IGI Global..

Keifer-Boyd, K. (2005). Children teaching children with their computer game creations. *Visual Arts Research, 31*(60), 117–128.

Ke, K. (2009). A qualitative meta-analysis of computer games as learning tools. In R. E. Ferdig (Ed.), *Handbook of Research on Effective Electronic Gaming in Education* (pp. 1–32). Kent, OH: Kent State University..

Kellar, M., Watters, C., & Duffy, J. (2005). Motivational factors in game play in two user groups. In *Proceedings of the DiGRA 2005 Conference: Changing Views—Worlds in Play*. Vancouver, Canada: DiGRA.

Kellough, R. D., & Kellough, N. G. (1999). *Secondary school teaching: A guide to methods and resources; planning for competence*. Upper Saddle River, New Jersey: Prentice Hall..

Keltner, D., Van Kleef, G., Chen, S., & Kraus, M. (2008). A reciprocal influence model of social power: Emerging principles and lines of inquiry. *Advances in Experimental Social Psychology*, *40*, 151–192. doi:10.1016/S0065-2601(07)00003-2.

Kemere, C., Santhanam, G., Yu, B. M., Afshar, A., Ryu, S. I., Meng, T. H., & Shenoy, K. V. (2008). Detecting neural-state transitions using hidden Markov models for motor cortical prostheses. *Journal of Neurophysiology*, *100*(4), 2441–2452. doi:10.1152/jn.00924.2007 PMID:18614757.

Kemper, T. D. (2011). *Status, power and ritual interaction: A relational reading of Durkheim, Goffman and Collins*. London: Ashgate Publishing, Ltd.

Kestenbaum, G. I., & Weinstein, L. (1985). Personality, psychopathology and developmental issues in male adolescent video game use. *Journal of the American Academy of Child Psychiatry*, *24*(3), 329–337. doi:10.1016/S0002-7138(09)61094-3 PMID:4008824.

Khatib, F., Cooper, S., Tyka, M. D., Xu, K., Makedon, I., & Popovic, Z. et al. (2011). Algorithm discovery by protein folding game players. *Proceedings of the National Academy of Sciences of the United States of America*, *108*(47), 1–5. doi:10.1073/pnas.1115898108 PMID:22065763.

Kickmeier-Rust, M. D., Hockemeyer, C., Albert, D., & Augustin, T. (2008). Micro Adaptive, Non-Invasive Knowledge Assessment in Educational Games. In *Proceedings of Second IEEE International Conference on Digital Games and Intelligent Toys Based Education Game and Intelligent Toy Enhanced Learning*.

Kickmeier-Rust, M. D., Steiner, C. M., & Albert, D. (2009). Non-invasive assessment and adaptive interventions in learning games. In *Proceedings of Intelligent Networking and Collaborative Systems 2009 INCOS 09 International Conference* (pp. 301–305). IEEE. doi:10.1109/INCOS.2009.30

Kickmeier-Rust, M. D., & Albert, D. (2010). Micro adaptivity: Protecting immersion in didactically adaptive digital educational games. *Journal of Computer Assisted Learning*, *7*, 95–105. doi:10.1111/j.1365-2729.2009.00332.x.

Kickmeier-Rust, M. D., Mattheiss, E., Steiner, C. M., & Albert, D. (2011). A Psycho-Pedagogical Framework for Multi-Adaptive educational games. *International Journal of Game-Based Learning*, *1*, 45–58. doi:10.4018/ijgbl.2011010104.

Kiili, K., & Ketamo, H. (2007). Exploring the learning mechanism in educational games. In *Proceedings of the ITI 2007 29th Int. Conf. on Information Technology Interfaces*. Cavtat, Croatia: IEEE.

Kiili, K. (2005). Digital game-based learning: Towards an experiential gaming model. *The Internet and Higher Education*, *8*, 13–24. doi:10.1016/j.iheduc.2004.12.001.

Kiili, K., & Lainema, T. (2008). Foundation for measuring engagement in educational games. *Journal of Interactive Learning Research*, *19*(3), 469–488.

Kiili, K., & Lainema, T. (2010). Power and flow experience in time-intensive business simulation game. *Journal of Educational Multimedia and Hypermedia*, *19*(1), 39–57.

Kim, B., Park, H., & Baek, Y. (2009). Not just fun, but serious strategies: Using meta-cognitive strategies in game-based learning. *Computers & Education*, *52*, 800–810. doi:10.1016/j.compedu.2008.12.004.

Kimmel, A. J. (1988). Ethics and values in applied social research. *Methods (San Diego, Calif.)*, *12*, 160. doi:doi:10.4135/9781412984096.

Kim, R. B., & Kim, J. P. (2011). Creative economy in Korea: A case of online game industry. *Actual Problems of Economics*, *124*(10), 435–442.

Kinnear, P. R., & Gray, C. D. (2008). *SPSS 16 made simple*. New York: Psychology Press..

Kinzie, M. B., & Joseph, D. R. D. (2008). Gender differences in game activity preferences of middle school children: Implications for educational game design. *Educational Technology Research and Development*, *56*(5–6), 643–663. doi:10.1007/s11423-007-9076-z.

Kipnis, D. (1976). *The powerholders*. Chicago, IL: University of Chicago Press..

Kirriemuir, J., & McFarlane, A. (2004). *Literature review in games and learning*. Bristol, UK: Furturelab..

Kirschner, P. A., Ayres, P., & Chandler, P. (2011). Contemporary cognitive load theory research: The good, the bad and the ugly. *Computers in Human Behavior*, 27(1), 99–106. doi:10.1016/j.chb.2010.06.025.

Klauer, K. C., Stgmaier, R., & Meiser, T. (1997). Working memory involvement in propositional and spatial reasoning. *Thinking & Reasoning*, 3(1), 9–47. doi:10.1080/135467897394419.

Klawe, M. M., & Phillips, E. (1995). *A classroom study: Electronic games engage children as researchers*. Paper presented at the meeting of Computer Support for Collaborative Learning (CSCL). Bloomington, IN.

Klingberg, T., Fernell, E., Olesen, P. J., Johnson, M., Gustafsson, P., & Dahlström, K. et al. (2005). Computerized training of working memory in children with ADHD--A randomized, controlled trial. *Journal of the American Academy of Child and Adolescent Psychiatry*, 44(2), 177–186. doi:10.1097/00004583-200502000-00010 PMID:15689731.

Klopfer, E., Osterweil, S., & Salen, K. (2009). *Moving learning games forward*. Retrieved from http://education.mit.edu/papers/MovingLearningGamesForward_EdArcade.pdf

Knight, P. T. (2001). A briefing on key concepts: Formative and summative, criterion and norm-referenced assessment. York: Learning and Teaching Support Network (LTSN) Generic Centre ASS007..

Knight, J. F., Carley, S., Tregunna, B., Jarvis, S., Smithies, R., & De Freitas, S. et al. (2010). Serious gaming technology in major incident triage training: A pragmatic controlled trial. *Resuscitation*, 81(9), 1175–1179. doi:10.1016/j.resuscitation.2010.03.042 PMID:20732609.

Knight, R. (2002). *Five easy lessons*. Harlow, UK: Addison Wesley..

Kobbe, L., Weinberger, A., Dillenbourg, P., & Harrer, A., Hämäläinen, Häkkinen, P., & Fisher, F. (2007). Specifying computer-supported collaboration scripts. *Computer-Supported Collaborative Learning*, 2, 211–224. doi:10.1007/s11412-007-9014-4.

Kober, S. E., Kurzmann, J., & Neuper, C. (2012). Cortical correlate of spatial presence in 2D and 3D interactive virtual reality: An EEG study. *International Journal of Psychophysiology: Official Journal of the International Organization of Psychophysiology*, 83(3), 365–374. doi:10.1016/j.ijpsycho.2011.12.003 PMID:22206906.

Kober, S. E., & Neuper, C. (2011). Sex differences in human EEG theta oscillations during spatial navigation in virtual reality. *International Journal of Psychophysiology: Official Journal of the International Organization of Psychophysiology*, 79(3), 347–355. doi:10.1016/j.ijpsycho.2010.12.002 PMID:21146566.

Koehn, D. (1997). Business and game-playing: The false analogy. *Journal of Business Ethics*, 16(12/13), 1447–1452. doi:10.1023/A:1005724317399.

Kolb, D. A. (1984). *Experiential learning: Experience as the source of learning and development*. Englewood Cliffs, NJ: Prentice Hall..

Kolodny, N., & Brunero, J. (2013). Instrumental rationality. In E. N. Zalta (Ed.), *The Stanford Encyclopedia of Philosophy*. Palo Alto, CA: Stanford University. Retrieved from http://plato.stanford.edu/archives/spr2013/entries/rationality-instrumental/

Kong, S. C., Pgata, H., Arnseth, H. C., Chan, C. K. K., Hirashima, T., & Klett, F. … Yang, S. J. H. (2009). Exploring variables affecting player's intrinsic motivation in educational games. In *Proceedings of the 17th International Conference on Computers in Education (CDROM)*. Hong Kong: Asia-Pacific Society for Computers in Education.

Kordaki, M. (2012). A computer card game for the learning of basic aspects of the binary system in primary education: Design and pilot evaluation. *Education and Information Technologies*, 16, 395–421. doi:10.1007/s10639-010-9136-6.

Kortmann, R., Bekebrede, G., Van Daalen, C. E., Harteveld, C., Mayer, I. S., & Van Dierendonck, D. (2012). Veerkracht—A game for servant-leadership development. In *Proceedings of the 43rd Annual Conference of the International Simulation and Gaming Association*. ISGA.

Ko, S. (2002). An empirical analysis of children's thinking and learning in a computer game context. *Educational Psychology*, 22(2), 221–233. doi:10.1080/01443410120115274.

Koster, R. (2002). *Online world timeline*. Retrieved on December 23, 2012 from http://www.raphkoster.com/gaming/mudtimeline.shtml

Koster, R. (2005). *Theory of fun for game design*. Scottsdale, AZ: Paraglyph Press..

Kotchoubey, B., Strehl, U., Holzapfel, S., Blankenhorn, V., Fröscher, W., & Birbaumer, N. (1999). Negative potential shifts and the prediction of the outcome of neurofeedback therapy in epilepsy. *Clinical Neurophysiology: Official Journal of the International Federation of Clinical Neurophysiology, 110*(4), 683–686. doi:10.1016/S1388-2457(99)00005-X PMID:10378738.

Krathwohl, D. R., Bloom, B. S., & Betram, B. M. (1973). *Taxonomy of educational objectives, the classification of educational goals: Handbook II: Affective domain*. New York: David McKay Co., Inc.

Kriz, W. C., & Hense, J. U. (2004). Evaluation of the EU-project simgame in business education. In W. C. Kriz, & T. Eberle (Eds.), *Bridging the gap: Transforming knowledge into action through gaming and simulation* (pp. 352–363). Munchen, Germany: Sagsaga..

Kriz, W. C., & Hense, J. U. (2006). Theory-oriented evaluation for the design of and research in gaming and simulation. *Simulation & Gaming, 37*(2), 268–283. doi:10.1177/1046878106287950.

Kropotov, J. D. (2009). *Quantitative EEG, event-related potentials and neurotherapy*. San Diego, CA: Elsevier Academic Press..

Krovi, R., Graesser, A. C., & Pracht, W. E. (1999). Agent behaviors in virtual negotiation environments. *Trans. Sys. Man Cyber Part C, 29*(1), 15–25. doi:10.1109/5326.740666.

Kuhn, T. S. (1962). *The structure of scientific revolutions*. Chicago: University of Chicago Press..

Kuit, M. (2002). *Strategic behavior and regulatory styles in The Netherlands energy industry*. Retrieved May 3, 2013, from http://www.narcis.nl/publication/RecordID/oai:tudelft.nl:uuid:f940a515-f967-4cf3-9a96-07cb69a61ae5

Kyllonen, P. C., & Christal, R. E. (1990). Reasoning ability is (little more than) working-memory capacity?! *Intelligence, 14*(4), 389–433. doi:10.1016/S0160-2896(05)80012-1.

Lainema, T., & Nurmi, S. (2006). Applying an authentic, dynamic learning environment in real world business. *Computers & Education, 47*, 94–115. doi:10.1016/j.compedu.2004.10.002.

Lake, A. (2011). *Game programming gems 8*. Boston, MA: Course Technology..

Lambropoulos, N., Romero, M., & Culwin, F. (2010). HCI education to support collaborative e-learning systems design. *eLearn Magazine, 9*.

Lannen, T., Brown, D., & Powell, H. (2002). Control of virtual environments for young people with learning difficulties. *Disability and Rehabilitation, 24*(11-12), 578–578. doi:10.1080/09638280110111342 PMID:12182797.

Lanzilotti, R., & Roselli, T. (2007). An experimental evaluation of Logiocando, an intelligent tutoring hypermedia system. *International Journal of Artificial Intelligence in Education, 17*(1), 41–56.

Lastowka, G., & Hunter, D. (2004). *The laws of virtual worlds*. Retrieved on December 23, 2012 from http://papers.ssrn.com/sol3/papers.cfm?abstract_id=402860

Lave, J., & Wenger, E. (1991). *Situated learning: Legitimate peripheral participation*. Cambridge, UK: Cambridge University Press. doi:10.1017/CBO9780511815355.

Law, E., & Von Ahn, L. (2011). Human Computation. *Synthesis Lectures on Artificial Intelligence and Machine Learning, 5*(3), 1–121. doi:10.2200/S00371ED-1V01Y201107AIM013.

Lawson, L. L., & Lawson, C. L. (2010). Video game-based methodology for business research. *Simulation & Gaming, 41*(3), 360–373. doi:10.1177/1046878109334038.

Lee, J. (1999). Effectiveness of computer-based instructional simulation: A meta analysis. *International Journal of Instructional Media, 26*(1), 71–85. Retrieved May 3, 2013, from http://www.questia.com/googleScholar.qst?docId=5001238108

Lee, M. J., & Ko, A. J. (2011). Personifying programming tool feedback improves novice programmers' learning. In *Proceedings of the Conference on International Computing Education Research (ICER)*. Providence, RI: ACM.

Leeb, R., Scherer, R., Friedman, D., Lee, F., Keinrath, C., Bischog, H., et al. (2007). Combining BCI and virtual reality: Scouting virtual worlds. In G. Dornhege, J. del R. Millán, T. Hinterberger, D. J. McFarland, & K.-R. Müller (Eds.), Toward brain computer interfacing (pp. 393–408). Cambridge, MA: MIT Press..

Lee, C.-Y., & Chen, M.-P. (2009). A computer game as a context for non-routine mathematical problem solving: The effects of type of question prompt and level of prior knowledge. *Computers & Education*, *52*(3), 530–542. doi:10.1016/j.compedu.2008.10.008.

Lee, D., & LaRose, R. (2007). A socio-cognitive model of video game usage. *Journal of Broadcasting & Electronic Media*, *51*(4), 632–650. doi:10.1080/08838150701626511.

Lee, K., & Ashton, M. C. (2004). Psychometric properties of the HEXACO personality inventory. *Multivariate Behavioral Research*, *39*(2), 329–358. doi:10.1207/s15327906mbr3902_8.

Lee, M. J., & Tedder, M. C. (2003). The effects of three different computer texts on readers' recall: Based on working memory capacity. *Computers in Human Behavior*, *19*(6), 767–783. doi:10.1016/S0747-5632(03)00008-6.

Leemkuil, H. (2006). *Is it all in the game? Learner support in an educational knowledge management simulation game*. Enschede, The Netherlands: University of Twente. Retrieved May 3, 2013, from http://users.gw.utwente.nl/leemkuil/PhDThesisLeemkuil2006.pdf

Leemkuil, H., de Jong, T., & Ootes, S. (2000). *Review of educational use of games and simulations*. Retrieved from http://kits.edte.utwente.nl/documents/D1.pdf

Leigh, J., DeFanti, T. A., Johnson, A. E., Brown, M. D., & Sandi, D. J. (1997). Global tele-immersion: Better than being there. In *Proceedings of ICAT '97*. Tokyo, Japan: ICAT.

Leite, I., Castellano, G., Pereira, A., Martinho, C., & Paiva, A. (2012). Long-term interactions with empathic robots: Evaluating perceived support in children. In S. S. Ge, O. Khatib, J.-J. Cabibihan, R. Simmons, & M.-A. Williams (Eds.), *Social Robotics* (pp. 298–307). Berlin: Springer. Retrieved from http://link.springer.com/chapter/10.1007/978-3-642-34103-8_30

Leite, I., Martinho, C., Pereira, A., & Paiva, A. (2009). As time goes by: Long-term evaluation of social presence in robotic companions. In *Proceedings of the 18th IEEE International Symposium on Robot and Human Interactive Communication,* (pp. 669–674). IEEE. doi:10.1109/ROMAN.2009.5326256

Leite, I., Pereira, A., Martinho, C., & Paiva, A. (2008). Are emotional robots more fun to play with? In *Proceedings of the 17th IEEE International Symposium on Robot and Human Interactive Communication,* (pp. 77–82). IEEE. doi:10.1109/ROMAN.2008.4600646

Leite, I., Pereira, A., Mascarenhas, S., Martinho, C., Prada, R., & Paiva, A. (2013). The influence of empathy in human–robot relations. *International Journal of Human-Computer Studies*, *71*(3), 250–260. doi:10.1016/j.ijhcs.2012.09.005.

Lempert, R. J., & Schwabe, W. (1993). *Transition to sustainable waste management, a simulation gaming approach*. Santa Monica, CA: Rand Corporation..

Lenhardt, A., Kahne, J., Middaugh, E., Macgill, A., Evans, C., & Vitak, J. (2008). Teens' gaming experiences are diverse and include significant social interaction and civic engagement. *Pew Internet & American Life Project*. Retrieved from: http://www.pewinternet.org/

Lennon, J. L. (2006). Debriefings of web-based malaria games. *Simulation & Gaming*, *37*(3), 350–356. doi:10.1177/1046878106291661.

Leuner, B. (1966). Emotional intelligence and emancipation: A psychodynamic study on women. *Praxis der Kinderpsychologie und Kinderpsychiatrie*, *15*(6), 196–203. PMID:5975008.

Levinsen, K. (2006). Collaborative on-line teaching: The inevitable path to deep learning and knowledge sharing? *Electronic Journal of E-learning*, *4*(1), 41–48.

Lewin, K. (1936). *Principles of topological psychology* (F. Heider, & G. Heider, Trans.). New York: McGraw-Hill. doi:10.1037/10019-000.

Lewis, M. W. (2007). Analysis of the roles of serious games in helping teach health-related knowledge, skills, and in changing behavior. *Journal of Diabetes Science and Technology, 1*(6). PMID:19885166.

Leyton-Brown, K., & Shoham, Y. (2008). Essentials of game theory. In R. J. Brachman, & T. Dietterich (Eds.), *Political science*. San Francisco, CA: Morgan & Claypool Publishers..

Lim, C. P., Nonis, D., & Hedberg, J. (2006). Gaming in a 3D multiuser virtual environment: Engaging students in science lessons. *British Journal of Educational Technology, 37*(2), 211–231. doi:10.1111/j.1467-8535.2006.00531.x.

Lindh, J., Hrastinski, S., Bruhn, C., & Mozgira, L. (2008). Computer-based business simulation games as tools for learning: A comparative study of student and teacher perceptions. In *Proceedings of the 2nd European Conference on Games-Based Learning (ECGBL)*. Barcelona, Spain: ECGBL.

Linehan, M., & Scullion, H. (2001). Challenges for female international managers: Evidence from Europe. *Journal of Managerial Psychology, 16*(3), 215–228. doi:10.1108/02683940110385767.

List, A., & Robertson, I. C. (2007). Inhibition of return and object-based attentional selection. *Journal of Experimental Psychology. Human Perception and Performance, 33*, 1322–1334. doi:10.1037/0096-1523.33.6.1322 PMID:18085946.

Liu, C., Agrawal, P., Sarkar, N., & Chen, S. (2009). Dynamic difficulty adjustment in computer games through real-time anxiety-based affective feedback. *International Journal of Human-Computer Interaction, 25*(6), 506–529. doi:10.1080/10447310902963944.

Lloyd-Fox, S., Blasi, a, & Elwell, C. E. (2010). Illuminating the developing brain: The past, present and future of functional near infrared spectroscopy. *Neuroscience and Biobehavioral Reviews, 34*(3), 269–284. doi:10.1016/j.neubiorev.2009.07.008 PMID:19632270.

Locke, E. A., & Latham, G. P. (1990). *A theory of goal setting & task performance*. Englewood Cliffs, NJ: Prentice-Hall, Inc.

Lofthouse, N., Arnold, L., & Hurt, E. (2012). Current status of neurofeedback for attention-deficit/hyperactivity disorder. *Current Psychiatry Reports, 14*(5), 536–542. doi:10.1007/s11920-012-0301-z PMID:22890816.

Loftus, G. R., & Loftus, E. F. (1983). *Mind at play: The psychology of video games*. New York: Basic Books..

Logan, F. A., & Wagner, A. R. (1965). *Reward and punishment*. Boston, MA: Allyn and Bacon..

Logie, R. H., & Della Sala, S. (2010). Brain training in schools, where is the evidence? *British Journal of Educational Technology, 41*(6), 127–128. doi:10.1111/j.1467-8535.2010.01101.x.

Loman, M. E., Johnson, A. E., Westerlund, A., Pollak, S. D., Nelson, C. A., & Gunnar, M. R. (2012). The effect of early deprivation on executive attention in middle childhood. *Journal of Child Psychology and Psychiatry, and Allied Disciplines, 54*(1), 37–45. doi:10.1111/j.1469-7610.2012.02602.x PMID:22924462.

Lopes, P. N., Salovey, P., Côté, S., Beers, M., & Petty, R. E. (2005). Emotion regulation abilities and the quality of social interaction. *Emotion (Washington, D.C.), 5*(1), 113. doi:10.1037/1528-3542.5.1.113 PMID:15755224.

Lopes, P. N., Salovey, P., & Straus, R. (2003). Emotional intelligence, personality, and the perceived quality of social relationships. *Personality and Individual Differences, 35*(3), 641–658. doi:10.1016/S0191-8869(02)00242-8.

LTS. (2009). *Curriculum for excellence: Technologies experiences and outcomes*. LTS..

LTS. (2011a). *Approaches to learning*. Retrieved January 28, 2012, from http://www.ltscotland.org.uk/learning-teachingandassessment/approaches/index.asp

LTS. (2011b). *The consolarium*. Retrieved January 28, 2012, from http://www.ltscotland.org.uk/usingglowandict/gamesbasedlearning/consolarium.asp

Lucas, K., & Sherry, J. L. (2004). Sex differences in video game play: A communication-based explanation. *Communication Research, 31*(5), 499–523. doi:10.1177/0093650204267930.

Luhmann, N. (1995). *Social systems*. Stanford, CA: Stanford University Press..

Lustig, C., Shah, P., Seidler, R., & Reuter-Lorenz, P. A. (2009). Aging, training, and the brain: A review and future directions. *Neuropsychology Review, 19*, 504–522. doi:10.1007/s11065-009-9119-9 PMID:19876740.

Lynch, R. A., Steen, M. D., Pritchard, T. J., Buzzell, P. R., & Pintauro, S. J. (2008). Delivering food safety education to middle school students using a web-based, interactive, multimedia, computer program. *Journal of Food Science Education, 7*, 35–42. doi:10.1111/j.1541-4329.2007.00046.x.

Mackenzie, N., & Knipe, S. (2006). Research dilemmas: Paradigms, methods and methodology. *Issues in Educational Research, 16*(2), 193–205.

MacLellan, E. (2001). Assessment for learning: The differing perceptions of tutors and students. *Assessment & Evaluation in Higher Education, 26*(4), 307–318. doi:10.1080/02602930120063466.

Maeder, C. L., Sannelli, C., Haufe, S., & Blankertz, B. (2012). Pre-stimulus sensorimotor rhythms influence brain-computer interface classification performance. *IEEE Transactions on Neural Systems and Rehabilitation Engineering: A Publication of the IEEE Engineering in Medicine and Biology Society, 20*(5), 653–62. doi:10.1109/TNSRE.2012.2205707

Magnenat-Thalmann, N., & Kasap, Z. (2009). Virtual humans in serious games. In *Proceedings of the International Conference on CyberWorlds,* (pp. 71–79). CW. doi:10.1109/CW.2009.17

Mahmoudi, B., & Erfanian, A. (2006). Electro-encephalogram based brain-computer interface: Improved performance by mental practice and concentration skills. *Medical & Biological Engineering & Computing, 44*(11), 959–969. doi:10.1007/s11517-006-0111-8 PMID:17028907.

Maier, F. H., & Grössler, A. (2000). What are we talking about? A taxonomy of computer simulations to support learning. *System Dynamics Review, 16*(2), 135–148. doi:10.1002/1099-1727(200022)16:2<135::AID-SDR193>3.0.CO;2-P.

Maitri, S. (2001). *The spiritual dimension of the enneagram: Nine faces of the soul*. Tarcher..

Malan, D. J. (2010). Reinventing CS50. In *Proceedings of the 41st ACM Technical Symposium on Computer Science Education*. ACM.

Malan, D. J., & Leitner, H. H. (2007). Scratch for budding computer scientists. In *Proceedings of the 38th SIGCSE Technical Symposium on Computer Science Education*. ACM.

Malone, T. W. (1980). What makes things fun to learn? A study of intrinsically motivating computer games. *Dissertation Abstracts International, 41*(5B), 1955.

Malone, T. W. (1981). What makes computer games fun? *Byte, 6*(12), 258–277.

Malone, T. W., & Lepper, M. (1987a). Intrinsic motivation and instructional effectiveness in computer-based education. In R. E. Snow, & M. J. Farr (Eds.), *Aptitude learning and instruction*. London: Lawrence Erlbaum Associates Publishers..

Malone, T. W., & Lepper, M. (1987b). Making learning fun: A taxonomy of intrinsic motivation for learning. In R. E. Snow, & M. J. Farr (Eds.), *Aptitude, learning, and instruction: III: Cognitive and affective process analysis* (pp. 223–225). Hillsdale, NJ: Lawrence Erlbaum Associates Publishers..

Maloney, J. H., Peppler, K., Kafai, Y. B., Resnick, M., & Rusk, N. (2008). Programming by choice: Urban youth learning programming with scratch. In *Proceedings of the 39th SIGCSE Technical Symposium on Computer Science Education*. ACM.

Mania, K., & Chalmers, A. (1998). A classification for user embodiment in collaborative virtual environments. In *Proceedings of the 4th International Conference on Virtual Systems and Multimedia*. Boca Raton, FL: IOS Press.

Marsella, S. C., & Pynadath, D. V. (2005). Modeling influence and theory of mind. In *Artificial Intelligence and the Simulation of Behavior* (pp. 199–206). IEEE..

Martin, A. J., & Jackson, S. (2008). Brief approaches to assessing task absorption and enhanced subjective experience: Examining short and core flow in diverse performance domains. *Motivation and Emotion, 32*(3), 141–157. doi:10.1007/s11031-008-9094-0.

Martin, R. A. (2007). *The psychology of humor: An integrative approach*. Academic Press..

Mascarenhas, S., Dias, J., Afonso, N., Enz, S., & Paiva, A. (2009). Using rituals to express cultural differences in synthetic characters. In *Proceedings of the 8th International Conference on Autonomous Agents and Multiagent Systems* (Vol. 1, pp. 305–312). Richland, SC: International Foundation for Autonomous Agents and Multiagent Systems. Retrieved from http://dl.acm.org/citation.cfm?id=1558013.1558055

Mascarenhas, S., Prada, R., Paiva, A., Degens, N., & Hofstede, G. J. (2013). Can I ask you a favour? A relational model of socio-cultural behaviour. In *Proceedings of the 12th International Conference on Autonomous Agents and Multiagent Systems (AAMAS 2013)*. AAMAS.

Mascarenhas, S., Dias, J., Prada, R., & Paiva, A. (2010). A dimensional model for cultural behavior in virtual agents. *Applied Artificial Intelligence*, *24*(6), 552–574. doi:10.1080/08839514.2010.492163.

Maslow, A. H. (1943). A theory of human motivation. *Psychological Review*, *50*(4), 370–396. doi:10.1037/h0054346.

Maslow, A. H. (1968). *Towards a psychology of being* (2nd ed.). New York: Van Nostrand Reinhold..

Matsuyama, H., Asama, H., & Otake, M. (2009). Design of differential near-infrared spectroscopy based brain machine interface. In *Proceedings of 18th IEEE International Symposium on Robot and Human Interactive Communication*, (pp. 775–780). IEEE. doi:10.1109/ROMAN.2009.5326215

Matthews, R., Turner, P. J., McDonald, N. J., Ermolaev, K., Manus, T. M., Shelby, R. A., & Steindorf, M. (2008). Real time workload classification from an ambulatory wireless EEG system using hybrid EEG electrodes. In *Proceedings: Annual International Conference of the IEEE Engineering in Medicine and Biology Society*. IEEE. doi:10.1109/IEMBS.2008.4650550

Ma, Y., Williams, D., Prejean, L., & Richard, C. (2007). A research agenda for developing and implementing educational computer games: Colloquium. *British Journal of Educational Technology*, *38*(3), 513–518. doi:10.1111/j.1467-8535.2007.00714.x.

Mayer, I. S. (2012). Towards a comprehensive methodology for the research and evaluation of serious games. In *Proceedings VS-Games 2012* (Vol. 15, pp. 1–15). Genoa, Italy: Procedia Computer Science. doi:10.1016/j.procs.2012.10.075

Mayer, I. S., Zhou, Q., Lo, J., Abspoel, L., Keijser, X., Olsen, E., et al. (2012). Integrated, ecosystem-based marine spatial planning? First results from international simulation-game experiment. In *Proceedings of Third International Engineering Systems Symposium*. Delft, The Netherlands: IEEE.

Mayer, I. S., Zhou, Q., Lo, J., Abspoel, L., Keijser, X., Olsen, E., et al. (2013). Integrated, ecosystem-based marine spatial planning: Design and results of a game-based quasi-experiment. *Ocean and Coastal Management, 82*, 7–26. doi:dx.doi.org/10.1016/j.ocecoaman.2013.04.006

Mayer, I. S. (2009). The gaming of policy and the politics of gaming: A review. *Simulation & Gaming*, *40*(6), 825–862. doi:10.1177/1046878109346456.

Mayer, I. S., Bekebrede, G., Harteveld, C., Warmelink, H. J. G., Zhou, Q., & Lo, J. et al. (2013). The research and evaluation of serious games: Towards a comprehensive methodology. *British Journal of Educational Technology*. doi:10.1111/bjet.12067.

Mayer, I. S., Carton, L., de Jong, M., Leijten, M., & Dammers, E. (2004). Gaming the future of an urban network. *Futures*, *36*(3), 311–333. doi:10.1016/S0016-3287(03)00159-9.

Mayer, I. S., & Veeneman, W. (Eds.). (2003). *Games in a world of infrastructures: Gaming simulation for research, learning and intervention*. Eburon Publishers..

Mayer, I. S., Warmelink, H. J. G., & Bekebrede, G. (2013). Learning in a game-based virtual environment: A comparative evaluation in higher education. *European Journal of Engineering Education*, *38*(1), 85–106. doi:10.1080/03043797.2012.742872.

Mayer, J. D., & Salovey, P. (1997). What is emotional intelligence? In P. Salovey, & D. Sluyter (Eds.), *Emotional development and emotional intelligence: Implications for educators* (pp. 3–31). New York: Basic Books..

Mayer, J. D., Salovey, P., & Caruso, D. R. (2002). *Mayer-Salovey-Caruso emotional intelligence test (MSCEIT)*. Toronto, Canada: Multi-Health Systems, Inc.

Mayer, J. D., Salovey, P., Caruso, D. R., & Sitarenios, G. (2003). Measuring emotional intelligence with the MSCEIT V2.0. *Emotion (Washington, D.C.)*, *3*, 97–105. doi:10.1037/1528-3542.3.1.97 PMID:12899321.

Mayer, R. E. (2005). Cognitive theory of multimedia learning. In R. E. Mayer (Ed.), *The Cambridge handbook of multimedia learning* (pp. 31–48). Cambridge, MA: Cambridge University Press. doi:10.1017/CBO9780511816819.004.

Mayer, R. E. (Ed.). (2005). *Cambridge handbook of multimedia learning*. New York: Cambridge University Press. doi:10.1017/CBO9780511816819.

Mayes, D. K., & Cotton, J. E. (2001). Measuring engagement in video games: A questionnaire. In *Proceedings of the Human Factors and Ergonomics Society 45th Annual Meeting* (pp. 692–696). Retrieved May 3, 2013, from http://www.scopus.com/inward/record.url?eid=2-s2.0-0442310948&partnerID=40&md5=b56e 3e59c17f58d-4d21a35d7755b9f6a

Maynard Smith, J. (1982). *Evolution and the theory of games*. Cambridge, UK: Cambridge University Press. doi:10.1017/CBO9780511806292.

Mazur, E. (1997). *Peer instruction*. Englewood Cliffs, NJ: Prentice Hall..

McAlpine, M., van der Zanden, L., & Harris, V. (2010). Using Games Based Technology in Formal Assessment of Learning. In *Proceedings of the 4th European Conference on Games-Based Learning*.

McClelland, D. C. (1961). *The achieving society*. New York: Free Press..

McDermott, L. (2001). Oersted medal lecture 2001: Physics education research – The key to student learning. *American Journal of Physics*, *69*(11). doi:10.1119/1.1389280.

McDermott, L. C. (1996). *Physics by inquiry*. London: J. Wiley..

McDougall, W. (1908). *An introduction to social psychology*. London: Dover Publications. doi:10.1037/12261-000.

McFarlane, A., Sparrowhawk, A., & Heald, Y. (2002). *Report on the educational use of games*. Retrieved from http://www.teem.org.uk/publications/teem_gamesined_full.pdf

McGonigal, J. E. (2011). *Reality is broken: Why games make us better and how they can change the world*. New York. The Penguin Press..

McGuinness, C. (2005). Teaching thinking: Theory and practice. *BJEP Monograph series II, Number 3 – Pedagogy – Teaching for Learning*, *1*(1), 107-126.

McGuinness, C. (2005). BJEP monograph series II, number 3 – Pedagogy. *Teaching for Learning*, *1*(1), 107–126.

McGurk, H., & MacDonald, J. (1976). Hearing lips and seeing voices. *Nature*, *264*(5588), 746–748. doi:10.1038/264746a0 PMID:1012311.

Mead, G. H. (1934). *Mind, self, and society*. Chicago: University of Chicago Press..

Meadows, D. L. (1999). Learning to be simple: My odyssey with games. *Simulation & Gaming*, *30*(3), 342–351. doi:10.1177/104687819903000310.

Medina, E. (2005). Digital games: A motivational perspective. In *Proceedings of DiGRA 2005 Conference: Changing View—World in Play*. Vancouver, Canada: DiGRA.

Mehrabian, A. (1969). Measures of achievement tendency. *Educational and Psychological Measurement*, *29*(2), 445–451. doi:10.1177/001316446902900222.

Mehrabian, A. (1970). The development and validation of measures of affiliative tendency and sensitivity to rejection. *Educational and Psychological Measurement*, *309*(2), 417–428. doi:10.1177/001316447003000226.

Meijer, S. A. (2009). *The organisation of transactions: Studying supply networkd using gaming simulation*. Retrieved from http://www.narcis.nl/publication/RecordID/oai:library.wur.nl:wurpubs/376893

Meijer, S. A., Mayer, I. S., Van Luipen, J., & Weitenberg, N. (2011). Gaming rail cargo management: Exploring and validating alternative modes of organization. *Simulation & Gaming*, *43*(1), 85–101. doi:10.1177/1046878110382161.

Melby Lervag, M., & Hulme, C. (2013). Is working memory training effective? A meta analytic review. *Developmental Psychology*, *49*(2), 270–291. doi:10.1037/a0028228 PMID:22612437.

Melis, E., & Monthienvichienchai, R. (2004). They call it learning style but it's so much more. In *Proceedings of World Conference on e-Learning in Corporate, Government, Healthcare, and Higher Education*. Chesapeake, VA: IEEE.

Mendelson, M. J., & Aboud, F. E. (1999). Measuring friendship quality in late adolescents and young adults: McGill friendship questionnaires. *Statistics*, *31*(2), 130–132.

Metcalfe, J. (2002). A region of proximal learning model of study time allocation. *Journal of Memory and Language*, *52*, 465–477.

Meyer, B. (2010). Comparative studies in game-based language learning: A discussion of methodology. In *Proceedings of the 9th European Conference on Elearning*, (pp. 362–369). IEEE.

Michael, D., & Chen, S. (2005). *Proof of learning: Assessment in serious games*. [Blog post]. Retrieved April 14th, 2013 from http://www.gamasutra.com/view/feature/2433/proof_of_learning_assessment_in_.php

Michael, D. R., & Chen, S. (2006). *Serious games that educate, train, and inform*. Boston, MA: Thomson Course Technology PTR..

Milgram, S. (1974). *Obedience to authority: An experimental view*. New York: Harper & Row..

Miller, D. J., & Robertson, D. P. (2010). Using a games console in the primary classroom: Effects of brain training programme on computation and self-esteem. *British Journal of Educational Technology*, *41*(2), 242–255. doi:10.1111/j.1467-8535.2008.00918.x.

Miller, D. J., & Robertson, D. P. (2011). Educational benefits of using game consoles in a primary classroom: A randomised controlled trial. *British Journal of Educational Technology*, *42*, 850–864. doi:10.1111/j.1467-8535.2010.01114.x.

Miller, D. J., & Robertson, D. P. (2011). Response to Logie and Della Sala: Brain training in schools, where is the evidence? *British Journal of Educational Technology*, *42*(5), 101–102. doi:10.1111/j.1467-8535.2011.01205.x.

Miller, L. M. (2005). Using learning styles to evaluate computer-based instruction. *Computers in Human Behavior*, *21*, 287–306. doi:10.1016/j.chb.2004.02.011.

Mills, C., & Dalgarno, B. (2007). A Conceptual Model for Game Based Intelligent Tutoring Systems. In Ascilite conference 2007..

Mishra, J., Bavelier, D., & Gazzaley, A. (2012). How to assess gaming-induced benefits on attention and working memory. *Games for Health Journal: Research. Development and Clinical Applications*, *3*(1), 192–198.

Mislevy, R. J., Steinberg, L. S., & Almond, R. G. (2003). On the structure of educational assessments. *Measurement: Interdisciplinary Research and Perspectives*, *1*, 3–67. doi:10.1207/S15366359MEA0101_02.

MIT. (2011). *Statistics on scratch users*. Retrieved May 5, 2011, from http://stats.scratch.mit.edu/

Mitchell, A., & Savill-Smith, C. (2004). *The use of computer and video games for learning: A review of the literature*. Ultralab..

Miyake, A., Friedman, N. P., Emerson, M. J., Witzki, A. H., Howerter, A., & Wager, T. D. (2000). The unity and diversity of executive functions and their contributions to complex frontal lobe tasks: A latent variable analysis. *Cognitive Psychology*, *41*(1), 49–100. doi:10.1006/cogp.1999.0734 PMID:10945922.

Moffat, S., Hampson, S., & Hatzipantelis, M. (1998). Navigation in a virtual maze: Sex differences and correlation with psychometric measures of spatial ability in humans. *Evolution and Human Behavior*, *19*(2), 73–87. doi:10.1016/S1090-5138(97)00104-9.

Monroy-Hernández, A., & Resnick, M. (2008). Empowering kids to create and share programmable media. *Interaction*, *15*(2), 50–53. doi:10.1145/1340961.1340974.

More, T. (1516). *Utopia*. Retrieved 17 April, 2012, from http://www.gutenberg.org/files/2130/2130-h/2130-h.htm

Moreno-Ger, P., Burgos, D., Martínez-Ortiz, I., Sierra, J. L., & Fernández-Manjón, B. (2008). Educational game design for online education. *Computers in Human Behavior*, *24*(6), 2530–2540. doi:10.1016/j.chb.2008.03.012.

Moreno-Ger, P., Torrente, J., Bustamante, J., Fernández-Galaz, C., Fernández-Manjón, B., & Comas-Rengifo, M. D. (2010). Application of a low-cost web-based simulation to improve students' practical skills in medical education. *International Journal of Medical Informatics*, *79*(6), 459–467. doi:10.1016/j.ijmedinf.2010.01.017 PMID:20347383.

Morillo Arroyo, D., Santos Rodríguez, P., Pérez Calle, D., Delgado Kloos, C., Ibáñez Espiga, M. B., & Hernández-Leo, D. (2010). Assessment in 3D Virtual Worlds: QTI in Wonderland, In Congreso Iberoamericano de Informática Educativa, 410-417..

Morsi, R., Richards, C., & Rizvi, M. (2010). Work In Progress - BINX: A 3D XNA Educational Game for Engineering Education. In *Proceedings of 40th ASEE/IEEE Frontiers in Education Conference, S1E-1*.

Mortagy, Y., & Boghikian-Whitby, S. (2010). A longitudinal comparative study of student perceptions in online education. *Interdisciplinary Journal of Elearning and Learning Objects*, *6*, 23–44.

Moseley, A., Culver, J., Piatt, K., & Whitton, N. (2009). *Motivation in alternate reality gaming environments and implications for learning*. Paper presented at the 3rd European Conference on Games Based Learning. Graz, Austria.

Muehlemann, T., Haensse, D., & Wolf, M. (2008). Wireless miniaturized in-vivo near infrared imaging. *Optics Express*, *16*(14), 10323–10330. doi:10.1364/OE.16.010323 PMID:18607442.

Mueller, C., Luehrs, M., Baecke, S., Adolf, D., Luetzkendorf, R., Luchtmann, M., & Bernarding, J. (2012). Building virtual reality fMRI paradigms: A framework for presenting immersive virtual environments. *Journal of Neuroscience Methods*, *209*(2), 290–298. doi:10.1016/j.jneumeth.2012.06.025 PMID:22759716.

Mulwa, C., Lawless, S., Sharp, M., Arnedillo-Sanchez, I., & Wade, V. (2010). Adaptive educational hypermedia systems in technology enhanced learning: A literature review. In *Proceedings of the 2010 ACM Conference on Information Technology Education*. Midland, MI: ACM.

Murray, H. A. (1938). *Explorations in personality*. Oxford, UK: Oxford University Press..

Murray, H. A. (1981). Proposals for a theory of personality. In E. S. Shneidman (Ed.), *Endeavors in psychology: Selections from the personology of Henry A. Murray* (pp. 125–203). New York: Harper and Row..

Musallam, S., Corneil, B. D., Greger, B., Scherberger, H., & Andersen, R. A. (2004). Cognitive control signals for neural prosthetics. *Science*, *305*(5681), 258–262. doi:10.1126/science.1097938 PMID:15247483.

Nabi, R. L., & Kremar, M. (2004). Conceptualising media enjoyment as attitude: Implications for mass media effects research. *Communication Theory*, *14*(4), 288–310. doi:10.1111/j.1468-2885.2004.tb00316.x.

Nadolski, R. J., Hummel, H. G. K., Van den Brink, H. J., Hoefakker, R., Slootmaker, A., Kurvers, H., & Storm, J. (2008). EMERGO: Methodology and toolkit for efficient development of serious games in higher education. *Simulation & Gaming*, *39*(3), 338–352. doi:10.1177/1046878108319278.

Nadolski, R. J., Van der Hijden, P., Tattersall, C., & Slootmaker, A. (2006). *Multi-user online serious games: Beleid, ontwerp en gebruik* [Multi-user online serious game: Policy, design and use]. Utrecht, The Netherlands: Stichting Digitale Universiteit..

Nadolski, R., Baalsrud Hauge, J., Boyle, E., Riedel, J., Mayer, I., & Moreno Ger, P. (2012). *Are you serious? Evidence for learning using games*. Berlin: Online Educa..

Nakamura, J., Rodman, G., & Kolko, B. (2000). *Race in cyberspace*. New York: Routledge..

Nambu, I., Osu, R., Sato, M., Ando, S., Kawato, M., & Naito, E. (2009). Single-trial reconstruction of finger-pinch forces from human motor-cortical activation measured by near-infrared spectroscopy (NIRS). *NeuroImage*, *47*(2), 628–637. doi:10.1016/j.neuroimage.2009.04.050 PMID:19393320.

Nan, W., Rodrigues, J. P., Ma, J., Qu, X., Wan, F., & Mak, P.-I. et al. (2012). Individual alpha neurofeedback training effect on short term memory. *International Journal of Psychophysiology: Official Journal of the International Organization of Psychophysiology*, *86*(1), 83–87. doi:10.1016/j.ijpsycho.2012.07.182 PMID:22864258.

Naranjo, C. (1997). *Transformation through insight: Enneatypes in life*. Hohm Press..

National Gaming Survey. (2009). *Detailed data of gaming in The Netherlands*. Retrieved February 24, 2012, from http://www.nationaalgamingonderzoek.nl

National Research Council. (2010). *Exploring the intersection of science education and 21st century skills: A workshop summary*. Washington, DC: National Academy Press..

National Science Board. (2010). *Preparing the next generation of STEM innovators: Identifying and developing our nations' human capital*. Retrieved from http://www.nsf.gov/nsb/publications/2010/nsb1033.pdf

Neisser, U. (1967). *Cognitive psychology*. New York: Appleton-Century-Crofts..

Neuper, C., Scherer, R., Reiner, M., & Pfurtscheller, G. (2005). Imagery of motor actions: Differential effects of kinesthetic and visual-motor mode of imagery in single-trial EEG. *Brain Research. Cognitive Brain Research*, *25*(3), 668–677. doi:10.1016/j.cogbrainres.2005.08.014 PMID:16236487.

Newell, A., & Simon, H. A. (1972). *Human problem solving*. Englewood Cliffs, NJ: Prentice-Hall..

NFER. (2009). *Teacher voice omnibus survey*. Retrieved August 24, 2012, from http://www.nfer.ac.uk/nfer/what-we-offer/teacher-voice/PDFs/futurelab.pdf

Nieborg, D. B. (2004). America's army: More than a game.[Munich, Germany: SAGA.]. *Proceedings of ISAGA*, *2004*, 883–891.

Nieborg, D. B. (2011). *Triple-A the political economy of the blockbuster video game*. Amsterdam: Universiteit van Amsterdam..

Niedermeyer, E., & Lopes da Silva, F. H. (2005). *Electroencephalography: Basic principles, clinical applications, and related fields*. Academic Press..

Nijboer, F., Furdea, A., Gunst, I., Mellinger, J., McFarland, D. J., Birbaumer, N., & Kübler, A. (2008). An auditory brain-computer interface (BCI). *Journal of Neuroscience Methods*, *167*(1), 43–50. doi:10.1016/j.jneumeth.2007.02.009 PMID:17399797.

Norman, D. A. (1988). *The design of everyday things*. New York: Doubleday..

Norman, D. A. (1999). Affordances, conventions, and design. *Interaction*, *6*(3), 38–41. doi:10.1145/301153.301168.

Normand, V., Babski, C., Benford, S., Bullock, A., Carion, S., & Farcet, N. et al. (1999). The COVEN project: Exploring applicative, technical, and usage dimensions of collaborative virtual environments. *Presence (Cambridge, Mass.)*, *8*(2), 218–236. doi:10.1162/105474699566189.

Nouchi, R., Taki, Y., Takeuchi, H., Hashizume, H., Nozawa, T., & Kambara, T. et al. (2013). Brain training game boosts executive functions, working memory and processing speed in the young adults: A randomized controlled trial. *PLoS ONE*, *8*(2), 1–13. doi:10.1371/journal.pone.0055518 PMID:23405164.

Novak, G. (1999). *Just-in-time teaching*. Englewood Cliffs, NJ: Prentice Hall..

Novak, J. (2005). *Game development essentials: An introduction*. Clifton Park, NY: Thomson/Delmar Learning..

Noy, A., Raban, D. R., & Ravid, G. (2006). Testing social theories in computer-mediated communication through gaming and simulation. *Simulation & Gaming*, *37*(2), 174–194. doi:10.1177/1046878105286184.

NSS. (2011). *NSS 2010 shows continued high levels of satisfaction among higher education undergraduate students*. Retrieved January 20, 2013 from http://www.hefce.ac.uk/news/hefce/2010/nssresult.htm

Nuttin, J., & Lens, W. (1985). *Future time perspective and motivation: Theory and research method*. Hillsdale, NJ: Erlbaum..

Nygaard, C., Courtney, N., & Leigh, E. (Eds.). (2012). *Simulations, games and role play in university education*. Fringdon Oxfordshire, UK: Libri Publishing..

Nyquist, J. B. (2003). *The benefits of reconstructing feedback as a larger system of formative assessment: A meta-analysis*. Unpublished Master of Science thesis, Vanderbilt University.

O'Brien, D. (2011). A taxonomy of educational games. In *Gaming and simulations: Concepts, methodologies, tools and applications* (pp. 1–23). Hershey, PA: IGI Global..

O'Brien, H. L., & Toms, E. G. (2008). What is user engagement? A conceptual framework for defining user engagement with technology. *Journal of the American Society for Information Science and Technology, 59*(6), 938–955. doi:10.1002/asi.20801.

O'Neil, H. F., Wainess, R., & Baker, E. L. (2005). Classification of learning outcomes: Evidence from the computer games literature. *Curriculum Journal, 16*, 455–474. doi:10.1080/09585170500384529.

O'Shaughnessy, T. E., & Swanson, H. L. (1998). Do immediate memory deficits in students with learning disabilities in reading reflect a developmental lag or deficit? A selective meta-analysis of the literature. *Learning Disability Quarterly, 21*(2), 123–148. doi:10.2307/1511341.

Oblinger, D. (2004). The next generation of educational engagement. *Journal of Interactive Media in Education, 8*, 1–18.

OECE. (2008). *Encouraging student interest in science and technology studies*. Paris: OECD Publishing..

Oei, A. C., & Patterson, M. D. (2013). Enhancing cognition with video games: A multiple game training study. *PLoS ONE, 8*(3), e58546. doi:10.1371/journal.pone.0058546 PMID:23516504.

Oh, S. H., & Kim, M. S. (2004). The role of spatial working memory in visual search efficiency. *Psychonomic Bulletin & Review, 11*(2), 275–281. doi:10.3758/BF03196570 PMID:15260193.

Okan, Z. (2003). Edutainment: Is learning at risk? *British Journal of Educational Technology, 34*(3), 255–264. doi:10.1111/1467-8535.00325.

Olsen, D., & Mateas, M. (2009). Beep! Beep! Boom! Towards a planning model of coyote and road runner cartoons. In *Proceedings of the 4th International Conference on Foundations of Digital Games* (pp. 145–152). IEEE.

Olsen, T., Procci, K., & Bowers, C. (2011). Serious games usability testing: How to ensure proper usability, playability, and effectiveness. In A. Marcus (Ed.), *Design User Experience and Usability Theory Methods Tools and Practice Proceedings First International Conference DUXU 2011*. doi:10.1007/978-3-642-21708-1

Oppermann, R., Rashev, R., & Kinshuk. (1997). Adaptability and adaptivity in learning systems. In A. Behrooz (Eds.), *Knowledge Transfer* (2nd ed.). London: pAce, London.

Ordeshook, P. C. (1986). *Game theory and political theory: An introduction*. Retrieved from http://books.google.com/books?id=faytzOKtquMC&pgis=1

Ormrod, J. E. (2008). *Educational psychology: Developing learners* (6th ed.). Upper Saddle River, NJ: Pearson..

Ortony, A., Clore, G. L., & Collins, A. (1990). *The cognitive structure of emotions*. Cambridge, UK: Cambridge University Press. Retrieved from http://www.amazon.com/Cognitive-Structure-Emotions-Andrew-Ortony/dp/0521386640

Oslin, J. L., Mitchell, S. A., & Griffin, L. L. (1998). The game performance assessment instrument (GPAI), some concerns and solutions for further development. *Journal of Teaching in Physical Education, 17*(2), 220–240.

Othmer, S., & Kaiser, D. (2000). Implementation of virtual reality in EEG. *Biofeedback, 3*(3).

Ott, M., & Tavella, M. (2009). A contribution to the understanding of what makes young students genuinely engaged in computer-based learning tasks. *Procedia - Social and Behavioral Sciences, 1*(1), 184–188. doi:10.1016/j.sbspro.2009.01.034

Overmars, M. (2004). Teaching computer science through game design. *Computer, 37*(4), 81–83. doi:10.1109/MC.2004.1297314.

Owen, A. M., Hampshire, A., Grahn, J. A., Stenton, R., Dajani, S., & Burns, A. S. et al. (2010). Putting brain training to the test. *Nature, 465*(7299), 775–778. doi:10.1038/nature09042 PMID:20407435.

Paiva, A., Dias, J., Sobral, D., Aylett, R., Woods, S., Hall, L., & Zoll, C. (2005). Learning by Feeling: Evoking Empathy with Synthetic Characters. *Applied Artificial Intelligence, 19*, 35–266. doi:10.1080/08839510590910165.

Palmer, G. (2005). *Physics for game programmers.* Berkeley, CA: Apress..

Palmer, H. (1988). *The enneagram: Understanding yourself and the others in your life.* New York: Haper & Row..

Papastergiou, M. (2009). Digital game-based learning in high school computer science education: Impact on educational effectiveness and student motivation. *Computers & Education, 52*, 1–12. doi:10.1016/j.compedu.2008.06.004.

Papert, S. (1980). *Mindstorms: Children, computers, and powerful ideas.* New York: Basic Books, Inc.

Pashler, H., McDaniel, M., Rohrer, D., & Bjork, R. (2008). Learning styles: Concepts and evidence. *Psychological Science in the Public Interest, 9*, 105–119. doi:doi:10.1111/j.1539-6053.2009.01038.x.

Passey, D. (1999). *Anytime, anywhere, learning project evaluation focus.* Lancaster, UK: Lancaster University/AAL..

Paul, S. T., Messina, J. A., & Hollis, A. M. (2006). A Technology Classroom Review Tool for General Psychology. *Teaching of Psychology, 33*(4). Aut, *2006*, 276–279.

Payne, W. L. (1985). *A study of emotion: developing emotional intelligence, self integration, relating to fear, pain and desire.* (Doctoral dissertation). The Union for Experimenting Colleges and Universities.

Peirce, N., Conlan, O., & Wade, V. (2008). Adaptive educational games: Providing non-invasive personalised learning experiences. In *Proceedings of the Second IEEE International Conference on Digital Games and Intelligent Toys Based Education.* IEEE.

Peppler, K. A., & Kafai, Y. (2007). *What videogame making can teach us about literacy and learning: Alternative pathways into participatory culture.* Paper presented at the 3rd International Conference of the Digital Games Research Association (DiGRA). Tokyo, Japan.

Pereira, G., Prada, R., & Santos, P. A. (2013). Bases of social power for agents. In *Proceedings of the 12th International Conference on Autonomous Agents and Multiagent Systems (AAMAS 2013).* AAMAS.

Perkins, D. N., & Salomon, G. (1989). Are cognitive skills context bound? *Educational Researcher, 18*(1), 16–25. doi:10.3102/0013189X018001016.

Pernin, J., Michau, F., Mandran, N., & Mariais, C. (2012). ScenLRPG, a board game for the collaborative design of Gbl scenarios: Qualitative analysis of an experiment. In *Proceedings of the 6th European Conference on Games Based Learning.* Cork, Ireland: IEEE.

Petersen, S. A., & Bedek, M. A. (2012). Challenges and opportunities in evaluating learning in serious games: A look at behavioural aspects. In M. Ma, M. Fradinho, J. B. Hauge, H. Duin, & K.-D. Thoben (Eds.), *Serious Games Development and Applications - Third International Conference, SGDA 2012* (LNCS), (vol. 7528). Berlin: Springer.

Pfeffer, J. (1981). *Power in organizations.* Boston: Pitman Marshfield..

Pfeifer, R., Bongard, J., & Grand, S. (2007). *How the body shapes the way we think: A new view of intelligence.* Cambridge, MA: MIT Press. Retrieved from http://books.google.pt/books?id=EHPMv9MfgWwC

Pfister, R. (2011). Gender effects in gaming research: A case for regression residuals? *Cyberpsychology Behavior and Social Networking, 14*(10), 603–607. doi:10.1089/cyber.2010.0547 PMID:21486141.

Pfurtscheller, G. (1992). Event-related synchronization (ERS): An electrophysiological correlate of cortical areas at rest. *Electroencephalography and Clinical Neurophysiology, 83*(1), 62–69. doi:10.1016/0013-4694(92)90133-3 PMID:1376667.

Pfurtscheller, G., & Lopes da Silva, F. H. (1999). Event-related EEG/MEG synchronization and desynchronization: Basic principles. *Clinical Neurophysiology: Official Journal of the International Federation of Clinical Neurophysiology, 110*(11), 1842–1857. doi:10.1016/S1388-2457(99)00141-8 PMID:10576479.

Phillips, L. H. (1997). Do frontal tests measure executive function? Issues of assessment and evidence of assessment and evidence from fluency tests. In P. M. A. Rabbitt (Ed.), *Methodology of Frontal and Executive Function*. Hove, UK: Psychology Press..

Piaget, J. (1932). *The moral judgment of the child*. London: K. Paul, Trench, Trubner & Co. ltd.

Piaget, J., & Inhelder, B. (1958). *The growth of logical thinking from childhood to adolescence*. New York: Basic Books..

Piatt, K. (2009). Using alternate reality games to support first year induction with ELGG. *Campus-Wide Information Systems*, *26*(4), 313–322. doi:10.1108/10650740910984646.

Pillay, H. (2002). An investigation of cognitive processes engaged in by recreational computer game players: Implications for skills of the future. *Journal of Research on Technology in Education*, *34*(3), 336–350.

Pillay, S., Brownlee, J., & Wilss, L. (1999). Cognition and recreational computer games: Implications for educational technology. *The Journal of Research on Computing in Education*, *32*(1), 203–216.

Pine, B. J., & Gilmore, J. H. (1999). *The experience economy, work is theatre and every business a stage*. Boston, MA: Harvard Business School Press..

Pinker, S. (2009). *How the mind works*. New York: Norton Publishers..

Pintrich, P. R., & Schunk, D. H. (1996). *Motivation in education: Theory, research and applications*. Englewood Cliffs, NJ: Prentice-Hall, Inc.

Piper, A. M. (2002, December). O'Brien, E. Morris, M.R., & Winograd, T. (2002). SIDES: A Cooperative Tabletop Computer Game for Social Skills Development. *Simulation & Gaming*, *33*(4), 526–532.

Pivec. (2009). *Game-based learning or game-based teaching*. Retrieved from http://emergingtechnologies.becta.org.uk/upload-dir/downloads/page_documents/research/emerging_technologies/game_based_learning.pdf

Pivec, M. (2007). Editorial: Play and learn: Potentials of game-based learning. *British Journal of Educational Technology*, *38*(3), 387–393. doi:10.1111/j.1467-8535.2007.00722.x.

Plessner, H. (1968). *Der kategorische konjunktiv*. Frankfurt/M.

Poggi, I., Pelachaud, C., De Rosis, F., Carofiglio, V., & De Carolis, B. (2005). GRETA: A believable embodied conversational agent. In O. Stock & M. Zancanaro (Eds.), *Multimodal Intelligent Information Presentation* (Vol. 27, pp. 1–23). Boston: Kluwer Academic Publishers. Retrieved from http://www.springerlink.com/index/vg369201254923n7.pdf

Posner, M. I. (1980). Orienting of attention. *The Quarterly Journal of Experimental Psychology*, *32A*, 3–25. doi:10.1080/00335558008248231 PMID:7367577.

Posner, M. I., & Peterson, S. E. (1990). The attention system of the human brain. *Annual Review of Neuroscience*, *13*, 25–42. doi:10.1146/annurev.ne.13.030190.000325 PMID:2183676.

Posner, M., & Raichle, M. (1994). *Images of mind*. New York: Scientific American Library..

Poulsen, M., & Køber, E. (2011). *The GAMEiT handbook: A framework of game based learning pedagogy*. Oslo, Norway: GAMEiT.

Poverty Is Not, A. Game (PING). (n.d.). *Serious game on poverty awareness*. Retrieved from http://www.povertyisnotagame.com/?lang=en

Power, S. D., Kushki, A., & Chau, T. (2012). Automatic single-trial discrimination of mental arithmetic, mental singing and the no-control state from prefrontal activity: Toward a three-state NIRS-BCI. *BMC Research Notes*, *5*(1), 141. doi:10.1186/1756-0500-5-141 PMID:22414111.

Prada, R., Raimundo, G., Dimas, J., Martinho, C., Peña, J. F., & Baptista, M. ... Ribeiro, L. L. (2012). The role of social identity, rationality and anticipation in believable agents. In *Proceedings of the 11th International Conference on Autonomous Agents and Multiagent Systems* (vol. 3, pp. 1175–1176). Richland, SC: International Foundation for Autonomous Agents and Multiagent Systems. Retrieved from http://dl.acm.org/citation.cfm?id=2343896.2343907

Prada, R., & Paiva, A. (2009). Teaming up humans with autonomous synthetic characters. *Artificial Intelligence, 173*(1), 80–103. doi:10.1016/j.artint.2008.08.006.

Prensky, M. (2002). The motivation of gameplay: The real twenty-first century learning revolution. *Horizon, 10*(1), 5–11. doi:10.1108/10748120210431349.

Prensky, M. (2006). *Don't bother me, mom, i'm learning! How computer and video games are preparing your kids for 21st century success and how you can help.* St. Paul, MN: Paragon House..

Prensky, M. (2007). *Digital game-based learning.* St Paul, MN: Paragon House Publishers..

Preschl, B., Wagner, B., Forstmeier, S., & Maercker, A. (2011). E-health interventions for depression, anxiety disorder, dementia, and other disorders in older adults: A review. *Cyber Therapy and Rehabilitation, 4*(3), 371–385.

Price, L. (2004). Individual differences in learning: Cognitive control, cognitive style, and learning style. *Educational Psychology, 24*, 681–698. doi:10.1080/0144341042000262971.

Price, M., Carroll, J., O'Donovan, B., & Rust, C. (2011). If I was going there I wouldn't start from here: A critical commentary on current assessment practice. *Assessment & Evaluation in Higher Education, 36*(4), 479–492. doi:10.1080/02602930903512883.

Prins, P. J. M., Dovis, S., Ponsioen, A., Brink, E. T., & van der Oord, S. (2011). Does a computerized working memory training with game elements enhance motivation and training performance in boys with ADHD? *Cyberpsychology. Behavior & Social Networking, 14*, 115–122. doi:10.1089/cyber.2009.0206.

Provenzo, E. F. (1991). *Video kids: Making sense of Nintendo.* Cambridge, MA: Harvard Business Press..

PWC. (2010). *Global entertainment and media outlook: 2010-2014.* Retrieved from http://www.pwc.com/

QAA (2006). Section 6: Assessment of students, Code of practice for the assurance of academic quality and standards in higher education. Retrieved May 8 2013 from http://www.qaa.ac.uk/.

QAA. (2011). *Chapter B6: Assessment of students and accreditation of prior learning.* Gloucester, UK: The UK Quality Code for Higher Education.

Quellmalz, E. S., Timms, M. J., Silberglitt, M. D., & Buckley, B. C. (2012). Science assessments for all: Integrating science simulations into balanced state science assessment systems. *Journal of Research in Science Teaching, 49*(3), 363–393. doi:10.1002/tea.21005.

Rademacher, R. J. (2009). *An assessment of current pure online physics courses.* Paper presented at the American Association of Physics Teachers Winter Meeting. Chicago, IL.

Rademacher, R. (2010b). A proposed framework for studying educational virtual worlds. In P. Zemliansky (Ed.), *Design and Implementation of Educational Games.* Hershey, PA: IGI Global..

Rademacher, R. (2011). Assessing serious games using the EE grid. In *Computer games education review.* Rotterdam, The Netherlands: Sense Publishers..

Rademacher, R. J. (2010a). Best practices in teaching and designing a pure online science classroom. In Y. Katz (Ed.), *Learning Management Systems Technologies and Software Solutions for Online Teaching: Tools and Applications.* Hershey, PA: IGI Global..

Raessens, J. (2009). Homo ludens 2.0. *Metropolis M,* (5), 64–69, 85–88.

Raessens, J. (2006). Playful identities, or the ludification of culture. *Games and Culture, 1*(1), 52–57. doi:10.1177/1555412005281779.

Rajendran, G., & Mitchell, P. (2007). Cognitive theories of autism. *Developmental Review, 27*(2), 224–260. doi:10.1016/j.dr.2007.02.001.

Ramler, I. P., & Chapman, J. L. (2011). Introducing statistical research to undergraduate mathematical statistics students using the guitar hero video game series. *Journal of Statistics Education*, *19*(3), 1–20.

Randel, J. M., Morris, B. A., Wetzelf, C. D., & Whitehill, B. V. (1992). The effectiveness of games for educational purposes: A review of the research. *Simulation & Gaming*, *25*, 261–276. doi:10.1177/1046878192233001.

Rankin, Y., Gold, R., & Gooch, B. (2006). Gaming as a Language Learning Tool. *Proceedings of the ACM SIGGRAPH Educators Program*, 2006.

Raphael, C., Bachen, C., Lynn, K. M., Baldwin-Philippi, J., & McKee, K. A. (2009). Games for civic learning: A conceptual framework and agenda for research and design. *Games and Culture*, *5*(2), 199–235. doi:10.1177/1555412009354728.

Ravaja, N., Turpeinen, M., Saari, T., Puttonen, S., & Keltikangas-Jarvinen, L. (2008). The psychophysiology of James Bond: Phasic emotional responses to violent video game events. *Emotion (Washington, D.C.)*, *8*(1), 114–120. doi:10.1037/1528-3542.8.1.114 PMID:18266521.

Raven, B. H. (1992). A power/interaction model of interpersonal influence: French and Raven thirty years later. *Journal of Social Behavior and Personality*, *7*(2), 217–244.

Raybourn, E. M. (2006). Applying Simulation Experience Design Methods to Creating Serious Game-based Adaptive Training Systems. *Interacting with Computers*.

Razak, A. A., Connolly, T. M., & Hainey, T. (2012). Teachers' views on the approach of digital games-based learning within the curriculum for excellence. *International Journal of Game-Based Learning*, *2*(1), 33–51. doi:10.4018/ijgbl.2012010103.

Rebolledo-Mendez, G., Avramides, K., & De Freitas, S. (2009). Societal impact of a serious game on raising public awareness: The case of FloodSim. *Methodology*, *148*(2), 15–22. doi: doi:10.1145/1581073.1581076.

Reed, M. S., Evely, A. C., Cundill, G., Fazey, I., Glass, J., & Laing, A. (2010). What is social learning ?. *Ecology and Society*, *15*(4).

Reeves, T. C. (2000). Alternative Assessment Approaches for Online Learning Environments in Higher Education. *Journal of Educational Computing Research*, *21*(1).

Reichlin, L., Mani, N., McArthur, K., Harris, A. M., Rajan, N., & Dacso, C. C. (2011). Assessing the acceptability and usability of an interactive serious game in aiding treatment decisions for patients with localized prostate cancer. *Journal of Medical Internet Research*, *13*(1), e4. doi:10.2196/jmir.1519 PMID:21239374.

Reid, M., Burn, A., & Parker, D. (2002). *Evaluation report of the Becta digital video pilot project*. Retrieved from http://partners.becta.org.uk/pagedocuments/research/dvreport 241002.pdf

Remmele, B. (2003). *Die entstehung des maschinenparadigmas*. Opladen: Leske & Budrich.

Remmele, B., Seeber, G., Krämer, J., & Schmette, M. (2009). Game-based teaching - Dimensions of analysis. In M. Pivec (Ed.), *Proceedings of the 3rd European Conference on Games-Based Learning* (pp. 325-331). Reading, MA: Academic Publishing Limited.

Resnick, L. (1987). *Education and learning to think*. Washington, DC: National Academy..

Resnick, M., Kafai, Y., & Maeda, J. (2003). *A networked, media-rich programming environment to enhance technological fluency at after-school centers in economically-disadvantage communities*. Academic Press..

Ribeiro, T., Vala, M., & Paiva, A. (2012). Thalamus: Closing the mind-body loop in interactive embodied characters. In *Proceedings of IVA* (pp. 189–195). IVA.

Ricks, T. R., Turley-Ames, K. J., & Wiley, J. (2007). Effects of working memory capacity on mental set due to domain knowledge. *Memory & Cognition*, *35*(6), 1456–1462. doi:10.3758/BF03193615 PMID:18035641.

Rieber, L. P., Smith, L., & Noah, D. (1998). The value of serious play. *Educational Technology*, *38*(6), 29–37.

Riedel, J. C. K. H., Pawar, K. S., & Barson, R. (2001). Academic & industrial user needs of a concurrent engineering computer simulation game. *Concurrent Engineering: Research & Applications*, *9*(3), 223–237. doi:10.1177/1063293X0100900304.

Riehle, D., & Bruckman, A. (2009). *Proceedings of the 5th International Symposium on Wikis and open collaboration 2009*. Orlando, FL: ACM.

Riso, D. R., & Hudson, R. (1996). *Personality types*. New York: Houghton Mifflin..

Ritterfeld, U., Cody, M. J., & Vorderer, P. (2009). *Serious games: Mechanisms and effects*. Retrieved from http://books.google.com/books?id=GwPf7tbO5mgC&pgis=1

Ritterfield, U., & Weber, R. (2006). Video games for entertainment and education. In P. Vorderer, & J. Bryant (Eds.), *Playing video games: Motives, responses, and consequences*. Hoboken, NJ: Lawrence Erlbaum Associates..

Rizzo, P., Veloso, M., Miceli, M., & Cesta, A. (1997). Personality-driven social behaviors in believable agents. In *Proceedings of the AAAI Fall Symposium on Socially Intelligent Agents* (pp. 109–114). AAAI. Retrieved from http://www.aaai.org/Papers/Symposia/Fall/1997/FS-97-02/FS97-02-026.pdf

Roberts, L., Birbaumer, N., Rockstroh, B., Lutzenberger, W., & Elbert, T. (1989). Self-report during feedback regulation of slow cortical potentials. *Psychophysiology*, 26(4), 392–403. doi:10.1111/j.1469-8986.1989.tb01941.x PMID:2798689.

Robertson, J., & Good, J. (2004). *Children's narrative development through computer game authoring*. Paper presented at the Meeting of the 2004 Conference on Interaction Design and Children: Building a Community. Baltimore, MD.

Robertson, J., & Oberlander, J. (2002). Ghostwriter: Educational Drama and Presence in a Virtual Environment. *Journal of Computer-Mediated Communication*, 8(1), October 2002.

Robertson, M. (2010). *Can't play, won't play*. [Blog post]. Retrieved January 20, 2013 from http://www.hideandseek.net/2010/10/06/cant-play-wont-play/

Robertson, J., & Howells, C. (2008). Computer game design: Opportunities for successful learning. *Computers & Education*, 50(2), 559–578. doi:10.1016/j.compedu.2007.09.020.

Rockwell, G. M., & Kee, K. (2011). The leisure of serious games: A dialogue. *Game Studies, 11*(2).

Rodrigues, S. H., Mascarenhas, S. F., Dias, J., & Paiva, A. (2009). I can feel it too! Emergent empathic reactions between synthetic characters. In *Proceedings of Affective Computing and Intelligent Interaction and Workshops, 2009*. ACII. doi:10.1109/ACII.2009.5349570.

Romero, M. (2010). Gestion du temps dans les activités projet médiatisées à distance. Ed.s Européenes Universitaires..

Romero, M. (2011). *Students' temporal perspectives, participation, temporal group awareness and grades: Are future oriented students performing better?* Paper presented at the FP7 IAPP Euro-CATCSCL Scientific Results' Workshop. Toulouse, France.

Romero, M., & Usart, M. (2012). Game based learning time-on-task and learning performance according to the students' temporal perspective. In *Proceedings of the 6th European Conference on Games Based Learning*. Waterford Institute of Technology.

Romero, M., Usart, M., Ott, M., & Earp, J. (2012). Learning through playing for or against each other? Promoting collaborative learning in digital game based learning. Retrieved from http://aisel.aisnet.org/ecis2012/93

Romero, M., & Usart, M. (2013). Time factor in the curriculum integration of game based learning. In *New pedagogical approaches in games enhanced learning curriculum integration*. Hershey, PA: IGI Global. doi:10.4018/978-1-4666-3950-8.ch013.

Romero, M., Usart, M., Popescu, M., & Boyle, E. (2012). Interdisciplinary and international adaption and personalization of the metavals serious games. *Lecture Notes in Computer Science, 7528*, 59–73. doi:10.1007/978-3-642-33687-4_5.

Ron-Angevin, R., & Díaz-Estrella, A. (2009). Brain-computer interface: Changes in performance using virtual reality techniques. *Neuroscience Letters, 449*(2), 123–127. doi:10.1016/j.neulet.2008.10.099 PMID:19000739.

Rosenberg, M. (1965). *Society and the adolescent self-image*. Princeton, NJ: Princeton University Press..

Rossi, L. (2009). Playing your network: Gaming in social network sites. In *Proceedings of DiGRA 2009: Breaking New Ground: Innovation in Games, Play, Practice and Theory*. DiGRA.

Rotter, J. (1966). Generalized expectancies for internal versus external control of reinforcement. *Psychological Monographs, 88*(609). PMID:5340840.

Rowe, J. P., Shores, L. R., Mott, B. W., & Lester, J. C. (2010). *Integrating learning and engagement in narrative-centered learning environments.* Academic Press. doi:10.1007/978-3-642-13437-1_17.

Rowntree, D. (1987). *Assessing students: How shall we know them?* New York: Taylor & Francis..

Rubinstein, A., & Salant, Y. (2012). Eliciting welfare preferences from behavioural data sets. *The Review of Economic Studies, 79,* 375–387. doi:10.1093/restud/rdr024.

Rudnianski, M. (1991). Deterrence typology and nuclear stability: A game theoretical approach. *Defense Decision Making,* 137-168.

Rudnianski, M. (2012). From argumentation to negotiation: The game of deterrence path. *Rivista Quadrimestrale,* (17).

Rudnianski, M., & Bestougeff, H. (2008). Deterrence and defeasibility in argumentation process for ALIS project. In *Computable Models of the Law* (pp. 219–238). Berlin: Springer. doi:10.1007/978-3-540-85569-9_14.

Rudnianski, M., & Lalonde, T. (2009). Argumentation and time in IPR issues: the ALIS project game of deterrence approach. *Game Theory and Applications, 14,* 114–140.

Ruiz, S., York, A., Stein, M., Keating, N., & Santiago, K. (2009). *Darfur is dying.* Retrieved from http://www.darfurisdying.com/

Rupnik, J. (2006). Finding community structure in social network analysis – Overview. *Journal of Mathematical Sociology.* Retrieved from http://eprints.pascal-network.org/archive/00003800/

Rusk, N. (2009a). *Scratch programming concepts.* Retrieved September 5, 2011, from http://info.scratch.mit.edu/sites/infoscratch.media.mit.edu/files/file/ScratchProgrammingConcepts-v14.pdf

Rusk, N. (2009b). *Scratch cards.* Retrieved September 5, 2011, from http://scratched.media.mit.edu/resources/scratch-cards

Ryan, R. M., Rigby, C. S., & Przybylski, A. (2006). The motivational pull of video games: A self-determination theory approach. *Motivation and Emotion, 30,* 347–363. doi:10.1007/s11031-006-9051-8.

Sakai, K., & Russell, D. (1994). *To expand, we divide: The practice and principles of Bunsha management.* Intercultural Group..

Salen, K. (Ed.). (2007). *The ecology of games: Connecting youth, games, and learning.* Cambridge, MA: MIT Press..

Salen, K., & Zimmerman, E. (2004). *Rules of play: Game design fundamentals.* Cambridge, MA: The MIT Press..

Salminen, M., & Ravaja, N. (2008). Increased oscillatory theta activation evoked by violent digital game events. *Neuroscience Letters, 435*(1), 69–72. doi:10.1016/j.neulet.2008.02.009 PMID:18325669.

Salmoni, A., Schmidt, R., & Walter, C. (1984). Knowledge of results and motor learning: A review and critical reappraisal. *Psychological Bulletin, 95*(3), 355–386. doi:10.1037/0033-2909.95.3.355 PMID:6399752.

Salomon, M., & Soudoplatoff, S. (2010). Why virtual-world economies matter. *Journal of Virtual Worlds Research, 2*(4), 14.

Salovey, P., & Mayer, J. D. (1990). *Emotional intelligence.* Retrieved on December 24, 2012, available from http://www.unh.edu/emotional_intelligence/EIAssets/EmotionalIntelligenceProper/EI1990%20Emotional%20Intelligence.pdf

Salovey, P., & Grewal, D. (2005). The science of emotional intelligence. *Current Directions in Psychological Science, 149*(16), 281–285. doi:10.1111/j.0963-7214.2005.00381.x.

Salthouse, T. A., Atkinson, T. M., & Berish, D. E. (2003). Executive functioning as a potential mediator of age-related cognitive decline in normal adults. *Journal of Experimental Psychology. General, 132*(4), 566–594. doi:10.1037/0096-3445.132.4.566 PMID:14640849.

Sanbonmatsu, D. M., Strayer, D. L., Medeiros-Ward, N., & Watson, J. M. (2013). Who multi-tasks and why? Multi-tasking ability, perceived multi-tasking ability, impulsivity, and sensation seeking. *PLoS ONE, 8*(1), e54402. doi:10.1371/journal.pone.0054402 PMID:23372720.

Sanchez, A., Cannon-Bowers, J., & Bowers, C. (2010). Establishing a science of game based learning. In J. A. Cannon-Bowers, & C. Bowers (Eds.), *Serious game design and development: Technologies for training and learning* (pp. 290–304). Hershey, PA: IGI Global. doi:10.4018/978-1-61520-739-8.ch016.

Sandford, R., & Williamson, B. (2005). *Games and learning: A handbook from Futurelab.* Retrieved from http://archive.futurelab.org.uk/resources/documents/handbooks/games_and_learning2.pdf

Sandford, R., Ulicsak, M., Facer, K., & Rudd, T. (2006). *Teaching with games: Using commercial off-the-shelf computer games in formal education.* Retrieved from http://archive.futurelab.org.uk/resources/documents/project_reports/teaching_with_games/TWG_report.pdf

Saucier, D., Bowman, M., & Elias, L. (2003). Sex differences in the effect of articulatory or spatial dual-task interference during navigation. *Brain and Cognition, 53*(2), 346–350. doi:10.1016/S0278-2626(03)00140-4 PMID:14607178.

Sawyer, B., & Smith, P. (2008). *Keynote address.* Paper presented at the Second European Conference on Games-Based Learning. Barcelona, Spain.

Sawyer, B. (2008). *Serious games taxonomy.* Sawyer, Ben Smith, Peter..

Schaaf, R. (2012). Digital game-based learning improve student time-on-task behavior and engagement in comparison to alternative instructional strategies? *Canadian Journal of Action Research, 13*(1), 50–64.

Schacter, D. L. (1987). Implicit memory: History and current status. *Journal of Experimental Psychology. Learning, Memory, and Cognition, 13*(3), 501–518. doi:10.1037/0278-7393.13.3.501.

Scharpf, F. W. (1997). Games real actors play? Actor-centered institutionalism in policy research. In P. Sabatier (Ed.), *Theoretical lenses on public policy.* Boulder, CO: Westview Press..

Schauster, E. (2012). The structuration of crisis management: Guiding a process of repair. *Journal of Professional Communication, 2*(1), 77–88.

Schell, J. (2008). *The art of game design: A book of lenses.* Boca Raton, FL: CRC Press..

Scheufele, D. A., Iyengar, S., Kenski, K., Hall, K., & Eds, J. (2002). The state of framing research: A call for new directions. In K. Kenski, & K. H. Jamieson (Eds.), *The Oxford handbook of political communication theories* (pp. 1–27). Oxford, UK: Oxford, University Press..

Schifter, K. (2012). *Minecraft in an English class.* Paper presented at 6th European Conference on Games Based Learning. Cork, Ireland.

Schmidt, J. T., & Werner, C. H. (2007). Designing online instruction for success. *Future Electronic Journal of e-Learning, 5*(1), 69-78.

Schmidt, C. (2010). *Neuroéconomie: Comment les neuro-sciences transforment l'analyse économique.* Odile Jacob..

Schmidt, R., Young, D., Swinnen, S., & Shapiro, D. (1989). Summary knowledge of results for skill acquisition: Support for the guidance hypothesis. *Journal of Experimental Psychology. Learning, Memory, and Cognition, 15*(2), 352–359. doi:10.1037/0278-7393.15.2.352 PMID:2522520.

Schmitz, B., Czauderna, A., & Specht, M. (2011). Game Based Learning for Computer Science Education, In Proceedings of the Computer Science Education Research Conference CSERC'11

Schneider, B., & Schmitt, N. (1992). *Staffing organizations* (2nd ed.). Prospect Heights, IL: Waveland Press..

Schneider, D. K. (2005). *Research design for educational technologists.* Geneva: AACE..

Schneider, W., Roth, E., & Ennemoser, M. (2000). Training phonological skills and letter knowledge in children at risk for dyslexia: A comparison of three kindergarten intervention programs. *Journal of Educational Psychology, 92*, 284–295. doi:10.1037/0022-0663.92.2.284.

Schoenau-Fog, H. (2011). The player engagement process: An exploration of continuation desire in digital games. In *Proceedings of DiGRA 2011 Conference: Think Design Play.* Digital Games Research Association.

Scholz-Reiter, B., & Delhoum, S. (2007). The effect of enhanced collaboration on the performance of subjects for the task of inventory control. In K. D. Thoben, J. Baalsrud Hauge, R. Smeds, & J. O. Riis (Eds.), *Multidisciplinary research on new methods for learning and innovation in enterprise networks*. Verlagsgruppe Mainz GmbH Aachen..

Schrage, M. (2000). *Serious play: How the world's best companies simulate to innovate*. Boston: Harvard Business School Press..

Schramm, W., Lyle, J., & Parker, E. (1961). *Television in the lives of our children*. Palo Alto, CA: Stanford University Press..

Schuster, A., & Yamaguchi, Y. (2010). Application of game theory to neuronal networks. *Advances in Artificial Intelligence*, , 1–13. doi:10.1155/2010/521606.

Schutte, N., Malouff, J., Post-Gordon, J., & Rodasta, A. (1988). Effects of playing video games on children's aggressive and other behaviors. *Journal of Applied Social Psychology*, *18*(5), 454–460. doi:10.1111/j.1559-1816.1988.tb00028.x.

Schuurink, E., Houtkamp, J., & Toet, A. (2008). Engagement and EMG in serious gaming: experimenting with sound and dynamics in the levee patroller training game. In P. Markopoulos, B. de Ruyter, W. Ijsselsteijn, & D. Rowland (Eds.), *Fun and games: Second international conference*, (pp. 139-149). Eindhoven, The Netherlands: Springer Verlag. doi:10.1007/978-3-540- 88322-7_14

Schwartz, K. (2013). *SimCityEDU: Using games for formative assessment*. [Blog post]. Retrieved April 4, 2013 from http://blogs.kqed.org/mindshift/2013/03/video-games-as-assessment-tools-game-changer/

Schwartz, R. G., & Teach, R. D. (2002). The congruence game: A team-building exercise for students of entrepreneurship. *Simulation & Gaming*, *33*(1), 94–108. doi:10.1177/1046878102033001006.

Scott, D. (1995). The effect of violent games on feelings of aggression. *The Journal of Psychology*, *129*(2), 121–132. doi:10.1080/00223980.1995.9914952 PMID:7760289.

Sedighian, K. (1997). *Challenge-driven learning: A model for children's multimedia mathematics learning environments*. Paper presented at the meeting of ED-MEDIA 1997: World Conference on Educational Multimedia and Hypermedia. Calgary, Canada.

Seitlinger, P., Bedek, M. A., Kopeinik, S., & Albert, D. (2012). Evaluating the validity of a non-invasive assessment procedure. In M. Ma, M. Fradinho, J. B. Hauge, H. Duin, & K.-D. Thoben (Eds.), *Serious games development*. Retrieved from http://www.springerlink.com/index/K66751M360805G62.pdf

Selnow, G. W. (1984). Playing videogames: The electronic friend. *The Journal of Communication*, *34*(2), 148–156. doi:10.1111/j.1460-2466.1984.tb02166.x.

Selwyn, N. (2008). *Education 2.0? Designing the web for teaching and learning: A commentary by the technology enhanced learning phase of the teaching and learning research programme*. Retrieved from http://www.tlrp.org/tel/files/2008/11/tel_comm_final.pdf

Senge, P. M. (1990). *The fifth discipline, the art and practice of the learning organization*. New York: Doubleday..

Senge, P. M., Roberts, C., & Ross, R. B. (1994). *The fifth discipline fieldbook, strategies and tools for building a learning organization*. Garden City, NJ: Doubleday..

Serrano, A., Marchiori, E. J., del Blanco, Á., Torrente, J., & Fernández-Manjón, B. (2012). A Framework to Improve Evaluation in Educational Games. In *Global Engineering Education Conference (EDUCON)*.

Serruya, M. D., & Kahana, M. J. (2008). Techniques and devices to restore cognition. *Behavioural Brain Research*, *192*(2), 149–165. doi:10.1016/j.bbr.2008.04.007 PMID:18539345.

Serway, R., Faughn, J., & Moses, C. (2003). *College physics*. Sydney, Australia: Thomson-Brooks/Cole..

Shaffer, D. W. (2006). Epistemic frames for epistemic games. *Computers & Education*, *46*(3), 223–234. doi:10.1016/j.compedu.2005.11.003.

Shams, L., & Seitz, A. R. (2008). Benefits of multisensory learning. *Trends in Cognitive Sciences*, *12*(11), 411–417. doi:10.1016/j.tics.2008.07.006 PMID:18805039.

Shaw, A. (2010). What is video game culture? Cultural studies and game studies. *Games and Culture, 5*(4), 403–424. doi:10.1177/1555412009360414.

Sheldon, L. (2011). *Gaming the classroom: Syllabus.* Retrieved January 20, 2013 from http://gamingtheclassroom.wordpress.com/syllabus/

Sheng, S., Magnien, B., Kumaragurg, P., Acquisiti, A., Cranor, L. F., Hong, J., & Nunge, E. (2007). Anti-Phishing Phil: The Design and Evaluation of a Game That Teaches People Not to Fall for Phish. In *Proceedings of the 3rd symposium on Usable privacy and security SOUPS '07*, Publisher: ACM Press.

Shernoff, D. J., Csikszentmihalyi, M., Schneider, B., & Shernoff, E. S. (2003). Student engagement in high school classrooms from the perspective of flow theory. *School Psychology Quarterly, 18*(2), 158–176. doi:10.1521/scpq.18.2.158.21860.

Sherry, J. (2004). Flow and media enjoyment. *Communication Theory, 14*(4), 328–347. doi:10.1111/j.1468-2885.2004.tb00318.x.

Sherry, J. L. (2001). The effects of violent video games on aggression. *Human Communication Research, 27*(3), 409–431.

Shiffrin, R. M., & Schneider, W. (1977). Controlled and automatic human information processing: Perceptual learning, automatic attending, and a general theory. *Psychological Review, 84*, 127–190. doi:10.1037/0033-295X.84.2.127.

Shin, N. (2006). Online learner's 'flow' experience: An empirical study. *British Journal of Educational Technology, 37*(5), 705–720. doi:10.1111/j.1467-8535.2006.00641.x.

Shipstead, Z., Redick, T. S., & Engle, R. W. (2012). Is working memory training effective? *Psychological Bulletin, 138*(4), 628–654. doi:10.1037/a0027473 PMID:22409508.

Shubik, M. (1999). *Political economy, oligopoly and experimental games: The selected essays of Martin Shubik volume one.* Cheltenham, UK: Elgar..

Shute, V. J., & Spector, J. M. (2008). SCORM 2.0 White Paper: Stealth Assessment in Virtual Worlds. In *Learning*.

Shute, V. J., Masduki, I., & Donmez, O. (2010). Conceptual Framework for Modeling, Assessing and Supporting Competencies within Game Environments. In Tech., Inst., Cognition and Learning, 8, 137–161.

Shute, V. J. (2011). Stealth assessment in computer-based games to support learning. In S. Tobias, & J. D. Fletcher (Eds.), *Computer games and instruction* (pp. 503–524). Charlotte, NC: Information Age..

Shute, V. J., & Ke, F. (2012). Games, learning, and assessment. In D. Ifenthaler, D. Eseryel, & X. Ge (Eds.), *Assessment in game-based learning: Foundations, innovations, and perspectives* (pp. 43–58). New York, NY: Springer. doi:10.1007/978-1-4614-3546-4_4.

Shute, V. J., & Kim, Y. J. (2010). Formative assessment: Opportunities and challenges. *Journal of Language Teaching and Research, 1*(6), 838–841. doi: doi:10.4304/jltr.1.6.838-841.

Shute, V. J., & Kim, Y. J. (2013). Formative and stealth assessment. In J. M. Spector, M. D. Merrill, J. Elen, & M. J. Bishop (Eds.), *Handbook of research on educational communications and technology* (4th ed.). New York, NY: Lawrence Erlbaum Associates, Taylor & Francis Group..

Shute, V. J., & Ventura, M. (2013). *Measuring and supporting learning in games: Stealth assessment.* Cambridge, MA: The MIT Press..

Shute, V. J., Ventura, M., Bauer, M., & Zapata-Rivera, D. (2009). Melding the power of serious games and embedded assessment to monitor and foster learning? Flow and grow. *Serious Games Mechanisms and Effects, 1*(1), 1–33.

Shute, V. J., Ventura, M., Kim, Y. J., & Wang, L. (2013). Assessing learning in video games. In W. G. Tierney, Z. Corwin, T. Fullerton, & G. Ragusa (Eds.), *Postsecondary play: The role of games and social media in higher education.* Baltimore, MD: John Hopkins University Press..

Shute, V. J., Ventura, M., Small, M., & Goldberg, B. (2013). Modeling student competencies in video games using stealth assessment. In R. Sottilare, X. Hu, & A. Graesser (Eds.), *Design recommendations for adaptive intelligent tutoring systems: Learning modeling* (Vol. 1). Washington, DC: Army Research Laboratory..

Sica, L. S., Delli Veneri, A., & Miglino, O. (2011). Exploring new technological tools for education: Some protime-on-taskypes and their pragmatical classification. In *E learning*. São Paulo, Brazil: Technological Research Institute of São Paulo..

Sigrist, R., Rauter, G., Riener, R., & Wolf, P. (2012). Augmented visual, auditory, haptic, and multimodal feedback in motor learning: A review. *Psychonomic Bulletin & Review*. doi: doi:10.3758/s13423-012-0333-8 PMID:23132605.

Silius, K., Miilumäki, T., Huhtamäki, J., Tebest, T., Meriläinen, J., & Pohjolainen, S. (2010). Students' motivations for social media enhanced studying and learning. *Knowledge Management & E-Learning: An International Journal*, 2(1), 51.

Silvern, S. B., Lang, M. K., & Williamson, P. A. (1987). Social impact of video game play. In *Meaningful Play, Playful Meaning: Proceedings of the 11th Annual Meeting of the Association for the Anthropological Study of Play*. Champaign, IL: Human Kinetics.

Silvern, S. B., & Williamson, P. A. (1987). The effects of video game play on young children's aggression, fantasy, and prosocial behavior. *Journal of Developmental Psychology*, 8(4), 453–462. doi:10.1016/0193-3973(87)90033-5.

Simon, H. A. (1982). *Models of bounded rationality*. Cambridge, MA: MIT Press..

Simon, H. A. (1991). Bounded rationality and organizational learning. *Organization Science*, 2(1), 125–134. doi:10.1287/orsc.2.1.125.

Simons, J., Vansteenkiste, M., Lens, W., & Lacante, M. (2004). Placing motivation and future time perspective theory in a temporal perspective. *Educational Psychology Review*, 16(2), 121–139. doi:10.1023/B:EDPR.0000026609.94841.2f.

Singer, J. A. (1990). Affective responses to autobiographical memories and their relationship to long-term goals. *Journal of Personality*, 58(3), 535–563. doi:10.1111/j.1467-6494.1990.tb00242.x.

Singh, A. K., Okamoto, M., Dan, H., Jurcak, V., & Dan, I. (2005). Spatial registration of multichannel multi-subject fNIRS data to MNI space without MRI. *NeuroImage*, 27(4), 842–851. doi:10.1016/j.neuroimage.2005.05.019 PMID:15979346.

Sitaram, R., Caria, A., & Birbaumer, N. (2009). Hemodynamic brain-computer interfaces for communication and rehabilitation. *Neural Networks: The Official Journal of the International Neural Network Society*, 22(9), 1320–1328. doi:10.1016/j.neunet.2009.05.009 PMID:19524399.

Sivilotti, P. A. G., & Laugel, S. A. (2008). Scratching the surface of advanced topics in software engineering: A workshop module for middle school students. *Learning*, 291-295.

Skadberg, Y. X., & Kimmel, J. R. (2004). Visitors' flow experience while browsing a website: Its measurement, contributing factors, and consequences. *Computers in Human Behavior*, 20, 403–422. doi:10.1016/S0747-5632(03)00050-5.

Skinner, B. F. (1938). *The behavior of organisms*. New York: Appleton Century Crofts..

Skinner, B. F. (1953). *Science and human behavior*. New York: MacMillan..

Slate, M., Sadagic, A., Usoh, M., & Schroeder, R. (2000). Small group behavior in a virtual and real environment: A comparative study. *Presence (Cambridge, Mass.)*, 9(1), 37–51. doi:10.1162/105474600566600.

Sliney, A., & Murphy, D. (2011). Using Serious Games for Assessment. In Serious Games and Edutainment Applications, 225-243..

Sliney, A., Murphy, D., & O'Mullane, J. (2009). Secondary Assessment Data within Serious Games. In Serious Games on the Move, 225-233..

Sloep, P. B., Van der Klink, M., Brouns, F., Van Bruggen, J., & Didderen, W. (Eds.). (2011). Leernetwerken, kennisdeling, kennisontwikkeling en de leerprocessen. Houten, The Nederland: Bohn, Stafleu, Van Loghum..

Smith, M. K. (2002). *Howard Gardner and multiple intelligences, the encyclopedia of informal education*. Retrieved on December 25, 2009 from http://www.infed.org/thinkers/gardner.htm

Smith, C. R., & Hutchinson, J. (1995). *Gender: A strategic management issue*. Sydney, Australia: Business & Professional Publishing..

Smith, E. R., & Mackie, D. M. (2000). *Social psychology* (2nd ed.). Philadelphia: Psychology Press..

Smith, L. H., & Renzulli, J. S. (1984). Learning style preferences: A practical approach for classroom teachers. *Theory into Practice*, *23*, 44–50. doi:10.1080/00405848409543088.

Soflano, M. (2013). *Adaptivity and Personalisation in Games-based Learning*. PhD thesis, University of the West of Scotland.

Sorger, B., Dahmen, B., Reithler, J., Gosseries, O., Maudoux, A., Laureys, S., & Goebel, R. (2009). *Another kind of bold response: Answering multiple-choice questions via online decoded single-trial brain signals*. London: Elsevier. doi:10.1016/S0079-6123(09)17719-1.

Sourina, O. (2013). *Emotion-based personalised digital media experience in co-spaces (EmoDEx Project)*. Retrieved January 5, 2013, from http://www3.ntu.edu.sg/home/EOSourina/projects.html

Spelke, E. S., Hirst, W. C., & Neisser, U. (1976). Skills of divided attention. *Cognition*, *4*, 215–230. doi:10.1016/0010-0277(76)90018-4.

Spires, H. A., Rowe, J. P., Mott, B. W., & Lester, J. C. (2011). Problem solving and game-based learning: Effects of middle grade students' hypothesis testing strategies on learning outcomes. *Journal of Educational Computing Research*, *44*(4), 453–472. doi:10.2190/EC.44.4.e.

Spronck, P., Ponsen, M., Sprinkhuizen-Kuyper, I., & Postma, E. (2006). Adaptive game AI with dynamic scripting. *Machine Learning*, *63*(3), 217–248. doi:10.1007/s10994-006-6205-6.

Squire, K., Barnett, B., Grant, J. M., & Higginbotham, T. (2004). Electromagnetism Supercharged! Learning physics with digital simulation games. In *Proceedings of the international conference on Learning sciences, 6*, 513–520.

Squire, K. (2002). Cultural framing of computer/video games. *The International Journal of Computer Game Research*, *2*(1).

Squire, K. (2004). *Replaying history: Learning world history through playing civilization III*. Bloomington, IN: Indiana University..

St. Clair-Thompson, H. L., & Gathercole, S. E. (2006). Executive functions and achievements in school: Shifting, updating and inhibition, and working memory. *Quarterly Journal of Experimental Psychology*, *59*(4), 745–759. doi:10.1080/17470210500162854 PMID:16707360.

Staddon, J. E. R., & Simmelhag, V. L. (1971). The superstition experiment: A reexamination of its implications for the principles of adaptive behavior. *Psychological Review*, *78*(1), 3–43. doi:10.1037/h0030305.

Standen, P., & Brown, D. (2005). Virtual reality in the rehabilitation of people with intellectual disabilities[Review]. *Cyberpsychology & Behavior*, *8*(3), 272–282. doi:10.1089/cpb.2005.8.272 PMID:15971976.

Stanovich, K. (2011). *Rationality and the reflective mind*. Oxford, UK: Oxford University Press..

Stanovich, K. E. (2009). *What intelligence tests miss: The psychology of rational thought*. New Haven, CT: Yale University Press..

Steinkuehler, C. A. (2005). *Cognition & learning in massively multiplayer online games: A critical approach*. Madison, WI: University of Wisconsin-Madison..

Steinkuehler, C., & Duncan, S. (2008). Scientific habits of mind in virtual worlds. *Journal of Science Education and Technology*, *17*(6), 530–543. doi:10.1007/s10956-008-9120-8.

Sternberg, R. J. (1985). *Beyond IQ: A triarchic theory of intelligence*. Cambridge, UK: Cambridge University Press..

Steunenberg, B., Schmidtchen, D., & Koboldt, C. (1999). Strategic power in the European Union: Evaluating the distribution of power in policy games. *Journal of Theoretical Politics*, *11*(3), 339–366. doi:10.1177/09516928 99011003005.

Stewart, K. M. (1997). Beyond entertainment: Using interactive games in web-based instruction. *Journal of Instruction Delivery Systems*, *11*(2), 18–20.

Stoney, S., & Oliver, R. (1999). Can higher order thinking and cognitive engagement be enhanced with multimedia?. *Interactive Multimedia Electronic Journal of Computer-Enhanced Learning, 1*(2).

Subrahmanyam, K., & Greenfield, P. M. (1994). Effect of video game practice on spatial skills in girls and boys. *Journal of Applied Developmental Psychology*, *15*, 13–32. doi:10.1016/0193-3973(94)90004-3.

Subrahmanyam, K., & Greenfield, P. M. (1996). Effect of video game practice on spatial skills in girls and boys. In P. M. Greenfield, & R. R. Cocking (Eds.), *Interacting with video* (pp. 95–114). Norwood, NJ: Ablex Publishing Corp.

Suits, B. (1978). *The grasshopper: Games, life and utopia*. Peterborough, Canada: Broadview Press..

Sung, Y.-T., Chang, K.-E., & Lee, M.-D. (2008). Designing multimedia games for young children's taxonomic concept development. *Computers & Education*, *50*(3), 1037–1051. doi:10.1016/j.compedu.2006.07.011.

Sutton-Smith, B. (1997). *The ambiguity of play*. Cambridge, MA: Harvard University Press..

Swaak, J., & de Jong, T. (1996). Measuring intuitive knowledge in science: The development of what-if test. *Studies in Educational Evaluation*, *22*(4), 341–362. doi:10.1016/0191-491X(96)00019-3.

Sweeney, L. B., & Meadows, D. L. (2001). *The systems thinking playbook*. Durham, NC: Pegasus Communication..

Sweetser, P., & Wyeth, P. (2005). GameFlow: A model for evaluating player enjoyment in games. *Computers in Entertainment*, *3*(3), 1–24. doi:10.1145/1077246.1077253.

Sweller, J. (1994). Cognitive load theory, learning difficulty, and instructional design. *Learning and Instruction*, *4*(4), 295–312. doi:10.1016/0959-4752(94)90003-5.

Sweller, J. (1999). *Instructional design in technical areas*. Camberwell, Australia: ACER Press..

Sweller, J., Van Merriënboer, J., & Paas, F. (1998). Cognitive architecture and instructional design. *Educational Psychology Review*, *10*(3), 251–296. doi:10.1023/A:1022193728205.

Szturm, T., Betker, A. L., Moussavi, Z., Desai, A., & Goodman, V. (2011). Effects of an interactive computer game exercise regimen on balance impairment in frail community-dwelling older adults: A randomized controlled trial. *Physical Therapy*, *91*(10), 1449–1462. doi:10.2522/ptj.20090205 PMID:21799138.

Tachibana, A., Noah, J. A., Bronner, S., Ono, Y., & Onozuka, M. (2011). Parietal and temporal activity during a multimodal dance video game: an fNIRS study. *Neuroscience Letters*, *503*(2), 125–130. doi:10.1016/j.neulet.2011.08.023 PMID:21875646.

Tajfel, H. (1972). La catégorisation sociale. *Introduction à la psychologie sociale, 1*, 272–302.

Tajfel, H. (Ed.). (1978). *Differentiation between social groups: Studies in the social psychology of intergroup relations*. Oxford, UK: Academic Press..

Taleb, N. N. (2007). *The black swan: The impact of the highly improbable*. New York: Random House..

Tallir, I. B., Lenoir, M., Valcke, M., & Musch, E. (2007). Do alternative instructional approaches result in different game performance learning outcomes? Authentic assessment in varying game conditions. *International Journal of Sport Psychology*, *38*(3), 263–282.

Tamborini, R., Eastin, M. S., Skalski, P., Lachlan, K., Fediuk, T. A., & Brady, R. (2004). Violent virtual video games and hostile thoughts. *Journal of Broadcasting & Electronic Media*, *48*(3), 335–358.

Tang, J.-Y., Chen, J.-H., Ku, D. T., Chao, L. R., Shih, T. K., & Weng, M. M. (2009). Constructing the 2D Adventure Game-Based Assessment System. In Lecture Notes in Computer Science, 2009, Volume 5686, Advances in Web Based Learning – ICWL.

Tannenbaum, P. H., & Zillmann, D. (1975). *Emotional arousal in the facilitation of aggression through communication* (L. Berkowitz, Ed.). Advances in experimental social psychologyNew York, NY: Academic Press. doi:10.1016/S0065-2601(08)60250-6.

Taylor, J. L. (1971). *Instructional planning systems, a gaming-simulation approach to urban problems.* London: Cambridge University Press. doi:10.1017/CBO9780511720789.

Telkemeyer, S., Rossi, S., Nierhaus, T., Steinbrink, J., Obrig, H., & Wartenburger, I. (2011). Acoustic processing of temporally modulated sounds in infants: Evidence from a combined near-infrared spectroscopy and EEG study. *Frontiers in Psychology*, *1*, 62. doi:10.3389/fpsyg.2011.00062 PMID:21716574.

Ten Brummelhuis, A., & Van Amerongen, M. (2010). *Vier in balans monitor 2010: ICT in het onderwijs: de stand van zaken.* Kennisnet. Retrieved February 2, 2011, from http://onderzoek.kennisnet.nl/vierinbalansmonitor

Terlecki, M., Brown, J., Harner-Steciw, L., Irvin-Hannum, J., Marchetto-Ryan, N., Ruhl, L., & Wiggins, J. (2011). Sex differences and similarities in video game experience, preferences, and self-efficacy: Implications for the gaming industry. *Current Psychology (New Brunswick, N.J.)*, *30*(1), 22–33. doi:10.1007/s12144-010-9095-5.

Terlecki, M., & Newcombe, N. (2005). How important is the digital divide? The relation of computer and videogame usage to gender differences in mental rotation ability. *Sex Roles*, *53*(5/6), 433–441. doi:10.1007/s11199-005-6765-0.

Ternier, S., Klemke, R., Kalz, M., Van Ulzen, P., & Specht, M. (2012). ARLearn: Augmented reality meets augmented virtuality. *Journal of Universal Computer Science - Technology for Learning across Physical and Virtual Spaces.*

Terras, M. M., & Ramsay, J. (2013). *A psychological perspective on the temporal dimensions of e-learning.* E-Learning and Digital Media..

Thaler, R. H., & Sunstein, C. R. (2008). *Nudge: Improving decisions about health, wealth, and happiness.* New Haven, CT: Yale University Press..

Thalmann, D., Hery, C., Lippman, S., Ono, H., Regelous, S., & Sutton, D. (2004). Crowd and group animation. In *ACM SIGGRAPH 2004 course notes* (p. 34). Retrieved from http://dl.acm.org/citation.cfm?id=1103934

The Critical Thinking Co. (2005). Retrieved from http://www.criticalthinking.com/company/articles/critical-thinking-definition.jsp

Thomas, J. M., & Young, R. M. (2010). Annie: Automated Generation of Adaptive Learner Guidance For Fun Serious Games. In IEEE Transactions on Learning Technologies, 3(4)..

Thomas, P., Labat, J.-M., Muratet, M., & Yessad, A. (2012). How to Evaluate Competencies in Game-Based Learning Systems Automatically? In Lecture Notes in Computer Science, 7315, Intelligent Tutoring System.

Thomas, K. W. (1976). Conflict and conflict management. In *Handbook of industrial and organizational psychology.* Chicago: Rand McNally..

Thorndike, R. K. (1920). Intelligence and its uses. *Harper's Magazine, 140*, 227-335.

Tillman, C., Eninger, L., Forssman, L., & Bohlin, G. (2011). The relation between working memory components and ADHD symptoms from a developmental perspective. *Developmental Neuropsychology*, *36*(2), 181–198. doi:10.1080/87565641.2010.549981 PMID:21347920.

Tobias, S., & Fletcher, J. D. (2011). *Computer games and instructions.* Charlotte, NC: Information Age Publishers..

Tobias, S., Fletcher, J. D., Dai, D. Y., & Wind, A. P. (2011). Review of research on computer games. In S. Tobias, & J. D. Fletcher (Eds.), *Computer games and instruction* (pp. 127–222). Charlotte, NC: Information Age Publishers..

Toms, M., Morris, N., & Ward, D. (1993). Working memory and conditional reasoning. *The Quarterly Journal of Experimental Psychology Section A*, *46*(4), 679–699. doi:10.1080/14640749308401033.

Torrente, J., & Lavín-Mera, P. Moreno-Ger, P., & Fernandez-Manjon, B. (2008). Coordinating Heterogeneous Game-based Learning Approaches in Online Learning Environments. *In Proceedings of Sixth International Game Design and Technology Workshop and Conference (GDTW2008)*, 27-36, Liverpool, UK.

Torrente, J., Del Blanco, Á., Marchiori, E. J., Moreno-Ger, P., & Fernández-Manjón, B. (2010). e-Adventure: Introducing educational games in the learning process. In *Proceedings of the IEEE EDUCON 2010 Conference*. Madrid, Spain: IEEE.

Torrente, J., Moreno-Ger, P., Fernandez-Manjon, B., & Sierra, J. L. (2008). Instructor-oriented Authoring Tools for Educational Videogames. In *Proceedings of 8th International Conference on Advanced Learning Technologies*.

Tran, B. (2008). *Expatriate selection and retention*. (Doctoral dissertation). Alliant International University, San Francisco, CA.

Trepte, S., & Reinecke, L. (2011). The pleasures of success: Game-related efficacy experiences as a mediator between player performance and game enjoyment. *Cyberpsychology Behavior and Social Networking*, *14*(9), 555–557. doi:10.1089/cyber.2010.0358 PMID:21342012.

Turkay, S., & Adinolf, S. (2012). What do players (think they) learn in games?. *Procedia - Social and Behavioral Sciences, 46*, 3345–3349.

Turkle, S. (1984). *The second self: Computers and the human spirit*. New York, NY: Simon & Schuster..

Turkle, S. (1995). *Life on the screen: Identity in the age of the internet*. New York: Simon and Schuster..

Turner, J. C. (1978). Social categorization and social discrimination in the minimal group paradigm. In H. Tajfel (Ed.), *Differentiation between social groups: Studies in the social psychology of intergroup relations*. Oxford, UK: Academic Press..

Turner, J. C., Oakes, P. J., Alexander, S., & McGarty, C. (1994). Self and collective: Cognition and social context. *Personality and Social Psychology Bulletin*, *20*(5), 454–463. doi:10.1177/0146167294205002.

Tuzun, H. (2007). Blending video games with learning: Issues and challenges with classroom implementations in the Turkish context. *British Journal of Educational Technology*, *38*(3), 465–477. doi:10.1111/j.1467-8535.2007.00710.x.

Tuzun, H., Yilmazsoylu, M., Karakus, T., & Inal, Y., KIzIlkaya, G., Tüzün, H., & YIlmaz-Soylu, M. (2009). The effects of computer games on primary school students' achievement and motivation in geography learning. *Computers & Education*, *52*(1), 68–77. doi:10.1016/j.compedu.2008.06.008.

Tykhonov, D., Jonker, C., & Meijer, S. A. (2008). *Agent-based simulation of the trust and tracing game for supply chains and networks, & social simulation*. Retrieved May 3, 2013, from http://jasss.soc.surrey.ac.uk/11/3/1.html

U.S. Department of Education, National Center for Education Statistics. (2000). *Internet access in U.S. public schools and classrooms: 1994–99*. Washington, DC: NCES..

UK Assessment Reform Group. (1999). *Assessment for learning: beyond the black box*. Cambridge: University of Cambridge School of Education..

Ulicny, B., & Thalmann, D. (2001). Crowd simulation for interactive virtual environments and VR training systems. In P. D. N. Magnenat-Thalmann & D. D. Thalmann (Eds.), *Computer Animation and Simulation 2001* (pp. 163–170). Vienna: Springer. Retrieved from http://link.springer.com/chapter/10.1007/978-3-7091-6240-8_15

Underwood, J. S., Kruse, S., & Jakl, P. (2010). Moving to the Next Level: Designing Embedded Assessments into Educational Games. In P. Zemliansky, & D. Wilcox (Eds.), *Design and Implementation of Educational Games: Theoretical and Practical Perspectives*. doi:10.4018/978-1-61520-781-7.ch009.

Usart, M., Romero, M., & Almirall, E. (2011). Impact of the feeling of knowledge explicitness in the learners' participation and performance in a collaborative game based learning activity. *Lecture Notes in Computer Science*, *6944*, 23–35. doi:10.1007/978-3-642-23834-5_3.

Vala, M., Ribeiro, T., & Paiva, A. (2012). A model for embodied cognition in autonomous agents. In *Proceedings of IVA* (pp. 505–507). IVA.

Van der Spek, E. D. (2011). (n.d.). *Experiments in serious game design: A cognitive approach*. Retrieved May 3, 2013, from http://www.narcis.nl/publication/RecordID/oai:dspace.library.uu.nl:1874/211480

Van der Spek, E. D., Wouters, P., & Van Oostendorp, H. (2011). Code red: Triage or cognition-based design rules enhancing decisionmaking training in a game environment. *British Journal of Educational Technology*, *42*(3), 441–455. doi:10.1111/j.1467-8535.2009.01021.x.

Van Houten, S. P. A. (2007, November 6). *A suite for developing and using business games: Supporting supply chain business games in a distributed context*. Retrieved from http://www.narcis.nl/publication/RecordID/oai:tudelft. nl:uuid:006a4dfd-8aba-47e5-8a15-c481eace87e1

Van Merriënboer, J., & Sweller, J. (2005). Cognitive load theory and complex learning: Recent developments and future directions. *Educational Psychology Review*, *17*(2).

van Meurs, R. (2011). Then you wait: The issue of dead time in social network games. In *Proceedings of DiGRA 2011 Conference* (Vol. 7). DiGRA.

van Reekum, C. M., Johnstone, T., Banse, R., Etter, A., Wehrle, T., & Scherer, K. R. (2004). Psychophysiological responses to appraisal dimensions in a computer game. *Cognition and Emotion*, *18*, 663–688. doi:10.1080/02699930341000167.

Van Rosmalen, P., & Westera, W. (2012). Introducing serious games with wikis: Empowering the teacher with simple technologies. *Interactive Learning Environments*. doi:10.1080/10494820.2012.707128.

van Ruijven, T. (n.d.). *Virtual emergency management training*. Delft, The Netherlands: Delft University of Technology.

Van Staalduinen, J. P. (2012). *Gamers on games and gaming: Implications for Educational game design*. Delft, The Netherlands: TU Delft..

VanDeventer, S. S., & White, J. A. (2002). Expert behaviour in children's video game play. *Simulation & Gaming*, *33*(1), 28–48. doi:10.1177/1046878102033001002.

Vannini, N., Enz, S., Sapouna, M., Wolke, D., Watson, S., & Woods, S. et al. (2010). FearNot! A computer-based anti-bullying-programme designed to foster peer intervention. *European Journal of Psychology of Education*.

Varoufakis, Y. (2008). Game theory: Can it unify the social sciences? *Organization Studies*, *29*(8-9), 1255–1277. doi:10.1177/0170840608094779.

Vartiainen, P. (2000). *Evaluation methods and comparative study*. Retrieved May 3, 2013, from http://cjpe.ca/distribution/20001012_vartiainen_pirkko.pdf

Ventura, M., Shute, V. J., & Zhao, W. (2013). The relationship between video game use and a performance-based measure of persistence. *Computers & Education*, *60*, 52–58. doi:10.1016/j.compedu.2012.07.003.

Verdaasdonk, E. G. G., Dankelman, J., Schijven, M. P., Lange, J. F., Wentink, M., & Stassen, L. P. S. (2009). Serious gaming and voluntary laparoscopic skills training: A multicenter study. *Official Journal of the Society for Minimally Invasive Therapy*, *18*(4), 232–238. doi:10.1080/13645700903054046.

Vermunt, J. D. (1994). *Inventory of learning styles in higher education*. Leiden, The Netherlands: Leiden University..

Vernon, D. (2005). Can neurofeedback training enhance performance? An evaluation of the evidence with implications for future research. *Applied Psychophysiology and Biofeedback*, *30*(4), 347–364. doi:10.1007/s10484-005-8421-4 PMID:16385423.

Vernon, D., Egner, T., Cooper, N., Compton, T., Neilands, C., Sheri, A., & Gruzelier, J. (2003). The effect of training distinct neurofeedback protocols on aspects of cognitive performance. *International Journal of Psychophysiology: Official Journal of the International Organization of Psychophysiology*, *47*(1), 75–85. doi:10.1016/S0167-8760(02)00091-0 PMID:12543448.

Veurink, N. L., Hamlin, A. J., Kampe, J. C., Sorby, S. A., Blasko, D. G., & Holliday-Darr, K. A. et al. (2009). Enhancing visualization skills-improving options and success (EnViSIONS). *Engineering Design Graphics Journal*, *73*(2), 1–17.

Vier in Balans Monitor. (2012). Retrieved December 5, 2012, from http://www.kennisnet.nl/fileadmin/contentelementen/kennisnet/Over.kennisnet/vier-in-balans-2012.pdf

Villringer, A., & Chance, B. (1997). Non-invasive optical spectroscopy and imaging of human brain function. *Trends in Neurosciences*, *20*(10), 435–442. doi:10.1016/S0166-2236(97)01132-6 PMID:9347608.

Virtual Reality at Ford Motor Company. (n.d.). Retrieved April 11, 2013, from http://www.youtube.com/watch?v=zmeR-u-DioE

Virvou, M., Katsionis, G., & Manos, K. (2005). Combining software games with education: Evaluation of its educational effectiveness. *Journal of Educational Technology & Society*, *8*(2), 54–65.

Vohs, K. D., Baumeister, R. F., Schmeichel, B. J., Twenge, J. M., Nelson, N. M., & Tice, D. M. (2008). Making choices impairs subsequent self-control: A limited-resource account of decision making, self-regulation, and active initiative. *Journal of Personality and Social Psychology*, *94*(5), 883. doi:10.1037/0022-3514.94.5.883 PMID:18444745.

Von Ahn, & Dabbish. (2004). Labeling images with a computer game. In *Proceedings of the SIGCHI Conference on Human Factors in Computing Systems* (pp. 319–326). Vienna, Austria: ACM.

Vorderer, P. Wulff, & Friedrichsen, M. (1996). Suspense: Conceptualizations, theoretical analyses, and empirical explorations. Mahwah, NJ: Routledge..

Vorderer, P., Klimmt, C., & Ritterfield, U. (2004). Enjoyment: At the heart of media entertainment. *Communication Theory*, *14*(4), 388–408. doi:10.1111/j.1468-2885.2004.tb00321.x.

Vorhaus, J. (1994). *The comic toolbox: How to be funny even if you're not.* Los Angeles, CA: Silman-James Press..

Vos, N., van der Meijden, H., & Denessen, E. (2011). Effects of constructing versus playing an educational game on student motivation and deep learning strategy use. *Computers & Education*, *56*(1), 127–137. doi:10.1016/j.compedu.2010.08.013.

Voyer, D., Voyer, S., & Bryden, M. P. (1995). Magnitude of sex differences in spatial abilities: A meta-analysis and consideration of critical variables. *Psychological Bulletin*, *117*(3), 250–270. doi:10.1037/0033-2909.117.2.250 PMID:7724690.

Vygotsky, L. S. (1978). *Mind in society: The development of higher psychological processes.* Cambridge, MA: Harvard University Press..

Wagner, D. Schmalstieg, D., & Billinghurst, M. (2006). Handheld AR for Collaborative Edutainment. *Advances in Artificial Reality and Tele-Existence.* Lecture Notes in Computer Science Springer Berlin / Heidelberg.

Wagner, P., Schober, B., & Spiel, C. (2008). Time students spend working at home for school. *Learning and Instruction*, *18*, 309–320. doi:10.1016/j.learninstruc.2007.03.002.

Walsh, A. (2012). *Final report on lemon tree, May 2012.* Retrieved April 4, 2013 from http://www.hud.ac.uk/tali/projects/tl_projects_11/lemon_tree/

Wang, H.-S., Chou, C.-H., Tsai, S.-N., & Hung, H.-J. (2012). The study of motivation and reasoning faculties of game-based learning in elementary school students. In *Proceedings of 2010 2nd International Conference on Education Technology and Computer (ICETC)*. ICETC.

Wang, Q., Sourina, O., & Nguyen, M. K. (2010). EEG-based serious games design for medical applications. In *Proceedings of 2010 International Conference on Cyberworlds* (pp. 270–276). Singapore: IEEE. doi:10.1109/CW.2010.56

Wang, T. (2012). *How must - see TV is now must - tweet TV.* Retrieved from http://www.youtube.com/watch?v=GCbhiBDsJDI&list=PL59D0CB455E1F5014&index=4

Wang, Q., Sourina, O., & Nguyen, M. K. (2011). Fractal dimension based neurofeedback in serious games. *The Visual Computer*, *27*(4), 299–309. doi:10.1007/s00371-011-0551-5.

Wassarman, H. S. (2002). The role of expectancies and time perspectives in gambling behaviour. *Dissertation Abstracts International. B, The Sciences and Engineering*, *62*(8B), 3818.

Watson, D., Clark, L. A., & Tellegen, A. (1988). Development and validation of brief measures of positive and negative affect: The PANAS scales. *Journal of Personality and Social Psychology*, *54*(6), 1063–1070. doi:10.1037/0022-3514.54.6.1063 PMID:3397865.

Webster, J., Trevino, L. K., & Ryan, L. (1993). The dimensionality and correlates of flow in human-computer interactions. *Computers in Human Behavior*, *9*, 411–426. doi:10.1016/0747-5632(93)90032-N.

Wegerif, R. (2002). *Literature review in thinking skills, technology and learning.* Retrieved from http://archive.futurelab.org.uk/resources/documents/lit_reviews/Thinking_Skills_Review.pdf

Weibel, D., Wissmath, B., Habegger, S., Steiner, Y., & Groner, R. (2008). Playing online games against computer-vs. human-controlled opponents: Effects on presence, flow, and enjoyment. *Computers in Human Behavior, 24*(5), 2274–2291. doi:10.1016/j.chb.2007.11.002.

Weiskopf, N. (2012). Real-time fMRI and its application to neurofeedback. *NeuroImage, 62*(2), 682–692. doi:10.1016/j.neuroimage.2011.10.009 PMID:22019880.

Weiss, C. H. (1997). Theory-based evaluation: Past, present, and future. *New Directions for Evaluation,* (76): 41–55. doi:10.1002/ev.1086.

Weng, M. M., Fakinlede, I., Lin, F., Shih, T. K., & Chang, M. (2011). A Conceptual Design of Multi-Agent based Personalised Quiz Game. In *Proceedings of 11ᵗʰ IEEE International Conference on Advanced Technologies.*

Wenzler, I. (2008). The ten commandments for translating simulation results into real-life performance. *Simulation & Gaming, 40*(1), 98–109. doi:10.1177/1046878107308077.

Weppel, S., Bishop, M., & Munoz-Avila, H. (2012). The design of scaffolding in game-based learning: A formative evaluation. *Journal of Interactive Learning Research, 23*(4), 361–392.

Westera, W., Nadolski, R. J., Hummel, H. G. K., & Wopereis, I. (2008). Serious games for higher education: A framework for reducing design complexity. *Journal of Computer Assisted Learning, 24*(5), 420–432. doi:10.1111/j.1365-2729.2008.00279.x.

White, M. (2008). *Level 10 human student: The effects of non-curricular role-playing game use on academic achievement and self-efficacy.* (Master's Thesis). University of New Brunswick, Fredericton, Canada.

White, M. (2012a). *New tutorials for digital games: Game design meets instructional design.* (Ph.D. Dissertation). Memorial University of Newfoundland, St. John's, Canada.

White, B. Y. (1984). Designing computer games to help physics students understand Newton's laws of motion. *Cognition and Instruction, 1*(1), 69–108. doi:10.1207/s1532690xci0101_4.

Whitebread, D. (1997). Developing children's problem-solving: The educational uses of adventure games. In A. Mc Farlane (Ed.), *Information technology and authentic learning: Realising the potential of computers in the primary classroom* (pp. 13–37). London: Routledge..

White, M. (2009). The senescence of creativity: How market forces are killing digital games. *Loading, 3*(4), 1–20.

White, M. (2012b). Designing tutorial modalities and strategies for digital games: Lessons from education. *International Journal of Game-Based Learning, 2*(2), 13–34. doi:10.4018/ijgbl.2012040102.

Whitlock, L. A., McLaughlin, A. C., & Allaire, J. C. (2012). Individual differences in response to cognitive training: Using a multi-modal, attentionally demanding game-based intervention for older adults. *Computers in Human Behavior, 28,* 1091–1096. doi:10.1016/j.chb.2012.01.012.

Whitson, J., & Dormann, C. (2011). Social gaming for change: Facebook unleashed. *First Monday, 16,* 10–13. doi:10.5210/fm.v16i10.3578.

Whitton, N. (2007). *An investigation into the potential of collaborative computer game-based learning in higher education.* (Unpublished doctoral dissertation). Edinburgh Napier University, Edinburgh, UK.

Whitton, N. (2010a). *Assessment of game-based learning.* Retrieved January 24, 2013 from http://www.transformingassessment.com/events_27_october_2010.php

Whitton, N. (2010b). *Learning with digital games: A practical guide to engaging students in higher education. New York, NY.* Abingdon: Routledge..

Wideman, H. H., Owston, R. D., Brown, C., Kushniruk, A., Ho, F., & Pitts, K. C. (2007). Unpacking the potential of educational gaming: a new tool for gaming research. *Simulation & Gaming, 38*(1), 10–30. doi:10.1177/1046878106297650.

Wieman, C., Perkins, K. K., & Adams, W. K. (2007). Interactive simulations for teaching physics: What works, what doesn't, and why. *American Journal of Physics, 76*(4-5).

Wiliam, D., & Thompson, M. (2008). Integrating assessment with instruction: What will it take to make it work? In C. A. Dwyer (Ed.), *The future of assessment: Shaping teaching and learning* (pp. 53–82). Mahwah, NJ: Lawrence Erlbaum Associates..

Williams, D., Martins, N., Consalvo, M., & Ivory, J. D. (2009). The virtual census: Representations of gender, race and age in video games. *New Media & Society, 11*(5), 815–834. doi:10.1177/1461444809105354.

Williams, D., & Skoric, M. (2005). Internet fantasy violence: A test of aggression in an online game. *Communication Monographs, 72*(2), 217–233. doi:10.1080/03637750500111781.

Williamson, B. (2009). *Computer games, schools, and young people: A report for educators on using games for learning*. Retrieved from http://archive.futurelab.org.uk/resources/documents/project_reports/becta/Games_and_Learning_educators_report.pdf

Wilson, A., Connolly, T. M., Hainey, T., & Moffat, D. (2011). Evaluation of introducing programming to younger school children using a computer game construction application. In *Proceedings of 5th European Conference on Games-based Learning*. Athens, Greece: IEEE.

Wilson, A., Hainey, T., & Connolly, T. (2012). Evaluation of computer games developed by primary school children to gauge understanding of programming concepts. In *Proceedings of the 6th European Conference on Games Based Learning*. Cork, Ireland: IEEE.

Wilson, K. A., Bedwell, W. L., Lazzara, E. H., Salas, E., Burke, C. S., & Estock, J. L. et al. (2009). Relationships between game attributes and learning outcomes: Reviews and research proposals. *Simulation & Gaming, 40*(2), 217–266. doi:10.1177/1046878108321866.

Winkel, M., Novak, D., & Hopson, H. (1987). Personality factors, subject gender and the effects of aggressive video games on aggression in adolescents. *Journal of Research in Personality, 2*(1), 211–223. doi:10.1016/0092-6566(87)90008-0.

Winter, D. G. (1988). The power motive in women—and men. *Journal of Personality and Social Psychology, 54*(3), 510–519. doi:10.1037/0022-3514.54.3.510.

Winter, D. G. (1992). Power motivation revisited. In C. P. Smith (Ed.), *Motivation and personality: Handbook of Thematic Content Analysis*. Cambridge, UK: Cambridge University Press. doi:10.1017/CBO9780511527937.022.

Wittgenstein, L. (1953). *Philosophical investigations*. Oxford, UK: Blackwell..

Wohn, D. Y., Lampe, C., Wash, R., Ellison, N., & Vitak, J. (2011). The S in social network games: Initiating, maintaining, and enhancing relationships. In *Proceedings of the 2011 44th Hawaii International Conference on System Sciences*. doi:10.1109/HICSS.2011.400

Wolfe, J., & Box, T. M. (1988). Team cohesion effects on business game performance. *Simulation & Gaming, 19*(1), 82–98. doi:10.1177/003755008801900105.

Wolpaw, J. R., Birbaumer, N., McFarland, D. J., Pfurtscheller, G., & Vaughan, T. M. (2002). Brain-computer interfaces for communication and control. *Clinical Neurophysiology: Official Journal of the International Federation of Clinical Neurophysiology, 113*(6), 767–791. doi:10.1016/S1388-2457(02)00057-3 PMID:12048038.

Wood, D., Bruner, J. S., & Ross, G. (1976). The role of tutoring in problem solving. *Journal of Child Psychology and Psychiatry, and Allied Disciplines, 17*, 89–100. doi:10.1111/j.1469-7610.1976.tb00381.x PMID:932126.

Wood, R. T. A., Griffiths, M. D., & Eatough, V. (2004). Online data collection from video game players: Methodological issues. *Cyberpsychology & Behavior, 7*(5), 511–518. doi: doi:10.1089/cpb.2004.7.511 PMID:15667045.

Wooldridge, M. (2002). *An introduction to multiagent systems*. Hoboken, NJ: John Wiley & Sons..

Woolfson, L. M. (2011). *Educational psychology: The impact of psychological research on education*. London: Prentice Hall, Pearson Education..

Wouters, P., van der Spek, E., & van Oostendorp, H. (2009). Current practices in serious game research: A review from a learning outcomes perspective. In Connolly, Stansfield, & Boyle (Eds.), Games-based learning: Techniques and effective practices. Hershey, PA: IGI Global..

Wouters, P., van der Spek, E. D., & van Oostendorp, H. (2011). Measuring Learning in Serious Games; A Case Study with Structural Assessment. *Educational Technology Research and Development*, *59*(6), 741–763. doi:10.1007/s11423-010-9183-0.

Wriessnegger, S. C., Kurzmann, J., & Neuper, C. (2008). Spatio-temporal differences in brain oxygenation between movement execution and imagery: A multichannel near-infrared spectroscopy study. *International Journal of Psychophysiology: Official Journal of the International Organization of Psychophysiology*, *67*(1), 54–63. doi:10.1016/j.ijpsycho.2007.10.004 PMID:18006099.

Wright, J. D., & Marsden, P. V. (Eds.). (2010). *Handbook of survey research* (2nd ed.). Bingley, UK: Emerald Group Publishing..

Wu, W.-H., Hsiao, H.-C., Wu, P.-L., Lin, C.-H., & Huang, S.-H. (2011). Investigating the learning-theory foundations of game-based learning: A meta-analysis. *Journal of Computer Assisted Learning*, *28*. doi:doi:10.1111/j.1365-2729.2011.00437.x.

Yan, N., Wang, J., Liu, M., Zong, L., Jiao, Y., & Yue, J. et al. (2008). Designing a brain-computer interface device for neurofeedback using virtual environments. *Journal of Medical and Biological Engineering*, *28*(3), 167–172.

Yee, N. (2006b). The psychology of massively multi-user online role-playing games: Motivations, emotional investment, relationships and problematic usage. In R. Schroeder, & A. Axelsson (Eds.), *Avatars at work and play: Collaboration and interaction in shared virtual environments* (pp. 187–207). London: Springer-Verlag. doi:10.1007/1-4020-3898-4_9.

Yee, N. (2006c). The demographics, motivations, and derived experiences of users of massively multi-user online graphical environments. *Presence (Cambridge, Mass.)*, *15*(3), 309–329. doi:10.1162/pres.15.3.309.

Yee, N. (2007). Motivations of play in online games. *Journal of CyberPsychology and Behavior*, *9*, 772–775. doi:10.1089/cpb.2006.9.772 PMID:17201605.

Yongyuth, P., Prada, R., Nakasone, A., Kawtrakul, A., & Prendinger, H. (2010). AgriVillage: 3D multi-language internet game for fostering agriculture environmental awareness. In *Proceeding of the International Conference on Management of Emergent Digital Ecosystems*. New York: ACM.

Yoo, S., Lee, J., O'Leary, H., Panych, L. P., & Jolesz, F. A. (2008). Neurofeedback fMRI-mediated learning and consolidation of regional brain activation during motor imagery. *International Journal of Imaging Systems and Technology*, *18*(1), 69–78. doi:10.1002/ima.20139 PMID:19526048.

Yoo, S.-S., Fairneny, T., Chen, N.-K., Choo, S.-E., Panych, L. P., & Park, H. et al. (2004). Brain–computer interface using fMRI: Spatial navigation by thoughts. *Neuroreport*, *15*(10), 1591–1595. doi:10.1097/01.wnr.0000133296.39160.fe PMID:15232289.

Young, M. F., Slota, S., Cutter, A. B., Jalette, G., Mullin, G., & Lai, B. et al. (2012). Our princess is in another castle: A review of trends in serious gaming for education. *Review of Educational Research*, *82*(1), 61–89. doi:10.3102/0034654312436980.

Zaibon, S. B., & Shiratuddin, N. (2010). Adapting Learning Theories in Mobile Game-Based Learning Development. In *Proceedings of IEEE International Conference on Digital Game and Intelligent Toy Enhanced Learning*.

Zakay, D. (2000). Gating or switching? Gating is a better model of prospective timing. *Behavioural Processes*, *50*, 1–7. doi:10.1016/S0376-6357(00)00086-3 PMID:10925031.

Zakay, D. (2012). Experiencing time in daily life. *The Psychologist*, *25*(8), 578–581.

Zapata-Rivera, D., VanWinkle, W., Doyle, B., Buteux, A., & Bauer, M. (2009). Combining learning and assessment in assessment-based gaming environments: A case study from a New York City school. *Interactive Technology and Smart Education*, *6*(3), 173–188. doi:10.1108/17415650911005384.

Zap, N., & Code, J. (2009). Self-regulated learning in video game environments. In R. E. Ferdig (Ed.), *Handbook of Research on Effective Electronic Gaming in Education* (pp. 738–756). Hershey, PA: IGI Global..

Zelazo, P. D., Qu, L., & Muller, U. (2004). Hot and cool aspects of executive function: Relations in early development. In W. Schneider, R. Schumann-Hengsteler, & B. Sodian (Eds.), *Young children's cognitive development: Interrelationships among executive functioning, verbal ability and theory or mind* (pp. 71–93). Mahwah, NJ: Erlbaum..

Zhang, X., & Furnas, G. (2002). Social interactions in multiscale CVEs. In *Proceedings of 4ᵗʰ International ACM Conference on Collaborative Virtual Environments*. Bonn, Germany: ACM.

Zhao, Q., Zhang, L., & Cichocki, A. (2009). EEG-based asynchronous BCI control of a car in 3D virtual reality environments. *Chinese Science Bulletin, 54*(1), 78–87. doi:10.1007/s11434-008-0547-3.

Zichermann, G., & Linder, J. (2010). *Game-based marketing: Inspire customer loyalty through rewards, challenges, and contests*. Hoboken, NJ: Wiley..

Zielke, M. A., Evans, M. J., Dufour, F., Christopher, T. V., Donahue, J. K., Johnson, P., et al. (2009). Serious Games for Immersive Cultural Training. In *Proceedings of IEEE Computer Graphics and Applications*.

Zillmann, D. (1988a). Mood management through communication choices. *The American Behavioral Scientist, 31*(3), 327–340. doi:10.1177/000276488031003005.

Zillmann, D. (1988b). Mechanism of emotional involvement with drama. *Poetics, 23*(1/2), 33–51.

Zillmann, D. (1996). The psychology of suspense in dramatic expositions. In P. Vorderer, H. J. Wagele, & R. Baron (Eds.), *The enneagram made easy* (pp. 199–232). New York: HarperOne..

Zillmann, M. (1994). *Behavioral expressions and biosocial bases of sensation seeking*. Cambridge, UK: Cambridge University Press..

Zimbardo, P. G., & Boyd, J. N. (1999). Putting time into perspective: A valid, reliable individual differences metric. *Journal of Personality and Social Psychology, 77*, 1271–1288. doi:10.1037/0022-3514.77.6.1271.

Zimbardo, P. G., Keough, K. A., & Boyd, J. N. (1997). Present time perspective as a predictor of risky driving. *Personality and Individual Differences, 23*, 1007–1023. doi:10.1016/S0191-8869(97)00113-X.

Zimmerman, B. J. (2002). Becoming a self-regulated learner: An overview. *Theory into Practice, 41*(2), 64–70. doi:10.1207/s15430421tip4102_2.

Zwikael, O., & Gonen, A. (2007). Project execution game (PEG), training towards managing unexpected events. *Journal of European Industrial Training, 31*(6), 495–512. doi:10.1108/03090590710772668.

Zyda, M. (2005). From visual simulation to virtual reality to games. *IEEE Computer*, 25-32.

About the Contributors

Thomas Connolly is Professor and Head of Creative Technologies at the University of the West of Scotland, Director of the Research Institute for Creative Technologies and Applied Computing (ICTAC) and Chair of the Centre for ICT in Education (ICTE). He has published over 150 papers in online learning, games-based learning, Web 2.0 technologies, and database systems. He is also Director of the Scottish Centre for Enabling Technologies (SCET), whose mission is to support large and small companies in the adoption of emerging technologies, particularly with the Creative Industries sector. In the past 5 years, he has managed over 150 projects with Scottish companies, increasing company turnover by over £65 million and creating 500 jobs and safeguarding a further 900 jobs.

Thomas Hainey is a Lecturer of Computer Games Technology at the University of the West of Scotland and an active researcher in the Centre of Excellence for Serious Games and a member of the GALA Network of Excellent in Serious Game. His doctoral thesis focused on the development and evaluation of a computer game to teach requirements collection and analysis at tertiary education level. His main research interests are evaluation of serious games, motivations for playing computer games for educational purposes, assessment and content integration for serious games, and emotional AI. He has a number of journal publications and conference publications in this area and has worked on a number of European projects associated with Serious Games.

Elizabeth Boyle is a reader in psychology at the University of the West of Scotland. Her research interests are in thinking, learning, language, communication, and motivation. More recently, she has followed up these interests in the area of e-learning and digital games with publications in the area of engagement and learning in digital games. Elizabeth has been involved in research on games, including the GALA project, a European network of academics and businesses interested in serious games, and the CHERMUG project, which aims to design and develop a game to teach research methods and statistics to nurses and social scientists.

Gavin Baxter is a Lecturer in Games Technology at the University of the West of Scotland. He is a member of the University's Information and Communication Technologies in Education (ICTE) Research Group. His research interests include the application of Web 2.0 and games technologies within Higher Education and Enterprises for the purposes of supporting learning, knowledge creation, and dissemination.

Pablo Moreno-Ger is an Associate Professor in the Department of Software Engineering and Artificial Intelligence at Complutense University of Madrid (UCM). He is a member of the e-UCM research group and his research interests cover the different technical, engineering, and educational challenges faced in the integration of educational games in the learning flow. Within that area, his research focuses on facilitating the participation and involvement of instructors, through the use of simplified authoring tools as well as through the development of automated tracking and reporting techniques that give instructors insight into how the students are learning. He has authored over 50 scientific publications related to these topics.

* * *

Yulia Bachvarova is currently working as a senior researcher at Cyntelix BV on FP7 EU projects related to serious games. Her main research interests are in incorporating pedagogical principles in serious games and the interrelation between pedagogical and engagement principles, designing metrics for the effectiveness of serious games for corporate training, Social Network Analysis, and Social TV. She worked previously with the University of Twente, The Netherlands, on automatic generation of multimodal interfaces, University of Lausanne, Switzerland, on the Swiss Virtual Campus federal programme and University of Sofia, Bulgaria, on EU projects in the field of e-learning.

Richard Beeby is Senior Lecturer and Leader of the Computer Games cluster group in the School of Computing at the University of the West of Scotland. He has over 25 years experience teaching in Higher Education and has served as a specialist reviewer in Computing for the Quality Assurance Agency both in the UK and overseas. He is part of the School's research group on ICT in Education and has particular interests in the teaching and assessment of programming and software development.

Geertje Bekebrede is an assistant professor in Policy, Organization, and Gaming in the Faculty of Technology, Policy, and Management, TU Delft, and a senior game designer at Tygron Serious gaming, The Netherlands.

Francesco Bellotti, Assistant Professor, is currently teaching Cyberphysical Systems and Entrepreneurship in the MSc Electronics Engineering. He is in the teaching committee of the Interactive and Cognitive Environments (ICE) Erasmus Mundus Ph. D. programme. His main research interests are in the field of serious games design and development, educational simulations, artificial intelligence, cooperative automotive systems, and HCI. He has been the responsible for the design and implementation WPs of several European FP and Italian industrial research projects. In the field of serious games he is in the coordination team of the Games and Learning Alliance (GaLA) FP7 EU network of excellence on serious games and of the eSG (Stimulating entrepreneurship through serious games in higher education) LLP project, and one of the co-organizers of the NewToo Knows Erasmus IP. He authored 150+ papers in international journals and conferences.

Dawn Blasko is an associate professor of psychology at the Pennsylvania State University at Erie. She received her M.S. and Ph.D. at Binghamton University, State University of New York in experimental psychology. She teaches research methods, cross-cultural psychology and cognitive psychology. Her research focuses on individual differences in linguistic and spatial reasoning. She was an early adopter of educational technology and more recently has focused on ways to develop serious games that can enhance learning in difference populations of learners. She has worked with the multi-university NSF funded project, EnVISIONS-Enhancing Visualization Skills-Improving Options aNd Success. The goal of the EnVISIONS project was to disseminate programs developed at Michigan Tech and Penn State Erie to broad range of institutions in order to develop a spatial visualization curriculum to improve student success and enhance the opportunities for women and minorities.

Holly Blasko-Drabik received her B. S. in psychology at Penn State Erie, the Behrend College in 2001. She attended the University of Central Florida when she completed her M.Sc in Modeling and Simulation and is currently completing her Ph.D. in Applied Psychology and Human Factors. Her dissertation involves developing and validating a method to assess the effectiveness of serious games and simulations. For the past several years, her research focus has focused on the use of virtual technology for simulation and training and on user interface and design. She has conducted several studies with the US Navy examining the important of communication and training methods in learning and recalling material. Her other research interests include studying individual differences in learning styles and working memory on the use of serious games. She has also taught human factors and engineering psychology at Penn State and designed a user interface for teaching and administrative software.

Stefano Bocconi graduated in Electrical Engineering at the Faculty of Florence, Italy. After working for several years in ICT companies, he went back to academia and obtained his Ph.D. in Computer Science at the CWI in Amsterdam, with a thesis titled "Vox Populi: Generating Video Documentaries from Semantically Annotated Media Repositories." Subsequently, he carried on research as a post doc in Model-Based Diagnosis at the Computer Science department, University of Turin, and on Semantic Web at the Knowledge and Reasoning department at the Free University Amsterdam. He is currently working as a senior researcher for Cyntelix, a company involved in several FP7 EU projects.

James Boyle is Professor of Psychology in the School of Psychological Sciences and Health at the University of Strathclyde where he is Director of Postgraduate Professional Training in Educational Psychology. His research interests include language development and language delay and the relationship between executive functions and the cognitive benefits of physical activity and serious games.

António Brisson is a PhD student at Instituto Superior Técnico, Technical University of Lisbon, and a research assistant at the GAIPS research group at INESC-ID. After finishing his MSc in Information Systems Computer Engineering where he developed I-Shadows an Affective and Interactive Drama, he decided to continue his research on the boundaries of theatre and interactive media. He is particularly interested in studying the contributions of cognitive research in improve theatre to interactive storytelling.

Joana Campos is a researcher at the Intelligent and Synthetic Characters Group of INESC-ID. J. Campos has a MSc in computer science from Instituto Superior Técnico (IST), Technical University of Lisbon, and she is pursuing a PhD in autonomous agents at IST. Her research interests include cognition-based agent modelling and affective elements applied to human-agent interaction.

André Carvalho is currently a Software Engineer at Altitude Software. He finished his MSc in Computer Graphics, Multimedia and Software Engineering at Instituto Superior Técnico, Technical University of Lisbon in 2012. His thesis dealt with computational humour and interactive storytelling, using autonomous agents with an underlying emotion framework, and was developed under supervision of Prof. Ana Paiva, as an intern at the GAIPS research group at INESC-ID.

Yaëlle Chaudy is a PhD student at the University of the West of Scotland. She obtained an MSc in computing from INSA Lyon (National Institute of Applied Science) and a bachelor in French as a Second Language from Stendhal University in Grenoble. Interested in both computing and education, she is now studying the integration of assessment in GBL applications.

João Dias is currently an assistant professor at the Computer Science Department of Instituto Superior Técnico – Technical University of Lisbon (IST-UTL), where he teaches courses on Introduction to Programming, Artificial Intelligence, Logic Programing, and Autonomous Agents and Multi-Agent Systems. He is also currently a researcher at the Intelligent Agents and Synthetic Characters Group (GAIPS) of INESC-ID. In his research, he is interested in developing and studying cognitive, emotional and social agents, and is currently exploring the use of emotional intelligence skills in agents to establish social relations with others in interactive scenarios.

Joana Dimas is a research assistant from GAIPS, Intelligent Agents and Synthetic Character Group at INESC-ID. She received her MSc degree in Psychology at Instituto Superior de Psicologia Aplicada, and is currently pursuing a PhD in Information Systems and Computer Engineering at Instituto Superior Técnico – Technical University of Lisbon, on the topic of Virtual Agent's Identity. Her main interests are the improvement of computer game characters and enhancement of player's experience through the combination of cognitive sciences and game design.

Elisabeth V. C. Friedrich studied Psychology at the University of Graz, Austria, and conducted her Masters thesis at the Laboratory of Neural Injury and Repair, Wadsworth Center, Albany, NY. She received her doctorate in natural science in 2012 at the University of Graz, Austria. Her main research interest is Brain-Computer Interfaces (BCI). She explored different mental tasks to control an EEG-based BCI, the impact of distraction on user performance as well as improvements of BCI usability for severely motor impaired individuals. She is currently involved in the EU GALA Network of Excellence (www.galanoe.eu).

Erwin Hartsuiker worked as a software developer for digital EEG systems (clinical neurophysiology, evoked potentials, and brain mapping) from 1986 to1992. He founded the Mind Media enterprise (Netherlands) in 1992 after he became interested in Psychophysiology, Bio- and Neurofeedback. For four years (1988-1992), he was also involved part-time in the computer games industry. Within Mind Media, he is active as senior software developer creating the first Microsoft Windows based data processing and multimedia software platform for Bio and Neurofeedback in 1994, which became a standard in the industry. This software was later renamed to BioTrace+. He also created a new line of portable wireless technology (NeXus-10) for physiological research and bio- and neurofeedback, which was introduced in the year 2004.

Jannicke Baalsrud Hauge is a research scientist at Bremer Institut für Produktion und Logistik (BIBA). She teaches risk management, decision-making, and collaboration in SC at the University of Bremen and Jacobs University. Main interest: Serious games, TEL, use of ICT in logistics. She has been responsible for and managed the BIBA contribution in several EU and national projects in the field of innovation, logistics, ICT for logistics and productions as well as education/training. She is responsible for the BIBA gaming lab. Her main research topic is logistics and risk management in production networks and the mediation of skills using educational games. She has been and is responsible for many WPs in EU and national projects on ICT applications, logistics and serious games and TEL. Authored 100+ papers.

Hans Hummel gained his PhD degree with research on process support within multimedia practicals. He was responsible for the development of various innovative, interactive programs for the acquisition of workplace-based competences for various domains. Amongst others, he led EMERGO project that has developed an approach and toolkit for developing Serious Games (awarded the Comenius Multimedia Award 2008). Hummel has seated in various program committees, is in the editorial board of various journals, and by now has published over 100 articles in peer-reviewed journals. Currently Hans holds both the position of associate professor at the CELSTEC and as chair on the lectorate Workplace learning and ICT' at the NHL University of Applied Science in Leeuwarden, The Netherlands.

Silvia Erika Kober works as a Research Assistant at the University of Graz. Born in Graz, Austria, she received her MSc in Psychology from University of Graz, Austria in 2009. She obtained the Ph.D. degree from the University of Graz, Austria, in 2012. Since 2007, she has worked at the Department of Psychology (Section Neuropsychology) at the University of Graz. She was involved in various nationally and internationally funded research projects. Currently, her work focuses on virtual reality experience and its neuronal underpinnings, virtual reality as rehabilitation tool, and EEG and NIRS based neuro-feedback applications.

Milos Kravcik has a diploma degree in computer science and a doctoral degree in applied informatics from the Comenius University in Slovakia. He has been dealing with Technology Enhanced Learning (TEL) since 1988 in various national and international projects, later also at the Fraunhofer Institute for Applied Information Technology in Germany and at the Open University in The Netherlands. Since 2010, he has been working as a Research Fellow at the RWTH Aachen University and his main research interests include personalized learning environments and self-regulated learning. He co-organized several TEL doctoral schools and serves also as executive peer-reviewer or editorial board member for several journals related to learning technologies.

Jürgen Kurzmann is an associate staff in the Department of Neuropsychology at the University of Graz. He holds a Master degree in Biomedical Engineering from the Graz University of Technology. Currently, he is writing his dissertation on real-time neurofeedback using near-infrared spectroscopy. Another focus of his research is studying the effects of neurofeedback on cognitive performance. Further research interests are mental rotation, motor imagery and brain-computer interfaces. With his technical background as an electronic and software engineer, he has developed several tools for biomedical signal processing. Combining technical engineering and psychological research is one of his favourite passions.

Iolanda Leite is a PhD candidate at Instituto Superior Técnico, Technical University of Lisbon. Her research interests include human-robot interaction and affective computing, concretely in the areas of multimodal perception of social and affective behaviour, user modelling, adaptive behaviour generation, and long-term human-robot interaction. She worked as a research assistant in EU-funded projects LIREC (Living with Robots and IntEractive Companions), MINDRACES (from Reactive to Anticipatory Cognitive Systems), and currently on EMOTE (Embodied-perceptive Tutors for Empathy based learning). In the fall of 2012, she was a visiting researcher at Disney Research, Pittsburgh.

Theodore Lim is an academic researching haptic-VR environments, Serious Games for engineering, neurometrics, knowledge engineering, and human factors. The emphasis of research is in conceptual design of products and integrated systems. Since 1997, he has developed automatic feature recognition algorithms and GPU methods for path planning both of which have since been commercialised. He has also been involved with a number of EU and EPSRC projects, the most recent in the domain of engineering learning via game ware for next generation engineering applications. Since 2009, he has applied games for teaching engineering design and manufacturing.

Heather Lum is a research associate of psychology at Penn State Erie, the Behrend College. She received her Ph.D. in applied experimental and human factors psychology from the University of Central Florida. Her research foci include human-robot interaction, human-animal interaction, and more broadly how individuals perceive and interact with technology. At Behrend, she is responsible for teaching human factors/engineering psychology, human-animal interaction courses, science, technology, and society courses, and the psychology of gaming. She is also the laboratory coordinator for the psychology program. In her downtime, she is a member of a local canine search and rescue team, which is responsible for finding lost individuals in Northwest Pennsylvania.

Carlos Martinho received his PhD degree in Computer Science and Engineering from Instituto Superior Técnico, Technical University of Lisbon. He is currently a Senior Researcher in the Intelligent Agents and Synthetic Character Group at INESC-ID and an Assistant Professor in the Computer Science and Engineering Department of IST. His research focuses on using artificial intelligence to enhance user experience with computer and video games. His research interests include autonomous synthetic characters, affective and anticipatory computing, and user adaptation in serious games. He has co-authored over 100 papers, served on the program committee of international conferences as ACII, IVA, and AAMAS, and as a reviewer for international journals such as *Computational Intelligence*, JAAMAS, and TAFFC. He is currently working in EU FP7 project SIREN, developing intelligent interactive software to support teaching conflict resolution skills to children, and in UTAustin–Portugal cooperation agreement project INVITE, developing autonomous characters with social identity awareness.

Samuel Mascarenhas received the MSc degree in computer science from the Instituto Superior Técnico, in 2009, Lisbon, Portugal. Since then, he is presently a PhD student at the same university, working as a research assistant at the Intelligent Agents and Synthetic Characters Group (GAIPS) / Inesc-ID Taguspark, in Porto Salvo, Portugal. His main research interests are in artificial intelligence, virtual agents and cognitive and affective sciences. In his PhD, he aims to study the integration of cultural aspects in virtual agents. This should improve their ability to act with other humans in social contexts, as human cultures are very different in terms of values, norms, symbols, gestures and rituals.

Igor Mayer is an associate professor in Public Administration and Gaming in the Faculty of Technology, Policy, and Management, and director of the Serious Gaming Research Center, TU Delft, The Netherlands.

Carol McGuinness is Professor of Psychology at Queen's University in Belfast, Northern Ireland. Her research interests are in the applications of cognitive psychology to classroom learning. Specifically, she has researched how teachers can promote the development of children's thinking skills, and the role of educational games in this context. She is director of the ACTS (Activating Children's Thinking Skills) project, which uses an infusion methodology for enhancing children's thinking skills across the curriculum, and has helped launched similar projects in Wales, England, and Scotland. She is author of the influential report, *From Thinking Skills to Thinking Classrooms,* which was commissioned by the UK Department of Education (1999) and acted as an advisor to the Northern Ireland Curriculum Council (CCEA) developing a Framework for Thinking Skills and Personal Capabilities, which is part of their statutory curriculum introduced in 2007.

Ricardo Javier Rademacher Mena obtained his PhD in particle physics in 2002 and immediately started teaching at local universities. Since then, he founded Futur-e-Scape, LLC, a company dedicated to leveraging emergent technologies toward physics education. He has also been extremely active in the world of online higher education having taught at several pure online schools as well as written on best practices for teaching science online. On top of running his company, teaching for offline institution, and teaching for online schools, he is also an avid electric bass player.

Alex Moseley is a National Teaching Fellow, and an Educational Designer and University Teaching Fellow at the University of Leicester, where he has had long experience as both practitioner and researcher of course design and development for higher education. He has particular interests in online and distance education, student engagement, and provision of effective research skills and student induction. His principle research area is in games based learning; he recently co-authored *Using Games to Enhance Teaching and Learning* (Routledge, 2012) and has suggested key features of online immersive games, which can be transferred to higher education to ensure high engagement and community development. He was part of the team behind the first charity Alternative Reality Game, Operation: Sleeper Cell, co-chairs the Association for Learning Technology special interest group on Games and Learning, and co-organises the Let's Change the Game cross-sector conference.

Rob Nadolski is assistant professor technology enhanced learning at the Centre for Learning Sciences and Technologies (CELSTEC) at the Open University of the Netherlands. His main interests are in competence-based education and serious games, especially enhancing learner support facilities by exploiting newest technologies (like sensors). He has done the design and project management of e-learning applications for acquiring complex cognitive skills as well as research on such applications (i.e., serious games) and has participated in various European and national projects. He now participates in the EU-project GaLA.

Christa Neuper obtained her Ph.D. degree from the University of Graz in 1984. From 1985-1986, she worked as Scientific Co-Worker at the Department of Psychology at the University of Graz. Between 1990 and 1994, she was University Assistant at the Institute for Biomedical Engineering, University of Technology Graz, and from 1994-2005, she worked as Senior Scientist at the Ludwig Boltzmann-Institute for Medical Informatics and Neuroinformatics, University of Technology Graz. Between 2002 and 2005, she was Assistant Professor at the Department of Psychology, University of Graz, where she has the rank of a full professor of 'Applied Neuropsychology: Human-Computer Interface' since 2005. Additionally, since 2010 she has the rank of professor at the Institute for Knowledge Discovery, Laboratory of Brain-Computer Interfaces at the University of Technology Graz. Her research topics are EEG-based brain-computer communication and neurofeedback, event-related brain oscillations and cognition, sensorimotor processing in motor actions and motor imagery, sense of presence in virtual realities, and neurophysiology of individual differences in cognition.

Manuel Ninaus is a research assistant and PhD-candidate at the Department of Psychology (Section Neuropsychology) at the University of Graz, Austria. He received his MSc in Psychology from University of Graz, Austria in 2012. Since 2010, he has worked as a Research Assistant at the Department of Psychology and at the University of Graz and is involved in national and international scientific projects. He is currently involved in the EU GALA Network of Excellence (www.galanoe.eu). His research topics are neuronal plasticity through learning, EEG-based neurofeedback and auditory mirror neurons. Furthermore, Manuel Ninaus has many years of experience with different neurophysiological methods such as EEG, NIRS, and fMRI.

Karen Orr is a Research Assistant in the Centre for Effective Education, within the School of Education at Queen's University, Belfast. Her research interests lie broadly within the areas of Psychology and Education, with a focus on attitude measurement, educational programme evaluation, and the use of interactive technologies in the classroom. Karen graduated with a PhD in Psychology in 2011. Her thesis ("Games-Based Learning Environments in the Classroom: Attitudes, Dialogue, and Thinking") focused on the measurement of teacher and pupil attitudes towards games for learning purposes, as well as an exploration of the thinking strategies employed by young people engaged with games in the classroom.

Ana Paiva is an Associate Professor at Instituto Superior Técnico, Technical University of Lisbon and the GAIPS research group leader at INESC-ID. She is well known in the area of Intelligent Agents, Virtual Agents, Affective Computing, and Artificial Intelligence Applied to Education. Her research is focused on the affective elements in the interactions between users and computers and in particular in the creation of affective behavior in synthetic virtual agents. Prof. Ana Paiva served as a member of numerous international conferences and workshops. She has (co)authored over 120 publications in refereed journals, conferences, and books, and coordinated the participation of INESC-ID in many international and national research projects. Prof. Ana Paiva is member of the IEEE, ACM, and AAAI.

Gonçalo Pereira is a PhD student at Instituto Superior Técnico (Technical University of Lisbon) and an assistant researcher at the GAIPS research group of INESC-ID. In 2009, he finished his MSc thesis on adaptive map generation for turn based strategic multiplayer browser games. After this in 2010, he started his PhD studies at the Intelligent Agents and Synthetic Characters Group (GAIPS). His research addresses the concept of social power, its dynamics, and how to integrate those in socially intelligent virtual agents.

Rui Prada is an assistant professor at the Computer Science Department of Instituto Superior Técnico – Technical University of Lisbon (IST-UTL), where he teaches courses on User Centred Design, Socially Intelligent Agents and Game Design and Development. He has a degree in Computer Science with a specialization in Artificial Intelligence. In December 2005, he obtained his doctoral degree, from IST-UTL, in Computer Science with his work on the believability of groups of autonomous synthetic characters. Since 1999, he is a researcher of INESC-ID, where he participated and coordinated several research projects. He develops his current research interests in the fields of Social Intelligent Agents and Computer Games at GAIPS (Intelligent Agents and Synthetic Characters Group) research group. He is co-founder and currently the president of the SPCVideojogos (Sociedade Portuguesa de Ciências dos Videojogos).

Judith Ramsay is a Chartered Psychologist and an Associate Fellow of the British Psychological Society. Judith is a Lecturer in Psychology at the University of the West of Scotland with research interests in the psychology of human-computer interaction.

Bernd Remmele is Professor for Economics Education at the WHL Graduate School of Business and Economics in Lahr, Germany. He gained his doctoral degree in sociology of knowledge. He has directed national and European projects dealing with educational gaming. Further research interests are the development of knowledge structures, educational standards, and business ethics.

Johann Riedel is a senior research fellow in the Centre for Concurrent Enterprise at Nottingham University Business School. Johann has over 140 publications. He has a B.Sc. in electrical and electronic engineering, M.Sc. in social and economic aspects of science and technology and a PhD in design management. His research has focused on innovation, design, engineering and the management thereof. He was one of the key designers of the advanced simulation game for Concurrent Engineering (COSIGA). He has also developed innovative evaluation strategies and methods to validate the learning process and outcomes of simulation based learning. This has included the evaluation cognitive/conceptual change, analysis of communication, and analysis of team processes – knowledge creation, problem solving, decision-making, and negotiation. He also has research interests in design of ICT products and services for the elderly. He has been working in the European Serious Games network of excellence (GaLA).

James Ritchie is a professor specialising in design, manufacture, and manufacturing management. With over 150 publications, his recent research includes product development applications including the use of virtual reality in design and manufacture, rapid prototyping, design process capability analysis and mechanical engineering knowledge and information capture. He has been involved in a large number of EPSRC-funded research projects and Knowledge Transfer Partnerships, all of which involve industrial companies, as well as EU-funded work. He is a member of Heriot-Watt University's Innovative Manufacturing Research Centre's Management Committee and Academic Director of the University's Advanced Manufacturing Unit.

Margarida Romero has a European Ph.D. in Educational Psychology by UMR CNRS (France) and Universitat Autonoma de Barcelona (Extraordinary Ph. D. Award in Psychology). She is a researcher in the FP7 Network of Excellence Games and Learning Alliance (GaLA) for ESADE (Spain) and Assistant Professor in Educational Technologies at the Université Laval (Canada). Her research aims to advance the understanding of the time factor in Computer Supported Collaborative Learning (CSCL) in the contexts of blended and online learning. Her research and teaching interests include also the educational technologies in primary, secondary and tertiary education, with a special focus on Game Based Learning and Serious Games.

Peter van Rosmalen (associate professor) has been active in educational technology since the early eighties as e-learning consultant for the financial and industrial sector. In 2000, he was co-founder and director of a company in e-learning and knowledge management. In 2003, he joined the Centre for Learning Sciences and Technologies at the Open University of The Netherlands. He participated both as a researcher and as a project manager in a large number of Dutch and European research and development projects on topics such as authoring tools, simulations, e-universities, computer-supported cooperative learning, adaptive e-learning, peer support, networked competence, language technologies for learning, and serious games. His current research activities include research on serious games, the application of language technologies in technology enhanced learning, creativity, and learner support services.

Michel Rudnianski holds a Master in History and a Doctorate in Systems Theory, which a specialization on Game Theory. Having developed then theory of Games of Deterrence, and applied it to a variety of fields, he is presently the Head of the MBA and Specialized Masters in Management Branch at the CNAM's Ecole Management and Society in Paris, and teaches decision making, negotiations, and strategy.

Mario Soflano is a Research Fellow at University of the West of Scotland. His doctoral thesis focused on Adaptivity and Personalisation in Games-based Learning. His background education is in computer science. His main interests are computer games technology, games design, educational technology, Web development, adaptive system, and mobile games / software development.

Melody M. Terras is a Chartered Psychologist and an Associate Fellow of the British Psychological Society. Melody is a Lecturer in Psychology at the University of the West of Scotland with research interests in the areas of language, learning disabilities, and psychologically driven applications of educational technology.

Ben Tran received his Doctor of Psychology (Psy.D) in Organizational Consulting/Organizational Psychology from California School of Professional Psychology (formerly known as the Marshall Goldsmith School of Management) at Alliant International University in San Francisco, California, United States of America. Dr. Tran's research interests include domestic and expatriate recruitment, selection, retention, evaluation, training, CSR, business and organizational ethics, organizational/international organizational behaviour, knowledge management, and minorities in multinational corporations. Dr. Tran has presented articles on topics of business and management ethics, expatriate, and gender and minorities in multinational corporations at the Academy of Management, Society for the Advancement of Management, and International Standing Conference on Organizational Symbolism. Dr. Tran has also published articles and book chapters with the *Social Responsibility Journal, Journal of International Trade Law and Policy, Journal of Economics, Finance and Administrative Science*, Financial Management Institute of Canada, and IGI Global.

Mireia Usart has a M.Sc. in e-learning by Universitat Oberta de Catalunya (UOC). She is a PhD candidate in the eLearn Center, Universitat Oberta de Catalunya (UOC). Her PhD paper was awarded 1st prize in eLSE 2012 conference. She is a researcher in the FP7 Network of Excellence Games and Learning Alliance (GaLA) for ESADE (Spain) and a research assistant in the eLearn Center (UOC). Her research aims to advance the understanding of the time factor, concretely time perspective, focused on Game-Based Learning in the contexts of formal adult learning.

Marco Vala is a researcher at the Intelligent Agents and Synthetic Characters Group (GAIPS) of INESC-ID, and a lecturer of information systems and computer engineering at Instituto Superior Técnico, Technical University of Lisbon. He received a diploma degree in information systems and computer engineering and an MSc in intelligent systems and multimedia, both from IST – Technical University of Lisbon. He participated in the EU-funded projects SAFIRA, ELVIS, VICTEC, eCircus, and LIREC. He has (co)authored over 20 publications in refereed journals, conferences, and books. Currently, his research focuses on embodied characters and intelligent bodily behaviour.

Harald Warmelink is an assistant professor in Policy, Organization and Gaming in the Faculty of Technology, Policy, and Management, TU Delft.

Matthew White received a B. A. and B. Ed. from Cape Breton University in 2006 and 2007, respectively. He then completed a M. Ed. in Instructional Design and Technology from the University of New Brunswick at Fredericton in 2008. His recent Ph. D. work was completed at Memorial University of Newfoundland, and dealt with how video game players assimilate new information and play skills. Dr. White joined Penn State Behrend in August 2012. Prior to working with us, he studied Usability and User Experience at the University of Prince Edward Island, and was a professional Game Designer for an independent development studio called Snow Day Games. A member of the Canadian Game Studies Association, Digital Games Research Association, and International Game Developer's Association, Dr. White's interdisciplinary work involves creating and playing games, as well as studying them and their larger effects and significance.

Nicola Whitton is a Research Fellow at Manchester Metropolitan University and a director of the Technology, Innovation, and Play for Learning research group. She has written widely in the area of games for adult learners, and recently managed projects in motivation and games for older learners and collaborative game design in schools. Her research interests particularly focus on the value of play for creating safe learning spaces.

Amanda Wilson is in the last year of her doctoral studies in the School of Computing at the University of the West of Scotland and an active researcher in the Centre of Excellence for Games-Based Learning. Her thesis is focused on Games-Based Construction Learning at Primary Education Level using Scratch to teach programming concepts and has produced a framework for the integration of Games-Based Construction Learning into Primary level classrooms to be used by Primary educationalists. Amanda has a number of journal and conference publications presenting qualitative and quantitative empirical evidence in the area of Games-Based Learning and Games-Based Construction. Amanda has organised events with a number of Primary Schools and utilised Scratch to motivate children to learn programming concepts and construct their own playable games.

Matthias Witte is currently working as a University Assistant at the University of Graz, Austria. He received his diploma in biology (M.Sc. equivalent) from the University of Freiburg, Germany, in 2007. Until 2012, he worked as a Research Associate at the MEG Center, Institute of Medical Psychology and Behavioral Neurobiology, University of Tübingen, Germany. He obtained a Ph.D. in neuroscience from the Graduate School of Neural and Behavioral Sciences/International Max Planck Research School Tübingen in 2012. His work is inspired by questions from motor control, applications in brain-computer interfaces, and multivariate decoding techniques in neuroimaging.

Guilherme Wood is Assistant Professor at the Department of Psychology at the University of Graz in Austria. Guilherme Wood received his master degree in Psychology from the Federal University of Minas Gerais (Brazil) and his PhD at the RWTH University Aachen, Germany. His research foci are neurofeedback, the impact of aging on cognition and brain function, neurocognitive aspects of number processing and the genetic correlates of cognitive and brain activity.

Qiqi Zhou is an assistant professor in Policy, Organization, and Gaming in the Faculty of Technology, Policy, and Management, TU Delft.

Index